MO

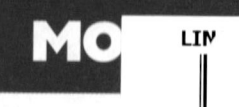

ARIZONA & THE GRAND CANYON

TIM HULL

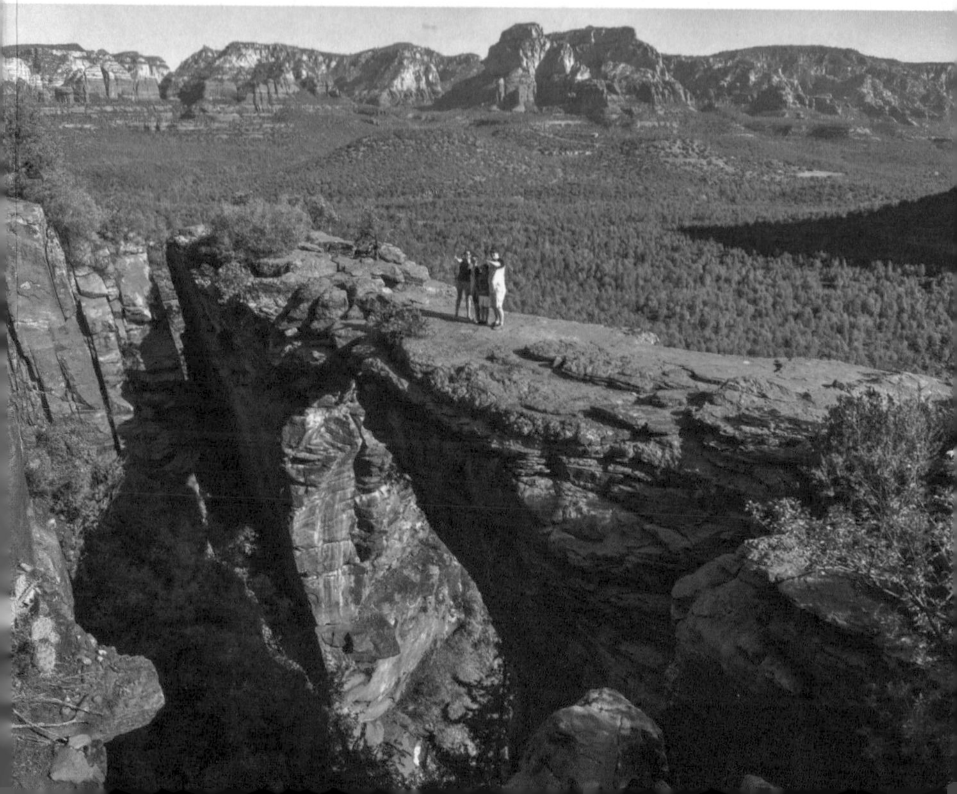

Contents

Although every effort was made to make sure the information in this book was accurate when going to press, research was impacted by the COVID-19 pandemic and things may have changed since the time of writing. Be sure to confirm specific details, like opening hours, closures, and travel guidelines and restrictions, when making your travel plans. For more detailed information, see p. 435.

DISCOVER

Arizona &
the Grand Canyon

Arizona is authentic. It's too hot to fake it, too rugged to tell tall tales, and too beautiful to commit to the hard sell. All of its institutions, its attractions, and even its mythologies were forged through hard experience, trial, and error.

This is even true of the land, built by the movement and explosion of the earth—canyons ripped open and mountains kicked up over millennia of shaking and oozing. This roiling has provided a wonderland of diversity, building—all at once—hot and verdant desert scrublands, cool evergreen mountain forests, dry sweeping grasslands, and red-rock, river-carved, fairy-tale canyons, all of which merge with a horizon lit most evenings with postcard-ready sunsets. It remains one of the most exotic destinations in North America, with endless variety, iconic scenery, and a dark history of which the world has never tired.

You will be surprised and changed by Arizona. Here you might see cliff dwellings created centuries ago by the state's Indigenous peoples or a gathering of just-built dream homes along a stretch of highway. This may be the perfect image for the dichotomies of this landscape: Everything here is either ancient or five minutes old.

Clockwise from top left: Sedona's world-famous Red Rock Country; hiking in Phoenix; Saguaro National Park cactus; a mule at the Grand Canyon; Cactus League baseball; view from Lookout Studio on the Grand Canyon's South Rim.

There's a reason all those road movies feature scenes in the Grand Canyon State. There's no better way to see all the state has to offer than to pile in a car and hit the open road. Less than a day's drive from anywhere, you can discover something unexpected, whether it be the calm and sunny ease of life along the lower Colorado River, where houseboats and water-skiers pass by great monuments to engineering, or a chance meeting with a rare tropical bird hiding out in the riparian mist of a sky island.

In many a traveler's imagination, this place is home to rattlesnakes, tumbleweeds, and vast tracts of arid wilderness. Luckily, Arizona has all of these; there are still trackless spaces to explore. But the face Arizona shows to most of the world belies the leaps this once isolated territory has made. The youngest state in the Lower 48 is one of the fastest-growing regions in the nation, and while near-constant growth makes for sometimes rancorous debates about land use and natural resources, it adds to Arizona a dynamism—a flux that perpetuates itself. It is never boring here; it is beautiful and unknowable. There is always something, or someone, being created anew, changing, and blooming.

Clockwise from top left: Mount Hayden on the North Rim of the Grand Canyon; the Colorado River; gila woodpecker on saguaro cactus in Saguaro National Park; Lowell Observatory in Flagstaff.

10 TOP
EXPERIENCES

1 **Experience a Wonder of the World:** Hike, bike, raft, or just gaze in awe at the **Grand Canyon** (page 243).

2 **Explore Red Rock Country:** Discover the sculpted red cliffs and buttes around **Sedona** (page 234).

>>>

3 **Take a Hike:** Trails crisscross Arizona, from the **deserts** to the **forests** to the **slickrock canyon lands** (page 21).

<<<

4 **Have a Ball at Spring Training:** Enjoy the Valley of the Sun in March while watching your favorite **Major League Baseball** teams play in intimate family-friendly ballparks (page 58).

>>>

5 **Relax at a Spa Resort:** Treat yourself to the high-style pampering and luxury for which Arizona resorts are known (page 96).

6 **Feast on Mexican Food:** Whether you're craving avocado enchiladas, street-style tacos, or a loaded Sonoran hot dog, Southern Arizona is the place to find it (page 147).

<<<

∧
∧
∧

7 **Take a Scenic Drive through Monument Valley:** Find an otherworldly landscape filled with the eroded sandstone buttes and spires of the Navajo Nation (page 327).

8 **Feel the Heat in the Sonoran Desert:** Explore this unique and surprising landscape at the **Arizona-Sonora Desert Museum** (page 121) and **Saguaro National Park** (pages 121 and 123).

<<<

9 **Journey back in Time on Old Route 66:** Drive the remains of the Mother Road to the Colorado River, passing through a time warp along the way (page 387).

>>>

10 **Wander around Historic Small Towns:** Peruse one-of-a-kind boutiques and art galleries in charming Old West towns like **Bisbee** (page 177) and **Jerome** (page 216).

<<<

Planning Your Trip

Where to Go

Phoenix, Scottsdale, and the Valley of the Sun

Arizona's **largest metro area** has 10 cities linked together to create a sprawling megalopolis of glass high-rises and labyrinthine stacked freeways spreading over a hot Sonoran Desert valley. Visitors and residents tend to refer to the whole area as the Valley of the Sun, or simply Phoenix, after the valley's largest city. There are pockets of urbanity out in the sprawl, like Scottsdale with its **art galleries,** high-style eateries, resorts, and **golf courses,** and Tempe with its college-town nightlife, shopping, and museums. This area has **some of the state's best resorts and restaurants,** nightlife, museums, and Arizona's largest airport. The rural desert outskirts are home to old mining towns, river canyons, and saguaro forests.

Tucson and Southern Arizona

Tucson, the state's second-largest city and the one with the most character and history, anchors this region of **saguaro forests,** sweeping grasslands, and quirky desert outposts. Towering **sky island** mountain ranges shoot up from the long desert seas, and the nearby Mexican border looms equally large in this region's culture and history. They also say a few of those myths and legends of the **Old West** actually happened here.

Flagstaff, Sedona, and Red Rock Country

Arizona's sap-scented high country begins

the colorful, bushy Sonoran Desert around Tucson

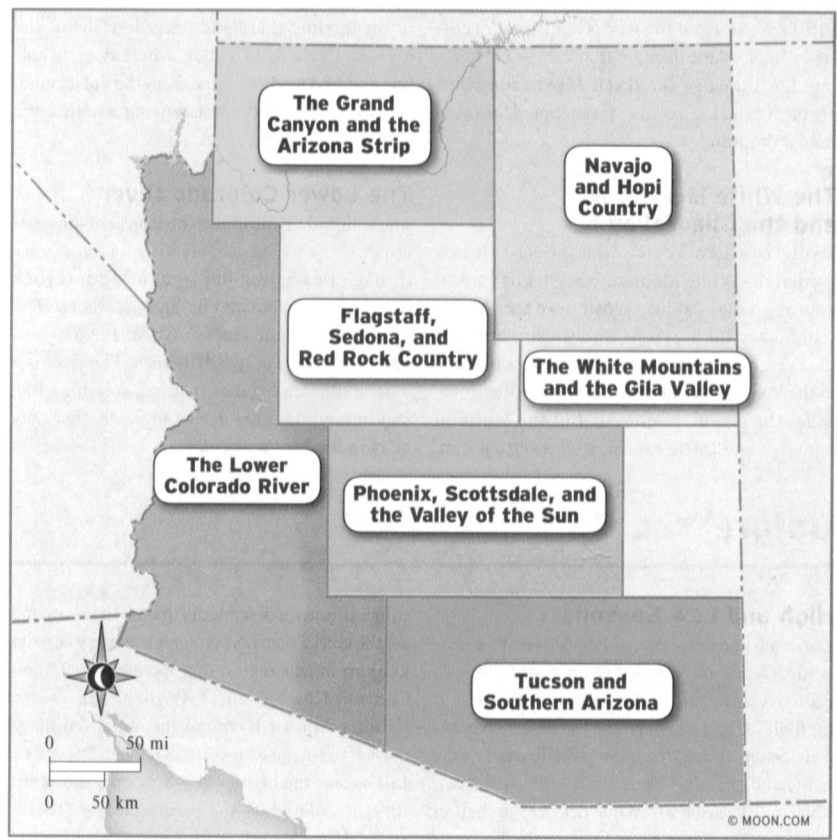

© MOON.COM

around mile-high **Prescott** and rises to a great ponderosa pine forest stretching north and east. Even higher is snowy **Flagstaff** and the bald-rock tip of the **San Francisco Peaks,** their slopes variegated by white and yellow aspens among the evergreens. Below the **Mogollon Rim,** the green edge of a great plateau, **Sedona** offers fine dining, self-healing, red-rock buttes, and shady streambeds.

The Grand Canyon and the Arizona Strip

The **Kaibab Plateau** rises in northwestern Arizona; river-cut more than a mile deep into the plateau is **Arizona's signature attraction**

and one of the world's most sought-after landscapes—the only canyon on earth deserving of the grand title. Beyond the canyon's forested rims is the lonely Arizona Strip, empty save for high, barren red cliffs, sagebrush plains, and the water-and-red-rock mazes of **Lake Powell.**

Navajo and Hopi Country

The **high-desert grasslands** in Arizona's northeastern plateau country are dotted with a few old cattle and **railroad towns,** trading posts, and an empty pastel-painted desert strewn with broken swirling-stone trees. The vast Navajo Nation is cut deep with **red-sandstone canyons** in which abandoned cliff-face cities and the tracks of dinosaurs create a timeless atmosphere that can be entrancing. On the edge of **Black Mesa,** the Hopi people live on high cold cliffs occupied for more than a thousand years.

The White Mountains and the Gila Valley

Rising in eastern Arizona near the New Mexico border, the White Mountains region has **small towns,** rental cabins, **trout streams,** coldwater lakes, hiking trails, and wolves. Much of the evergreen mountainous wilderness is home to the **Western Apache,** and their culture pervades the region, as does that of the Mormon pioneers and cattle ranchers who settled here in the territorial era and never left. Below the highlands, the Gila Valley, where deserts collide and **hot springs** burst from the hot ground, spreads out along the last flowing remains of a once-mighty desert river.

The Lower Colorado River

The Colorado River flows the length of far western Arizona to Mexico, creating a river border through this barren hot land of **jagged rock mountains** populated by bighorn sheep. The views are long and empty save for the toughest **cacti, scrubs,** and **wildflowers.** The river is a blue-and-green band of rustling, splashing life, and living things are drawn to it, whether they be **rare birds** or water-skiers.

Before You Go

High and Low Seasons

Spring is the best time to be on Arizona's lowland deserts, including Phoenix and Tucson. February-May, the weather is gorgeous, often in the high 70s and 80s. Spring is the desert's bloomtime, when all the dormant **wildflowers** come to life and the spiny cacti burst with vivid color. It's also the season for Major League Baseball in Arizona; fans of the game flock to the Valley of the Sun for **Cactus League spring training** games in March. The desert-country tourist season is definitely at its high point during spring.

It typically stays **triple-digit hot** on Arizona's deserts from **summer well into October,** so fall isn't really a recognized season here. By November the weather cools off, and then, seemingly overnight, it starts to get cold. December-February a kind of **winter** comes to the desert, when the **snowbirds** flock to Arizona from the Midwest, the Northeast, and Canada, crowding the roads, stores, and restaurants of Tucson and the Valley of the Sun.

In **summer,** the high country is warm, tending toward hot during the day, and cool, clear, and star-filled at night. In late summer the rains come: afternoon downpours that clean the air and get the creeks rising. Summer is the **busy tourist season** in this region that includes the Grand Canyon, North-Central Arizona, and Indian Country. You are bound to encounter crowds at most of the major attractions. October-December, **fall** blesses the highlands with **cool, pleasant days,** crisp nights, and turning leaves. This is an ideal time to visit North-Central Arizona and the Grand Canyon. Above 7,000 feet elevation, the cold and the snow have been known to arrive as early as November, but **ski season** doesn't usually get going in the White Mountains and Flagstaff until January. In winter, especially in a wet year, expect to find the mountain country crowded on the weekends with skiers and snowboarders.

Reservations and Permits

A trip to Arizona requires a certain amount of **advance planning,** at least **six months** if you're going to be spending time in the **Grand Canyon** (page 245), and more if you want to stay in the inner canyon's only lodge, **Phantom Ranch** (page 293). If you're hoping to **raft**

heat warning trail signage in Phoenix

down the Colorado (page 292), start planning at least a year in advance. Renting houseboats, for example on Lake Powell (page 310), also requires booking six months in advance. Bring your passport along if you're planning to cross the U.S.-Mexico border.

You must have a car, and you'll need to be prepared for a lot of time in it. Towns, sights, and attractions are scattered throughout the state, and most are far from the two urban centers of Phoenix and Tucson.

What to Pack

Your luggage should include a few essential items, no matter the season. These include a good pair of hiking or walking shoes. Day hikers or at least a pair of tough running shoes or trainers are a necessity. At nearly every national park or national monument, there's some kind of short hike in order to really appreciate what you're seeing. A water bottle is always nice to have around, and you'll probably want to include a small pack for carrying snacks and water on day hikes or sightseeing excursions. Sunscreen is a necessity in any season; if you're not in a hot desert, you're in mountain country, where the sun shines hard and dangerous. A hat is a must, and one with a brim wide enough to cast a shadow on your neck is recommended. Think about bringing along a pair of binoculars; they are always handy when spotting bighorn sheep, petroglyphs, and rare birds.

Even if you're going to be in the desert in the summer, bring along a light jacket. In some of the outer and higher regions the nights will be much cooler. In the high country, layers will serve you best. It is often warm in the day and cold at night, even in summer.

As for style, think casual and utilitarian. If you're going to be staying or dining at any of the top resorts, a few fancy outfits might be in order. Otherwise, jeans and T-shirts, shorts and tank tops, flip-flops, rock sandals, and general outdoor style are the norm.

Arizona Road Trip

The best way to see Arizona is from behind the wheel of your own car. A road trip through the heart of the American Southwest provides a unique opportunity to explore this exotic region from the ground up.

Day 1: Scenic Drive to Cave Creek
70 MILES / 1.5 HOURS

Arrive at **Phoenix Sky Harbor International Airport** and head to a hotel in central Phoenix, a resort in **Scottsdale,** or **Tempe.** Introduce yourself to the desert by taking a scenic drive along AZ 51 about 35 miles or 45 minutes out to **Cave Creek** and **Carefree.** Have dinner at **El Encanto** in Cave Creek before heading back.

Day 2: Phoenix, Scottsdale, and Prescott
100 MILES / 2 HOURS

Get an early start and spend the morning touring the **Heard Museum,** the **Phoenix Art Museum,** or **Taliesin West.** Leave the city via I-17 to **Prescott.** Stop for a late lunch and a slice of pie midway at the **Rock Springs Café,** north of Phoenix along I-17. Spend the night at one of downtown Prescott's historic hotels or bed-and-breakfasts. Have dinner at the **Raven Café** and hit up a few **Whiskey Row** watering holes.

Day 3: Prescott and Jerome
35 MILES / 1 HOUR

Get up early and eat breakfast at **The Local.** Walk around downtown Prescott and tour the museums, shops, and galleries. Be sure to visit the **Sharlot Hall Museum.** Head north on scenic

entrance to the Heard Museum featuring *Earth Song* by Allan Houser

Best Hikes

The Grand Canyon State's varied landscapes, not to mention the great canyon itself, are a hiker's paradise, crisscrossed with hundreds of well-maintained and well-used trails of various lengths and difficulties. From an easy walk in the desert to a multiday expedition deep into the canyon's depths, the hikes listed below are among the best of the best.

- **White House Ruin Trail** (Canyon de Chelly National Monument; 2.5 mi round-trip, 2-3 hours, elevation gain 550 ft, moderate): High sandstone walls tower above as you descend into the Navajo Nation's Canyon de Chelly, where the otherworldly White House Ruin awaits, carved into the cliffs (page 332).

- **Brown Mountain Trail** (Tucson Mountain Park; 4.8 mi round-trip, 2-3 hours, elevation gain 260 ft, moderate): This trail winds through the saguaro forests on Tucson's wild western edge, rising to traverse a ridgeline with spectacular views of the surprisingly verdant Sonoran Desert (page 131).

- **West Fork of Oak Creek Trail** (north of Sedona; 6.5 mi round-trip, 2-3 hours, elevation gain 200 ft, easy): A rare example of a high-desert streamside forest environment, dark green evergreens mingle with red rocks and trickling water to create an exotic Southwestern Eden (page 239).

- **Mount Humphrey Trail** (Snowbowl Ski Area, Flagstaff; 9 mi round-trip, 5-6 hours, elevation gain 3,833 ft, difficult): This hike is challenging, but the effort is richly rewarded when you're

Bright Angel Trail

looking out over Arizona from its highest point, 12,000 feet above sea level (page 195).

- **Bright Angel Trail to Phantom Ranch** (Grand Canyon Village; 9.6 mi one-way, overnight, elevation gain 4,380 ft, moderate-difficult): Obtain a permit and head down the ancient Bright Angel Trail to the Colorado River and Phantom Ranch, in the mystical depths of the Grand Canyon. It takes a bit of planning, but this is truly the hike of a lifetime (page 288).

AZ 89A to **Jerome.** Stay at the **Jerome Grand Hotel** and have dinner at **The Asylum.**

Day 4: Jerome and Sedona
28 MILES / 40 MINUTES
Have brunch at **The Clinkscale** and take a walk around Jerome. Head down AZ 89A to **Sedona.** Check into your hotel, and then head out to explore the red rocks, galleries, and shops of Sedona.

Eat dinner at **Creekside American Bistro & Bar.**

Day 5: Sedona and the Verde Valley
52 MILES / 1.25 HOURS
Spend the day shopping, hiking, sightseeing, and exploring Sedona and the **Verde Valley.** Check out **Montezuma Castle National**

Monument, 26 miles from town, or hike into red-rock country or take a Jeep tour through the red lands.

Day 6: Oak Creek Canyon and Flagstaff
30 MILES / 1 HOUR

Eat breakfast at the **Coffee Pot Restaurant** in Sedona, then head north on AZ 89A through **Oak Creek Canyon**. Stop for a hike or to splash around in the water at **Slide Rock State Park.** Continue north to **Flagstaff**, about an hour's drive from Sedona. Check into one of the historic hotels downtown. Stroll and shop downtown, then have dinner and beers at **Beaver Street Brewery.**

Day 7: Flagstaff and the High Desert
130 MILES / 3 HOURS

Wake up and head out to visit the **Museum of Northern Arizona** in Flagstaff, three miles north of downtown on U.S. 180, then drive a circuit to take in **Wupatki, Sunset Crater Volcano, and Walnut Canyon National Monuments** via U.S. 89 and the Loop Road. From here, drive east for an hour on I-40 to **Winslow.** Check into **La Posada.** Have dinner in the **Turquoise Room,** and order a box lunch from the restaurant for the next day.

Day 8: The High Desert and Navajo Country
175 MILES / 3.5 HOURS

Spend the morning touring the **Painted Desert** and **Petrified Forest National Park** near **Holbrook,** 52 miles or an hour from Winslow on I-40. Then take I-40 to U.S. 191 north to **Chinle** on the Navajo Reservation, a distance of 123 miles, 2.5 hours. Stay at the **Thunderbird Lodge** near **Canyon de Chelly** or at one of the chains in Chinle.

Day 9: Canyon de Chelly and Monument Valley
150-180 MILES / 3-4 HOURS

Spend the morning hiking into **Canyon de Chelly** to the **White House Ruin** and driving

upper and lower levels of White House Ruin in Canyon de Chelly

the scenic rim roads, or hire a Navajo guide and go deeper into the canyon. After lunch, head north on U.S. 191, west on U.S. 160, then north on U.S. 163 to Kayenta, a distance of 75 miles or 1.5 hours. Get a hotel room in Kayenta, drive through Monument Valley late in the afternoon, and watch the sun set. Monument Valley is 50 miles or 1 hour from Kayenta.

Day 10: The Grand Canyon
155 MILES / 3 HOURS

Eat breakfast in Kayenta at the Blue Coffee Pot Restaurant and then head west on U.S. 160 past Tuba City to U.S. 89, then south to Cameron, 100 miles or 1.5 hours. Take AZ 64 west 30 miles to Grand Canyon National Park and make your way to the east entrance. Check out the Desert View sights, then drive to Grand Canyon Village and have lunch at El Tovar. Spend the night at El Tovar or the Bright Angel Lodge. Get up early and hike down one of the South Rim trails as far as you feel like going. If you're not a hiker, take a mule ride to the river and back. Spend the remainder of the day looking around the rim and staring into the canyon.

Day 11: Heading to Tucson
340 MILES / 5 HOURS

This day will be spent mostly in the car driving from the high country to Tucson and Southern Arizona. Leave the Grand Canyon early through the South Entrance and take I-40 East to I-17 South. In Phoenix, follow the signs to I-10 south to Tucson. You'll probably arrive in the late afternoon. Check into the Hotel Congress or Hotel McCoy, or one of the area's bed-and-breakfasts, and then head to Mi Nidito for a Mexican-food dinner.

Day 12: Tucson and the Border Region
135 MILES / 2 HOURS

Get up early and spend the morning walking around Saguaro National Park West and visiting the nearby Arizona-Sonora Desert Museum. Have lunch at the museum's café, or at the Coyote Pause Café five miles south. Then continue south to see the mission San Xavier del Bac. Drive back to your hotel in Tucson, about an hour's drive, and relax.

Day 13: Southeastern Arizona
50-150 MILES / 1-3 HOURS

This day is a Southern Arizona grab bag. Drive through the San Pedro Valley or the Mountain Empire. Do some wine-tasting in Elgin, shop in Bisbee, or drive the dirt roads into the Huachuca Mountains and up to the Coronado National Memorial. Visit Chiricahua National Monument, Cochise Stronghold, Patagonia, Madera Canyon, Kartchner Caverns, or Tombstone. A full busy day will allow you to make three or four major stops, depending on your interests and the amount of time you spend at any one place. You'll likely arrive back at your hotel in Tucson late.

Day 14: Tucson and Back to Phoenix
116-156 MILES / 2-3 HOURS

Wake up early and take a stroll through one of Tucson's downtown neighborhoods or 4th Avenue and the University District. On your way north on I-10 to the airport in Phoenix, a distance of 116 miles, stop at Picacho Peak State Park for a last hike. With more time, you could take a short detour off of I-10 to Casa Grande Ruins National Monument, 20 miles off of I-10, a 30-minute drive, for a last look at Indigenous Arizona.

Ancient Indigenous Cultures

Arizona and the Southwest were home to many Indigenous cultures that are no longer around to tell their stories. The ruins of the Hohokam, Ancestral Puebloans, Salado, Sinagua, and others are protected throughout the state by federal law. You could make a whole trip out of visiting these fascinating structures, learning about the cultures that once scraped more than subsistence out of the uncaring land.

THE HOHOKAM AND SALADO

Use Phoenix and the Valley of the Sun as your base to see what was left behind by the Hohokam and Salado tribes.

- **Pueblo Grande Museum and Archaeological Park:** Learn how the Hohokam coaxed an empire out of the Salt River Valley at the ruins and museum in the middle of the city, near the canals the Hohokam built to irrigate the desert (page 46).

- **Tonto National Monument:** Take the backcountry route called the **Apache Trail**, east of the city, and witness a well-preserved cliff dwelling once inhabited by the Salado tribe rising above slopes crowded with saguaros (page 101).

- **Casa Grande Ruins National Monument:** Between Phoenix and Tucson, this monument is the largest example of Hohokam architecture left, the huge molded-dirt apartment building called Casa Grande (page 102).

THE SINAGUA

Use Sedona or Flagstaff as your base for visiting the awesome structures of North-Central Arizona's vanished Sinagua.

- **Wupatki National Monument:** Just north of Flagstaff, this monument preserves the ruins of several red-sandstone great houses (page 192).

- **Walnut Canyon National Monument:** East of Flagstaff is a lost world where a long-gone culture once built a busy village on the rim and along the walls of a hidden canyon (page 194).

Casa Grande Ruins National Monument

- **Montezuma Castle National Monument:** This Verde Valley cliff dwelling is one of the best preserved in the Southwest (page 223).

THE ANCESTRAL PUEBLOANS

The abandoned cliff cities of the Ancestral Puebloans are on display in the Navajo Nation.

- **Navajo National Monument:** While visiting Tsegi Canyon, you can spot the ruins called **Betatakin** from the rim, nestled in a rock alcove above a bottomland forest (page 323).

- **Keet Seel:** Sign up for a 16-mile round-trip hike below the rim of Tsegi Canyon to spend the night near the spectacularly preserved ruins hidden deep in the canyon (page 323).

- **Canyon de Chelly National Monument:** Also on Navajo land, don't miss this area where you can hike down a slickrock trail and stand in awe before the **White House Ruin** (page 332).

Grand Canyon Adventure

In the Grand Canyon, you don't need to be a seasoned backcountry adventurer to experience nature at its most primal. This itinerary includes one night below the rim and thus requires you to secure reservations and permits far in advance. The best time to go is spring or October.

Day 1

Take an early-morning flight into **Phoenix Sky Harbor International Airport,** rent a car, and drive north to **Williams** (170 mi). Park your car and catch the **Grand Canyon Railway** to **Grand Canyon National Park's South Rim.** Check into a cabin at **Bright Angel Lodge,** and then explore and go sightseeing around **Grand Canyon Village,** getting acclimated to the huge gorge in front of you. Eat dinner at **El Tovar.**

Day 2

Tour the South Rim, visiting the **Desert View Watchtower, El Tovar,** and the **Hopi House.** Have dinner at one of the casual eateries on the South Rim and get a good night's sleep—you'll need it.

If you've got kids ages 4-12, before you start sightseeing, take them to the **Grand Canyon Visitor Center** and get them in the **Junior Ranger** program. The ranger will give them age-appropriate booklets, and throughout the day they'll earn a Junior Ranger badge and patch by fulfilling the fun and educational requirements, which include attending one of the ranger-led programs offered throughout the day.

Day 3

If you are hiking, get a very early start down either the **Bright Angel Trail** or the **South Kaibab Trail.** Don't carry your own bags. Spend a few extra bills to have the mules do it, so you can enjoy the hike and really see the scenery. If you're riding with a mule train to the bottom, show up at the appointed time and place

Rain clouds enhance the beauty and mystery of the Grand Canyon.

Back to the Old West

The conquistadores, miners, ranchers, outlaws, and mythmakers of the Old West all left an imprint on Arizona, and their descendants do what they can to keep them from fading back into the deserts and the canyons.

SOUTHERN ARIZONA

Southern Arizona represents the northern extreme of the Spanish crown's New World empire, while southwestern Arizona is full of the legends and kitsch of the Old West. Here you will find the following:

- **Tubac Presidio State Historic Park:** Visit the small park that preserves the memories and artifacts of Spain's empire (page 165).

- **Coronado National Memorial:** Tour the remote monument in the Huachuca Mountains that marks the trail used by Coronado as he trudged north toward the Seven Cities of Cibola (page 174).

Main Street in Bisbee

- **Tombstone:** Examine several forensic exhibits on that world-famous seconds-long gunfight that took place in the town's dusty streets (page 175).

- **Bisbee:** Visit an example of an Old West mining town rich with antiques stores and artisanal boutiques (page 177).

- **Yuma Territorial Prison State Historic Park:** See what awaited those outlaws and bandits who ran afoul of territorial law (page 404).

NORTH-CENTRAL ARIZONA

- **Riordan Mansion State Historic Park:** Peek into the private lives of two 19th-century Flagstaff lumber barons featured at this state park (page 188).

- **Jerome:** Explore the history of the state's mining booms in this preserved mountainside town (page 216).

- **Zane Grey Cabin:** Pay your respects to one of the Old West's greatest mythmakers. Here you can see an exact replica of Grey's hunting cabin (the real one burned down in 1990), complete with period decorations and furniture, and learn all about the prolific author's passion for Arizona's Mogollon Rim region (page 241).

- **Pipe Spring National Monument:** Discover what it was like to live on a lonely fortified ranch in the late 1800s at this Arizona Strip sight (page 302).

South Kaibab Trail

and saddle up. You'll arrive at **Phantom Ranch** near the **Colorado River** late in the day. (You have to reserve a cabin and meals at the cantina up to a year beforehand. A mule trip will be all-inclusive, but if you're hiking, you'll need to make separate reservations.) Take a shower, explore Phantom Ranch, dip your feet in **Bright Angel Creek,** walk to the river, and relax in the inner gorge. Eat a hearty meal at the cantina and attend a ranger-led program before collapsing into bed.

Day 4

Get up early, eat breakfast at the cantina, and spend the day exploring the **inner gorge,** the river, and Phantom Ranch. Ask a ranger for recommendations on the best day hikes and sights in the inner canyon.

Day 5

Wake up early, eat breakfast, and head out, either on a mule or on foot. It'll take you most of the day to get out of the canyon. If you're hiking and you came down the Bright Angel Trail, head up the South Kaibab for a different view. If you came down the South Kaibab, hike out using the Bright Angel so you can see the lush **Indian Garden.** When you make it out of the canyon, treat yourself to a nice dinner and relax and recover for the rest of the day.

Day 6

Spend the morning seeing the canyon for the last time and shopping for souvenirs. Catch the train back to Williams and check into the **Grand Canyon Hotel.** Have dinner at **Rod's Steak House** in Williams, then head back to the hotel to swim or soak in the hot tub.

Day 7

Head south to Phoenix after breakfast at the **Pine Country Restaurant** in Williams. Stop for a late lunch just outside of the city at **Rock Springs Café.** Catch your flight home at Sky Harbor.

Best Scenic Drives

landscape along the Arizona Strip

Grab some road snacks. Make that perfect highway mix of songs that go well with long, empty views. Then hit the road for some of the most scenic landscapes in the country.

THE DESERT

Open spaces and strange scenery abound on these routes through the hot rocky deserts of western Arizona.

- **Historic Route 66:** Drive the remains of the Mother Road on the dry northwestern plains, where you can jump back to a slower time, passing through Kingman, stopping at the **Historic Route 66 Museum,** and spending some time in Seligman, the center of a Route 66 cultural zrebirth (page 387).

- **Joshua Tree Forest Parkway:** Take U.S. 60 northwest from Phoenix through Wickenburg and keep going when it turns to U.S. 93, known for its stands of Joshua trees (page 396).

THE FOREST

You'll be driving uphill on these scenic drives; watch as the vegetation changes from desert to a transitional bushy scrub to highland evergreen forests, all while you sit comfortably behind the wheel.

- **The Apache Trail:** This drive takes you past Indigenous ruins and old mining towns, and the forest comes up quickly as you leave the central scrublands and rise along a twisty highway—make sure to stop for a photo op at majestic **Salt River Canyon** (page 100).

- **AZ 89A from Prescott to Jerome:** Take AZ 89A up over forested **Mingus Mountain,** stopping to enjoy a sweeping view of the Verde River Valley below when you reach the pass at the top of the hill. A little farther on you're in the old copper-mining town of **Jerome,** now home to boutiques and restaurants (page 216).

- **Swift Trail Parkway:** Negotiate a twisting forest road from the desert Gila Valley to the top of **Mount Graham** at over 10,000 feet, the highest of Southern Arizona's sky islands—it's the equivalent of driving from Mexico to Canada in an hour (page 370).

THE PLATEAU

The vast and sparsely populated Colorado Plateau has many lonely scenic roads. On some the traffic is so thin that you could take a nap on the center stripe.

- **Vermilion Cliffs Highway:** Perhaps the loneliest of Arizona's lonely routes, this scenic road snakes across the **Arizona Strip** in northwestern Arizona, just south of the border with Utah, and passes towering red-rock cliffs and vast bunchgrass plains (page 302).

- **Valley Drive:** This loop road in **Monument Valley Navajo Tribal Park** on the Navajo Reservation, with its strangely eroded sandstone spires, buttes, and mesas rising from the sweeping red-dirt plains, is an essential Southwest drive. An added bonus is the short drive—which is almost as scenic—to the valley from **Kayenta** (page 327).

Beat the Heat

Most people who don't live in Arizona would say that it's primarily a desert state of cacti, tumbleweeds, and rattlesnakes. Of course, that's only a part of the story. More than one-third of the Grand Canyon State—including the South and North Rims of the Grand Canyon—is covered in evergreen forests. This itinerary, which starts in Flagstaff, the capital of the state's forested northland, will take you through these forests along cool, secluded, tree-lined highways and to the top of the tallest mountains in the state. The best time to go is summer, when the deserts are too hot for comfort.

Day 1

Arrive in **Flagstaff** the night before and stay at one of the historic hotels downtown (the **Weatherford Hotel** or **Hotel Monte Vista**). Wake up early, have breakfast at the **Morning Glory Café,** and head out to the **San Francisco Peaks.** Hike through the pine-and-aspen forest on the **Mount Humphrey Trail** to the top of Arizona, at 12,600 feet. If you're not into hiking, ride the **Scenic Chairlift** at **Arizona Snowbowl** up to 11,500 feet. After a day in the forest, relax at one of the restaurants or bars in downtown Flagstaff.

Day 2

Get up early and drive to **Williams,** where you'll park your car and hop on the **Grand Canyon Railway.** The historic train will drop you at the forested South Rim of the Grand Canyon, where you can spend the day looking into the canyon, exploring the charming buildings in Grand Canyon Village, and walking along the **Rim Trail** or taking a bike ride to **Hermit's Rest.** Catch the train back to Williams, have dinner at **Rod's Steak House,** and stay the night at **The Lodge on Route 66.**

downton Flagstaff

Ecofriendly Hotels

Bright Angel Lodge

Sustainability should have an expansive definition in arid lands. It should include the usual responsible practices—water conservation, recycling, moving toward renewables, and so forth—but also go farther to embrace cutting-edge building materials and methods; refurbishing and repurposing old buildings; desert-adapted native landscaping; and dedication to local farmers, artisans, and traditions. Although there really is no truly green or sustainable hotel in Arizona, these excellent places are moving in the right direction.

- **Arizona Grand Resort,** near Phoenix's South Mountain Park, offers sumptuous guest rooms and inviting pools for relaxing and recovering in the Valley of the Sun. The hotel's parent, Classic Hotels & Resorts, is a member of the 1% for the Planet alliance and strives to use sustainable and recycled materials and organic local foods (page 75).

- **Hotel McCoy** makes new use of a forgotten old mid-century motor court in Tucson. The hotel is filled with Tucson-only art; serves only local beer, wine, and coffee; and has been retrofitted with low-flow plumbing fixtures (page 154).

- **Miraval, Life in Balance Resort & Spa,** at the base of Tucson's Santa Catalina Mountains, is known the world over as a magical desert paradise dedicated to health and healing. Less known is that the high-end resort operates an on-site water-treatment facility, allowing it to reuse nearly 100 percent of the precious resource (page 157).

- **Bright Angel Lodge,** on the Grand Canyon's South Rim, and most of the other accommodations in Grand Canyon National Park are eco-friendly options thanks to the robust recycling and water-conservation efforts of park concessionaire Xanterra (page 275).

Day 3

Rise early once again and take AZ 89A through **Oak Creek Canyon** to **Sedona,** stopping along the way to admire the babbling forested creek. Have dinner at **Creekside American Bistro & Bar** and stay overnight in Sedona.

Day 4

Have breakfast in Sedona, hit AZ 179 south from Sedona to I-17, and then pick up AZ 260 east to the **Mogollon Rim** region. Drive through the forest along AZ 87, stopping in the small forest communities of **Pine, Strawberry,** and **Payson** to shop, hike, and eat. Check out the **Zane Grey**

Scenic Chairlift at Arizona Snowbowl

Cabin in Payson, and consider stopping at the gorgeous **Tonto Natural Bridge State Park.** Stay at the **Majestic Mountain Inn** in Payson and have dinner at **Macky's Grill.**

Day 5

Get an early start for a drive across the **Mogollon Rim** to the **White Mountains** region. Drive slowly across the rim along Forest Road 300 for 51 miles to the **Mogollon Rim Visitor Center,** where there's a paved trail and some breathtaking views, stopping often to explore and enjoy the forest along the escarpment. Stay the night in Show Low or Pinetop-Lakeside in the White Mountains region.

Day 6

Rise early and lace up your hiking boots for a trek either to the top of **Mount Baldy,** the second-highest peak in the state, or **Escudilla Mountain,** the third-highest peak. Escudilla is the easier hike, and along the way you'll see some of the most beautiful old-growth forests in the state. Have dinner at the **Goob's Pizza** in Springerville and rest up for your last forest drive of the trip.

Day 7

Gas up the car and head south along the **Coronado Trail,** a twisting 120-mile forested two-lane from the mountains down to the desert. Stop often to admire the wildflowers growing along the road, and keep a vigilant watch for wildlife. If you feel up to it, there are many hiking trails along the route that lead into the forest.

Phoenix, Scottsdale, and the Valley of the Sun

If you spend enough time in the desert basin known as the Valley of the Sun (often just "the valley"), there will undoubtedly come a time when you will ask yourself, "Why would they build a megalopolis *here*?"

This question will likely come up during the month of July or thereabouts, when it's 110°F in the shade and you're slogging to your car through a heat-storing parking lot somewhere. Don't lose heart, though. There is much in this mostly urbanized valley to do and see, eat and watch, find and buy.

A loose affiliation of cities and suburbs anchored by Phoenix and spreading to the wild northern Sonoran Desert along its edges, the Valley of the Sun is one of the largest metro areas in the nation and

Highlights

Look for ★ to find recommended sights, activities, dining, and lodging.

© MOON.COM

★ **Heard Museum:** This renowned institution is filled with artistic, ceremonial, and daily-life artifacts from both ancient history and modern Native American communities (page 38).

★ **Phoenix Art Museum:** See some of the most spectacular art in the West—and of the Western world (page 40).

★ **Taliesin West:** Architect Frank Lloyd Wright's desert masterpiece is a rare example of how humans can settle on the wild desert without marring or destroying it in the process (page 86).

★ **The Apache Trail and Vicinity:** Drive through the wild Sonoran Desert east of Phoenix, passing old mining towns, Indigenous ruins, Saguaro-lined lakes, and plunging canyons (page 100).

★ **Casa Grande Ruins National Monument:** Explore the mysterious remains of a crumbling Hohokam great house (page 102).

Greater Phoenix

(303)

Lake Bonita

Beardsley Canal

N LAKE PLEASANT RD

Deadman Wash

To Lake Pleasant Regional Park

SEE "SCOTTSDALE AND VICINITY" MAP

Apache Wash

Cave Creek

(17)

New River

Aqua Fria R.

Skunk Creek

Scatter Wash

Thunderbird Park

W UNION HILLS DR

N 51ST AVE
N 43RD AVE
N 35TH AVE

(101)

N 19TH AVE
N 7TH AVE
N 7TH ST

E UNION HILLS DR

(60)

N 99TH AVE

(101)

W BELL RD

W GREENWAY RD

(17)

Lookout Mountain Preserve

Luke Air Force Base

LITCHFIELD RD
N DYSART RD
N EL MIRAGE RD

N 111TH AVE
N 107TH AVE
N 103RD AVE
N 99TH AVE

Arizona Canal

W THUNDERBIRD RD

W CACTUS RD

W PEORIA AVE

★ SAHUARO RANCH

W OLIVE AVE

Cave Creek

(51)

Phoenix Mountains Preserve

Luke Air Force Base

(101)

N 91ST AVE

N 83RD AVE
N 75TH AVE

W NORTHERN AVE

CUFF ▼ W GLENDALE AVE

(60)

N 67TH AVE

Grand Canal

Aqua Fria R.

N 59TH AVE

N 51ST AVE

W BETHANY HOME RD

W CAMELBACK RD

N 43RD AVE

W INDIAN SCHOOL RD

SEE "CENTRAL PHOENIX" MAP

N 32ND ST

HEARD MUSEUM ★

N 36TH AVE

W THOMAS RD

PHOENIX ART MUSEUM ★

W McDOWELL RD

(10)

W VAN BUREN ST

E MONROE ST

E BUCKEYE RD

N 27TH AVE

SEE "PHOENIX" MAP

(10)

PHOENIX-GOODYEAR AIRPORT ✈

W LOWER BUCKEYE RD

(60)

(17)

PHOENIX SKY HARBOR INTERNATIONAL AIRPORT ✈

(60)

W BROADWAY RD

Salt River

W SOUTHERN AVE

SEE "SOUTH VALLEY" MAP

Western Canal

Gila River

W BASELINE RD

S 75TH AVE

Gila River

W ESTRELLA DR

0   2.5 mi

0   2.5 km

© MOON.COM

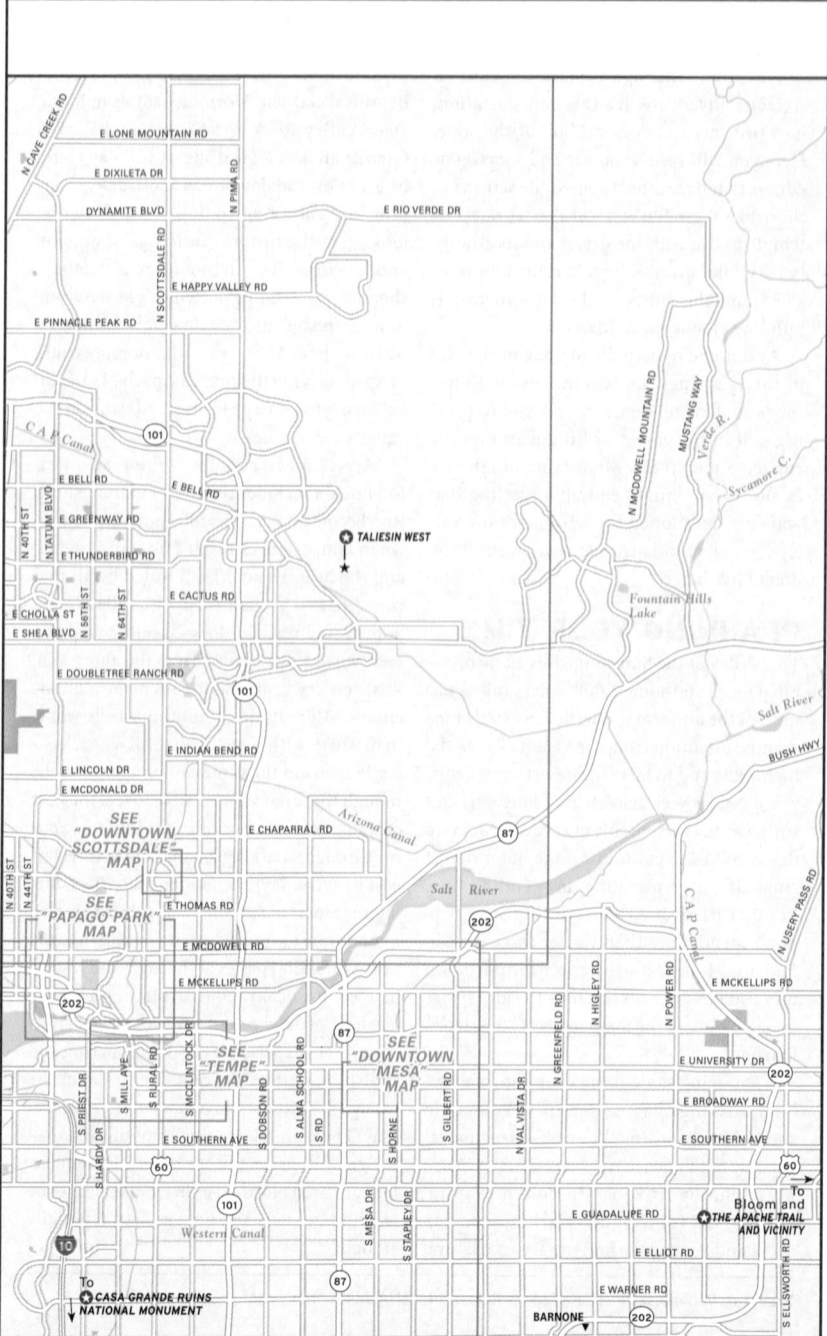

boasts world-class hotels, restaurants, museums, theaters, sports, and shopping.

Phoenix is the logical place to begin an Arizona adventure; it's the transportation, government, and cultural hub of the state. Here you will see the hubris and shortsightedness that have often typified the settling of the urban West. But you will also see novel attempts to live with the desert and its strange beauty, like Frank Lloyd Wright's Taliesin West and the ruins of the ancient canal-building Hohokam civilization.

And if you're here during one of the two or three "springs" that soothe the long summer's violent tendencies, and you're playing golf in December or hiking around the rugged Superstition Mountains in January in shorts, you might end up forgetting that you ever questioned the wisdom of the valley's founders and instead ask yourself, "Why don't I live here?"

PLANNING YOUR TIME

The Valley of the Sun comprises 10 incorporated cities and some 2,000 square miles, but most of the uniform sprawl deserves only pinpointed attention from the visitor. To see the highlights and to taste the desert-city thrills, you'll need a week at least, but a long weekend suffices for a memorable once-over. An extra day could be spent touring the outer desert rings. If you're planning on spending time in other parts of Arizona during your trip, don't spend more than two or three days in Phoenix. It is best used as a transportation hub and jumping-off station—the ideal place to begin but not the main focus of an Arizona journey.

That being said, going deep into the valley's offerings has its rewards. You could spend a week touring the area's museums, especially the Phoenix Art Museum, the Heard Museum, the Arizona Museum of Natural History, the contemporary art museums in Mesa and Scottsdale, and the art and natural history museums at Arizona State University. You could spend a full day or two checking out the excellent Phoenix Zoo, Phoenix Botanical Garden, Mormon Temple in Mesa, Deer Valley Rock Art Center, and Pueblo Grande archaeological site. A full day could be given over to downtown Scottsdale, shopping and eating, or to downtown Phoenix, looking at the historic buildings, shopping, and lunching. An afternoon spent strolling, shopping, and dining on Tempe's Mill Avenue or in Glendale's historic downtown is never a waste of time. Another full day or more could be spent driving the rugged Apache Trail and exploring the dusty old mining towns on the valley's outer edges.

May-October, about half the year, a visit to Phoenix includes the risk of extreme heat. Risk becomes ridiculous folly June-September, when temperatures reach 110°F and higher, and the heat-island effect created by all that concrete and asphalt turns the valley into a monstrous oven that doesn't really cool down even when the moon replaces the angry sun. It is, yes, dry heat, and it does make a difference—90°F with high humidity feels worse than 110°F with none at all. Still, experiencing Phoenix in the summer is uncomfortable, though these days it's possible to feel the heat only on rare occasions: say, walking from your car through a parking lot and into a store. It is best to avoid daytime outdoor activities during the worst of summer, but summer is also a good time to find a deal. If you can take the heat, you'll find prices at the high-end resorts in town drastically reduced, offering a chance for those of us who aren't movie stars and millionaires to experience a little pampering and stylish lounging. The best days to be in the valley are October-November and February-May. These are the "spring" months, when all is right and perfect in the desert. December-January aren't too bad either, but expect to be wearing sweaters and light jackets, especially at night.

Previous: Phoenix skyline; Casa Grande Ruins National Monument; Heard Museum entrance.

ORIENTATION

Phoenix sits at the center of a large basin surrounded by rugged mountain ranges: the McDowell Mountains to the northeast, the White Tank Mountains to the west, the Sierra Estrella to the southwest, the Superstition Mountains to the east, and the South Mountains to the south. In the northeastern portion of the metro area, the Phoenix Mountains provide a convenient landmark in an otherwise rather flat and repetitive urban landscape. The mountains surrounding the Salt River Valley are rocky and dry, topped by cactus and creosote; these are much shorter and hotter than the 9,000-foot and higher sky islands of the southern Sonoran region. The Salt River used to run through the whole basin, but the Roosevelt Dam and other factors long ago dried the river.

Although there are many incorporated towns across the basin, for the purposes of the traveler, the valley can be conveniently sliced into a few general regions that make the megalopolis easier to digest. These include **Downtown and Central Phoenix**, where you'll find many of the valley's sights and stops, bounded roughly by 7th Street on the east and 7th Avenue on the west, and by I-17 on the south and Camelback Road on the north; the **east valley**, which includes **Tempe, Arizona State University,** and **Mesa; Scottsdale** and the **north valley,** which includes Scottsdale, just to the northeast of central Phoenix, and the small resort towns of Carefree and Cave Creek; and the **west valley,** which includes Glendale. Even longtime residents rarely distinguish between the towns when they're deciding which restaurant or shopping center to patronize, though it is true that if you live in Tempe or Scottsdale, you're not often found in Glendale. Unless you're paying close attention, you won't notice right away that you've left one city and entered another. The area's many freeways make getting around fairly easy, though you should expect traffic jams everywhere during the rush hours, roughly 6am-10am and 4pm-7pm on weekdays.

I-10 runs east-west through the center of the valley and then turns south along the eastern flank of central Phoenix, skirting Sky Harbor International Airport and heading southeast to Tucson and beyond. I-17 runs east-west from its interchange with I-10 near 7th Street in the east, and then, around 7th Avenue in the west, it moves north through the northwest valley all the way to Flagstaff. The Loop 202 freeway runs mostly east-west through the east valley, continuing east from where the I-10 turns south, and Loop 101 runs north-south and east-west in a loop around the northern, western, and eastern edges of the city.

Sights

DOWNTOWN AND CENTRAL

Downtown Phoenix, the center of the sprawling desert megacity, is roughly bounded by 7th Street on the east, 7th Avenue on the west, Fillmore Street on the north, and Jackson Street on the south. It's the historic heart of the city where you'll find many of the area's best museums, restaurants, theaters, sports arenas, shops, hotels, and parks.

The whole downtown area comes alive 6pm-10pm or later every month during the **First and Third Friday Art Walks.** This is the time to see downtown at its most vibrant and creative, as more than 100 galleries and art spaces throw open their doors and put on shows and special performances, and thousands of Phoenicians mingle in the streets of up-and-coming neighborhoods. Along Roosevelt Row there's usually a block party, with street performers, live bands, and vendors selling all manner of handmade and one-of-a-kind items. The art walks are self-guided.

Contact the good folks who put on this popular event at **Artlink** (602/256-7539, www.artlinkphoenix.com); maps and other information are available on its website.

Heritage Square

Phoenix was founded by Anglo Americans, most of whom were Victorians through and through, despite their isolation out here in adobe land. With the coming of the railroad in the 1880s, building materials other than mud and rocks became available, and the homes in the valley began to reflect this; suddenly the adobe huts of the early years were replaced by redbrick and lumber homes, some of them as big and ornate as anything in the East. The remains of Phoenix's Victorian past can be seen at this downtown collection of museums and restaurants known as **Heritage Square** (115 N. 6th St., 602/262-5071, http://heritagesquarephx.org), especially through a tour of the **Rosson House** (602/262-5029, http://heritagesquarephx.org, 10am-4pm Fri.-Sat., noon-4pm Sun., $12 adults, free under age 5), a refurbished Victorian showcase built in 1895 at a cost of about $8,000. The tour takes about 1 hour and will likely disabuse you of any lingering notions that what passed for the good life in late-19th-century North America didn't find its way out to the frontier.

Arizona Science Center

Kids and adults alike will enjoy the popular, futuristic-looking silver-winged **Arizona Science Center** (602/716-2000, www.azscience.org, 10:30am-4pm daily, $20 adults, $15 under age 17, planetarium $6 adults, $5 children) in Heritage Square, where you can move a ball with your brain, lie on a bed of nails, and ride a bike across a line rope like a trapeze artist (with a net below, of course). Even teenagers will like this excellent museum, which has a permanent collection of more than 300 hands-on exhibits and a planetarium. There are exhibits on the human body and the brain, solar energy, and the science of flight, plus hands-on displays about gravity and other natural forces.

A few exhibits are somewhat Arizona-specific, but most of the museum is general and geared toward kids. On a weekday during school hours you're liable to run into a rowdy school tour group. There's also an on-site café that's a bit pricey but offers sandwiches and snacks without a lot of grease. Several of the center's more exciting attractions cost extra.

★ Heard Museum

If you're planning on spending any time in Arizona's other regions, a stop at the **Heard Museum** (2301 N. Central Ave., 602/252-8848, www.heard.org, 10am-4pm Tues.-Sun., $17 adults, $9 ages 6-12) will enhance your trip. This essential Arizona museum provides a rich perspective on the cultures, religions, and histories of the state's Indigenous people.

The museum was the 1929 brainchild of one of the valley's most influential couples, Dwight and Maie Heard. Dwight Heard was the onetime publisher of the *Arizona Republican,* now the *Arizona Republic,* the state's largest newspaper both then and now. There was hardly a civic improvement in Phoenix's early-20th-century history that didn't have Dwight's hand in it, including the Roosevelt Dam. It was primarily Maie who developed the museum, however, as Dwight died just before its official opening.

Today the museum has 10 galleries featuring the art, artifacts, and historical narratives of each of the state's tribes. The large display on the Hopi is particularly comprehensive and includes Barry Goldwater's kachina collection. Several galleries feature contemporary art by Native Americans and others. Sculptures dot the grounds while artists demonstrate their methods to onlookers. There are also galleries for kids with hands-on displays about Native American culture, many of them featuring the various ingenious methods Indigenous people developed to live well in an arid country. If you're in the market for Native American art (or if you just like looking at it), especially that produced by Hopi and Navajo artists, don't miss the museum's store, which has a good selection of books as well.

Phoenix

© MOON.COM

SEE "CENTRAL PHOENIX" MAP

To Tradiciones

To La Tolteca

WELCOME DINER

MCDOWELL RD

N 11TH ST
N 10TH ST
N 9TH ST
N 7TH ST
N 5TH ST
N 2ND ST
N 1ST ST
N CENTRAL AVE
N 3RD AVE
N 4TH AVE
N 5TH AVE
N 6TH AVE

E VAN BUREN

S 7TH ST
S 7TH ST
LINCOLN ST
BUCHANAN ST
JACKSON ST
JEFFERSON ST

MRS. WHITE'S GOLDEN RULE CAFE

SEE DETAIL

Heritage and Science Park

Chase Field

WILLETTA ST
MORELAND ST
PORTLAND ST

TAMMIE COE CAKES
OBON
THE LOST LEAF
ROOSEVELT ROW
ROOSEVELT
GARFIELD
ROOSEVELT TAVERN

PHOENIX ART MUSEUM

BURTON BARR CENTRAL LIBRARY

FOUNDRE PHOENIX

Japanese Friendship Garden

W PORTLAND ST

FAIR TRADE CAFE

Arizona Center

DISTRICT AMERICAN KITCHEN & WINE BAR

3RD
FILLMORE ST
MONROE ST
WASHINGTON

PHOENIX SYMPHONY HALL

SHERATON

THE CHURCHILL
MATT'S BIG BREAKFAST
WESTWARD HO
FAIR TRADE CAFE
2ND ST
1ST ST

WYNDHAM

HERBERGER THEATER

HANNEY'S

Civic Space Park

TURF RESTAURANT
AMSTERDAM
PHOENIX PUBLIC MARKET
N 1ST AVE

MCKINLEY ST

LOLA COFFEE

CIBO

N 3RD AVE
N 5TH AVE

BUDGET LODGE

AMERICA'S BEST VALUE INN

N 6TH AVE

LUHRS TOWER

Patriot's Square

HOTEL SAN CARLOS

ORPHEUM THEATRE

WELLS FARGO HISTORY MUSEUM

HISTORIC CITY HALL

S CENTRAL AVE
S 1ST AVE
S 3RD AVE

THE DUCE

FIRST PRESBYTERIAN CHURCH

DODGE THEATRE

Sandra Day O'Connor Courthouse

7TH AVE

AZTECA

N 9TH AVE
N 11TH AVE

University Park

PAPAGO FWY
W LATHAM ST
W PORTLAND ST
ROOSEVELT ST
GRAND AVE

N 13TH AVE

LYNWOOD ST
WILLETTA ST
CULVER ST
W MORELAND ST

8TH AVE
MORELAND ST

S 9TH AVE
ADAMS ST
W WASHINGTON ST
S 11TH AVE

Library Park

E VAN BUREN ST
W BUREN ST

N 15TH AVE
W 16TH AVE
W 17TH AVE
N 19TH AVE

FILLMORE ST
POLK ST

S 15TH AVE
S 17TH AVE

Bolin Memorial Park

ARIZONA CAPITOL MUSEUM & WESLEY BOLIN MEMORIAL PLAZA

W JEFFERSON ST
W MADISON ST
S LINCOLN ST

0   400 yds
0   400 m

ST. MARY'S BASILICA

ROSSON HOUSE
CHILDREN'S MUSEUM OF PHOENIX
NOBUO

PHOENIX MUSEUM OF HISTORY

ARIZONA DOLL & TOY MUSEUM
PIZZERIA BIANCO
BAR BIANCO
ARIZONA SCIENCE CENTER

Heritage and Science Park

E MONROE ST
N 5TH ST
N 7TH ST
WASHINGTON ST

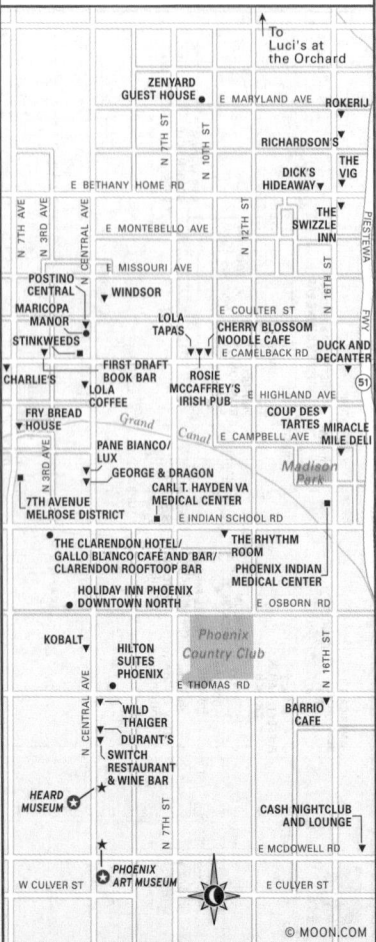

Central Phoenix

To Luci's at the Orchard

ZENYARD GUEST HOUSE
E MARYLAND AVE
ROKERIJ
N 7TH ST
N 10TH ST
RICHARDSON'S
DICK'S HIDEAWAY
THE VIG
E BETHANY HOME RD
THE SWIZZLE INN
N 7TH AVE
N 3RD AVE
CENTRAL AVE
E MONTEBELLO AVE
N 12TH ST
PIESTEWA FWY
E MISSOURI AVE
N 16TH ST
POSTINO CENTRAL
WINDSOR
E COULTER ST
MARICOPA MANOR
LOLA TAPAS
CHERRY BLOSSOM NOODLE CAFE
DUCK AND DECANTER
STINKWEEDS
E CAMELBACK RD
FIRST DRAFT BOOK BAR
ROSIE MCCAFFREY'S IRISH PUB
E HIGHLAND AVE
51
CHARLIE'S
LOLA COFFEE
FRY BREAD HOUSE
Grand
Canal
COUP DES TARTES
MIRACLE MILE DELI
E CAMPBELL AVE
PANE BIANCO/ LUX
Madison Park
GEORGE & DRAGON
CARL T. HAYDEN VA MEDICAL CENTER
N 3RD AVE
7TH AVENUE MELROSE DISTRICT
E INDIAN SCHOOL RD
THE CLARENDON HOTEL/ GALLO BLANCO CAFÉ AND BAR/ CLARENDON ROOFTOOP BAR
THE RHYTHM ROOM
HOLIDAY INN PHOENIX DOWNTOWN NORTH
PHOENIX INDIAN MEDICAL CENTER
E OSBORN RD
KOBALT
HILTON SUITES PHOENIX
Phoenix Country Club
N 16TH ST
N CENTRAL AVE
E THOMAS RD
WILD THAIGER
BARRIO CAFE
DURANT'S
SWITCH RESTAURANT & WINE BAR
HEARD MUSEUM
N 7TH ST
CASH NIGHTCLUB AND LOUNGE
E MCDOWELL RD
W CULVER ST
PHOENIX ART MUSEUM
E CULVER ST

© MOON.COM

The Courtyard Café (602/251-0204, 11am-3pm daily, $10-20), in the museum's enchanting shady courtyard, serves appetizing Southwestern-tinged salads, sandwiches, and soups, plus coffee, beer, and wine.

★ Phoenix Art Museum

The state's largest and best art museum and one of the better collections in the Southwest, the **Phoenix Art Museum** (1625 N. Central Ave., 602/257-1222, www.phxart.org,

10am-7pm Wed., 10am-5pm Thurs.-Sun., $23 adults, $5 ages 6-17, prices vary with the number of open galleries) is the high-water mark of the valley's sometimes rather shallow cultural stream. Here you will find exactly what you'd expect from an art museum in the West as well as much that will likely surprise you.

What you'd expect is an excellent collection of Western American art; the museum has that very definitely and is home to the Cowboy Artists of America annual show and sale. There are important and representative works by Eanger Irving Couse, whose arresting *The Captive* should not be missed, as well as Fredric Remington and other well-known Western artists. One particular highlight is an otherworldly Arizona landscape by the fantasist illustrator Maxfield Parrish, who manages to capture that strange, fantastical vibe the desert sometimes gives off. There's also a worthy collection of Latin American art, featuring paintings by Frida Kahlo, Rufino Tamayo, and others, along with Spanish-era art and religious items. The eclectic modern and contemporary galleries manage to be challenging without becoming ridiculous, and there are interesting displays on fashion and Asian art. The miniatures gallery should not be overlooked, with its little model-room displays on interior design through the ages. Plan on spending several hours or even half a day here.

After you've spent time in the galleries, you can grab a bite or a drink at the museum's restaurant, **Palette** (11am-8pm Wed., 11am-3:30pm Thurs.-Sat., 11am-3:30pm Sun., $15-20), which serves sandwiches, salads, and desserts made with local organically grown ingredients as well as a fine selection of Arizona-made beer and wine. The gift shop sells a wide selection of prints, books, and the usual museum-store fare. Art lovers would do well to check the museum's website before traveling, as several large special exhibitions are put on every year.

1: Rosson House in Heritage Square **2:** close-up of *Intertribal Greeting* sculpture by Doug Hyde in the Heard Museum

1

2

Arizona Capitol Museum and Wesley Bolin Memorial Plaza

A neoclassical copper-domed monument to power on the western edge of downtown, the Arizona Capitol, built in 1901, is no longer the center of day-to-day legislative work here at the bustling state capitol complex. It's now the **Arizona Capitol Museum** (1700 W. Washington St., 602/926-3620, 9am-4pm Mon.-Fri., 10am-2pm Sat. Sept.-May, free), with displays on the state's political history, its flora and fauna, its symbols and industries. Definitely worth seeing are the large paintings with heroic and mythical depictions of Arizona's past, painted by famous local artist Lon Megargee in 1913-1914 to celebrate statehood, and a few exhibits of historic furniture and other items from the territorial days. Just east of the capitol is a large plaza crowded with monuments to various heroes of Arizona and U.S. history, including a large equestrian statue of Padre Kino and a black-wall memorial to the state's Vietnam War veterans. This is a good place for a springtime walk, but it isn't worth visiting in the summer unless you have a particular interest in Arizona history. If you do, neither of these sights should be missed.

Hall of Flame Fire Museum

The **Hall of Flame Fire Museum** (6101 E. Van Buren St., 602/275-3473, www. hallofflame.org, 10am-6pm Tues.-Sat., $15 adults, $13 ages 6-17, $9 ages 3-5) has an engaging collection of relics from the history of firefighting. The almost one-acre museum near Papago Park includes the **National Firefighting Hall of Heroes,** a tribute to firefighters killed in the line of duty, and a display on the history of wildland firefighting, a particularly important occupation in the flame-prone forests of Arizona.

Burton Barr Library

Take a quick ride up through the "Crystal Canyon," the five-story glass atrium that divides this star of Phoenix's underrated architecture scene, to the fifth floor's **Great Reading Room** for an expansive view of the Valley of the Sun that nearly beats any vista you'd gain by hiking into the desert mountains. Along the way, make sure to check out the art on the walls—it's an amazing collection, with paintings by some of the Southwest's most famous artists.

Architect Will Bruder designed Phoenix's main library branch, the **Burton Barr Library** (1221 N. Central Ave., 602/262-4636, www.phxlib.org, 9am-5pm Mon., 1pm-5pm Tues.-Thurs., 9am-9pm Fri.-Sat., free), to suggest one of the great sandstone buttes of Monument Valley on the Navajo Reservation. Step in around noon on June 21, the summer solstice, when round skylights with special lenses project illusory flames; people usually gather to watch the event. The 43,000-square-foot Great Reading Room is one of the nation's largest, and it offers workstations and Wi-Fi. Throughout this beloved local landmark, the sleek, modern, modular furnishings and exposed wires and cables create a futuristic-utilitarian atmosphere that clashes evocatively with those bookshelves full of ancient stories—all of it washed in filtered desert light. A second-floor room holds the library's **Arizona Collection,** a place to get lost in the fascinating history of the Grand Canyon State. The ground floor holds the **Central Gallery,** a space featuring exhibits by mostly local artists, and nearby there's a small store selling used and discarded books at very fair prices.

Civic Space Park

This expanse of green space downtown, hovered over by the unique net-sculpture *Her Secret Is Patience,* by artist Janet Echelman, is hopefully an example of the direction urban design in the desert is headed. Opened in 2009, the **Civic Space Park** (424 N. Central Ave., 602/262-4734, 5am-11pm daily), right next to the light-rail station on Central Avenue, has solar panels, still-developing shade trees, and pervious concrete that captures rain runoff.

1: Arizona Capitol Museum **2:** fountain in downtown Phoenix **3:** Burton Barr Library **4:** Children's Museum of Phoenix

The valley's rainstorms are often short and violent, especially during the summer monsoon rainy season. With all the paved surfaces that have replaced the thirsty desert floor, not much of the rushing rainwater soaks into the ground. Instead, it runs off quickly into the gutters and is wasted. The pavers and pervious concrete here allow more water to seep in, making the field of cool and inviting green grass a gift for outdoor loungers rather than a waste of precious resources. Solar panels on the roofs of several shade structures provide the electricity for ghostly blue lights that illuminate Echelman's sculpture, inspired by the life-giving clouds that so infrequently visit the valley's wide skies, and suspended by cables 38 feet above the ground. A kid-entrancing **Splash Pad** (daily Memorial Day weekend-Oct. 1) also lights up with purplish hues after the sun goes down, making nighttime ideal for a visit.

St. Mary's Basilica

St. Mary's Basilica (231 N. 3rd St., 602/354-2100, www.saintmarysbasilica.org, 9am-4pm Mon.-Fri.), the white-stone and red-tile Spanish Revival church downtown, whose tall cross-topped towers have been points on the valley's skyline for nearly a century, is one of several vital sights in Arizona for the religious soul, though at just under 100 years old, it's also one of the youngest (San Xavier del Bac and Mission Tumacacori in Southern Arizona were founded in the 1600s). The current building, which replaced an older church on the same spot, held its first mass in 1915. The soaring interior, lined and lit by dozens of stained-glass windows (the largest collection in the state), should be seen by anyone interested in religious architecture. Before visiting Arizona in 1987, Pope John Paul II, who drew thousands of Catholics from the state's rural hinterlands and across the valley to a huge mass at Sun Devil Stadium, made St. Mary's a "minor basilica" (an important church with special ceremonial rights). On the east side of the building the

Via Assisi Gift Shop (10am-3pm Thurs.-Fri., 10am-6:30pm Sat., 9am-1pm Sun.) sells Catholic gifts.

Children's Museum of Phoenix

Arizona's children's museums have a knack for reusing grand old buildings that have been tossed aside by the renewal-mad developers of the urban Southwest. Tucson's small museum for kids took over a stately old Carnegie library, while the larger **Children's Museum of Phoenix** (215 N. 7th St., 602/253-0501, www.childrensmuseumofphoenix.org, 9am-4pm daily, $16 over age 1) is housed in the **Historic Monroe School Building,** designed in 1913 by noted California architect Norman Marsh. Half the fun of taking kids to these hands-on play centers is experiencing the soul of a beautiful old space. Of course, that's not what the kids will say. They'll enjoy scrambling up and all over the 37-foot-high pile of steel, tubes, planks, and passageways called **The Climber,** serving plastic food in the make-believe restaurant, pretending to be a firefighter, doing a shift feeding and changing lifelike dolls in the nursery, or throwing paint in imitation of abstract expressionist master and Monroe Elementary School alumnus Jackson Pollock. Don't expect to make a quick visit. The hands-on, interactive, and deceptively educational activities here will appeal to kids under 10.

Japanese Friendship Garden

A perfect slice of green Japan in the middle of downtown Phoenix, the **Japanese Friendship Garden** (1125 N. 3rd Ave., 602/256-3204, www.japanesefriendshipgarden.org, 10am-4pm Tues.-Sun. Oct.-May, $10 adults, free under age 7) celebrates the valley's relationship with Himeji, Japan, Phoenix's sister city, with a sculpted and manicured "strolling garden" with a trickling creek, rushing waterfall, and crowded koi pond. Called Ro Ho En in Japanese, the 3.5-acre refuge holds four different vegetation zones and more than 50 different kinds of plants that

The Lost Hohokam Culture

The Sonoran Desert is neither a wasteland of shifting dunes nor a place to make it through at all costs but never to stop and settle. While such may be the popular conception of a desert, first-time visitors to Central and Southern Arizona are often surprised to see so much vegetation, so much diversity, and so much evidence of eons of human habitation.

That's not to say it has always been easy to live here; prior to the damming of the Southwest's rivers, a drought or a flood could wipe out a lifetime's worth of progress, and you never really knew with any confidence if the annual rains would come too heavy, too light, or not at all. There are usually two rainy seasons in the Sonoran Desert: In midsummer the Mexican Monsoon sends moisture north every late afternoon, and in winter the rains come again, hopefully. The twice-a-year rains, though scant compared to nearly every other place (the whole 100,000-square-mile desert gets less than 15 inches per year), allow for myriad dryland-adapted plants and animals to thrive.

People too have thrived here for thousands of years, taking advantage of the once-perennial desert rivers like the Gila, the Salt, the Santa Cruz, and the San Pedro. Because of damming, overuse, and other factors, none of these waterways is much of a river anymore, but each of them long ago provided a healthy, if unpredictable, lifeline for the complex culture of the Hohokam, desert farmers who lived in the Sonoran river valleys from the beginning of the common era (AD 1) to about 1450. They disappeared from the valleys about 100 years before the Spanish arrived, leaving behind great mud ruins and more than 1,000 miles of irrigation canals built with stone and wooden tools.

The Hohokam culture went through several stages before reaching its golden age around 1150-1450, also called the classic period. During this time, the tribe's irrigation farming of the Salt River Valley produced a surplus of maize, beans, squash, and cotton, and the culture grew more complex, the buildings bigger, and the population denser. Ball courts like those found in Mesoamerica were built in Hohokam villages, and pottery became more beautiful and less strictly utilitarian. At the culture's high point, there were as many as 40,000 Hohokam people living in the valley, irrigating 100,000 acres of farmland using canals that were still intact and usable when Anglos arrived in the 19th century. Evidence of this golden age can be seen at ruins like Pueblo Grande in Phoenix and Casa Grande between Phoenix and Tucson.

Around 1450, it all fell apart. This is roughly the time the Ancestral Puebloan cultures of the Four Corners region also ended abruptly, and the theories about both collapses are similar, though by no means universally accepted. The culprits include soil salinization, disease, warfare, flood, drought, climate change, internal unrest, overpopulation, and various combinations thereof. The O'odham cultures, formerly called the Pima and Papago Indians, tell stories about how their ancestors overthrew the Hohokam cities along the Salt River because they had grown arrogant. Many archaeologists believe that the Hohokam were the ancient forebears of today's Sonoran Desert tribes, and oral tradition among the Hopi of northeastern Arizona links that culture to the Hohokam as well.

gradually rise into a "mountain zone" above a large pond topped with water lily beds. A creek trickles down from the mountains and spills into the pond over a 12-foot waterfall. It's an enchanting place for a stroll on a warm breezy fall day in the desert (the garden closes for the torrid summer months). Easy paved paths snake around the deceptively secluded property, past sculpted trees, hanging lanterns, and bamboo fences, and over stone footbridges to the pond, which swarms with large multicolored koi. The garden also has a traditional Japanese tea garden and an elegant teahouse, where once a month you can vie for a seat at a traditional **Japanese Tea Ceremony** (www.japanesefriendshipgarden.org/tea, $65 pp). It's essential to call ahead for a reservation: The garden hosts just four ceremonies each time, with only five guests per ceremony.

Pueblo Grande Museum and Archaeological Park

The valley's ubiquitous construction cranes can usually be seen at work from the smooth dirt mound tops of the ancient Hohokam ruins at **Pueblo Grande Museum and Archaeological Park** (4619 E. Washington St., 602/495-0900, www.pueblogrande.org, 9am-4:45pm Tues.-Sat., $6 adults, $3 under age 17), a canal-side city that reached the peak of its power and population just before it was abandoned around 1450. You'll also see the remains of one of the hundreds of canals the Hohokam dug through the valley to harness the Salt River—canals that formed the basis for modern agricultural pursuits as well. A short trail takes you to various points around the main ruins, which looks like a well-worked mound of dirt. Particularly interesting is the collection of Hohokam model homes along the trail, built according to what archaeologists think domestic structures may have looked like in the valley's ancient past. The contrast with today's tract homes and McMansions is striking, to say the least. Though not as large as the spectacular Casa Grande to the east, Pueblo Grande, the rare ruins of a city center, is recommended to anyone interested in the Hohokam and to learn how past cultures have tried to live with the desert rather than against it. A small informative museum has displays on who the Hohokam were, how they developed, and where they went.

Encanto Park

A lush duck-pond park east of the city center, **Encanto Park** (2605 N. 15th Ave., 602/261-8991, 5:30am-11pm daily) was once the place to go on a hot Phoenix afternoon, and it's still a peaceful, green, trickling-water oasis within the heat-island sprawl. It borders one of the valley's most tourable residential neighborhoods, the **Encanto-Palmcroft Historic District.** With its winding manicured streets, each home more elegant and each lawn better landscaped than the next, this was Phoenix's first and best garden-style suburb, planned and built in the 1920s by Dwight Heard. It's fun to drive slowly through the neighborhood to see the style and grace that upper-middle-class merchants and city leaders once brought to valley living. The Spanish Colonial Revival and Monterrey Revival homes and the tall palms lining many of the streets—nonnative to Arizona—give the whole neighborhood a dreamy pre-World War II California feel. Over at the park, kids will enjoy the old-school county fair-style rides at **Enchanted Island Amusement Park** (602/254-1200, www.enchantedisland.com, $5 per ride, $21.75 all-day pass, $5 Splash Zone water feature); check the website for hours, as they change often.

Wrigley Mansion

A mere "winter cottage" to William Wrigley Jr., of the chewing-gum Wrigleys, the shining-white 16,000-square-foot **Wrigley Mansion** (2501 E. Telawa Trail, 602/955-4079, www.wrigleymansion.com), perched on a hill overlooking central Phoenix, is still one of the valley's most beloved reminders of the pre-World War II cityscape. Wrigley, who also owned the Arizona Biltmore resort just down the hill, built the home in 1931 in a kind of California-Spanish Colonial style with a lot of art deco flourishes. Composer and founder of the legendary Village Recording Studio in Los Angeles, George "Geordie" Hormel bought the 24-room palace in the 1990s and, after a costly refurbishing, opened a bar and restaurant inside. The place is a club that offers memberships for a range of prices, following the letter if not the spirit of the zoning laws. Out-of-town guests can choose a $5 one-month trial membership that allows you to have brunch ($54 pp), lunch ($16-46), or dinner ($20-60) at **Geordie's at Wrigley Mansion** (2501 E. Telawa Trail, 602/955-4079, 11am-3pm and 5pm-9pm Tues.-Sat., 10am-2pm Sun.), a fantastic restaurant in the mansion that serves Arizona-bred meat and other locally sourced dishes. It's essential to call ahead for brunch reservations. A lounge and wine bar are also open to members. The most interesting part of a visit to this landmark hilltop, which bicyclists like to climb on weekend mornings, is the one-hour **tour** (10am and 3pm Tues.-Sat., arrive 15 minutes early, summer hours vary, reservations required, $17), which reveals all the details and flourishes that you couldn't otherwise see. They also offer a lunch-tour package.

Tovrea Castle and Carraro Cactus Garden

Perched on a cactus-covered hilltop just west of the I-10 freeway nearing the east valley and resembling a many-tiered cake made of stone, the Phoenix landmark **Tovrea Castle** (5025 E. Van Buren St., 602/256-3221, www.tovreacastletours.com) is mostly seen from the seat of a car as you fly by at 75 miles per hour. It was built in 1928 by San Francisco businessman Alessio Carraro in a typical fit of passion for the desert but soon sold to Della Tovrea. The unique home was Tovrea's winter getaway while she lived in Prescott with her second husband, a newspaper publisher, and she used it as her full-time residence after he died until her own death in 1969. The city of Phoenix purchased the large cactus garden, the home, and some adjacent property in the 1990s and led a multimillion-dollar effort to renovate the property. It has since become very popular; to see the home you must enter a lottery to purchase a tour ticket (1.5 hours, $22).

Phoenix Zoo

The excellent **Phoenix Zoo** (455 N. Galvin Pkwy., 602/273-1341, www.phoenixzoo.org, 7am-2pm daily June-Aug., 9am-5pm daily Sept.-Oct., 9am-4pm daily Nov.-Jan. 14, 9am-5pm daily Jan. 15-May, $30 adults, $20 ages 3-13) in Papago Park was called the "Maytag Zoo" when it first opened in 1962 in honor of its main booster, Robert Maytag, a scion of the appliance family. Today it's the nation's largest privately owned nonprofit zoo, hosting more visitors every year than any other valley attraction. You'll see all the usual suspects, from the mountain lions and bighorn sheep that stalk Arizona's wildlands to the rare Arabian oryx, which the zoo is credited with saving from near extinction. As you walk along three paved trails through the zoo's clean lush grounds, you'll commune with lions, elephants, camels, giraffes, and too many birds to name. You can catch a ride on a camel, walk through the frenetic Monkey Village, and stare for as long as you want at the invariably sleepy big cats. A newer exhibit lets you get up close and personal (sort of) with stingrays and even sharks. Don't miss Baboon Kingdom, where you can watch those exceedingly humanlike creatures interact (often hilariously), and be sure to walk the Arizona Trail, where you'll witness what you're missing out in the desert. Plan on spending at least half of the day.

Desert Botanical Garden

A 50-acre garden in Papago Park, the **Desert Botanical Garden** (1201 N. Galvin Pkwy., 480/941-1225, www.dbg.org, 7am-8pm daily, $15-30 adults, $10-14 ages 3-17) is the best place to go to learn about the desert's unique flora—other than the wild desert itself, of course. Actually, the garden might be even better than the raw desert—you aren't risking your life by coming here in the summer, and there are signs everywhere explaining what each bush and thorn-heavy succulent is called and why. There are several special exhibitions each year, including art installations by visiting artists. You can eat at the excellent **Gertrude's** (480/719-8600, www.gertrudesrestaurant.net, 10:30am-8pm Mon.-Fri., 8am-8pm Sat.-Sun., $10-18), or purchase a strange alien cactus for yourself. If you have any interest in the desert Southwest's unique and always threatened plantlife, spend a few hours strolling the garden's easy pathways. Visiting in the summer can be trying, but it's not completely out of the question, as all that plantlife gives off a cooling vibe and a shady feeling, even when the sun is incessant.

1
2
3
4

TEMPE AND THE EAST VALLEY

Tempe, a college town along the banks of the Salt River, is home to **Arizona State University,** the state's largest and one of the largest public land-grant schools in the Southwest. The east valley includes **Mesa,** a seemingly unending sprawl east of Tempe that is the third-largest city in Arizona and the part-time home to thousands of snowbirds and RV parks. Mesa was founded in the late 19th century by Mormon pioneers from Utah and has the state's largest Latter-day Saints temple.

Arizona Sealife Aquarium

The colorful family-oriented **Arizona Sealife Aquarium** (5000 Arizona Mills Circle, Tempe, 480/478-7600, www.visitsealife.com, 10am-7:30pm Mon.-Sat., 10am-6pm Sun., $25 adults, $20 ages 3-12) at Tempe's Arizona Mills mall is pricey for what it is. If you don't have kids with you, it's not worth the admission. That being said, kids up to about age 12 will likely enjoy this innovative, educational, and eye-catching attraction. The 26,000-square-foot space features a series of galleries with aquariums in different shapes and sizes holding more than 5,000 creatures of the sea, including eerie black rays, sharp-toothed sharks, and goofy sea horses. There's a tidal pool display that allows kids to touch a few creatures, and several super-fun observation bubbles get them up close and surrounded on all sides by sealife. At the end of the trail, after you've passed through each gallery and looked into all 30 tanks, there's a big indoor climbing-and-sliding apparatus that will likely keep you on-site for another hour or so.

Arizona Heritage Center at Papago Park

So much of what travelers and historical re-enactors find most interesting about Arizona history—cowboys, placer miners, and improbable gunfights in the streets—happened before the dawn of the 20th century. For many people the state's history stops at the O. K. Corral. But many of the more peculiar events that have occurred in the last state among the Lower 48 happened in the 1900s, not the 1800s. The **Arizona Heritage Center at Papago Park** (1300 N. College Ave., 480/929-9499, www.arizonahistoricalsociety. org, 10am-2pm Tues.-Sat., $12 adults, $8 ages 7-17, free under age 7, 2-for-1 admission 1st Tues. of each month) explains the state's 20th-century urban history, including how the Valley of the Sun became one of the largest cities in the country, and the state's essential role during World War II. Among displays covering Arizona's singular culture, the one on the memorable local cartoon show hosts Wallace and Ladmo will have longtime Arizonans chuckling with recognition. Don't miss the exhibit on the mass escape of German prisoners of war from nearby Camp Papago Park: In December 1944, after digging a 176-foot tunnel in the hard desert soil, 25 German POWs got away, but the cruel desert expanses proved to be too much for most of them.

Tempe Town Lake

Tempe Town Lake (620 N. Mill Ave., 480/350-8625, www.tempe.gov/lake, free), a large city-center waterway just off Tempe's main street, represents an ambitious long-term attempt to bring back a bit of the Salt River. It's a pleasant place to stroll, jog, bike, pedal-boat, and kayak, or you can lounge around on the grass at **Tempe Beach Park,** where there's always something going on. Rent a pedal boat or a kayak, or take an electric-boat cruise on the lake. Kids can put on their swimsuits and dash around the cool water features at **Splash Playground** (10am-7pm daily, free), where they'll also learn about water and why it's so important in the desert. At the western edge of the park, near the inflatable dam that holds the lake together, check out the **Tempe Center for the Arts** (700 W. Rio Salado Pkwy., 480/350-2822,

---

1: Desert Botanical Garden 2: Tovrea Castle and Carraro Cactus Garden 3: kayakers paddling across Tempe Town Lake 4: Phoenix Zoo

Tempe

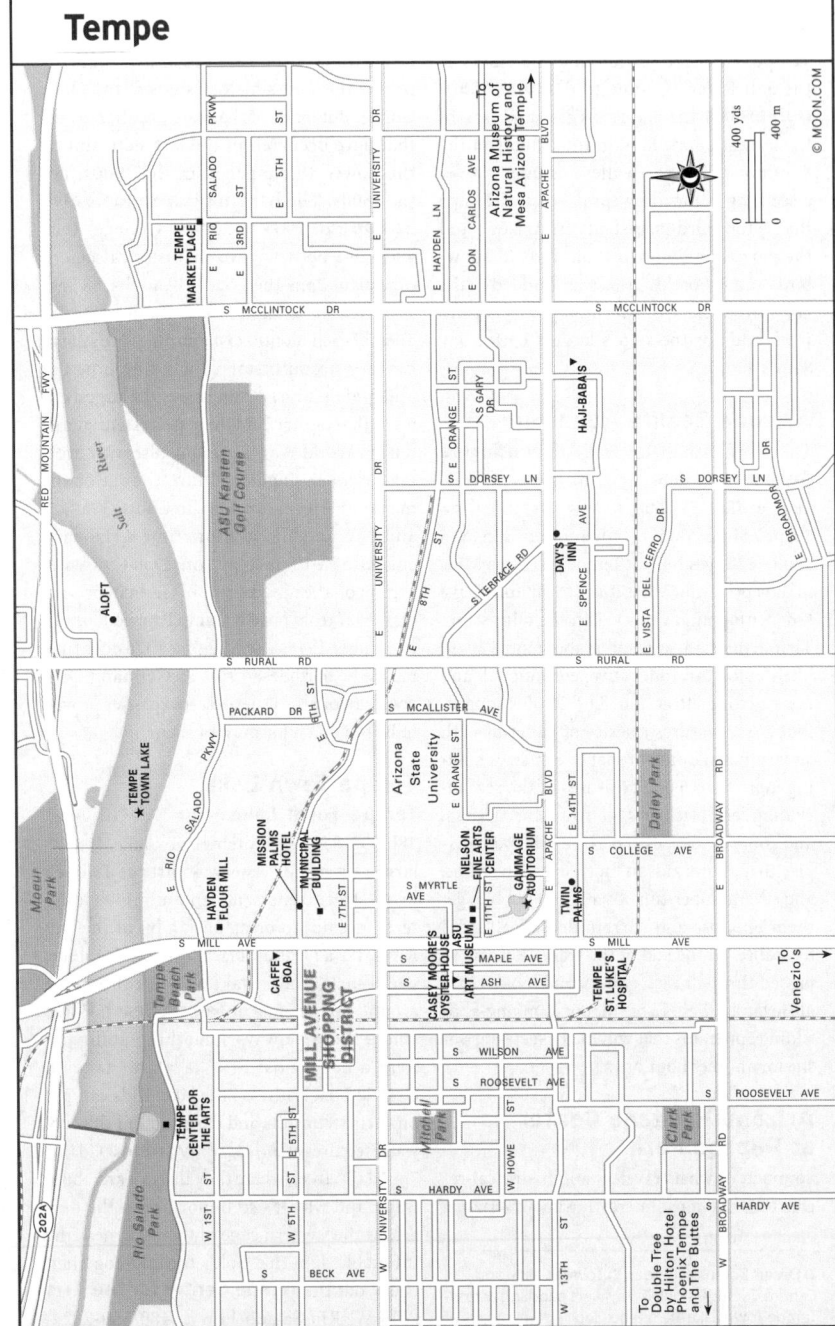

© MOON.COM

To Arizona Museum of Natural History and Mesa Arizona Temple

Salt River

RED MOUNTAIN FWY

ASU Karsten Golf Course

TEMPE MARKETPLACE

ALOFT

HAJI-BABA'S

DAY'S INN

Moeur Park

TEMPE TOWN LAKE

Arizona State University

MISSION PALMS HOTEL

HAYDEN FLOUR MILL

MUNICIPAL BUILDING

NELSON FINE ARTS CENTER

GAMMAGE AUDITORIUM

Daley Park

TWIN PALMS

CAFFE BOA

Tempe Beach Park

MILL AVENUE SHOPPING DISTRICT

CASEY MOORE'S OYSTER HOUSE

ASU ART MUSEUM

TEMPE ST. LUKE'S HOSPITAL

To Venezio's

TEMPE CENTER FOR THE ARTS

Mitchell Park

Clark Park

Rio Salado Park

To Double Tree by Hilton Hotel Phoenix Tempe and The Buttes

0   400 yds
0   400 m

www.tempe.gov), which hosts Broadway-style shows, local theater, music, and dance performances. The Tempe Center for the Arts also has an excellent art gallery, **The Gallery at TCA** (10am-6pm Tues.-Wed., 10am-7:30pm Thurs.-Fri., 11am-7:30pm Sat., free), featuring exhibitions of exciting work by local and regional artists.

Arizona State University (ASU)

A large and innovative public research university, **Arizona State University** (University Dr. and Mill Ave., 480/965-9011, www.asu. edu) has its sprawling, shady main campus in Tempe but belongs to the entire Valley of the Sun. With more than 40 programs ranked among the top 25 in the United States, a few high-profile sports teams, and, like its rival in Tucson, a role in space exploration, ASU is known around the world. Its focus, though, is primarily local: The university is training a new generation to meet the challenges of climate change, ground zero of which is the great arid Southwest. Students in the first-of-its-kind ASU School of Sustainability work with Phoenix-area governments, groups, and businesses on sustainability issues, and the campus itself is among the most ecofriendly in the country. ASU's main campus is listed as number 5 on *Sierra* magazine's Cool Schools Report and number 7 on the Sustainable Campus Index.

ASU has about 50,000 students, several times the population of most Arizona towns. The school graduates about 20,000 every year, and many of Arizona's leaders, lawyers, teachers, artists, and architects were trained here. The main Tempe campus is a pleasant place to stroll and people-watch, and it's worth a visit if only to see Frank Lloyd Wright's **Grady Gammage Auditorium.** But the best reason to stop by is to visit the **ASU Art Museum** (51 E. 10th St., 480/965-2787, www. asuartmuseum.asu.edu, 11am-5pm Tues.-Wed. and Fri.-Sat., 11am-8pm Thurs., free), a small but memorable museum focused on contemporary art in various media. Housed in an amazing building designed by architect Antoine Predock, who also designed the Arizona Science Center downtown, the museum's permanent collection includes prints by Hogarth, Goya, and Posada and paintings by O'Keeffe, Hopper, Siqueiros, Tamayo, and other notable artists. There's free parking in front of the museum off Mill Avenue.

Mesa Contemporary Arts Museum

Mesa Contemporary Arts Museum (1 E. Main St., 480/644-6500, www.mesaartscenter. com, 10am-5pm Tues.-Wed. and Fri.-Sat., 10am-8pm Thurs., noon-5pm Sun., free) is highly recommended to anyone who wants to witness the most current moment in painting, sculpture, and other media. Three galleries in this cool, spare space inside the **Mesa Arts Center** show revolving exhibitions primarily featuring artists from the Southwest, California, and Mexico, but rarely what most would think of as Southwestern-style art. The shows are typically provocative and singular. This museum, along with a similar contemporary space in nearby Scottsdale, is must-see proof that the valley isn't exactly the cultural graveyard it can sometimes appear to be.

Arizona Museum of Natural History

The valley's only natural history museum, the **Arizona Museum of Natural History** (53 N. MacDonald, 480/644-2230, www. azmnh.org, 10am-5pm Tues.-Fri., 11am-5pm Sat., 1pm-5pm Sun., $13 adults, $7 ages 3-12, $8 students) has quite a few hulking dinosaur skeletons in its Dinosaur Hall, and its three-story Dinosaur Mountain is definitely something to see, but the most interesting exhibits here are related to the history of the Southwest, including models of a Spanish-era mission and a territorial jail. The exhibition about Arizona in the movies is fascinating, and the exhibit on the Hohokam people is one of the best around. This is a great place to stop prior to traveling to other parts of the state, a kind of one-stop lesson on the nature and

Downtown Mesa

people of Arizona and the Southwest through the ages—especially recommended to parents hoping to sneak a little education into a Southwestern vacation.

Arizona Temple Visitors Center

If you're not a member of the Church of Jesus Christ of Latter-day Saints, you can't go inside the beautiful **Arizona Temple** (525 E. Main St., Mesa, 480/964-7164, www.lds.org, 9am-9pm daily, free), set on 20 green acres near the original Mesa town site. But those interested can stop by and see the outside, which some say resembles the biblical Temple of Herod. Construction on the LDS temple, the first in Arizona, a state that has welcomed Mormon settlers for generations, began in 1922, and the

building was dedicated in 1927. The grounds include a cactus garden and reflecting pools, and the visitors center has some displays and a film about the LDS church.

SOUTH VALLEY
Mystery Castle

From the early 19th through the mid-20th centuries, U.S. doctors had a simple, if life-altering, prescription for patients suffering from tuberculosis and other chest ailments: seek dry air. As a result, the mountains and deserts of the interior West, especially the arid Southwest, became a popular place for the dying to live out their final days. Phoenix's early boosters did much to attract these "health seekers" to the Valley of the Sun and thus shouldered Arizona and the desert lands

South Valley

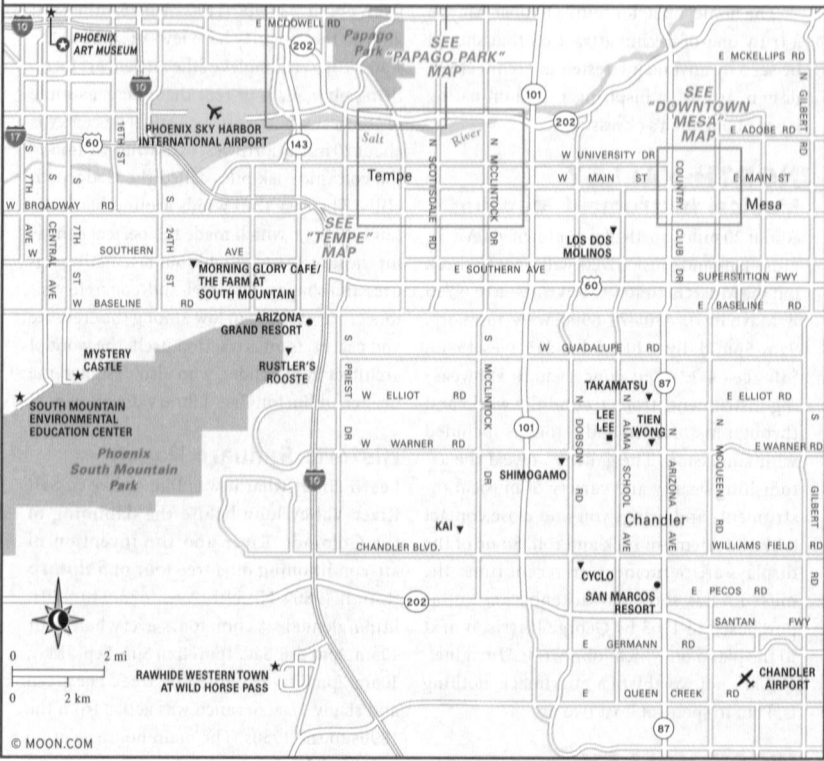

© MOON.COM

early on with a reputation as a wide-open infirmary for the diseased and aged—a reputation the state still can't shake entirely, thanks to its many retirement communities. The American West is littered with the failed and half-realized dream projects of those living in a kind of surrealistic gulf between this and the afterworld, and this 18-room, stacked-stone **Mystery Castle** (800 E. Mineral Rd., 602/268-1581, www.mymysterycastle.com, 11am-3:30pm Thurs.-Sun. Oct.-May, $10 adults, $5 ages 5-12, free under age 5) near South Mountain is one of the more fantastical among them.

Something of a masterpiece of folk architecture, the odd home was built by the tubercular Boyce Luther Gulley, who came to the valley in 1930 from Seattle, leaving his wife

and daughter behind. He spent the remaining years of his life cobbling together the sprawling fairy-tale house out of stones found around the property and salvaged materials like telephone poles and railroad ties, believing he was constructing a walk-in sand castle for his daughter. His methods, and the resulting structure, were not that different from the mesa-top stone homes built for centuries by the Hopi people of northeastern Arizona, whose methods and aesthetic were copied by Mary Colter, one of the Southwest's finest designers and architects, when she built the famous stone structures that line the South Rim of the Grand Canyon. Gulley's project was unfinished when he died in 1945, but his wife and daughter, Mary Lou Gulley, moved in anyway. Mary Lou and the home were famously featured in a 1948 article in *Life* magazine.

The home, open for tours October-May, is a truly one-of-a-kind attraction that should be seen by anyone interested in architecture, design, art, or an inspiring and illuminating story of one man's obsession.

NORTH VALLEY
Musical Instrument Museum

About 20 miles north of downtown via AZ 51, musicians and music lovers will want to check out the **Musical Instrument Museum** (4725 E. Mayo Blvd., 480/478-6000, www.mim.org, 9am-5pm daily, $20 adults, $15 ages 13-19, $10 ages 4-12) and concert hall, showcasing instruments from around the world and through history. An audio tour is included with admission. The galleries reveal the astonishing beauty and variety of musical instruments and brings you into close contact with the totems of rock and roll. Some of the displays are permanent. In recent times the museum has shown a Rickenbacker guitar purchased in 1963 by George Harrison next to the piano on which John wrote "Imagine." If that's not worthy of a pilgrimage, nothing is. Plan to spend at least two hours.

WEST VALLEY
Deer Valley Petroglyph Preserve

ASU scholars are researching the forms and meanings of the petroglyphs that cover the Southwest at the **Deer Valley Petroglyph Preserve** (3711 W. Deer Valley Rd., 623/582-8007, http://dvrac.asu.edu, 9am-5pm Tues.-Sat. Oct.-Apr., 8am-2pm Tues.-Sat. May-Sept., $9 adults, $5 ages 7-12) in the far northwest valley. The more than 1,500 works of rock art on this 46-acre preserve were scraped and scratched by the Hohokam and other tribes that once inhabited the valley, believed to date from about AD 900-1100. A 0.25-mile trail around the property has views of some of the state's finest examples of the ancient art form. Bring binoculars or rent them here, as some of the best work is off the trail. The center is about 20 miles northwest of downtown among the volcanic rock piles called the Hedgepeth Hills. The easy trail winds around black basalt boulders, which made the perfect canvas for the largely inscrutable but fascinating figures and shapes. The steel-and-concrete visitors center, tucked in low among the creosote and cactus, is an attraction itself, the work of architect Will Bruder, who also designed the masterful Burton Barr Library downtown.

Historic Sahuaro Ranch

Learn about what it was like to live in Salt River Valley long before the damming of the Colorado River and the invention of air-conditioning on a free tour of **Sahuaro Ranch** (9802 N. 59th Ave., 623/930-4201, http://glendaleaz.com, tours every half hour 10am-2pm Fri.-Sat., 1pm-4pm Sun. Sept.-May, 10am-2pm Fri.-Sat. June-July, free). The green and shady 17-acre ranch was active from the 1890s to the 1930s. The main house went up in 1891 and the orchard, palm groves, and rose garden create a lushness that is a world away from the rocky deserts all around. The ranch comprises 13 original buildings and is listed on the National Register of Historic Places. Don't forget to say hello to the peacocks wandering around. The old ranch is a city park and a great place to walk and have a picnic. Free guided tours take off every half-hour from the main porch. The ranch is closed in August, and it's not a good idea to go during summer.

Sports and Recreation

Phoenicians love to get outdoors—with more than 300 sunny days a year, they really don't have a choice in the matter. They keep their parks and recreation areas immaculate. There are well-trod desert hiking trails a short drive from just about anywhere in town, but Phoenix's official sport is golf, and there are many courses to choose from and play on year-round.

HIKING AND BIKING

The valley's best hiking trails are in a few easily accessible the urban desert preserves, close to the bustle and yet almost secluded.

Phoenix Mountains

The **Piestewa Peak Summit Trail** (2701 E. Squaw Peak Lane, www.phoenix.gov, 5am-11pm daily), a 1.2-mile one-way hunched-over climb up to what was, prior to the Iraq War, one of the more politically incorrect landmarks in the state—Squaw Peak. The term *squaw* has long had negative connotations for Native Americans, so in 2003 the peak was renamed Piestewa Peak, after Lori Piestewa, a Navajo soldier who was killed in Iraq. You are sure to run into a crowd on the trail on any given day, but if the weather is clear, you can see all of the valley and beyond spread out before you. The Piestewa Peak Summit Trail is an easy, if vertical, hike, and kids won't have a problem with it.

A little bit tougher is the hike up **Camelback Mountain** (www.phoenix.gov), just a little higher than nearby Piestewa Peak at 2,704 feet. Within the **Echo Canyon Recreation Area** (5959 Echo Canyon Dr., 602/256-3220, sunrise-sunset daily), the 1-mile-long one-way **Summit Trail** is a popular hike, and you may have to wait for a parking spot on weekends. You gain more than 1,000 feet of elevation on the way up, so it's not to be taken lightly. There are parts of the trail that are hewn out of slickrock, with handrails alongside. From the top you can see everything.

South Mountain Park and Preserve

Forming the valley's southern border, the obviously named South Mountains can't be missed—they are the ones with all the communication towers and antennae shooting up from their peaks like pins in a hard-rock cushion. The 16,000-acre **South Mountain Park and Preserve** (10919 S. Central Ave., www.phoenix.gov, 5am-7pm daily, trails 5am-11pm daily) is popular with valley residents as an exercise field; bicyclists in particular enjoy climbing the twisting paved road to the lookout peak and then shooting rocket-like back down to the desert floor. One feels a little bad cruising slowly behind them on the curvy drive up to Dobbins Point, the park's highest accessible point at 2,300 feet, a favorite pastime of less-active Phoenicians and their visitors. There are several dry rocky trails through the rugged cactus-and-creosote desert, most of them accessed off the main road to the top and most of them up-and-down routes that aren't too difficult.

Right after the main entrance, there's a trail-map station across from the Civilian Conservation Corps-built rock house, in which you'll find public restrooms. Nearly 58 miles of trails are open to hikers, mountain bikers, and horses. Mountain bikers will find some fun, moderately tough single-track here. For an easy representative loop hike or bike ride, try a 3.5-mile round-trip jaunt on the **National Trail** to Hidden Valley. The trail is rough and rocky, and slick from wear in some places, but the views are spectacular and the saguaros plentiful. Pick up the trail at the top of the Summit Road at the Buena Vista Lookout. The National Trail crosses the entire park, if you're feeling ambitious.

Papago Park

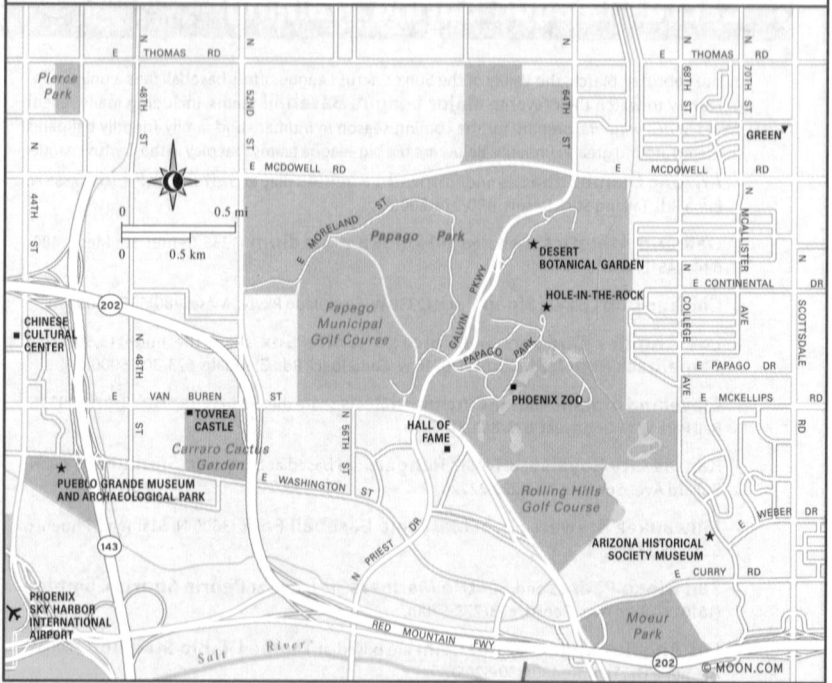

Papago Park

A twisting red-rock desert park just east of central Phoenix, **Papago Park** (625 Galvin Pkwy., 602/495-5458, www.phoenix.gov) is a fun place to tear around on a mountain bike for a while or scramble up to **Hole-in-the-Rock,** a big hole in a jutting-rock hill through which the valley opens up beautifully. It's an easy climb up a very short trail, and then you can sit in the little smooth notch—archaeologists will tell you it lines up perfectly with a building at Pueblo Grande a few miles to the southwest—and look out over the land. Facing west, this is a particularly good spot for viewing sunset. Walking trails crisscross the park, and there are dozens of picnic tables and even a lagoon for fishing.

1: Camelback Mountain 2: Hole-in-the-Rock at Papago Park

GOLF

Seen from the air, the Valley of the Sun appears to be stamped illogically with wide swaths of short green grass, all dotted with artificial duck ponds and sandy beach interruptions. The 300-plus days of sunshine allow for year-round golf—the waking dream of your average Rust Belt duffer. As such, an inordinate amount of desert has been rolled over with grass, creating a golfer's paradise and constituting a fairly questionable use of natural resources. Golf lovers will disagree, especially during a bright morning round in November with the raw desert mountains beautifully framing the impossibly green fairways. There are dozens of courses throughout the valley, many linked to famous resorts. The valley also has some of the most popular municipal courses in the nation, each of them a bargain compared to the fancier places and

Cactus League Spring Training

In late February-March, the Valley of the Sun's Cactus League offers baseball fans a unique opportunity to watch their favorite **Major League Baseball** teams, including many recent World Series winners, prepare for the coming season in intimate and family-friendly ballparks scattered around greater Phoenix. Below are the big-league teams that play in the Cactus League:

- **Arizona Diamondbacks** and **Colorado Rockies** play at **Salt River Fields** (7555 N. Pima Rd., Talking Stick Resort, 480/270-5000).

- **Oakland Athletics** are based at **Hohokam Stadium** (1235 Center St., Mesa, 480/644-4451).

- **Chicago Cubs** play at **Sloan Park** (2330 W. Rio Salado Pkwy., Mesa, 480/668-0500).

- **Los Angeles Dodgers** and **Chicago White Sox** share the huge 13,500-seat **Camelback Ranch Stadium** (10710 W. Camelback Rd., Glendale, 623/302-5000).

- **Cleveland Indians** and the **Cincinnati Reds** share the **Goodyear Ball Park** (1933 S. Ball Park Way, Goodyear, 623/882-3120).

- **Kansas City Royals** and **Texas Rangers** are based at **Surprise Stadium** (15850 N. Bullard Ave., Surprise, 623/222-2222).

- **Milwaukee Brewers** play at **Maryvale Baseball Park** (3600 N. 51st Ave., Phoenix, 623/245-5555).

- **San Diego Padres** and **Seattle Mariners** are based at **Peoria Sports Complex** (16101 N. 83rd Ave., Peoria, 623/773-5700).

- **Los Angeles Angels of Anaheim** are based at **Tempe Diablo Stadium** (2200 W. Alameda Dr., Tempe, 480/350-5205).

- **San Francisco Giants** play at **Scottsdale Stadium** (7408 E. Osborn Rd., Scottsdale, 480/312-2580).

competing just fine when it comes to lushness and creative design. Many of the municipal courses host more than 100,000 rounds of golf per year, so it's a good idea to book tee times in advance. You might want to book before traveling—the city's golf course web pages allow for easy online reservations up to eight days in advance.

Perhaps the valley's most environmentally thoughtful course is the municipal **Cave Creek Golf Course** (15202 N. 19th Ave., 602/866-8076, www.phoenix.gov, $12-31 residents, $13-43 nonresidents), a par-72 built on a reclaimed landfill, though you won't notice—it's green, tree-lined, and the valley's most popular public course. One of the oldest courses in the state, built in 1935 near Encanto

Park, the city center's lush and attractive oasis, **Encanto Golf Course** (2755 N. 15th Ave., 602/253-3963, www.phoenix.gov, $12-31 residents, $13-43 nonresidents) is a par-70 municipal course lined, like its titular park, with tall shaggy palm trees. At Papago Park in the east valley, the green of the links at **Papago Golf Course** (5595 E. Moreland St., 602/275-8428, www.papagogolfcourse.net, $51-72, including cart) contrasts perfectly with red-rock hills all around. The par-72 municipal course is very popular and hosts the Phoenix Open qualifying rounds.

HORSEBACK RIDING

There's nothing like a leisurely horseback ride among the saguaro forests to make you feel

Your favorite team's website has all the schedules and links to purchase tickets. Tickets for most of the teams are relatively abundant and affordable, usually starting around $10-15 for lawn or nosebleed seats and up to $60-70 for great seats. Add $5-10 for parking at the stadium. Many of the ballparks offer package deals that include opportunities to take batting practice and work out with the team.

Depending on the popularity of the team, tickets may sell out quickly, while for others you may be able to get a ticket on the day of. If you're set on seeing a particular match-up, get your tickets as soon as they go on sale. The hottest ticket in town is the Chicago Cubs at Sloan Park, a beautiful, state-of-the-art facility with 15,000 seats, the largest in the Cactus League. There's a waiting list for spring training season tickets to see the Cubs, but it's free to get on it (http://chicago.cubs.mlb.com/chc/sloan-park/spring-training-waiting-list). For individual Cubs games, single tickets go on sale every January. Spring training tickets in general go on sale in January, though it could be earlier—check directly with your team's website.

Most of the teams' workouts are open to the public, and if you arrive about 30 minutes before the games, there are usually opportunities to get player autographs. With daytime highs through February-March typically in the mid-70s to low 80s, and the sky always so clear and blue, it's a lot of fun to watch a game, have a beer or two, and kick back on the cool grass next to the couples and families out for a day off.

Before heading to the ballpark, pack your sunglasses and sunscreen—you will need both. Also bring a reusable water bottle. All the ballparks have plenty of water fountains for refills. You will get thirsty out there in the sun, and refillable is the ecofriendly and pocket-friendly way to go.

Many of the ballparks are surrounded by shiny urban entertainment complexes, with all kinds of shopping, hotels, and restaurants close by. As the Cactus League is very popular, plan ahead and book your accommodations early (and expect to pay a high-season rate), just after tickets go on sale.

A great place to start planning your spring training vacation is at www.cactusleague.com, which has all the information and schedules, or you can call individual stadiums for ticket information.

like a real cowpoke, and there's no better way to meet a real cowboy or cowgirl than to hire one to guide you on a trail ride. The desert preserves around the valley are filled with trails perfect for riding, and there are myriad companies offering one-hour to all-day rides through the unforgettable scenery. You can book an early-morning ride to see the desert come alive or a sunset ride to watch it settle down, colorfully as always. There's usually a weight limit of 225-250 pounds, and kids generally need to be age eight or older. Most of the companies offer full-day rides with lunch or evening rides with dinner around a campfire. Call ahead and make a reservation. Horseback riding in the valley is not recommended during the summer months; most places are closed for summer.

The best stables, and the closest to downtown, are the Ponderosa Stables (10215 S. Central Ave., 602/268-1261, www.arizona-horses.com) in South Mountain Park, just before the park's main entrance. It offers 1- to 2-hour trail rides ($50-80) along the park's many trails among the saguaro, creosote, and petroglyphs. The stables are open year-round but suspend rides when the temperatures reach 100°F, which generally means they are closed during the day for a good part of the summer and open in the early evening for sunset rides. The guides are friendly and knowledgeable, and if you don't like to hike or tear around on a mountain bike, this is the best way to see South Mountain.

SALT RIVER TUBING

A leisurely, convivial float down the Salt is a desert-living tradition, especially during the unrelenting summer. **Salt River Tubing and Recreation** (480/984-3305, www. saltrivertubing.com, 9am-6:30pm daily May-Sept., last rental 3pm, $19 pp, includes shuttle to launch, cash only) rents out tubes all summer, shuttling seekers of cool water to a launch on the Salt River just below Saguaro Lake, east of the city in the Tonto National Forest. You can rent an extra inner tube to hold your ice chest and stock it with cans of beer and soda (no glass allowed) and sandwiches; make sure to include some water. The party can get a bit drunken and adult some days, especially on weekends. Kids must be at least age eight and four feet tall. There are some fun rapids and a fast current in places, depending on the water release schedule at the lake, but mostly it's a slow and sunny float along a thin band of shallow, cool green-blue water, flanked by rock- and saguaro-lined canyon walls and thick riparian greenbelts. There are several beach landings along the way where floaters stop and picnic. Don't expect to be alone, and don't count on quiet all the time; a few waterborne revelers along the way will typically blast music, hoot, and yell, depending on how much beer is left. You can choose 2-, 3-, and 5-hour trips on weekdays; a 6-hour trip is offered on weekends. To get to the rental office, head north for 15 miles from U.S. 60 on the Power Road in Mesa. Call ahead: trips are subject to weather and water flow.

SPECTATOR SPORTS

Everybody in the valley is from somewhere else, or so the conventional wisdom says. The metropolis is indeed a transient city in a transient state; people are always moving in and out, and the new replaces the barely old at a whirlwind clip. This reality is both good and bad for the city's several major-league sports

clubs. There's always a built-in crowd of local devotees, and casual fans will usually turn out in droves when one of the big Midwestern or Eastern teams is in town. When the Chicago Cubs come to visit every summer, it's sometimes difficult to see the Diamondbacks fans among all those blue shirts. That being said, most of the local teams have been able to ingratiate themselves with longtime residents and new arrivals alike simply by doing what a sports team is supposed to do: win.

The Arizona Diamondbacks

Major League Baseball's **Arizona Diamondbacks** (602/462-6500, http:// arizona.diamondbacks.mlb.com) was franchised in 1998 and had a World Series trophy in the clubhouse by 2001. With one of the best scouting programs in the game, lately the D-Backs have skewed younger, introducing future superstars to big-time playoff baseball and beginning a new tradition of smart, fast, and fundamental baseball that has locals filling the seats at downtown **Chase Field** (401 E. Jefferson St., 602/462-6799 or 800/821-7160, tours 9:30am, 11am, and 12:30pm Mon.-Sat. year-round, $7 adults, $5 under age 12), one of the few ballparks in the world with a retractable roof. The roof is closed during most of the season with the air conditioners blasting—the only way baseball can be played in the desert without killing the athletes. Individual game tickets range $5 for nosebleed seats to $215 for a clubhouse box. A decent seat costs $15-40. Although the team is popular in the valley, tickets can usually be purchased the day of the game at the ballpark. If one of the big Midwestern or Eastern teams is in town, like the Chicago Cubs or the Detroit Tigers, you will need to plan far ahead.

The Phoenix Suns

The quick play of the **Phoenix Suns** (602/379-7900, www.nba.com/suns, $25-55) has made the NBA basketball team a beloved institution in Arizona. The Suns also have a long and storied history, with the likes of

Charles Barkley, Danny Ainge, and Dennis Johnson, and of course Shaquille O'Neal, once wearing the purple and orange. The Suns often battle the LA Lakers for supremacy in the Western Conference's Pacific League, and the stands at the huge **Talking Stick Resort Arena** (201 E. Jefferson St.) downtown are always packed with fans.

The Arizona Cardinals

The National Football League's **Arizona Cardinals** (602/379-0102, www.azcardinals. com, $47-148) play in the **University of Phoenix Stadium** (1 Cardinals Dr., Glendale), a flying saucer-shaped building in Glendale, drawing a rabid crowd of football fans from across the state.

ASU Sports

The various teams that play under the name **ASU Sun Devils** (480/965-2381, www. thesundevils.cstv.com, box office 9am-5pm Mon.-Fri., 9am-noon Sat. Aug. 16-Apr.) are typically pretty good and often, especially in baseball and football, very good. The students and the many Arizona State University alumni around the valley really get into it, and tickets for the bigger games aren't easy to come by. Barry Bonds played college baseball here, as did many other big leaguers.

Entertainment

NIGHTLIFE

There are a lot of young people in Phoenix—in many ways it is a very young city. There are also a lot of retirees and even a few people in between. They all manage to come together when the sun goes down. Like so many desert creatures, they love the nightlife. There's upscale and dive-scale, sports bars and ultracool lounges, rock bars, honky-tonks, and hookahs. Hidden somewhere out in that hot sprawl is a place that offers what you want. The best way to identify both the new and the classic is with the *Phoenix New Times*, an alternative weekly you'll find free everywhere.

Downtown and Central
BARS AND PUBS

Bookish types just might meet their soul mate at **First Draft Book Bar** (300 W. Camelback Rd., 602/274-0067, www.changinghands. com, 9am-10pm Mon.-Sat., 9am-8pm Sun.), a craft beer and wine bar inside the midtown Phoenix location of the legendary **Changing Hands Bookstore,** which has been one of the brightest literary lights in Arizona for a few generations. The charming bar has a wide selection of craft beer, much of it from

Arizona, on tap and in cans and bottles. The menu includes cider, mead, sangria, mimosas, kombucha, coffee drinks, light breakfasts, small plates, sandwiches, and snacks. The bookstore sells new and used books and has an intelligent selection. Come for happy hour (3pm-6pm Mon.-Fri., 9am-3pm Sat.-Sun.).

Ready-made Irish and English "pubs" have popped up all over the country these days, but central Phoenix's **George & Dragon Pub** (4240 N. Central Ave., 602/241-0018, www. georgeanddragonpub.net, 11am-2am daily) is the real deal, and it has been around forever. A fabulous selection of beers on tap—heavy on the delicious brews of the British Isles—a well-stocked jukebox, billiards, and good eats (the bangers and mash are particularly tasty) make this authentic pub a perfect place to spend an hour or ten.

The Vig Arcadia (4041 N. 40th St., 602/553-7227, www.thevig.us, 11am-close daily), with its refined interior of redbrick walls, pale wood tables, and chocolate-brown booths, is one of the best hangouts in the valley. Spend the afternoon or evening drinking on the cool, shady, laid-back patio, playing bocce ball, and sampling the wonderful food.

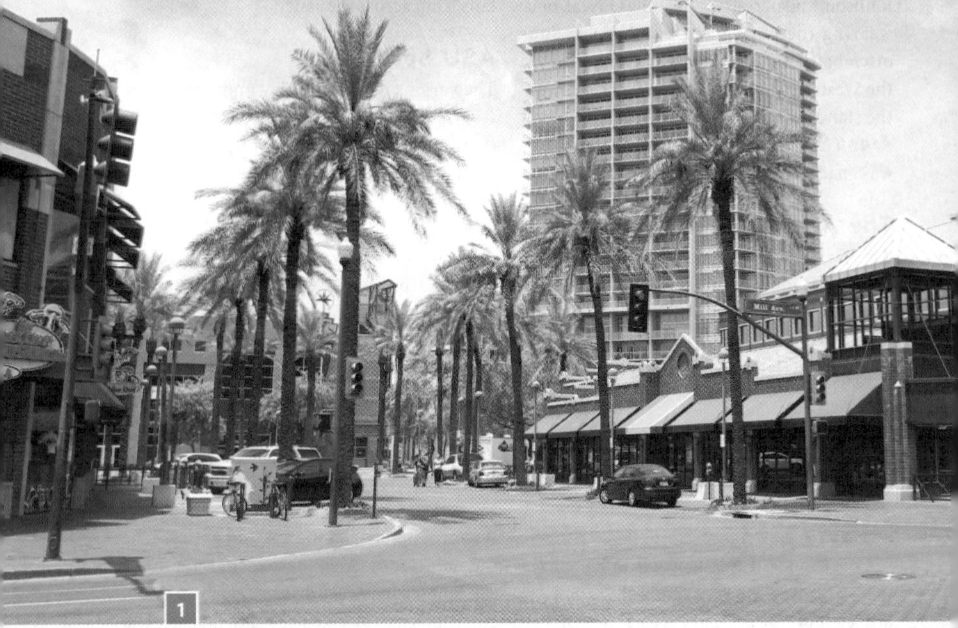

1

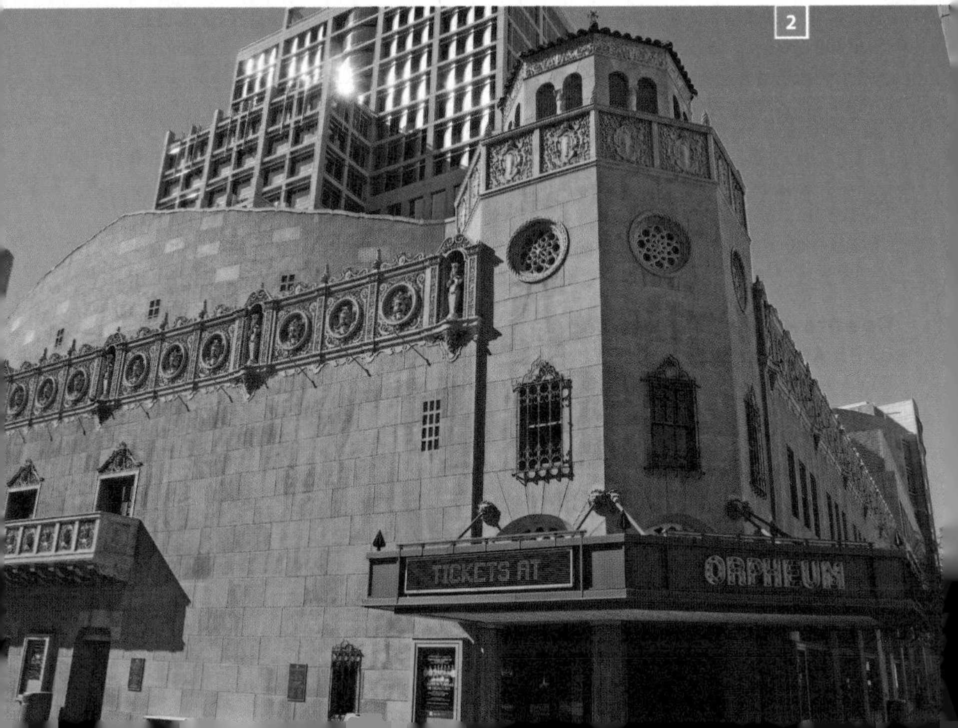

2

Nearby, **The Little Woody** (4228 E. Indian School Rd., 602/955-0339, www.littlewoodyaz.com, 4pm-2am daily) is a fun laid-back spot featuring craft cocktails, Arizona beers on tap, and a large whiskey menu. It also has a small menu of appetizers, paninis, and flatbreads, a happy hour (4pm-7pm daily), and live DJs (from 9pm Thurs.-Sun.). Check out the game room, with darts, Skee-Ball, and other old-school diversions.

The **Ice House Tavern** (3855 E. Thomas Ave., 602/244-1179, www.icehousetavernphx.com, 1:30pm-2am Mon.-Thurs., 11am-2am Fri.-Sun., sometimes open earlier for college football games) is a casual and fun local hang-out to grab a beer, watch the game, and then stick around and dance to a local garage band. The bar has an ice-hockey theme, and you can watch through a big window as skaters attempt to stay up at the Arcadia Ice Arena.

Head over to the **Valley Bar** (130 N. Central Ave., 602/368-3121, www.valleybarphx.com, 4pm-2am Mon.-Fri., 6pm-2am Sat.-Sun.) for a large dose of Valley of the Sun culture and history at this fun, inventive, and local-proud bar and dungeon-like live music venue. Just a block from the Adams Street light-rail stop, you can kick back in The Rose Room, a cozy lounge named after Rose Mofford, Arizona's first female governor (who always wore her hair in a fantastic beehive), and sample cocktails named after Arizona politicians past and present. Along with a basement stage for live bands and a game room with pool tables, pinball, and video games, the bar also has food to offer (until 1am Fri.-Sat., midnight Sun.-Thurs.): sandwiches, small plates, and flatbread pizzas.

LOUNGES AND WINE BARS

Housed in an old department store downtown that was hailed as a local masterpiece of the International Style when it opened in 1947, the retro-modernist lounge and restaurant **Hanny's** (40 N. 1st St., 602/252-2285, www.hannys.net, 11am-1:30am Mon.-Fri., 5pm-1:30am Sat.-Sun.) is an essential bar-hopping stop for anyone who appreciates urban renewal done the right way. This sophisticated lounge serves food—gourmet pizzas, appetizers, and sandwiches—until 1am and a large menu of creative, expertly mixed, though expensive cocktails, wine, and beer until 1:30am.

For a top-notch glass of wine, a plate of cheese and olives with bruschetta, and a quiet, laid-back, but elegant atmosphere, head to **Postino** (3939 E. Campbell Ave., 602/852-3939, www.postinowinecafe.com, 11am-11pm Mon.-Thurs., 11am-midnight Fri., 9am-midnight Sat., 11am-10pm Sun.), where they'll squeeze an orange and mix you one of the best mimosas you've ever had. The wine program changes frequently, and they offer a decent selection of beers, most of them in bottles.

Just across Camelback Road from the Biltmore Fashion Park, the upscale **MercBar** (2525 E. Camelback Rd., 602/508-9449, www.mercbar.com, 4pm-2am Mon.-Thurs., 7pm-2am Fri.-Sun.) claims to be "just a bar," but it is far beyond that: It is a civilized and darkly inviting lounge. You might not want to leave once you sit down at a small round table in a deep leather chair and taste one of the signature concoctions the expert bartenders mix up. It's pricey, and you should wear your slickest duds, but it is worth it for the atmosphere and the tasty mixes. This is an ideal place to stop for a before- or after-dinner cocktail if you are on a hot date and want to impress.

With its rustic exposed brick and wood floors contrasting against a mid-century modern and urban-hip decor, the **SideBar** (701 W. McDowell Rd., 602/254-1646, www.sidebarphoenix.com, 4pm-2am Mon.-Thurs., 3pm-2am Fri.-Sun.), at the southwest corner of 7th Avenue and McDowell Road, has atmosphere to spare. They also take their mixing seriously, with fresh-squeezed juices, perfectly balanced simple syrups, and a range of top-shelf booze both familiar and exotic.

Stop in at **Carly's Bistro** (128 E. Roosevelt St., 602/262-2759, www.carlysbistro.com,

10:30am-1am Mon.-Wed., 10:30am-2am Thurs.-Fri., 10am-2am Sat., 10am-1am Sun.) for a glass of real absinthe, a perfectly made White Russian with soy milk, or a carafe of sangria for the table. This bistro and hangout has a good selection of beers and a warm atmosphere that will keep you sampling from their exciting cocktail menu. Don't forget about **Durant's** (2611 N. Central Ave., 602/264-5967, www.durantsaz.com, 11am-10pm Mon.-Thurs., 11am-11pm Fri., 5pm-11pm Sat., 4:30pm-10pm Sun.), where they have more than excellent steaks and prime rib: They also serve one of the best martinis in town, with an old-school upscale mood perfect to start a night on the town.

Skydeck/Clarendon Rooftop Bar (401 W. Clarendon Ave., 602/252-7363, http://goclarendon.com, 5am-10pm daily Oct.-early July), on the roof of the Clarendon Hotel, offers amazing views of the valley in an ultra-posh atmosphere, but it's not always easy to get up there. They enforce a strict numbers limit, but it's worth a try for the peace you'll feel looking out over the desert city as the sun dips away, cocktail in hand.

GAY AND LESBIAN

The vibe at **Charlie's** (727 W. Camelback Rd., 602/265-0224, www.charliesphoenix.com, noon-4am Mon.-Thurs. and Sat., 2pm-4am Fri., noon-2am Sun.) is down-home. The home of the Arizona Gay Rodeo Association is all about shuffling your cowboy boots across the floor and getting in on a good line dance, and the DJs often (but not always) spin country hits rather than Lady Gaga. They also have drag shows, proms, and tons of other special events.

In Park Central Mall, **Kobalt** (3110 N. Central Ave., Suite 125, 602/264-5307, www.kobaltbarphoenix.com, 11am-2am Mon.-Fri., 10am-2am Sat.-Sun.) claims to have the best selection of karaoke music in town. This is a fun, trendy, and popular place; it has a kind of a local watering-hole vibe, hosts all kinds of fun games, offers drink specials, and has a comfortable open patio.

In 2019, the popular Cash Country Inn changed its tune, moving to a new location and evolving into the **Cash Night Club and Lounge** (1730 E. McDowell Rd., 602/244-9943, www.cashnightclub.com, 9pm-2am Thurs.-Sun.), a dance club for the valley's LGBT community, while holding on to the welcoming atmosphere for which it has been known. Now you're more likely to hear hip-hop and Latin music over country-western, and there's a lot of beautiful people and fancy dancing—the whole place has a much more upscale vibe than it did before.

LIVE MUSIC

The **Crescent Ballroom** (308 N. 2nd St., 602/716-2222, www.crescentphx.com, 11am-1am or 2am Mon.-Fri., 5pm-1am or 2am Sat.-Sun.) downtown brings the best artists to the valley, from classic rockers to beloved alternative cult-leaders and contemporary singer-songwriters. It's an intimate little place just a block west of the Van Buren light-rail station. There are no bad seats here; if you're not standing in front of the stage watching spit fly out of the singer's mouth, you're perched mid-center on a small set of bleachers, gulping a martini. The Ballroom's restaurant, **Cocina 10** (11am-midnight Mon.-Fri., 5pm-midnight Sat.-Sun.) serves excellent overstuffed burritos with a variety of fillings to choose from. Parking is $5 at a lot next to the Ballroom; bring exact change, or better yet, just take the light rail.

A hip wood-and-brick lounge in a converted home, **The Lost Leaf** (914 N. 5th St., 602/258-0014, www.thelostleaf.org, 5pm-2am daily) at 5th and Roosevelt Streets offers dozens of beers (many of them Arizona-brewed), meads, ciders, sakes, and wines (also many from Arizona), and hosts the best bands and musicians you've never heard of nearly every night. All the shows are free, and it also costs nothing to look at the astounding, confusing, and haunting art on the walls.

The **Rhythm Room** (1019 E. Indian School Rd., 602/265-4842, www.rhythmroom.com,

7pm-2am daily) is an excellent venue to catch local and national touring acts playing blues, rock, and country, and on any given night there's likely to be some roots-heavy band tearing up the stage.

Right next to Stand Up Live in downtown's CityScape development, Copper Blues (50 W. Jefferson St., 480/719-5005, www.copperblueslive.com, 11am-10pm Mon.-Tues., 11am-11pm Wed., 11am-midnight Thurs., 11am-2am Fri., 4pm-2am Sat., 4pm-10pm Sun., happy hour 3pm-6pm Mon.-Fri., 4pm-6pm Sat.-Sun.) has more than 60 beers on tap, which you can sample while live local and regional bands rock your socks off. Most of the shows are free, and so are three hours of parking with validation. Copper Blues also serves excellent stone-oven pizzas with all kinds of creative toppings, plus sandwiches, burgers, salads, and much more ($10-20). This fun, laid-back place is right next to the light-rail stops at Jefferson and 1st Avenue and Washington and Central Avenue, and it has a comfortable patio for enjoying those perfect Valley of the Sun nights.

COMEDY

Located in the thick of all the downtown action in the bustling CityScape development, Stand Up Live (50 W. Jefferson St., 480/719-6100, www.standuplive.com, $10-30) brings A-list comedians to the valley and serves frosty drinks for you to blow out your nose while laughing. Check the club's online calendar for upcoming shows. A ticket to a show comes with a three-hour parking validation, but it's also easy to take the light rail to either the Jefferson and 1st Avenue Station or the Washington and Central Avenue Station.

Tempe and the East Valley

Head over to Mill Avenue in Tempe to party with the ASU crowd; there are several clubs, bars, and restaurants along Mill, and there's bound to be a fashionable, fun, and beautiful crowd anywhere you stop.

BARS AND PUBS

Casey Moore's (850 S. Ash Ave., 480/968-9935, www.caseymoores.com, 11am-2am daily) is a favorite among ASU students, faculty, and still-partying alumni, with a patio, a large selection of beers, and huge plates of oysters.

For one of the best handcrafted beers in the valley, try the Four Peaks Brewing Company (1340 E. 8th St., 480/303-9967, www.fourpeaks.com, 11am-midnight Mon.-Thurs., 11am-2am Fri., 9am-2am Sat., 9am-midnight Sun.) near campus; you can also find Four Peaks beers at most of the better bars and restaurants in the valley.

The Handlebar (6805 Mill Ave., 480/474-4888, www.handlebaraz.com, 11am-2am daily) is a fun, laid-back, bicycle-centric bar along Tempe's bustling main street, Mill Avenue. It has 24 beers on tap, many of them made in Arizona, as well as a huge patio perfect for hanging out on a warm winter day and a kitchen open late that serves brats, sandwiches, burgers, and other delicious food.

LIVE MUSIC

The Yucca Tap Room (29 W. Southern Ave., 480/967-4777, http://yuccatap.com, 6am-2am daily) is a legendary ASU-area bar that hosts local and touring rock bands and musicians in a dive-bar setting near campus. A leader in the renowned Tempe music scene of the 1990s, the Yucca Tap Room is still one of the best places in the valley to see live music.

The Tempe Tavern (1810 E. Apache Blvd., 480/794-1706, http://tempetavern.com, 10am-2am daily), just south of ASU on Apache Boulevard, puts on local and regional bands, from rock to punk to hip-hop, for a mixed crowd. The restaurant serves pretty good burgers, wings, onion rings, salads, and sandwiches until midnight.

PERFORMING ARTS

The excellent Phoenix Symphony (602/495-1999, www.phoenixsymphony.org) puts on dozens of pops and classics concerts throughout the year at downtown's beautiful **Symphony Hall** (75 N. 2nd St.). The hall is also home to the **Arizona Opera Company** (602/266-7464, www.azopera.org), which presents mostly well-known classic operas with creative set designs and top-notch performers. A few blocks away, the spectacular **Arizona Federal Theatre** (400 W. Washington St., 602/379-2800, www.arizonafederaltheatre.com) welcomes a constant stream of headlining national acts, including an impressive array of big-name comedians and rock bands.

Perhaps the best seat in the valley is at the intimate **Celebrity Theatre** (440 N. 32nd St., 602/267-1600, www.celebritytheatre.com). The round stage makes every seat in the house perfect, and a wide variety of performers appear every year—jazz bands, crooners, rappers, classic rock, and nearly everything else. The acts aren't usually as big as the ones that play the Arizona Federal Theatre or the huge outdoor **Ak-Chin Pavilion** (2121 N. 83rd Ave., 602/254-7200, www.cricket-pavilion.com), but you'll want to check the website; if any band or performer you like is playing at Celebrity Theatre, definitely think about going.

The valley's premier live theater venue is the **Herberger Theater Center** (222 E. Monroe St., 602/254-7399, www.herbergertheater.org) downtown—you'll know you've found it when you see the fascinating dancing nude sculptures out front. Here you can see original productions by the **Arizona Theatre Company** (502 W. Roosevelt, 602/256-6995, www.aztheatre.org), one of the nation's finest regional companies and one that is never daunted by difficult, unique work.

Even if you don't have tickets to see one of the many theatrical, musical, or live performances at the classic **Orpheum Theatre** (203 W. Adams St., 602/262-6225, http://orpheum-theater.com), you might want to step into the gorgeous old venue for a look around. The theater, one of the valley's oldest, retains its 1927 glory. If style, beauty, and design are

the ultimate criteria, this is probably the best venue in the valley.

CINEMA

For art-house and independent films, Tempe's **Harkins Valley Art** (509 S. Mill Ave., 480/446-7272, www.harkins.com) is the best venue in the valley, showing the films you won't see at the multiplex in a cool, if a bit rickety, old building on Mill Avenue.

COMEDY

Tempe Improv (930 E. University Dr., 480/921-9877, www.tempeimprov.com) welcomes some of the best comedians in the country to its stage, from local talents and touring up-and-comers to *Saturday Night Live* favorites. There's a two-drink minimum, but it's easy to oblige with their long list of cocktails, and the bar-and-grill food is a cut above the usual dinner-theater fare. You must be 21 or older to attend most shows, but some are 18 and over.

CASINOS

For Vegas-style gaming and entertainment, you can't do much better than **Wild Horse Pass Resort and Casino** (5040 W. Wild Horse Pass Blvd., 800/946-4452, www.wildhorsepass.com), the biggest Native American casino in the region. The 100,000-square-foot casino, hotel, and resort on the Gila River Indian Community Reservation, just off I-10 in the southeast valley, has 875 slot machines willing to take your money, plus live and video poker and blackjack tables. Wild Horse Pass also has a buffet for when you need to refuel and live entertainment for when you lose all your money and need a little cheering up.

FESTIVALS AND EVENTS

Downtown comes alive during the monthly **First and Third Friday Art Walks** (6pm-10pm), when more than 100 galleries and art spaces hold special events and locals mingle in the streets. The event is organized by Artlink, which also maintains the Phoenix Urban Guide (http://phoenixurbanguide.com), where you can learn about other events going on in the city.

At the end of December and the first days of January, the valley celebrates college football with the Fiesta Bowl Parade, Fiesta Bowl Block Party, and, of course, the Fiesta Bowl (www.fiestabowl.org) at University of Phoenix Stadium in Glendale. In February the popular VNSA Book Sale (602/265-6805, www.vnsabooksale.org) has more than 600,000 used books for sale at the fairgrounds.

In March the Heard Museum Guild Indian Fair & Market (602/253-8848, www.

heardguild.org) includes more than 600 artists, and spring training and Cactus League (www.cactusleague.com) bring professional baseball teams to the valley for a game every day of the month. In April NASCAR Subway Fresh Fit 500 (www.nascar.com) roars into town, bringing the popular auto sport's top drivers with it.

In October the Arizona State Fair and the Heard Museum Spanish Market keep locals and visitors busy, and in November the cars return for the NASCAR Checker Auto Parts 500. In December, don't miss the popular Pueblo Grande Museum Indian Market (602/495-0901, www.pueblogrande.com).

Shopping

DOWNTOWN AND CENTRAL
Shopping Districts

The upscale Biltmore Fashion Park (24th St. and Camelback Rd., 602/955-8400, www.shopbiltmore.com) along Camelback Road is the valley's finest shopping mall, with Saks Fifth Avenue, Ralph Lauren, and dozens of other high-end shops. You'll want to spend the whole day here if you're a shopping enthusiast with money to burn, and there are several restaurants to choose from for a memorable lunch or dinner.

On 7th Avenue between Camelback and Indian School Roads, in the Melrose District, you'll find retro boutiques, thrift stores, and hip home-decor shops. The busy and stroll-worthy Roosevelt Row (Roosevelt St. between Grand Ave. and 16th St.) has a host of funky locally owned boutiques, cafés, bars, artist studios, and galleries and a pedestrian-friendly vibe that sets it apart from the valley's strip-mall wastelands. The district hosts the Second Saturday Sidewalk Sale (10am-8pm 2nd Sat. of the month), with lots of street vendors and live music and people-watching; and during the popular downtown

event known as First and Third Fridays (6pm-10pm) this area gets busy and vibrant with revelers, shoppers, and art lovers.

The Churchill (901 N. 1st St., http://thechurchillphx.com, 10am-10pm Mon.-Thurs., 10am-2am Fri.-Sat.) is a cluster of local shops, restaurants, and bars housed in stylishly refurbished and recycled packing crates that sees itself as a community-driven gathering place; each tenant is required to complete at least four hours a month of community service. The shops face a 9,000-square-foot shaded courtyard, a great place to meet friends. The complex includes several excellent eateries and watering holes, as well as a few artisanal and lifestyle shops. Make sure to check out the shop called State Forty Eight, which sells Arizona-only clothing and other products.

It's a 30-minute drive to the Farm at Agritopia in Gilbert, a former (and, to some extent, current) agriculture community. It's an 11-acre organic farm in a Stepford-esque subdivision that looks as if it were built in the Midwest in the early 20th century. A Farm Store sells farm products, and the eye-catching Barnone AZ (3000 E. Ray Rd.,

Gilbert, 480/988-1238, http://barnoneaz.com, 7am-9pm Sun.-Wed., 7am-11pm Thurs.-Sat.) is an interesting and illuminating gathering of valley craftspeople in a large Quonset hut, including a few innovative farm-to-table eateries and bars, a beauty salon, a gunmaker, a flower shop, a paper shop featuring unique Arizona items, a winemaker, a sign maker, and more.

Farmers Markets

The most popular farmers market in the valley is the **Downtown Phoenix Public Market** (721 N. Central Ave., 602/253-2700, http://phxpublicmarket.com), which gathers hundreds of vendors together downtown to sell locally grown fruits and vegetables, locally prepared foods, arts and crafts, and other items that you can't get anywhere else. There's also usually live music and a lot of interesting people to meet. At the northeast corner of Central Avenue and McKinley Street, the **Open-Air Market** (721 N. Central Ave., 8am-noon Sat. May-Sept., 8am-1pm Sat. Oct.-Apr.) happens all year, even in summer and the rainy season.

TEMPE AND THE EAST VALLEY

If the clothes at the Biltmore's Saks are too expensive, drive over to Tempe and the **Arizona Mills** (5000 Arizona Mills Circle, 480/491-7300, www.arizonamills.com, 10am-9pm Mon.-Sat., 11am-6pm Sun.), an outlet mall that has a Saks outlet (called Off 5th) and dozens of other outlet shops, including Ann Taylor, Kenneth Cole, and many more. This mall is huge and clean and has a fun gaming center for the kids and several restaurants.

Take a stroll along **Mill Avenue,** where you'll find all kinds of hip shops and boutiques; while Mill used to be quite a bit funkier than it is today, the bigger corporate stores that overtook it about a decade ago still have a lot of good shopping to offer.

WEST VALLEY
Shopping Districts
Historic Downtown Glendale (59th Ave.

and Glendale Ave.) and the nearby **Catlin Court Historic District** (bounded by Gardenia Ave., 59th Ave., Palmaire Ave., and 58th Ave.) in the northwest valley offer the valley's quaintest shopping. The streets of downtown Glendale are lined with gas lamps and crowded antiques stores, while Catlin Court is a historic residential neighborhood whose white picket fence-fronted bungalows have been turned into boutiques and restaurants. This area is a must-visit for those who enjoy walking in picturesque small-town settings and finding unique items to take home.

Bookstores

The valley isn't exactly a book-hunter's paradise, but there are a few stores worth checking out. The best bookstore in town is the legendary **Changing Hands Bookstore** (6428 S. McClintock Dr., 480/730-0205, www.changinghands.com, 10am-9pm Mon.-Fri., 9am-9pm Sat., 10am-6pm Sun.) in Tempe, which sells an excellent mixture of new and used books. The statewide chain **Bookmans,** selling all manner of used media, including books, CDs, DVDs, games, and much more, has two well-stocked locations nearby, one in the north valley (8034 N. 19th Ave., 602/433-0255, www.bookmans.com, 9am-10pm daily) and one in the east valley in Mesa (1056 S. Country Club Dr., 480/835-0505, www.bookmans.com, 9am-10pm daily). All Bookmans locations offer free Wi-Fi.

Music

If you prefer browsing in the real world for your CDs and you still enjoy the warm sounds and cover art of vinyl records, there are a few places in the valley not to miss. At the Arizona and Nevada chain **Zia Records** (1940 W. Indian School Rd., 602/241-0313, www.zianation.com, 10am-midnight daily) you'll find stacks of new and used CDs in all genres, plus movies, books, and magazines, and a relatively large selection of used vinyl.

Stinkweeds (12 W. Camelback Rd., 602/248-9461, www.stinkweeds.com, 11am-9pm Mon.-Sat., noon-6pm Sun.), at the northwest corner of Central Avenue and Camelback Road, has been a valley favorite since 1987, when we had little choice other than brick-and-mortar stores to buy our music and the biggest worry of the independent record store was the coming of the superchains. This stubborn little store, which specializes in independent record labels and hard-to-find music, offers hours of browsing potential for new and used CDs and vinyl.

Food

In many ways, Phoenix and the Valley of the Sun began as clean slates, uncluttered by too much history and tradition, available for residents and visitors to scrawl on at will, creating amalgams and collages by cross-pollinating everything they'd seen or heard or tasted before arriving in the desert. The new always finds a foothold here, right up until it is replaced by something else. This is especially true of dining life. While the details may be changing all the time, the lifestyle remains constant: creative and eclectic, with a particular dedication, like the valley's residents now and through history, to fusion.

The daily *Arizona Republic* (www. azcentral.com) keeps an excellent up-to-the-second guide to the valley's constantly changing dining scene on its website. The alternative weekly *Phoenix New Times* (www. phoenixnewtimes.com) publishes entertaining and knowledgeable reviews and listings on valley eateries.

It's always a good idea to call ahead and attempt to make a reservation, even though for most places you probably won't need one. This is especially smart in the valley, where you may have to drive some distance in traffic to get anywhere. Many restaurants change their hours of operation during summer, so call ahead if there's any doubt. At most of the area's fancier places, reservations are recommended, if not required. Only the highest-end restaurants have anything approaching a dress code, and that is usually business casual, but with a jacket. The vast majority of valley hosts and hostesses won't bat an eye at your jeans or even your flip-flops, especially during summer.

DOWNTOWN AND CENTRAL
Mexican

Aunt Chilada's Squaw Peak (7330 N. Dreamy Draw Dr., 602/944-1286, www. auntchiladas.com, 11am-11pm Mon.-Thurs., 11am-2am Fri., 10am-1am Sat., 10am-11pm Sun., $10-18) serves delicious Mexican food in a historic building in the shadow of the Phoenix Mountains. The **Barrio Café** (2814 N. 16th St., 602/636-0240, www.barriocafe. com, 11am-10pm Tues.-Thurs., 11am-10:30pm Fri., 5pm-10:30pm Sat., 11am-9pm Sun., $12-22) gets quite a bit more creative, serving rare (for Arizona) modern Mexican cuisine from many different regions. This is not the place for chimichangas and chicken enchiladas. Try the slow-roasted pork, and somebody at the table should order Oaxacan black mole, one of Mexico's famous sauces created by nun-chefs in the 19th century. The bar has over 200 varieties of tequila.

American and Southwestern

An innovative indoor marketplace and food court, ★ **The Churchill** (901 N. 1st St., http://thechurchillphx.com, 10am-10pm Mon-Thurs., 10am-2am Fri.-Sat., prices vary) is the place to please different tastes in your group. Constructed from 19 refurbished shipping containers, this large and exciting gathering place in the Roosevelt Arts District downtown has seven different restaurants and bars around a 9,000-square-foot courtyard with tables. All the eateries are locally owned, and the variety is impressive: pizza, açaí bowls, a Mexican spot serving dishes from Jalisco and Michoacán, a bar with

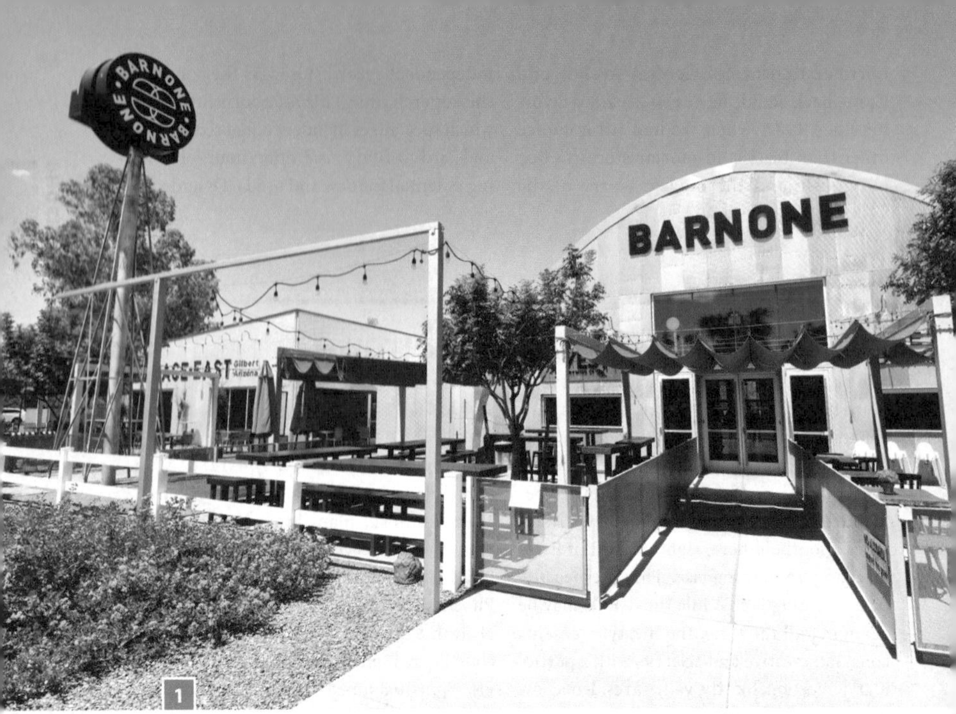
BARNONE
BARNONE
1

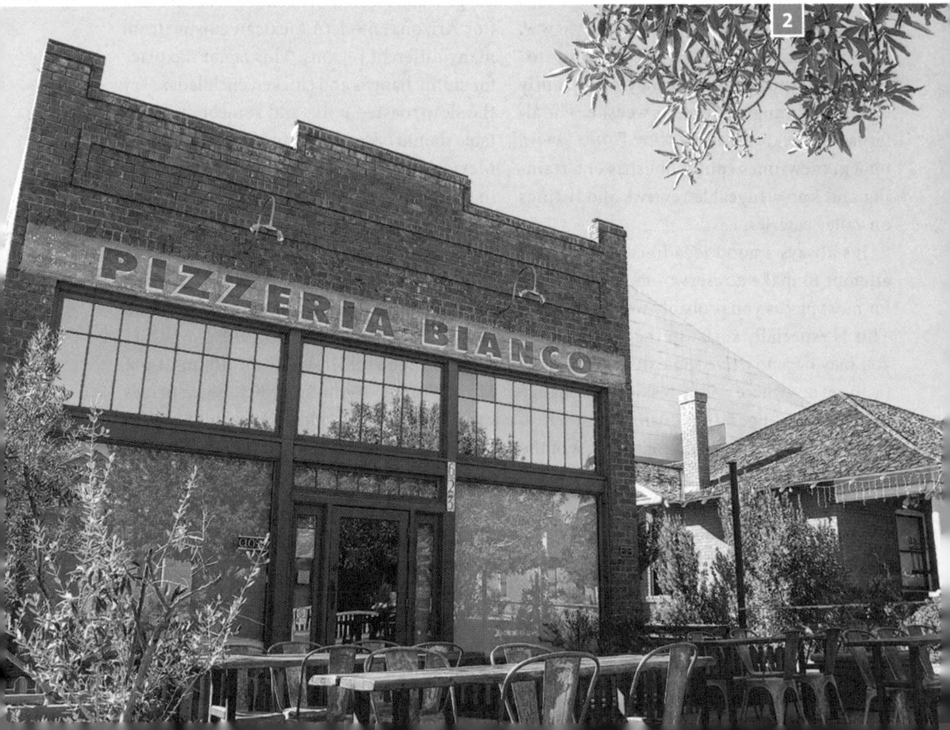
PIZZERIA BIANCO
2

craft cocktails and local beer and wine, and much more.

Quiessence (6106 S. 32nd St., 602/276-0601, www.quiessencerestaurant.com, 5pm-close Tues.-Sat., $43-45), an enchanting restaurant in a converted farmhouse, is set among the gardens and organic crops at **The Farm at South Mountain** (near Southern Ave. and 32nd St.), a 10-acre former pecan orchard that features gardens, three restaurants, shops, markets, and events. With its green-grass patio, Quiessence serves seasonally inspired cuisine with ingredients from local farms, gardens, ranches, and streams. The menus change daily and include fish, beef, and vegetable dishes as well as unique delicious cocktails. This is an ideal place to spend an adventurous, fun, and, yes, educational night with friends, sampling the many foods that are grown, raised, and made in-state, like feta from Snowflake, Arizona.

Another excellent farm-to-table option is **Gertrude's** (1201 Galvin Pkwy., 480/719-8600, www.gertrudesrestaurant.net, 10:30am-8pm Mon.-Fri., 8am-8pm Sat.-Sun., $10-18) at the Desert Botanical Garden. With its wonderful patio and lush, cool garden setting, Gertrude's is a great place for a long valley lunch over a few bottles of wine. It offers a revolving seasonal menu of American dishes with international flavors, sourced and inspired by Arizona growers.

Windsor (5223 N. Central Ave., 602/279-1111, http://windsoraz.com, 11am-11pm Mon.-Thurs., 11am-2am Fri., 9am-midnight Sat., 9am-10pm Sun., $14-20) serves excellent burgers, sandwiches, and specials, such as a delicious potpie and perfectly prepared fried chicken, all in a stylish central location with a patio and a hip youngish clientele. Don't miss one of the best decorating flourishes in the valley—a whole wall decorated with old cassette tapes from the 1980s-1990s.

A winner of the James Beard Foundation's America's Classics Award, **The Fry Bread House** (4545 N. 7th Ave., 602/351-2345, 10:30am-7pm Mon.-Sat., $6-11) has been serving Tohono O'odham cuisine in the valley for more than 30 years, with an emphasis on the eponymous Southwestern staple in both its sweet and savory forms, including fry bread tacos and burritos, amazing red- and green-chili stews, tamales, and other unforgettable dishes.

Luci's at the Orchard (7100 N. 12th St., Bldg. 2, 602/633-2442, http://lucisorchard.com, 7am-8pm daily, $10-16) celebrates the history of the Valley of the Sun with details alluding to those famous Five C's of Arizona: cattle, copper, cotton, citrus, and climate. The charming, stylish ranch-style restaurant, coffeehouse, and juice bar has an orchard-adjacent patio and a splash-pad for the kids. Serving scratch-made worldly creations for breakfast, lunch, and dinner, this is a wonderful place to eat all three.

Breakfast and Lunch

For an excellent cup of certified fair-trade organic coffee and a bowl of hearty oatmeal—say, after a brisk hike in the desert—head to ★ **Fair Trade Café** (1020 N. 1st Ave., Roosevelt Row, 602/354-8150, www.azfairtrade.com, 6am-10pm daily, $3.50-8.50) downtown. The café has a relaxing patio, local art on the wall, and light, healthy, and delicious breakfast and lunch options. All the baked goods are made in-house from scratch. Vegetarians and vegans will find much to ponder, including a hummus sandwich and a veggie burrito. The café uses organic, local, and sustainable produce, and all of the cups, napkins, and lids are made with recyclable materials.

The tasteful diner **Matt's Big Breakfast** (825 N. 1st St., 602/254-1074, www.mattsbigbreakfast.com, 6:30am-2:30pm Tues.-Sun., $8-14) always seems to have a line outside, especially on weekends, because it serves some of the best breakfast food in the valley. The scratch-prepared, deceptively simple classic breakfasts will keep you full for most of the day.

1: Barnone AZ eatery and shop complex 2: Pizzeria Bianco

Be prepared to wait for a table at tiny **Lo-Lo's Chicken & Waffles** (1220 S. Central Ave., 602/340-1304, www.loloschickenandwaffles.com, 10am-9pm Mon.-Fri., 8am-9pm Sat., 8am-6pm Sun., $5-13), a classic and popular soul-food joint on Central Avenue. Lo-Lo's serves crispy Southern-fried chicken and big waffles, macaroni-and-cheese, greens, and many other Southern favorites. You may find yourself liking the huge "jar of drank" the best: a fruit jar filled with red Kool-Aid, the finest drink on the planet. There's also a Lo-Lo's in Scottsdale (3133 N. Scottsdale Rd., 480/945-1920) that has the same hours.

Italian and Pizza

Another valley winner of the prestigious James Beard Award, Chris Bianco operates ★ **Pizzeria Bianco** (623 E. Adams St., Heritage Square, 602/258-8300, www.pizzeriabianco.com, 11am-9pm Mon.-Thurs., 11am-10pm Fri.-Sat., $11-20) out of a historic brick building at downtown's Heritage Square. The pizza is the best in the valley, and, according to many food critics, among the best in the nation as well. This is a small, romantic, hip place, and it takes a while to get a table and a while to get your pizza. It is all worth it. Go here if you love pizza. Next door, **Bar Bianco** (602/528-3699, 11am-9pm Mon.-Thurs., 11am-10pm Fri.-Sat.) has a wide selection of wine and a warm atmosphere, with picnic tables on a grassy candlelit patio. Pizzeria Bianco also has a location in the Town & Country shopping center (4743 N. 20th St., 602/368-3273, 11am-9pm daily).

Steaks and Chops

Durant's Fine Foods (2611 N. Central Ave., 602/264-5967, www.durantsaz.com, 11am-10pm Mon.-Thurs., 11am-11pm Fri., 5pm-11pm Sat., 4:30pm-10pm Sun., $50-75) downtown is the archetypal retro-haute steak house and lounge, where you can get a juicy slice of prime rib, a perfectly cooked steak, and an expert martini served by professional tuxedoed waitstaff. Durant's has been serving the same food in the same location for more than 50 years and has a loyal following, so make reservations.

Vegetarian

★ **Loving Hut** (3239 E. Indian School Rd., 602/264-3480, www.lovinghut.us, 11am-2:30pm and 5pm-9pm Tues.-Sat., 4pm-8pm Sun., $8-13) is 100 percent vegan, but you wouldn't know it unless they told you so. The delicious and spicy Asian-style dishes are prepared with all kinds of faux-meat protein that adds depth and zest. Vegetarians and vegans will be in ecstasy here. Loving Hut is closed the last Sunday of every month.

TEMPE AND THE EAST VALLEY
Mexican

The food at **Casa Reynoso** (3138 S. Mill Ave., 480/966-0776, www.casareynoso.com, 11am-8:30pm Tues.-Thurs., 11am-9:30pm Fri.-Sat., 11am-8pm Sun., $10-17) is prepared from old family recipes passed down from an older place in the Central Arizona mining region of Globe-Miami. The Mexican food here is a bit more authentic than your average chimichanga hut, and the hacienda-style building gives the place an Old Mexico aura that makes for a fun night out just slightly north of the border.

American and Southwestern

Located at the Sheraton Grand at Wild Horse Pass, **Kai** (5594 West Wild Horse Pass Blvd., reservations noon-5pm Tues.-Sat. 602/385-5726, other times 602/225-0100, www.wildhorsepassresort.com, 5:30pm-9pm Tues.-Thurs., 5:30pm-9:30pm Fri.-Sat. early Sept.-late July, $46-56) is one of the most unusual five-star restaurants in the West, with a fascinating Native American-inspired menu. Dress is business casual: no T-shirts, shorts, hats, or open-toed sandals for men, and denim is not preferred.

Burgers and Steaks

Rustler's Rooste (8383 S. 48th St.,

602/431-6474, www.rustlersrooste.com, 5pm-10pm daily, $17-30) is a cowboy-style steak house that seeks to recreate a rough-hewn ranch mess hall near South Mountain. Get pots of cowboy beans and steaming ears of corn, thick steaks, an always-celebratory atmosphere, and expansive views of the desert and city. This place is great for families and has a relatively inexpensive kids' menu offering small steaks and ribs. If you're just visiting Arizona, this may be your one chance to try fried rattlesnake.

The **Pedal Haus Brewery** (730 S. Mill Ave., 480/314-2337, http://pedalhausbrewery. com, 11am-11pm Mon.-Thurs., 11am-1am Fri.-Sat., 11am-10pm Sun., $13-19) is a cavernous restaurant-brewery off Mill Avenue with a huge stylish patio and front-row booths for watching the lonely brewmaster work his trade. Like all working breweries, this one has that wet-hops smell, but it's soon replaced by the beefy deliciousness of the burgers and sandwiches. There's also a large selection of vegan and gluten-free options. The decor is about bikes and beer, two things that Tempe residents enjoy and celebrate. The brewery offers a dozen handmade beers, delicious and inventive in their variety.

Indian

Perhaps the best Indian food in the state is at **Delhi Palace** (933 E. University Dr., Suite 103, 480/921-2200, www.delhipalacetempe. us, 11am-2:30pm and 5pm-10pm Mon.-Fri., 11am-3pm and 5pm-10pm Sat.-Sun., $10-17), near ASU, offering well-prepared standards. The service can be patchy, but you will never leave unsatisfied, especially after partaking in the lunch buffet (11am-2:30pm Mon.-Fri., 11am-3pm Sat.-Sun.).

Italian

Caffe Boa (398 S. Mill Ave., 480/968-9112, www.cafeboa.com, 11am-10pm Sun.-Wed., 11am-11pm Thurs.-Sat., 10am-3pm Sun., $10-28) serves the east valley's best Italian and Mediterranean food in an intimate setting in the busy Mill Avenue District. The panini here are particularly good for lunch, and there's a new dinner menu every month, always featuring delectable and creative pasta dishes grounded in tradition.

Middle Eastern

★ **Haji-Baba Middle Eastern Food** (1513 E. Apache Blvd., 480/894-1905, 10am-8pm Mon.-Sat., noon-4:30pm Sun., $10-15), a storefront in a strip mall just south of the ASU campus in Tempe, serves without a doubt the best Middle Eastern food in Arizona. The baba ghanoush is amazing, as are the hummus, gyros, kebabs, and falafel. The place is laid-back and casual, with a busy grocery store operating behind a thin partition; it's often packed, and the service can be a bit lackadaisical, but the food is perfect.

Vegetarian

The folks at **Green** (2240 N. Scottsdale Rd., 480/941-9003, www.greenvegetarian. com, 11am-9pm Mon.-Sat., $9-10), a "New American Vegetarian" restaurant, use mock meats and fresh vegetables and sauces to create 100 percent vegan meals. This is a place that even avid meat eaters will enjoy. They've got the best vegan chili fries and vegan chicken wings in town, and the "no harm chicken parm sandwich" is so tasty that it's difficult to believe *no* harm was done in its creation.

The **Udupi Café** (1636 N. Scottsdale Rd., 480/994-8787, www.udupiaz.com, 11am-3pm and 5pm-9:30pm Sun.-Thurs., 11am-3pm and 5pm-10pm Fri.-Sat., $9-16) is a fantastic option for vegetarians and vegans who like Indian food. The casual restaurant concentrates on dishes from different regions of the subcontinent, offering delicious vegetarian vindaloos, curries, and the like. Udupi will typically make a dish vegan for you if it isn't already on offer as such. It also has an excellent lunch buffet daily ($10 pp).

WEST VALLEY

While strolling and shopping in downtown Glendale, stop by **Cuff** (5819 W. Glendale

Ave., 623/847-8890, www.cuffglendale.com, 11am-9pm Mon.-Thurs., 11am-10pm Fri.-Sat., $11-15), a casual but sophisticated bistro and bar with an eclectic menu of burgers, sandwiches, salads, tacos, brisket, shrimp and grits, and more. Vegetarians and vegans will like this spot (offerings include green-chili jackfruit tacos and black-bean burgers), and several dishes can be made vegan and gluten free. Try the relaxing and well-stocked bar during happy hour (3pm-6pm Mon.-Fri.).

If you're in the northwest valley around breakfast time, don't miss **Kiss the Cook Restaurant** (4915 W. Glendale Ave., 623/939-4663, http://kissthecookrestaurant.com, 6am-2:30pm Mon.-Fri., 7am-3pm Sat., 7am-1pm Sun., $5-9), which serves favorites like omelets, homemade biscuits, and pancakes in an antique-shop interior.

Accommodations

The accommodations scene in the valley is ruled by the big chains and resorts. If you're hoping to find something a bit more distinctive and independent, expect to pay for it accordingly. The best time to find bargains is in summer, when nearly every big hotel and resort slashes its prices to attract business to the infernal desert.

Downtown Phoenix is a great place to stay for most visitors. It's centrally located and home to the best accommodations, restaurants, and nightlight in the valley. It's also relatively pedestrian friendly and convenient to Tempe's main street, Mill Avenue, by light rail. Scottsdale's downtown and Old Town neighborhoods are also good options, with fun places to stay and some areas that are pedestrian friendly—but never really cheap. If you're visiting Arizona State University or one of its students, you can stay in the lively areas of Tempe around the university campus and Mill Avenue.

If you're staying at one of the resorts on the edges of the city, expect to do a lot of driving to get to most of the sights around the valley.

DOWNTOWN AND CENTRAL
$50-100
The best deal in town is the **Hosteling International Phoenix** (1026 N. 9th St., 602/254-9803, www.phxhostel.org, $30-85), but you really have to be a hostel kind of person to enjoy it. You can stay in a dorm room or pay extra for a private room, but you share the baths and kitchen area. There's a shady courtyard, coin-operated laundry, and a common area with a piano; the staff is friendly and laid-back, and the house is located downtown in the Roosevelt Row arts district.

$100-250
The historic ★ **Hotel San Carlos** (202 N. Central Ave., 602/253-4121, www.hotelsancarlos.com, $189-300) sits right downtown with a facade that brings back the golden age of big-city hotels. Opened in 1928, the San Carlos was a favorite stop of Hollywood stars during the first half of the 20th century, and it was one of the first high-rise hotels in the Southwest, with full air-conditioning and electric elevators. The hotel now celebrates its glory days with themed rooms and memorabilia. Rooms are comfortable and chic, and the whole place has a kind of overstuffed, retro-cool ambience that you'll get nowhere else. Despite being charmingly old-school, Hotel San Carlos has an ecofriendly soul: It's a member of the Arizona Green Chamber of Commerce, which works to promote sustainable economic development, and is certified "Green Platinum" by the national Green Business Bureau. The certification is the result of the hotel's efforts to make sustainability an integral part of daily operations.

The Clarendon Hotel (401 W. Clarendon

Ave., 602/252-7363, www.theclarendon.net, $179-250) is a popular hangout owing to an amazing rooftop deck that overlooks the city and desert. It also has gorgeous, spacious rooms with cool and comfortable beds and a pool area to beat any in the valley.

Over $250

The ★ **Arizona Biltmore** (2400 E. Missouri Ave., 602/955-6600, www.arizonabiltmore. com, $459-518 plus $45 per night resort fee), covering 39 acres at the base of the Phoenix Mountains, is the valley's most famous, and still in most ways its best, resort. Other places may come and go, but this Frank Lloyd Wright-inspired (and, many contend, de-signed—Wright received a consulting fee on the project) "Jewel of the Desert" just keeps getting better with age. There are 738 guest rooms, including one- and two-bedroom suites, seven swimming pools, seven tennis courts, two 18-hole golf courses at the country club next door, a spa, an enormous outdoor chess set, and three restaurants.

Located near South Mountain Park, the ★ **Arizona Grand Resort** (8000 S. Arizona Grand Pkwy., 602/438-9000, www. arizonagrandresort.com, $250-400) has well-appointed comfortable suites, a water park for the kids, a golf course for the adults, a health club, a spa, six pools, and seven restaurants. It's a great place to take the family for an un-forgettable getaway. The resort is "Certified Green" by the Arizona Hotel & Lodging Association.

The **Foundre Phoenix** (1100 N. Central Ave., 602/875-8000, http://foundrehotels.com, $210-349) rises at the corner of Central and Portland downtown, and even if you can't af-ford to stay here (it's cheaper in the summer, expensive in the high season), you should take a look inside, especially if you're an art lover. This place takes its walls so seriously that it has a curator on staff. You will find work by major Arizona artists throughout this strange and wonderful place. The loft-style rooms are individually decorated with a kind of indus-trial craftsman style. This is probably the

hippest, coolest hotel in Phoenix; check it out if only to see the huge and cheeky painting of the great Burt Reynolds. The hotel has won best of Phoenix awards from several local and national magazines. Parking is $25 per night.

The **Royal Palms** (5200 E. Camelback Rd., 602/840-3610, www.royalpalmshotel. com, $450-709), right by the Phoenician at the base of Camelback Mountain, is a lush hide-out with all the amenities and then some. The rooms are decorated with antiques and other stylish touches; the grounds resemble some king's well-kept gardens, with Camelback Mountain shining in the background. This wonderful resort offers comfortable rooms, private casitas, and sprawling villas, plus the usual pool, spa, fitness center, and excellent gourmet dining. The Royal Palms is Certified Green by the Arizona Hotel & Lodging Association.

The kids will love the **Pointe Hilton at Squaw Peak** (7677 N. 16th St., 602/997-2626, www.pointehilton.com, $250-300) for its **Hole-in-the-Wall River Ranch**, a four-acre watery playground of linked pools, wa-terslides, spas, cabanas, and all sorts of other watery fun. This is a very nice place that is also relatively affordable, especially during summer, when they offer cut-rate deals that no family in need of a vacation should pass up.

Also a great place for families is the **Pointe Hilton Tapatio Cliffs Resort** (11111 N. 7th St., 602/866-7500, www.pointehilton.com, $250-300), which has a gorgeous series of pools and cabanas called the **Falls Water Village**, with several waterfalls, whirlpools, a waterslide, and hidden romantic spots to soak up the sun. There's also a golf course, a spa, and several restaurants. The Tapatio Cliffs is Certified Green by the Arizona Hotel & Lodging Association.

TEMPE AND THE EAST VALLEY
$100-250

★ **Graduate Tempe** (225 E. Apache Blvd., 480/967-9431, www.graduatehotels. com, $180-200) is right across from the ASU

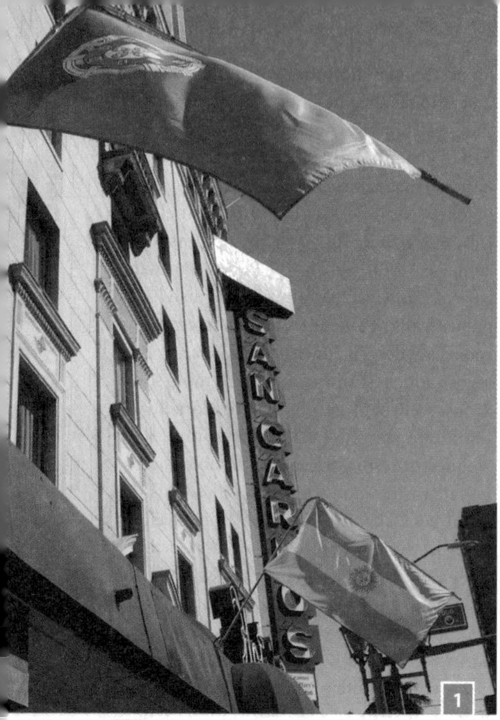

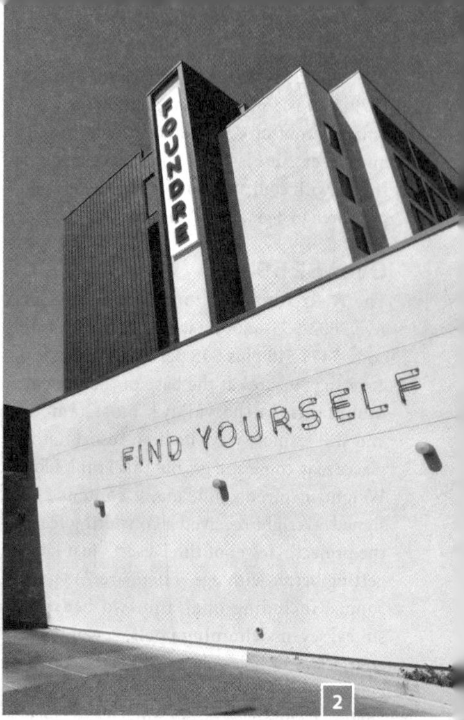
FOUNDRE
FIND YOURSELF

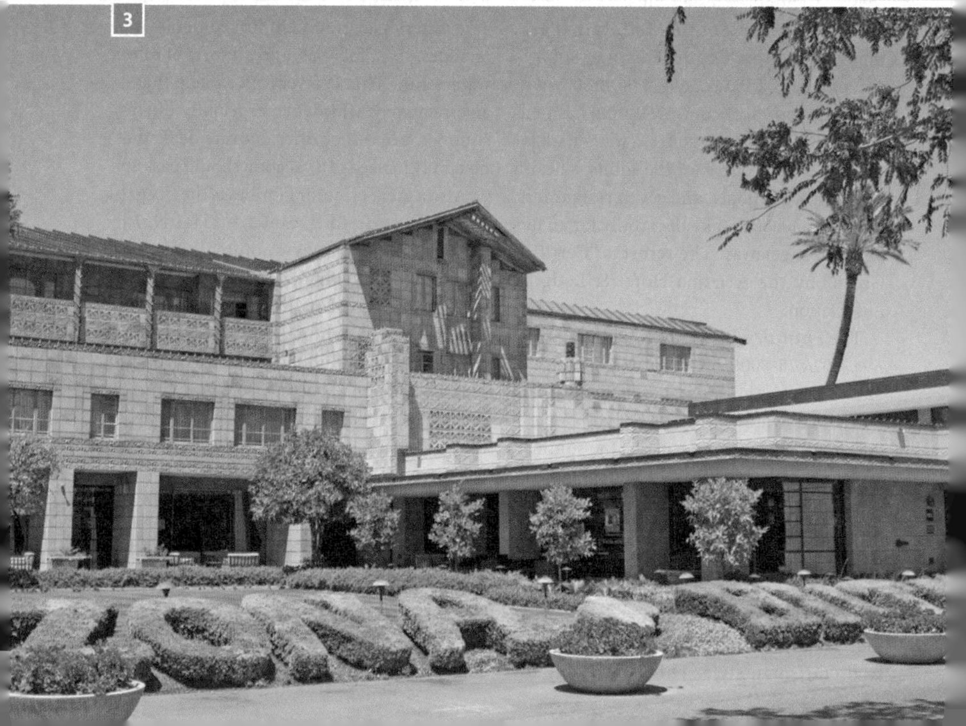

campus and close to all the action in Tempe. It's a stylish art-filled place with distinctive, comfortable, and memorable rooms. The hotel also has two restaurants, a large pool, and free use of bikes for exploring the campus. This is also a pet-friendly hotel—dogs stay free and are welcomed in style. This a great place to stay if you're visiting ASU or shopping and partying on Mill Avenue.

The **DoubleTree by Hilton Hotel Phoenix Tempe** (2100 S. Priest Dr., Tempe, 480/967-1441, http://doubletree3.hilton.com, $169-200) is a favorite among visiting ASU parents. It isn't the only valley hotel to call itself Frank Lloyd Wright-inspired, but it is certainly the most affordable. This high-end but not-too-pricey resort has tasteful Old Southwest-style rooms and common areas, acres of saltillo tile, and sharp rustic-looking decor all around. It has a big glistening blue pool (heated in winter), a great restaurant and lounge with complimentary finger foods at happy hour, and service that rivals much pricier places.

The **Tempe Mission Palms** (60 E. 5th St., Tempe, 480/894-1400, www.missionpalms. com, $199-322) in downtown Tempe is a beautiful property with a huge pool and tennis courts on the roof overlooking the entire valley. It has its own cozy bar and restaurant and is within walking distance to the shops and restaurants on Mill Avenue. The rooms have a Southwest style, and the courtyards are lush and watered. This is one of the most luxurious places to stay in Tempe and a bit less pricey than similarly appointed places in Phoenix and Scottsdale. The Mission Palms is Certified Green by the Arizona Hotel & Lodging Association.

As its name suggests, **The Buttes** (2000 Westcourt Way, 602/225-9900, www.marriott. com/phxtm, $200-450) overlooks the east valley from atop a 25-acre promontory in Tempe.

This gorgeous resort offers free Wi-Fi, sumptuously comfortable rooms, two large swimming pools with a waterslide, a full-service spa, and all manner of other fun and relaxing amenities.

Over $250

Near Tempe Town Lake, **Aloft** (951 E. Playa Del Norte Dr., 480/621-3300, www.alofttempe. com, $284-299) is a contemporary chic destination with complimentary spa products in your room and a plug-and-play station to charge your gadgets. The hotel offers free Wi-Fi, superbly comfortable beds, a hip bar, oversize showerheads in sleek walk-in showers, and so much style that you'll want to take photos of your room and the lobby.

WEST VALLEY

The historic ★ **Wigwam Hotel** (300 E. Wigwam Blvd., Litchfield Park, 623/935-3811, http://wigwamarizona.com, $220-350), which opened in 1929 and still has some of its original adobe casitas, offers a bit of classic Arizona in the west valley. The citrus trees that used to crowd the valley before the population boom still live on at this retro resort, and the whole place smells like oranges and lemons. It's far from the action but worth the drive for the classic touches and historic feel. The resort has the Red Door Spa, a golf course, and all the other amenities you'd expect from a legendary desert hideaway.

At Glendale's **Westgate** complex, just a few miles west of historic downtown on Glendale Avenue, you'll find several big chain hotels right next to the stadiums—homes of the NFL's Arizona Cardinals and the NHL's Phoenix Coyotes. The Westgate center also has a host of mid-range and upscale shopping and eating options, all conveniently located right next to the stadiums.

1: Hotel San Carlos 2: Foundre Phoenix 3: Arizona Biltmore

Information and Services

TOURIST INFORMATION

The Downtown Phoenix Visitor Center (125 2nd St., 877/225-5749, www.visitphoenix. com, 8am-5pm Mon.-Fri.) has stacks of information and literature, and the helpful staff will answer all your questions.

MEDIA

The two best newspapers in the valley, and in the state, for that matter, are the daily *Arizona Republic* (www.azcentral.com), the largest newspaper in Arizona, and the weekly *Phoenix New Times* (www. phoenixnewtimes.com), the best source for investigative reporting, off-center opinions, and cultural coverage.

HOSPITALS AND EMERGENCY SERVICES

If you get hurt in the valley or have any kind of emergency medical situation, the simplest thing to do is call 911. There are several top-notch hospitals around the valley, and many of them have satellite centers in every major subregion around the basin. **St. Joseph's Hospital and Medical Center** (350 W. Thomas Rd., 602/406-3000) is a Catholic hospital started by the Sisters of Mercy in the late 19th century and is consistently ranked one of the top hospitals in Arizona. It operates a Level 1 trauma center, one of just a few in Arizona.

St. Luke's Medical Center (1800 E. Van Buren St., 602/251-8100, www. stlukesmedcenter.com) is located near downtown Phoenix and has an updated and state-of-the-art emergency room that includes an innovative Chest Pain Emergency Center dedicated to preventing heart attacks. **Maricopa Medical Center** (2601 E. Roosevelt St., 602/344-5011, www.mihs.org) is one the nation's top hospitals, offering a full range of services, including a Level 1 trauma center and an infant ICU.

Transportation

The information in this section applies to the entire Valley of the Sun, not just Phoenix proper. If you spend time in the sprawling valley, you'll soon realize that it is easier to view it as one big city rather than many midsize cities. Although each of the cities around the valley has something unique to offer, in terms of transportation, the differences are negligible. If you're going to be in the valley more than a day, you are going to need a car. The bus system is reliable and comfortable, but it is not realistic to employ it for sightseeing tours. The light-rail system moves past most of the downtown and central sights, restaurants, and accommodations.

AIR

Phoenix Sky Harbor International Airport

Phoenix Sky Harbor International Airport (PHX, 3400 E. Sky Harbor Blvd., 602/273-3300, www.skyharbor.com) is one of the Southwest's largest, with two terminals served by 17 domestic and international airlines offering flights to about 80 domestic and 22 international destinations, mostly in Mexico and Canada. If you're traveling to Arizona by air, you will likely land at Sky Harbor.

AIRPORT TRANSPORTATION

Sky Harbor is just five miles east of downtown Phoenix. If you're leaving the airport in a rental car, head east on Sky Harbor Boulevard to AZ 143. Go south on AZ 143 and after about two miles take Exit 1B and get on I-10 going west. It should take about 10 minutes, or up to 20 in traffic, to get downtown from the airport. If you're headed to Tempe and Arizona State University, take Sky Harbor Boulevard east to North Priest Drive. Turn right onto North Priest and then left on West University Drive. The airport is about five miles from campus, which could take up to 15 minutes in traffic.

The **Metro Light Rail** goes to the airport ($2)—take the light rail to the 44th Street and Washington Valley Metro Station to get to terminals 2-4. From the Metro station, you can catch the free **Sky Train** to get to the terminals and the economy parking lots. The Sky Train runs day and night, and there's never a wait of more than five minutes or so. There's also a **free shuttle** that travels from the economy parking lots to the terminals.

SuperShuttle (602/244-9000, www. supershuttle.com) offers rides to the airport from destinations all over the valley. Sky Harbor contracts with the shuttle giant to provide the service, and the ride is typically reliable and not unpleasant. You have to make a reservation. Shuttles run every 15 minutes 9am-9pm daily. Expect to pay $12-38 for the first person in your party, depending on how far you are from the airport, and $7 for each additional passenger regardless of where you are. Catch the shuttle from terminal 2 on the north curb; from terminal 3, wait at the north or south curbs; and from terminal 4, head down to the first floor and wait at the north or south curb.

Three **taxicab** companies contract with Sky Harbor to provide transportation at a set rate ($5 1st mile, $2.30 each additional mile, $23 per hour traffic delay, $15 minimum fare, $1 per trip surcharge): **Apache Taxi** (480/557-7000), **AAA/Yellow Cab** (480/888-8888), and **Mayflower Cab** (602/955-1355).

You can meet a taxi on the north curb outside terminal 2's door 8, on the north curb of terminal 3, outside door 8, or on the first floor of terminal 4 on the north curb, outside door 7.

You can get a taxi to take you anywhere in the valley; however, considering the long distances involved, they can quickly get expensive. On the weekends you'll find taxis waiting outside of popular drinking and partying areas like downtown Phoenix, Scottsdale, and Tempe, but most of the time you have to call and arrange for a pickup. Ultimately, taxis are not really an efficient way of getting around the valley.

Uber, Lyft, and other ride-share companies serve Sky Harbor as well. Each terminal has a specified pickup location.

CAR

The easiest way to get to, from, and around Phoenix and Arizona is by car. The best way to see the wonderland that is Arizona is in your own car, preferably with your road-trip mix on the stereo.

I-10 passes through the valley's heart on its way to the California coast. Phoenix is 372 miles east of Los Angeles, a straight five-hour drive on I-10. Continue east on I-10 another 100 miles or so and you're in Tucson, Arizona's second city. The valley is connected to east-west I-40 by I-17, which runs north 150 miles from central Phoenix to Flagstaff, an I-40 town and one of the gateways to the Grand Canyon. The trip north from the desert of Phoenix to the cool pines of Flagstaff takes just over two hours.

Car Rental

It is easy to rent a car at the airport, but the exorbitant airport taxes and fees make doing so a bad idea; the price shock will ruin your trip. Sky Harbor provides a free **Rental Car Shuttle** from the baggage claim at each terminal to the **Rental Car Center** (1805 E. Sky Harbor Circle South, 602/683-3741), just west of the airport. All the major rental companies are represented at the center, including

Hertz (602/267-8822 or 800/654-3131, www. hertz.com) and Budget (800/527-7000, www. budget.com).

It's more economical to head outside the airport to rent a car. Try the locally owned Phoenix Car Rental (2934 E. McDowell Rd., 602/269-9310; 3625 W. Indian School Rd., 602/269-9310, www.rentacarphoenix.com). The McDowell Road site is about seven miles from the airport. You can arrange for them to pick you up.

LONG-DISTANCE BUS

Phoenix's Greyhound bus station (2115 E. Buckeye Rd., 602/389-4200) is located near Sky Harbor International Airport. Groome Transportation (928/350-8466, http:// groometransportation.com, $49 one-way) offers several daily trips between Flagstaff's Amtrak station and Sky Harbor International Airport.

TRAIN

The Amtrak *Sunset Limited* (800/872-7245, www.amtrak.com), which runs the southern route of dry desert Southwest three times a week from New Orleans, stops in Maricopa, Arizona, about 30 miles east of Phoenix.

However, transportation options from Maricopa to Phoenix are tough to come by and expensive.

PUBLIC TRANSPORTATION

Bus

Valley Metro (602/253-5000, www. valleymetro.org), the valley's public transportation authority, runs bus service ($2 per ride) everywhere, including Glendale, Scottsdale, Tempe, and Mesa.

Metro Light Rail

The best thing to happen to the valley since affordable air-conditioning, the sleek Metro Light Rail (602/253-5000, www.valleymetro. org) is transforming the city's one-person, one-car culture into something more sustainable. The current system is nearly 30 miles long, beginning in the northwest at Montebello Avenue and 19th Avenue, where there's a large parking lot, and traversing the valley all the way to Mesa in the east. Along the way the futuristic people-mover stops at or near most of the valley's top sights, including downtown's Heard and Phoenix Museums and Tempe's Mill Avenue and

Metro Light Rail

Town Lake. It's a great way to get around and see the sights without a car and finding parking, although this strategy is recommended only in winter-spring. Fares start at $2 per ride, $4 for an all-day pass, and the last trip begins at 11pm Sunday-Thursday and 2am Friday-Saturday. See the website for a complete map and fare schedule.

Scottsdale

Scottsdale suffers somewhat from its reputation as being high-toned, high-dollar, and maybe even a little pretentious. This isn't the case, however, in most corners of the city, which has won numerous national awards for being generally livable, clean, and attractive. It's true that you see more Beemers and Jags within Scottsdale's city limits than in other parts of the valley (save Paradise Valley, a mostly residential community that is one of the richest in the nation), but a day's visit here will likely reveal that there is much more to Scottsdale than beautiful rich people and their high-walled resorts.

SIGHTS

Downtown

Visitors to Scottsdale, a citrus-growing suburb turned international resort destination and art center, primarily come to stroll, shop, and eat in the city's bustling downtown area (www.downtownscottsdale.com), which includes Old Town, Fifth Avenue, and the Arts District, among others. There are dozens of Native American and Western art galleries and trading posts, boutiques selling Southwestern-style items both authentic and touristy, contemporary art galleries with a flair for the most current styles, restaurants from hamburger huts to highbrow gourmet destinations, and lots of coffeehouses and cool watering holes.

Downtown Scottsdale is roughly defined by Chaparral Road on the north, Osborn Road on the south, Miller Road on the east, and 68th Street on the west. Within these boundaries there are several distinct districts, though they meld into one another. The attractions are art-searching, shopping, eating and drinking, and strolling and people-watching. In the Arts District, between Goldwater Boulevard and Scottsdale Road, you'll find a collection of art galleries to rival any other artsy block in the Southwest; the neighborhood is home to a popular art walk every Thursday night. On Fifth Avenue you'll find more than 80 boutiques and shops selling mostly Southwestern and Native American items. You'll also find **Bob Parks's Horse Fountain,** a collection of wild galloping stone horses jumping out of a large fountain. There are several kiosks scattered around downtown that are stuffed with pamphlets, free magazines, and handouts about visiting Scottsdale.

HISTORIC OLD TOWN SCOTTSDALE

The stretch of downtown where Scottsdale's founder, Eastern banker Albert G. Utley, first staked out a town site (roughly bounded by Scottsdale Rd., Brown Ave., Indian School Rd., and 2nd St.) has a collection of shops and eateries, some of them with Old West-style facades and hitching posts out front. The main shopping, sauntering, and people-watching area is along Main Street just before Brown Avenue. In the old days, Main Street was lined with homes, but in the 1940s Scottsdale began selling itself as "The West's Most Western Town," and the homes were turned into businesses with faux frontier-era facades. Main Street ends at the 21-acre **Scottsdale Civic Center Mall,** prime strolling grounds with lots of grass, shade-giving trees, and public art both silly and thought-provoking. Just as you reach the mall, off Main Street, look for the **Little Red Schoolhouse,** also known as the **Scottsdale Historical Museum** (7333 E. Scottsdale Mall, 480/945-4499, www.

Scottsdale and Vicinity

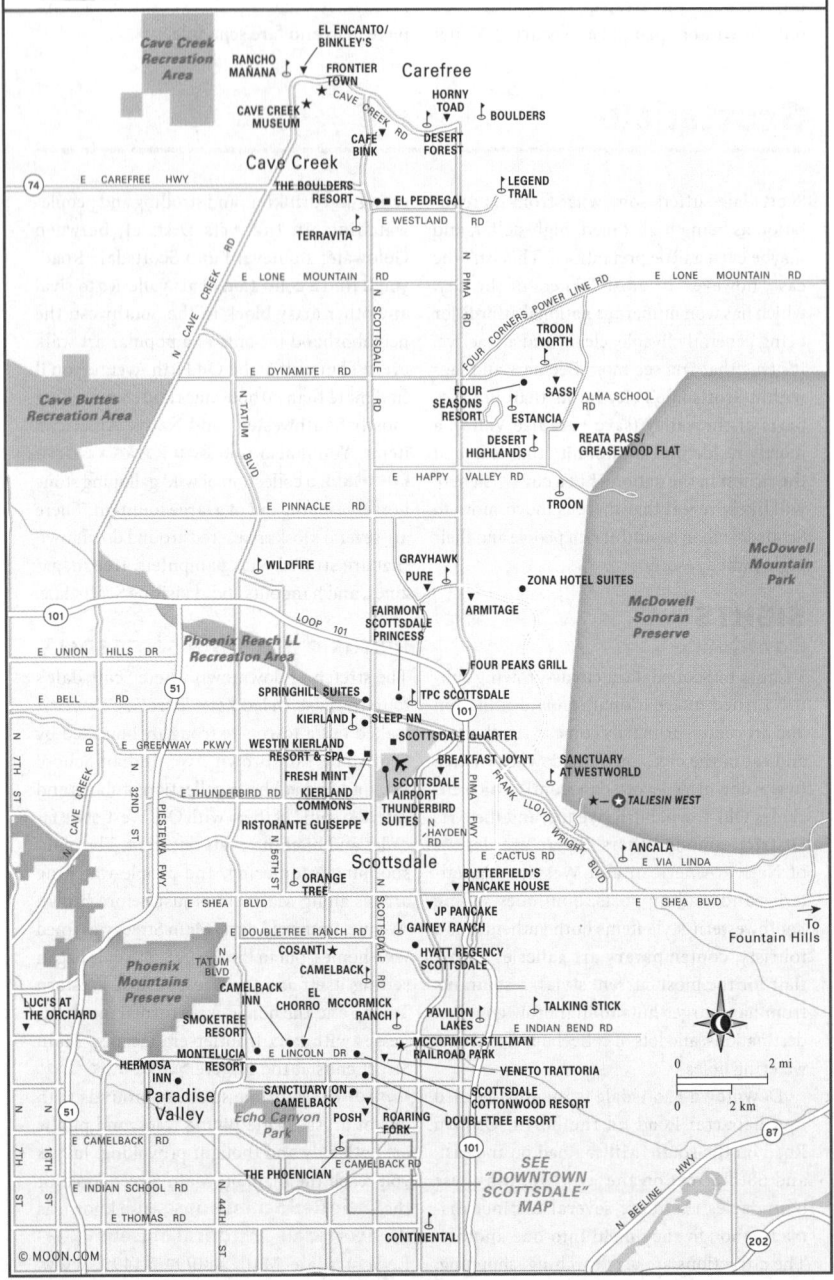

Cave Creek
Recreation
Area

EL ENCANTO/
BINKLEY'S

RANCHO
MAÑANA

FRONTIER
TOWN

Carefree

HORNY
TOAD

BOULDERS

CAVE CREEK RD

CAVE CREEK
MUSEUM

DESERT
FOREST

CAFÉ
BINK

Cave Creek

74   E CAREFREE HWY

THE BOULDERS
RESORT

EL PEDREGAL

LEGEND
TRAIL

TERRAVITA

E WESTLAND   RD

N CAVE CREEK RD

E LONE   MOUNTAIN   RD

N PIMA   RD

FOUR CORNERS POWER LINE RD

E LONE   MOUNTAIN   RD

Cave Buttes
Recreation Area

E DYNAMITE   RD

N TATUM   BLVD

N SCOTTSDALE   RD

TROON
NORTH

SASSI

ALMA SCHOOL
RD

FOUR
SEASONS
RESORT

ESTANCIA

DESERT
HIGHLANDS

REATA PASS/
GREASEWOOD FLAT

E   HAPPY   VALLEY   RD

E PINNACLE   RD

TROON

McDowell
Mountain
Park

101

WILDFIRE

GRAYHAWK
PURE

ZONA HOTEL SUITES

McDowell
Sonoran
Preserve

E UNION   HILLS DR

LOOP 101

Phoenix Reach LL
Recreation Area

FAIRMONT
SCOTTSDALE
PRINCESS

ARMITAGE

51

E BELL   RD

FOUR PEAKS GRILL

N 7TH ST

N CAVE CREEK RD

N 32ND ST

PIESTEWA FWY

SPRINGHILL SUITES

TPC SCOTTSDALE

101

KIERLAND

SLEEP NN

E GREENWAY PKWY

WESTIN KIERLAND
RESORT & SPA

SCOTTSDALE QUARTER

SANCTUARY
AT WESTWORLD

FRESH MINT

FRANK LLOYD WRIGHT BLVD

E THUNDERBIRD RD

KIERLAND
COMMONS

SCOTTSDALE
AIRPORT

BREAKFAST JOYNT

★ ◑ TALIESIN WEST

RISTORANTE GUISEPPE

N 56TH ST

THUNDERBIRD
SUITES

N PIMA RD

N HAYDEN RD

Scottsdale

E CACTUS RD

ANCALA

E VIA LINDA

ORANGE
TREE

BUTTERFIELD'S
PANCAKE HOUSE

E SHEA BLVD

To
Fountain Hills

E SHEA   BLVD

JP PANCAKE

GAINEY RANCH

E DOUBLETREE RANCH RD

N SCOTTSDALE RD

Phoenix
Mountains
Preserve

N TATUM BLVD

COSANTI ★

CAMELBACK

HYATT REGENCY
SCOTTSDALE

LUCI'S AT
THE ORCHARD

CAMELBACK
INN

EL
CHORRO

MCCORMICK
RANCH

PAVILION
LAKES

TALKING STICK

E INDIAN BEND RD

SMOKETREE
RESORT

E LINCOLN DR

MCCORMICK-STILLMAN
RAILROAD PARK

0   2 mi

HERMOSA
INN

MONTELUCIA
RESORT

VENETO TRATTORIA

0   2 km

51

Paradise
Valley

SANCTUARY ON
CAMELBACK

Echo Canyon
Park

POSH

SCOTTSDALE
COTTONWOOD RESORT

ROARING
FORK

DOUBLETREE RESORT

87

E CAMELBACK   RD

N 16TH ST

N 7TH ST

THE PHOENICIAN

E CAMELBACK RD

101

N 44TH ST

SEE
"DOWNTOWN
SCOTTSDALE"
MAP

N BEELINE HWY

E INDIAN SCHOOL RD

E THOMAS RD

© MOON.COM

CONTINENTAL

202

scottsdalemuseum.org, 10am-2pm Wed.-Sun. Sept.-June, 10am-5pm Wed.-Sun. Oct.-May, free). Inside this charming brick structure, built in 1909 and used as the town's school, city hall, courthouse, and library at various times over the years, there are several exhibits on Scottsdale's history. At 10am every Tuesday January-March, a docent leads a one-hour **Downtown Historic Walking Tour** that begins at the schoolhouse. All around Old Town and in the other touristy districts of downtown, you'll see quite a few horses doing draft duty in front of some restored carriage or wagon, loaded down with couples and kids.

SCOTTSDALE MUSEUM
OF CONTEMPORARY ART

It's fitting that the only art museum in Arizona dedicated strictly to the new and the now is in Scottsdale, one of the magnetic centers of art in the Southwest. You won't find any howling coyotes or Kokopelli here; the works are edgy, sometimes confusingly avant-garde, and always interesting. **SMoCA** (7374 E. 2nd St., 480/874-4666, www.smoca.org, noon-5pm Tues.-Wed. and Fri.-Sun., noon-9pm Thurs., $10 adults, $7 students, free under age 15, free Thurs.) is located just across the street from the Center for the Arts and has five galleries in a spare, modern space that used to be a movie theater. Special shows and exhibitions rotate often, and there's always at least one gallery showing work from the museum's permanent collection.

WESTERN SPIRIT: SCOTTSDALE'S
MUSEUM OF THE WEST

Located in downtown Scottsdale's arts district, **Western Spirit: Scottsdale's Museum of the West** (3830 N. Marshall Way, 480/686-9539, http://scottsdalemuseumwest.org, 9:30am-5pm Tues.-Sat., 11am-5pm Sun., $20) should be visited by anyone interested in the art, culture, and history of the Old West. Focused on the art and images of the Western frontier, it offers several unique exhibitions each year on subjects such as the Cowboy Artists of America, the Grand Canyon in painting, Native American pottery, Western films, and more.

OLD ADOBE MISSION

The **Old Adobe Mission** (7655 E. Main St., 480/947-4331, www.olphaz.com, 10am-4pm daily Nov.-Apr., free), a small chapel in the heart of the Old Town district, was built in 1933 by a group of Mexican and Yaqui families. If it looks a bit like a miniature San Xavier del Bac, that's because it's supposed to: Architect Robert Evans allegedly had Tucson's famous "White Dove of the Desert" in mind when he designed this little Mission-style gem. It was built by volunteers with some 14,000 adobe bricks made from a mixture of dirt, straw, and horse manure. Local tinsmith Barnebe Herrera made—and signed—the church's stained-glass windows. There's often a volunteer on-site to talk about the building, its history, and the important effort to save it.

Central Scottsdale
and Paradise Valley
COSANTI

Known for his visionary utopian architecture, the late Paolo Soleri, founder of the living architecture research facility in Central Arizona called Arcosanti, was a powerful figure in the valley, if only because he represented what could be when it comes to humans living in resource-sparse environments. His round, organic, fairy-world structures, which seem to have been waiting there in the desert for some mad genius to tell them to rise up, are part Frank Lloyd Wright (who brought Soleri to the valley to study at Taliesin West), part Native American, and part artistic fantasy. His Paradise Valley desert complex, established in 1956, has a gallery, studio, living spaces, and a foundry, where students make the famous **Soleri Windbells,** sold throughout the world to fund the ongoing urban design experiments at Arcosanti. You can watch the bells being made most weekday mornings. An ideal way to visit **Cosanti** (6433 E. Doubletree Ranch Rd., 480/948-6145, www.cosanti.com, 9am-5pm Mon.-Sat., 11am-5pm

Downtown Scottsdale

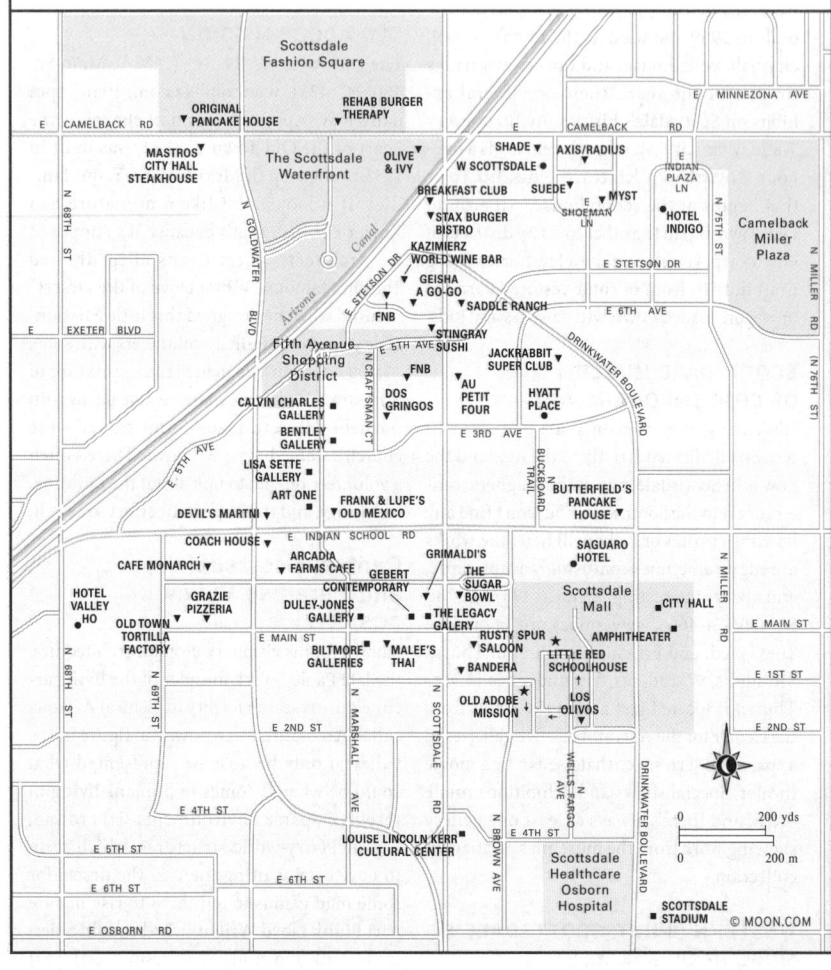

Sun., free) is to combine it with a tour of Taliesin West, which is located about eight miles northeast.

MCCORMICK-STILLMAN RAILROAD PARK

Kids and train enthusiasts will love **McCormick-Stillman Railroad Park** (7301 E. Indian Bend Rd., 480/312-2312, www. therailroadpark.com, generally 10am-6pm daily, free), dedicated to the old iron horse.

Rides on the train and carousel cost $3 each. A replica of a Colorado narrow-gauge railroad called **The Paradise and Pacific Railroad** makes you feel like a giant as it moves around a one-mile track running through the green park. There are also several old trains in the park that are worth a look as well as a museum

1: desert in bloom in the McDowell Sonoran Preserve 2: Old Adobe Mission 3: fountain in Old Town Scottsdale 4: Gilbert Ortega Gallery & Museum, featuring Native American arts

featuring exhibits on the history of the railroad and how it changed the valley—housed in a 1914 Santa Fe Railroad baggage car. Another highlight is a presidential Pullman car used by Eisenhower and FDR. Don't skip a ride on the restored old carousel—it's pure joy. The park's hours vary slightly by season, so call ahead or visit the website to verify.

North Scottsdale

ODYSEA IN THE DESERT

A family entertainment complex, **OdySea in the Desert** (9500 E. Via De Ventura, off AZ 101 Loop, 480/291-8000, http://odyseainthedesert.com) has a pleasant courtyard with a soaring metal structure, a fountain, and several restaurants, bars, and shops to hang out in and peruse before or after you check out the sea creatures at the huge **OdySea Aquarium** (480/291-8000, www.odyseaaquarium.com, 9am-7pm Mon.-Wed., 9am-8pm Thurs.-Sat., 9am-6pm Sun., $22 adults, $15 ages 3-12) or the butterflies and reptiles at **Butterfly Wonderland** (www.butterflywonderland.com, 480/800-3000, 9am-5pm daily, $22 adults, $15 ages 3-12). Kids will love the **Laser and Mirror Maze** (480/270-6200, www.odyseamirrormaze.com, 10am-7pm Sun.-Fri., 10am-8pm Sat., $4-13), a fun playland with challenging games that have you scooting around to avoid green lasers, like a secret agent or cat burglar. The complex also has super-fun **bumper boats** (10am-6pm daily, $4 per ride).

HUHUGAM KI MUSEUM

In an adobe building on the **Salt River Pima-Maricopa Indian Community,** two of the state's river-bred tribes preserve their history and cultural customs. "Huhugam Ki" means "House of the Ancestors," and the ancestors they are talking about are the mysterious Hohokam, who irrigated and grew crops in the Salt River Valley hundreds of years ago. The **Huhugam Ki Museum** (10005 E. Osborn Rd., 480/362-7400, www.srpmic-nsn.gov, 9:30am-4:30pm Mon.-Fri., free) tells the stories and histories of the Pima

people, now commonly referred to in their own language as the Akimel O'odham (River People)—cousins to Southern Arizona's Tohono O'odham (Desert People)—and the Maricopa, or Xalychidom Piipaash, a tribe that migrated to the valley from the banks of the Gila and Colorado Rivers, through exhibits, old photographs, pottery, and other artifacts. The Akimel O'odham are known for their basket-making, and a highlight of a visit to this small museum is the live demonstrations of the intricate art by tribal members.

★ TALIESIN WEST

Architect Frank Lloyd Wright spent the money he made from his masterpiece Fallingwater on a large swath of desert northeast of Scottsdale, and from about 1937 onward he spent a portion of each year living in the desert with his apprentices and building what would become **Taliesin West** (12621 Frank Lloyd Wright Blvd., 480/860-2700, recorded tour info 480/860-8810, www.franklloydwright.org, 9am-4pm Thurs.-Mon.). If every house built in the desert used the natural landscape in the same way as this wondrous complex does, the valley would be a much different, better place today. Familiar Wright motifs, like his ubiquitous compression-and-release entranceways, Oriental touches, and native-rock-and-mortar aesthetic, are on display at this truly unique and important attraction.

You can see Taliesin only by tour, and the guides are knowledgeable and enthusiastic about Wright's work and legacy. Since the complex is still used and lived in today by fellows of Taliesin Associated Architects, a group carrying on the spirit of Wright's work, some buildings may be off-limits during a given tour. You have various tours from which to choose. The most popular is the 60-minute **Insights Tour** (11am-4pm Thurs.-Mon., $40 adults, $19 ages 6-12), which includes a look at the living quarters and beautiful Garden Room. The **Guided by Wright Audio Tour** (9am-10:30am Thurs.-Mon., $40 adults, $19 ages 6-12) is

Frank Lloyd Wright in the Valley of the Sun

In 1940 Frank Lloyd Wright published an essay in *Arizona Highways* in which he eloquently pleaded for a different kind of architecture for the desert, one not based on previous models but on the unique colors and contours of the desert itself: "The ever advancing human threat to the integral beauty of Arizona might be avoided if the architect would only go to school in the desert," he wrote, "and humbly learn harmonious contrasts or sympathetic treatments that would, thus, quietly, belong."

Certainly the best of the very few real-world examples of what Wright had in mind is his own **Taliesin West,** Wright's most famous desert building. He designed a few other distinctive structures in the valley, and some of them are accessible to fans of the nation's greatest architect. In addition to a church and an auditorium, Wright built nine private homes in the valley, eight of which still exist.

Many critics and scholars include the 1928 **Arizona Biltmore** (2400 E. Missouri Ave., Phoenix), then as now the state's most stylish resort, on the short list of public structures Wright designed in the valley. Though the architect of record is his former apprentice, Albert Chase McArthur, Wright was paid a consulting fee on the project and left his mark on the design, as anyone with knowledge of Wright's quirks and obsessions will see during a stroll around the magnificent "Jewel of the Desert."

Wright created the design for the north valley's **First Christian Church** (6750 N. 7th Ave., 602/246-9206, www.fccphx.com) in 1950 as part of the Classical University commission that never got off the ground. In 1972, church leaders obtained the unused plans and started construction on the sanctuary, considered by many the best example of Wright's church architecture. You can stop in for a look around, or attend one of the services (9am and 10:30am Sun.).

Wright originally designed Arizona State University's **Grady Gammage Memorial Auditorium** (1200 S. Forest Ave., Tempe, 480/965-5062) as an opera house for Baghdad, Iraq. In 1957, when Wright was 90 years old, the king of Iraq commissioned him to design several public buildings. Unfortunately, the king was killed the next year, so the project fell apart. Later, the design for the Baghdad opera house was changed a bit to become Gammage Auditorium. It is not one of the critics' favorites—it's a bit puffy and sappy for some tastes—but the acoustics, as in all of Wright's performance spaces, are absolutely perfect.

Journalist Lawrence Cheek wrote a slim but comprehensive book about Wright's desert work, *Frank Lloyd Wright in Arizona* (Rio Nuevo, 2006), which should be read by anybody interested in Wright's Western masterpieces.

an hour-long self-paced tour; you'll walk around the grounds on your own, listening to a recording of Wright himself talking, along with other guides. The tour schedules change; call ahead. Arrive a little early so you can check out the excellent bookstore and gift shop, which sells Wright-inspired knickknacks and just about every book ever published by or on the master.

CAREFREE AND CAVE CREEK

Drive north on Scottsdale Road (about 15 miles from Phoenix) through a beautiful, if disappearing, stretch of desert to these tiny resort-style towns full of galleries, antiques stores, restaurants, and artisanal shops—a perfect daylong escapade to the valley's northeastern outer reaches. Along the way, watch for the large signs on the side of the road pointing out various representative Sonoran Desert flora. In January and March, the **Carefree Fine Art & Wine Festival** attracts artists, artisans, and wine lovers from across the nation. This drive is very popular with motorcycle groups, and on any given weekend (though not so much in the summer) the area is likely to be somewhat crowded.

SPORTS AND RECREATION

Scottsdale is a bit greener than many desert cities, and there are quite a few parks and open spaces within the relatively small area of the town. One of the best of these is the long multiuse trail that winds through the center of the mostly residential neighborhoods along Hayden Road from Indian Bend Road south to Tempe—about 13 miles of greenspace for bikers, joggers, walkers, and skaters called the Indian Bend Wash Greenbelt (Scottsdale Parks and Recreation, 7340 Scottsdale Mall, 480/312-7957, www.scottsdaleaz.gov). Along this unique flood-control system, which channels intermittent desert floods—mostly in the late-summer monsoon season—into Indian Bend Wash while at the same time creating a fine exercise and recreation belt through the length of the town, you'll see a steady stream of bikers, in-line skaters, and joggers, especially in the morning. The path passes through several city parks and golf courses as it makes its way south all the way to Tempe Town Lake. There's not a set-aside signed starting block for the greenbelt, but a good place to pick it up is at Chaparral Park (5401 N. Hayden Rd., 480/312-2353).

Hiking and Biking

MCDOWELL MOUNTAIN REGIONAL PARK

If you'd like to get out of the city and into the desert, head out to McDowell Mountain Regional Park (16300 McDowell Mountain Park Dr., 480/471-0173, www.maricopa.gov), a 21,000-acre desert preserve northeast of Scottsdale with miles of desert hiking, biking, and equestrian trails, an excellent setting for getting to know the Sonoran Desert. From Scottsdale, take Shea Boulevard east to Fountain Hills Boulevard, which heads north and turns into McDowell Mountain Road, leading into the park. If you've got some extra time, think about stopping in the retirement haven of Fountain Hills and seeing the world's biggest fountain; continue on Shea past Fountain Hills Boulevard, and

then turn north on Saguaro Boulevard, which leads right past Fountain Park and The Fountain and then meets with Fountain Hills Boulevard, which leads to the preserve.

Inside the park, there are various trails for hiking, biking, and horseback riding; one of the more popular short hikes is the 3-mile North Trail. The 15-mile Pemberton Trail is the toughest and longest hike in the park.

MCDOWELL SONORAN PRESERVE

McDowell Sonoran Preserve (various trailheads around Scottsdale, 480/312-7013, www.scottsdaleaz.gov, sunrise-sunset daily, free) in Scottsdale holds back the sprawling cityscape from some 27,000 acres of beautiful desert around the McDowell Mountains. The area is northeast of the city center and has dozens of varied trails for hiking, all of them fairly near each other. The largest and most developed trailhead is the Gateway Access Area (18333 N. Thompson Peak Pkwy.), about 15 miles north of downtown Scottsdale via the AZ 101 Loop. Other access areas with trails include Lost Dog Wash (12601 N. 124th St.), 14 miles north of downtown via the 101 Loop; Quartz (10215 E. McDowell Mt. Ranch Rd.), also 14 miles north on the 101; Ringtail (12300 block of N. 128th St.), 14.5 miles north on the 101; Sunrise (12101 N. 145th Way), 16 miles north of downtown via the 101; and WestWorld (15939 N. 98th St.), 13 miles from downtown on the 101.

The Gateway Loop Trail (Gateway Access Area) is a relatively easy 4.5-mile loop through a beautiful Sonoran Desert setting—and an excellent primer on desert hiking. More difficult is the Tom Thumb Trail (23015 N. 128th St.), a 4.5-mile climb to a promontory that provides spectacular views of the desert and the city. The Brown's Ranch Trail (30301 N. Alma School Pkwy.) is an easy 3-mile hike through an old ranch property.

Golf

There are about 200 golf courses in the Valley of the Sun, and about 50 of them are in Scottsdale, a town as famous for its golf as for its galleries and resorts. You'll likely find the golf courses in Scottsdale a bit more challenging and considerably more beautiful and dramatic than those in surrounding communities, but they are also considerably more expensive. For a true golf lover, though, this is where you'll want to splurge. Book a tee time before traveling if you want to play any of Scottsdale's courses.

Kierland Golf Club (15636 N. Clubgate Dr., 480/922-9283, www.kierlandgolf.com) is a gorgeous 27-hole, par-36 desert course along Scottsdale Road just south of Frank Lloyd Wright Boulevard. It's part of the Weston Kierland Resort and Spa but is open to the public. The greens are shocking against the hard desert scenery, which has been left to itself along the edges of the greenery, making for a uniquely Arizona golfing experience. It's not cheap, at $170-190 in high season, $44-74 during the hottest days of summer. The course offers some twilight-hour prices that are significantly cheaper, however. You can book a tee time online.

The fabulous **Troon North Golf Club** (10320 E. Dynamite Blvd., 480/585-5300, www.troonnorthgolf.com) in the far northeast valley is a much-sought-after golfing experience for duffers the world over. It's probably the most beautiful public course in the valley. There are two courses, both lined with desert boulders and saguaro; the Monument Course, the better of the two, is so named because of the 14-foot boulder rising off the fairway. Expect to pay $50-80 in summer and around $200 in high season.

Starfire at Scottsdale Country Club (11500 N. Hayden Rd., 480/948-6000, www.starfiregolfclub.com) is a more centrally located course—head north on Hayden Road and you'll find it—and more reasonably priced than some of the fancier desert courses north of the city. The 27-hole course, lined with eucalyptus and palm trees, was designed by Arnold Palmer and is moderately challenging. Expect to pay about $20 for a round in summer, $40-50 during high season.

TPC of Scottsdale (17020 N. Hayden Rd., 480/585-4334, http://tpc.com) is where the PGA pros play one of the most popular tournaments of the year in late January; the **Waste Management Open** (www.phoenixopen.com), formerly the Phoenix Open, is one of the oldest tournaments on the pro tour and draws some of the biggest crowds of any tournament. In the off-season you're likely to see one of the local PGA tour members practicing on the two exquisite courses. The Scottsdale Princess Resort is linked with the club. To stay and play is to engage in the height of luxury and enjoy challenging golf. Greens fees run more than $200 in high season and about $80 in deep summer, with discounts for evening play.

Spas

Scottsdale is known far and wide as a place to pamper your body and soul. There are dozens of spas in this upscale desert burg, and many of them are associated with the city's many world-famous resorts. A half- or full day at one of these spas may be just what you need. It's going to cost you; check the websites for current pricing, but don't expect rates under $100 to get started. During the summer months, most of the spas, like their parent resorts, cut prices to attract business to the hot valley. Call ahead for a reservation in any season.

The **Phoenician Spa** (6000 E. Camelback Rd., 480/843-2392, www.thephoenician.com, 7am-7pm daily) takes your health and comfort seriously. They offer 75 different treatments at this 22,000-square-foot spa that will put you through a vigorous workout, give you a facial, massage, and a makeover, and then send you on your way after you've stopped at the "waters bar" and found your center in the meditation room.

The **Spa at Camelback Inn** (5402 E. Lincoln Dr., 800/922-2635, www.camelbackspa.com, 6:15am-7:30pm daily, appointment required) has a gorgeous spa, with plunge pools, Turkish baths and saunas, and a beautiful pool area where you can rent a spa cabana for a day of relaxation. They offer all manner of body wraps and facial treatments, massages, and other bodywork in a truly stunning setting. They also have exercise classes, personal training and consultations, and a spa restaurant serving healthy and wholesome foods.

At **The Sanctuary Spa at Sanctuary Resort** (5700 E. McDonald Dr., Paradise Valley, 480/607-2326, www.sanctuaryoncamelback.com, 6am-8:30pm daily), you can get a variety of Asian treatments, such as the medicinal herb massage called *luk pra kope*, as well as acupuncture, Reiki, shiatsu, and Thai reflexology. This refined tranquil space on the grounds of the Sanctuary Resort also offers a host of other treatments, including Swedish massage, facials, makeovers, and personal training.

If you're in downtown Scottsdale and need of a massage, facial, and sauna, stop into **The Lamar Everyday Spa** (5115 N. Scottsdale Rd., 480/945-7066, www.thelamar.com, 10am-7pm Sun.-Thurs., 9am-7pm Fri.-Sat.), with massages, facials, pools and saunas, and all the other soothing treatments in a friendly coed atmosphere that was voted one of the valley's best places for a romantic date. The prices are generally a bit lower than those of the resort spas.

ENTERTAINMENT
Nightlife

Scottsdale is known as a playground for the beautiful and the rich, and some quarters of town focus on dancing to repetitive beats and peeking into VIP rooms to espy some minor celebrity. But there are a lot of down-to-earth watering holes and scenes here too. Last call is usually 2am, per the state legislature, but many bars and clubs stay open for hours afterward, offering late-night menus and after-hours fun. Dress is generally casual unless you're going to the highest of the high-end places. Most of the restaurants listed in the Food section double as nightspots as well.

Downtown's **Entertainment District** (roughly bounded by Camelback Rd.,

Scottsdale Rd., Miller Rd., and 6th Ave.) is a good place to start your night on the town in Scottsdale, and you'll likely find enough clubs, bars, and lounges to keep you busy for a while.

BARS AND PUBS

The **Living Room at the W Scottsdale** (7277 E. Camelback Rd., 480/970-2100, 4pm-midnight Sun.-Thurs., 4pm-2am Fri.-Sat.) provides a perfect introduction to the high-end Scottsdale nightlife scene, with its moneyed and tanned patrons, high-priced handcrafted cocktails, and swanky modernist-fusion interiors. You might even see a few celebrities staying at the hotel.

If you're looking for something a bit rowdier, try the cowboy-dive **Rusty Spur Saloon** (7245 E. Main St., 480/425-7787, www.rustyspursaloon.com, 10am-1am Mon.-Thurs., 10am-2am Fri.-Sat.), a historic Scottsdale saloon housed in a building that opened in 1921 as a bank. The vault is still here, but they keep booze in it now, and there's all kinds of cool old Western memorabilia on the walls and a relaxed neighborhood-joint atmosphere. They serve heaping plates of rib-sticking bar food and offer live bands.

Rockbar (4245 N. Craftsman Circle, 480/331-9190, www.rockbarscottsdale.com, 3pm-2am daily) in Old Town Scottsdale is a fun place to see local and touring rock bands, kick back a cocktail or two, and chomp some excellent pizza. Check the bar's website for a schedule of bands.

CASINOS

The **Salt River Pima-Maricopa Indian Community** operates two casinos in Scottsdale, though both require a bit of a drive from downtown. **Casino Arizona at Salt River** (524 N. 92nd St., 480/850-7777, www.casinoarizona.com), east of the AZ 101 Loop at McKellips Road, has 900 slots, 34 gaming tables, keno, and a showroom that hosts touring acts and a review featuring look- and sound-alike music superstars.

Casino Arizona at Talking Stick (9700 E. Indian Bend Rd., 480/850-7777, www. talkingstickresort.com), about one mile east of the AZ 101 Loop on Indian Bend Road, has 700 slots and 50 gaming tables. If you're in town for spring training, the casino is right next to the spring home of the Arizona Diamondbacks.

Performing Arts

The Scottsdale Center for the Performing Arts (7380 E. 2nd St., 480/499-8587, www. scottsdaleperformingarts.org) is a huge complex of theaters, classrooms, and grassy knolls right downtown. Inside, the Virginia G. Piper Theater and a few smaller spaces host a wide range of theater, dance, comedy, and music—mostly classical and jazz. Acts like Laurie Anderson and Arlo Guthrie have performed here, as have jazz legend Dave Brubeck and many others.

Festivals and Events

More than 100 artists, many of them internationally known in art circles, participate in the popular Arizona Fine Art Expo (Scottsdale Rd. and Jomax Rd., www.arizonafineartexpo. com) January-March, during which you can stroll in and out of galleries and cabanas set up street-side and watch the artists at work. Also in January, the famous Barrett-Jackson Antique Auto Auction (7400 E. Monte Cristo Ave., 480/421-6694, www.barrett-jackson.com) gets underway, selling auction-style the most expensive and spectacular automobiles in existence. Hundreds of white tents go up at Scottsdale Road and the AZ 101 Loop January-March for the Celebration of Fine Art (www.celebrateart.com), while inside, juried artists create their works before your eyes and sell them directly.

The Scottsdale Arabian Horse Show (Westworld, 16601 N. Pima Rd., www. scottsdaleshow.com) brings equestrian enthusiasts from all over the world to town in February, and in March the Scottsdale Arts Festival (75th St. and Main St., www. scottsdaleperformingarts.org) attracts 10,000 visitors to the Scottsdale Center for the Performing Arts for three days of art sales, demonstrations, and performances. In April, just before it starts to get hot, the shining stars of the eating scene gather for the Scottsdale Culinary Festival (www. scottsdaleculinaryfestival.org).

SHOPPING

Shopping Centers and Districts

If you're a serious shopper with serious money, don't miss the upscale centers for which this part of the valley is famous. It's fun to walk around these always well-landscaped and fashionable shopping centers, bustling with beautiful people and stocked with luxury items from all over the globe, to get an idea of how the other 1 percent lives. Scottsdale's busy downtown areas provide the best shopping in town, and nearby Scottsdale Fashion Square (7014 E. Camelback Rd., 480/945-5495, www.fashionsquare.com, 10am-9pm Mon.-Sat., 11am-6pm Sun.) is the largest enclosed mall in the Southwest, featuring high-end department stores, boutiques, and restaurants.

Kierland Commons (6166 N. Scottsdale Rd. at Greenway Pkwy., 480/348-1577, www. kierlandcommons.com, 10am-5pm Mon.-Sat., noon-6pm Sun.) has about 70 upmarket shops and eateries, including Anthropologie and Crate & Barrel.

The Shops at Gainey Village (Scottsdale Rd. and Doubletree Ranch Rd., www. theshopsgaineyvillage.com, 10am-6pm Mon.-Sat., noon-6pm Sun.) is perhaps the most stylish of them all, featuring unique boutiques, interior design shops, and furniture stores with custom-made items you won't find anywhere else.

Close to downtown, check out Scottsdale Quarter (15059 N. Scottsdale Rd., 480/270-8123, http://scottsdalequarter.com, 10am-9pm daily), a civilized and therapeutic wonderland of high-end retail and restaurants. Along the Arizona Canal, the Scottsdale Waterfront (7135 E. Camelback Rd., 480/247-8071, http://

scottsdalewaterfrontshopping.com, hours vary) has mid-range stores, shops, restaurants, and a pleasant atmosphere for strolling and people-watching.

Downtown
CLOTHING

It might be hard to swallow Scottsdale's claim as "The West's Most Western Town" when you are, say, sipping a cocktail in some urban-chic lounge. But when you visit **Saba's Western Wear** (3965 N. Brown Ave., 480/947-7664, 10am-7pm Tues.-Fri., 10am-6pm Sat., 11am-5pm Sun.), a fixture in Old Town since back when it was merely "town," you might start to sympathize. Members of the Saba family, longtime valley merchants with nine stores, including one just across the street, still sell the finest, most authentic working-cowpoke Western wear you can find—plus an unparalleled selection for the equally authentic urban cowboy and cowgirl.

NATIVE AMERICAN ARTS

Scottsdale has long been known as one of the three or four top places in the Southwest to see and buy Native American arts. There are several galleries and shops along Main Street downtown, and the **Gilbert Ortega Gallery & Museum** (3925 N. Scottsdale Rd., 480/990-1808, 10am-6pm Sun.-Tues., 10am-9pm Wed.-Sat.) is worth a perusal.

For Hopi kachina dolls, Hopi and Zuni pottery, and Zuni fetishes, don't miss the **River Trading Post & Traditional Pueblo Arts** (7033 E. Main St., Suite 102, 480/444-0001, www.rivertradingpost.com, 11am-5pm Tues.-Sat., noon-4pm Sun.). This museum-like shop has a superior collection of Navajo rugs, sculptures, and frontier-era furniture. The **Old Territorial Indian Arts** (7100 E. Main St., Suite 3, 480/945-5432, www. oldterritorialshop.com, 10am-4pm Mon.-Sat.) is a classic gallery that has been selling and showing wonderful antique Navajo rugs, Hopi pottery and kachina dolls, and Native American jewelry, folk art, and baskets, for more than 40 years.

FARMERS MARKET

Every Saturday the **Old Town Farmers Market** (7am-11am Sat. late Oct.-late May), in the city parking facility at the corner of Brown Avenue and 1st Street, features local farmers and artists, food artisans, and food lovers selling and promoting their unique wares.

GALLERIES

Scottsdale is second only to Santa Fe as a center for the Southwestern art scene. The **Scottsdale Arts District** (west of Scottsdale Rd. to 70th St., north along Marshall Way to 5th Ave.) has more than 100 galleries, many of them featuring the work of classic Southwestern artists and contemporary masters. But it's not all about regional expectations; be prepared to see a lot that defies preconceived notions about what Southwestern art is and should be. It's not all about Southwestern art; several galleries display instead a general contemporary style that is always intriguing.

One of the best ways to see all that the downtown Scottsdale art scene has to offer is the famed Thursday night **Scottsdale Artwalk** (480/377-9366, 6:30pm-9:30pm Thurs.). Every Thursday for three hours (and sometimes longer), the galleries along Main Street, Marshall Way, Stetson Drive, and 6th Avenue throw open their doors to hundreds of art lovers, and you can walk along the lit-up streets, stop in for a drink at one of the area's many watering holes, and dip in and out of dozens of galleries. The weekly event has been going on since 1976 and is one of the nation's oldest art walk events. For more information, and for a complete list of galleries, check out the **Scottsdale Gallery Association** website (www.scottsdalegalleries.com).

The **Wilde Meyer Gallery** (4142 N. Marshall Way, 480/945-2323, www. wildemeyer.com, 10am-5:30pm Mon.-Fri., 10am-6pm Sat.) shows an eclectic mix of paintings by mostly contemporary artists, many of whom have infused the Southwestern landscape with a surreal sensibility. The work here is some of the most exciting and baffling in the Arts District. At the Trailside Galleries (7330 Scottsdale Mall, 480/945-7751, www.trailsidegalleries.com, 10am-5:30pm Mon.-Sat.) on Scottsdale Mall, which has been around since 1963, you'll find mostly realistic Western art in the form of bucking-bronc bronzes, noble Native American chiefs, and tired old cowboys lounging on their saddles. They also have a fine collection of landscape paintings. At Bonner David Galleries (7040 E. Main St., 480/941-8500, www.bonnerdavid.com, 10am-5:30pm Mon.-Wed. and Fri.-Sat., 10am-9pm Thurs.) you'll find a thrilling mix of abstracts, landscapes, and realistic sculpture.

FOOD

Scottsdale has many of the valley's poshest restaurants, and the scene is always changing and evolving. You'll find enough variety here to make your head and your palate spin. It's not all high-toned and intimidating, though; most of the best restaurants here are serious about food, design, and service, but they don't take themselves too seriously. Many of Scottsdale's restaurants serve late-night menus and have busy bars as well as packed dining rooms. Reservations are always a good idea.

Mexican

Don't leave Cave Creek without stopping for lunch or dinner at El Encanto (6248 E. Cave Creek Rd., 480/488-1752, http://elencantorestaurants.com, 11am-9pm Wed.-Sun., $12-20), serving what is perhaps the valley's best Mexican food from comfortable booths that look out on an enclosed Spanish-style courtyard with a pond with elegant swans. Try the prickly pear margarita, sweet and delicious with a perfect kick.

Downtown's Old Town Tortilla Factory (6910 E. Main St., 480/945-4567, www.oldtowntortillafactory.com, 5pm-9pm Sun.-Thurs., 5pm-10pm Fri.-Sat., $17-29) has an enchanting patio and serves gourmet Southwestern-style creations with pork, fish, chicken, shrimp, and beef. The tortillas are

made on-site in several different flavors and are served hot and fresh. The excellent margarita menu offers mango, raspberry, blue agave, and other creative takes, along with the classic original.

American and Southwestern

★ Arcadia Farms Café (7014 E. 1st Ave., 480/941-5665, www.arcadiafarmscafe.com, 7am-3pm daily, $10-20) is a casual farm-to-table spot that sources a large portion of its ingredients from local and organic farms and food purveyors. Menu offerings include a warm chopped vegetable salad; a chicken and vegetable quesadilla; and chicken, wild mushroom, and leek crepes. The café's on-site market sells a variety of local foods.

A leading light of the locavore movement in the valley, ★ Rancho Pinot (6300 N. Scottsdale Rd., Suite 101, 480/367-8030, www.ranchopinot.com, 5:30pm-9pm Tues.-Sat., $29-40) serves a seasonally based always-fresh menu of truly feel-good food. Chef Chrysa Robertson started the Phoenix chapter of Slow Food and has been a pioneer in sustainable local cuisine for three decades. The menu changes often but generally features small plates like grilled quail with polenta and stuffed squash blossoms, and large plates like spinach fettucine and grilled lamb chops with mint pesto. This is Arizona-bred eating at its best.

★ Lon's at the Hermosa (5532 N. Palo Cristi Rd., 602/955-7878, www.lons.com, 7am-10am, 11:30am-2pm, and 5:30pm-10pm Mon.-Fri., 7am-2pm and 5:30pm-10pm Sat.-Sun., $29-52) offers "comfort cuisine" carefully prepared with regional flair and ingredients, including many grown in the organic gardens on the grounds of this boutique resort, built in the original desert studio of renowned valley artist Lon Megargee. The desert hideaway atmosphere enhances the spectacular New American cuisine. The tortilla soup is a classic, and you must try the "truffle-scented" macaroni-and-cheese.

Chef Charleen Badman of FnB (7125 E. 5th Ave., Suite 31, 480/284-4777, www.fnbrestaurant.com, 5pm-10pm Mon.-Sat., 5pm-9pm Sun. Sept.-May, 5pm-10pm Wed.-Sat. June-Aug., $32-40, credit cards only) won a 2019 James Beard Award for Best Chef Southwest, a category for which she's been in the running four years in a row. FnB has also been lauded by national magazines and newspapers as a leader in Arizona's culinary scene. The menu changes often but always features wonderful and strange dishes with ingredients sourced from local farms and food artisans. Reservations are a must.

Rehab Burger Therapy (7210 E. 2nd St., 480/621-5358, http://rehabburgertherapy.com, 11am-9pm Sun.-Tues., 11am-10pm Wed.-Thurs., 11am-11pm Fri.-Sat., $8-18) serves a wide selection of creative craft-burgers in a casual atmosphere. The burgers go very well with a big basket of sweet potato fries. They also serve salads, wings, and sandwiches that will not disappoint. Rehab has locations in Phoenix and Tempe as well.

An ultracool lounge and restaurant, **AZ 88** (7353 Scottsdale Mall, 480/994-5576, www.az88.com, 11:30am-12:30am daily, $15-32) has delicious simple dishes like hamburgers and chicken sandwiches, DJs spinning many nights, and consistently interesting art on the walls, changed out regularly.

The **Sugar Bowl** (4005 N. Scottsdale Rd., 480/946-0051, www.sugarbowlscottsdale.com, 11am-10pm Sun.-Thurs., 11am-midnight Fri.-Sat., $6-12) has been a Scottsdale institution since it opened in 1958, serving delicious and filling sandwiches, soups, chili, burgers, and dogs as well as decadent ice cream treats in a family atmosphere. Bill Keane, who lived in nearby Paradise Valley, featured the Sugar Bowl several times in his famous *Family Circus* cartoon.

ACCOMMODATIONS

In Scottsdale, world-class accommodations and pampering are available to those who have the resources to buy them; those who don't can still find middle ground, and there are even a few places for the budget-minded traveler. If you don't mind braving the heat, summer prices at the top resorts and getaways dip down into the real world.

$100-250

The **3 Palms** (7707 E. McDowell Rd., 800/450-6071, www.scottsdale-resort-hotels.com, $115-275) is a middle-brow resort-style lodging in Scottsdale, offering most of the comforts and style of the more expensive places with just a slightly less ritzy sheen. This boutique hotel has cool contemporary interior design in all the rooms and a large pool area perfect for lounging in the hot sun while sipping drinks. The **Aloft Scottsdale** (4415 N. Civic Center Plaza, 480/941-9400, www.marriot.com, $199-215) is an upscale boutique hotel with tasteful rooms featuring big comfortable beds and retro-chic couches. The pool area and the outdoor lounge are perfect places to gather for drinks around a fire.

Papago Inn (7017 E. McDowell Rd., 480/947-7335, $160-180) is a centrally located boutique hotel with lush grounds, a big blue pool, and a throwback style with a lot of mid-century desert-style touches. It's a comfortable and affordable place to stay in the middle of all the action in Scottsdale and the valley. A room comes with free Wi-Fi, a fridge, and a free breakfast buffet.

Over $250

The spectacular ★ **Sanctuary Camelback Mountain Resort and Spa** (5700 E. McDonald Dr., Paradise Valley, 480/607-2326, www.sanctuaryoncamelback.com $550-700) is on 53 acres of preserved and manicured desert in Paradise Valley, with elegant private casitas tucked among the rocks, all watched over by the jagged dry mountain and with the valley spread out below. Inside the casitas' wood and limestone interiors are huge beds and deep tubs, and the spa and exercise regime will have you rejuvenated in no time if lounging by the pool in your own private cabana doesn't do the trick. Voted by *Condé Nast Traveler* readers as the best resort in the nation, the Sanctuary is a prime example of all a desert resort can be.

A beautiful structure in the middle of downtown Scottsdale, the ★ Hotel Valley Ho (6850 E. Main St., 480/248-2000, www.hotelvalleyho.com, $350-525) recalls mid-20th-century hip high-end style. It's within easy walking distance of the restaurants, bars, and galleries. The upscale atmosphere is infectious, and after a few hours you'll feel like you deserve it all. The hotel has a wonderful pool for lounging, with cabanas and daybeds, and a relaxing spa for pampering. Hotel Valley Ho is Certified Green by the Arizona Hotel & Lodging Association.

In Old Town, within easy walking distance of the best Scottsdale has to offer, stylish upscale Saguaro (4000 N. Drinkwater Blvd., 480/308-1100, http://thesaguaro.com, $194-356) has a spa and gym, a gorgeous pool, a fantastic restaurant, and enough elegance and luxury to stick in your memory long after you've returned home.

Built up over many decades from the Paradise Valley studio of famed valley artist Alonzo "Lon" Megargee, the Hermosa Inn (5532 N. Palo Cristi, 602/955-8614, www.hermosainn.com, $400) is one of the most enchanting places to stay in Arizona. With 34 detailed high-rustic hacienda-style rooms, a gorgeous pool and myriad hidden outdoor spaces, and the surrounding desert scenery, it's truly a desert original. The 1930s Arizona details, reflecting Megargee's time, add to the pervading romance and enchantment.

The Scott Resort & Spa (4925 N. Scottsdale Rd., 480/945-7666, www.thescottresort.com, $275-330) is a sumptuous garden-like place downtown with secluded and secret lagoons, hot tubs, and cozy cabanas, along with leather chairs and flat-screen TVs in the rooms and a full-service spa. The Scott is Certified Green by the Arizona Hotel & Lodging Association, and the resort's parent company is a member of the 1% for the Planet alliance.

A five-diamond resort in downtown Scottsdale, the Fairmont Scottsdale Princess (7575 E. Princess Dr., 480/585-4848, www.fairmont.com/scottsdale, $500-700) has unbelievably comfortable and richly decorated rooms, suites, and casitas as well as golf courses, three restaurants, and one of the top spas in the nation. The Fairmont is Certified Green by the Arizona Hotel & Lodging Association.

Out in the wild desert of Carefree, The Boulders Resort and Golden Door Spa (34631 N. Tom Darlington Dr., Carefree, 480/488-9009, www.theboulders.com, $550-700) has been named the country's top spa more than a dozen times. This unique desert property offers gorgeous suites, casitas, villas, and haciendas in a secluded setting away from the city. It goes far beyond the norm in comfort, style, and recreation.

The Phoenician (6000 E. Camelback Rd., 480/941-8200, www.thephoenician.com, $365-775), along the Camelback Corridor, has an excellent golf course, high-end style, and the Center for Well-Being spa. The Phoenician is Certified Green by the Arizona Hotel & Lodging Association.

Well-appointed guest rooms at the Camelback Inn (5402 E. Lincoln Dr., 480/596-7040, $415-525) have French doors that open onto private patios. The long pool, with luxurious lounging areas, overlooks unspoiled desert scenery, and the spa offers relaxation and balance in a secluded peaceful setting.

The Four Seasons Resort Scottsdale at Troon North (10600 E. Crescent Moon Dr., 480/515-5700, www.fourseasons.com, $600-800), just below jagged Pinnacle Peak, is a stunning resort that takes full advantage of its desert setting, with casitas set among the creosote and saguaros. The whole place has a whitewashed hacienda look, with exposed vigas, ironwork touches, and fireplaces. Many of the rooms have balconies that overlook the desert, and the pool area is spectacular, watched over by the landmark peak.

The Westin Kierland Resort & Spa (902 E. Greenway Pkwy., 480/624-1000, www.kierlandresort.com, $500-700) makes a great choice for families looking for different resort experiences: golf, spa treatments, and a

Luxurious Retreats

Arizona is known around the world for the high-luxury resort accommodations offered in Scottsdale, Phoenix, Tucson, Sedona, and elsewhere. The best of these spa resorts appear to require their own zip code and guidebook, and those who frequent them can spend weeks in Arizona without venturing beyond the gates. Here are some of the best of the bunch:

- **Wigwam Hotel:** Southwestern elegance at its best is on display at this historic resort west of Phoenix, where you can experience all of today's luxuries while immersed in stylish reminders of yesterday (page 77).

- **Sanctuary Camelback Mountain Resort and Spa:** On 53 acres around Camelback Mountain in Paradise Valley, this aptly named sanctuary has amazing views of the desert, upscale lodgings, and opportunities for renewal (page 94).

- **Miraval, Life in Balance Resort & Spa:** This ultraexclusive desert hideaway at the base of Tucson's Santa Catalina Mountains has lots of green and shady spots for yoga and meditation, and it also has a big green heart. Among many other sustainable practices, Miraval operates its own treatment facility and reuses 99 percent of its water (page 157).

- **Hacienda del Sol Guest Ranch Resort:** Nestled in the foothills of the Santa Catalina Mountains above Tucson, this resort dates to 1929 and embodies the rustic glamour and high-style Southwest of yesteryear, as well as modern amenities, including a spa, stables, and an excellent on-site restaurant (page 157).

- **Amara Resort and Spa:** Set among the red rocks of Sedona, this oasis-like hideaway is the perfect place to relax the body and renew the spirit (page 233).

super-fun waterslide, the holy trinity of modern family happiness. The Westin Kierland is Certified Green by the Arizona Hotel & Lodging Association.

Cave Creek

Not surprisingly, this mid- to high-end burg has not a few bed-and-breakfasts. The **Spur Cross Bed & Breakfast** (38555 N. School House Rd., Cave Creek, 480/473-1038, www.spurcrossbnb.com, $139-250) rents four nice rooms with outside entrances and has a hot tub and Wi-Fi.

INFORMATION

The **Scottsdale Convention & Visitors Bureau** (www.experiencescottsdale.com) operates a **tourist center** at **Scottsdale Fashion Square** (7014 E. Camelback Rd., 480/421-1004, 800/782-1117, 9am-6pm Mon.-Sat., 10am-5pm Sun.).

TRANSPORTATION

The best way to get from Phoenix to Scottsdale is to take one of the surface streets east from downtown; that way you'll get to see more of the ground-level city instead of breezing past everything on the freeways. If you take Camelback Road east from downtown Phoenix, you'll run into downtown Scottsdale. If you're heading from Scottsdale to Tempe, take Scottsdale Road south, and you'll run into the college town.

Valley Metro (602/253-5000, www.valleymetro.org), the valley's public transportation authority, provides bus service ($2 per ride) throughout the area, including to Glendale, Scottsdale, Tempe, and Mesa.

Each downtown district in Scottsdale runs into the next and is easy to walk to, and there's a **free trolley** (every 15 min. 11am-6pm Fri.-Wed., 11am-9pm Thurs.) that will take you all around the downtown area.

Around the Valley of the Sun

On the far eastern edge of the spreading cityscape, the desert holds a strong line in the Tonto National Forest. In this cactus, creosote, and mesquite wilderness, dashed with fallen slabs and boulders covered in faded-green dry lichen, you will experience the real Central Arizona outback, a rugged and storied stretch of the upper Sonoran Desert. Driving the Apache Trail (AZ 88), a mostly dirt route that takes you deep into the desert, past several artificial lakes to one of the state's huge reclamation-era dams, is a highlight. You can then loop around to U.S. 60, where you'll cruise through several old mining towns and past the jagged Pinal Mountains before heading back into the city. Or detour north for about 40 miles on U.S. 60 from Globe to get a jaw-dropping look at Salt River Canyon. All along the way there are pull-offs and stops, trailheads, and historic markers. You can tour these eastern and northeastern reaches of the valley in one long day, unless you want to hike; then you'll need to mount a separate expedition.

If you're headed to Southern Arizona from the valley along I-10, veer off the main route for a few hours and visit the mysterious Casa Grande, the largest remaining Hohokam ruins. Or stop at Picacho Peak State Park just off the interstate to hike along a ragged rock spine towering over the desert.

About 60 miles northwest of the city on U.S. 60 you'll find the old mining town of Wickenburg, which still has a bit of Old West charm. Continue north on AZ 89 for a twisting and scenic mostly two-lane drive through the chaparral and scrub midlands, through a lush ranching region, and up to the pine forests of Prescott. And if you're taking the quick route to the northland along I-17, consider stopping at Arcosanti, an ongoing experiment in architecture and living.

THE SUPERSTITION MOUNTAINS

These rugged desert mountains rise 5,000 feet off the desert floor and are the main component of the 160,000-acre **Superstition Wilderness Area** in the Tonto National Forest. The Superstitions pale in comparison to other Arizona mountains both in elevation and diversity, but they are an ideal place to get an introduction to the Sonoran Desert and spend some time in the wilderness close to the city. The trails are rocky and quite worn in places; the landscape is rough gray-green desert, crowded with mobs of saguaro reaching into the huge and always clear-blue sky, carpeted with creosote, brittlebush, prickly pear, and other desert familiars. In February-March, especially after a winter of plentiful rainfall, and again April-June, large patches of the desert pop with purple, red, yellow, and blue as dormant plants explode into bloom. This is the best time to be in the Superstitions; don't go in the heat of summer.

It is possible to get very far from the city by going far into the wilderness area. Most visitors, however, stick to the well-trodden but still impressive sights along the popular **Peralta Trail,** a moderately difficult 6-mile round-trip hike that leads to a saddle with a fine view of Weavers Needle, a fantastically eroded butte. From Phoenix, take U.S. 60 east through Gold Canyon, then turn east on Peralta Road and drive about 8 miles to the trailhead for Peralta and the **Dutchman's Trail,** an 18-mile journey through the wilderness area. Expect to pay a user fee ($6 per vehicle) in the Tonto National Forest. For more on hiking in the Superstitions, check out the Tonto online **trail guide** (www.fs.fed.us/r3/tonto).

Lost Dutchman State Park

A stop at small **Lost Dutchman State Park** (6109 N. Apache Trail, 480/982-4485,

The Valley of the Sun

Sitgreaves National Forest

White Mountain Apache Indian Reservation

To Whiteriver and Show Low

To Whiteriver and Show Low

San Carlos

San Carlos Lake

To Safford

To Tucson

Canyon

Apache Mountains

Salt River

Globe

Pinal Mountains

Pinal Mountain

Pioneer Pass

Kearny

Winkelman

To Holbrook and Show Low

Christopher Creek

MOGOLLON RIM VISITOR CENTER

Young

Sierra Anchas

Tonto National Forest

Claypool

Miami

Oak Flat

Superior

To Tucson

260

Payson

Rye

Punkin Center

Theodore Roosevelt Lake

Roosevelt

Burnt Corral

188

THE APACHE TRAIL AND VICINITY

Boyce Thompson Arboretum State Park

79

CASA GRANDE RUINS NATIONAL MONUMENT

To Tucson

Tonto Natural Bridge State Park

Mazatzal Peak 7,894ft

Mazatzal Mountains

Four Peaks 7,657ft

Apache Trail

Canyon Lake

Tortilla Flat

Lost Dutchman State Park

Superstition Mountains

Florence Junction

Florence

Coolidge

To Picacho Peak State Park and Tucson

Bartlett Lake

Horseshoe Lake

Verde River

Apache Junction

Mesa

Chandler

Casa Grande

Prescott National Forest

Ft McDowell

Fountain Hills

TALIESIN WEST

Scottsdale

Tempe

SCOTTSDALE RD

Gila River Indian Reservation

GILA INDIAN CENTER

Cave Creek

Carefree

Seven Springs

Spur Cross Ranch Conservation Area

Cave Creek Regional Park

DESERT BOTANICAL GARDEN

PHOENIX ART MUSEUM

South Mountain Park

ARCOSANTI

To Flagstaff

BLOODY BASIN RD

Black Canyon City

Lake Pleasant Regional Park

SEE "GREATER PHOENIX" MAP

Sun City

Peoria

Glendale

PHOENIX

HEARD MUSEUM

Bradshaw Mountains

Sunset Point

CASTLE HOT SPRINGS RD

Hells Canyon Wilderness

Circle City

White Tank Mountain Regional Park

Goodyear

Estrella

Estrella Mountain Regional Park

Sierra

Gila River

15 mi

15 km

Prescott National Forest

To Prescott

Stanton

Octave

Yarnell

Wickenburg

White Tank Mountains

Buckeye

Gila

Gila Bend Indian Reservation

Gila Bend

85

To Ajo

To Kingman

Congress

JOSHUA FOREST PKWY

DESERT CABALLEROS WESTERN MUSEUM

To Quartzsite

To Yuma

http://azstateparks.com, sunrise-10pm daily, $7 per vehicle) at the base of the Superstitions is a good way for families and day hikers to see the range and to spend some time walking around the desert on relatively easy trails. The park has 70 campsites (no hookups $15-20, electric $25-35) with showers as well as tables and grills, perfect for picnics. The **Treasure Loop Trail** is an easy way to see the park and get an idea of what the desert is like at 2,000 feet elevation. It's a 2.4-mile (round-trip) moderate and well-marked hike, starting at either picnic area. Using the **Siphon Draw Trail,** you can climb up to about 5,000 feet elevation, first to a high overlook spot called the Flatiron and then on to the top of Superstition Peak, a hard 5-mile round-trip hike that rewards with some striking desert views.

Superstition Mountain Museum

The small **Superstition Mountain Museum** (4087 N. Apache Trail, 480/983-4888, www.superstitionmountainmuseum.org, 10am-5pm daily, $7), at the beginning of the Apache Trail just outside Apache Junction, makes an interesting stop if you have an extra half hour to an hour. The displays on local mining legends, especially the infamous whopper about the **Lost Dutchman Mine** (which people still hunt for today, believing that 1890s prospector "Dutchman" Jacob Waltz died before revealing the route to the world's richest gold mine somewhere deep in the Superstitions), and other Old West history lessons will enhance and contextualize the backcountry drive you're about to take.

Goldfield

Heading out of Apache Junction, the Apache Trail passes the Old West-show tourist trap **Goldfield** (4650 N. Mammoth Mine Rd., 480/983-0333, www.goldfieldghosttown.com, 10am-5pm daily, $4-10), a rebuilt 1890s town on the site of what used to be a mining camp with about 5,000 people, settled after gold was discovered in the Superstitions and depopulated soon after the mining stopped. It's a kind of mining-camp theme park now, with a working narrow-gauge railroad, theme shops along a boardwalk main street, a couple of cowboy-style restaurants, a saloon, a mine tour, gold panning, staged gunfights, and Jeep tours into the Superstitions. Kids will likely enjoy this attraction; everybody else should move on down the trail.

horseback riding trail through a desert park near Superstition Mountains

★ THE APACHE TRAIL AND VICINITY

A tour of the **Apache Trail** (AZ 88, which converges with AZ 188 at Roosevelt Lake) and the **Old West Highway** (U.S. 60), a 120-mile round-trip loop along the wild edges of the sprawl-choked valley, begins just outside Apache Junction and eventually winds around the Superstition Mountains to Roosevelt Dam, and then on through the Pinal Mountains and a few old mining towns.

Although much of the Apache Trail is dirt, you can drive the whole loop in a regular car, though an SUV or a similar high-clearance vehicle is better in terms of comfort. In places the route follows the course of the Salt River, the damming of which first made all that sprawl possible and also created several desert lakes, each improbably beautiful and surrounded by an arid army of saguaros peering down from jagged-rock cliffs into the mirage-like waters, wondering what all the fuss is about. The Apache Trail itself came about as a result of the dam, built as it was to cart materials and workers to and from the great construction site, though the route had been regularly traversed by Indigenous inhabitants long before the reclamation project began.

The best place to eat and get gas is at Globe, at the trail's end. However, if you find yourself in a bind, there's a good fun restaurant at Tortilla Flat, plus restaurants and gas at each of the marinas along the route. Make sure you bring water with you, and check your tires and fluids before you go.

Apache Junction, a sprawling suburb east of Phoenix at the base of the Superstition Mountains, marks the beginning of the Apache Trail from the west, and the trail ends at Tonto National Monument, 49 miles from Apache Junction. To reach Apache Junction from downtown Phoenix, go 40 miles east on U.S. 60, a drive of about an hour. The well-marked Apache Trail is AZ 88, right off of U.S. 60. The route described runs clockwise from Apache Junction.

At the time of writing, portions of the Apache Trail between Tortilla Flat and Apache Lake Marina remain closed due to the 2019 Woodbury Fire and subsequent flooding; consult the **Arizona Department of Transportation** website (http://azdot.gov; search for "Apache Trail" or "SR 88") for the latest updates. Depending on conditions, it may not be possible to complete the entire loop in one go, thought it may be possible to see more of the sights with a counterclockwise route.

Needle Vista to Tortilla Flat

The wild portion of the Apache Trail really gets started about 8 miles outside Apache Junction at **Needle Vista,** which provides a sweeping view of the rough country and a good look at Weavers Needle, a distinctive rock formation. There are restrooms here. Continuing east on the paved road, you next come to **Canyon Lake,** about 12 miles from Apache Junction. The smallest of the Salt River Project lakes, and the first you come to along the trail from Phoenix, Canyon Lake has 950 surface acres and 28 miles of shoreline. The headquarters here is the **Canyon Lake Marina and Campground** (16802 NE AZ 88, 480/288-9233, www.canyonlakemarina. com), which has a restaurant and campground with sites for tents and RVs with hookups, tables, grills, fire rings, and showers (waterfront campsite $55, 2 tents, 6 people, 1 vehicle per site; pull-through RV site with hookups $70; other sites $10; $20 per additional vehicle). You're allowed to ride personal watercraft and water-ski on Canyon Lake, and there's even an excursion steamboat and a dinner cruise.

About five more miles east and you're at the old **Superstition Restaurant and Saloon** (20909 E. Apache Trail, 480/984-1776, 10am-6pm Mon.-Fri., 8am-6pm Sat.-Sun., $8-20) at **Tortilla Flat** (http://tortillaflataz. com), once a stage stop and is now . . . well, a stage stop, with burgers, homemade chili, Mexican food, beers, and saddle-topped barstools popular with Harley riders, who haunt the trail in large numbers on the weekends. This strange, charming little place, restored from the original but still romantically rustic, is named after a butte nearby that looks a bit like stacked tortillas.

Apache Lake

Continuing on the trail another five miles east, a saguaro and scrub forest spreads out on either side, boulders strewn about and rising from the earth, the Superstitions looming like the petrified rock remains of giant jagged teeth; then the route descends precipitously just before it turns to dirt and washboards near spectacular Fish Creek Canyon, where you'll probably want to stop and take a few photos. Then it's on to the next of the desert lakes, Apache Lake, where the **Apache Lake Marina and Resort** (AZ 88, 928/467-2511, www.apachelake.com) rents clean and basic lakeside rooms at the **Apache Lake Motel** ($90-105), including suites with kitchenettes. The 17-mile-long lake is popular with Phoenicians who enjoy waterskiing, riding personal watercraft, and fishing for small- and largemouth bass.

Roosevelt Dam and Roosevelt Lake

After Apache Lake, the dirt trail follows a narrow band of river below the dam. Then it climbs a bit, and that sheer rock wall holding back the river comes into sight, about five miles from the last lake. You can stop here, read some plaques about the dam, and look at it from a promontory. Then the road passes the large **Roosevelt Dam Bridge** and the highway heading north to Payson and the Rim Country. The largest of the Salt River Lakes with a peak fill of 22,000 surface acres, Roosevelt Lake can be accessed through the **Roosevelt Lake Marina** (28085 N. AZ 188, 602/977-7170, www.rlmaz.com). You can rent a kayak here (2-person $60 full day), skid around on personal watercraft, or explore hidden coves and fishing spots.

Tonto National Monument

Pass Roosevelt Lake, heading south on AZ 88, which doubles as AZ 188 along this stretch, to get to **Tonto National Monument**

(8am-5pm daily, 928/467-2241, www.nps.gov, $10), picturesque cliff-side ruins once inhabited by the Salado people about 1150-1450. It's so well preserved it appears—from far away, at least—as if people could still live here in the cool shade of a natural rock alcove high above the saguaro and cholla. The paved **Lower Ruin** trail is about one mile round-trip, most of it straight up, and open to the public. The visitors center below the ruins has some interesting artifacts of the Salado people and a good bit of information on this often overlooked tribe. Tonto is about 49 miles from Apache Junction and marks the end of the Apache Trail from the west and its beginning from the east.

Globe

Just before the junction with U.S. 60, hungry travelers can try **Guayo's on the Trail** (14249 S. AZ 188, Globe, 928/425-9969, www.guayosrestaurants.com, 10:30am-9pm Mon. and Wed.-Sat., 10:30am-8:30pm Sun., $7-15), which serves outstanding traditional Mexican food based on old family recipes. This casual place has been around since 1938, and it's very popular with Apache Trail travelers, especially the motorcycle crowd.

At the junction, head east on U.S. 60, called the Old West Highway, for about four miles to the quaint old downtown of Globe, which is ripe for discovery—sort of like Bisbee before the craft boom.

Just outside downtown, kids will have fun climbing around the largely rebuilt Hohokam and Salado ruins at **Besh-Ba-Gowah Archaeological Park** (1324 Jess Hayes Rd., 928/425-0320, www.globeaz.gov, 9am-4:30pm daily, $5 adults, free under age 12). Unlike most ruins in Arizona, these modest reconstructed pit houses and courtyards are open for scrambling and exploring, and there's a small but interesting museum with exhibits on the lifestyles of those ancient tribes.

Salt River Canyon

Take a detour north on AZ 77, which doubles as U.S. 60 for this stretch, from Globe along the edge of the Apache Mountains for about 40 miles to spectacular **Salt River Canyon,** one of the more impressive roadside natural wonders in a state chock-full of them. Once used as a hideout by the Apache during the Indian Wars, this 2,000-foot-deep jagged desert gorge is where the Salt River runs free and wild. There's a parking area before the bridge where you can learn about the canyon and take pictures, and easy paved trails lead down to the river. If you've got a 4WD vehicle, you can head off on a riverside Jeep trail and explore the canyon in more depth. The traffic on AZ 77 near the canyon bridge can get heavy and frustrating, especially on the weekends.

Superior and Boyce Thompson Arboretum State Park

After stopping in Globe, head back west on a scenic stretch of U.S. 60. Along the way is **Superior.** Like Globe, it has an old downtown with a few really cool but disused buildings, long ago fancy hotels and shops, that could be expensively hipped up for the ever-growing retro-loving crowd.

Just three miles west of Superior along U.S. 60 is the **Boyce Thompson Arboretum** (37615 U.S. 60, 520/689-2811, http:// ag.arizona.edu/bta, 6am-3pm daily May-Sept., 8am-5pm daily Oct.-Apr., $15 adults, $5 ages 5-12). A stroll around the unique arboretum is the perfect capstone to an Apache Trail tour. It was developed in the early 20th century by wealthy mining magnate and do-gooder Colonel William Boyce Thompson. He built his own dreamland here, a kind of desert-country Hearst Castle, and endeavored to grow several different ecosystems on his property. Here you can walk on well-trodden easy paths leading through otherworldly cactus gardens, across a cottonwood-covered stream, along the shores of a desert lake, and even through an Australian eucalyptus forest, all surrounded by the huge boulder-mountains of the Central Arizona outback. This is not recommended in summer.

West to Phoenix

Phoenix is about 60 miles west of the arboretum via U.S. 60, a scenic stretch that skirts the edge of the Superstition Mountains and passes through Florence Junction and Gold Canyon. There's not much to look at along the route back to Phoenix save for awesome desert scenery. U.S. 60 becomes the Superstition Freeway once you're back in the city.

FROM PHOENIX TO TUCSON

The small towns southeast of the metro area are a rural snapshot in a state of flux, adapting to the city's spread and trying to hold on to some kind of identity as commuters move in and take over. The southeast, known to most Arizonans as the area you have to drive through to get from Phoenix to Tucson, was once dedicated to agriculture, though these days many of those fields are covered not with cotton but with stuccoed homes and RV parks. The area is prone to blowing dust storms, especially during the summer rainy season.

★ Casa Grande Ruins National Monument

A fragile molded-mud apartment building just outside the old farming town of Coolidge, **Casa Grande Ruins National Monument** (1100 W. Ruins Dr., 520/723-3172, www.nps. gov/cagr, 9am-5pm daily, free) is all that remains of one of the largest ancient structures ever built in North America. There are still a lot of unanswered questions about how and why Casa Grande grew to dominate the Salt River Valley and beyond at its peak in about 1350, and even more questions about what caused its catastrophic decline around 1450. It's an amazing sight—almost like a huge human-size sand castle covered by a towering metal roof to keep out the elements. The monument's excellent museum interprets and explains what we do know about the Hohokam

---

1: Tonto National Monument **2:** historic Rock Springs Café

people, those ancient arid-land agricultur-ists who inspired the valley's modern-day settlers to attempt to turn the desert into an Eden. Casa Grande is an easy 10- to 15-minute detour off I-10 via Exit 211, halfway between Phoenix and Tucson; watch for signs.

Picacho Peak State Park

Small **Picacho Peak State Park** (just off I-10 Exit 219, 520/466-3183, http://azstateparks.com, 5am-10pm daily, trails close at sunset, $7 per car, camping $25-30), about 40 miles north of Tucson and 60 miles south of Phoenix, sits in the shadow of a dramatic 1,500-foot rock upcropping in the middle of an otherwise mostly flat desert plain. **Picacho Peak** has always been a natural landmark in this part of the state, and nearby, in 1862, soldiers fought Arizona's only Civil War battle, reenacted at the park every year. There are several good trails that lead up and along the rough spine of the peak; the area is particularly popular in spring, when the *bajada* stretching out from the cliff sides is often carpeted with multicol-ored wildflowers. Try the four-mile round-trip **Hunter Trail,** a rather difficult and steep route to the top that begins on the north side and requires the use of steel cables anchored into the rock in some places. The three-mile round-trip **Sunset Vista Trail** is a bit eas-ier but longer, starting on the south side and heading to the top. Either way, the views from the top are amazing and well worth the climb.

WICKENBURG

This old mining town northwest of the valley on U.S. 60 still has a bit of Old West charm and makes for a fun day trip from Phoenix or a couple of hours' detour during a drive north. If you're headed to Prescott from Phoenix, consider taking the back way along U.S. 60 through Wickenburg, then on to AZ 89 north, cruising along a twisting rural two-lane through a sleepy but scenic mining and ranching region that most visitors miss.

Sights

Fans of Western art will want to spend an hour or so at the **Desert Caballeros Western Museum** (1 N. Frontier St., 928/684-2272, www.westernmuseum.org. 10am-5pm Mon.-Sat., noon-4pm Sun. Sept.-May, 10am-5pm Tues.-Sat., noon-4pm Sun. June-Aug., $12), a decent regional art museum that has some unique exhibits on life in the Old West.

Hikers and birders shouldn't miss the beautiful riparian area at the 770-acre **Hassayampa River Preserve** (49614 U.S. 60, www.maricopacountyparks.net, 7am-7am Wed.-Sun. summer, 8am-5pm Wed.-Sun. winter, free) just outside Wickenburg. At the preserve you can walk along a creek beneath cottonwoods and willows and watch for all manner of water-loving birds darting among the bushes.

Food

A good place to stop for lunch in Wickenburg is **Anita's Cocina** (57 N. Valentine Dr., 928/684-5777, http://anitascocina.com, 8am-9pm Mon.-Fri., 7am-9pm Sat.-Sun., $8-16), a popular place with locals, where they serve delicious and inexpensive Mexican favorites in a casual atmosphere.

NORTH ON I-17

If you've got a little time to spare on a drive north to Prescott, Sedona, or Flagstaff along I-17, there are a few interesting diversions to tempt you.

A 23,000-acre desert preserve in the far northwest valley, **Lake Pleasant Regional Park** (41835 N. Castle Hot Springs Rd., Morristown, 602/506-2930, ext. 1, www.maricopacountyparks.net) offers limit-less opportunities for boating, fishing, hik-ing, and swimming. The reservoir spreads across the desert, fluctuating in depth and surface area; it's at its highest in March-April as the highland snows melt, and lowest in November, long after the summer rains. You can rent a kayak or a stand-up paddle board at the **Pleasant Harbor Marina** (9am-5pm daily, entry $7, rentals $20-30 per hour), where there's also a restaurant and store. This beau-tiful desert area is unbearable in summer but becomes a veritable paradise in spring. To get to the marina from downtown Phoenix, head north for 25 miles on I-17, then take Exit 223A to head west 11 miles to the lake via AZ 74.

Farther north on I-17, the **Agua Fria National Monument** (623/580-5500, www. blm.gov, free) offers a relatively easy hike through a lush riparian area that includes access to a petroglyph site. The trailhead is about 40 miles north of downtown Phoenix via I-17. Take Exit 256 for Badger Springs and follow the dirt road for about a mile east to the parking area at the trailhead. The trail runs through Badger Springs Wash, which may be filled with some water outside mid-summer, and follows the wash for about two miles one-way.

As the ever-reaching imprint of the valley's insatiable growth begins to disappear and the midland desert scrublands open up, veer off at Exit 262 for Cordes Junction and follow the signs to take a tour of the fascinating "urban laboratory" being built by the followers of the late artist Paolo Soleri at **Arcosanti** (928/632-7135, www.arcosanti.org, 9am-5pm daily, tours $15-30). The sweeping high-desert locale adds to its evocative otherworldliness. The one-hour and two-hour tours take you through the settlement as a guide explains the history and philosophy of the project. There's a small café and a gift shop where you can buy one of the world-famous handmade bells that support this ongoing experiment in "arcology"—an architectural theory that seeks to lessen our imprint on the earth by bringing together architecture and ecology.

Food

Off I-17 at Exit 242, ★ **Rock Springs Café** (35769 S. Old Black Canyon Hwy., 623/374-5794, www.rockspringscafe.com, 7am-9pm Sun.-Thurs., 7am-10pm Fri.-Sat., $10-21) is an old cowboy-style saloon, historic general store, soda fountain, and café that serves locally famous hamburgers, steaks, barbecue, and homemade pies that you'll want to send home in a refrigerated crate. The whole place has a dark wood-and-stone air of historic authenticity, and it's been the site of a dusty travelers' wayside since the late 19th century.

Tucson and Southern Arizona

The Sonoran Desert's soft greens and yellows can appear monotonous. But look closely and you'll find staggering variety. So it is with the culture in Tucson and Southern Arizona.

If there's a melting pot in the United States, it bubbles here. While traveling the region, it's difficult to escape constant reminders that not too long ago this land was considered not the southern end of the United States but rather the northern end of Mexico. The Anglo and Hispanic settlers have since come to terms with each other, for the most part, and their mixing has created a unique culture that can only be described as Southwestern. While this true Southwestern experience can be explored in a few other places, nowhere is it more authentic and dynamic than in Southern Arizona. Proof of this is in the region's food,

Highlights

Look for ★ to find recommended sights, activities, dining, and lodging.

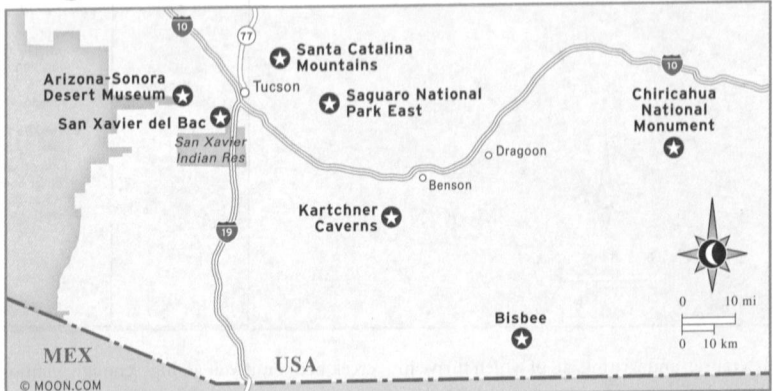

★ **Arizona-Sonora Desert Museum:** See the region's animals—mountain lions, wolves, bighorn sheep, and other rare Sonoran creatures—up close (page 121).

★ **Saguaro National Park East:** Drive, walk, or ride a bike through the Sonoran Desert's unique saguaro forests (page 123).

★ **Santa Catalina Mountains:** Drive to the top of a sky island peak and cool off in the high green forests (page 125).

★ **San Xavier del Bac:** See Arizona's answer to the Sistine Chapel, a white jewel of a mission on the desert (page 129).

★ **Kartchner Caverns:** Enter an otherworldly cave still being formed by slowly dripping water (page 174).

★ **Bisbee:** Explore an old mining boomtown, now an enclave for artists and antiques shops (page 177).

★ **Chiricahua National Monument:** Marvel at the "Land of Standing-Up Rocks," a forest of hoodoos high in the evergreen mountains (page 182).

Tucson and Southern Arizona

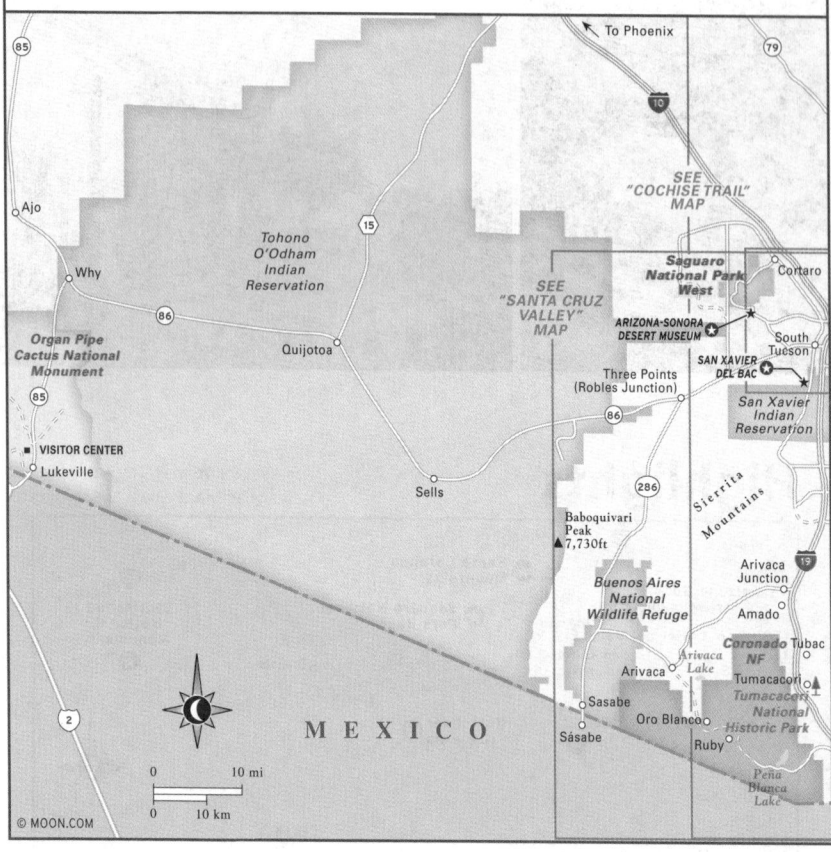

art, music, and writing, all of which thrive in the arid climate and cultural complexity.

The landscape is dominated by desert, stretching out like a vast forgotten sea. It rains here only rarely, yet in spring the land bursts with otherwise dormant wildflowers, like a one-night-only command performance, and during the summer monsoon season this so-called arid region is positively lush. At higher elevation on one of the region's sky islands you will be hunting for tropical birds in a misty creek bed, or, if you go high enough, clamping on a pair of skis. Take a short drive south and you'll experience the dynamic border region with all its bustling and color. Go east and you'll find the remains of the Old West at its most iconic. Look a little closer and you'll find the new as well, in the artists and artisans who find Southern Arizona's quaint towns like Tubac and Bisbee so inviting. This is a fascinating region, and one in which you might find yourself happily lost.

Previous: Saguaro National Park; Santa Catalina Mountains; San Xavier del Bac.

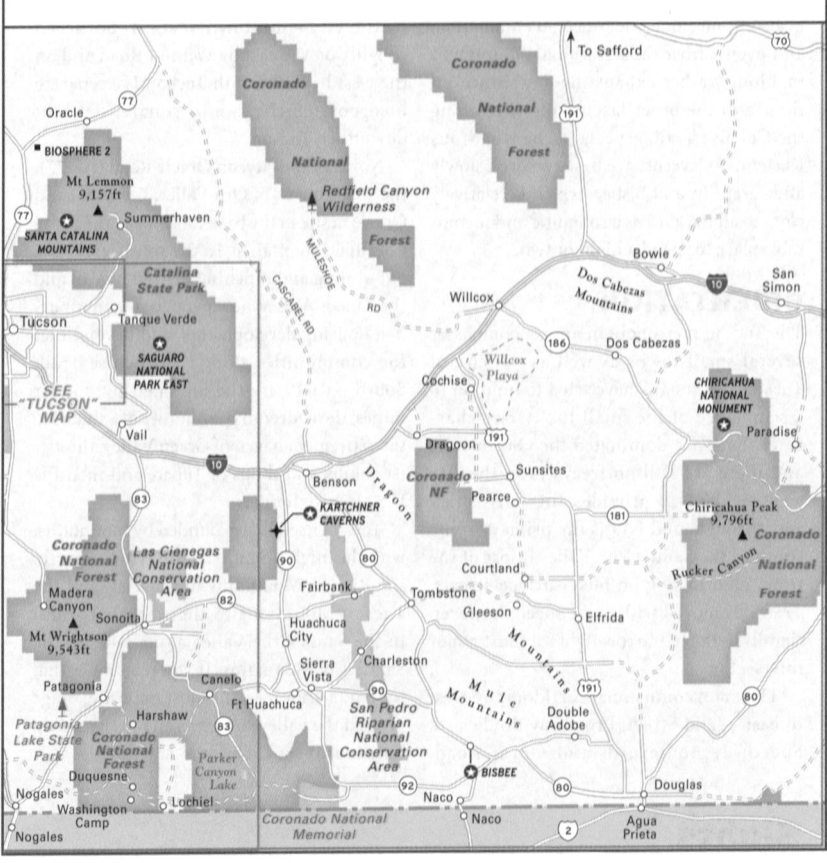

PLANNING YOUR TIME

You can do Tucson and Southern Arizona in one busy week; to sample some of the sky island trails and hideaways, take two weeks. The best times to visit are March-May and September-November. The weather is very hot in the desert in summer but perfect in the mountains, and in July-August count on near-daily late-afternoon thunderstorms. Hot and humid during the day, the months of the monsoon are a wonderful time to be alive in the Sonoran Desert. It's best to use Tucson as a base and explore the outlying areas by car unless you have more than a week or two to

explore. All of the major sights in this region are within a few hours of the city.

Tucson's charms deserve at least three days of concentration. Spend a full day visiting the west side's Saguaro National Park, Tucson Mountain Park, the Arizona-Sonora Desert Museum, and San Xavier del Bac, and another day hanging around downtown and 4th Avenue, sampling the desert's urban side. Then head up the Sky Island Highway to Mount Lemmon to see a completely different view of Southern Arizona from the forested mountain heights. You can visit the Santa Cruz Valley and the Border Region, and even take a stroll into Mexico at Nogales, in a long day trip from Tucson. You can also drop by Bisbee, Tombstone, the Amerind Foundation, and even Chiricahua National Monument in a long, rather exhausting day. However, these and the other fascinating sites along the Cochise Trail, especially the wondrous Kartchner Caverns, are best explored slowly and carefully, and Bisbee, which is relatively close to all the sites, is a romantic and memorable place to spend a night or two.

ORIENTATION

The Tucson metropolitan area encompasses several small towns as well as the city of Tucson. Tucsonans have tried to hold on to a semblance of the small funky city character that once dominated the Old Pueblo, and there are still no freeways in the city as a result. I-10 provides the only quick way through, and I-19 is the primary route south to the Santa Cruz Valley. Most of the time, plan to slog on busy surface streets. Traffic is moved with some speed, however, thanks to the left-arrow lights at most major intersections.

The main commercial corridors run west to east—22nd Street, Broadway Boulevard, Speedway Boulevard, and Grant Road.

Dozens of hotels, motels, and restaurants can be found along any of these main roads in the city's midtown section, bordered roughly on the east by Wilmot Road and on the west by I-10. South Tucson is a separate incorporated city, a mile square, south of downtown Tucson.

North of the city, on Oracle Road (AZ 77), the small towns of Oro Valley, Catalina, and Oracle nestle in the back foothills of the Santa Catalina Mountains. To the southeast is the old mining and ranching district of Vail and the Rincon Valley, now peppered with suburban housing developments, and beyond that the communities along the Cochise Trail. South on I-19 are the big open-pit copper mines, the bedroom community of Sahuarita, the retirement haven of Green Valley, the artist colony and shops of Tubac, and then the U.S.-Mexico border.

Tucson itself is surrounded by mountains, with the mighty Santa Catalinas to the north, the Rincon Mountains to the east, and the Tucson Mountains to the west. Far south in the Santa Cruz Valley along I-19 are the Santa Rita Mountains. If you remember that the Santa Catalinas, the most imposing range around the valley, are generally to the north, Tucson isn't too difficult to navigate.

Sights

DOWNTOWN AND CENTRAL

Downtown Tucson is where the city first rose from the desert. The general area can be expanded to include 4th Avenue and the historic neighborhoods of El Presidio, Armory Park, and Barrio Historico, as well as those around the University of Arizona. The Sun Link Streetcar serves all of these areas, and most of them are pedestrian friendly—something rare in a Southwestern cityscape. The streetcar also goes to the west-side Mercado San Agustin and MSA Annex, both part of the greater downtown area.

Tucson Museum of Art and Historic Block

The permanent collection at the **Tucson Museum of Art** (140 N. Main Ave., 520/624-2333, www.tucsonmuseumofart.org, 10am-5pm Tues.-Sat., noon-5pm Sun., $12 adults, $10 seniors, $7 students) features mysterious artifacts of the Americas prior to Columbus's arrival, the art of the U.S. West, and contemporary art, often with a Latin and Southwestern flavor. This is a good place to introduce yourself to that tricultural mixing that makes Southern Arizona unique. The museum's several special exhibitions each

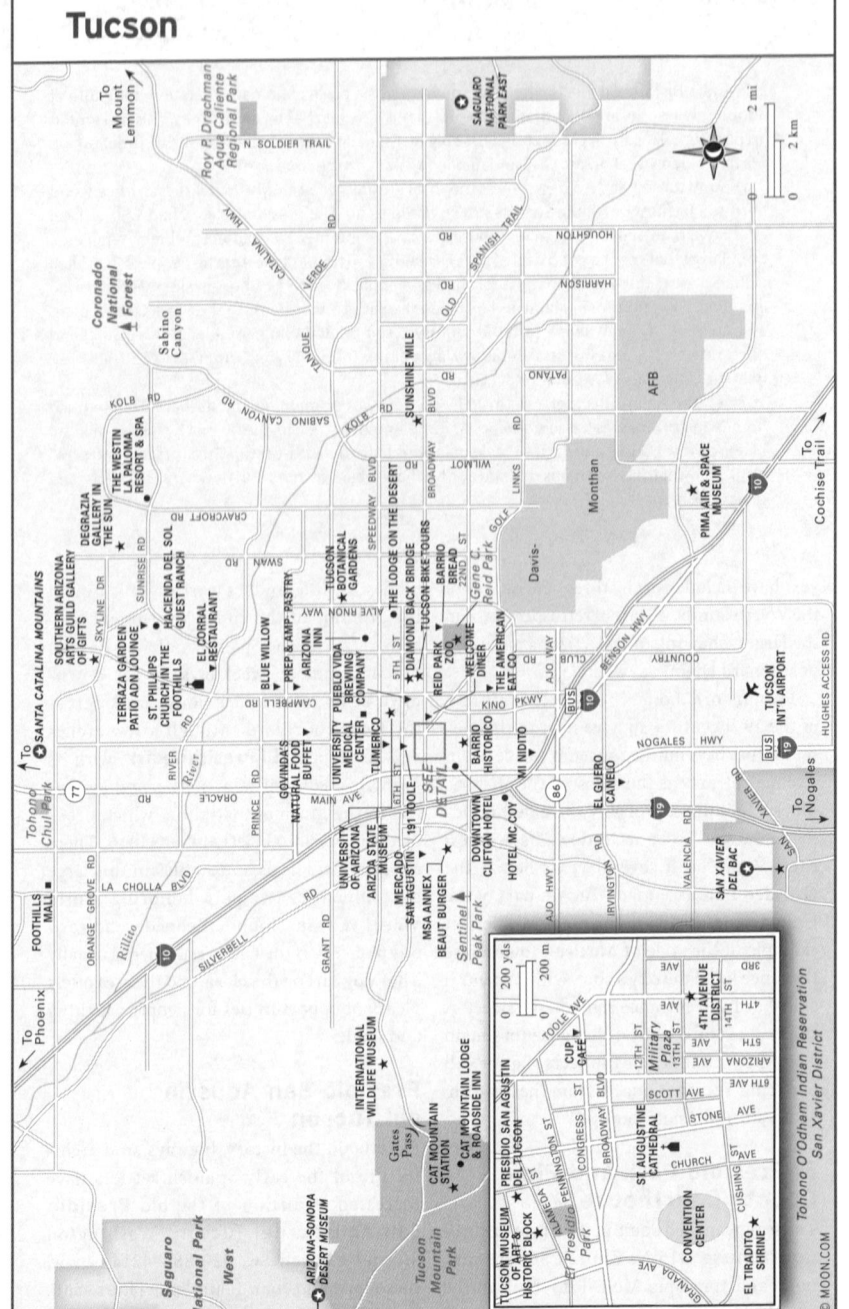

El Presidio Historic District

El Presidio Historic District is where Tucson began as a place of human habitation, a mixture of adobe row houses and Victorian mansions that is several chapters in the city's history writ in architecture. The district is bounded roughly by Granada Avenue on the west, 6th Street on the north, Church Street on the east, and Alameda Street on the south.

Though turned back to desert now, the royal Presidio de San Agustín del Tucson once stood here, the farthest north the Spanish crown dared to go. The presidio, or fort, had 12-foot-high adobe walls and covered 11 acres, housing a small contingent of soldiers and their families, a population that spent a good deal of its time fearing and fighting the Apache people. Much later, archaeologists discovered that the fort had been built close to a Hohokam site that flourished about AD 700-900, proving humans had made their lives on the banks of the Santa Cruz River for as long as nearly anywhere else in the country. A self-guided tour pamphlet of this district and other downtown-area historic sites is available at the Tucson Visitor Center (811 N. Euclid Ave.), near the University of Arizona's Main Gate.

When the Americans took over in 1856, the fort was dismantled and its walls used to build homes and businesses for new arrivals. As more Anglos settled in, the district became a mixture of adobe row houses and Eastern-style mansions for early-20th-century Tucson's rich and powerful. Many of these old mansions and adobes have been restored and now serve as offices and private residences.

year have included art by three generations of the Wyeth family, a Warhol retrospective, and the largest showing of the Arizona paintings of Maynard Dixon anywhere.

Five historic homes built in the last half of the 19th century survive next to the museum. Just beyond the museum's wide Main Avenue entrance is the oldest of the Historic Block's buildings, probably the oldest building in Tucson, La Casa Cordova. Its two west rooms were built several years before the Gadsden Purchase made Tucson part of the United States in 1854. The home is a perfect example of the style of Mexican townhouse that once lined the city's core, with its central courtyard and entrance right on the street. A shady courtyard behind the museum's main building, the Plaza of Pioneers, has a wall honoring Tucson pioneers from the Spanish, Mexican, and Anglo periods.

El Presidio Park and Pima County Courthouse

The sea-green tiled dome of the **Pima County Courthouse** (115 N. Church St., 8:30am-noon and 1pm-5pm Mon.-Fri.), built in the late 1920s, is a landmark of the Old Pueblo's modest skyline, and it's worth a walk around the grounds of the city's government bee-hive to take in the Spanish Colonial Revival touches and, on weekdays, to see downtown at its most industrious. Walk across the front courtyard through a few arches and you'll be in **El Presidio Park,** with its fountains, conquistador statue, and memorial to the Mormon Battalion, which occupied the presidio briefly in late 1846. There are also memorials and statues in this large government-center park honoring World War II veterans, John F. Kennedy, and various pioneers of the Old West. There's usually a hot-dog cart on the plaza, and the area offers plenty of opportunities for people-watching and shade.

Presidio San Agustín del Tucson

Experts on the history, lifeways, and architecture of the early Spanish settlers have recreated a portion of the old **Presidio San Agustín del Tucson** (Washington St. and Church St., 520/884-4214, www. tucsonpresidio.com, 10am-3pm Thurs.-Sun. May-Sept., 10am-4pm Wed.-Sun. Oct.-Apr.,

$5, ages 6-14 $1). Within the adobe walls there's a large mural depicting daily life in and around the fort. There are a few dark, cool adobe rooms set up in period style to show what life was like on the far lonely northern edge of the Spanish Empire in 1775, when an Irishman working for the Spanish rode north from Tubac to establish the fort. During the week, parking is available in a nearby parking garage on Alameda Street; metered parking is available on nearby streets.

Barrio Historico

The photogenic Sonoran-style row houses in the **Barrio Historico** (bounded by Stone Ave., I-10, Cushing St., and 18th St.) on the southwest edge of downtown are well adapted to the desert environment. Their front entrances hug the property line (unlike their Anglo counterparts, with large front and back yards) to make space for central courtyards hidden from the street, which provide a shaded outdoor living space within the home. Many of the adobes here have been lovingly and colorfully restored and now serve as offices, working galleries, and private residences. Sometimes called Barrio Viejo (the Old Neighborhood), the barrio has been on the National Register of Historic Places since the 1970s. It dates from the mid-1850s and, as its dominant architecture suggests, has traditionally been a Mexican enclave. Once, several neighborhoods sprawled out here to create a large quarter referred to as Barrio Libre (Free Neighborhood). Much of the quarter was razed in the late 1960s to make way for the "urban renewal" program that built the Tucson Convention Center. The best examples of the adobe row houses can be found along Myer and Main Avenues and Cushing Street. Along Myer Avenue, look for the old Teatro Carmen, a Spanish-language theater that opened in 1915. The adobe building, which over the years served as a movie house, a boxing arena, and an Elks Lodge, still retains the charm and historic interest that once pervaded this district.

El Tiradito Shrine

Roadside shrines are common in Southern Arizona, even in the most out-of-the-way places, but only one is dedicated to a folk saint who was, by the church's standards, an unredeemed sinner. **El Tiradito** (The Castaway, 221 S. Main Ave.) dates to the 1870s, when Juan Oliveras, a young shepherd, fell in love with his mother-in-law, and the two gave in to an illicit passion. They were discovered by her ax-wielding husband, who killed Oliveras and tossed his dead body away on the land that now holds the shrine (such is the tradition, anyway). The church wouldn't allow the doomed lover to be buried on consecrated land, so the people of the barrio interred him where he was "cast away" and erected a shrine. Some say that if you make a wish at the shrine by night, leave a lit candle, and find it still burning in the morning, your wish will come true—this is why El Tiradito is sometimes called the "Wishing Shrine."

St. Augustine Cathedral

Facing Stone Avenue on the eastern edge of the Barrio Historico, **St. Augustine Cathedral** (192 S. Stone Ave., 520/623-6351, http://cathedral-staugustine.org, 7am-4pm Mon.-Fri., see website for mass times), dedicated to Tucson's patron saint, was built in 1896 and remodeled several times over the years. The facade has stone-carved yucca, saguaro, and horned toad flourishes, and there are statues of the Virgin Mary and the titular saint near the big heavy-wood entrance. Catholics or anyone interested in regional variations on the mass should attend the lively weekly mariachi mass (8am Sun.). Inside, one of the bells formerly used in the original Spanish-era cathedral is preserved in the vestibule.

Tucson Children's Museum

Housed downtown in Tucson's original Carnegie Library, the **Tucson Children's Museum** (200 S. 6th Ave., 520/792-9985, www.childrensmuseumtucson.org, 9am-5pm Tues.-Sun., $9, free under age 1), a nonprofit interactive learning center, is a local family favorite. Parents will appreciate the creativity and attention to detail. There are 12 permanent exhibits, all hands-on and featuring some kid-mesmerizing subjects like dinosaurs, electricity, ocean life, and trains. There's also a beautiful garden that was planted by Tucson's most famous chef, Janos Wilder. It's not always easy to find parking because the museum has no lot of its own; there are metered spaces ($1 per hour) around the museum.

Southern Arizona Transportation Museum

When the railroad reached the isolated town of Tucson in the 1880s, it transformed the city and the region. The small **Southern Arizona Transportation Museum** (414 N. Tooele Ave., 520/623-2223, www.tucsonhistoricdepot.org, 11am-3pm Tues.-Thurs. and Sun., 10am-4pm Fri.-Sat., free) at the refurbished 1940s rail depot downtown explains all the myriad ways the railroad, and later the car and the interstate highway system, changed Tucson and the Southwest, opening it up to visitors and settlers and linking it more to the United States than with Mexico, as it had been before the train's arrival. There's a lifelike statue of Wyatt Earp and Doc Holliday nearby and a plaque that tells the story of a bit of revenge or murder that went down right here back in the violent old days of the territory.

The Diamondback Bridge

Artist Simon Donovan designed this work of public art (spanning Broadway Blvd. near Euclid Ave.) in 2002 to be a memorable entrance to a downtown that has been undergoing a slow revitalization for at least 20 years. **The Diamondback Bridge,** spanning Broadway Boulevard just as the busy street dips into the central city, has since become a popular local landmark. In 2003 it won the prestigious American Public Works Project of the Year award. The 300-foot-long bridge looks like a monster-size rattlesnake taking it easy, albeit with its jaw perpetually stretched open, and cost about $2.7 million to build. There's a small pleasant park on either end of the snake. The easiest way to see it is to pull over at Euclid Avenue and Broadway Boulevard, park, and walk across. Just after the snake bridge, as you enter downtown, you'll see huge black-and-white photographs on both sides of the underpass. These are from the 1940s-1950s of Tucsonans walking, shopping, and generally bustling about downtown.

Sunshine Mile

Pass under the Diamondback Bridge heading east and you're at the start of the **Sunshine Mile** (http://sunshinemile.com) along Broadway Boulevard between Euclid Avenue and Country Club Road. Starting with a soaring 1964 Googie diner, now an excellent farm-to-table restaurant, the Sunshine Mile features a host of well-preserved **mid-century modern architecture.** Built up during the postwar boom years along the city's main east-west corridor, this stretch is for anyone interested in 20th-century car culture and the clean lines and optimistic space-age details of classic American architecture. Most of the eye-catching storefronts still host locally owned businesses. Particularly interesting examples include the Kelly Building (2343 E. Broadway Blvd.), the Chase Bank (3033 E. Broadway Blvd.), and Broadway Village, a charming shopping plaza just opposite the bank. A delightful example of the regional amalgam called Sonoran Modern, Broadway Village was designed by Tucson's favorite architect, Josias Joesler.

4th Avenue District

Lined with chic thrift stores, clothing boutiques, smoke shops, restaurants, and cocktail lounges, **4th Avenue** is an ideal place to people-watch, and there are some really good places to eat as well as treasures to be found in the quirky shops. Twice a year, in fall and spring, the area closes to vehicular traffic for

1: giant tiki head on Tucson's 4th Avenue
2: University of Arizona campus **3:** Tucson Mountain Park

a street fair featuring artisan booths, concerts, and greasy food galore. Between downtown and the University District, 4th Avenue is a short walk from campus, and on Friday-Saturday nights expect hordes of college kids out looking for inebriation. It's best to avoid driving in this area on weekend nights.

Tours

Tucson Bike Tours (215 N. Hoff Ave., 520/488-4446, http://tucsonbiketours.com, 9am, noon, 3pm, 6pm daily Oct.-early May, 2.5 hours, $50) offers invigorating and informative bike tours around Tucson's historic neighborhoods, including downtown, Barrio Viejo, and 4th Avenue. Your guide leads you on an easy 9- to 11-mile ride over flat and well-paved streets, pointing out interesting and historical details along the way. You'll ride a comfortable Civia neighborhood cruiser with a single gear and hand brakes. It's easy, safe, and a lot of fun.

UNIVERSITY OF ARIZONA (UA)

Since it rose from the desert in 1885 as the first institution of higher learning in the Arizona Territory, the fate of the University of Arizona and that of its host pueblo have been linked. It's difficult to imagine what Tucson would be without the shady central campus. A land-grant school that has educated countless Arizona leaders and residents, UA has nearly 37,000 students—more populous than most Arizona towns. The school is world-renowned for its arid-land research, and it has a center for integrative medicine founded by best-selling healer-doctor Andrew Weil. It's also the place where anthropology, archaeology, and many other disciplines were revolutionized through the discovery of tree-ring dating.

The university is active in the U.S. space program, specifically in Mars exploration. Check out the displays on the HiRISE Mars camera, the *Phoenix* Mars lander, and the *Cassini* mission to Saturn at the **Sonett Visitor Center** (University Blvd. and Cherry St., 520/626-7432, 9am-5pm Mon.-Fri., free).

On campus you'll find a number of museums and galleries, and the entire campus is an arboretum: the green central campus claims to be the "oldest continually maintained green space in Arizona." Flora enthusiasts can stroll the campus and take in a cactus garden, a collection of rare tropical trees, and various arid-land species that have been brought to UA from all over the world. If you want to learn more about the campus's natural wonders, go by the **Campus Arboretum** (Herring Hall, 520/621-7074, http://arboretum.arizona.edu, 9am-5pm Mon.-Fri., free). Don't miss the **Joseph Wood Krutch Cactus Garden** in the center of the campus's long, grassy mall.

Kids will enjoy the hands-on exhibits, laser shows, and sky-watching at **Flandrau: The UA Science Center** (1601 E. University Blvd., 520/621-4516, www.flandrau.org, 9am-5pm Mon.-Thurs., 9am-10pm Fri., 10am-10pm Sat., noon-5pm Sun., $16 adults, $12 ages 4-17); admission includes entry to the science center, mineral museum, and one planetarium show. Downstairs at Flandrau, you'll find the **UA Mineral Museum** (520/621-4516, www.uamineralmuseum.org, 9am-5pm Mon.-Thurs., 9am-10pm Fri., 10am-10pm Sat., noon-5pm Sun., free), which displays a wondrous collection of rocks from Arizona and beyond.

There are also numerous public art installations on campus. One that should not be missed is the hulking commentary *Border Dynamics,* created by artists Alberto Morackis and Guadalupe Serrano. It's not always easy to find parking on campus, and it's impossible during sporting events. Visitors can pay to park at the Park Avenue Garage (Park Ave. and Helen St.) and at the Main Gate Parking Garage (Euclid Ave. and E. 2nd St.).

Arizona Historical Society Museum

Just south of the main gate wall along North Campus Drive is the **Arizona Historical Society Museum** (949 E. 2nd St., 520/628-5774, www.arizonahistoricalsociety.org,

10am-2pm Tues.-Sat., $12 adults, $6 ages 7-13), the largest of the Arizona Historical Society's three Tucson museums. Exhibits include Arizona's role in space as well as a full-scale reproduction of the cramped canvas-tent home early miners lived in and a walk through a dark underground mine. There's also an old Studebaker on display; this make of car was once so popular with Arizona's sheriffs that the car company sent an author to the young state to write a public relations pamphlet that included exciting stories of frontier law enforcement. This is an interesting stop for Arizona history buffs, and there are several hands-on exhibits for the kids.

Arizona State Museum

Established in 1893, the **Arizona State Museum** (1013 E. University Blvd., 520/621-6302, www.statemuseum.arizona.edu, 10am-4pm Mon.-Sat., $8) is the oldest anthropology museum in the Southwest. Here you'll find several rooms of fascinating displays on the state's various Native American tribes and the world's largest collection of Southwest Indian pottery, including many contemporary pieces that prove pottery-making is certainly not a lost art. Every year in February the museum's grassy grounds play host to the Southwest Indian Art Fair, one of the more important and well attended of such events in the Southwest. A permanent exhibition inside the stately old building explains the origins and histories of 10 of Arizona's Native American groups, including the Hohokam, the O'odham, and the Apache, each of whom once thrived in Southern Arizona. Park in the garage at either Euclid Avenue and Second Street or North Tyndall Avenue and Fourth Street; both are free on weekends.

University of Arizona Museum of Art

The permanent collection of the **University of Arizona Museum of Art** (UA campus, near Park Ave. and Speedway Blvd., 520/621-7567, http://artmuseum.arizona.edu, 9am-5pm Tues.-Fri., noon-4pm Sat.-Sun., $8)

houses works by Tintoretto, Piazzetta, Goya, Brueghel, Rodin, Picasso, Hopper, Pollock, Rothko, O'Keeffe, and many more. Asian and Latin American traditions are also well represented. Special shows often feature the work of well-known local, national, and Mexican artists. The museum has an impressive collection of Spanish medieval art, the signature piece of which is the 26-panel *Retablo of Ciudad Rodrigo,* an altarpiece depicting the sweep of biblical events from Genesis through the life of Christ to the Last Judgment.

Center for Creative Photography

UA's **Center for Creative Photography** (1030 N. Olive Rd., 520/621-7968, www.creativephotography.org, 10am-4:30pm Tues.-Sat., free) has one of the largest photography collections in the world; it holds the archives of Ansel Adams, Edward Weston, and other major artists. The center mounts a few exhibitions a year, so check the website before traveling to see what's on display. You can make an appointment by phone to personally view a few of the 80,000 prints accessible to the public.

MIDTOWN
Reid Park Zoo

Take Broadway Boulevard east to Randolph Way at Reid Park to Tucson's small but prestigious **Reid Park Zoo** (1100 S. Randolph Way, 520/791-4022, www.tucsonzoo.org, 9am-4pm daily winter, 8am-2pm daily summer, $10.50 adults, $8.50 seniors, $6.50 ages 2-14). The zoo specializes in giant anteater breeding and preservation, and there are several of these strange beasts to look at here. The zoo also features elephants, bears, various big cats, and much more.

Make sure to take the kids to the **Giraffe Encounter** (10am-10:45am Mon.-Fri. winter, 9:30am-10:15am Mon.-Fri. summer, $3 pp), where you can feed the long-necked residents, who stick out their long purple tongues, dripping with saliva, to capture the morsel. If you get to the zoo early enough, you might catch

Howard Hughes in Tucson

Many have heard about those weird few years that Howard Hughes spent hiding out on the top floor of a Las Vegas hotel, going mad. There are hints that the Old Pueblo could have been the site of Hughes's infamous hideout rather than Vegas. Bob Maheu, Hughes's right-hand man and official public face during the Vegas years, told Geoff Schumacher, author of the 2008 book *Howard Hughes: Power, Paranoia, and Palace Intrigue*, that in the mid-1960s, before moving to Vegas, Hughes first considered moving to Tucson, where he'd already set up a manufacturing plant in 1951.

Hughes loved the desert, considering it free of the germs that stalked him. There's a great scene in *The Aviator* in which the young Hughes, played by Leonardo DiCaprio, sees a stand of saguaros in a film he's watching and whispers something like, "so clean." Ultimately, though, Hughes soured on the desert around Las Vegas due to his inability to stop nuclear testing at the Nevada Test Site, fallout from which he obsessively feared.

Though he never moved to Tucson, Hughes did have a presence here. Hughes Aircraft built the Falcon, the world's first air-to-air guided missile, and many other missiles and weapons here, employing thousands of workers. Hughes Missile Systems was eventually bought by Raytheon, which is today Southern Arizona's largest private employer.

a glimpse of the elegant black jaguar lounging in the cool of the morning.

A gift shop sells all kinds of zoo-related stuffed animals, shirts, and books, and a fast-food-style eatery serves hamburgers, corn dogs, and the like. The zoo is small enough that little kids aren't likely to get too tired out. Plan about three hours, less if you don't have kids. Check out the cameras on the zoo's website to get a preview of the some of the animals.

Tucson Botanical Gardens

Gardeners and anybody who appreciates beauty should stop at the **Tucson Botanical Gardens** (2150 N. Alvernon Way, 520/326-9686, www.tucsonbotanical.org, 8:30am-4:30pm daily winter, 7:30am-4:30pm daily summer, $15 adults, $8 ages 4-17), a midtown oasis, for a few hours. Easy walking trails wind around the six-acre property, which feels secluded and hidden away even though it's right in busy midtown. Benches throughout allow contemplation of the various gardens, each showcasing a different gardening tradition. A cactus and succulent garden has examples of cacti from nearby deserts and around the world, and the xeriscape garden demonstrates how you can grow desert-adapted plants without using a lot of water.

October-March you can see **Butterfly Magic,** a live tropical butterfly exhibit. Call ahead for times and availability. Different tours of the gardens (included in admission) are offered throughout the month, and not every tour is offered every day, so call ahead or check the website. The **Garden Gallery** has rotating art shows (8:30am-4:30pm daily).

Mini Time Machine Museum of Miniatures

Built by passionate collectors, the charming **Mini Time Machine Museum of Miniatures** (4455 E. Camp Lowell Dr., 520/881-0606, www.theminitimemachine. org, 9am-4pm Tues.-Sun., $11.50 adults, $8 ages 4-17) in midtown is a great place to take kids, who generally find all the tiny objects and detailed dioramas endlessly fascinating. They'll also like the Enchanted Tree, with its big face and fairy-tale trunk life. The museum has a permanent collection of 300 miniatures, both contemporary and antique, and presents special exhibits from time to time that explore a particular theme or style in depth and, of course, in miniature.

Take Speedway Boulevard west under I-10. The road becomes Gates Pass Road and then runs into Kinney Road. Follow the signs to each of the following sights, some of Tucson's most representative attractions. You can do it in one long day, though the Desert Museum and Saguaro National Park stand up to a full day each. To get to the Desert Museum, take Speedway Boulevard west for 12 miles through the desert and turn right onto Kinney Road. The International Wildlife Museum is along the way, as is Old Tucson.

Sentinel Peak and Tumamoc Hill

Also called "A" Mountain for the large white letter "A" repainted on its face every year by University of Arizona students, a tradition that began in 1915, **Sentinel Peak** (1000 S. Sentinel Peak Rd., 8am-8pm Mon.-Sat., 8am-6pm Sun.) served the early populations of the Tucson Valley with springwater and black basalt. When Father Kino first rode into the valley in the 1690s, he found the Indigenous population living in the small peak's shadow, and it was surely an important landmark in the basin for eons before that. During the presidio days it earned its name as a promontory from which soldiers would scan the desert for Apaches. Now there's a park on the peak, reached by a winding paved road. Take Congress Street west under I-10 and follow the signs. There are a few short trails around the park, a little rock shelter to sit under, charcoal barbecues, and some great views of the valley.

The hill just to the north of Sentinel Peak, called **Tumamoc Hill** (Tumamoc Hill Rd.), is home to a desert laboratory founded in 1903. For thousands of years Indigenous residents of the Tucson Valley farmed on and around Tumamoc Hill, as evidenced by numerous archaeological sites here. Among the legends of the Tohono O'odham is the story of a giant horned lizard that threatened to devour the tribe had not the god I'itoi, in response to prayers, turned the great reptile into a hill, hence the name Tumamoc (horned lizard) Hill.

International Wildlife Museum

As you drive west toward Gates Pass and the Tucson Mountains, off on the north side of the road, partly obscured by the thick desert, a large castle-like building holds the impressive taxidermy collection of the private nonprofit **International Wildlife Museum** (4800 W. Gates Pass Rd., 520/629-0100, www. thewildlifemuseum.org, 9am-5pm Mon.-Fri., 9am-6pm Sat.-Sun., $10 adults, $5 ages 4-12). The more than 400 stuffed and preserved mammals, birds, insects, and spiders include "Big Terror," a stuffed tiger who still looks a bit hungry. The mighty beast was killed in 1969 in India, after he'd reportedly devoured 8-12 people. This is a fun and educational place to bring kids, but if you have limited time, skip it in favor of the Arizona-Sonora Desert Museum a few miles up the road, where the mountain lions, rattlesnakes, beavers, and scorpions are all indigenous, and alive.

Tucson Mountain Park and Gates Pass Scenic Overlook

Robert Gates was a typical Southwestern frontier entrepreneur: He did a little mining, a little ranching, a bit of saloon keeping, and some homesteading. In 1883, in order to connect his Avra Valley mine with his other interests in Tucson, he set about building a precipitous route over the Tucson Mountains, and in the process set the stage for local officials, 50 years later, to establish one of the largest public parks of its kind in the nation. The 37-square-mile Sonoran Desert preserve called **Tucson Mountain Park** (Speedway west from downtown over Gates Pass to Kinney Rd., 7am-10pm daily, free) features one of the largest saguaro forests in the world and has 62 miles of trails for hiking and mountain biking, as well as a rifle and pistol range, three large picnic areas with grills, ramadas, and the world-renowned Arizona-Sonora Desert Museum.

If all these activities seem a bit sweaty and active for your taste, at least make it to the top of the road named for the man who conquered the comparatively low Tucson Mountains at **Gates Pass.** You can drive to

the pass and park in a large lot, which offers restrooms, a ramada, and two little stacked-rock huts decorated inside with eons of graffiti. There are short trails out to a promontory from which you can see the whole sweeping expanse of the desert below. It's one of the best views in Arizona—a state that has no shortage of sweeping views. If you want to stay the night at the park, the **Gilbert Ray Campground** (8451 W. McCain Loop, off Kinney Rd., 520/883-4200, $10-20) has sites with RV hookups, picnic tables, restrooms, and a dumping station.

TOP EXPERIENCE

★ Arizona-Sonora Desert Museum

A big part of the fun of a visit to the **Arizona-Sonora Desert Museum** (2021 N. Kinney Rd., 520/883-2702, www.desertmuseum. org, 7:30am-5pm daily Mar.-Sept., 7:30am-5pm Sun.-Fri., 7:30am-10pm Sat. June-Aug., 8:30am-5pm daily Oct.-Feb., $24 adults, $12 ages 3-12) is getting there. Driving west out of Tucson over dramatic Gates Pass, you'll see thousands of saguaros standing tall on the hot, rocky ground below, surrounded by pipe cleaner-like ocotillo and fuzzy cholla, creosote, and prickly pear.

But the saguaro forests of Tucson Mountain Park and Saguaro National Park West, both of which surround the Desert Museum, are only one of several distinctive desert life zones you'll see and learn about at this world-famous museum and zoo, where native mammals, birds, reptiles, amphibians, fish, and arthropods live in displays mimicking their open-desert habitats. This is the best place to learn about both the general structure and the minute details of the surrounding desert, and it is probably your only realistic chance to see all of the unique creatures that call it home.

Easy trails wind through the beautiful 21-acre preserve, passing exhibits of semidesert grasslands and mountain woodlands similar to those on the Sonoran Desert's high mountain ranges. The Desert Loop Trail leads through a lowland scrub and cacti landscape with javelinas and coyotes. In Cat Canyon, a bespeckled ocelot sleeps in the shade, and a bobcat lounges on the rocks. A mountain lion can be seen close up through a viewing window, and a black bear strolls along an artificial stream and sleeps on a rock promontory. There are also rare Mexican wolves, white-tailed deer, bighorn sheep, and adorable prairie dogs in their commune.

A riparian habitat has beavers and otters, water lovers that were once abundant in the Southwest. There's a desert garden exhibit, a cactus and succulent garden, and a butterfly and wildflower display. There are also displays on desert fish and dunes, and a walk-in aviary with dozens of native birds. Docents throughout the complex help with questions and give presentations on special topics. All this plus a restaurant, snack bars, and a gift shop that sells excellent Pueblo Indian crafts make this Tucson's very best attraction. If you're planning on doing any exploring in the desert, do so after a trip to the Desert Museum, where you'll get a comprehensive minicourse in desert ecology.

TOP EXPERIENCE

Saguaro National Park West

This is where the icon of arid America holds court. The split **Saguaro National Park** (www.nps.gov/sagu, 7am-sunset daily, visitors center 9am-5pm daily, $25 per car, valid for seven days, good at both sections) has a western section at the base of the Tucson Mountains and a larger eastern section at the base of the Rincon Mountains. Both are worth visiting, but if you have time for only one, go to the eastern section, which is older and larger. (Then again, there are a few other sights around the western portion, while the eastern is a bit on its own, save for nearby

---

1: Arizona State Museum **2:** a bobcat at the Arizona-Sonora Desert Museum **3:** ancient petroglyphs in Saguaro National Park West **4:** Saguaro National Park visitors center

Colossal Cave.) Together they protect about 91,300 acres of magnificent Sonoran Desert landscape, including large and crowded saguaro forests surrounded by a thick underbrush of ocotillo, prickly pear, cholla, mesquite, and paloverde. If you want to see an accessible and wondrous example of the Sonoran Desert at its best, there are few better places to go.

The saguaro ("sa-WAH-ro") is much more than a strange-looking plant to the original inhabitants of the Sonoran Desert, be they cactus wrens, coyotes, screech owls, or the Tohono O'odham people. Adapted to the arid environment, in which the rains come but twice a year, it anchors an entire busy community of living things, providing food and shelter to all sorts of desert creatures.

The great cactus-tree grows slowly, and only during the summer rainy season. After living shaded and protected by a mesquite tree for 15 years, a saguaro is still only about a foot tall. These green ribbed giants can live to be 150 years old or more. When it reaches 75 it begins to sprout its identifying arms, so when you see a tall and fat one with many arms—there are many in both sections of the park—know that it is a venerable old plant.

The place to start your tour of the western park is the **Red Hills Visitor Center** (2700 N. Kinney Rd., 520/733-5158), where you can learn about the ancient symbiotic friendship between the Tohono O'odham and the saguaro. You'll find a guide to the park's 40 miles of trails, and you can book a tour with a naturalist and peruse the bookstore stocked with titles on local history and nature.

A good way to see the park, especially in the heat of summer, is to drive the six-mile **Bajada Loop** through a thick saguaro forest. The route is graded dirt and can get dusty; you can also walk or bike the loop. Drive the loop and stop at the **Valley View Overlook Trail,** an easy one-mile round-trip trail off the loop road that rises to an expansive view of the Avra Valley, the saguaro-lined desert, and the skulking rock mountains. A half-mile round-trip walk to the **Signal Hill Picnic Area**

offers a look at ancient petroglyphs. Both trails can be accessed off the Bajada Loop drive and are well marked. There are also a few very short paved walks around the visitors center featuring interpretive signs about the saguaro and other desert fauna.

Ironwood Forest National Monument

A 129,000-acre wild Sonoran Desert preserve about an hour's drive northwest of Tucson, **Ironwood Forest National Monument** (520/258-7200, www.blm.gov, free) is a great place to encounter the desert up close. Its namesake tree will likely appear a bit underwhelming to the uninitiated. The gray-green monotony of the surface-level desert blurs the vision, and one bushy little tree tends to look a lot like another. But the truth is in the details: The ironwood, which can live as long as 800 years, anchors a deceptively busy desert ecosystem, providing shade and succor for a host of flora and fauna unique to the region. Like most of Arizona's national monuments monitored by the Bureau of Land Management (BLM), Ironwood Forest is vast and empty, inviting to hikers, hunters, and campers. There's no visitors center, campgrounds, or rangers. It is a perfect place for a long drive through the desert on dirt roads, mostly smooth and accepting of regular cars, although coming in an SUV is best.

More than Saguaro National Park, Ironwood is a place where the wild desert is there to discover—unvarnished, uncultivated, and unforgiving. It's not a good idea to venture out here in summer. The easiest way to see it is to drive slowly along the dirt roads that traverse part of the monument, stopping to look into the details. The best way is to take I-10 north to Avra Valley Road and follow it until it turns to dirt around the waste piles of the Silverbell Mine. Follow the road through the monument, passing the mine, the Silverbell Mountains, Ragged Top Mountain, and Wolcott Peak. Take Silverbell Road out of the monument and back to I-10. The trip can take all day if you stop to look around.

Archaeologists say that people have been living here for 5,000 years, although these days there are only campers and hunters in this glorious desert outback.

EAST AND NORTH OF DOWNTOWN

The north end of Tucson, on the *bajada* and the foothills of the Santa Catalinas, is known for its high-end accommodations and Mission Revival and Spanish Colonial homes, many of them designed by famed architect Josias Joesler. The mighty mountains, reaching nearly 10,000 feet elevation and an entirely different world from the desert below, rise northeast of downtown and are easily reached by taking Grant Road east from midtown to Tanque Verde (Catalina Hwy.) and then the Mount Lemmon Highway north into the range. To the east you'll find caves, mountains, and saguaros as far as the eye can see.

TOP EXPERIENCE

★ Saguaro National Park East

The eastern portion of **Saguaro National Park** (3693 S. Old Spanish Trail, 520/733-5153, 7am-sunset daily, visitors center 9am-5pm daily, $25 per car, valid for seven days, good at both sections) is backed by the 8,600-foot Rincon Mountains. The visitors center has a bookstore and exhibits about the desert. The easiest way to see this section is to stroll, bike, or drive slowly along the paved Cactus Forest Drive, an eight-mile one-way that begins at the visitors center and winds up and across the *bajada*. The desert here is gorgeous, especially after a rainstorm or early in the morning during the bloom months. The 100 miles of trails include one that goes to Rincon Peak, above 8,000 feet. The park's newspaper guide has a full description of the major trails.

Vista del Rio Cultural Resource Park

Before the Spanish arrived in Southern Arizona and even before the Tohono O'odham and the Apache ruled this desert, it was home to the Hohokam people, arid-land farmers who lived in the Sonoran Desert's river valleys, building a highly complex culture that survived for centuries. Though the Tucson Valley doesn't have any spectacular Hohokam ruins on the order of Casa Grande, halfway between Tucson and Phoenix, **Vista del Rio Cultural Resource Park** (7575 E. Desert Arbor St., dawn-dusk daily, free), a four-acre archaeological park on the east side, preserves the humbler ruins of a village occupied by the Hohokam about AD 1000-1150. Even if you're less than fascinated by the dirt-mound ruins, this is a quiet and peaceful park with walking paths and sitting areas, perfect for relaxation and contemplation among the ghosts of a long-lost nation.

Colossal Cave Mountain Park

Sure it's a "dead cave," and certainly it has become a poor cousin to the living underground wonderland that is Kartchner Caverns State Park just a few dozen miles to the southeast, but **Colossal Cave Mountain Park** (16721 E. Old Spanish Trail, 520/647-7275, www.colossalcave.com, 8am-5pm daily, entry $5 per car, cave tours $20 adults, $10 ages 5-12) near Vail, about a half-hour drive through the desert east of Tucson, has many charms. The cave has been used as a shelter, an altar, a hideout, and a tourist attraction by various Native American bands and colonists for the last 1,000 years—this according to ancient artifacts and historic local newspaper accounts. In the 1930s the Civilian Conservation Corps (CCC) built a few structures near the cave's entrance in that inimitable native-stone style and installed lights and railings through a half mile of the sprawling grotto. The typical tour follows this route, while the guide narrates a general natural history of the cave with a bit of human history (including a tale of outlaws) peppered in. It's interesting and really fun, especially with kids.

After the cave tour, there's a gift shop, a café, and long views of the desert. A few miles down the road, still within the park, the mid-1870s **La Posta Quemada Ranch** offers more activities, particularly for children. In addition to pony rides ($5), a petting zoo ($5), trail rides ($38-87), and a gift shop, the ranch features a large sundial, displays on the cave and the CCC's work in the park, and a habitat for desert tortoises Shelly and Cienega. It's unlikely you'll see either tortoise unless you arrive in the morning, especially during the hotter months. There are plenty of shady and peaceful places to picnic, and you can even camp ($7.50) if you make a reservation.

Trail Dust Town

The best way to visit **Trail Dust Town** (6541 E. Tanque Verde Rd., 520/296-5442, www. traildusttown.com, 5:30pm-9pm daily, $2.50-6 per attraction), an Old West-themed family attraction on the east side, is to wrap it up with a cowboy steak-and-beans dinner at Pinnacle Peak Steak House. If you don't have kids, rethink the entire venture. I'm not saying that there's nothing for the adult at Trail Dust Town; anyone interested in big-screen notions of Old West culture might get a kick or two here—there's some movie set-style buildings, a miniature train that circles the property, a few on-cue gunfights in the dusty streets, and various shops and displays featuring touristy gifts and frontier artifacts. There's also a gold-panning game, a shoot-out gallery, and a lot of other commotion. If you have young children, you and the spouse can sit in the saloon and wait for your table while the kids explore the attractions.

St. Philips Church in the Foothills

St. Philips Church in the Foothills (4440 N. Campbell Ave., 520/299-6421, www. stphilipstucson.org) was originally designed in 1936 by Josias Joesler, a Swiss-born architect who designed many other foothills structures and who is responsible for the amalgam of native and revival architecture sometimes known as the Tucson style. Joesler's structures usually mimic Mexican, Spanish, and Moorish styles with upscale flourishes, many of them stylish desert haciendas on the *bajada*

of the Catalinas, an area long reserved for the region's wealthy. A longtime Tucson architect said that Tucson, at least when it came to architecture, divorced itself from Mexico (and thereby Spain and its Moorish traditions) too quickly; these styles, with their courtyards, native materials, and passive solar heating, are ideal for living in the Sonoran Desert, certainly much better than the cheaply built tract homes that proliferate in the valley these days. Very few Tucsonans build homes in the Joesler style anymore, as it is out of the financial question for most, and that's too bad.

St. Philip's is along the busy River Road corridor and yet retains a peaceful atmosphere, with gardens and fountains behind thick, silent walls. The building and grounds have been added to and changed over the years, but always with respect paid to the original vision. Church officials welcome visits from students of architecture and anybody else who wants to look around. It's best not to go on a Sunday if you're just looking, and to arrive before 4pm Monday-Friday if you want to talk to someone about the church and its history.

Tohono Chul Park

Tohono Chul Park (7366 N. Paseo del Norte, 520/742-6455, www.tohonochulpark. org, 8am-5pm daily, $15 adults, $13 seniors, $6 ages 5-12), a 49-acre desert preserve, is worth the short drive north on Oracle Road into Tucson's sprawl. Turn left on Ina Road, then right on Paseo del Norte, and you'll find native-plant gardens with easy trails punctuated by interpretive signs. The **Ethnobotanical Garden,** with rows of maize and other crops once planted by the O'odham people and Spanish settlers, demonstrates the different methods used by each group to coax subsistence out of the dry ground.

If you stay quiet and sit by one of the many fountains or other water features on the grounds, you might get a glimpse of the many bobcats and javelinas that call the preserve home. One night a year, in June-July, the garden's **night-blooming cereus** comes to life, an event so rare and spectacular that there's a hotline (520/575-8468) for visitors to keep up to date on the expected bloom timing.

There are gift shops and galleries on the property, and exhibits generally feature Native American and Hispanic folk art and fine art. **The Garden Bistro** (520/797-1222, 8am-4:30pm daily brunch, $15-20) has an excellent Southwestern-inspired brunch menu; it's the perfect place to lounge before or after exploring the grounds, sipping a mimosa or a prickly pear margarita.

Roy P. Drachman Agua Caliente Regional Park

Approaching the shock of wet greenery among the otherwise gray-green of the foothills, it's easy to see why this spring-fed oasis has been a popular spot for humans for the last 5,000 years. **Roy P. Drachman Agua Caliente Regional Park** (12325 E. Roger Rd., 520/749-3718, 7am-sunset daily, visitors center and art gallery 1pm-4pm Wed.-Fri., 8am-4pm Sat.-Sun. Nov.-Apr.), a 100-acre public park with a visitors center, gallery, nature shop, and wildlife-attracting spring-fed ponds, has been a stopover for hunter-gatherers and the farming Hohokam people as well as a ranch and a resort built to exploit the supposedly curative powers of the springs. Much of the vegetation, as along with the fish and the log-lounging turtles you'll see everywhere, is decidedly nonnative. The shaggy palms encircling the ponds like some spice-road camp were planted long ago, but the 200-year-old mesquite tree next to the former ranch house, a tree that hosts a whole ecosystem of its own, is native and one of the oldest mesquites in the valley. This is a contemplative, peaceful spot, a good place for a walk, a picnic, or a long talk by the 87°F ponds, with lazy turtles listening in.

DeGrazia Gallery in the Sun

A lot of art lovers turn up their noses at Ettore "Ted" DeGrazia. His little sad-eyed Native American children are ubiquitous here, on mugs and Christmas ornaments and whatever else. All the work can look the same and seems to offer little in the way of depth. A visit to the **DeGrazia Gallery in the Sun** (6300 N. Swan Rd., 520/299-9191, http://degrazia.org, 10am-4pm daily, $8 adults, $5 ages 12-18), the amazing foothills home and gallery that he largely built himself, changes many opinions of the artist. When you see the home he built and get a close look at the more serious paintings that hang throughout the gallery—epic cycles about the Mexican Revolution, the "founding" of the Southwest by Cabeza de Vaca and his doomed companions, and the lives and traditions of the Tohono O'odham people, to name just a few—you may conclude that DeGrazia actually created some of the most enduring impressionistic visions in the Southwest.

Born in Southern Arizona, DeGrazia attended UA and published his first work in *Arizona Highways* magazine. He went on to study in Mexico with muralists Diego Rivera and José Clemente Orozco. He died in 1982 at age 73, but the DeGrazia Foundation carries on his memory at the Gallery in the Sun, his first studio and gallery in Tucson, built in honor of Padre Kino and dedicated to Our Lady of Guadalupe. A mission on the grounds features DeGrazia murals with a roof open to the sky. The gallery has a gift shop stocked with DeGrazia reproductions for sale. Even if you can't muster an appreciation of this admittedly overexposed artist's work, go for the native architecture and design at Gallery in the Sun, which may be DeGrazia's greatest work of art.

★ Santa Catalina Mountains

Drive about 40 miles (1 hour) up a twisty, paved two-lane from the desert floor northeast of midtown and you're at nearly 10,000 feet elevation—the trip, it is often said, is like traveling from Mexico to Canada in one short scenic drive. It wasn't until the 1930s that Tucsonans could reach the cool heights in great numbers, when former U.S. postmaster general Frank Hitchcock called in some federal favors and secured money and prison labor to begin building a road into the mountains. The indomitable Civilian Conservation

Corps eventually finished the job, and in the 1940s real estate agents began selling lots in what is now **Summerhaven,** a little cabin village at 7,840 feet with a few gift shops and cafés. Just up from the village are the 22 runs of **Ski Valley** (10300 Ski Run Rd., 520/576-1321, snow report 520/576-1400, www.skithelemmon.com, 10am-4:30pm Mon. and Thurs.-Fri., 9am-5pm Sat.-Sun., $30-60), the nation's southernmost ski hill. In a good year the season runs roughly mid-December-early April. The chairlift ($15 adults, $12 youths) operates year-round, and it's fun to ride it to the green and cool mountaintop in the summer while the rest of the world sweats below.

Dozens of trails are on the range, along with several public restrooms, campgrounds, and lookout points. The trails in the Santa Catalina Mountains move through dense pine and aspen forests, along high ridges overlooking the hazy valley and the city spread out below, and through mazes of boulders and along trickling creeks. It's very different up here in the forest from the desert valley below, and it snows here in the winter, limiting access by car for brief periods throughout the season. It's a good idea to stop at the **Palisade Visitor Center** (520/749-8700, 8:30am-4:40pm daily) at 7,200 feet, which has trail maps, a bookstore, and displays about the mountain's ecology.

Don't expect to be alone when you're exploring the Catalinas; this is an extremely popular area among locals for picnicking and hiking, especially in spring-summer. While the weekends are sometimes bumper to bumper, on weekdays, even in summer, it's possible to avoid large crowds.

Sabino Canyon

Sabino Creek starts as springs high up in the mountains, gathering snowmelt and runoff as it descends into the foothills. It rushes through Sabino Canyon with sometimes deadly vigor, creating a riparian oasis of cottonwoods, willow, walnut, sycamore, and ash. Saguaro, barrel cactus, prickly pear, and cholla dominate the rocky canyon slopes away

from the creek's influence. It is a truly spectacular place that should not be missed.

Sabino Canyon Recreation Area (8am-4:30pm daily, $8 per car), about 13 miles northeast of downtown Tucson, is easily accessible, user-friendly in the extreme, and much used—best estimates say 1.25 million people visit every year. Many locals use the canyon's trail system for daily exercise, and hikers, picnickers, and sightseers usually pack the canyon every day year-round.

A paved road rises four miles up into the canyon, crossing the nearly always running creek in several places. During Southern Arizona's summer and winter rainy seasons, it is nearly impossible to cross the small bridges without getting your feet wet. The Forest Service closed the road to cars in 1978. It's a relatively easy walk along the road to the top of the canyon, which offers access to trails that go far into the Santa Catalinas. If you don't feel like walking, the **Sabino Canyon Shuttle** (http://sabinocanyoncrawler.com, 9am-4pm daily, $12 adults, $7 ages 3-12, free under age 2), an ecofriendly electric tram, runs 30-minute narrated trips into the canyon all day, pausing at nine stops along the way to pick up or drop hikers at various trailheads.

From the last tram stop 3.8 miles up in the canyon, hikers can take an easy stroll down the road, crossing the creek at nearly every turn, or try the **Phoneline Trail,** winding along the canyon slopes and overlooking the riparian beauty below. Perhaps the most popular trail in the entire Tucson Valley is the hike through nearby **Bear Canyon** to **Seven Falls,** a wonderful series of waterfalls and collecting pools. You can access the **Bear Canyon Trail** from just outside the visitors center, or take the shuttle to a trailhead 1.5 miles on. To the falls it's a total of 3.8 miles one-way and worth every step, though it is moderately difficult, rocky, and rather steep. The Bear Canyon shuttle

1: Sabino Creek in Sabino Canyon **2:** Tohono Chul Park **3:** Biosphere 2 **4:** San Xavier del Bac

($4 adults, $2 ages 3-12) leaves the visitors center every hour on the hour 9:15am-4:15pm daily.

The **Sabino Canyon Visitors Center and Bookstore** (520/749-8700, www.fs.fed.us/r3/coronado, 8am-4:30pm daily) has trail guides and sells gifts and books. There are restrooms, drinking fountains, and dozens of tucked-away picnic areas throughout the canyon, and many of the trails link up with one another, so it is easy to cobble together a loop hike that will take you through the various life zones. The canyon is open sunrise-sundown every day, and bikes are allowed in the canyon only before 9am and after 5pm, never on Wednesday or Saturday, and never on trails that lead into the **Pusch Ridge Wilderness Area.**

To get to the canyon from midtown, take Speedway Boulevard east until it turns into Tanque Verde Road, then turn north on Sabino Canyon Road to the recreation area, just north of Sunrise Road.

Catalina State Park

Catalina State Park (AZ 77, mile marker 81, 520/628-5798, http://azstateparks.com, 5am-10pm daily, $7 per car), a popular desert reserve just north of Tucson in the saguaro-dotted foothills of the Santa Catalinas, is heavily used, especially on weekends. Hikers shouldn't be surprised to pass large families carrying coolers up the trail.

The 5,500-acre park has eight trails—most of them easy to moderate—along with picnic areas, charcoal grills, and a small gift shop. It's an easily accessible place to see the desert, lush here thanks to the runoff and snowmelt that barrel down from the mountains through boulder-strewn washes. In early spring and late summer there are many natural pools that fill with runoff, some of them deep enough to be called swimming holes.

The seven-mile **Romero Canyon Trail** leads to an array of natural pools, and you don't have to hike the whole trail. If you want to get off the beaten track a little, veer right about a mile into the trail near a bench, pick

your way down into the wash, and then follow a footpath up the wash that leads to some out-of-the-way less-used pools. For an easy walk, take the 0.5-mile round-trip **Romero Ruin Interpretive Trail** to an ancient Hohokam site. The ranger station and gift shop has a guide to all the park's trails, some of which link up to other trails all the way up into the mountains.

Biosphere 2

In the early 1990s eight scientists took up residence in **Biosphere 2** (32540 S. Biosphere Rd., 520/838-6200, www.b2science.org, 9am-4pm daily, $25 adults, $15 ages 5-12), a 3.14-acre simulation of the earth (which would, of course, be Biosphere 1), in hopes of lasting two years and gaining important knowledge about how humans will survive in the future. They weren't able to remain self-contained, owing to problems with the food supply, but two members of the team did fall in love. The unique laboratory may yet save the world, however, as the UA is now running experiments under the dome and researching ways to combat climate change.

A self-guided tour with narration via the Biosphere's app takes about 1.5 hours. While the science is fascinating—there are actually small savannas, rain forests, deserts, and even an ocean under the glass—many who embark on the tour seem more fascinated by the doomed experiments in togetherness. Indeed, the tour takes you into the Biospherians' apartments, kitchen, and garden. The Biosphere is in a beautiful 35-acre desert setting about 30 minutes north of Tucson near the small town of Oracle.

Oracle

This small historic town about 30 miles north of Tucson on the northeastern slopes of the Santa Catalina range has a few historic buildings and a proliferation of high desert-dwelling artists. The **Acadia Ranch Museum** (825 Mount Lemmon Rd., 4pm-6pm Thurs., 1pm-4pm Sat., free) tells the colorful history of the ranch—once a sheep ranch and later a sanatorium for sufferers of TB and other ailments—and of the town, which today has about 3,500 people, many of them artists and other desert runaways. The **Oracle Union Church** (695 E. American Ave.) is on the National Register of Historic Places and worth a look, as is a nearby state park. There are several restaurants, including a historic steak house, and even a few little B&Bs, if you'd rather stay out here in the relative cool of 4,000 feet elevation.

SOUTH OF DOWNTOWN

Head south from downtown and you reach South Tucson, a largely Latino community incorporated as a separate city. The airport is farther south, and to the southeast is the Pima Air and Space Museum, on the southwest edge of Davis Monthan Air Force Base. To the southwest, reached via I-19, is San Xavier del Bac.

Pima Air and Space Museum

One of the largest museums of its kind in the West, the **Pima Air and Space Museum** (6000 E. Valencia Rd., 520/574-0462, www.pimaair.org, 9am-5pm daily, $16.50 adults, $13.75 seniors and military, $10 ages 5-12) has interesting exhibits and an impressive number of decommissioned aircraft that tell the story of our fascination with defying gravity. Nearly 300 rare airplanes, many of them military, rest on the grounds and in six hangars.

The Air and Space Museum is operated by the same group that operates the Titan Missile Museum near Green Valley, and for one price you can see both attractions. Warplane enthusiasts will want to take the hour-long bus tour to the **Aerospace Maintenance and Regeneration Center (AMARC)** to see the hundreds of dust-gathering planes ending their days in this "boneyard."

★ San Xavier del Bac

Founded in 1692 by Father Eusebio Francisco Kino and then built slowly over decades by other priests, missionaries, and Native Americans, the mission **San Xavier del Bac** (1950 W. San Xavier Rd., 520/294-2624, www.sanxaviermission.org, 7am-5pm daily, free) sits pure white against the perpetually blue sky about nine miles south of Tucson on the Tohono O'odham's San Xavier Indian Reservation. It is considered by many to be the foremost example of mission architecture remaining in the United States, blending elements of Moorish, Byzantine, and late Mexican Renaissance architecture.

Few Arizona landmarks have received as much worldwide attention as the "White Dove of the Desert," which has been called America's answer to the Sistine Chapel. Mass is still celebrated daily in the church (check the website for times), but non-Catholic visitors are welcome.

Most days there are tables and booths set up in the mission's plaza selling burritos, fry bread, and other delicious eats, and across from the mission to the south is a small shopping area called **San Xavier Plaza,** with a snack bar and several shops selling Native American crafts.

Statues and paintings of St. Francis Xavier and the Virgin of Guadalupe decorate the cool, dark interior of the domed church. A continuous videotape about the mission runs throughout the day as a self-guided tour, and there's a gift shop that sells religious items and books about the history of the mission and the region. A small museum presents the history of the area's Indigenous inhabitants and the construction and ongoing rehabilitation of the mission. The mission is continually being worked on, but the seemingly ever-present scaffolding doesn't detract from its grandeur.

Stay mindful that San Xavier, in addition to being a very popular tourist attraction, is an active Catholic church and an important community resource for the Tohono O'odham Nation. Be respectful and follow the posted rules of conduct, especially if you happen to be visiting during mass or other ceremonies. Always ask before photographing private homes, religious ceremonies, and people you do not know.

TUCSON
SIGHTS

Sports and Recreation

It's certainly true that Tucson is an active, out-doorsy, sunburned kind of place. On any given weekday, let alone during the crowded busy weekends, you'll see Tucsonans decked out in colorful Lycra, pedaling with all their might up and down the steep mountain roads and along the bike routes through the city; you'll also see them hiking on desert trails among the saguaro forests and exploring the sky island mountain ranges that encircle the valley. If you're coming to Tucson to find similar action, you won't have to look far.

PARKS

Some might say there is neither a river nor a park at **Santa Cruz River Park** (south from Grant Rd. to 29th St.), but it's as good a vantage as any other from which to view what remains. The Santa Cruz, like most Southwestern desert rivers, was never a deep swollen river, but at least it had perennial flow. It sustained a few different Indigenous communities for eons and was the green and cool home of beavers, otters, native fish species, and other riparian life. Now look at it. It's not all our fault; the region is prone to long droughts, and most desert rivers have wildly fluctuating or intermittent flows. But it was largely the pumping of groundwater throughout the region that sent the river underground a few generations ago. Every now and then, if the late-summer monsoon comes on strong, the water rises and flows past this pleasant artificial green space just west of downtown, where you can ride your bike, take an early-morning jog, or just gaze at the dry rocky bed.

A 131-acre green space on the southern end of midtown, **Gene C. Reid Park** (900 S. Randolph Way, 520/791-4873, www.tucsonaz. gov, 6am-10:30pm daily) is probably the city's favorite nondesert playground, with plenty of shade from imported trees and cool Bermuda grass for lounging and forgetting. Among dozens of other attractions are two small duck-topped lakes (no swimming), a band shell and amphitheater for concerts under the stars, and an off-leash dog park. The playground equipment involves cool submarine-style passageways, twisting slides, fire poles, and sky-reaching swing sets, and several layers of soft woodchips and some bouncy outdoor foam flooring provide soft landings. Hi Corbett Stadium is on the park's grounds, as are the Reid Park Zoo, a large modern recreation and aquatics center, a tennis facility, and a golf course.

Kids love the splash pad (mid-Apr.-Oct., free) at **Brandi Fenton Park** (3482 E. River Rd., http://brandifentonmemorialpark.org), between River Road and the Rillito, and it's a worry-free good time for parents as well. Just push the button, and for 15 minutes at a time cool water sprays out of fountains, falls from buckets, and bubbles and sprays up out of the ground, allowing water-resistant tykes to get the hang of a wet face before tackling the pool.

HIKING

Tucson and its surrounding sky island ranges have hiking trails for all experience levels. Desert trails tend to be rather flat and rocky, while the mountain trails are steep and usually offer some spectacular views.

The **Arizona Trail** (various trailheads around Southern Arizona, www.aztrail.org) is a 1,000-mile network of mostly existing trails to follow on foot, horse, or mountain bike (not allowed in the Grand Canyon and some other federal wilderness areas along the way), from the border with Mexico to the border with Utah. There are 43 "passages" that make up the trail, each between 11 and 35 miles; more than a dozen of these are in Southern Arizona, within easy reach of Tucson. The trail through Southern Arizona traverses all of the region's biomes, from the scrubby desert to the dry grasslands to the cool green mountains—it's a great way to get to know all

The Lemmon Rock Lookout

Arizona still has 72 active or semiactive fire lookouts, meaning they are staffed at least intermittently, especially during fire season or times of high risk and emergency. Only Oregon, with 106, and Florida, with 130, have more, according to the Forest Fire Lookout Association, a group that advocates for the preservation of lookouts and their traditions. What's more, Arizona has a higher ratio of active to standing lookouts than most states—72 active or semiactive out of 83 still standing. Contrast that with California, where 198 lookouts still stand but just 50 of those are active.

Only a small handful of lookouts classified as active are still staffed full-time for the entire fire season, roughly April 1-September 1, and one of these rare huts happens to be lashed to a rock overhang in the Santa Catalinas above Tucson, overlooking the Wilderness of Rocks and, beyond that, the unfurled basin and range territory as far as the urban haze will allow. The Lemmon Rock Lookout, at 8,820 feet elevation, has been occupied about five months a year since 1928. On the face of the 14-by-14-foot lookout shack, the side that looks down on the vast pine and boulder land below, someone long ago stenciled the words "No Diving," as if aware of the risks of so much time with oneself.

Fire lookouts like Lemmon Rock started to proliferate in the 1930s with the advent of the Civilian Conservation Corps (CCC) and the U.S. Forest Service's all-or-nothing suppression policy. Responding to several huge and unprecedented backcountry forest fires that plagued the nation during the early 20th century, government foresters enacted the 10am policy, decreeing that every fire on public lands must be quelled by 10am the morning after its initial spark. The fire lookout was an integral component. In many ways, we are paying for it now with overgrown drought-ridden forests just waiting for dry lightning or a tossed cigarette to burn and rip through the million-dollar homes we build in the forest hoping old Smokey the Bear will keep us safe from nature's cycles. Around the same time, the stock market crashed, and so did the job market, hence the birth of the New Deal and the CCC, which put thousands of out-of-work Americans in the national forests to build trails, firebreaks, and, in some of the remotest areas in the country, fire lookouts. Lemmon Rock was built by a CCC crew in the early 1930s, replacing a more primitive lookout on Mount Lemmon that had stood since 1913.

You can look at the Lemmon Rock Lookout yourself, and during the summer months, sit down and have a high-altitude chat with the friendly current occupant of the little hut. To get here, drive up the **Sky Island Highway** to **Ski Valley** and park at the trailhead parking lot at the top of Mount Lemmon (keep going past the ski slopes and take the dirt road after the pavement ends). Once you park, pick up the short **Lemmon Rock Trail.**

of the natural wonders around Tucson. The nonprofit **Arizona Trail Association** (www.aztrail.org) is responsible for upkeep and trail building, and their website has a complete map and detailed descriptions of the trail.

Some of the best desert hiking in the region can be found at **Tucson Mountain Park** (www.pima.gov), a sprawling saguaro-crowded park west of the city. Here the trails are rocky and sandy, moderately flat, and thickly lined with desert vegetation. The nearly five-mile round-trip **Brown Mountain Trail** leads through a cactus forest along the sandy bottomlands between the mountains, then rises gradually to a ridgeline

that looks out on the hard country all around. Keep an eye out for lazy desert tortoises, known to sun themselves on the trail early in the morning. You can access the trailhead at the Brown Mountain Picnic Area or the Juan Santa Cruz Picnic Area, both just southeast of the Arizona-Sonora Desert Museum off Kinney Road. Just before you reach the valley after the steep descent from Gates Pass, there's a parking lot and trailhead where you can pick up the 5.5-mile **David Yetman Trail,** named for the host of the PBS show *The Desert Speaks*. There's another trailhead at Camino de Oeste—and if you leave a car at both ends you won't have to do a 10-mile there-and-back trudge. Pima County's Natural Resources Department keeps a map of the trails around Tucson Mountain Park on their website.

The dozens of trails around 9,157-foot **Mount Lemmon and the Santa Catalina Mountains** (Coronado National Forest, 520/670-4522, www.fs.usda.gov/coronado, $5 per car), about an hour's drive up the winding Sky Island Highway from central Tucson and into another world entirely, are beloved among Tucsonans sweating away in the hot valley, dreaming of scrambling around the evergreen forests and cool streams on the mountain. Since there are so many trails that lead into and branch off one another, consider the following eight-mile loop, composed of portions of several trails, designed to take you through some of the best areas: At Summerhaven, turn onto the Sabino Canyon Parkway and follow it down to **Marshall Gulch;** leave your car at the small streamside parking lot. Start on Trail 3 (Marshall Gulch Trail) behind the restrooms and follow it up through the shady forest for 1.2 miles to Marshall Saddle, at 7,920 feet elevation. At Marshall Saddle, branch off on Trail 44, which will take you down about 700 feet in elevation into the beautiful **Wilderness of Rocks** for 1.7 miles. At the junction, take Trail 12 (Lemmon Rock Lookout Trail) as it rises for about two miles to near the peak of Mount Lemmon (9,157 feet), where you'll be among metal antennas essential to life down below. Along the way you can stop at the Mount Lemmon Lookout, with one the best views in the region. You'll see the ski lift near the top, but don't get on. Instead, hike along **Radio Ridge** using the Mount Lemmon Trail (Trail 5) for 1 mile to its junction with Trail 93 (Aspen Trail). Follow that downhill for 1.3 miles and you're back at Marshall Saddle, where it's 1.2 miles back to the car. The climbs on this loop can be a bit brutal, but you're definitely rewarded for the effort. For information on other trails and more suggestions, stop by the Palisades Visitor Center, on your way up the hill, where you can talk to rangers and pick up a map of the trail system.

Both sections of **Saguaro National Park** (Red Hills Visitor Center, 520/733-5153, www.nps.gov/sagu) offer superior desert hiking. In the **Tucson Mountains** district west of town, a strenuous but beautiful hike up to 4,687-foot **Wasson Peak,** the highest in the Tucson Mountains, is a great way to spend a Sonoran Desert morning. You can get there by picking up the **King Canyon Trail** just across Kinney Road near the Arizona-Sonora Desert Museum. It's about 3.5 miles to the top of the peak, hiking on switchbacks through typical *bajada* desert; make it a loop by heading down the **Hugh Norris Trail** to its junction with the **Sendero Esperanza Trail** and taking the **Gold Mine Trail** back to the car. The whole adventure is 7.5 miles total. There are easier and less steep trails around the park. An easy one with kids is the 0.5-mile **Signal Hill Petroglyphs Trail,** a modest climb to a collection of boulders with several petroglyphs on display. If you continue from here on the flat easy trail, you'll go through some wonderful desert with a good chance to see wildlife. In the park's eastern section, at the base of the **Rincon Mountains,** there are several 3- to 5-mile loop hikes that will take you through all the best parts of the sprawling cactus forests; for a 2-mile round-trip walk, the **Cactus Forest Trail** is an easy, mostly flat trail among the green-armed giants. The visitors centers at both the western and eastern sections have complete trail guides and rangers who can advise on the best routes. The park's website has detailed maps and trail guides as well.

BIKING

The **3rd Street Bike Route** is an easy flat way to get from midtown to downtown on a bike—it goes from Wilmot on the eastern edge of midtown all the way through the University of Arizona to downtown. The **Rillito River Park Bike Route** is a flat and easy 11-mile route following the sandy-bottomed Rillito

---

1: golfing in Gene C. Reid Park **2:** The Loop, a popular bike route around the city

THE LOOP of
Congress Street
Santa Cruz River Park

Road	0.6 mi.
y Boulevard	1.0 mi.
d	2.5 mi.
k	3.0 mi.

River, a great route for exercise and commuting across the north end of Tucson. The river is dry on top, but it's a relatively green and shady path that runs from near I-10 to Craycroft Road. Along the way it passes several parks, always hugging the parched riverbed, colored here and there with seeping lushness. The Rillito Park Bike Route is one of the more popular sections of an ambitious project called **The Loop** (www.pima.gov/TheLoop), which, when complete, will comprise 130 miles of connected paths for bikers and walkers. At the time of writing, about 120 miles of The Loop were complete, connecting the Rillito River Park with Santa Cruz River Park downtown, and with other parks on the east and south sides. Pima County has a map of the entire Loop on its website, and paper maps are available at most library branches and at the visitors center downtown.

Serious road cyclists proliferate in Tucson, and a few teams even do their winter training here. One of their favorite rides on a warm weekend morning is the **Dan Yersavich Memorial Bikeway** along Old Spanish Trail from Broadway all the way to Saguaro National Park East. Another favorite route is the long, hard climb up the Catalina Highway, also called the **Brad P. Gorman Memorial Bikeway,** and into the cool heights of the mountains. The ride up and over Gates Pass and into the Tucson Mountains region west of downtown is another favorite.

Tucson's downtown and central neighborhoods can be easily explored by bike. For rentals, check out the **Tugo Bike Share** (http://tugobikeshare.com), a program sponsored by local business Tucson Electric Power. There are 36 stations in 13 neighborhoods—about 330 bikes! A 30-minute station-to-station trip costs $4, or you can take an unlimited number of 3-hour trips over 24 hours for $15. For locations, check the website.

GOLF

It's not easy to justify the existence of golf courses in the arid Southwest from a perspective that recognizes the region's rather obvious resource deficiencies. For golfers, what most see as the region's primary deficiency—its aridity—is instead its greatest attribute, allowing them to play 36 holes on Thanksgiving morning with their envious visitors from Chicago. The city of Tucson operates five public courses in town, all of them excellent, though older and less dramatic than the resort and private courses invading the desert. The city's humbler courses come with the added benefit of being ecologically defensible: They are all irrigated with reclaimed water. The city maintains a helpful website (www.tucsoncitygolf.com) with maps of all the courses, rates (generally $25-75 for 18 holes, depending on season, time of day, and residency), and bookable tee times. All the city courses have clubhouses, lighted driving ranges, carts, pros, and pro shops. The two most popular courses in Tucson's municipal system are **Randolph Golf Course** and **Dell Urich Golf Course** (600 S. Alvernon Way, 520/791-4161, www.tucsoncitygolf.com, 5am-7pm daily, $23-72 for 18 holes, rates depend on season and residency), side-by-side courses at midtown's Reid Park. Randolph, the city's flagship course and the longest at 6,500 yards from the regular tees, has been the site of numerous PGA and LPGA tournaments and is green, spacious, and tree-lined. Dell Urich, a par-70 course south of Randolph, opened in 1996 and is probably the most popular in town. Both make for easy-access, in-town, and relatively inexpensive play year-round.

HORSEBACK RIDING

The horse has been an integral part of daily life Southern Arizona since the Spanish introduced it to the Southwest in the 1500s. The animal transformed the lives and cultures of the Indigenous peoples virtually overnight, and today there is a distinct subculture of "horse people" in the Old Pueblo whose lives are dedicated to enjoyment of the equestrian kind. Quite a few such people will rent you a usually friendly, docile horse and guide you deep into the desert on trails once traversed by conquistadores, ranchers, and Native Americans. Most places require that kids be at least six years old to ride, and most have a 230-pound maximum weight limit, but call ahead to make sure. Spring rides are the best, especially when the desert is in bloom. Summer is different—go early in the morning, or book one of the many fun evening or nighttime rides. Always wear long pants and closed-toe shoes, and always bring a hat, though it doesn't have to be the cowboy type.

About 13 miles southeast of town, in the shaggy cactus-and-scrub desert not far from Saguaro National Park East, the friendly folks at **All Around Trail Horses** (520/298-8980, http://fareharbor.com/horsingaroundarizona, 8am-5pm daily winter, 8am-noon and 4pm-6:30pm daily summer, $70-200) will take you out and make you feel like a real cowhand. The desert is beautiful and thick, and if you go when the cacti are blooming, you are in for a spectacular show. Call ahead for a reservation.

SPECTATOR SPORTS

The biggest sports draws in the region are the teams of the **University of Arizona.** With perennial powerhouses in basketball, volleyball, and baseball, and a Pac-10 football team that holds its own in a tough division, there's always something to cheer for on campus. Tickets are in high demand; for information call the UA's **McKale Center** (520/621-2287, www.arizonaathletics.com).

FC Tucson (Kino Sports Complex, 2801 N. Ajo Way, 520/600-3095, www.fctucson.com) is the Old Pueblo's scrappy USL League 1 soccer team. They are a lot of fun to watch, and most of the seats are just $10. The team plays late April-early October, and the action on the field is exciting as promising young talents compete furiously for a future in the beautiful game.

Entertainment

NIGHTLIFE

Tucson's most vibrant nightlife is on three blocks within easy walking, or stumbling, distance of each other: Congress Street downtown, 4th Avenue, and Main Gate Square near the UA. There are always plenty of cabs waiting around outside the bars in these neighborhoods, especially on weekends. When school is in session, these areas are typically packed with students. But Tucson's nightlife and entertainment scene is fairly casual and mixed, drawing college kids, postcollege slackers and go-getters, thirtysomething urban workers, hip parents who still haunt the alt-rock shows, and professors and professionals of indeterminate age. There's really something for everybody.

Second Saturdays

Once a month on **Second Saturdays** (www.2ndsaturdaysdowntown.com, 5pm-10:30pm 2nd Sat. of the month), the streets of downtown Tucson come alive as thousands of Old Pueblo residents head to the city's traditional heart to meet and mingle. The event features street vendors, performers, food, bands, art shows, and more, and downtown stores, bars, clubs, and restaurants along Congress Street are usually hopping with activity. This is the best time to see downtown Tucson at its most active.

Bars, Pubs, and Lounges
DOWNTOWN AND UNIVERSITY DISTRICT
The Tap Room (311 E. Congress St., 520/622-8848, www.hotelcongress.com, 11am-2am daily) has been around since 1919 and still packs them in, especially when there's a band playing at Club Congress, to which the Tap Room serves as a kind of hideout from the crush and noise. But if you belly up here of an afternoon, or on a slow midweek night, you'll

notice the details: the retro booths and stools; the scratchy juke in the corner; and especially the cowboy-life art of Pete Martinez, one of several lauded Western artists who once called Tucson home. Martinez, who lived in Tucson from 1935 until his death in 1971, was neighbor to the painter and illustrator Maynard Dixon and friend to Ted DeGrazia, and he reportedly spent a good deal of his time drinking at the Tap Room. People always used to say that he would from time to time trade his work for his drinks, and that's how they got on the bar's walls. But the management says that's just a rumor, and that the artist gifted the paintings to his favorite bar.

The **Playground Bar & Lounge** (278 E. Congress St., at 5th Ave., 520/396-3691, http://playgroundtucson.com, 4pm-2am Mon.-Fri., noon-2am Sat.-Sun.) is a hip fun place to hang out, drink and eat, listen to DJs, and meet locals and students downtown. This sleek space with old chain-and-wood swings decorating the ceiling has an urban vibe combined with the historic warmth of a tastefully refurbished old building. The wonderful rooftop patio should not be missed, nor the long views of the Old Pueblo. For sports fans, there's often a soccer game on the big TVs.

Scott & Co. (49 N. Scott Ave., 520/624-4747, www.47scott.com, 4pm-11pm Tues.-Thurs., 4pm-midnight Fri.-Sat., 4pm-8pm Sun.) is the bar at downtown's popular bistro. The emphasis here is on drinks, and the expert bartenders take their jobs very seriously. The menu of unique and creative drinks, many of them updated twists on classic cocktails, changes often, but the ingredients are always top-shelf and house-made.

The place to sample some of the best microbrews in the Old Pueblo is **Borderlands Brewing Co.** (119 E. Toole Ave., 520/261-8773, http://borderlandsbrewing.com, noon-9pm Wed.-Thurs., noon-10pm Sat., noon-5pm Sun.). The brewers use local ingredients and follow in the footsteps of beer-loving Germans who settled in the Southwest in the 1800s. They serve several different beers in a beautifully refurbished old redbrick

warehouse near the train tracks, including a superior IPA, a prickly pear wheat beer, and a rich "noche dulce" porter. A food truck is usually parked outside while a local band rocks the house inside. Check out the jaguar mural by artist Kati Astraeir across the street.

Pueblo Vida Brewing Company (115 E. Broadway Blvd., 520/623-7168, http://pueblovidabrewing.com, 4pm-10pm Mon.-Thurs., 1pm-10pm Fri., noon-11pm Sat., noon-8pm Sun.) serves amazing craft beers, brewed on-site, in a fun and convivial tap room with lots of windows and sunlight. This is very much a representative downtown Tucson hangout: it is particularly dog friendly, allowing well-behaved pups to join the party, and caters to the cycling crowd, letting you park your ride inside. Bring your own food or have some delivered from one of the nearby restaurants. They also sell many of their craft brews in four-pack cans to go.

A laid-back and comfortable beer-and-wine bar in a refurbished historic space on 4th Avenue, **Ermanos Craft Beer and Wine Bar** (220 N. 4th Ave., 520/445-6625, http://ermanosbrew.com, 11am-midnight Mon.-Thurs., 11am-1am Fri.-Sat., 11am-10pm Sun.) offers 25 wines, 34 draft beers, and a wide assortment of bottles and cans—a list so varied that you're guaranteed to discover something new and possibly life-altering. The scratch food here is several steps above the usual pub fare, including panko-crusted avocado fries, and a five-cheese grilled cheese sandwich ($15-25), with jackfruit asada and other excellent vegetarian options.

Bar Toma at **El Charro** (311 N. Court Ave., 520/622-1922, www.elcharrocafe.com, noon-9pm Sun.-Thurs., noon-10pm Fri.-Sat.), one of the Old Pueblo's oldest and best-loved restaurants, has patio seating and a small but stylish bar that is a laid-back and civilized place to drink a margarita or five.

Mr. Head's Art Gallery and Bar (513 N. 4th Ave., 520/792-2710, noon-2am daily)

1: Mr. Head's Art Gallery and Bar **2:** Congress Street in downtown Tucson

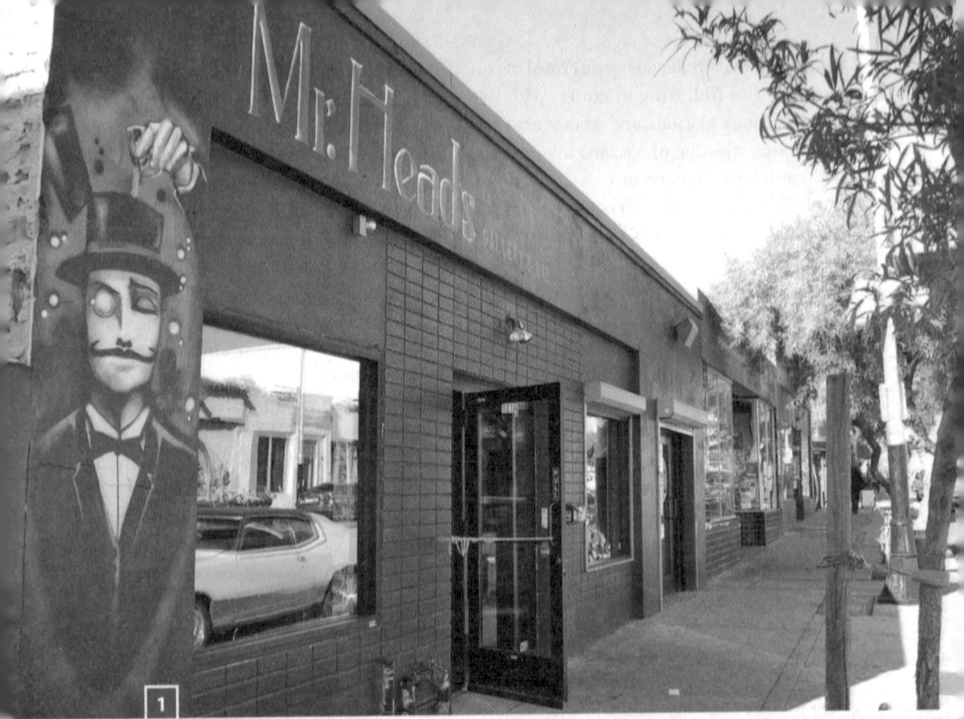

1

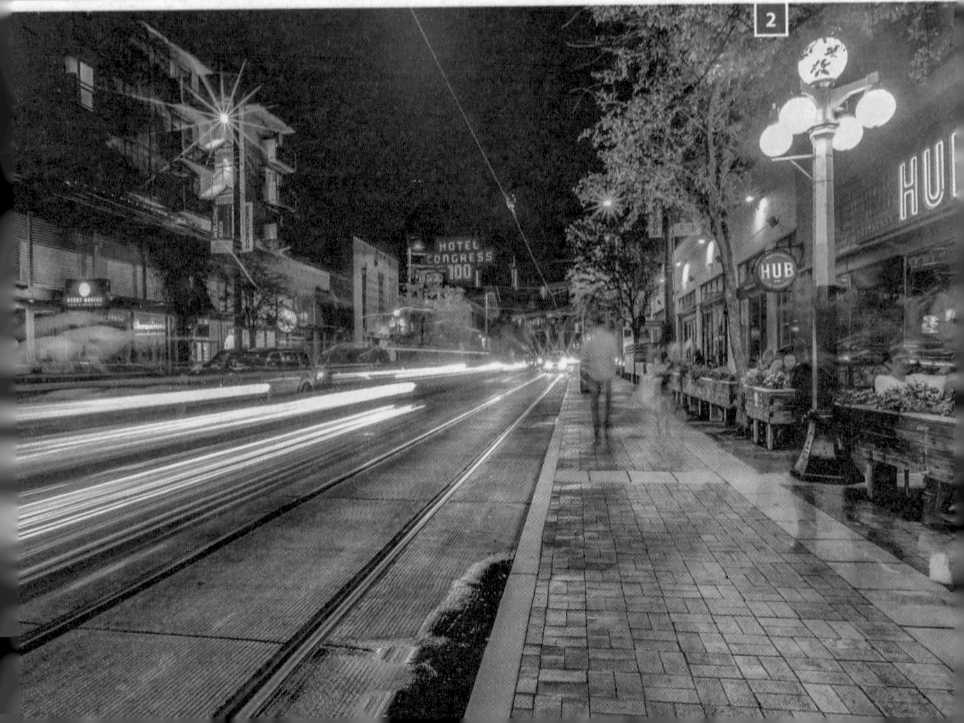

2

draws a mixed 4th Avenue-style crowd of college kids and frolicking urbanites with live bands; curious, glorious, and strange artwork; and a large selection of Arizona microbrews. The patio is particularly nice.

Not exactly a hangout for revolutionaries in the Che Guevara mode, **Che's Lounge** (350 N. 4th Ave., 520/623-2088, www.cheslounge. com, noon-2am daily) is instead a small inviting hangout for a vast array of 4th Avenue denizens, from college kids to fortysomethings. Local and touring bands regularly play on the lounge's patio.

Next to Brooklyn Pizza on 4th Avenue, **Skybar** (536 N. 4th Ave., 520/622-4300, www.skybartucson.com, 9am-2am daily) is a "solar powered café by day" and an "astronomy bar by night." The open airy bar, with a patio to watch all the people sauntering along 4th Avenue, is ideal for kicking back with a drink and a slice of New York-style pizza from next door (they'll bring it to you). The "astronomy bar" title comes from the telescopes they set up come nightfall, allowing patrons to peer into the nearly always clear skies above Tucson. They also show deep-space images on a big screen. Happy hour prices are 5pm-8pm daily, and throughout the week are theme nights as well as live music, DJs, open mic nights, and dance parties.

MIDTOWN

The Tucson Valley played a major role in the Cold War: For years ICBMs ringed the city, locked and loaded beneath the desert and aimed at various targets in the USSR. While there's a museum south of town where you can learn all about the Old Pueblo's atomic age bona fides, **The Shelter** (4155 E. Grant Rd., 520/326-1345, 3pm-2am daily) is the best place to celebrate, so to speak, the era and its two coolest cold warriors. It's dark and cool like a shelter should be, with plenty of good booze and always a campy cult film playing silently on a TV in the corner. The walls are covered with Jack and Bobby, and the pinball machines ding and flap.

The **Casa Film Bar** (2905 E. Speedway Blvd., 520/326-6314, www.casafilmbar.com, 10am-1am daily) is a fun bar inside Tucson's last and favorite video store, still going strong thanks to the city's significant population of microbrew-loving film nerds. It's a great place to hang out, knock back a few local and regional beers, order in pizza from a nearby restaurant, watch a foreign film on the TV screens, and meet like-minded locals.

Tucson Hop Shop (3230 N. Dodge Blvd., 520/908-7765, www.tucsonhopshop.com, 2pm-9pm Mon.-Thurs., noon-11pm Fri.-Sat., noon-8pm Sun.) is a laid-back and stylishly utilitarian beer and wine bar in the Metal Arts Village, a small collection of artists' studios and shops near the Rillito River bike path, The Loop. This "bicycle friendly business" encourages patrons to ride and to bring the kids along too. The outdoor beer garden is a great place to kick back after a long ride. The metal building is cool and comfortable inside, with plenty of seating, records on the turntable, and beer-loving bartenders. About 20 beers are on tap from around the world, including a few from Arizona.

FOOTHILLS

An eminently tasteful and upscale place to drink, the **Cascade Lounge at Loews Ventana Canyon Resort** (7000 N. Resort Dr., 520/299-2020, www.loewshotels.com, 3pm-10pm Mon.-Thurs., 3pm-midnight Fri.-Sat., 11am-10pm Sun.) has warm earthy colors, thick and comfortable furniture, flattering low lighting, and 30-foot windows offering commanding views from Ventana Canyon's high perch in the Catalina Foothills. One of Tucson's most romantic night spots, Cascade offers a nightly happy hour (5:30pm-7pm) with affordable drinks and small plates, and music Wednesday-Saturday.

Sipping a martini among stylish and stimulating surroundings while watching the desert city fade to black from high above the valley is just as much a typical Tucson experience as scrambling up a rocky trail shadowed by saguaros. One of the best places to do the former is the **Azul Lounge** (3800 E. Sunrise Dr.,

520/742-6000, www.westinlapalomaresort. com, 2pm-midnight daily), an upscale but not forbidding lounge at the **Westin La Paloma Resort** in the Catalina Foothills. Decorated all in blue and washed by music that registers but doesn't get in the way, the lounge offers top-notch cocktails and delicious small plates, complemented with a view that can't be beat. The least expensive time to go is during happy hour (5pm-7pm Mon.-Fri.).

Live Music

Most of the bars, pubs, and lounges in downtown and along 4th Avenue host local bands and performers throughout the week.

The city's premier spot for touring alternative rock and alt-country bands is **Club Congress** (311 E. Congress St., 520/622-8848, www.hotelcongress.com, 9pm-1am Sun.-Mon., 10pm-1am Tues.-Sat., cover varies), inside the historic Hotel Congress. Most nights if there's not a band playing, there's a DJ and dancing. Music geeks and college-town rock-and-rollers frequent the shows, and it's a kind of headquarters for the thriving downtown music scene—the stage new local bands aspire to get to. If you're not in the mood for sweaty crowds, guitars, or breakbeats, there's a quieter lounge in the lobby, but the music is the club's reason for being, and thank the gods for that.

The nicest Quonset hut you've ever danced in, **The Hut** (305 N. 4th Ave., 520/623-3200, 4pm-2am Mon.-Fri., noon-2am Sat.-Sun., cover varies) books in the weird and the rocking in equal measure, with roots, rock, blues, reggae, and even spoken-word performance art filling the faux-tropical bar most nights. It has a kind of slum-tiki vibe, laid-back and beach-bound with a lot of frozen drinks on the menu. Don't miss taking a picture of the three-story cement tiki head out front.

Head up to the foothills to see a tight jazz band at the **Terraza Garden Patio and Lounge** on the enchanting grounds of the historic **Hacienda del Sol Guest Ranch Resort** (5501 N. Hacienda del Sol Rd., 7am-10:30pm daily). The large and usually bustling patio hosts jazz trios and quartets, singers, and pianists every night of the week. During the popular happy hour (3pm-6pm daily), when the expensive drinks ($15 for a craft cocktail, try the "Day Spa," one of the bar's signature drinks) and tapas are slightly less expensive, you're likely to meet some locals, some tourists, and maybe even a few European travelers. On a cool evening, sit out on the couches by the fire and look at the looming Santa Catalina Mountains—then you'll know what Tucson is all about.

THEATERS AND VENUES

A furbished theater from the 1920s, the **Rialto** (318 E. Congress St., 520/740-1000, www.rialtotheatre.com, box office noon-6pm Mon.-Fri.) books an eclectic list of acts, from Steve Earl to 2 Chainz. It's a great place to catch your favorite alt-rock and alt-country bands on tour. Across Congress Street from the Hotel Congress downtown, over the years the historic building has been a vaudeville house, a Spanish-language cinema, and for five years in the 1970s, a porn theater.

191 Toole (191 E. Toole Ave., 520/445-6425, http://191toole.com, times and prices vary by show) hosts hard-working touring bands and other performers in a cavernous old space downtown. You can buy tickets to specific shows at the door one hour before show time, or at the Rialto Theater box office. From the 1930s to the 1970s, the **Fox Theatre** (17 W. Congress St., 520/624-1515, www.foxtucsontheatre.org, box office 11am-6pm Mon.-Fri., 11am-2pm Sat.) was the place to go to see Hollywood's latest offering, and the theater's art deco style nearly matched the glamour on the screen. Along with many other once-famous and much-used buildings downtown, the Fox fell into disrepair until the late 1990s, when a group raised money to refurbish the old movie house. Now the theater, beautifully restored to its original grandeur, shows classic films several times a month and hosts concerts and events.

The downtown **Temple of Music and Art** (330 S. Scott Ave., 520/884-4875) is a beautiful

The Day of the Dead

In the Arizona borderlands these days it's difficult to find a boutique, gift shop, or gallery that doesn't sell *calavera* (skeletons doing human things) statues, paintings, T-shirts, and all manner of other consumer goods featuring the Day of the Dead aesthetic. Generally these art objects recreate the work, or at least the spirit of the work, of Posada, a late-19th-early-20th-century Mexican printmaker and illustrator whose broadsides and newspaper illustrations employed the *calavera* and Day of the Dead traditions in social commentary. While Posada's work had the immediacy of journalism, it has outlasted its original intent and is more popular today than ever before. His style and overt political commentary influenced Diego Rivera and other Mexican muralists of the first half of the 20th century.

skeleton statue

The Day of the Dead, El Día de los Muertos, falls on November 2, but the celebrations begin on November 1 or even earlier. It roughly coincides with the traditional Catholic holidays of All Saints Day and All Souls Day, but the tradition is far older than the Spanish conquest. Like most Latin American rites, it is a deep-time amalgam of pre-Columbian and Spanish traditions whose origins reach far back.

The Day of the Dead reminds us that death and the dead have a profound influence on the living. The celebrations vary from region to region and from the big city to rural areas. Generally they include feasts in graveyards with a dead relative's favorite dishes prepared and set aside. There are also parades and marches, candles and altars, sugar skulls, and sweet breads shaped like skulls and skeletons.

For many years the Day of the Dead has been marching north, and it now rivals Cinco de Mayo as the Southwestern Anglo's favorite Mexican import. But the spectacles surrounding the holiday have long been a subject of fascination for tourists. As far back as the 1970s, Mexican observers were complaining that in places like Mixquic and Patzcuaro, towns famous for their Day of the Dead celebrations, "cameras had come to outnumber candles in the cemeteries."

Throughout November there's usually a traditional Day of the Dead altar at **Tolteca Tlacuilo** in Tucson's Old Town Artisans complex, and the **Tucson Museum of Art** typically celebrates with a family event on November 2, with music, food, arts and crafts, an altar, a parade, and big-headed puppets.

old theater and playhouse built in 1927. It is the main stage for the **Arizona Theatre Company** (www.arizonatheatre.org) and hosts concerts and shows throughout the year.

PERFORMING ARTS

The **Arizona Theatre Company** (330 S. Scott Ave., 520/622-2823, www.arizonatheatre.org) puts on an excellent season of plays September-May at the Temple of Music and Art, and the **Arizona Opera** (520/293-4336, www.azopera.org) presents some of the best regional opera in the country October-April at the **TCC Music Hall** (260 S. Church Ave.). The **Tucson Symphony** (520/882-8585, www.tucsonsymphony.org) holds concerts September-May also at the TCC Music Hall.

CINEMA

The best theater in town is **The Loft Cinema** (3233 E. Speedway Blvd., 520/795-0844, www.loftcinema.com), showing art-house, classic, cult, and foreign films, and offering free showings of classic films on Sunday afternoons and Monday nights. There's always something worth seeing at this remodeled old theater, and you can buy a beer and a slice of pizza to go with all the soul-searching on the big screen.

Roadhouse Cinema (4811 E. Grant Rd., 520/468-7980, http://roadhousecinemas.com) in midtown shows all the big movies and serves great food, microbrews, and cocktails while you watch. Perhaps the best thing about Roadhouse is the comfortable chairs that lean back and cradle you to sleep if you're not attentive. The food here is pretty good—finger foods and burgers and fries, quesadillas and jalapeño popcorn—and the servers go out of their way to stay out of the way while the movie is on. You have to reserve seats, and they are often sold out, so plan ahead. There's also a Roadhouse in Scottsdale.

COMEDY

Touring stand-up comedians from around the country stop at **Laffs Comedy Club** (2900 E. Broadway, Suite 154, 520/323-8669, www.laffscomedyclub.com, $12.50-17.50). Thursday night is open mic, and comedians hit the stage 8pm and 10:30pm Friday-Saturday. The club also serves food and drinks.

CASINOS

Take I-19 south to Pima Mine Road for the fun **Desert Diamond Casino & Hotel** (7350 S. Nogales Hwy., 520/294-7777 or 866/332-9467, www.desertdiamondcasino.com) on Tucson's south side, operated by the Tohono O'odham tribe. It has slot machines, blackjack, poker, keno, and bingo along with several restaurants and a hotel. **The Agave Restaurant** (11am-9pm daily) serves wonderful eclectic lunches and dinners. There's also a constant stream of talent moving through Desert Diamond's intimate concert venues, often hosting top-name acts like Willie Nelson and Bob Dylan.

West of I-19 on Valencia Road, the Pascua Yaqui tribe operates **Casino Del Sol** (800/344-9435, www.casinodelsol.com), a Mediterranean-influenced fun land with poker, slots, bingo, blackjack, and keno. The complex has several places to eat and drink, including an excellent upscale steak house. Stick around after the gaming for a concert in the casino's amphitheater, which regularly hosts major touring acts.

THE ARTS

Creativity is well represented in Tucson, with probably more artists and artisans living in or near the Old Pueblo than in any other Arizona locale save the Navajo and Hopi Reservations. Some top galleries in Tucson also have sister galleries in Santa Fe, New Mexico, or Sedona in Northern Arizona. You don't have to appreciate the sometimes overly romantic depictions of the Old West to enjoy art in Tucson. There are all kinds of galleries, especially in the downtown area, that show art from a more experimental and contemporary Southwest, and there are few cowboys left these days. But if you do love Western and Southwestern art, from the conservative to the experimental, there are few better places. Head to the foothills around Campbell and Skyline for galleries showing the best of the genre. Check with the **Tucson-Pima Arts Council** (www.tucsonpimaartscouncil.org) for a complete calendar of all the arts-related stuff going on.

Galleries

For anyone enraptured by the classic art of the Southwest—from the photographs of Edward Curtis to the modernist paintings of Maynard Dixon; from the ceremonial kachinas of the Hopi people to the elegant yellow-brown pottery of Nampeyo—**Mark Sublette's Medicine Man Gallery** (6872 E. Sunrise, 520/722-7798, www.medicinemangallery.com, 10am-5pm Tues.-Sat. May-Sept., 10am-5pm Mon.-Sat. Oct.-late Nov., 10am-5pm Mon.-Sat., 1pm-4pm Sun. late Nov.-Apr.) is an absolute must-visit. The huge gallery also features the **Maynard Dixon Museum,** with a wide selection of often obscure paintings, illustrations, and ephemera from throughout the great artist's career. There's also a contemporary art gallery here featuring the best in new Western art by the likes of the fabulous Navajo artist Shonto Begay.

True to a long tradition of repurposing old buildings in downtown Tucson, **MOCA Tucson** (265 S. Church Ave., 520/624-5019, www.moca-tucson.org, noon-5pm Wed.-Sun., $8 winter, $5 summer) used to be a fire station. MOCA puts on several exhibits each year, mixing paintings, photography, and installations. When they say contemporary, they mean it: You will see art done this afternoon by working, struggling, and inspired artists confronting aesthetic and social themes in all kinds of interesting and confusing ways. It's a small museum but worth the time.

More than 70 local artists display and sell their work at the **Southern Arizona Arts Guild (SAAG) Gallery of Gifts** (2905 E. Skyline Dr., 520/437-7820, http://southernarizonaartsguild.com, 10am-7pm Mon.-Wed., 10am-8pm Thurs.-Sat., 11am-6pm Sun.) at La Encantada shopping center. The large gallery has paintings and photography by Sonoran Desert artists as well as ceramics, jewelry, handbags, and textiles created by Tucson's notable arts community. With an emphasis on decorative and Southwestern-themed pieces, this is a great spot to look for a unique souvenir or gift.

FESTIVALS AND EVENTS

In January the multicultural **Family Arts Festival** (Tucson-Pima Arts Council, 520/624-0595, www.familyartsfestival.org) features exhibits, concerts, and performances. February is dominated by the biggest local event of them all, the **Tucson Gem & Mineral Show** (520/322-5773, www.tgms.org), which brings thousands of visitors to the Old Pueblo. February also welcomes **La Fiesta de Los Vaqueros** (800/964-5662, www.tucsonrodeo.com), Tucson's famed rodeo and parade—the longest nonmechanized parade in the world. The **Southwest Indian Art Fair and Market** (520/621-6302, www.statemuseum.arizona.edu) in February

brings the region's top jewelers, potters, weavers, and carvers from the Navajo, Hopi, Zuni, and other tribes.

In March, Civil War enthusiasts recreate the Battle of Picacho Pass during the **Civil War in the Southwest** (http://azstateparks.com). Also in March, the Tohono O'odham hold their annual gathering at Mission San Xavier del Bac during the **Wa:k Powwow** (520/294-5727, www.powwows.com). Cinephiles file into town in April to catch the **Arizona International Film Festival** (520/628-1737, www.azmac.org).

The Tucson Kitchen Musicians put on their signature event, the always fun (and free) **Tucson Folk Festival** (www.tkma.org), in May. With the heat of June come prayers and dances for rain on **Día de San Juan,** a series of festivals and rituals celebrating John the Baptist and the saint's historical relationship with the desert's summer rainy season.

Ski Valley on Mount Lemmon celebrates **Oktoberfest on Mount Lemmon** (520/885-1181) a month early, in September. In early October, the Tucson Historic Preservation Foundation sponsors **Tucson Modernism Week** with events that celebrate the Old Pueblo's mid-century style (http://preservetucson.org). Another October event is the **Tucson Culinary Festival** (www.tucsonculinaryfestival.com), which features top local and national chefs and lots of good food.

The **All Souls Procession** (www.allsoulsprocession.org), held the first weekend in November, has brought the artful traditions of the Day of the Dead to downtown Tucson since 1990. The celebration, organized by the nonprofit arts group Many Mouths One Stomach, culminates in a colorful and rather spooky nighttime parade through the downtown streets, featuring ghouls, ghosts, skeletons, big-headed puppets and myriad other walking works of art. Throughout the weekend, art shows and other events take place at venues around the city—all celebrating the impermanence of life and the glory of human-made art.

Shopping

In the Old Pueblo you just might find that authentic artifact that has long eluded you. Here you'll find merchants with Mexican imports, folk arts, Western Americana, and Native American jewelry; boutiques with clothes you'll find nowhere else; and galleries featuring the work of artists from Tucson and the rest of the world.

SHOPPING CENTERS AND DISTRICTS

Main Gate Square (University Blvd., 520/622-8613, www.maingatesquare.com, hours vary by shop) is right next to the University of Arizona and frequented by students, with 52 stores and restaurants like Urban Outfitters and American Apparel mixed in with local shops and bars, all of them skewing young for the university crowd. Walk around and have lunch; there's always something new opening or moving in. Be careful about parking—instead of braving the back-in-only metered parking, go to the **Main Gate Parking Garage** (815 E. 2nd St.) and leave your car in shade and safety.

The **Lost Barrio** (Park Ave., south of Broadway Blvd., www.thelostbarrio.com, 10am-6pm Mon.-Sat., noon-4pm Sun.) is a series of rustic old warehouses tucked away on Park Avenue just before you enter downtown from Broadway. Six shops sell unique items such as handcrafted and imported furniture, folk arts, antiques, and locally sourced home decor. The oldest and best is **Rustica**, which has gorgeous Mexican and Peruvian furniture and Talavera pottery.

Even if you don't have any room in your budget for pottery, Mexican folk arts, and turquoise jewelry, visit historic **Old Town Artisans** (201 N. Court Ave., 520/623-6024, www.oldtownartisans.com, 9:30am-5:30pm Mon.-Sat., 11am-5pm Sun. Sept.-May, 10am-4pm Mon.-Sat., 11am-4pm Sun. June-Aug.)

downtown, across from the Tucson Art Museum. Six shops and galleries are in the 150-year-old adobe structure, each opening onto the verdant Mexican-style courtyard with a fountain and tables. There's a good restaurant here as well, and festivals and live music are often in the courtyard, a fine place to sit and rest with a beer. The import shop **Tolteca Tlacuilo** (186 N. Meyer Ave., 520/623-5787, www.toltecatlacuilo.com, 10am-4pm Mon.-Sat., 11am-4pm Sun. June-mid-Sept., 9:30am-5:30pm Mon.-Sat., 11am-5pm Sun. mid-Sept.-May) sells some of the best Día de los Muertos items in town.

There are nearly 20 shops and restaurants at **Plaza Palomino** (southeast corner of Swan Rd. and Fort Lowell Rd., 520/320-6344, www.plazapalomino.com, 10am-6pm Mon.-Sat.), an upscale midtown shopping center, including purveyors of Native American arts and crafts, Southwestern-style items and home decor, furniture, jewelry, fine art, and high-style women's clothing.

West of downtown, the **Mercado San Agustin** (100 S. Av. del Convento, 520/461-1107, http://mercadosanagustin.com, daily, hours vary by shop) is a stylish open-air market and shopping center in the burgeoning west-side Mercado District, featuring a Mexican-style bakery that sells knee-buckling doughnuts as well as a Sonoran snow-cone spot. Boutiques, a great restaurant, and a bright and sunny coffee spot are popular with locals. On Saturday-Sunday morning there are usually a host of resting cyclists and active families having fun in the shade. Just a few steps outside the Mercado is the **MSA Annex** (267 S. Av. del Convento, 520/461-1107, http://mercadodistrict.com, hours vary by shop), home to 13 locally owned businesses, all of them housed in stylishly rusted recycled shipping containers. With added floors and windows and doors, of course, the surprisingly elegant and eye-pleasing boutiques and restaurants face shaded open spaces with tables and chairs. Don't miss the tiny bike shop and the charming store that sells Tucson-specific items.

The ideal upscale shopping experience is in the foothills at **La Encantada** (2905 E. Skyline Dr., at Campbell Ave., 520/299-3556, 10am-7pm Mon.-Wed., 10am-8pm Thurs.-Sat., 11am-6pm Sun.), with posh shops like Tiffany & Co., Louis Vuitton, Crate & Barrel, and dozens more in a lush two-level outdoor setting.

Drive west from downtown over dramatic Gate's Pass and through the saguaro forests to **Cat Mountain Station** (2740 S. Kinney Rd., 520/578-4272, www.catmountainstation. com, 8am-8pm daily), an oasis of taste and style close to the Tucson Desert Museum and Saguaro National Park. The enchanting station, with gorgeous desert landscaping and a shady courtyard, hosts a Buffalo Exchange boutique offering fashionable secondhand clothing, along with a store selling handmade jewelry and local art, a Southwestern art gallery, and a shop featuring handmade Tucson-only gifts and souvenirs. There's also a restaurant and bed-and-breakfast, and a small observatory for guided tours of the inky-black desert sky.

ANTIQUES

The **Grant Road Antique District** (Grant Rd. between Campbell Ave. and Craycroft Rd.) has over half a dozen antiques and resale shops, the best of which is the **American Antique Mall** (3130 E. Grant Rd., 520/326-3070, www.americanantiquemall.com, 10am-5pm Tues.-Sat.). A visit here gives a good idea of the kinds of antiques, collectibles, and generally interesting junk available at most of the Old Pueblo's resale places—a crowded mix of cowboy-life and Southwestern collectibles and kitsch; Native American jewelry and artifacts (not all of them authentic); furniture from the common to the rare, handmade and colonial,

retro and modern; old but not necessarily collectible books (*a lot* of Westerns); and all the varied possessions and ephemera left behind by several generations of snowbirds and retirees who spent their final days warm and content in the desert. Though it is not really recognized locally as such, there is a kind of **Speedway Antiques District** along both sides of busy Speedway Boulevard, roughly between Country Club Road and Wilmont Road, with half a dozen or more shops, small and large, selling used furniture, antiques, and other used and historic treasures.

CLOTHES

"Vintage clothing for New Bohemians" is how the founder of **The Buffalo Exchange** (2001 E. Speedway, 520/795-0508, www. buffaloexchange.com 10am-8pm Mon.-Fri., 10am-7pm Sat., 11am-6pm Sun.) describes her first store in Tucson. Now the chain has spread to college towns and bohemian enclaves from Tempe to Brooklyn, but it all started in midtown Tucson in the early 1970s. This boutique has a few Tucson locations and offers some of the most unique used clothes you'll ever find.

NATIVE AMERICAN ARTS

First opened in 1952 by Tom Bahti, father of current owner Mark Bahti, **Bahti Indian Arts** (4330 N. Campbell Ave., Suite 72, at River Rd., 520/577-0290, www.bahti.com, 9:30am-6pm Mon.-Sat., 9am-4pm Sun.), though no longer in its original location, is now the oldest shop of its kind in the Old Pueblo. The small shop at St. Philip's Plaza sells some of the finest examples of Navajo, Hopi, and Pueblo textiles, kachinas, jewelry, basketry, pottery, paintings, sculptures, and fetishes in the state, as well as an assortment of art and artifacts from tribes outside the Southwest. Mark is a noted expert on Native American arts, as was his father. He sells many useful books and guides at his store, including his own *Silver + Stone: Profiles of American Indian Jewelers*.

Morning Star Traders (2020 E. Speedway Blvd., 520/881-2112, www. morningstartraders.com, 10am-6pm Mon.-Sat.) has a fabulous collection of the high-end Indian arts—kachinas, Navajo textiles, pots and baskets, carvings, and historical artifacts—from the Southwest and other traditions. The friendly knowledgeable folks at Mac's Indian Jewelry (2400 E. Grant Rd., 520/327-3306, www.macsindianjewelry.com, 9am-5pm Mon.-Fri., 10am-5pm Sat.), longtime purveyors of Native American art and crafts in Tucson, will help you find that playful kachina doll, delicately wrought basket, or substantial silver-and-turquoise heirloom you've always wanted.

FOLK ARTS

The Old Pueblo has its fair share of resident artists, and, contrary to popular belief, not all of them are struggling to find the most evocative pose for a sunset-lit cowboy atop his horse. Native Seed Search (3061 N. Campbell Ave., 520/622-5561, www.nativeseeds.org, 10am-5pm daily) has uniquely Southwestern items, from heirloom seeds for nearly lost regional crops to one-of-a-kind gifts and videos and handmade crafts and soaps like yucca root—all with a link to the region and its past. A perfect gift to take home is one of the gift baskets, with all kinds of locally and regionally produced foods, soaps, and balms. This store also has an excellent selection of books about Tucson and the Southwest.

The concept of upcycling is relatively new, but it makes a lot of sense in our cluttered world. The artists selling their wares at the charming 4th Avenue boutique Popcycle (422 N. 4th Ave., 520/622-3297, www. popcycleshop.com, 11am-6pm Mon.-Thurs., 11am-7pm Fri.-Sat., 11am-5pm Sun.) take old pop-culture artifacts—record albums, found art, advertising, and other detritus of the culture—and create new and exciting items. You won't believe what a creative mind can come up with, given a bit of time spent in the attic or a thrift store.

BOOKS, MAPS, AND OUTDOOR SUPPLIES

Book lovers can't miss Bookmans (6230 E. Speedway Rd., 520/748-9555, www.bookmans. com, 9am-10pm daily), a Southern Arizona original, now with clones throughout the state. There are three Bookmans in Tucson, all featuring thousands of used books, CDs, videos, DVDs, and video games, but the relatively new Speedway location has become the firm's flagship store. Prices are cheap compared to smaller boutique-style used bookstores, and the selection is absolutely without compare. This is one of the West's best used bookstores.

The Book Stop (214 N. 4th Ave., 520/326-6661, www.bookstoptucson.com, 10am-7pm Mon.-Thurs., 10am-10pm Fri.-Sat., noon-5pm Sun.) is one of the last independent bookstores in Tucson. Open since the late 1960s, it's been on 4th Avenue since 2007. A decent selection of used and out-of-print books includes a substantial section on the Southwest. The books are a bit pricey in comparison to the bigger Bookmans, but when you're inside this classic store, nestled deep in the heady world of dusty old books, you feel a million miles away from the present.

You'll find topographical maps and hiking guides, bedrolls, backpacks, outdoor clothing, and everything else for a desert adventure at the locally owned Summit Hut (5251 E. Speedway Blvd., 520/325-1554, www. summithut.com, 9am-8pm Mon.-Fri., 9am-6:30pm Sat., 10am-6:30pm Sun.).

Food

The Old Pueblo's culinary scene is famously dominated by the ranch-land comfort food available at the dozens of Mexican eateries in town, most of them serving classic variations of cuisine formed in Mexico's arid northern states and the hot, dry coastlines of the nearby Sea of Cortez. While such home-style Mexican food represents one of the most popular in the country, in Tucson it has a kind of authenticity and diversity of taste that's available nowhere else—except an hour's drive across the border. UNESCO apparently agrees with this assessment: In 2015 it named Tucson a "City of Gastronomy."

You could spend a lifetime here eating carne asada, chiles rellenos, and enchiladas, but you'd not only gain more weight than you'd like but also miss out on sampling the work of some of the most creative, adventurous chefs and restaurateurs in the Southwest. The amorphous hodgepodge that is Southwestern-inspired American cuisine thrives in Tucson through an impressive array of mid- to high-end locally owned restaurants. If none of the spots below sends you craving, check out the list of locally owned eateries at Tucson Originals (http://tucsonoriginals.com).

To be totally honest, when you've got year-round outdoor patio dining—with gentle heaters when it's chilly, and water-spitting "misters" when it's hot—and the sky above is ever blue and clear, and the views from that patio are of looming high mountains and sweeping desert valleys, the quality of the food in front of you often becomes a secondary issue. Whenever you can, barring unlikely rain or cold, ask to sit on the patio or in the Spanish-style courtyard—scores of restaurants have them, and alfresco dining in, say, February is one of the great joys of desert living.

Fast Food

A homegrown enterprise, **Eegee's** (21 locations in Tucson, www.eegees.com) has been a favorite since 1971. The most popular items on the menu are the frozen drinks—multi-flavored shaved ice in a Styrofoam cup goes down easy on a hot summer day in the desert. My favorite is still the one they started with: lemon. They serve excellent deli-style sandwiches—many of them hot—french fries, and similar fare. The ranch fries, a heap of sliced deep-fried potatoes smothered in ranch dressing and topped with bacon bits, are a delight if you can risk the coronary. There's one of these Tucson-only joints on a corner near you wherever you are in the Old Pueblo.

DOWNTOWN AND UNIVERSITY DISTRICT
Mexican and Latin American

Do you like loud music while you eat, waitresses who kiss and hug their customers, and a bit of attitude with your chiles rellenos? The food is so spectacular at ★ **The Little One** (151 N. Stone Ave., at Alameda St., 520/612-7830, http://thelittleoneaz.com, 9am-2pm Mon.-Fri., $9-13, cash only) you might be willing to put up with just about anything to get the simple Mexican and Latin American fare at this beloved lunch spot. Make sure to tip big; a large percentage of everything goes to various good causes.

The carne asada and the Mexican (also called Sonoran) hot dogs are the specialties of the house at ★ **El Guero Canelo** (5201 S. 12th Ave., 520/295-9005, www.elguerocanelo.com, 10am-11pm Sun.-Thurs., 10am-midnight Fri.-Sat., $4-7), which replicates better than any other Old Pueblo restaurant the tastes and atmosphere of casual eating south of the border. If you're a fan of hot dogs, try the Sonoran variation—a skinny grilled dog hidden in a thick, rich, soft white bun, lathered

From *Machacas* to Menudos: Mexican Cuisine in Arizona

Because so many Arizona residents are from somewhere else, you'll find all the world cuisines well represented in even the most out-of-the-way places. However, one style reigns supreme: Mexican food. The cuisine of Mexico is popular throughout the United States these days, and travelers to Arizona and the border region are likely to have at least a passing knowledge of the favorites. But Tucson and Nogales (especially if you cross "the line" and try one of the restaurants in the tourist section of Nogales, Sonora, Mexico) are the best places in the state to eat Mexican food. In Tucson you'll find dozens of restaurants featuring a variety of regional Mexican foods, but the most prevalent is the style of northern Mexico, "El Norte"—after all, it wasn't that long ago that this region was not the extreme south of the United States but rather the extreme north of Mexico.

A ranching frontier, northern Mexico (specifically the states of Sonora and Chihuahua) has a cuisine based on beef, beans, cheese, and chilies—the comfort foods of

Mexican cuisine

Mexico. You are more likely to find flour tortillas in northern Mexico than in the central and southern regions, as the desert and semidesert land is harder on corn than on wheat. A popular ranch-land delicacy is *machaca,* also called *carne seca*—dried, shredded beef available at nearly every restaurant as a filling for burritos and tacos or on its own. Many Tucson restaurants are famous for their carne asada, or grilled meat—thin strips of beef spiced and grilled and then stuffed in tacos or burritos or served on their own with rice and beans. Another popular northern dish is menudo, available at many taco stands and restaurants around Tucson as well as Phoenix. It's a kind of soup made with tripe, hominy, and cow's foot that's said to cure hangovers—it is often offered only on the weekends.

Originating in Hermosillo, the capital of the Mexican border state of Sonora, the so-called Sonoran hot dog is a decadent variation of the great American street food. You can find them all over Tucson and Phoenix at restaurants and from vendors on street corners. The classic version is a grilled hot dog wrapped in bacon and then couched in a fluffy Mexican-style bun (*bolillo*), topped with beans, salsa, tomatoes, onions, creamy mayonnaise, and mustard.

Throughout Southern Arizona it's also easy to find excellent Mexican seafood. Tucson is only a few hours from the Sea of Cortez, and many locals have vacation homes along the desert coast. Places serving fish tacos, shrimp cocktail, and other seafood abound. There are also a few restaurants in the state that serve a more complex, gourmet version of Mexican cuisine. At these places, you'll be able to sample the intricate moles and chicken and pork dishes of central and southern Mexico.

with beans, mayo, salsa, and whatever else you want to add. It's amazing, but it rarely sparks ambivalence—people either love it or hate it. The restaurant has two additional locations, in North Midtown (2480 N. Oracle Rd., 520/882-8977) and Eastside (5802 E. 22nd St., 520/790-6000).

El Charro Café (311 N. Court Ave., 520/622-1922, www.elcharrocafe.com, 11am-8:30pm daily, $6-18) makes the city's most beloved Mexican food in a building once lived in by Julias Finn, a French stonemason who came to Tucson to work on the cathedral. The restaurant has a bar, ¡Toma!, with half-price drinks and appetizers (delicious Mexican favorites like cheese crisps and quesadillas) 3pm-6pm daily.

American and Southwestern

The ★ **Cup Café** (311 E. Congress St., 520/798-1618, http://hotelcongress.com, 7am-10pm Sun.-Thurs., 7am-11pm Fri.-Sat., $9-27) serves an eclectic blend of American food with several ethnic traditions. Inside the Hotel Congress downtown, the Cup is a popular weekend breakfast destination and a perfect choice for lunch or dinner. The menu features dishes such as dates stuffed with chorizo and wrapped in bacon, fish tacos, and burgers with Arizona-raised beef (also a wonderful veggie burger). Not only does the restaurant have a range of unique and memorable creations, many are gluten-free and vegan.

In a glorious and lovingly refurbished 1964 Googie building on the eastern edge of downtown, the ★ **Welcome Diner** (902 E. Broadway Blvd., 520/622-5100, http://welcomediner.net, 8am-9pm Sun.-Thurs., 8am-10pm Fri.-Sat., $8-16) puts on a feast of style, flavor, and goodness. Its mid-century style stands out even along Tucson's Sunshine Mile, a stretch of classic mid-century architecture along Broadway Boulevard. And that's just the outside. Inside, the chicken and biscuits, fried green tomato sandwiches, burritos with native tepary beans, full bar, and friendly people will keep you around. Delicious and creative dishes are made with organic local produce, chicken, bread, coffee, tortillas, and more.

Hidden behind a nondescript storefront on downtown's Scott Avenue, **47 Scott** (47 N. Scott Ave., 520/624-4747, www.47scott.com, 4pm-close Mon.-Fri., 10am-10pm Sat., 10am-9pm Sun., $10-30) has a romantic brick-walled patio that's lit subtly after dark. The menu is adjusted seasonally but generally is a familiar appetizing take on New American comfort food. Order the phyllo-wrapped chicken—a juicy breast cased in toasted phyllo dough, stuffed with goat cheese and spinach, drizzled with a rich and hearty chicken jus, flanked by smashed potato cakes and sage carrots. It's a wonderful kind of deconstructed chicken potpie.

The **Hub Restaurant and Ice Creamery** (266 E. Congress St., 520/207-8201, http://hubdowntown.com, 11am-midnight daily, $12-18) has hipster style and the soul of a great American diner. The food is certainly a few cuts above the usual countertop fare: fries smothered in prime rib, chicken potpie, and pastrami sandwiches. So is the decor: white faux-leather booths, thick ropes like vines on the redbrick walls, and upside-down house lamps hanging from the exposed rafters.

Italian and Pizza

There's nothing better than a greasy slice (from $3) of authentic New York-style pizza after a night of hitting the bars, and **Brooklyn Pizza** (534 N. 4th Ave., 520/622-6868, www.brooklynpizzacompany.com, 11am-11pm Mon.-Sat., noon-10pm Sun. slices 11pm-2:30am Fri.-Sat., $7-22) serves them late into the night on weekends. The pizza rivals anything you can find back East, and the meatball subs, calzones, and gelato are the best in town. What's more, this little pizza place is completely solar powered.

Caruso's (434 N. 4th Ave., 520/624-5765, www.carusositalian.com, 4pm-close Tues.-Thurs., 11:30am-close Fri.-Sun., $12-18) has been serving delicious Italian favorites on 4th Avenue since 1938. Sit on the shaded patio next to a trickling fountain and enjoy the pasta dishes and pizzas. It's nothing fancy—just well-prepared Italian favorites in a laid-back atmosphere with, of course, checkered tablecloths and fat bottles of chianti.

Some of the most toothsome pizza in town is served by **Reilly Craft Pizza and Drink** (101 E. Pennington St., 520/882-5550, www.reillypizza.com, 11am-11pm daily, $13-19) out of a tastefully refurbished circa-1908 downtown building that once housed a funeral home. The restaurant kept the funeral home's name and sign but little else. With an urban-cool interior and sophisticated menu, Reilly is a standout in the ever-expanding downtown culinary scene. The craft pizzas have a thick-but-light toasted crust and come with a variety of toppings far removed from the usual slice-on-the-corner variety (fennel pollen, truffle cheese, eggplant, fontina). Reilly also serves pasta dishes and extraordinary salads. Try the one with watermelon and goat cheese.

Vegetarian

Head over to the west-side MSA Annex near the Mercado San Juan to find a bustling complex of shipping crates made into stores and eateries. One of them, ★ **Beaut Burger** (267 S. Av. del Covento, 520/344-5907, www.beautburger.com, 11:30am-8:30pm daily, $6-9), serves an array of fantastically tasteful scratch-made veggie burgers—made from grains, beans, vegetables, walnuts, and spices.

A bright café on the southern edge of downtown, **Café Desta** (758 S. Stone Ave., 520/370-7000, www.destacafe.com, 11am-9pm daily, $12-17) serves exceptional Ethiopian cuisine, much of it vegan, and has a full coffee bar. Bring your own bottle of wine and a few friends and try the vegan signature plate (serves 3, $30), a sampling of several spicy and exotic dishes featuring mushrooms, lentils, cabbage, onions, collard greens, spinach, and more, served with rice and the spongy Ethiopian *injera* flatbread (which is also vegan). If you have carnivores in tow, Desta also has flavorful beef, lamb, and fish.

Small and always busy, **Tumerico** (402 E. 4th St., 520/270-2055; 2526 E. 6th St., 520/240-6947, www.tumerico.com, 9am-8pm Thurs.-Sat., 9am-3pm Sun., $13-18) has two locations offering unique and inspiring plant-based Mexican food in a casual counter-service setting. The chef, who started out selling her creations from a cooler at local events, makes plant-based dishes a world away from the usual cheese-and-sauce-smothered hot plate. The small regularly changing menu often includes classic dishes with a vegetarian twist, such as jackfruit tacos, green enchiladas, and vegan tamales, all made with local ingredients. Try the Tumerico lemonade; it's amazing. Take a free yoga class (9am

Sat.-Sun.) at the 4th Street location (corner of 4th Ave. and 4th St.).

MIDTOWN
Mexican

The Arizona home of the Sonoran hot dog is ★ **El Guero Canelo** (2480 N. Oracle Rd., 520/882-8977, www.elguerocanelo.com, 10am-11pm Sun.-Thurs., 10am-midnight Fri.-Sat., $4-7), which has been serving authentic and fast Mexican street food in the Old Pueblo for two decades, including what many believe to be the city's best Sonoran dogs—a grilled beef hot dog wrapped in bacon, nestled deep in a thick rich bun, smothered in beans, onions, mustard, mayo, and salsa. It's a decadent meal because it's nearly impossible to have just one. Another must-try is the carne asada tacos, and don't forget to wash it all down with a bottle of Mexican soda. It also has two other locations: Southside (5201 S. 12th Ave., 520/295-9005), and Eastside (5802 E. 22nd St., 520/790-6000).

A recognized leader among the Old Pueblo's many purveyors of the Sonoran hot dog, **BK Carne Asada & Hot Dogs** (2680 N. 1st Ave., 520/207-2245, www.bktacos.com, 9am-11pm Sun.-Thurs., 9am-midnight Fri.-Sat., $4-13), with a cozy midtown location, is the perfect place to have, say, 30 of the bacon-wrapped bean-heaped dogs, and maybe a few dozen carne asada tacos, and an indeterminate number of cold beers. BK also serves awesome "caramelos." A local creation, they're a sort of grilled tortilla sandwich, usually overstuffed with meat, cheese, chilies, and other staples. They also have a Southside location (5118 S. 12th Ave., 520/295-0105, 9am-midnight Sun.-Thurs., 9am-2:30am Fri.-Sat.).

American and Southwestern

The genius baker behind ★ **Barrio Bread** (18 S. Eastbourne Ave., 520/327-1292, http://barriobread.com, 9am-5pm Tues.-Fri., 9am-2pm Sat.), Don Guerra, was a semifinalist for the 2019 James Beard Award. Yeah, he's that good. He's also fascinated with local and heritage grains and uses them to make some of the

best bread in Arizona. In Broadway Village along Broadway Boulevard's Sunshine Mile, Barrio Bread features a dizzying selection of fresh loaves, including the signature Heritage loaf made with a blend of Southwestern heritage flours and embossed with a charming saguaro. Guerra also bakes a loaf called the pan de Kino using white Sonora wheat. Padre Kino first brought this kind of wheat to Southern Arizona in the late 1600s, and it's still grown and milled locally for Barrio Bread at a small farm in nearby Marana. You'll know you've found it when you see the line out the door.

The best greasy spoon in Tucson, and perhaps the greasiest, is ★ **Frank's/Francisco's** (3843 E. Pima St., 520/881-2710, 6am-2pm and 5pm-10pm Mon.-Thurs., 6am-2pm and 5pm-midnight Fri., 7am-2pm and 5pm-midnight Sat., 8am-2pm and 5pm-10pm Sun., $5-10), whose motto is "Elegant Dining Elsewhere." You can sit at a rickety table or belly up to the bar and watch your hash browns cook on the grill. The breakfast menu has all you'd expect, with the addition of highly recommended Mexican favorites. There's nothing like getting all spiced up early in the morning. At night Frank's becomes Francisco's, serves Michoacán-style Mexican food, and gives away free slow-cooked pinto beans to go.

Try either of the two midtown locations of **Prep & Pastry** (2660 N. Campbell Ave., 520/326-7737; 6450 E. Grant Rd., Unit 160, 520/838-0809, www.prepandpastry.com, 7am-3pm daily, $8-14) for a breakfast any day and brunch on the weekends. The chefs use local and seasonal ingredients to create inspired and unique breakfast dishes like herb-cheddar biscuits smothered in duck fat gravy, spicy tri-tip, scrambled egg and arugula on a croissant, asparagus toast, and of course plain old pancakes—it's a bright and busy spot for foodies. Brunch is fantastic and popular; get your name on the waiting list early by going to the website.

Cielos at Lodge on the Desert (306 N. Alvernon Way, 520/320-2000, www.lodgeonthedesert.com, 7am-10:30am, 11am-2pm, and 5pm-10pm daily, $12-36) has become one of the city's most esteemed eateries. The midtown restaurant and bar, deep within the boutique hotel's property, exudes a kind of Old West high-walled coziness that pairs perfectly with a regional take on New American cuisine. It has a daily happy hour (3pm-7pm).

High-piled gourmet burgers in a casual setting seems like a stroke of genius when you bite into your towering, inventive **Monkey Burger** (5350 E. Broadway Blvd., 520/514-9797, www.monkeyburgerrestaurant.com, 11am-9pm Mon.-Sat., noon-7pm Sun., $6-10). They offer a dozen or so signature burgers and a few not-so-usual sides (fried pickles, sweet potato fries, roasted corn on the cob), plus draft beer and thick shakes.

Huge and delicious omelets are at the **Blue Willow** (2616 N. Campbell Ave., 520/327-7577, www.bluewillowtucson.com, 8am-3pm Sun.-Tues., 8am-8pm Wed.-Sat., $13-22), in a cute old house with a large covered patio in Campbell Avenue's busy commercial district. The emphasis is on the fresh, homemade, and all-natural. A gift shop sells funny stickers, buttons, and knickknacks about politics and gender issues.

Vegetarian

Govinda's Natural Food Buffet (711 E. Blacklidge Dr., 520/792-0630, www.govindasoftucson.com, 5pm-9pm Tues., 11:30am-2:30pm and 5pm-9pm Wed.-Sat., 11am-2:30pm Sun., $11-13) puts out a tasty, expertly prepared, and inexpensive all-you-can-eat vegetarian and vegan buffet. On Thursday nights everything is vegan, and on Tuesdays authentic Indian food is served. Sunday brunch (11am-2:30pm) features pancakes, home fries, and scrambled tofu. The restaurant is at the Chaitanya Cultural Center, its name referring to one of Krishna's many incarnations; you will be among Tucson's Hare Krishna community in a peaceful and

---

1: Beaut Burger **2:** Coyote Pause Café **3:** The Parish restaurant **4:** The American Eat Co.

always friendly atmosphere that may spark a meditative mood—post-buffet, of course.

WEST OF DOWNTOWN
American and Southwestern

The ideal place to refuel after exploring the desert of Tucson Mountain Park, Saguaro National Park, and the Arizona-Sonora Desert Museum, **Coyote Pause Café** (2740 S. Kinney Rd., 520/883-7297, www. coyotepausecafe.com, 7:30am-2:30pm daily, $6-12) is a casual diner-style eatery serving classic American rib-stickers with a few nods to the territory. It's in a refurbished 1950s-era desert outpost called Cat Mountain Station, an easy drive from all of the main west-side attractions. The Coyote Burger, with house-made prickly pear barbecue sauce (you might want to take home several bottles) and thick crunchy onion rings, will restore your energy. A number of vegetarian, vegan, and gluten-free dishes include a spicy locally inspired Sonoran Veggie Burger.

SOUTH OF DOWNTOWN
Mexican

If you only have the time or inclination to eat at one of Tucson's famous Sonoran-style Mexican restaurants, consider ★ **Mi Nidito** (1813 S. 4th Ave., 520/622-5081, www.minidito.net, 11am-10:30pm Wed.-Thurs. and Sun., 11am-2am Fri.-Sat., $10-18); Bill Clinton did. While on a short stopover in Tucson during his presidency, Clinton, known for his love of comfort food, stopped at Mi Nidito (My Little Nest), sampling pretty much one of everything. His order is still preserved as a special on the menu. This bright South 4th Avenue restaurant, with its tropical decor and friendly, albeit always harried, staff, is the best among dozens of similar eateries in the Old Pueblo. *Tucson Weekly* readers invariably name it among the top Sonoran joints in town in the annual Best of Tucson poll, and you shouldn't be surprised to see a line of people waiting to be seated at 10:45am on a Wednesday. On a weekend night, figure on

at least a half-hour wait on the porch, waiting anxiously for your name to ring out.

American and Southwestern

Head south on 6th Avenue from downtown to South Tucson (2 miles from Congress St.) and ★ **The American Eat Co.** (1439 S. 4th Ave., 520/867-8700, http://americaneatco. com, 11am-9pm Mon.-Thurs., 11am-10pm Fri.-Sat., prices vary by restaurant), a food court featuring 10 local businesses, including a coffeehouse, a beer-and-wine bar, and a butcher shop. The counter-service restaurants offer an eclectic selection of burgers, ribs, pizza, poke bowls, and more. There's also a spot serving Chicano comfort food. Take your food to go or sit with the locals at the large family-style tables.

FOOTHILLS
American and Southwestern

An admirable restaurant in an incomparable setting, the **Flying V Bar and Grill** (7000 N. Resort Dr., 520/299-2020, www. loewshotels.com, 5:30pm-9pm Mon.-Thurs., 5pm-10pm Fri.-Sat., 5pm-9pm Sun., $18-45) at Loews Ventana Canyon, a gorgeous Catalina Foothills destination resort, combines all the best elements of Tucson's dining scene in one place: awesome views, a romantic terrace, guacamole made to order tableside by a "guacamoliere," and inspired comfort food with a dollop of Southwestern flavor.

An upscale pub on the edge of the foothills, **Union Public House** (4340 N. Campbell Ave., 520/329-8575, www.uniontucson.com, 11am-2am Mon.-Sat., 10am-2am Sun., $12-35) has outstanding food and one of the best patios in town, looking out on St. Philip's Plaza, with its shady trees and trickling fountain. The menu features creative variations on comfort classics—potpie, chicken and waffles, fish-and-chips, burgers, and flatbread pizzas.

For those who could exist on beef alone, and who believe that beef is best served ground, in patty form, and between two warm buns, there is **Zinburger** (1865 E. River Rd., 520/299-7799, www.zinburgeraz.

com, 11am-10pm Sun.-Thurs., 11am-11pm Fri.-Sat., $10-13), a gourmet homage to the good old burger joint. Try the Samburger, with maple bacon, American cheese, and Thousand Island dressing—a kind of dressed-up Big Mac. The sides alone are worth a visit: sweet-potato chips, zucchini fries, double truffle fries. Thick shakes, crème brûlée, and bananas Foster are among the perfectly paired desserts offered in this sleek and bright burger house.

A unique pairing of South-by-Southwest food styles, **The Parish** (6453 N. Oracle Rd., 520/797-1233, www.theparishtucson.com, 11am-midnight Sun.-Thurs., 11am-2am Fri.-Sat., $14-29) calls itself a "Southern fusion gastropub." That generally means New Orleans meets Tucson, and it's a meeting that anybody who loves food will want to be present for. Try the crawfish hush puppies; you may end up eating a dozen. Or sample the house-made pork rinds, or the bacon popcorn—and that's just the appetizers. The entrées include steaks, fish, and burgers, all prepared with Southern methods and just a dash of Southwestern spice. The Parish also has a creative cocktail menu and a wide selection of beers on tap.

Steaks and Chops

★ **El Corral Restaurant** (2201 E. River Rd., 520/299-6092, www.elcorraltucson.com, 5pm-10pm Mon.-Thurs., 4:30pm-10pm Fri.-Sun., $19-32) is a charming historic choice for prime rib, thick steaks, and a big bowl of cowboy beans. In a low-ceilinged stone-and-wooden-beam territorial ranch house with flagstone floors, this restaurant has been a Tucson institution since 1926. The setting is almost as inviting as the sizzling beef and ribs, with Technicolor portraits of movie-house cowboys on the walls and several rooms that offer romantic fireside dining.

Accommodations

There aren't a lot of inexpensive accommodations in Tucson worth taking a chance on. The best choice for budget travelers is the lone hostel, in a clean and friendly house near downtown. On the I-10 frontage road just west of downtown is a long row of chain hotels, some of them inexpensive. This isn't the Old Pueblo's most charming district, however. Throughout midtown and the east side there are dozens of big chain hotels, and many more around the south side near the airport.

For most travelers and casual visitors, downtown and the University District are the best places to stay. This area is best for walking, sightseeing, eating, and drinking, and close to I-10 and the road out to Saguaro National Park and the Arizona-Sonora Desert Museum. Midtown has the largest selection of accommodations, mostly chains of varied quality and price. For a truly memorable Tucson experience, consider staying in one of the small (though often relatively pricey) B&Bs and inns in one of the city's many historic neighborhoods, such as the El Presidio and Sam Hughes neighborhoods; the latter is a residential neighborhood on the eastern edge of the University of Arizona campus popular with students and professors. The northwest side and foothills have most of the high-end resorts, most of which are at least a half-hour drive from the city center.

During the summer months, late May-late September, most lodgings slash their prices—some by as much as 50 percent, but most by around 20 percent. During those torpid quiet months, you might be able to afford to live like a robber baron for a few days. It pays to explore the websites of the larger chains listed below; most offer many different packages, one of which will likely save you some money. If you're coming to town in February-March, book early and plan to pay a bit more; those perfect-weather months feature several very popular festivals, events, and conventions in the Old Pueblo, and most places are booked solid.

DOWNTOWN AND UNIVERSITY DISTRICT
$100-250

Built in 1919 and extensively remodeled since, ★ **Hotel Congress** (311 E. Congress St., 520/622-8848 or 800/722-8848, www. hotelcongress.com, $109-149) is a historic downtown hotel that offers charm and atmosphere; it's listed on the National Register of Historic Places and is in the center of downtown's bar and music scene. Guest rooms are a bit creaky, but the beds are comfortable, and the historic atmosphere makes up for the lack of sumptuous amenities. It's the best value in town if you value personality in your sleeping quarters. There is noise some nights from Club Congress downstairs (a slight thumping comes through the walls). The club is a venue for alternative and alt-country bands from across the nation, and the Tap Room bar will make you feel like a ranch hand on a day off. The Cup Café, off the beautiful old lobby, has an eclectic mix of gourmet and Southwestern-style food for breakfast, lunch, and dinner. Room rates are about $10 less in summer, beginning at the end of May. The Congress has been a leader in sustainability for many years. The hotel is Certified Green by the Arizona Hotel & Lodging Association and has been retrofitted with water-saving technology. The Congress is also a member of One-Less Straw, a nonprofit that helps keep plastic straws out of landfills and the oceans.

About a mile south of downtown and with easy access to I-10, the ★ **Hotel McCoy** (720 W. Silverlake Rd., 844/782-9622, http:// hotelmccoy.com, $93-149) offers clean, comfortable rooms, some with kitchenettes, in a resurrected mid-century motor court made into a traveler's haven with creative zest, retro style, and a local vibe and value that are hard to resist. Tucson-made art fills the rooms and the lobby, which has a bar with all local beer and wine, and in the morning, a nutritious,

filling, free oatmeal bar. It's not in a scenic location, but it's close to everything and the staff work hard to make the hotel sustainable and affordable. Not only have they made fine use of an old building, they installed low-flow water fixtures, drip irrigation, drought-tolerant landscaping, and LED lighting. If you stay for three or more nights, you can choose to skip housekeeping in exchange for a $10 gift certificate. Hopefully this place represents the future of mid-priced, locally flavored, and ecofriendly independent accommodations.

Small independent **Downtown Clifton Hotel** (485 S. Stone Ave., 520/623-3163, http:// downtowntucsonhotel.com, $109) is perfectly located in a lovingly restored 1947 motor lodge, near the intersection known as five points. It's close to all of downtown's historic walkable neighborhoods. The spacious clean and comfortable rooms, remodeled with polished concrete floors and brick walls, have free Wi-Fi, minifridges, microwaves, and smart TVs. Guests get a free meal at the nearby 5 Points Café and Market.

The enchanting **El Presidio Inn Bed & Breakfast** (297 N. Main Ave., 520/623-6151, www.elpresidiobbinn.com, $142-179), in the Julius Kruttschnitt House, built in 1886 and remodeled over the years in various architectural styles, is one of the city's best small inns. It's located in Snob Hollow in the historic El Presidio neighborhood, on the block with the mansions of Tucson's wealthy pioneers. The inn has a cool, lush, and peaceful garden courtyard with a babbling fountain, cobblestone walkways, and shade-casting trees. The inn has four rooms, two of which—the Carriage House and the Gate House—open onto the courtyard and have kitchenettes.

Over $250

The Blenman Inn (204 S. Scott Ave., 877/670-9022, www.theblenmaninn.com, 2-night minimum stay Oct.-May, $199-325) is in the historic home known as the Blenman House, built in 1878 in Tucson's El Presidio district. There are six large rooms elegantly decorated in Old World style with big sweeping beds and clawfoot stand-alone bathtubs. There's also a pool, a hot tub, and gorgeous gardens. They only allow kids over age 13, and don't allow pets or smoking.

MIDTOWN
$100-250

A charming Spanish Revival B&B in midtown's quiet tree-lined Sam Hughes neighborhood, the **Sam Hughes Inn Bed and Breakfast** (2020 E. 7th St., 520/861-2191, www.samhughesinn.com, $90-145) is within walking distance to the University of Arizona and close to downtown and midtown. The inn has four distinctively decorated rooms with free Wi-Fi and private baths. The enclosed courtyard out back is green, cool, and perfect for relaxing and watching the sun dip away.

Originally built in 1931, **The Lodge on the Desert** (306 N. Alvernon Way, 520/325-3366, www.lodgeonthedesert.com, $179-199) has a beautiful stylish lobby and restaurant on top of its great hacienda-style rooms offering free Wi-Fi, comfortable beds, and big cushy bathrobes. The grounds are green and private, and the patio lounge is one of the best in the city.

Over $250

The historic ★ **Arizona Inn** (2200 E. Elm St., 520/325-1541, www.arizonainn.com, $169-379), a boutique hotel in central midtown founded in the 1930s by Arizona's first congresswoman and still owned and operated by her family, is the best place to stay in Tucson—as long as you have fairly deep pockets. Several different kinds of rooms are decorated in the inimitable 1930s Southwestern style. The grounds and lobby have a lot of charm—there's a 60-foot pool, old-school tennis courts, and many quiet little corners in the verdant retreat-like setting behind high pink walls.

WEST OF DOWNTOWN

If you want to stay out in the desert west of downtown Tucson, near Saguaro National Park and the Arizona-Sonora Desert Museum,

try ★ **Cat Mountain Lodge and Roadside Inn** (2727 S. Kinney Rd., 520/578-6085, www.catmountainlodge.com, $218-298), an enchanting desert oasis with both lodge and roadside motel rooms, including rooms inspired by Frida Kahlo and Diego Rivera. The tasteful and regionally decorated rooms include free Wi-Fi and minifridges, and come with free breakfast or lunch at the nearby Coyote Pause Café. Many rooms open onto a shady and peaceful courtyard, and an on-site observatory offers star tours for an extra fee. Striving to be sustainable and ecofriendly, the owners built the lodge using the latest green materials and repurposed a neglected structure to build the roadside inn. Tanks on the property harvest rainwater for the landscaping, and the lodge is Certified Green by the Arizona Hotel & Lodging Association. Don't forget to introduce yourself to the resident desert tortoise, Juan Wayne.

FOOTHILLS
Resorts

Visitors and émigrés have sought healing in Southern Arizona since at least the early 19th century. Any tubercular patient lucky enough to flee the crowded tenements of the Northeast or the malarial bottomlands of the South was invariably advised to seek the high dry air of the Southwest. Physicians of the era had little else but this somewhat specious advice to offer the scores of Americans who suffered from tuberculosis, fevers, dysentery, and other ailments of the chest and the blood.

Scholar Billy Jones, in his book *Health-Seekers in the Southwest 1817-1900*, estimates that some 20-25 percent of those who moved to the Southwest during the migrations of the 19th-20th centuries did so hoping to cure some ailment, creating a "health frontier" that, in Tucson, resulted in the haphazard construction of vast tent cities on the outskirts of town populated by consumptives and often destitute people not long for the world.

Medical science has since cured most of the diseases that once brought sickly travelers to the desert, but today's visitors seek health

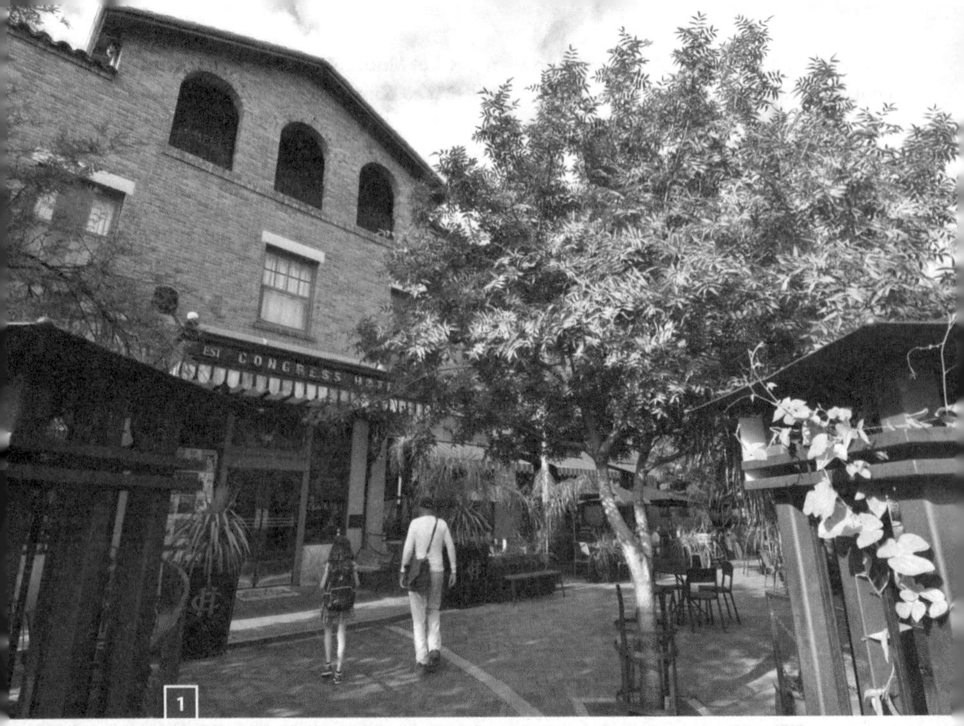

1

2
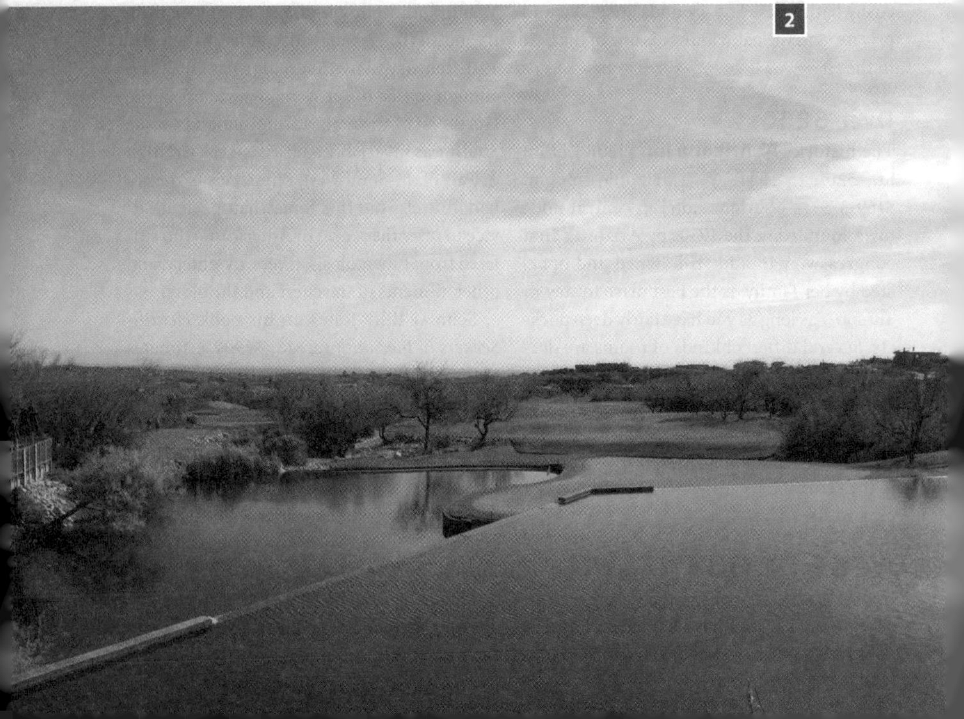

of a different kind. Tucson has long rivaled its ritzy northern neighbors Scottsdale and Sedona as a place where the afflicted, both physically and psychically, can find solace. The high season at most resorts in Tucson lasts late September-late May or early June. During the hot summer months many resorts drop their rates precipitously, but you may find service standards lowered, the staff lackadaisical, and even some amenities and features shut down. And you will not want to do much outdoors after 10am.

★ **Miraval, Life in Balance Resort & Spa** (5000 E. Via Estancia Miraval, Catalina, 520/825-4000 or 800/232-3969, www. miravalresorts.com, $579-1,300) is a magical desert hideaway where everybody wants to help you get fit, well, happy, and tuned in. The Santa Catalina Mountains tower over 400 acres of bushy desert and elegant sustainable buildings with guest rooms and suites featuring beehive fireplaces and private patios. There are myriad quiet spaces made by nature for meditation, yoga, and spiritual contemplation, and you'll eat gourmet food made with organic ingredients grown on the property.

Founded in 1929 and displaying elegant Spanish Colonial architecture, ★ **Hacienda del Sol Guest Ranch Resort** (5601 N. Hacienda del Sol Rd., 520/299-1501 or 800/728-6514, www.haciendadelsol.com, $445-594) reflects more than any other local lodging (save perhaps the Arizona Inn) the beauty and rustic chic of the high-style Southwest of yesteryear. Each distinctive room comes with custom-made furniture and a unique story. The Tracy-Hepburn Casita, with two bedrooms, two baths, and a kitchen, is where Spencer Tracy and Katharine Hepburn used to stay. The small, comparatively inexpensive Historic Rooms look out on the lush courtyard, and two inviting outdoor pools and hot tubs look out over the bushy desert toward the looming Santa Catalina Mountains. Like its younger foothill

neighbors, this resort has a full-service spa, riding stables, and an excellent restaurant and patio bar.

Perhaps Tucson's most famous resort, **Canyon Ranch** (8600 E. Rockcliff Rd., 520/749-9000 or 800/742-9000, www. canyonranch.com, from $1,100 pp) is not a mere resort; it's more of a life-affirming pleasure dome from which you're meant to emerge changed for the better. Pamper yourself silly with spa treatments and schedule appointments with a staff nutritionist, spiritual guide, acupuncturist, and physician. A personal trainer will work with you on keeping in shape in the long term, while a meditation class will help you get in tune with your spirituality. After one of your three daily healthy gourmet meals, you can attend lectures and classes and retreats on various healthful-living topics. For an experience so potentially meaningful, it's not surprising that you're going to have to spend accordingly.

One of the best things about **Loews Ventana Canyon Resort** (7000 N. Resort Dr., 520/299-2020 or 800/234-5117, www. loewshotels.com, $136-429) is its view—anywhere you stand on the grounds provides a long clear look beyond the sweeping golf course off to the valley below. With a fabulous restaurant, a top-notch spa, tennis courts, hiking trails, and one of the most scenic golf courses in the Southwest, it's no wonder this world-renowned hotel and spa was rated number 31 of the top 100 golf resorts in the nation by *Condé Nast Traveler* magazine. The resort also has a popular stargazing program and a desert setting you won't soon forget. Ventana Canyon is Certified Green by the Arizona Hotel & Lodging Association.

Guests of **The Westin La Paloma Resort & Spa** (800 E. Sunrise Dr., 800/937-8461, www.westinlapalomaresort.com, $215-374) are allowed to use the facilities of the nearby country club, which has a 27-hole Jack Nicklaus-designed golf course. The guest rooms here are spacious and have private

---

1: Hotel Congress **2:** Loews Ventana Canyon Resort

patios looking over the desert and huge sink-in beds; some have fireplaces and sunken spa tubs. The resort's **Elizabeth Arden Red Door Spa** will pamper you after a few sets on one of 10 championship tennis courts. There are also indoor racquetball courts, a huge pool area, Pilates and yoga studios, and an exercise room. La Paloma is Certified Green by the Arizona Hotel & Lodging Association.

First built as a private home in 1912, the hacienda-style **Westward Look Resort** (245 E. Ina Rd., 520/297-1151 or 800/722-2500, www.westwardlook.com, $329-344)

has Southwestern charm to spare. Built up and remodeled over time, the older, adobe portions still have the exposed vigas made from wood brought down from Mount Lemmon. The 241 guest rooms and suites have the usual high-end luxuries, and the resort offers horseback riding, tennis, spa treatments, and 80 acres of desert foothills grounds with nature trails, stargazing programs, and exhibits about the desert's natural history and Indigenous peoples. Westward Look is Certified Green by the Arizona Hotel & Lodging Association.

Information and Services

VISITORS CENTER

Near the University of Arizona's Main Gate area, the **Tucson Visitor Center** (811 N. Euclid Ave., at University Blvd., 800/638-8350, www.visittucson.org, 8am-5pm Mon.-Fri., 9am-4pm Sat.-Sun.) has advice, maps, brochures, and other resources for travelers.

FOREST CONTACTS

Most of the public land in Southern Arizona is administered by the **Coronado National Forest.** The main office in Tucson (300 W. Congress St., 520/388-8300, www.fs.usda.gov/coronado, 8am-4:30pm Mon.-Fri.) can direct you to a specific field office. The **Bureau of Land Management** (12661 E. Broadway Blvd., 520/258-7200, www.az.blm.gov, 8am-4pm Mon.-Fri.) controls much of the public land that is not within the national forest. If you have any trouble with wild animals or

need to report a poaching incident, call the **Arizona Game and Fish Department** (555 N. Greasewood Rd., 520/628-5376, www.azgfd.gov, 8am-5pm Mon.-Fri.).

HOSPITALS

Dial 911 for emergencies anywhere in Southern Arizona. **University Medical Center** (1501 N. Campbell Ave., 520/694-0111) has the region's only Level 1 trauma center.

MEDIA

The morning daily newspaper *Arizona Daily Star* (www.azstarnet.com) has a local focus but isn't provincial. The alternative tabloid *Tucson Weekly* (www.tucsonweekly.com) is the place to go for news on arts, entertainment, politics, and local news. You'll find it free throughout the city.

Transportation

AIR

Small but efficient **Tucson International Airport** (TUS, 7250 S. Tucson Blvd., 520/573-8100, www.flytucson.com), with free Wi-Fi, hosts six airlines, including American, Delta, Southwest, and Alaska, that fly daily to 18 cities, including Atlanta, Chicago, Minneapolis, Houston, Albuquerque, Denver, Salt Lake, Las Vegas, Seattle, San Francisco, Los Angeles, and San Diego. From other cities you'll likely you'll transit at **Sky Harbor International Airport** in Phoenix. If you find yourself at Sky Harbor and don't feel like boarding the absurdly short 45-minute flight, you can rent a car and make the easy 1.5-hour drive on I-10. Or call **Groome Transportation** (520/795-6771, http://groometransportation. com/arizona, $45 one-way), which offers many daily Phoenix-Tucson trips.

CAR

A car is necessary to visit Tucson the way it deserves to be visited. To get out into the desert, you need your own vehicle, though it need not be 4WD.

The main route to and from Tucson is I-10, which acts as an in-town freeway as well. Tucson is far from I-40, the main east-west route to the north. It's a four-hour, 263-mile drive from Tucson to I-40 at Flagstaff, one of the best gateway cities to the Grand Canyon. Phoenix is 100 miles from Tucson up I-10, a drive of about two hours. The Old Pueblo is connected to its former owner, Mexico, via I-19, a straight one-hour, 70-mile drive south through the beautiful Santa Cruz Valley.

Car Rental

If you're flying to Tucson and don't have someone to chauffeur you around the sprawling city, you'll need to rent a car. The airport has several providers, including local **A.P.S. Auto Rental** (3747 E. Speedway Blvd., 520/750-9776, www.tucsonautorental.com,

9am-5pm Mon.-Sat.), which rents used but well-maintained compacts, sedans, SUVs, and passenger vans. The lot is about 10 miles (20 minutes) from the airport.

LONG-DISTANCE BUS

Bus service from Tucson to all points on the map is at the **Greyhound Bus Station** (801 E. 12th St., near Broadway Blvd. and Euclid Ave., 520/792-3475, www.greyhound.com).

TRAIN

The **Amtrak Station** (400 N. Toole Ave., 520/623-4442, www.amtrak.com) downtown is served by the *Sunset Limited* and *Texas Eagle* lines.

PUBLIC TRANSPORTATION
Bus

The city of Tucson operates the **Sun Tran** (4220 S. Park Ave., 520/623-4301, www.suntran.com, 6am-7pm Mon.-Fri., 8am-5pm Sat.-Sun., $1.25) bus line, with stops all over the Old Pueblo. Children under five ride free.

Modern Streetcar

The **Sun Link Modern Streetcar** (www.sunlinkstreetcar.com, 7am-10pm Mon.-Wed., 7am-2am Thurs.-Fri., 8am-2am Sat., 8am-8pm Sun., $1.50 one-way, 24-hour pass $4) is a sleek light-rail system that traverses several city-center neighborhoods. It has transformed the Old Pueblo's downtown and entertainment districts since it opened in 2014.

The railcars shoot through the streets of downtown, 4th Avenue, and Main Gate Square near the University of Arizona to the Mercado District west of I-10—connecting the neighborhoods. The seven streetcars, each with 180-passenger capacity, run the route every 10-15 minutes in the daytime and every 20 minutes in the evening, making 17 stops along the way.

Cab and Shuttle

Cab rides can get expensive in Tucson because everything is so spread out. Expect to spend $20 for a ride from midtown to restaurants and bars downtown or on 4th Avenue. **Uber** and **Lyft** also operate in Tucson and may be cheaper.

Cool Cabs (520/308-1536, www. thecoolcab.com) operates locally and provides rides to and from the airport for a fair price. You can reserve a ride on its website or call them. Also try **Yellow Cabs** (520/300-0000, www.yellowcabaz.com), which also accepts reservations or calls. Expect to pay $30-40 depending on where you're headed in town. Unless you're staying near the airport, the ride will be at least 10-15 miles and take 20-30 minutes.

Groome Transportation (520/795-6771, http://groometransportation.com, $45) offers 18 daily trips between Tucson and Phoenix Sky Harbor International Airport.

Santa Cruz Valley

Heading south from Tucson on I-19, you enter the Santa Cruz Valley, a storied landscape through which the Spanish took some of their first steps into the vast north.

This is the land of the trailblazing priest Eusebio Kino, who in the later 1600s traveled through Pimeria Alta, the "land of the upper Pima," as the Spanish called this region, referring to one of the many Indigenous populations that called the valley home for eons before Europeans arrived. The Tohono O'odham people, formerly called the Papago, live here; their San Xavier Indian Reservation stretches out west of I-19. Kino, a Jesuit with a penchant for roughing it, founded several missions in Pimeria Alta, two of which, on the Arizona side of the border, still stand and still hold masses. One of the oldest continually inhabited villages in North America can be found at Tubac, now an artist colony and tourist stop where they celebrate the legacy of the Basque adventurer Juan Bautista de Anza II, who attempted to tame the valley and its hostile Apaches and eventually led the expedition west that established San Francisco, California.

The valley has always been a ranching area, even during Kino's time, and after the Gadsden Purchase several Anglo ranches were established and thrived for generations. Much of the former ranch land has been sold to establish conservation areas and wildlife refuges in this rare ecosystem. During the Cold War, intercontinental ballistic missiles (ICBMs) were cocked and ready in underground missile silos throughout the valley, an era celebrated with a museum. The area has also long been home to large open-pit copper mines, and the towering tailings piles rise like ziggurats to the west of the retirement community of Green Valley. And in Ambos Nogales—the name meaning, roughly, "both Nogaleses"—you'll witness the teeming U.S.-Mexico border region in all its fascinating chaos.

The Santa Rita Mountains to the east attract subtropical birds migrating from Mexico and points farther south to their sky island heights, a fact that in turn attracts birding enthusiasts from around the world. You can hike to the top of 9,453-foot Mount Wrightson and see the whole world on a clear day, or stay in one of Madera Canyon's small lodges and take a tour of an observatory where scientists are trying to discover the beginnings of the universe.

GREEN VALLEY AND SAHUARITA

Sahuarita is a bedroom community about 15 miles south of Tucson, the site of the largest pecan-growing operation in the world. Green Valley is one of Arizona's best retirement communities, home to 25,000 year-round residents and many more part-time

Santa Cruz Valley

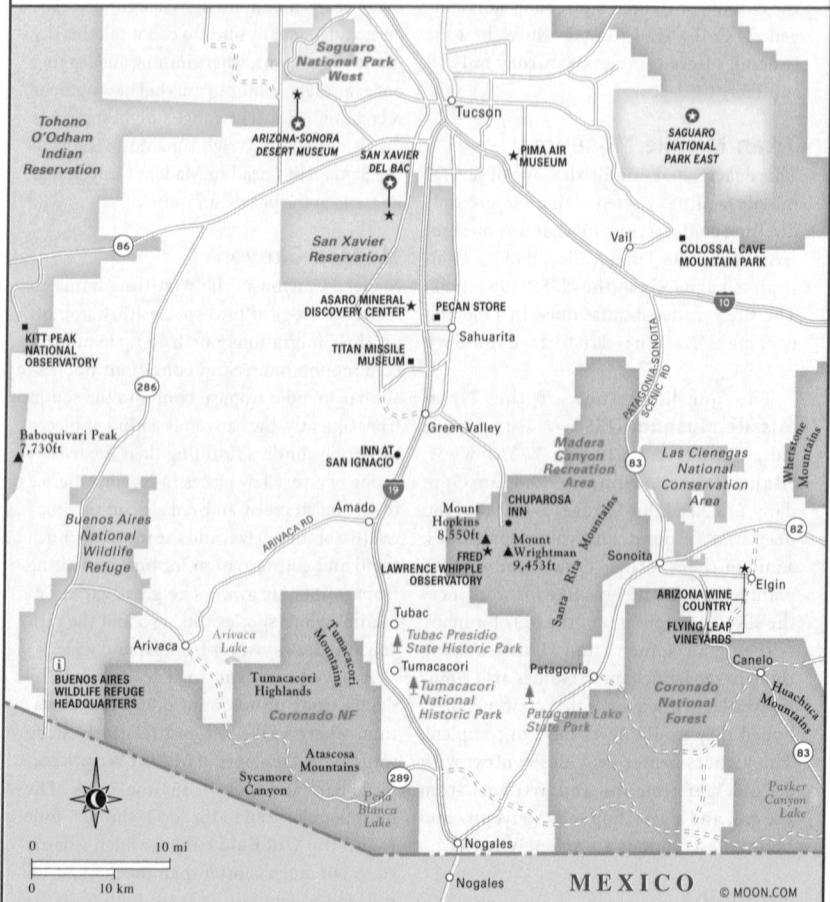

snowbirds from the frozen north. Together the two towns make up a relatively large population center between the dry Santa Cruz River to the east and the copper mines to the west.

Asarco Mineral Discovery Center

Take Exit 80 from I-19 and drive west of the casino to reach the **Asarco Mineral Discovery Center** (1421 W. Pima Mine Rd., Sahuarita, 520/625-8233, www.asarco.

com, 9am-3pm Tues.-Sat., exhibitions free, mine tour $10 adults, $7 ages 5-12). This illuminating sight, using exhibits, old mining equipment, and films, explains how all the huge piles of dirt flanking the valley's west side got there.

The copper in the Santa Cruz Valley takes a lot of earth-moving to get at; a one-hour bus tour will take you up into the hills to the sprawling Mission Mine to show you how it's done. From the bus you'll see the vast pit and the postapocalyptic landscape created by large-scale copper mining, and you'll drive through a working mill. Back at the Discovery Center, a gift shop sells souvenirs. Call ahead to make sure the tour is being offered; it runs Saturday only in summer.

Titan Missile Museum

This deactivated missile site, one of several missile facilities staffed with underground-dwelling cold warriors in what was once referred to as the Titan Valley, had its Titan II aimed squarely at the USSR 1963-1982. The site was decommissioned in 1986 and became a National Historic Landmark in 1994.

The one-hour tour of the **Titan Missile Museum** (1580 W. Duval Mine Rd., Sahuarita, 520/625-7736, www.titanmissilemuseum.org, 9:45am-5pm daily, $13.50 adults, $10 ages 5-12) takes you deep underground, and volunteer guides, some of them former crew members, explain what daily life was like for workers at the silo. The highlight of the tour for many is seeing an actual Titan II still waiting there in the launch duct. Guides also simulate the launch sequence that crew members hoped they would never have to complete. The visitors center provides context with a Cold War timeline and artifacts from the era, and a gift shop sells souvenirs and books. Reservations are strongly advised.

Shopping

Drive east on Sahuarita Road past the pecan groves—roll down your windows and feel how much cooler the trees make the air—and you'll come to the **Pecan Store** (1625 E. Sahuarita Rd., Sahuarita, 520/791-2062 or 800/327-3226, www.pecanstore.com, 10am-4pm Mon.-Fri.), an outlet of Farmers Investment Corp., which operates one of the largest pecan-growing and packaging operations in the world—some 400,000 trees on 5,000 acres—and sells, of course, pecans and pecan accessories.

SANTA RITA MOUNTAINS

Black bears, mountain lions, ring-tailed cats, deer, and too many birds to count call this sky island range home, where mining and logging once were legitimate pursuits but now outdoor recreation rules. The range's highest peak is 9,453-foot Mount Wrightson. Most visitors to the Santa Ritas head to Madera Canyon and its trails to the peak's summit.

Madera Canyon

Madera Canyon is the part-time home to many subtropical bird species that stop off on their migrations north to mate along a cool mountain creek in conditions not dissimilar to more tropical climes to the south. Consequently, the canyon is a kind of mecca for serious birders fulfilling their life lists. It is one of a very few places in North America to see the fat green-and-red elegant trogon, a relative of the quetzal and the source of much thrill and consternation for birders visiting from points far away. The great variety of hummingbird species flitting about the canyon also draws visitors from far and wide.

A paved two-lane road leads from the desert floor up to about 6,000 feet elevation, where well-used and relatively steep trails climb the slopes of **Mount Wrightson** to its bare and rocky 9,453-foot peak. The most popular trail to the top is the 10.8-mile round-trip **Old Baldy Trail,** which is fairly steep but much shorter than the gradual 16-mile round-trip **Super Trail.** Both trails are well marked, heavily used, and start near the Mount Wrightson Picnic Area at the top of the canyon. Both trails also take you over **Josephine Saddle,** at about 7,000 feet elevation, and **Baldy Saddle,** not far below the peak at 8,000 feet, which make good places to stop and rest. At Josephine Saddle make sure to look at the makeshift memorial to a group of Boy Scouts who got caught in a snowstorm on the mountain in the 1950s and never returned. If you're coming up the Super Trail, stop and rest at Sprung Spring just before you reach the saddle, which has delicious mountain water trickling from a spigot.

To see the lushness that a little trickling water can inspire, hit the 5.8-mile **Bog Spring-Kent Spring Loop,** which leads over some old mining roads in the lower reaches of the canyon onto some fairly steep and skinny trails along a windswept ridge, providing spectacular views of the valley below. The trail eventually leads deep into the forest, where sycamores thrive on the edges of green and spongy clearings. Also try the 4.4-mile one-way **Nature Trail,** a fairly steep but relatively easy way to see the entire canyon, from the desert grasslands at its entrance at the **Proctor Parking Area,** where you can pick up the trail, all the way to the woodlands at the top. Small signs along the way point out notable flora and fauna, and the highest point on the trail, high above the canyon floor, offers a unique perspective.

The average summertime temperature in the canyon is about 85°F, cooler by 15-20 degrees on any given summer day than it is down in the valley. It gets cold in the high country October-April, and it regularly snows in deep winter. Madera Canyon is an extremely popular day-use area and hiking destination for Tucson and Santa Cruz Valley residents, so expect to see quite a few people on the trails and using the three developed picnic areas, all of which have tables, restrooms, and charcoal grills. You can pick up a trail map at any of the lodges in the canyon, or you can get one at the welcome station at the canyon's entrance, but it is staffed irregularly. There's a $5 per car user fee, or you can purchase a $20 annual pass.

Mount Hopkins Fred Lawrence Whipple Observatory

The Smithsonian Institution operates the **Fred Lawrence Whipple Observatory** atop 8,550-foot Mount Hopkins, where astronomers take advantage of the dark Southern Arizona sky to scan space for very faint objects. The **MMT,** the largest single-mirror telescope in North America, is one of four you can see up close during a six-hour tour of the facility (Mon., Wed., and Fri. mid-Mar.-Nov., $10 adults, $5 ages 6-12, no children under 6). It's a good idea to make reservations far in advance. The **visitors center** (520/670-5707, www.cfa.harvard.edu, 8:30am-4:30pm Mon.-Fri.) near Amado has displays about the work being done on the mountain and the history of the telescope.

Accommodations and Camping

Madera Canyon used to be dotted with summer homes and getaway cabins, but beginning in the 1970s the U.S. Forest Service tore them down and converted the treasured ecosystem into a federal recreation area. Now only a scattered few homes remain on historic mining claims. Three of the lasting structures are lodges that welcome visitors year-round. As you're driving up the canyon's only road, you first come upon the **Santa Rita Lodge** (520/625-8746, www.santaritalodge.com, $138-182), offering several casitas and freestanding cabins with private decks. The lodge, the oldest in the canyon, has beautiful grounds along Madera Creek, where feeders attract birds and there are benches for viewing. There's also a gift shop, but no food, so bring your own or plan to eat in Green Valley, about 12 miles away. March-May the lodge can fix you up with an experienced birding guide (by appointment, $20 pp). The tours start early and last about four hours.

Next you'll see the A-frame **Madera Kubo** (520/625-2908, www.maderakubo.com, $145-160), with four cozy cabins and a gift shop but no food. Near the top of the canyon is the ★ **Chuparosa Inn** (520/393-7370, www.chuparosainn.com, 2-night minimum, $200-275), with four beautiful rooms, a great bird-watching area, a barbecue, and friendly hosts. The Chuparosa serves a hearty continental breakfast, but you're on your own for lunch and dinner.

If you prefer to rough it, the **Bog Springs Campground** (turn left off Madera Canyon Rd. at the sign, 520/281-2296, www.fs.usda.

gov/coronado, $10) has campsites year-round on a first-come, first-served basis.

Information

The area is managed by the Coronado National Forest Nogales Ranger District (303 Old Tucson Rd., Nogales, 520/281-2296, 8am-4:30pm Mon.-Fri.). The forest's main office in Tucson (300 W. Congress St., 520/388-8300, www.fs.usda.gov/coronado, 8am-4:30pm Mon.-Fri.) has information on this area as well. From I-19, exit at Ruby Road, then turn east.

BUENOS AIRES WILDLIFE REFUGE

This remote 118,000-acre refuge preserves large swaths of endangered semidesert grassland, home to the pronghorn. The refuge's flagship program was once the reintroduction of the rare masked bobwhite quail to the grasslands, but the program was transferred to a private organization in 2007. Its proximity to the U.S.-Mexico border has caused some trouble on the refuge, and portions are indefinitely closed to the public because of smuggling activity.

One the most accessible portions of the refuge is the Arivaca Cienega, a swamp-like desert wetland just outside the tiny village of Arivaca. The easy two-mile loop trail includes boardwalks over the wetter portions; birds, frogs, and snakes abound. Take Arivaca Road about 20 miles from I-19's Exit 48 until you see the sign for the Cienega, just east of Arivaca. At the western end of town, turn at the Y and drive 2.5 miles to Arivaca Creek, also managed by the refuge, where there's easy creek-side hiking among cottonwood and mesquite. Far off to the northwest in the Baboquivari Mountains is Brown Canyon, a riparian area accessible only with a guide and by appointment.

To get to refuge headquarters (520/823-4251, www.fws.gov, 7:30am-4pm Mon.-Fri. June-mid-Aug., 7:30am-4pm daily

1: Mount Wrightson 2: in the Santa Rita Mountains

mid-Aug.-May), go through Arivaca to AZ 286, head south four miles, and then turn left at milepost 7.5. There's also a satellite office that's open intermittently in downtown Arivaca, next to the mercantile.

TUBAC AND TUMACACORI

These two villages along the Santa Cruz River are steeped in the history of the Spanish expeditions in Pimeria Alta. Padre Kino established the mission at Tumacacori in 1691, and Tubac, a Piman village, became a mission farm and ranch. By the 1730s Spanish colonists had arrived from the south to farm and ranch the fertile river valley. In 1751 the violent Piman revolt convinced the Spanish crown to establish the Presidio San Ignacio de Tubac, founded the next year. The famous Basque Juan Bautista de Anza II was the second commander of the presidio, and in 1776 led the first of two overland journeys to establish a fort at San Francisco, California, taking along about 60 colonists from Tubac. In 1860, silver strikes nearby briefly made Tubac the largest town in the Arizona Territory. It eventually fell into obscurity but was discovered again as an artist colony during the second half of the 20th century, and today its many galleries and shops are a draw for travelers and locals alike.

Crowds flock to Tubac during the weeklong Tubac Festival of the Arts in February, during which artisans and artists from around the country set up booths. Music and the smell of greasy delicious food fill the village.

Tubac Presidio State Historic Park

Arizona's first state park, founded in 1959, Tubac Presidio State Historic Park (520/398-2252, http://azstateparks.com, 9am-5pm daily, $5 adults, $2 ages 7-13) preserves the history and foundations of the Presidio San Ignacio de Tubac. You can see the fort's original foundation and peruse a museum that explains what life was like for Native Americans, settlers, and soldiers. Guided tours and hands-on interpretation programs are available on request. The park's annual **Anza Days** celebration (3rd week of Oct.) honors the fort's most famous commander with historical re-creations, music, and food. The Tubaquenos, a historical reenactment society, put on living history demonstrations at the park (1pm-4pm Sun. Oct.-Mar.).

Tumacacori National Historic Park

Padre Kino founded **Mission San Jose de Tumacacori** in 1691, and much of it still stands today on 310-acre **Tumacacori National Historic Park** (Frontage Rd., 3 miles south of Tubac, 520/398-2341, www. nps.gov/tuma, 9am-5pm daily, $5 over age 16). Explore the mission and its grounds, including an old graveyard, an orchard, and a recreated Piman shelter. A museum tells the history of the mission and Pimeria Alta, and most days you can buy tortillas and refried beans made right before your eyes in the traditional fashion. A gift shop sells a wide assortment of books on local history.

The mission at Tumacacori still holds masses on holidays, but the two other missions protected by the park are mostly in ruins. The ruins of **Mission San Cayetano de Calabazas,** normally closed, can be visited on monthly guided tours ($10 pp); reservations are required (520/398-2341).

Juan Bautista de Anza National Historic Trail

Between the presidio and the mission is a 4.5-mile portion of the **Juan Bautista de Anza National Historic Trail,** the route used by colonists and their stock animals from northern Mexico to Northern California in 1775-1776. It makes an easy and shady riverside hike, though there's often a lot of trash along the route as a result of illegal migration and seasonal flooding of the northward-flowing Santa Cruz River. The route crosses private ranch land, and you're bound to see cattle. It leads from just outside the state park to just outside the national park, and it's the route used historically to travel between the two landmarks.

Shopping

Tubac has more than 100 shops and galleries, many of them selling Mexican and South American imports. Pick up an illustrated map of the shopping district at any of the shops or at the visitors center.

Food

Open since 1944 and still run by the same family, **Wisdom's Café** (1931 E. Frontage Rd., Tumacacori, 520/398-2397, www. wisdomscafe.com, 11am-8pm Tues.-Sat., $11-25) may be the best restaurant in the Santa Cruz Valley, serving Mexican food from handed-down family recipes. Don't miss the famous fruit burrito for dessert. Head south on Frontage Road toward the mission and look for the big chicken statue out front.

Accommodations

Historic upscale **Tubac Golf Resort and Spa** (1 Av. de Otero, Tubac, 520/398-2211, www.tubacgolfresort.com, $259-329) has casitas and guest rooms of various sizes and styles, two restaurants, a pool, a hot tub, and spa treatments. Once part of the sprawling Otero cattle ranch, it opened on 500 lush acres along the Santa Cruz River in 1959. Bing Crosby was one of the original owners. New owners completed a $40 million restoration of the historic gem in 2007. Check the website for package deals; prices drop considerably in summer.

The **Tubac Country Inn** (12 Burruel St., Tubac, 520/398-3178, www.tubaccountryinn. com, $135-175) is in the heart of the village and offers suites with kitchenettes, TVs, and Wi-Fi.

Tumacacori Highlands

This huge wilderness of semidesert grasslands, rugged mountains, and riparian canyons west of the valley can best be accessed using Ruby Road (take Exit 12 from I-19), just south of Tumacacori. West about 11 miles is **Peña Blanca Lake,** where bass and cat-fish can be caught but not eaten because of their high mercury content. There's a boat ramp and a trail around the lake. Branch off on Forest Road 39 for the **White Rock Campground,** with year-round campsites ($5) but no water. Continue another five miles along Forest Road 39 to the trailhead for the **Atascosa Lookout Trail.** The popular steep trail to the 6,255-foot peak, a six-mile round-trip, takes you to a decommissioned fire look-out. For a few months in 1968 it was staffed by writer **Edward Abbey.**

On Forest Road 39, about 10 miles in from Peña Blanca Lake, a sign points to the trail-head for the **Sycamore Canyon Trail,** which leads deep into a watered canyon. Steep walls are dotted with saguaro, white sycamore trees shade the creek bed, and jagged rocks jut out from above. It's a five-mile one-way hike to the U.S.-Mexico border, marked by a barbed-wire fence. The trail isn't always well marked as the creek often overtakes it, and you will certainly have to wade in places. During the rainy season, some sections may be impass-able. The canyon is a major corridor for drug smuggling, and you are likely to see a lot of trash and other evidence of the trade.

The Border Region

Anywhere you are in Cochise or Santa Cruz Counties, you're never more than a few miles from Mexico. Small towns like Bisbee and Douglas each have a Mexican twin right across the line, and traffic between the two generally flows pretty easily, although they are fraternal twins; the Mexican counterparts are larger and more populous. The easiest way to visit our neighbors to the south for the day is to walk across the border at the Mariposa Port of Entry in Nogales, Arizona, about an hour south of Tucson on I-19. The Arizona side of what locals call Ambos Nogales (Both Nogaleses) is a sleepy government center and produce-warehousing town of about 20,000, while the sprawling industrial city just across the border has about 300,000 residents. Most visitors stick to the tourist-friendly blocks just beyond the port of entry.

Farther west you'll find the desert home-land of the Tohono O'odham people, and to the east the grasslands and cottonwood forests of the Mountain Empire.

NOGALES
Nogales, Mexico, Tourist District
Nogales, Sonora, Mexico, is a modern ship-ping center for manufactured goods and produce, but it's also a very popular tourist destination. It's easy to get here: Just walk across the international border in downtown Nogales, Arizona, after parking at one of the many pay lots (about $4 per day) near the port of entry. There's a tourist area of about a square mile just south of the border, with res-taurants, curio shops, and drugstores. You can drive into Mexico, but the lines of cars driving north into the United States are long and slow. If you need a ride, there are cabs everywhere; drivers speak English and accept U.S. dollars.

There's lots of leather and silver items for sale in the tourist section, as well as Mexican handicrafts, Day of the Dead items, ceram-ics, Mexican vanilla, and cheap booze. There are *farmacias,* dentists, and doctor offices on every block, and their services are generally offered for a fraction of the price of their U.S. counterparts.

Nogales, Arizona
This small town, like its cross-border sister named for the walnut trees that once thrived in the area, has long been Santa Cruz County's seat. The beautiful old shiny-domed neoclas-sical **Santa Cruz County Courthouse** (2150 N. Congress Dr.), built in 1904 of locally quar-ried stone, lends it a historic feel that belies

the constant activity of a border town. The 1914 Old City Hall building now houses the Pimeria Alta Historical Society (Grand Ave. and Crawford St., 520/287-4621, 10am-4pm Wed.-Sun., free), with several interesting exhibits and artifacts on the history of the region. The town's historic downtown along Morley Avenue has a few stores that were established in the early 1900s and are still run by descendants of pioneer merchants.

Food

With dozens of authentic Mexican restaurants within an easy walk across the border, don't spend too much time eating on the Arizona side. If you insist, try the steaks and Sonoran-style food at Las Vigas Steak Ranch (180 W. Loma St., at Fiesta Market, off Arroyo Blvd., 520/287-6641, 10:30am-8:30pm Tues.-Thurs., 10:30am-9:30pm Fri., 9am-9:30pm Sat., 8am-8pm Sun., $19-25) or the excellent Mexican seafood at Cocina La Ley (226 W. 3rd St., 520/287-4555, http://cocinalaley.com, 8am-4pm daily, $5-15).

Across the border, the main north-south street is Obregón, two blocks west of the border-crossing station. Popular restaurants include La Roca (84010 Plutarco Elias Calles, 520/313-6316, www.larocarestaurant.com, 11am-6pm Mon.-Tues., 11am-midnight Wed., 8am-midnight Thurs.-Sat., 8am-6pm Sun. June-Oct., 11am-midnight Mon.-Wed., 8am-midnight Thurs.-Sat., 8am-6pm Sun. Nov.-May, $16-22), east of the railroad tracks in downtown; El Toro, a steak house, about two miles south of the border on López Mateos; and La Palapa, a no-frills seafood place 1.5 miles south on López Mateos. The Oasis has an outdoor balcony overlooking where two main thoroughfares, López Mateos and Obregón, merge; it is reminiscent of Times Square, but much smaller. Sit here to enjoy shrimp in a warm cheese sauce and watch the traffic.

Accommodations

There are several chain hotels in Nogales, Arizona, along Mariposa Road and along Grand Avenue, both major thoroughfares. If you're looking for something special, the historic Hacienda Corona de Guevavi (348 S. River Rd., 520/287-6503, www.haciendacorona.com, $199-239), along the Santa Cruz River, once hosted John Wayne and other stars. The inn features murals by Salvador Corona, a famous artist and bullfighter, and offers B&B-style guest rooms and stand-alone casitas. It has a swimming pool and offers horseback riding, stargazing, and many other activities.

Information

For visitor information, go to the Nogales-Santa Cruz Chamber of Commerce (23 W. Kino Park Place, 520/287-3685, www.nogaleschamber.com, 9am-5pm Mon.-Fri.).

There's a U.S. Consulate (Calle San José s/n, Fraccionamiento Los Álamos, Nogales, Sonora, tel. +52/631-980-0522, U.S. tel. 844/528-6611, 8am-3pm Mon.-Fri.; after-hours emergencies: Mex. tel. +52/555-080-2000, U.S. tel. 301/985-8843) in Nogales, Sonora, on Calle San José, about five miles south of the border. You must have a valid passport or passport card to cross into and return from Mexico.

THE WESTERN DESERT

Tohono O'odham Nation

Southwest of Tucson is the vast desert homeland of the Tohono O'odham people. You can head out to this 4,400-square-mile borderland reservation via AZ 286 west of Tucson, but there isn't much here except gorgeous, mostly untouched desert. Straddling the border, the reservation is a popular, albeit deadly, corridor for undocumented migrants heading north, and dozens die crossing the area every year. Only the O'odham know how to live out here.

KITT PEAK NATIONAL OBSERVATORY

About 90 minutes west of Tucson along AZ 86 and AZ 386 (follow the signs), you'll find one of Southern Arizona's famous observatories.

Kitt Peak National Observatory (AZ 386, 520/318-8726, www.noao.edu, 9am-3:45pm daily) operates 23 telescopes—the world's largest collection—atop the 6,875-foot peak in the reservation's Quinlan Mountains. Docent-led tours (10am, 11:30am, 1:30pm daily, $2 adults, $1 over age 6) last about an hour, or pick up a pamphlet and take a self-guided tour. The visitors center has exhibits on astronomy and a gift shop selling star- and planet-related items and O'odham baskets. Far to the south, look for 7,700-foot Baboquivari Peak, the home of I'itoi, the tribe's sacred elder-brother god.

EVENTS

During the first weekend in February, O'odham cowboys join in the All Indian Rodeo and Fair, during which locals set up food booths, play music, march in a parade, dance, and show off and sell their crafts.

FOOD

The reservation capital, Sells, is a small outpost 58 miles southwest of Tucson on AZ 86. There's a supermarket, a few businesses, and a school. Try the chimichangas and other Mexican, American, and Native American fare at the Papago Café (AZ 86, 520/383-3510, 8am-9pm Mon.-Fri., $5-10, cash only) along AZ 86.

Continue through the thick desert west on AZ 86 and then north on AZ 85 and you'll hit Ajo, a copper mining town with a few restaurants. It's a good place to see the scars that strip-mining leaves on the land.

Organ Pipe Cactus National Monument

Along the border, south of Ajo on AZ 85, past the tiny town of Why, you'll find rugged and beautiful Organ Pipe Cactus National Monument. It protects pretty much all the organ pipe cacti in North America, along with many other cactus species, and is a popular place for spring wildflowers. The Kris Eggle Visitor Center (520/387-6849) is open 8am-5pm daily. There's a campground ($12)

with 208 sites that offers drinking water but no hookups or facilities. The 21-mile Ajo Mountain Drive, a twisty dirt road that's usually passable, will take you into the monument's center, where you can see the many-armed cacti up close.

THE MOUNTAIN EMPIRE: PATAGONIA, SONOITA, AND ELGIN

With an average elevation of 4,000-5,000 feet and average annual rainfall around 20 inches, the grasslands and creek beds of the Mountain Empire on the eastern side of the Santa Rita range are much cooler than Tucson, and the landscape is unlike any other in Arizona. The towns here are tiny but serve an increasingly popular tourist spot; small out-of-the-way inns are plentiful. In the center of Patagonia, the largest town in the area (pop. 800), is a yellow train depot, built in 1900, and there's a butterfly garden nearby. A few shops sell unique locally made items and other treasures.

Transportation

There are two ways to get to the grassland seas and cottonwood forests of the Mountain Empire, a historic ranching and mining district between the Santa Rita, Patagonia, Mustang, and Huachuca Mountains. If you're coming from the Santa Cruz Valley, take AZ 82 from Nogales 19 miles northeast to Patagonia and then on to Sonoita, where AZ 83 branches north to I-10. If you're coming from Tucson, take I-10 east to AZ 83.

Telles Grotto Shrine

Just southwest of Patagonia along AZ 82, near milepost 15.9, is shrine built into the rock face of the mountain. It's worth taking a few minutes to climb the steps and look inside, where there will likely be candles burning and messages written to the dead. The shrine was built in the 1940s by the Telles family, whose matriarch vowed she would construct and maintain the shrine if her five boys returned safely from World War II. They did, and the shrine is still in use today.

Patagonia Lake State Park

About seven miles south of Patagonia on AZ 82 is Southern Arizona's largest lake, 2.5-mile-long **Patagonia Lake** (400 Patagonia Lake Rd., 520/287-6965, http://azstateparks.com, 4am-10pm daily, $15-20 per car), where you can rent a boat; swim; lie around Boulder Beach; water-ski (not on weekends); fish for bass, bluegill, and catfish; and hike in the 5,000-acre Sonoita Creek State Natural Area. The campground has 72 campsites and 34 hookups ($27 with water and electric, boat sites $17-20), and there are boat launches, restrooms, showers, a dump station, and a camp supply store. In March, crowds come to see the annual Mariachi Festival. From Nogales, head 12 miles northeast on AZ 82, then turn left at the sign and drive 4 miles to the park entrance.

Patagonia-Sonoita Creek Preserve

The Nature Conservancy protects a Fremont cottonwood-Gooding willow riparian forest—one of the best and last remaining examples of this lush landscape in Arizona—on about 750 acres along perennial Sonoita Creek. A small green paradise, the **Patagonia-Sonoita Creek Preserve** (150 Blue Heaven Rd., Patagonia, 520/394-2400, www.nature.org, 7:30am-4pm Wed.-Sun. Oct.-Mar., 6:30am-4pm Wed.-Sun. Apr.-Sept., $6 pp) has six miles of easy trails along the creek and through the forest of 100-foot-tall, 130-year-old cottonwoods—the biggest and oldest in the country. The birding is excellent, and it's not uncommon to see deer, bobcats, toads, and frogs in this verdant preserve. Friendly Conservancy volunteers lead nature walks (9am Sat.). This is an extremely rare ecosystem, once abundant in Southern Arizona but now all but disappeared.

Wine Country

With soil and growing conditions often likened to those in Burgundy, France, the Sonoita-Elgin grasslands have become a well-known wine-making region. It's fun to drive through the open landscape to sample wines, but consider taking along a designated driver.

In Sonoita, just east of the crossroads, on the east side of AZ 82, you'll find a tasting room at **Dos Cabezas Wineworks** (3248 AZ 82, 520/841-1193, www.doscabezas.com, 10:30am-4:30pm Thurs.-Mon.).

About eight miles east, on the road to Elgin, is the tasting room at **Callaghan Vineyards** (336 Elgin Rd., 520/455-5322, www.callaghanvineyards.com, 11am-4pm Thurs.-Sun.). Right down the street is the tasting room at **Flying Leap Vineyards and Distillery** (342 Elgin Rd., 888/431-5777, www.flyingleapvineyards.com, 11am-4pm daily), which creates some of the best wines in Arizona. Sample the innovative wines, including a refreshing rosé and an excellent malbec, made in partnership with a vineyard in Chile. The wines are made by a group of former fighter pilots using grapes grown on-site. The **Village of Elgin Winery** (471 Elgin Rd., 520/455-9309, www.elginwines.com, 9am-8pm Thurs.-Sat.), near town, also offers tastings. In April, locals turn out in Elgin for the annual **Blessing of the Vine Festival.**

Another tasting room is located three miles south of Elgin at **Sonoita Vineyards** (290 Elgin-Canelo Rd., 520/455-5893, www.sonoitavineyards.com, 10am-4pm daily).

Food and Accommodations

The Velvet Elvis Pizza Co. (292 Naugle Ave., Patagonia, 520/394-2102, 4pm-8:30pm Wed., 11:30am-8pm Thurs.-Sat., 11:30am-8:30pm Sun., $5-25) serves fabulous pizza among interesting pictures of the King and the Virgin. The **Steak Out Restaurant & Saloon** (AZ 82 and AZ 83, Sonoita, 520/455-5205, www.azsteakout.com, 5pm-9pm Mon.-Thurs., 5pm-10pm Fri., 11am-10pm Sat.-Sun.,

---

1: Tumacacori National Historic Park in Santa Cruz Valley **2:** Flying Leap Vineyards and Distillery **3:** Allen Street in Tombstone **4:** Kitt Peak National Observatory

$10-25) has pretty good steaks, ribs, and other hearty favorites.

The Sonoita Inn (3243 AZ 82, Sonoita, 520/455-5935, www.sonoitainn.com, $109-149) at the crossroads of AZ 82 and AZ 83, has 18 rooms with Western ambience, all with great views of the grasslands and mountains.

Southeastern Arizona

The small towns in southeastern Arizona offer many sights and attractions, mostly of the Old West variety, and are good bases for exploring the spectacular natural areas around them, mostly of the riparian and mountainous variety.

THE COCHISE TRAIL

Named after the indomitable Apache chief Cochise, who waged war against the United States in the 1860s and 1870s, the region was also home to the most famous Apache of them all, the warrior and medicine man Geronimo, the last of his kind to surrender to the reservation. Miners, ranchers, outlaws, and even a few gunfighters lived here too, and their brief reign is celebrated in touristy Tombstone. But many people come for the vistas, the birds, and the trails that can be found in the accessible Huachuca and Chiricahua mountain ranges.

Transportation

The Cochise Trail and its environs are best traveled by car. If you want to avoid the interstate, a good road trip is to head east of Tucson on I-10 and then south on AZ 83, through the grasslands of the Mountain Empire to the heights of the Coronado National Memorial (on some dirt roads), into the Huachuca Mountains, and then on to the San Pedro River Valley. Exit at AZ 90, AZ 80, or U.S. 191 to make loop drives to all the best sights in the area.

Sierra Vista and Fort Huachuca

Much of the war against the Apaches was fought from Fort Huachuca, founded in 1877 in a canyon that had historically served as an escape route for the West's final holdout tribe. Currently the fort is a major center for military intelligence training. Both stories are told at two museums here. The Fort Huachuca Museum (Bldg. 41401, 520/533-5736, 9am-4pm Tues.-Sat., $5 donation) has exhibits about army life on the Southwestern frontier, the infamous battles with the Chiricahua Apaches, and the Buffalo Soldiers—African American cavalry men whose story is one of the most fascinating of the West. Two doors down from the Fort Huachuca Museum, the U.S. Army Intelligence Museum (9am-4pm Tues.-Sat., $5 donation) tells the 200-year story of the army's underrated intelligence corps. Check the website or call before visiting to learn about procedures for accessing the military base where the museums are located.

The military town of Sierra Vista, the largest in the valley and the fort's host, sits at the base of the Huachuca Mountains and has little charm. There are a lot of well-known chain hotels and restaurants, and it's close to the southern end of the San Pedro River. It makes a good base to spend time in the mountains, but otherwise it's just a drive-through.

FOOD AND ACCOMMODATIONS

There is no shortage of chain hotels and restaurants in Sierra Vista, especially along Fry Boulevard, the town's main drag. If you want to stay in the mountains—and who wouldn't?—there are several bed-and-breakfasts nestled in the range's canyons. The riverside Casa de San Pedro (8933 S. Yellow Lane, Hereford, 520/366-1300 or 888/257-2050, www.bedandbirds.com,

The Cochise Trail

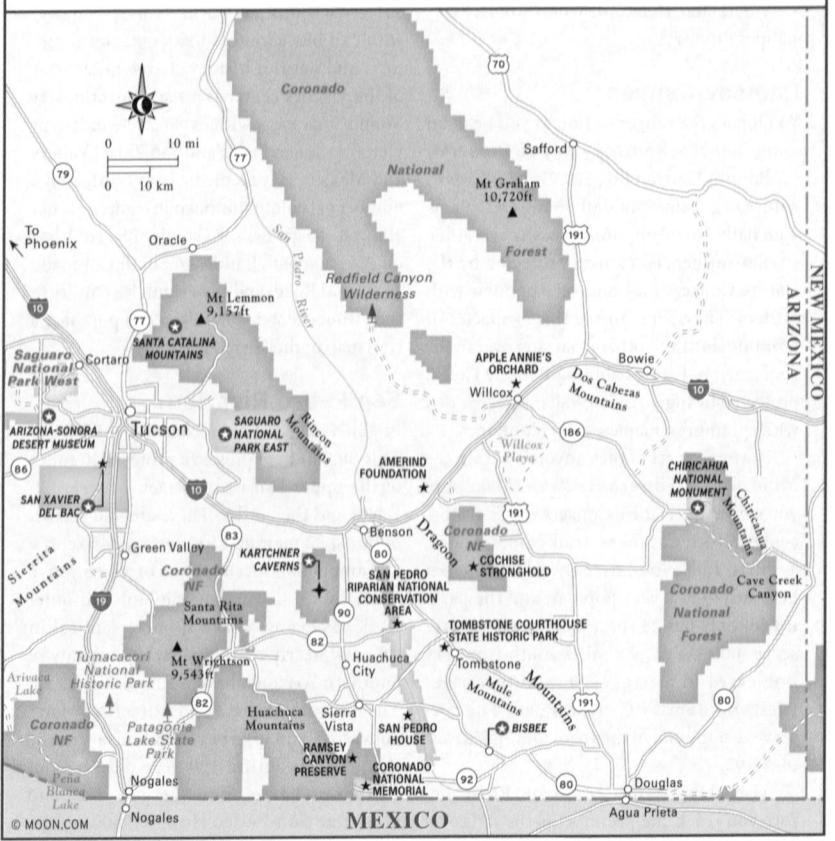

$175-295) is a territorial-style home with a central courtyard, a pool, a hot tub, and all kinds of activities geared toward birders and nature lovers. **Ramsey Canyon Inn** (29 Ramsey Canyon Rd., Hereford, 520/378-3010, www.ramseycanyoninn.com, $135-175), just outside the Ramsey Canyon Preserve, has six rooms named for hummingbird species, delicious breakfasts, and a setting that can't be beat.

INFORMATION

Check out the **Sierra Vista Convention and Visitors Bureau** (1011 N. Coronado Dr., 520/417-6960 or 800/288-3861, http:// visit.sierravistaaz.gov, 9am-5pm daily) for information about this area.

Huachuca Mountains

Ranging in elevation from 3,934 feet at the base to 9,455 feet at the top of Miller Peak, the Huachucas are another of Southern Arizona's signature sky island ranges. You'll see the transition from semidesert grasslands up into arid scrub, then mixed oak forests, and cool ponderosa pine forests in the higher reaches. There are dozens of trails in the range, plus rough roads that lead deep into the outback. If you're looking to put together a backpacking or camping adventure, talk to the staff at the **Coronado National Forest Sierra Vista Ranger District** (4070 S. Av. Saracino, Hereford, 520/378-0311, 8am-4:30pm Mon.-Fri.).

Ramsey Canyon

You'll pass the ranger station as you head up to the 300-acre **Ramsey Canyon Preserve** (27 Ramsey Canyon Rd., 520/378-2785, www.nature.org, 8am-5pm daily Mar.-Oct., 9am-4pm daily Nov.-Feb., $6), an easily accessible stream-influenced canyon protected by the Nature Conservancy and very popular with birders. They come to see the 14 species of hummingbird and others that stop over in the cool canyon, fed by babbling Ramsey Creek, protected by high canyon walls, and crowded with sycamores, maples, and columbines.

The upper part of the canyon is within the **Miller Peak Wilderness Area.** Make sure you stop at the Nature Conservancy's visitors center, which has maps, trail guides, books, T-shirts, and helpful friendly volunteers. Get here early—it is very popular, and the parking lot only has 23 spaces. To reach the preserve, take AZ 92 six miles south from Fry Boulevard in Sierra Vista, and turn right (west) on Ramsey Canyon Road. The preserve is at the end of the road, four miles west of AZ 92.

Also along Ramsey Canyon Road, before you reach the preserve, is the **Arizona Folklore Preserve** (520/378-6165, www.arizonafolklore.com), a quaint little theater along the creek where Arizona State Balladeer and nationally known folkie Dolan Ellis and others put on acoustic folk concerts (2pm Sat.-Sun.). The shows are popular, so call ahead for a reservation.

Coronado National Memorial

Named in honor of the Spanish conquistador Francisco Vázquez de Coronado, who trudged north in 1540 searching for the Seven Cities of Cibola—which turned out to be nothing more than a few hardscrabble pueblos—this beautiful landscape along the U.S.-Mexico border, on the southern end of the Huachuca

Mountains, has a **visitors center** (Coronado Memorial Rd., 5 miles from AZ 92, 520/366-5515, www.nps.gov/coro, 9am-5pm daily) with exhibits about its namesake, local history, and natural history. Three miles west of the visitors center is a scenic overlook at Montezuma Pass, with expansive windswept views of the San Pedro and San Rafael Valleys and Mexico. Have a picnic here or hike on a number of trails to the lookout; camping is not allowed. To get here, go south of Sierra Vista on AZ 92 about 20 miles to South Coronado Memorial Road, and turn right; it's 5 miles to the visitors center, where you can purchase a trail map of the Huachucas ($5).

San Pedro Riparian National Conservation Area

This 58,000-acre preserve protects 40 miles of the upper San Pedro River, between St. David and the border. There are 400 species of birds, 82 mammal species, and 45 reptile and amphibian species, some of which you're likely to see if you stay vigilant and quiet while exploring. Beavers, once plentiful in the now nearly extinct riparian habitats of Southern Arizona, have been reintroduced. The **Friends of the San Pedro River** have converted a 1930s-era ranch house—in the shade of a beautiful 120-year-old Fremont cottonwood tree—into the gift shop and bookstore **San Pedro House** (9800 AZ 90, 520/508-4445, 9:30am-4:30pm daily), where you can pick up information and pamphlets for a self-guided river walk and other trails as well as get advice from the volunteers. You'll also find the **Murray Springs Clovis Site and Trail,** a kind of stone-age butcher shop frequented by the Clovis people 8,000-11,000 years ago. Scientists have dug up the fossils of several huge extinct mammals here, some of which are housed at the Museum of Natural History in New York.

★ Kartchner Caverns

Kartchner Caverns (2980 AZ-90, Benson, reservations 520/586-2283, information 520/586-4100, http://azstateparks.com,

8am-6pm daily, free with tour, $7 per vehicle up to 4 people, $2 per additional person) were discovered in the early 1970s by two cave-loving University of Arizona students. Gary Tenen and Randy Tufts knew right away that they had shimmied down a sinkhole in the Whetstone Mountains into caving immortality: The small wet cave, still forming drip by drip and thus deemed "alive," is one of the most spectacular water-on-rock formations of its kind. The explorers managed to keep their find a secret for several years in an effort to protect it from less responsible cavers. They called it Xanadu, after the English poet Samuel Taylor Coleridge's famous unfinished poem "Kubla Khan," a name given to the Throne Room's 58-foot main column, formed not so much by drips as by torrents of water flowing into the cave over millennia, producing the largest cave column in Arizona.

Eventually Tenen and Tufts told the property owners what they'd found, and the Kartchner family quickly joined those who wanted to see the cave preserved. A pre-tour film in the park's **Discovery Center** tells the whole story and explains what makes this cave unique. There's also an interesting museum and a gift shop; just outside the Discovery Center, a native-plant butterfly garden is worth a stroll.

There are two different tours you can take through the caverns. The **Big Room Tour** (1.75 hours, Oct. 15-Apr. 15, $23 adults, $13 ages 7-13, no children under 7) isn't offered in summer because a large colony of bats returns to the big room, as they have for eons, to give birth and rear their single pups. The **Rotunda/Throne Room Tour** (1.5 hours, year-round, $23 adults, $13 ages 7-13) is more than enough to satisfy even the most discerning spelunker.

Because the cave is still "alive," much is made of its conservation. Visitors are warned repeatedly not to touch any of the formations, and guides are not shy about telling kids to stand back and keep their hands to themselves. The tour information is repetitive if you've just watched the pre-tour movie.

If a tour of the cave isn't enough, the park offers campsites ($15-50) with electric hookups, water, a dump station, and restrooms with showers, as well as camping cabins ($35-75).

Benson

The **Horseshoe Café** (154 E. 4th St., Benson, 520/586-3303, 6am-8pm Mon.-Sat., 6am-2pm Sun., $5-15) serves pretty good steaks, burgers, and Mexican favorites—including big, sloppy, and tasty burritos. It's been around since 1938 and is right on Benson's main drag; it's decorated with all kinds of portraits of horses and a few antiques. Author Neil Miller, in his recent history of the nearby caverns, reports that every time Gary Tenen and Randy Tufts would visit their secret cave during the many years they kept the discovery a secret, they'd invariably stop at the Horseshoe for a bite to eat before returning to Tucson. For some reason, nobody in the restaurant seemed to think it was strange that the two spelunkers always came in covered in mud.

TOMBSTONE

Just outside the green and lush Mormon village of St. David, AZ 80 rises onto the dry scrubby plane where Ed Schieffelin struck silver in 1879, defying the soldiers who'd predicted he'd find only his own tombstone out here.

The town of the same name became one of the largest, rowdiest, and most deceptively sophisticated locales in the Southwest for a time, a place where legends were created daily by overheated journalists and where a 30-second gunfight of dubious legality became a defining frontier myth. These days about 1,600 residents call Tombstone home, many of them retirees or workers in some capacity for the town's tourism industry, which attracts visitors, many from Europe, year-round.

Boothill Graveyard

Reportedly, many of Tombstone's gunfighters, along with their victims, lie alongside prostitutes, settlers, and obscure passers-through in the hilltop **Boothill Graveyard**

(7:30am-6pm daily, donations welcome). You can walk among the more than 300 uniformly bland and refurbished graves and read short messages on some of them that illuminate what death was like on the frontier. It doesn't feel authentic in the least, despite claims to the contrary, but it is free. Boothill is just off AZ 80 at the north end of town.

Allen Street and National Historic District

Closed to cars and lined with wood-plank sidewalks, Western kitsch shops, and even a few genuine historical attractions, Allen Street *is* Tombstone to most people. There are several saloons and restaurants; faux-gunfighters and saloon girls (some of them with somewhat anachronistic tattoos) mill about next to the working stagecoach replicas of **Old Tombstone Historical Tours** (520/457-3018, http://oldtombstonetours. net, 9am-5pm daily, $10 adults, $5 children). The National Historic District includes several streets off of Allen Street, including Toughnut, Fremont, and 6th Streets.

Within this historic district is the **Tombstone Epitaph Museum** (5th St., 520/457-2211, 9:30am-5pm daily, free), where you can see the original press used to print the perfectly named *Epitaph*, first published in 1880 and still going, and other printing-related exhibits. The **O.K. Corral and Historama** (Allen St., 520/457-3456, www.ok-corral.com, 9am-5pm daily, $6, with gunfight $10) has all the information you'll need on the famous, albeit short, gunfight between the Earps and the Clantons. You can see a historical reenactment of the fight and watch a show on the major events in Tombstone history.

Among the saloons in the district, the **Crystal Palace Saloon** and **Big Nose Kate's Saloon** are worth a look, with Kate's being a fine place to knock back a few and look at all the pictures on the walls. Both are on Allen Street. One of the best sights on Allen is the **Bird Cage Theatre** (Allen St. and 6th St., 520/457-3421, 8am-6pm daily, $6 adults, $5

ages 8-18), an 1881 dance hall, brothel, saloon, theater, and casino that has been spectacularly preserved. A self-guided tour takes you through the building, which looks much as it did when it closed in 1889. At Fremont and 6th Streets, the **Tombstone Western Heritage Museum** (520/457-3800, 9am-5pm Mon.-Sat., 12:30pm-5pm Sun., $5 adults, $3 ages 8-18) has many relics of Tombstone's past, including a few personal items once owned by the Earps.

Tombstone Courthouse State Historic Park

A more sober treatment of Tombstone's history is presented inside the preserved 1882 **Tombstone Courthouse** (3rd St. and Toughnut St., 520/457-3311, http:// azstateparks.com, 9am-5pm daily, $7 adults, $2 ages 7-13). The museum features artifacts, pictures, and ephemera from the territorial days, and there's a rebuilt gallows in the building's courtyard. Particularly interesting are the two nearly forensic accounts of the gunfight, with slightly differing details.

Rose Tree Museum

Planted way back in 1885, this Lady Banks rose, sent all the way from Scotland to Tombstone as a gift, is believed to be the world's largest rose tree at 8,700 square feet, listed in *Guinness World Records*. The white blossoms are usually at their best in early April. The small **Rose Tree Museum** (4th St. and Toughnut St., http:// tombstonerosetree.com, 11am-5pm Sun.-Fri., 10am-5:30pm Sat., $5) exhibits photos and furniture owned by the tree's planter, who moved to the territory in 1880. There's also an excellent bookstore with a lot of books about the history of the region.

Festivals and Events

In March, Tombstone celebrates its founder during **Ed Schieffelin Territorial Days.** In April the **Tombstone Rose Tree Festival** shines light on the record-making rose tree, and in May Tombstone's most famous citizen gets his own party during **Wyatt Earp**

Days. The anniversary of that infamous gunfight warrants a celebration every year in October. Contact the Tombstone Chamber of Commerce (109 S. 4th St., 520/457-9317, www.tombstonechamber.com, 8am-4:45pm Mon.-Fri.) for more information.

Food

Nellie Cashman Restaurant (5th St. and Toughnut St., 520/457-2212, 7:30am-9pm daily, $3-9), the oldest restaurant in Tombstone, is named for the so-called "angel of the camp," known throughout the mining camps of the West for her work aiding sick and distressed miners. She opened a hotel and restaurant in Tombstone in 1882. Today the spot serves delicious and filling home-style breakfasts and burgers, sandwiches, and salads for lunch and dinner.

Accommodations

There are a few easy-to-locate chain hotels in Tombstone and a variety of bed-and-breakfasts. The Tombstone Boarding House B&B (108 N. 4th St., 520/457-3716 or 877/225-1319, $59-89) offers comfortable rooms in two adobe houses that date to the 1880s.

One of the nicer options in this small town is the Tombstone Grand Hotel (580 W. Randolph Way, 855/904-7263, http://tombstonegrand.com, $98-150), which offers clean and comfortable rooms with fridges as well as free breakfast and a pool.

Information

Stop by the Visitor Information Center (4th St. and Allen St., 520/457-3929, 10am-4pm daily), where you'll find a nearly overwhelming amount of information about the town and its sights.

TOP EXPERIENCE

★ BISBEE

The most charming town in Cochise County began life in the 1880s as a copper mining camp. Eventually several billion pounds of the ore would be taken out of the ground here, and by 1910 Bisbee was said to be the biggest city between the Midwest and the West Coast. Flooding in the 1,000-foot-deep tunnels and the boom-and-bust nature of the mining economy closed the mines by the 1970s, and the town, with its labyrinthine staircases and cozy little bungalows built precariously on the slopes of the Mule Mountains, was nearly moribund when it was discovered by hippies, artists, and artisans, a group that funkified the town into what it is today. Retired miners, retirees from elsewhere, county government workers, and descendants of the pioneers also call Bisbee home.

Old Town Bisbee, centered around Main Street and Brewery Gulch, is stuffed full of shops, galleries, restaurants, historic landmarks, and some of the best old hotels in the West. Perhaps the most fun to be had in Bisbee is just walking around, climbing the scores of off-kilter steps, and exploring back alleys and narrow streets. Art lovers should check out the Art Alley, in which Bisbee's many homegrown artists have hung their work. Enter this amazing outdoor gallery-alley from Brewery Gulch, directly across from the Old Bisbee Brewing Company.

Mining History Sights

On AZ 80, just north of the junction with AZ 92, you can stop at a turnout along the side of the road and witness the Lavender Pit Mine and the huge tailings surrounding the largest open-pit mine in the state, now closed.

Bisbee is still proud of its history as the queen of all mining towns, and you can learn all about it at the Bisbee Mining and Historical Museum (Copper Queen Plaza, Main St. and Brewery Gulch, 520/432-7071, www.bisbeemuseum.org, 10am-4pm daily, $8 adults, $3 ages 4-16), housed in the building formerly occupied by the headquarters of the Copper Queen Consolidated Mining Company. Now an affiliate of the Smithsonian Institution, the museum has exhibits on local history and culture during the territorial era, with an emphasis on the history and science of copper mining.

You can see for yourself what it was like descending into the earth every day to coax the ore out of the mountain on the 75-minute **Queen Mine Tour** (478 N. Dart Rd., 520/432-2071 or 866/432-2071, www.queenminetour.com, 9am, 10:30am, noon, 2pm, and 3:30pm daily, $14 adults, $6.50 ages 6-12). Retired miners lead these tours and will regale you with stories of what it was really like underground as you ride deep beneath the earth on an old mine car, wearing a yellow slicker, a hard hat, and a headlamp. It's about 47°F in the shaft, so think about taking something warm to wear.

Events

Like most of the old mining towns in Arizona and northern Mexico, much of Old Town Bisbee is perched precariously on the sides of a mountain, and the early residents installed steps all over town to reach their homes. These days the steps are more atmospheric than useful; they contribute much to Bisbee's quaint character. Every October, people from all over the world gather in Old Town to run up and down these stairs during the **Bisbee 1,000 Stair Climb** (www.bisbee1000.org, $55-100). You too can join in, but the event fills up fast, so register early.

Shopping

Old Town Bisbee has dozens of unique shops, and there always seem to be new ones opening. There are jewelry stores, shops selling local and Mexican folk art, a bookstore with new and used books that include a large selection by local authors, and several multilevel antiques and junk shops that you can get lost in for hours.

Food

The best breakfast in town can be found at the **Bisbee Breakfast Club** (75A Erie St., 520/432-5885, www.bisbeebreakfastclub.com, 7am-3pm daily, $10-14), serving huge American-style breakfasts along with Mexican spice in a refurbished old building on the historic block next to the huge pit. You might have to wait to get a table, but the food is worth it.

Conveniently located right in the middle of old town in the Copper Queen Plaza, an indoor shopping area with a bookstore and a few other shops, the **Bisbee Table** (2 Main St., 520/432-6788, www.bisbeetable.com, 11am-9pm daily, $11-39) is a perfect place to have a long lunch before or after you walk around and explore. It serves amazing New American comfort food such as creative burgers and salads, big baskets of fries and onion rings, and a fried chicken sandwich that is a classic of the genre, along with an excellent selection of beer, wine, and cocktails.

Santiagos (5 Howell Ave., 520/432-1910, www.santiagosmexican.com, 11am-9pm daily, $10-26), a small and often busy Mexican restaurant in Old Town Bisbee, serves impeccable dishes in a new traditionalist style. Everything here is familiar (ceviche, chiles rellenos, enchiladas), but it's so well made— the ingredients fresh and local, the sauces soothing and surprising all at once—that you'll swear you never had its like before. They also make a huge mean margarita.

Be warned: When you visit the **Old Bisbee Brewing Company** (200 Review Alley, 520/432-2739, www.oldbisbeebrewingcompany.com, noon-10:30pm Mon.-Thurs., noon-11:30pm Fri.-Sat.), well situated in Bisbee's old "Brewery Gulch," if it is pleasant out, which it so often is, as you imbibe the delicious beers brewed on-site, sitting in the sun on the patio looking over the quaint old town, you probably aren't going anywhere for a while. The brewery also serves bratwurst and vegetarian chili.

Accommodations

There are all manner of accommodations in Bisbee, and bed-and-breakfasts proliferate along the narrow twisty roads of Old Town.

1: old mining town of Bisbee **2:** an outdoor gallery in a Bisbee alleyway **3:** Bisbee Grand Hotel

The Bisbee Grand Hotel (61 Main St., 520/432-5900 or 800/421-1909, www. bisbeegrandhotel.com, $94-175) is in a Victorian building in Old Town, with small well-decorated themed guest rooms with private baths. A full breakfast is served on the veranda. It has Wi-Fi and a saloon frequented by travelers and locals. The Copper Queen Hotel (11 Howell Ave., 520/432-2216, www. copperqueen.com, $140-200) is an institution in Bisbee, built in 1902 and still in beautiful shape but almost certainly haunted, as anyone in Bisbee will tell you. It has a solar-heated pool, a saloon, and a restaurant.

For a truly unique experience, rent one of the 1950s vintage trailers at Shady Dell RV Park (1 Old Douglas Rd., 520/432-3567, www. theshadydell.com, $95-115), each beautifully refurbished and decorated. Many have interiors of polished chrome and wood and include black-and-white TVs and phonographs complete with 45 singles from the era.

The oldest brick building in Bisbee now houses the elegant, friendly, and truly memorable small boutique Letson Loft Hotel (26 Main St., 520/432-3210, www.letsonlofthotel. com, $125-150), in the heart of Old Town. Romantic, high-end, but affordable, in a gorgeously remodeled and tastefully decorated space, all the guest rooms have modern amenities and are quiet and cozy despite the location in the thick of the action along Bisbee's narrow shop-lined main drag. Some of the rooms look down on the street, giving the guest a sense of what the town was like in its busy urban heyday.

Information

At the Bisbee Chamber of Commerce & Visitor Center (1 Main St., Copper Queen Plaza, 520/432-5421 or 866/224-7233, www. bisbeearizona.com, 9am-5pm Mon.-Fri., 10am-4pm Sat.-Sun.) you'll find brochures on self-guided walking tours and loads of information on what to do and see.

Parking isn't easy, especially on weekends, so it's a good idea to find a space, leave your vehicle, and explore the town on foot.

WILLCOX AND VICINITY

Though the former railroad and ranching town has seen better days, the canyons, mountains, and grasslands around Willcox are worth the 80-mile drive east on I-10 from Tucson. Willcox today has a few boarded-up buildings and abandoned motels along its main thoroughfare, but its historic downtown holds some interest and is worth a mosey. The famous singing cowboy Rex Allen grew up in the area; a museum and an annual festival honor him. Willcox is also known as the place where Wyatt's brother, Warren Earp, met with a bullet in 1900, later to be buried in the Historic Willcox Cemetery.

Historic Downtown and Railroad Avenue

This area used to be where life in Willcox happened, and even today it's the most interesting part of town. There's a shady, grassy park with a big bronze statue of local hero Rex Allen, and across the street on Railroad Avenue the singing cowboy's life and career are celebrated at the Rex Allen Arizona Cowboy Museum (150 N. Railroad Ave., 520/384-4583 or 877/234-4111, www.rexallenmuseum. org, 10am-1pm Mon., 11am-3pm Tues.-Sat., $2), which also displays a Cowboy Hall of Fame honoring area ranchers and cowboys. Every Monday the museum features free concerts by local musicians.

Just down the sidewalk is the Willcox Commercial Store, which claims to be the oldest continually operating store in the state. The Willcox Rex Allen Theater (134 N. Railroad Ave., 520/384-4244), a 1935 art deco movie house, still runs new movies daily, and at the end of Railroad Avenue is the Southern Pacific Depot, built in 1880 and now used by the city of Willcox. The depot's lobby has exhibits on the history of the area and the railroad, and Rex Allen narrates a video played on a loop (8:30am-4:30pm Mon.-Fri.). The small town honors its most famous son with Rex Allen Days the first week in October every year.

Just around the corner from Railroad

Avenue, the **Chiricahua Regional Museum** (127 E. Maley St., 520/384-3971, 10am-5pm Mon.-Sat., $2 pp, $3 per couple, $5 per family) exhibits mining artifacts, weapons used by Native Americans and the U.S. Cavalry, and rocks and minerals found in the region. There's also an excellent display on the history of the Chiricahua Apache people.

Apple Annie's Orchard

The Sulphur Springs Valley outside of Willcox has the perfect growing conditions for the apple, peach, pear, and Asian pear orchards at **Apple Annie's Orchard** (2081 N. Hardy Rd., Willcox, 520/384-2084, www.appleannies.com, 8am-5pm daily July 3-Oct.). Every year people flock to the "U-pick" farm to pick and purchase fruit by the bucketful. The farm also serves delicious hamburgers and cowboy beans for lunch, and you can buy all kinds of homemade preserves, sauces, condiments, and pies in the farm store. Take I-10 to Exit 340, turn west on Ft. Grant Road, and travel 5.5 miles to the Apple Annie's sign.

Amerind Museum

On your way east on I-10, get off at the Dragoon Road exit (Exit 318) to visit the **Amerind Museum** (2100 N. Amerind Rd., Dragoon, 520/586-3666, www.amerind.org, 10am-4pm Tues.-Sun., $12 adults, $10 ages 10-17), an excellent little museum in beautiful Texas Canyon. Established in 1937, the Amerind Foundation (a contraction of "American" and "Indian") preserves and studies Native American cultures from prehistory to the Chiricahua Apache people and beyond. It is commonly thought to hold one of the best private ethnological collections in the nation. The museum is fascinating, and the location, among the imposing boulders of Texas Canyon, makes it worth the stop.

Cochise Stronghold

A bit farther east on I-10, Exit 331 takes you to the **Cochise Stronghold,** the former hideout of Cochise and his band in the strange Dragoon Mountains. The great Apache chief is said to be buried somewhere out here, but nobody knows precisely where. As you look around, it seems an ideal place to hide, with bluffs from which to watch the plains for the oncoming army. There are a few easy trails at the Stronghold, including a short nature

Chiricahua National Monument

trail and a paved history trail with information about the Chiricahua Apache people. A few campsites ($10) are sheltered by the same high boulders that once kept the Chiricahua hidden. If you want to hike deeper into the canyon, try the six-mile round-trip Cochise Stronghold Trail that branches off the nature trail. To get here, head southeast from I-10 on U.S. 191 and then west on Ironwood Road for nine miles. The last four miles are a dirt road.

★ Chiricahua National Monument

This place has to be seen to believed. Precarious rock spires jut into the sky in a strange wonderful landscape, called the "Land of Standing-Up Rocks" by the Apache people. About 38 miles southeast of Willcox (120 miles from Tucson) on AZ 186, the Chiricahua National Monument (520/824-3560, www.nps.gov, 8am-4:30pm daily, free) protects one of the most unusual areas in Arizona. There's a visitors center two miles from the monument entrance on paved two-lane Bonita Canyon Road. Drive six gorgeous miles up to Massai Point and one of the most spectacular overlooks this side of the Grand Canyon.

The visitors center has an excellent free guide with information on all the trails within the monument, and there's a free hikers' shuttle available. You can camp at the Bonita Campground (no hookups, $12) 0.5 miles from the visitors center. Bring your own food and water; none is available for miles. For information and advice on getting out into the less accessible regions of the Chiricahua range, contact the Douglas Ranger District (1192 W. Saddleview Rd./U.S. 191, Douglas, 520/364-3468, 8am-4:30pm Mon.-Fri.), 2.2 miles north of AZ 80 on U.S. 191 in Douglas.

Flagstaff, Sedona, and Red Rock Country

Famed Red Rock Country, one of the world's most celebrated landscapes, is between Flagstaff, the hub of the northland, and the quaint town of Prescott, with posh Sedona at the center.

The landscape is a red, pink, and green-dotted geologic canvas, with the green bursts of Oak Creek Canyon and the often ignored but gorgeous Verde Valley right nearby. Just to the north is the Mogollon Rim, a 200-mile-long cliff that marks the southern border of the vast plateau. The Rim, as it's called locally, drops 2,000 feet in some places and provides some inspiring views. Those same views inspired the likes of the writer Zane Grey, who called the area home on occasion.

Exploring this region, you'll find a different Arizona that the clichéd ideas about the state don't account for. Don't miss contemplating

Highlights

Look for ★ to find recommended sights, activities, dining, and lodging.

★ **Museum of Northern Arizona:** Learn about the people, plants, animals, and geology that make the northlands such a fascinating landscape (page 189).

★ **Sunset Crater Volcano and Wupatki National Monuments:** Explore the foothills of a silent black-rock crater and the 800-year-old red-rock apartment buildings rising from the dry scrublands (page 192).

★ **Walnut Canyon National Monument:** In this enchanting lush canyon the Sinagua people built limestone-and-clay apartments into the cliff sides (page 194).

★ **Jerome:** This haunted mining town is now a funky mountain getaway, with bed-and-breakfasts, hotels, eclectic restaurants, and one-of-a-kind boutiques (page 216).

★ **Montezuma Castle National Monument:** See the mysterious ruins of the Southern Sinagua culture's high point—a cliff-wall castle molded out of limestone (page 223).

★ **Oak Creek Canyon:** Drive along a shady creek with red and white rock walls towering on each side, where birds, butterflies, and people flock to the babbling water sliding over pink slickrock (page 236).

★ **Hiking in Red Rock Country:** Find otherworldly scenery and maybe even some inner peace on the high-desert trails around Sedona (page 236).

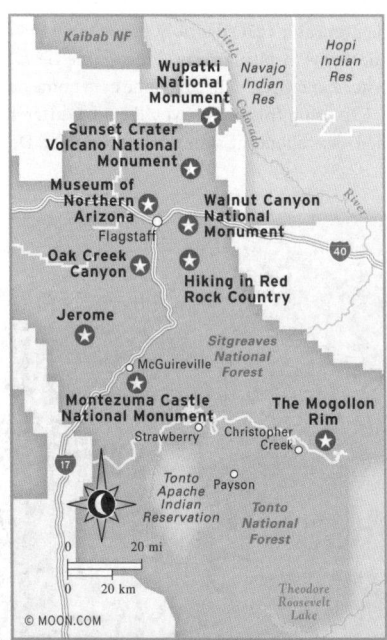

★ **The Mogollon Rim:** Sit on the very edge of the Colorado Plateau overlooking a deep-green sea of pine treetops, with all of lowland Arizona spread out before you (page 240).

Flagstaff, Sedona, and Red Rock Country

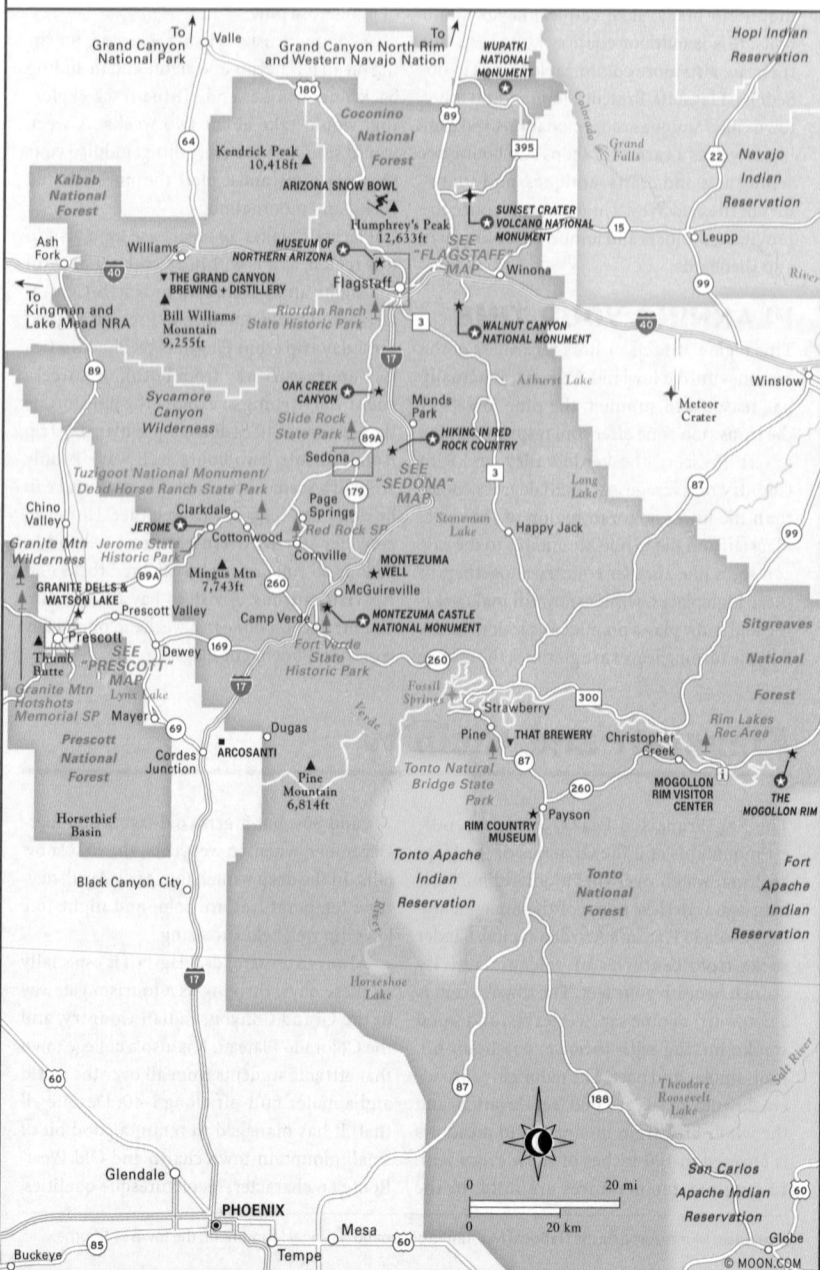

To Grand Canyon National Park
Valle
Grand Canyon North Rim and Western Navajo Nation
To
WUPATKI NATIONAL MONUMENT
Hopi Indian Reservation

180
Coconino National Forest
89
395
Colorado
Grand Falls

64
Kendrick Peak 10,418ft
ARIZONA SNOW BOWL
22
Navajo Indian Reservation

Kaibab National Forest
Humphrey's Peak 12,633ft
SUNSET CRATER VOLCANO NATIONAL MONUMENT
15
Leupp

Ash Fork
Williams
MUSEUM OF NORTHERN ARIZONA
SEE "FLAGSTAFF" MAP
99
River

40
THE GRAND CANYON BREWING + DISTILLERY
Flagstaff
Winona

To Kingman and Lake Mead NRA
Bill Williams Mountain 9,255ft
Riordan Ranch State Historic Park
WALNUT CANYON NATIONAL MONUMENT
40
Winslow

89
Sycamore Canyon Wilderness
OAK CREEK CANYON
Munds Park
Ashurst Lake
Meteor Crater

Slide Rock State Park
89A
HIKING IN RED ROCK COUNTRY
3
87
99

Tuzigoot National Monument/ Dead Horse Ranch State Park
Sedona
SEE "SEDONA" MAP
Long Lake

Chino Valley
Clarkdale
Page Springs
179
Red Rock SP
Stoneman Lake
Happy Jack

Granite Mtn Wilderness
Jerome State Historic Park
JEROME
Cottonwood
Cornville
MONTEZUMA WELL

89A
Mingus Mtn 7,743ft
260
McGuireville
Sitgreaves

GRANITE DELLS & WATSON LAKE
Prescott Valley
Camp Verde
MONTEZUMA CASTLE NATIONAL MONUMENT
National

Prescott
Dewey
169
Fort Verde State Historic Park
260
Forest

Thumb Butte
SEE "PRESCOTT" MAP
17
Fossil Springs
300
Rim Lakes Rec Area

Granite Mtn Hotshots Memorial SP
Lynx Lake
Mayer
69
Strawberry
THAT BREWERY
Christopher Creek

Prescott National Forest
Dugas
ARCOSANTI
Pine
87
260
Payson
MOGOLLON RIM VISITOR CENTER
THE MOGOLLON RIM

Cordes Junction
Pine Mountain 6,814ft
Tonto Natural Bridge State Park
RIM COUNTRY MUSEUM
Fort Apache Indian Reservation

Horsethief Basin
Black Canyon City
Tonto Apache Indian Reservation
Tonto National Forest

17
Horseshoe Lake

60
87
188
Theodore Roosevelt Lake
Salt River

Glendale
San Carlos Apache Indian Reservation
60

Buckeye
85
PHOENIX
Mesa
60
Tempe
Globe

0   20 mi
0   20 km
© MOON.COM

the ruins of the Sinagua culture scattered all over this land. And bring your hiking boots, mountain bikes, skis, canoes, kayaks, and tents; this is outdoor country at its best. But there are also more comfortable things to do: Sedona, Flagstaff, Prescott, Jerome, and other towns offer unique accommodations and dining as well as a variety of shops and boutiques selling arts and crafts, antiques, and souvenirs of the arid West's high country, once the province of miners and lumberjacks, ranchers and shepherds.

PLANNING YOUR TIME

This region attracts visitors regardless of the season—unlike lowland Arizona, it actually has seasons. In summer, the pine forests of the transition zone offer cool respite from the desert: Prescott, the Verde Valley, and Rim Country on average are 10-20 degrees cooler than the lower Sonoran region of the state. Flagstaff and the White Mountains to the east can seem like another country altogether; in these high places, winter snowfall makes skiing and snow play a popular attraction. In the fall, the turning leaves are glorious; the orange and yellow of the scattered deciduous trees look like flares among the dominant stands of ponderosa pine.

A comprehensive trip to the region, touching on all its charms and sights and including backcountry hikes and off-the-track exploring, would take about two weeks. A week would suffice to see everything, indulge your sensual whims, and explore the pinelands, red rocks, and mountaintops.

Flagstaff makes an ideal base for a visit to this region, as it is within a two-hour drive of the sights and adventures in North-Central Arizona. The quaint town of Prescott is good for a day trip from Flagstaff or Phoenix (it's two hours each way from both), or a weekend if you're going to explore the pine forests that surround it. Sedona, a popular day trip from Phoenix (two hours each way), is only an hour's scenic drive from Flagstaff and can be done in a long day from either. However, consider staying overnight or a weekend in Sedona so you can explore the red rocks and riparian canyons. A visit to Payson and Rim Country is best done in a weekend or as a day trip from Phoenix or Flagstaff.

Flagstaff and Vicinity

The San Francisco Peaks, Arizona's tallest mountains and the Olympus of the Hopi kachina, watch over this highland hub, the long-ago waterless home of the Sinagua and the Colorado Plateau's Arizona capital. Cinder rocks from centuries of volcanic activity crunch beneath your feet. The town's scent is a potpourri of pine sap, wet leaves, and wood smoke mixing with incense, patchouli oil, train smoke, and beer. The redbrick, railroad-era downtown sits at 7,000 feet elevation, and the whole area from mountains to meadows is covered in 100 inches of snow every year. In summer, temperatures are mild, in the 70s and 80s, but it gets cold fast September-December, when, in wet years, the first snow falls. In the deep winter, into early April, daytime temperatures are cold, and nighttime lows dip well below freezing.

Always a crossroads, Flagstaff is especially so these days, thriving as a tourism gateway to the Grand Canyon, Indian Country, and the Colorado Plateau. It is also a college town that attracts students from all over the world and a major pull-off along I-40. Despite all that, it has managed to retain a good bit of small mountain-town charm and Old West-Route 66 character. Its picturesque qualities,

---

Previous: Montezuma Castle National Monument; Wupatki National Monument; the town of Jerome.

Flagstaff

Coconino
National
Forest

To
Arizona Snowbowl,
San Francisco Peaks,
and Grand Canyon

ELDEN TRAILS
BED & BREAKFAST

180

MUSEUM OF
NORTHERN ARIZONA

ARIZONA
HISTORICAL SOCIETY-
PIONEER MUSEUM

89

Buffalo
Park

McPherson
Park

FLAGSTAFF
MEDICAL
CENTER

WEST HISTORIC ROUTE 66

To
WALNUT CANYON
NATIONAL MONUMENT

180

Thorpe
Park

SEE
INSET

40

LOWELL
OBSERVATORY

Flagstaff

WEST HISTORIC ROUTE 66

GREYHOUND
BUS LINES

RIORDAN MANSION
STATE HISTORIC PARK

BUSTER'S

Northern
Arizona
University

40

To
Sedona

SLADE MASH RD

17

To
Phoenix

PULLIAM
AIRPORT

Coconino

National

Forest

0   1 mi

0   1 km

To
Payson

© MOON.COM

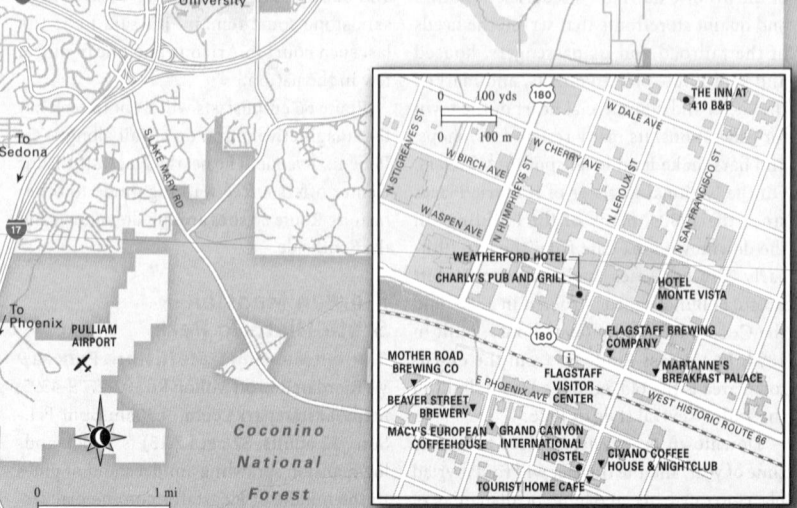

0   100 yds   180
0   100 m

N STIGREAVES ST

W BIRCH AVE

W CHERRY AVE

W DALE AVE

THE INN AT
410 B&B

W ASPEN AVE

N HUMPHREYS ST

N LEROUX ST

N SAN FRANCISCO ST

WEATHERFORD HOTEL

CHARLY'S PUB AND GRILL

HOTEL
MONTE VISTA

180

FLAGSTAFF BREWING
COMPANY

MOTHER ROAD
BREWING CO

FLAGSTAFF
VISITOR
CENTER

MARTANNE'S
BREAKFAST PALACE

E PHOENIX AVE

WEST HISTORIC ROUTE 66

BEAVER STREET
BREWERY

MACY'S EUROPEAN
COFFEEHOUSE

GRAND CANYON
INTERNATIONAL
HOSTEL

CIVANO COFFEE
HOUSE & NIGHTCLUB

TOURIST HOME CAFE

combined with myriad opportunities for outdoor adventuring, make Flagstaff a major northland draw in its own right.

Founded on July 4, 1876, Flagstaff didn't really get going until the Santa Fe Railroad arrived in the 1880s, establishing the present-day downtown area and allowing for the ranching and lumber industries to exploit the surrounding forests and grasslands. Today Flagstaff is home to about 77,000 residents, surrounded by 2 million acres of the Coconino National Forest. Although tourism and the service industry are the town's major lifelines these days, the railroad is still very much a part of Flagstaff. As many as 80 trains a day chug through the heart of town, dividing it in two and often stopping traffic. The wail of train horns is so ubiquitous that many residents don't even notice. There's something romantic and evocative about being in a warm bed on a cool star-bright forest night and hearing the plaintive whine of a westbound train.

SIGHTS

Historic Downtown Flagstaff

Flagstaff has managed to hold on to many of the historic downtown redbrick buildings and quaint storefronts that served the needs of the railroad and its passengers, housed and kept Route 66's argonauts, and marked the social and commercial heart of the town for generations. Its many restaurants, shops, and bars make it an ideal spot for travelers. On the National Register of Historic Places since the 1980s, many of the buildings in the downtown area date from the late 19th-early 20th centuries, including the Babbitt Brothers Building, constructed in 1888, and the Coconino County Courthouse, built in 1894. Just across Route 66 from the downtown area is the old Santa Fe Depot, built in the Tudor Revival style in 1926.

Downtown is a pleasant place to be any time of year, and the traveler will find myriad places to eat, drink, and hunt for all manner of artistic and handmade treasures. Take a half day or so and walk along Humphreys Street,

Beaver Street, Leroux Street, San Francisco Street, and Route 66 (also called Santa Fe Avenue) across from the train depot, ducking into shops, galleries, watering holes, and eateries. Heritage Square (Aspen Ave. between Leroux St. and San Francisco St., 928/853-4292, www.heritagesquaretrust.org) hosts live music, outdoor movies, and arts-and-crafts fairs on weekends in the warmer months.

Southside Historic District

After exploring downtown, walk south of the tracks, where there are more shops, restaurants, and bars in the Southside Historic District. Just south of downtown and bordered by Route 66 and the Santa Fe Railroad, the Rio de Flag, and Northern Arizona University (NAU), it's a bit shaggier than downtown and offers a look at Flagstaff's left-of-center scene. The neighborhood was added to the National Register of Historic Places in 2010.

Check out the ruins of the Historic Basque Handball Court (east side of San Francisco St.) built in 1926 by Jesus Garcia, who emigrated from Spain to Flagstaff in 1912. The building has been wonderfully restored and is now an excellent restaurant and bakery. The ruins of the 40-foot-high sandstone court remain. It's said to be the last such court in Arizona and one of only a few in the nation.

Route 66 enthusiasts will want to seek out the imaginative mural on a wall along West Phoenix Avenue. The nearby Flagstaff Visitor Center offers a free walking guide to other historic Route 66 sites around downtown and the Southside.

Riordan Mansion State Historic Park

Riordan Mansion State Historic Park (409 W. Riordan Rd., off Milton Rd., 928/779-4395, http://azstateparks.com, 9:30am-5pm Fri.-Sun., $2 adults, $2 ages 7-13) is a rock-and-log mansion sprawling amid a stand of pines in the middle of Flagstaff's commercial section and abutting the NAU campus. Its origin is an American success story that would have been perfectly depicted in Technicolor. Two brothers, Michael and Timothy Riordan, make it big on the western frontier, denuding the Arizona northland of its harvestable lumber. The boys are rich, powerful, and run in Flagstaff's founding circles, helping to build a lasting community out of a rough arid wilderness. The close brothers marry close sisters, Caroline and Elizabeth Metz, and the two fledgling families get on so well that they decide to build a 40-room, 13,000-square-foot masterpiece and live in it together. They hire El Tovar designer Charles Whittlesey to design two mansions in one, each shooting off in separate directions and linked by a pool hall and communal space. They decorate their majestic home with Stickley furniture, stained glass, and enough elegant details to draw crowds of visitors for the next 100 years. And everybody lives happily ever after.

The park offers hour-long **tours** (10am, noon, 2pm, and 4pm, admission and tour $12 adults, $7 ages 7-13, reservations strongly advised) of the arts and crafts treasure, one of the best examples of the distinctive architecture that left a stylish stamp on the Southwest in the late 19th-early 20th centuries. Only a small portion of the structure is included in the tour, but it's full of original furniture and displays about the family and life in Flagstaff's formative years.

Lowell Observatory

The hilltop campus of **Lowell Observatory** (1400 W. Mars Hill Rd., 928/774-3358, www.lowell.edu, 10am-10pm Mon.-Sat., 10am-5pm Sun., $17 adults, $12 Sun., $10 ages 5-17, $6 Sun.), just west of downtown, occupied by tall pines and a few small white-domed structures with round concrete bases, has had a good deal of influence over the science of astronomy since its founders began searching the clear skies over Flagstaff in 1894. The historic viewpoint has been involved in contemporary ideas about the beginning of the universe as well.

Vesto Slipher discovered in 1912-1914 that other galaxies are moving away from us, a

phenomenon measured by changes in the light spectrum called redshift. This in turn helped Edwin Hubble and others confirm that the universe is expanding, providing the first observable evidence for the Big Bang. Another historic distinction came a few years later, in 1930, when 24-year-old Clyde Tombaugh looked out from atop Mars Hill and discovered Pluto.

Today the campus welcomes the public with 45-minute tours (on the hour 10am-4pm daily summer, 1pm-4pm daily winter) that include a look through a solar telescope to view spots and flares on the sun, a visit to the Pluto Telescope building, and some fascinating historical documents and artifacts. The **Steele Visitor Center** shows a movie about the observatory and has interesting exhibits on astronomy. If you visit at night, you can take part in sky-viewing sessions with staff astronomers.

Lowell is worth the trip for its historical import (one of the oldest observatories in the nation, it was deemed a National Historic Landmark in 1965), craftsmanship (it incorporates local materials in the domes' interiors), and picturesque location in the shadowy pines at the edge of Flagstaff's Thorpe Park. Don't miss **Percival Lowell's tomb,** a neoclassical observatory-shaped mausoleum that honors the observatory's founder.

★ Museum of Northern Arizona

A couple of well-educated and adventurous easterners, Mary and Harold Colton, an artist and a zoologist, respectively, who first came to Northern Arizona on their honeymoon, founded the **Museum of Northern Arizona** (3101 N. Fort Valley Rd./U.S. 180, 928/774-5213, www.musnaz.org, 10am-4pm Tues.-Sat., 11am-4pm Sun., $15 adults, $10 ages 10-17), three miles north of downtown, in 1928 to preserve and encourage the Indigenous arts and crafts of the Colorado Plateau. Since then, this essential museum has become the cultural and scientific center of the Four Corners region, collecting,

interpreting, and displaying the natural history, art, and artifacts of timeless landscapes and human cultures.

The museum's main building is itself a dark-wood and river-rock work of art, set among the pines along the shallow Rio de Flag, with arts and crafts-era touches such as the handmade tile borders by Hopi potter Sadie Adams around the main entrance. Inside are comprehensive exhibits on the Four Corners region's ancient and current biomes and its buried and blowing strata, plus one of the better introductions you'll find to Ancestral Puebloan and Puebloan cultures, with displays from the Basket Makers up to the Hopi and Navajo people of today. Volunteer docents are eager to discuss and supplement any of the exhibits. The collection of Pueblo Indian pottery, jewelry, kachina, and basketry is the museum's high point, but the galleries showing contemporary Hopi and Pueblo art, including oil paintings, watercolors, and sculpture, tend to open one's eyes to the vibrancy of the region's current cultural moment. Those who appreciate design should stroll into the lounge to see the arts and crafts flourishes in this cozy living-room setting. There's also a beautiful and relatively easy **nature trail** on the museum's forested grounds. Maps to the half-mile trail are available at the front desk.

Arizona Historical Society-Pioneer Museum

Stop at the **Arizona Historical Society-Pioneer Museum** (2340 N. Fort Valley Rd., 928/774-6772, www.arizonahistoricalsociety. org, 10am-5pm Mon.-Sat., 10am-4pm Sun., $6 adults, $3 ages 7-17), near the Museum of Northern Arizona, to see how the early Anglo settlers lived in Flagstaff and Northern Arizona. It's rather fascinating, after just learning about the ancient plateau lifeways of the Hopi and other tribes, to see how a

completely different culture adapted to the same relatively harsh conditions. The building itself is something to see: It's the old Coconino County Hospital for the Indigent, built in 1908. The museum has several displays on, among other things, frontier farming, education, transportation, and medicine, including a bedroom kept exactly as a hardworking nurse would have left it a century ago. There's also a retired steam train and various old farming implements parked on the beautiful forested grounds, where the museum puts on a host of events in spring and summer.

Coconino Center for the Arts

Not a few artists and artisans lurk among the tall pines in Flagstaff, and many more sit atop the Hopi mesas nearby, carving kachinas out of cottonwood root, while others walk the wide empty roads of Navajo land and then recreate the landscape. Throughout the year the local arts group Flagstaff Cultural Partners gathers them for a series of art exhibitions and concerts at the **Coconino Center for the Arts** (2300 N. Fort Valley Rd., 928/779-2300, http://flagartscouncil.org, 11am-5pm Tues.-Sat., donation), a sleek, modern gallery that looks futuristic among the trees and contrasts with the historical architecture of the nearby Museum of Northern Arizona and the Pioneer Museum. Check the website for an up-to-date calendar of events at the "cultural hub of Flagstaff."

The Arboretum at Flagstaff

A 200-acre botanical garden and research station spotlighting the flora (and if you're lucky, the fauna) typical of the Colorado Plateau, **The Arboretum at Flagstaff** (4001 S. Woody Mountain Rd., 928/774-1442, www.thearb.org, 9am-4pm Wed.-Mon. Apr. 15-Oct., $10 adults, $5 ages 3-17) offers 50-minute guided walking tours (11am and 1pm daily) and shows off birds of prey (noon and 2pm Thurs.-Sat.). The forested property on the volcanic lands southwest of downtown Flagstaff has easy winding trails, tall, shaggy trees, a pond, a tree-ring

1: Sunset Crater Volcano National Monument **2:** the telescope at Lowell Observatory **3:** Riordan Mansion State Historic Park **4:** Wupatki National Monument

Who Were the Sinagua...
and Where Did They Go?

The Sinagua people left their architecture and masonry all over North-Central Arizona: the red-rock apartment buildings rising from the cinder plains below the San Francisco Peaks, the sandstone-cliff hideouts of Walnut Canyon, the limestone castles in the lush easy-living Verde Valley, and the brick-stone rooms leaning against Sedona's red walls.

We don't really know what they called themselves, but according to tradition, we call them the Sinagua, Spanish for "without water"—which alludes to the name used by early Spanish explorers for this region of pine-covered highlands still stuck somehow in aridity: *Sierra Sin Agua* (mountains without water).

Their cultural development followed a pattern similar to that of the Ancestral Puebloans in the Four Corners region. They first lived in pit houses bolstered by wooden beams and made a living from small-scale dryland farming, hunting, and gathering piñon nuts and other land-given seasonal delicacies. They made strong and stylish baskets and pottery (though they didn't decorate theirs in the manner of the Ancestral Puebloans and others); they were weavers, craftspeople, and traders.

Around AD 700 a branch of the Sinagua migrated below the Mogollon Rim to the Verde Valley and began living the good life next to fish-filled rivers and streams that flowed year-round; these migrants are now called the Southern Sinagua, and the people who stayed behind are the Northern Sinagua. When, around AD 1064, the volcano that is now Sunset Crater, northeast of Flagstaff, erupted, there were Sinagua villages well within reach of its spewing ash and lava, though archaeologists have found evidence that nearby pit houses had been disassembled and moved just before the eruption, leading to the assumption that they probably knew the big one was coming.

maze, and much more. A few hours here and you'll be able to recognize and appreciate the unique plants and animals that flourish in this high-and-dry plateau country. The arboretum is about four miles south of Route 66 on Woody Mountain Road, only the first mile of which is paved; the rest is navigable in any vehicle.

Elden Pueblo Heritage Site

The **Elden Pueblo Heritage Site** (Townsend-Winona Rd., off U.S. 89, 928/527-3452, free), a Sinagua ruins in the shadow of 9,280-foot Elden Mountain, on Flagstaff's eastern edge, was once a bustling trading center related to the more dramatic Wupatki and Walnut Canyon settlements to the north and east. These easily accessible volcanic-rock ruins were first studied in 1926 by the great Southwestern archaeologist and ethnologist Jesse Walter Fewkes, who also supervised digs at Casa Grande in Southern Arizona and Mesa Verde in southern Colorado. The

settlement in its heyday (about 1100-1275) had 60-70 rooms and hosted a fairly well-connected population: Archaeologists have found macaw skeletons and other evidence of trade with the far south. The site is still being studied and excavated, often with the help of students and volunteers. Tall ponderosa pines guard the ruins along the ADA-accessible 250-yard dirt path that circles the site. This is a perfect first stop on a daylong tour of the Sinagua ruins around Flagstaff. There's a sign for the parking lot on Townsend-Winona Road, one mile north of the Flagstaff Mall on the west side of U.S. 89.

★ Sunset Crater Volcano and Wupatki National Monuments

Sunset Crater Volcano isn't a volcano anymore but a nearly perfectly conical pile of cinder and ash that built up around the former volcano's main vent. Sunset Crater erupted, probably several times, between 1049 and

The eruption would not be the end of the Sinagua—quite the contrary. The reasons are debated—it could have been that crops grew to surplus because a post-eruption cinder mulch made the land more fertile, or it could be that the years following the big blow were wetter than normal, or it could be both—but after the eruption, Sinagua culture became more complex and soon went through a boom time. Roughly 1130-1400, Sinagua culture flourished as the Sinagua lands became an important stop in a trade network that included Mexico to the south, the Four Corners region to the north, and beyond. At pueblo-style ruins dating from this era, archaeologists have found shells, copper bells, and macaw bones, all from Mexico. Sinagua architecture became more Puebloan, and villages often had Mexican-style ball courts and kivas similar to those of the Ancestral Puebloans. The famous ruins throughout the region date from this era.

Then it all ended: Owing to drought, disease, war, civil strife, a combination of these, or some other strange tragedy we may never learn about, by the early 1400s the Sinagua culture was on the run. By 1425, even the seemingly lucky farmers of the Verde Valley had abandoned their castles. The survivors and stragglers mixed with other tribes, their kind never to be seen again. Lucky for us they were such good builders.

To learn more about the Sinagua, check out the easy-to-read booklet *Sinagua,* written by Rose Houk, part of the Western National Park Association's series Prehistoric Cultures of the Southwest. This and others in the series are available at Wupatki and other Sinagua sights near Flagstaff and in the Verde Valley. There are also displays on the Northern and Southern Sinagua at all the ruins near Flagstaff and in the Verde Valley. The information above comes from various museum displays and Houk's excellent booklet.

1100. The eruptions transformed this particularly arid portion of the not exactly lush Colorado Plateau, and now huge cinder barrens, as surprising as an alien world the first time you see them, stretch out along the loop road leading through these popular national monuments. You can't climb the crater cone anymore, after years of scarring by the crowds, but you can walk across the main lava field at the crater's base, a cinder field with scattered dwarfed crooked pines and bursts of rough rock-adapted flowers and shrubs, all the while craning up at the 1,000-foot-high, 2,550-foot-wide cone.

Along with turning its immediate environs into a scorched but beautiful wasteland, the volcano's eruptions may have inadvertently helped the Sinagua people thrive for a brief time in this formidable environment, the subject of Sunset Crater's sister monument, Wupatki. The series of eruptions spewed a ton of ashfall over 88 square miles, and closer to the source the ash created a kind of rich mulch that, combined with a few years of above-average rainfall, may have stimulated a spike in population growth and cultural influence. Archaeological findings suggest that the five pueblos in the shadow of the crater, especially the large Wupatki, were at the center of a trading crossroads and were the most important population center for 50 miles or more, with about 2,000 people living within a day's walk of the sprawling red-rock apartment building by 1190. Times seem to have been good for about 150 years, and then, owing to a variety of factors, everybody left. The Hopi and other Pueblo people consider Wupatki a sacred place, one more in a series of former homes their ancestors kept during their long migrations to Black Mesa. Today you can walk among the red and pink ruins, standing on jutting patios, looking out over the dry land, wondering what that waterless life was like, and marveling at the adaptive, architectural, and artistic genius of those who came before.

The monuments sit side by side on an arid sweep covered with clump grass, humps of volcanic remains, pine stands, and, if you're lucky, blankets of yellow wildflowers, about 12 miles north of Flagstaff on U.S. 89. Turn onto the Sunset Crater-Wupatki Loop Road, which leads across the cinder barrens, through the forest, onto the red-dirt plains and the ruins, and then back to U.S. 89. One ticket is good for both monuments.

Heading north from Flagstaff, you'll reach the **Sunset Crater Volcano National Monument Visitor Center** (6082 Sunset Crater Rd., 928/526-0502, www.nps.gov/sucr, 9am-5pm daily, $25 per vehicle for 7-day pass to both monuments) first, about two miles from U.S. 89. Take a few minutes to look over the small museum and gift shop; there are several displays about volcanoes and the history of the region. Pick up the guidebook ($1, or free if you recycle it) to the one-mile loop **Lava Flow Trail** out onto the **Bonito Lava Flow,** and head up the road a bit to the trailhead. This is an easy walk among the cinder barrens, a strange landscape with a kind of ruined beauty about it—only squat pines will grow, but there is surprising life throughout, small niches in which color can find a foothold. The trail skirts the base of the great crater cone and takes about an hour.

Another 16 miles on the loop road leads to **Wupatki National Monument Visitor Center** (25137 N. Wupatki Loop Rd., 928/679-2365, www.nps.gov/wupa, 9am-5pm daily, $25 per vehicle for 7-day pass to both monuments), a total of 21 miles from the junction, near the last of the five pueblos, the titular Wupatki. The other pueblos before Wupatki are reached by two separate short trails, each with its own parking lot along the loop road. At Wupatki, you can purchase a guidebook ($1, or free if you recycle it) to the half-mile **Wupatki Pueblo Trail,** which leads around the village complex and back to the visitors center. If you don't have time to see all five pueblos, head straight to Wupatki, the biggest and best of them all.

★ Walnut Canyon National Monument

Not far from Wupatki, another group of Sinagua people farmed the forested rim and built stacked limestone-and-clay apartments into the cliff sides of Walnut Canyon, a 20-mile-long, 400-foot-deep gathering of nearly every North American life zone in one relatively small wonderland. Near the rim, a huge island of rock juts out of the canyon innards, around which residents constructed their dwellings, most of them facing south and east to gather warmth. Depending on how much sunlight any one side of the island received, the Sinagua could count on several seasons of food gathering, from cactus fruit to piñon nuts and wild grapes. A creek snakes through the canyon's green bottomlands, encouraging cottonwoods and willows. The Sinagua lived in this high dry Eden for about 125 years, leaving for good around 1250. This is an enchanting and mysterious place that should not be missed.

VISITING THE MONUMENT

Take I-40 east from Flagstaff for 7.5 miles to Exit 204. Then it's three miles south to the canyon rim and the **Walnut Canyon Visitor Center** (928/526-3367, www.nps.gov/waca, 9am-5pm daily, $15 pp for 7-day pass), where there are a few displays, a small gift shop, and a spectacular window-view of the canyon. An hour or more on the **Island Trail,** a one-mile loop past 25 cliff dwellings (close enough to examine in detail) and into several different biomes high above the riparian bottomlands, is essential, but it's not entirely easy; you must climb down (and back up) 240 rock-hewn steps to get to the island, descending 185 vertical feet. Once you're on the island, though, it's an easy, mostly flat walk, and one you won't soon forget. There's also a short trail on the rim with some great views.

RECREATION
Hiking

Head north on U.S. 180 eight miles to the San Francisco Peaks for the best hikes in the area. There are dozens of lesser hikes around the peaks, but the most memorable essential hike in these sylvan volcanic lands is the **Mount Humphrey Trail** (Snowbowl Rd./Forest Rd. 516). The tough hike leads to the highest reaches of Humphreys Peak at 12,633 feet—the very top of Arizona and near the sacred realms wherein the Hopi kachina dwell and watch. The 10-mile round-trip is strenuous but beautiful and rewarding. The trail moves through a shady aspen forest and up above the tree line to a windy and rocky alpine stretch where only ancient bristlecones grow. The view from the wind-battered peak is unspeakably thrilling. Plan on the hike taking 5-6 hours, and be careful of altitude sickness if you're a habituated lowlander. The trailhead is signed 7.4 miles up Snowbowl Road.

The **Kachina Trail** (Snowbowl Rd./Forest Rd. 516), which begins at the first parking lot on the right, 7 miles up Snowbowl Road, is one of the most popular trails in the peaks. It's a moderate 10-mile round-trip hike across the south face of the peaks at 9,500 feet, through thick stands of conifers and aspens with sweeping views at every corner, and across an ancient lava flow. This is a particularly beautiful route in the fall, with fiery yellows and reds everywhere.

Contact the **Coconino National Forest** (1824 S. Thompson St., 928/527-3600, www.fs.usda.gov/coconino, 8am-4pm Mon.-Fri.) for information on hiking in the San Francisco Peaks, and see the national forest's website for other hikes in the volcanic highlands and more detailed trail descriptions.

Mountain Biking

Mountain biking is very popular in Flagstaff, and many of its trails are up-and-down exciting and technical to the point of mental and physical exhaustion. Enthusiasts will want to head straightaway to the series of moderate-to-difficult interconnected trails of the **Mount Elden Trail System,** northeast of town along U.S. 89. There are enough loops and mountainside single-tracks in this area to keep you busy for a while.

The **Flagstaff Biking Organization** (http://flagstaffbiking.org) offers information on northland biking events and issues. The experts at **Absolute Bikes** (202 E. Rte. 66, 928/779-5969, www.absolutebikes.net, 9am-7pm Mon.-Fri., 9am-6pm Sat., 10am-4pm Sun. Apr.-Dec., 10am-6pm Mon.-Sat., 10am-4pm Sun. Jan.-Mar.) have info on some of the best local trails on their website. They also have a store in the nearby slickrock paradise of Sedona, and they rent out mountain bikes in both areas.

Arizona Snowbowl

On the slopes of the San Francisco Peaks, the **Arizona Snowbowl** (Snowbowl Rd., off U.S. 180, 928/779-1951, www.arizonasnowbowl.com, all-day lift tickets $75) offers skiers and snowboarders 2,300 feet of vertical drop and 32 scenic trails that cover 777 acres. In wet years the first snow usually falls in December, but in recent drought-ridden years the snow has stayed away until late in the season. The resort prevailed in a dispute with Native Americans over artificial snow and now makes powder from reclaimed water when Mother Nature won't play along. The Hopi and other regional tribes consider the mountains sacred.

In the summer, the ski lift becomes the **Scenic Chairlift** (10am-4pm Fri.-Mon., $19 over age 12, $15 ages 6-12), lifting passengers slowly up to 11,500 feet, where you need a jacket in July. From here the hazy flatland stretches out for eternity.

Flagstaff Nordic Center

A complex of trails and sledding hills, the **Flagstaff Nordic Center** (U.S. 180, mile marker 232, 928/220-0550, www.flagstaffnordiccenter.com) is a popular place for cross-country skiing, sledding, snowshoeing, and all manner of snow play as long as there's snow on the Coconino National Forest at the base of the peaks. Equipment rentals, lessons, and races are available.

There's even more to do here in the summer. The high-meadow trails offer excellent hiking and biking during the cool mountain days, and if you just can't stand to leave, camp in a yurt or rustic cabin ($50-60) for an unforgettable night in the starlit forest, with the majestic San Francisco Peaks watching over your slumber.

ENTERTAINMENT
Nightlife
BARS, BREWPUBS, AND LOUNGES

Most of Flagstaff's favorite nightspots can be found in and around the historic downtown, the Southside Historic District, and on the edges of the Northern Arizona University campus. Naturally the nightlife is full of college students, but you'll find plenty of older locals and travelers in the mix.

The **Monte Vi** (100 N. San Francisco St., 928/779-6971, www.hotelmontevista.com, 1pm-2am daily) is a genial and historic place to sip cocktails or cry into your beer, with live music, karaoke, and pool tables. It's in what feels like the low-ceilinged basement of the Monte Vista Hotel, built in 1927. On entering this little old-school joint, down the steps from the hotel lobby, you can smell fourscore years of spilled beer and general revelry imprinted deeply into the walls and floor. They say there are even a few ghosts still hanging around, unwilling to go home. Also off the Monte Vista's lobby is the more modern-minded **Rendezvous** (100 N. San Francisco St., 928/779-6971, www.hotelmontevista.com, 5pm-2am Mon.-Wed., 2pm-2am Thurs.-Sun.), a coffeehouse and cocktail lounge with an impressive selection of spirits and creative cocktail creations. The coffee is superior, but don't be surprised if you start drinking early after looking at all those bottles as you sip your brew. The sleek, elegant interior and big windows that look out on bustling downtown Flagstaff encourage lounging and a "let's have another" attitude.

Charley's Pub (23 N. Leroux St., 928/779-1919, www.weatherfordhotel.com, 8am-10pm daily) and **The Gopher Hole Pub** (5pm-close daily), both in the historic Weatherford Hotel downtown, are historic

and fun places to have a beer or cocktail, hang out for happy hour, and watch live rock and blues bands.

Along Route 66 in downtown, **Flagstaff Brewing Company** (16 E. Rte. 66, 928/773-1442, www.flagbrew.com, 11am-2am daily) offers expertly crafted microbrews in a pub-style setting where locals and travelers meet and mix. Try the dark-as-midnight Sasquatch Stout and sit on the patio, letting the strong beer and high-country air adjust your outlook on the laid-back mountain town.

Mother Road Brewing (7 S. Mikes Pike St., 928/774-9139, www.motherroadbeer.com, 2pm-9pm Mon.-Fri., noon-9pm Sat.-Sun.), just across the train tracks on the Southside, has a casual tasting room, a patio with a fire pit (dogs and kids allowed), a rotating menu of creative small-batch beers, and an on-site food truck.

Beaver Street Brewery (11 S. Beaver St., 928/779-0079, http://beaverstreetbrewery.com, 11:30am-9pm Sun.-Thurs., 11:30am-10pm Fri.-Sat.), on the historic Southside, serves award-winning microbrews and fantastically delicious pizzas in a bar-and-grill setting. IPA lovers should not miss the HopShot IPA. Connected on the inside and owned by Beaver Street Brewery, a fun atmosphere prevails at **Brews & Cues** (11am-1am Sun.-Wed., 11am-2am Thurs.-Sat.), where a few games of eight ball provide the perfect complement to the tasty ales.

Flagstaff is a ski town, and the Southside's **Altitudes Bar & Grill** (2 S. Beaver St., 928/214-8218, www.altitudesbarandgrill.com, 11am-10pm daily) celebrates that fact with its snow-sports decor and "Skishots," a convivial way to get hammered quickly. A friendly bartender, perhaps with a full cold-weather beard and a wool cap, serves three or four shots of your favorite spirit affixed to an old ski. You and your drinking buddies must cooperate to sink them, a task that becomes increasingly tricky as the night progresses. Altitudes also offers a good selection of local beers and live

1: hiker in the San Francisco Peaks 2: The Orpheum

1

ORPHEUM
19 MODEST MOUSE - SOLD OUT
20 GEORGE CLINTON & PFUNK
29 END OF SUMMER REGGAE BASH
9/2 CRACKER - CAMPER VAN BEETHOVEN

2

music and serves a sufficiently tasty American grill-style menu until 10pm. **Civano Coffee House & Nightclub** (2 N. Leroux St., 928/447-7700, www.civano. com, 7am-2pm Sun.-Mon., 7am-10pm Tues.-Thurs., 7am-12:30am Fri., 7am-2pm and 6pm-12:30am Sat.) is a stylish and friendly coffeehouse-style restaurant severing tasty breakfast dishes and sandwiches by day ($10-15) but, come Friday-Saturday nights, it transforms into an LGBTQ nightclub with a packed calendar of fun times, theme nights, and special events.

LIVE MUSIC

Flagstaff is a laid-back town, with its share of mountain men, bohemians, and creative types. Northern Arizona University's 20,000 students, many from abroad, help give the old frontier town a dash of do-it-yourself cosmopolitanism. It's not surprising, then, that the area attracts headlining acts and smaller indie favorites to its bars and theaters. If you're a fan of alternative pop, alt-country, classic country, bluegrass, classic rock, and just plain rock-and-roll, it's a good idea to check the websites of the following venues before making your travel plans. Odds are some funky act will be playing.

The Orpheum (15 W. Aspen St., 928/556-1580, www.orpheumpresents.com), a retro-cool theater and bar that was Flagstaff's first movie house, hosts modern music from Ozomatli to Modest Mouse and shows classic and first-run movies on special nights each month. True to Flagstaff's crunchy reputation, the venue hosts a party every year on Jerry Garcia's birthday. The **Pepsi Amphitheater** (2446 Fort Tuthill Loop, 928/774-0899, www. pinemountainamphitheater.com), out in the pines at Fort Tuthill Park, is the region's best outdoor venue and attracts great bands, many of the bluegrass and country persuasion. **Prochnow Auditorium** (Knoles Dr., North Campus, NAU, 928/523-5638 or 888/520-7214) at Northern Arizona University books national and international acts in an intimate setting.

Festivals and Events

Flagstaff hosts a variety of cultural events, mostly during its cool spring and warm summer.

During Flagstaff's year-round **First Friday Artwalk** (6pm-9pm), downtown comes alive with local art, crafts, music, and food. Students and townies mix it up and celebrate the vibrancy of the northland's culture at this fun monthly street festival. A walking guide to participating galleries is available on the **Flagstaff Art Council's website** (http://flagartscouncil.org). In the summer, it joins forces with **Downtown Friday Nights/First Friday** (1st Fri. of the month May-Oct.), a monthly street festival with live bands, art walks, food, and crowds seeking fun. The party is centered at Heritage Square.

In May, world-renowned authors come to town for lectures, signings, readings, and panel discussions at the **Northern Arizona Book Festival** (928/380-8682, www. nazbookfest.org).

The **Museum of Northern Arizona Heritage Program** (928/774-5213, www. musnaz.org) puts on several important and well-attended cultural festivals each year, featuring Native American arts and crafts markets, food, history displays, and entertainment: the **Zuni Festival of Arts and Culture** in late May; the **Hopi Festival of Arts and Culture** in early July; the **Navajo Festival of Arts and Culture** in early August; and, in late October, **Celebración de la Gente,** marking Día de los Muertos (Day of the Dead).

The second week in September, just before it starts to get cold in the north country, Flagstaff ushers in **Route 66 Days** (www. flagstaffroute66days.com), celebrated with a parade, a classic car show, and all manner of special activities along the downtown portion of the Mother Road.

In October the **Flagstaff Mountain Film Festival** (www.flagstaffmountainfilms.org) screens the year's best independent films with an environmental, outdoor-adventure, and social-justice bent at The Orpheum.

If you find yourself in the northland on New Year's Eve, head over to the historic downtown **Weatherford Hotel** (23 N. Leroux St.) for the popular local party known as the **Pine Cone Drop.** Among rocking bands and general revelry, the hotel lowers a six-foot-tall lit-up pinecone from its roof, as if this little railroad town in Arizona were Times Square. Thousands attend to meet the new year with cheer and watch the fireworks. The pinecone drops twice: once at 10pm to coincide with the party on the East Coast and again at midnight.

SHOPPING

The best place to shop for distinctive gifts, souvenirs, decorations, clothes, and outdoor gear is Flagstaff's historic downtown. You'll find Native American arts and crafts, Western wear, New Age items, art galleries specializing in handmade objects, antiques stores, and more.

Outfitters

Famous old **Babbitt's** (12 E. Aspen Ave., 928/774-4775, www.babbittsbackcountry. com, 9am-8pm Mon.-Sat., 10am-6pm Sun.) sells top-notch outdoor gear. The store's 1880s-era local sandstone building once housed the state's largest general store, built by a pioneer family of traders. The knowledgeable staff can help you plan a backcountry adventure and will recommend the best gear for the conditions; they also have an excellent map and book section.

Another locally owned outfitter downtown, **Aspen Sports** (15 N. San Francisco St., 928/779-1935, http://aspensportsflagstaff. com, 10am-6pm Mon.-Thurs., 10am-7pm Fri.-Sat., 10am-5pm Sun.), sells the best in outdoor, hiking, skiing, snowboarding, and trekking gear and has an experienced staff of experts, all of whom would likely rather be skiing or climbing; in this wilderness those are the folks you want on your side.

Books

Arizona's original used-media supercenter, **Bookmans** (1520 S. Riordan Ranch Rd., 928/774-0005, www.bookmans.com, 9am-10pm daily) is the best bookstore in Northern Arizona bar none, with a huge selection of used books, CDs, vinyl records, DVDs, and musical instruments.

Galleries

Stop by the **West of the Moon Gallery** (14 N. San Francisco St., 928/774-0465, www. westofthemoongallery.com, noon-5pm Mon.-Sat., noon-4pm Sun.) to see the best work of contemporary painters, artists, and artisans from around the region, including both classic and experimental work from Navajo artists. This is one of several places in Arizona to see and purchase the luminous, swirling, mysterious paintings of Shonto Begay, one of the best Native American artists working today.

FOOD

Flagstaff has a fairly sophisticated restaurant scene, with places serving cuisine from all over the world as well as creative and inspired Southwestern fare. The downtown and Southside areas have the best local eateries, including many dedicated to sustainability and using locally and regionally sourced ingredients.

Mexican

★ **MartAnne's** (112 E. Rte. 66, 928/773-4712, http://martannes.com, 7:30am-9pm Mon.-Sat., 7:30am-3:30pm Sun., $5-13) is a lively spot downtown along Route 66. It calls itself the "house that chilaquiles built," referring to the signature breakfast dish: scrambled eggs mixed with cheese and corn chips and smothered in red or green sauce. Eyeing the art on the walls—lots of *calaveras* (skeletons) and Frida Kahlo-style masterpieces—will keep you busy until your breakfast burritos or enchiladas arrive. This a great place anytime, and serves breakfast all day.

American and Southwestern

The **Tourist Home Café** (52 S. San Francisco, www.touristhomecafe.com, 928/779-2811, 6am-3pm daily, $10-16) is a bright and airy counter-service eatery on the Southside serving from-scratch baked goods, breakfast burritos, sandwiches, and salads. With tables inside and outside, the wonderfully refurbished 1926 boarding house for Basque shepherds isn't a place to just get take out. The bakery entices to a criminal degree, and the "breakfast bar" with twisted mimosas and Bloody Marys may convince you not to rush off.

For the best burgers in the northland, head to **Diablo Burger** (20 N. Leroux St., Suite 112, 928/774-3274, www.diabloburger.com, 11am-9pm daily, $13-16), with a small but stellar menu of beef raised locally. All the finely crafted creations, such as the Cheech (guacamole, jalapeños, and spicy cheese) or Vitamin B (blue cheese with bacon and a beet), come on Diablo's branded English muffin-style buns alongside a mess of Belgian fries. Diablo also has a terrific veggie burger.

Brandy's Restaurant and Bakery (1500 E. Cedar Ave., Suite 40, 928/779-2187, www.brandysrestaurant.com, 7am-3pm daily, $10-15) often wins the "Best Breakfast" honors from readers of the local newspaper. The homemade breads and bagels make everything else taste better. Try the Eggs Brandy, two poached eggs on a homemade bagel smothered in hollandaise sauce. For lunch there are excellent sandwiches (try Brandy's Reuben), burgers, and salads. Brandy's also serves beer, wine, and mimosas.

Offering creative Southwestern fusion for brunch, lunch, and dinner from a cozy historic home near downtown, **Josephine's Modern American Bistro** (503 N. Humphreys St., 928/779-3400, www.josephinesrestaurant.com, 11am-2pm and 5pm-9pm Mon.-Fri., 11:30am-2pm and 5pm-8:30pm Sat., 9am-2pm Sun., $10-30) is one of the best places in town for brunch.

Charly's Pub and Grill (23 N. Leroux St., 928/779-1919, www.weatherfordhotel.com, 8am-10pm daily, $13-26), inside the Weatherford Hotel, serves Navajo tacos, enchiladas, burritos, and a host of other regional favorites for breakfast, lunch, and dinner. The

Navajo taco, a regional delicacy featuring fry bread smothered in chili and beans, might be the best outside the reservation. Try it for breakfast topped with a couple of fried eggs. Charly's also has more conventional but appetizing bar-and-grill food such as hot high-piled sandwiches, juicy burgers, steaks, and prime rib.

In a historic building a few blocks north of downtown, **Brix Restaurant & Wine Bar** (413 N. San Francisco St., 928/213-1021, http://brixflagstaff.com, 5pm-9pm Tues.-Sun., $27-46) serves creative and memorable food using local and sustainable ingredients. The menu changes often based on what's new at Arizona's small farms, ranches, and dairies. The New American-meets-Italian cuisine that results is typically spectacular. There's also a great wine list, a slew of creative cocktails, and desserts that should not be missed.

In the Southside District, the **Tinderbox Kitchen** (34 S. San Francisco St., 928/226-8400, www.tinderboxkitchen.com, 5pm-10pm daily, $18-44) serves a revolving menu of gourmet takes on familiar American favorites and has an elegant lounge (4pm-close daily) where you can wait for your table with a martini. The chef uses seasonal ingredients, and there's always something new and exciting—venison served with blue cheese grits, bacon creamed corn, or jalapeño mac-and-cheese. It's one of those places where the chef is lacking in neither ingredients or imagination.

Thai

Dara Thai (14 S. San Francisco St., 928/774-0047, www.darathaiflagstaff.com, 11am-10pm Mon.-Sat., $11-19) has been a beloved local institution since 1992. It's part of a small regional chain with sister restaurants in Williams, Anthem, Santa Fe, and Taos. Close to campus, it's popular with students and locals for its rich, tasty, and perfectly spiced dishes.

Pizza

Named Flagstaff's favorite pizza since 2002, **Fratelli Pizza** (119 W. Phoenix

Ave., 928/774-9200, www.fratellipizza.net, 10:30am-9pm daily, $10-20) swears by its stone deck oven and eschews the conveyer belt mentality of the chains. The results are sublime. Try the popular Flagstaff, with basil pesto, sun-dried tomatoes, and artichoke hearts. You can also build your own pie from dozens of fresh toppings or stop in for a huge slice ($4). Fratelli also serves salads, antipasti, and calzones and offer a decent selection of beer and wine. There's also a location on **4th Street** (2120 N. 4th St., 928/714-9700, 10:30am-9pm daily).

The wonderful **Pizzicletta** (203 W. Phoenix Ave., 928/774-3242, www.pizzicletta.com, 5pm-close Tues.-Sun., $13-17), in the Southside neighborhood, offers soppressata rather than pepperoni and prosciutto di Parma rather than ham. Among the carefully chosen list of toppings are almonds and charred kale. But it's the dough that makes the pizza here so good. Pizzicletta also serves fantastic bread, beer, wine, and house-made gelato.

Diners

For a big breakfast of eggs, bacon, and potatoes, or an omelet stuffed with cheese, a hot cup of coffee, and friendly service, head over to the **Downtown Diner** (7 E. Aspen Ave., 928/774-3492, 6am-6pm daily, $5-15) right across from Heritage Square. This clean little greasy spoon also has good burgers, shakes, and hot dogs. There's similar fare at local favorite **Miz Zip's Route 66 Diner** (2924 E. Rte. 66, 928/526-0104, 6am-9:30pm Mon.-Sat., 7am-2pm Sun., $5-15, cash only) on Flagstaff's east side. Open since the 1950s, it still serves the same diner classics of the golden age, such as hot open-faced sandwiches smothered in rich gravy, juicy burgers, and filling breakfasts.

The **Crown Railroad Café** (3300 E. Rte. 66, 928/522-9237, http://thecrownrailroadcafes.com, 6am-9pm daily, $8-12) celebrates the golden era of the railroad. Sit among model trains, iron road memorabilia, and Navajo blankets while enjoying the huge three-egg

Route 66 omelet, expertly prepared huevos rancheros, and a fresh homemade biscuit.

Vegetarian

A cozy little spot on San Francisco Street, the **Morning Glory Café** (115 S. San Francisco St., 928/774-3705, http://morningglorycafeflagstaff.com, 10am-2:30pm Tues.-Fri., 9am-2:30pm Sat.-Sun., $8-11, cash only) serves natural, tasty vegetarian eats. Try the hemp burger for lunch, and don't miss the blue corn pancakes for breakfast. With local art on the walls, free Wi-Fi, and friendly service, this is an ideal place to get to know the laid-back Flagstaff vibe. There are a lot of vegan and gluten-free options here.

South of the tracks, **Macy's European Coffee House** (14 S. Beaver St., 928/774-2243, www.macyscoffee.net, 6am-8pm daily, $5-10) is the best place to get coffee and a quick vegetarian bite to eat, or just hang out and watch the locals file in and out.

ACCOMMODATIONS

Being an interstate town close to several world-renowned sights, Flagstaff has all the chain hotels. A good value and a unique experience can be had at one of the historic downtown hotels. Along Route 66, as you enter town from the east, there are a large number of chain and locally owned small hotels and motels, including several old-school motor inns, and a few places that are likely inexpensive for a reason. East Flagstaff, while it lacks the charm of the downtown area, is an acceptable place to stay if you're just passing through. If you're a budget traveler and don't mind students, hippies, and international travelers, try the hostels in Flagstaff's Southside Historic District.

$50-100

In an old 1930s building in the Southside neighborhood, the **Grand Canyon International Hostel** (19 S. San Francisco St., 888/442-2696, www.grandcanyonhostel.com, $26-78) is a clean and friendly place to stay on the cheap, where you're likely to meet

1

2

3

4

some lasting friends, many of them foreign travelers tramping around the Colorado Plateau. The hostel offers bunk-style sleeping arrangements and private rooms, mostly shared baths, a self-serve kitchen, Wi-Fi, a free breakfast, and a chance to join in on tours of the region. It's a rustic but cozy and welcoming hippie home-style place to stay.

The same folks operate the **Motel DuBeau** (19 W. Phoenix St., 800/398-7112, www.modubeau.com, $80-110), a clean and charming hostel-inn with eight private rooms. It offers a free breakfast, Wi-Fi, and a friendly atmosphere in a classic motor hotel built in 1929. Make sure to spend some time at the on-site **Nomad's Global Lounge** (4:30pm-10pm Mon.-Thurs., 4pm-11pm Fri.-Sat., 4pm-9pm Sun.), kicking back with a few cold ones and a few new friends.

$100-250

The historic ★ **Hotel Monte Vista** (100 N. San Francisco St., 928/779-6971 or 800/545-3068, www.hotelmontevista.com, $105-175 Apr. 15-Nov. 5, $70-140 Nov. 6-Apr. 14) is a retro-swanky redbrick high-rise, built in 1927, and once served high-class and famous travelers heading west on the Santa Fe Railroad. These days it offers comfortable and convenient guest rooms with historic charm, cable TV, and private baths, as well as hostel-style rooms with shared baths. There's a cocktail lounge and a sleek coffee bar off the lobby, which you will hear during the night (especially on the first two floors). As with many of the grand old railroad hotels, there are lots of tales about the Hollywood greats who stayed here and the restless ghosts who stayed behind. Parking is not easy downtown, so if you have a large vehicle, consider staying somewhere else.

The hosts at ★ **Elden Trails Bed & Breakfast** (6073 Snowflake Dr., 928/266-0203, www.eldentrailsbedandbreakfast.com, $167-194 d, additional adults $40 pp) are

committed to living a sustainable-as-possible lifestyle, including growing a lot of their own food in a large garden and greenhouse full of native plants and organic crops. Both eco-tourists and foodies will feel at home in this comfortable and inspiring B&B at the base of Mount Elden, five miles east of downtown Flagstaff. It's a small place: just one detached studio suite that sleeps four adults. A healthy, organic (and if you prefer, vegan) breakfast is served in the studio's sunny nook, and your new home-away-from-home sits amid tall pines and hiking trails. Make reservations far in advance.

One of two historic hotels downtown, the **Weatherford Hotel** (23 N. Leroux St., 928/779-1919, www.weatherfordhotel.com, $80-205) is basic but romantic, like stepping back in time. There are no TVs or phones in the standard guest rooms. "European-style" rooms share a bath. While the whole place is a little creaky, the location and the history make it a fun place to rest. With live music at the hotel's two pubs and the odd wedding or private party in the historic ballroom, the Weatherford can sometimes get noisy: It's not for those looking for tranquility.

A wonderful little place with so much detail and stylishness, **The Inn at 410 Bed and Breakfast** (410 N. Leroux St., 928/774-0088 or 800/774-2008, www.inn410.com, $199-230) has eight artfully decorated guest rooms in a classic old home on a quiet tree-lined street just off downtown. Breakfasts are interesting and filling, often with a Southwestern tinge, and tea is served every afternoon. Booking far in advance, especially for a weekend stay, is a must.

The stately **England House Bed and Breakfast** (614 W. Santa Fe Ave., 928/214-7350 or 877/214-7350, www.englandhousebandb.com, $149-219) is in a quiet residential neighborhood near downtown at the base of Mars Hill, home to the famous Lowell Observatory. This beautiful old Victorian has been sumptuously restored, and it is fully booked most weekends. If you're just passing through, the innkeepers

---

1: England House Bed and Breakfast 2: Diablo Burger 3: Civano Coffee House & Nightclub 4: the historic Hotel Monte Vista

are happy to show you around, after which you will probably make a reservation for some far future date. They pay as much attention to their breakfasts as they do to details of the decor. This is one of the best little inns in the region.

Forest Inns

Base Camp at Snowbowl (6355 N. U.S. 180, 928/774-0729 or 800/472-3599, www. arizonasnowbowl.com, $109-179) has 26 small cabins, large cabins with kitchenettes, and a few hotel-style rooms, plus a good bar and grill on-site. Significantly remodeled in 2021, the cabins are comfortable and come with free Wi-Fi, televisions, and heaters (but no air-conditioners). The cabins are seven miles northwest of downtown, near the road up the peaks to the Snowbowl. It's dark out here, and you can see all the stars in the galaxy on many nights. This lodge is a good bet for skiing or other snow-related activities, and a great option for hikers in summer. Make reservations in advance for ski season, as there are few other places to stay in the immediate area. The drive from Flagstaff is 10-20 minutes, longer in inclement weather. Prices are considerably lower on weekdays.

Three miles northeast of town in the forest at the foot of Mount Elden, the **Starlight Pines Bed and Breakfast** (3380 E. Lockett Rd., 928/527-1912 or 800/752-1912, www. starlightpinesbb.com, $99) has four guest rooms stuffed with antiques and style in a Victorian-era home. There's a porch swing, deep tubs perfect for bubble baths, and fresh-cut flowers in every room—but no TVs. They'll even bring breakfast to your room. This is a perfect place for couples looking for a romantic mountain getaway.

For a touch of wilderness adventure with all the comforts, try the **Arizona Mountain Inn** (4200 Lake Mary Rd., 928/774-8959, www.arizonamountaininn.com), offering 17 rustic but comfortable family-perfect cabins ($135-600) in the pines not far from town as well as four B&B-style rooms ($120-160). Dogs are welcome in most guest rooms and cabins.

INFORMATION

The **Flagstaff Visitor Center** (1 E. Rte. 66, 928/774-9541 or 800/379-0065, www. flagstaffarizona.org, 8am-5pm Mon.-Sat., 9am-4pm Sun.), in the old train depot in the center of town, has all kinds of information on Flagstaff and the surrounding area.

TRANSPORTATION
Air

Flagstaff's small **Pulliam Airport** (FLG, 928/556-1234, www.flagstaff.az.gov), about five miles south of downtown, has five flights daily to and from Sky Harbor in Phoenix on **American Airlines** (800/443-7300, www. aa.com). It's a 50-minute flight, compared to a 2.5-hour drive from Phoenix, and generally costs about $550. Flying is not the best option, as you must rent a car to properly explore the northland. If you are coming from Phoenix, it's best to rent a car there and make the scenic drive north.

Car

The best and, really, only easy way to see Flagstaff and the surrounding country is by car. From **Phoenix,** take I-17 north for 2.5 hours (144 mi), and you're in another world. The scenic route to Flagstaff off I-17 starts at AZ 260 in the Verde Valley, about 1.5 hours (100 mi) north of Phoenix near Cottonwood. Get off the interstate at Exit 287 and head west toward Cottonwood. About 12 miles on, take AZ 89A north, through Sedona and Oak Creek Canyon, all the way to the mountains and the pines. It's only 50 miles from Cottonwood to Flagstaff but takes an hour or more to drive the scenic route through the verdant riverside valley and past the otherworldly red rocks of Sedona. You can also pick up AZ 89A at the Village of Oak Creek, 39 miles from Flagstaff, and take it straight north through Sedona and Oak Creek Canyon. This route is spectacular, as it includes about eight miles of travel on AZ 179 past some of the Sedona area's most famous eroded-rock attractions. Get off the interstate at Exit 298 for AZ 179 and pick up AZ

89A eight miles north at Sedona. From there, Sedona and Flagstaff are separated by about 30 slow miles of winding two-lane road with amazing views.

Once in "Flag," as the locals sometimes call this mountain town, you're ideally situated to visit a long list of unique attractions. Chief among these is Grand Canyon National Park's **South Rim,** a mere 80 scenic miles away. Take U.S. 180 north from downtown, driving through the pine forest in the shadow of the towering San Francisco Peaks. Pick up AZ 64 at the tiny windswept roadside stop known as Valle, about 50 miles from Flagstaff. From there it's a straight shot across a barren plain to the South Rim gate. The whole trip takes about 1.5 hours, making Flagstaff a logical place to base your Grand Canyon visit if you don't want to stay in the park.

A trip to the **North Rim** from Flagstaff takes quite a bit longer. Take U.S. 89 north across the volcanic cinder lands, through the western edge of the vast Navajo Reservation, and into the lonely landscape near the Utah border known as the Arizona Strip. After about two hours (123 mi), pick up U.S. 89A heading west at Bitter Springs. Cross the Colorado River at Marble Canyon and skirt the edge of Vermilion Cliffs National Monument toward the Kaibab Plateau, climbing to the forested highlands and Jacob Lake, the center of plateau life. The 50-mile drive from Bitter Springs to Jacob Lake usually takes an hour or more. When you pass the hotel and restaurant at Jacob Lake, you have another 45 miles to go on AZ 67, a drive that takes an hour or more through a mountain forest of evergreens and aspen, with patches blackened by fire. The whole gorgeous, unforgettable, 208-mile drive will take at least four hours. It's not a great idea for a day trip from Flagstaff unless you want to spend all day in the car; a better idea is to take two days and stay overnight in the park or at Jacob Lake.

The sights closest to town are **Meteor Crater,** 45 miles east on I-40; **Sunset Crater,** 14 miles north on U.S. 89; **Wupatki,** 39 miles north on U.S. 89; and **Walnut Canyon,** a quick 10.5-mile drive east on I-40. These places attract visitors from around the world and are easy to find. You can't miss them if you follow the signs along the highways. The **Navajo Nation**'s reservation begins about 50 miles north of Flagstaff along U.S. 89, and **Lake Powell** spreads across the hard land 136 miles to the north on the same route. The **Petrified Forest** and **Painted Desert** are about 115 miles east on I-40.

The 467-mile drive from Los Angeles to Flagstaff typically takes about seven hours, most of it on I-40. If you're starting from Las Vegas, take U.S. 93 past Hoover Dam and over the Colorado River to I-40. The 252-mile drive takes about four hours.

CAR RENTAL

Most of the major car-rental companies have a presence at Flagstaff's small **Pulliam Airport** (928/556-1234, www.flagstaff. az.gov), about five miles south of downtown. **Avis Downtown Flagstaff Car Rental** (175 W. Aspen Ave., 928/714-0713, www.avis.com, 7am-6pm Mon.-Fri., 8am-4pm Sat., 9am-1pm Sun.) is in the middle of all the action at the corner of Aspen Avenue and Humphreys Street. **Budget** (175 W. Aspen Ave., 800/527-7000, www.budget.com, 7am-6pm Mon.-Fri., 8am-4pm Sat., 9am-1pm Sun.) operates in the same facility. **Enterprise Rent-A-Car** (213 E. Rte. 66, 928/526-1377, www.enterprise.com, 8am-6pm Mon.-Fri., 9am-noon Sat.) is on the eastern edges of town along I-40.

If you're looking for a mythic Southwestern experience, stop by **EagleRider Flagstaff** (800 W. Rte. 66, 928/637-6575, www. eaglerider.com, 8am-6pm daily, $109-145 per day) and rent a Harley-Davidson.

Long-Distance Bus

Flagstaff's **Greyhound Bus Lines** (800 E. Butler Ave., 928/774-4573, www.greyhound. com) station is in the industrial wasteland that is East Butler Avenue. The company offers bus service to Flagstaff from most points on the map.

Shuttle

Groome Transportation aka Arizona Shuttle (928/350-8466, http://groometransportation.com) offers several daily trips between Flagstaff's Amtrak station and Sky Harbor International Airport ($49 one-way). The company also offers rides from Flagstaff to the Grand Canyon three times daily (Mar.-Oct., round-trip $60 adults) as well as from Flagstaff to Sedona, the Verde Valley, and Williams (one-way $35-43).

Train

Amtrak's *Southwest Chief* (800/872-7245, www.amtrak.com), which mirrors the old Santa Fe Railroad's *Super Chief* route of the grand Fred Harvey days, stops twice daily, once eastbound, once westbound, at Flagstaff's classic **downtown depot** (1 E. Rte. 66), the former Santa Fe headquarters and also the town's visitors center. The route crosses the country from Chicago to Los Angeles, entering the Southwest through northern New Mexico and Northern Arizona.

Public Transportation

Flagstaff's city bus, the **Mountain Line** (928/779-6624, www.mountainline.az.gov, $1.25 per ride, $2.50 day pass), runs 6am-10pm weekdays and 7am-8pm weekends to stops all over town.

Bike

Flagstaff is a bicycle-friendly city with a well-established and active bike culture. You'll see a lot of people riding mountain bikes around town, even in the winter. It's pretty easy to get around most of the town on a bike on a network of multiuse paths laid out in the **Flagstaff Urban Trails and Bikeways Map,** available for free at the **Flagstaff Visitor Center** downtown. You can pedal from downtown to the east side of town using the popular **Route 66 Trail** while avoiding the always busy traffic along Route 66. The 4.4-mile paved trail runs along the south side of Route 66 east from downtown and is popular with bike commuters. The ambitious 42-mile **Flagstaff Loop Trail** is about half finished. The trail will someday circle the town and feed smaller spoke-like paths to various points in town.

Prescott

With more than 700 buildings on the National Register of Historic Places and a rough Old West history full of political chicanery and violence, Prescott has much to recommend to visitors, especially those fascinated by the 19th-century Anglo West and Victorian architecture. Prescott has become "Everybody's Hometown," a slogan printed on signs and flags throughout the picturesque downtown. Prescott has a sizable population of well-off retirees and a hard-to-miss group of young back-to-nature bohemian residents, many of them students at Prescott College, a private liberal arts school.

Prescott's lasting draw for those living in the lowlands is its four-season climate—hot in summer, perfect in spring, cool in fall, and cold, sometimes even snowy, in winter. The Prescott National Forest hugs the outskirts of town in a sappy embrace, traversed by hundreds of trails and ideal for all manner of outdoor retreats and recreation.

SIGHTS
Downtown and the Courthouse Plaza

Most of Prescott's charm is centered on a few blocks in the **downtown area** (Gurley, Montezuma, Cortez, and Goodwin Streets), among dozens of shops, boutiques, antiques stores, and art galleries, many with an Old West theme, and most in the middle to high end of the price range, as well as the town's best restaurants and bars, frequented by visitors and locals alike. The whole scene surrounds the tall-pillared stone **Yavapai County Courthouse,** built in 1916 of locally quarried stone, and its grassy grounds lined by imported trees. There's always something going on—square dancing, craft shows, live theater, families or couples lounging on the grass with a picnic, kids playing with Frisbees, and exercisers doing laps on the cobblestone walkways, led by their dogs.

Large **bronze statues** grace three sides of the plaza: a cowboy supine fireside with his horse watching over him, a lifelike war memorial with sinewy soldiers, and a huge equestrian scene featuring Bucky O'Neill, frontier Renaissance man and Spanish-American War victim. This famous area landmark was sculpted by Solon Borglum, whose brother Gutzon sculpted Mount Rushmore. Downtown is definitely the place to be in Prescott, and you could spend an entire day and night just strolling around, shopping, eating, drinking, people-watching, looking at old buildings, and sucking in the clean mile-high air, never bothering to see the rest of the town, which is much bigger (pop. 40,000) than the quaint plaza and downtown suggest.

While no longer the capital of the entire territory, Prescott is seat of the Yavapai County, and as such the downtown's government buildings can get busy on weekdays. On weekends the road and foot traffic slow a little. Tourists and day-trippers crowd the center of town, especially during summer and the many festivals and shows held on the plaza year-round. There are parking spaces along the downtown streets and a public garage just west of the plaza on Gurley Street. It's best to find a parking space and keep it as long as you can.

Sharlot Hall Museum

Named for its brilliant founder, Sharlot M. Hall, a writer, editor, poet, and historian in a time when Western women didn't usually do such things, the **Sharlot Hall Museum**

(Gurley St., 2 blocks west of the plaza, 928/445-3122, www.sharlothallmuseum.org, 10am-5pm Mon.-Sat., noon-4pm Sun. May-Sept., $12 adults, $5 ages 13-17, free under age 13) has beautiful grounds and interesting exhibits on the town's wild frontier days, balanced by a good portion of the quotidian details and artifacts of hard life on the Southwestern edge of American civilization. The grassy complex, spread over three acres with rose gardens and recreated frontier structures, features the refurbished Victorian gem called the **Bashford House** and the log-cabin residence of the state's first governor. A rose garden honors Prescott's pioneer women, the fascinating biographies of whom are available for perusal in a file at the museum. It's an easy walk from downtown to the Sharlot Hall Museum, worth it if only to see the pretty green grounds and the mansions of another age.

Fort Whipple Museum

The Sharlot Hall Museum also operates the small **Fort Whipple Museum** (500 N. AZ 89, Bldg. 11, VA campus, 928/445-3122, 10am-4pm Thurs.-Sat., free) about four miles north of downtown on the tree-lined campus of the Veterans Administration Hospital, formerly home to Fort Whipple, a major base for General Crook's war against the Apache. The museum, housed in an old Victorian home once used as officers' quarters, displays the memorabilia and daily items of frontier military life and puts on historical reenactments the third Saturday of February, May, August, and November.

Museum of Indigenous People

For 70 years, 1920-1990, the builders of this little pueblo-esque building a few miles east of downtown off Gurley Street—a group of Prescott businesspeople who called themselves the Smoki People—covered their half-naked bodies in a shade of brownish-red and sold tickets to an annual fairground performance of dances and ceremonies based on Hopi religion, including even the famous Snake Dance with its live props. The group's

Prescott

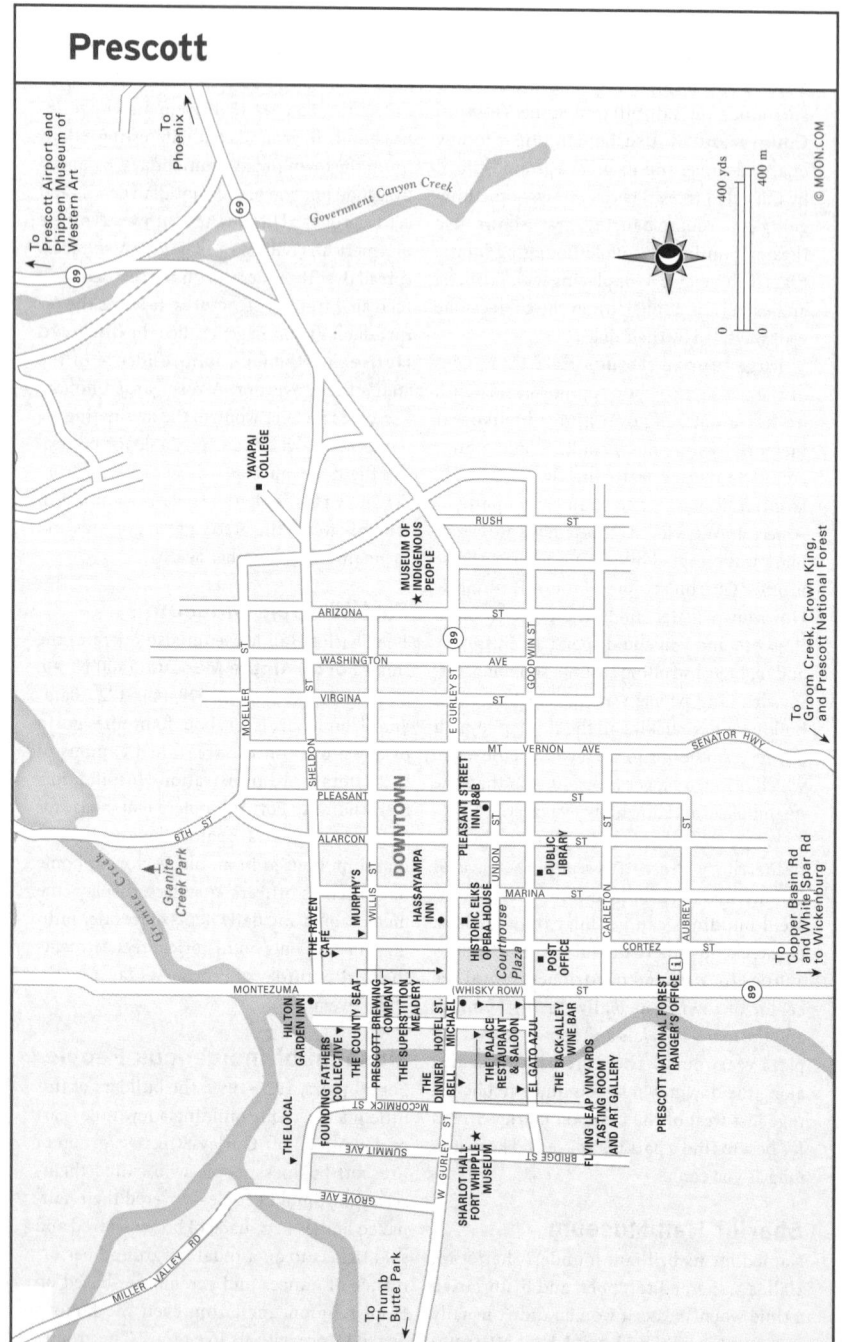

© MOON.COM

To Prescott Airport and Phippen Museum of Western Art

To Phoenix

Government Canyon Creek

YAVAPAI COLLEGE

MUSEUM OF INDIGENOUS PEOPLE

To Groom Creek, Crown King, and Prescott National Forest

RUSH ST

ARIZONA ST

WASHINGTON AVE

VIRGINA ST

MT VERNON AVE

SENATOR HWY

GOODWIN ST

E GURLEY ST

MOELLER ST

SHELDON ST

6TH ST

PLEASANT ST

ALARCON

DOWNTOWN

PLEASANT STREET INN B&B

UNION ST

MARINA ST

CARLETON ST

PUBLIC LIBRARY

AUBREY ST

THE RAVEN CAFE

MURPHY'S

WILLIS ST

HASSAYAMPA INN

HISTORIC ELKS OPERA HOUSE

Courthouse Plaza

POST OFFICE

CORTEZ ST

To Copper Basin Rd and White Spar Rd to Wickenburg

MONTEZUMA

(WHISKY ROW)

PRESCOTT NATIONAL FOREST RANGER'S OFFICE

HILTON GARDEN INN

THE COUNTY SEAT

PRESCOTT BREWING COMPANY

THE SUPERSTITION MEADERY

HOTEL ST. MICHAEL

THE PALACE RESTAURANT & SALOON

EL GATO AZUL

THE BACK-ALLEY WINE BAR

FLYING LEAP VINYARDS TASTING ROOM AND ART GALLERY

THE LOCAL

FOUNDING FATHERS COLLECTIVE

THE DINNER BELL

McCORMICK ST

SUMMIT AVE

W GURLEY ST

BRIDGE ST

SHARLOT HALL FORT WHIPPLE MUSEUM

GROVE AVE

W GURLEY ST

MILLER VALLEY RD

To Thumb Butte Park

Granite Creek Park

Granite Creek

400 yds

400 m

museum preserved and displayed some excellent examples of Pueblo, Navajo, and Yavapai arts, crafts, and artifacts, along with items from tribes throughout the West. Not exactly a politically correct organization, the Smoki People were protested out of existence in 1990 by the Hopi, who were fed up with having their sacred culture co-opted and mocked by Anglos. The whole story is told through a fascinating and frank exhibit in the **Museum of Indigenous People** (147 N. Arizona St., 928/445-1230, www. museumofindigenouspeople.org, 10am-4pm Mon.-Sat., 1pm-4pm Sun., $7 adults, free under age 12), formerly called the Smoki Museum, now dedicated to interpreting the Smoki phenomenon—extremely popular among the locals for many years—and preserving some of the wonderful treasures collected. This is a quirky and illuminating attraction, and the building itself should be seen by lovers of unique structures. The museum is part of the Prescott Armory Historic District, which includes nearby Ken Lindley Field, the old Prescott National Guard Armory, and the Citizens' Cemetery, each of which is of passing interest to history buffs and enthusiasts of quirky architecture.

The Phippen Museum of Western Art

Prescott's only art museum, **The Phippen Museum of Western Art** (4701 AZ 89 N., 928/778-1385, www.phippenartmuseum.org, 10am-4pm Tues.-Sat., 1pm-4pm Sun., $10 adults, free under age 12) is an essential stop for those who appreciate the Cowboy Artists of America school of painting and bronze sculpture. The museum's namesake, the artist George Phippen, was that famous group's cofounder and first president, and the collection features many of the luminaries of the movement as well as Native American arts and crafts and about four Western-related special exhibits every year. The drive out to the hilltop museum is as stimulating as all the oil paintings of cattle drives and bronze bucking broncos inside. A scenic seven miles

north from downtown, the building overlooks a little dry-grass valley just past the strangely piled giant boulders of Granite Dells and the reedy confines of Watson Lake.

RECREATION
Prescott National Forest

The **Prescott National Forest** (www. fs.usda.gov/prescott), more than a million acres of desert scrub, chaparral, piñon, juniper, and pine-carpeted rolling hills, dry-grass flatlands, and rocky mountains, is the western edge of the largest ponderosa pine forest in the world, the beginning of the great Arizona Pine Belt that stretches across and below the Mogollon Rim all the way to New Mexico.

Just a few miles from downtown, the forest around Prescott is a perfect place for a high-altitude hike over pine needle-strewn trails, an afternoon picnic, a cool-breeze glide across a tucked-away forest lake, or an overnight camping trip beneath the tall, sap-scented woods. The forest has long been used for small-scale mining, ranching, and outdoor recreation, and in some places it shows its wear and tear. There are more homes in this forest than one usually sees on federal land, mostly owing to the fact that owners of mining claims are allowed to build on public lands, and there are a lot of still-active mining claims in those mineral-laden mountains. Old mining and logging roads are now used by mountain bikers and hikers, and, in some areas, off-road vehicle enthusiasts.

Just outside downtown, the forest's **headquarters** (344 S. Cortez St., 928/443-8000, 8am-4:30pm Mon.-Fri.) has a kiosk with free single-sheet descriptions and maps of every trail in the forest. It's a good idea to stop here if you're going to be doing anything in the forest—there's simply too much information to pass up. Rangers at the office can answer any questions.

Lynx Lake Recreation Area (day use 6am-8pm daily Apr.-Sept., 7am-6pm daily Oct.-Mar., parking $5), just north of town off AZ 69, is a 55-acre lake surrounded by ponderosa pines and stocked with trout. You can float

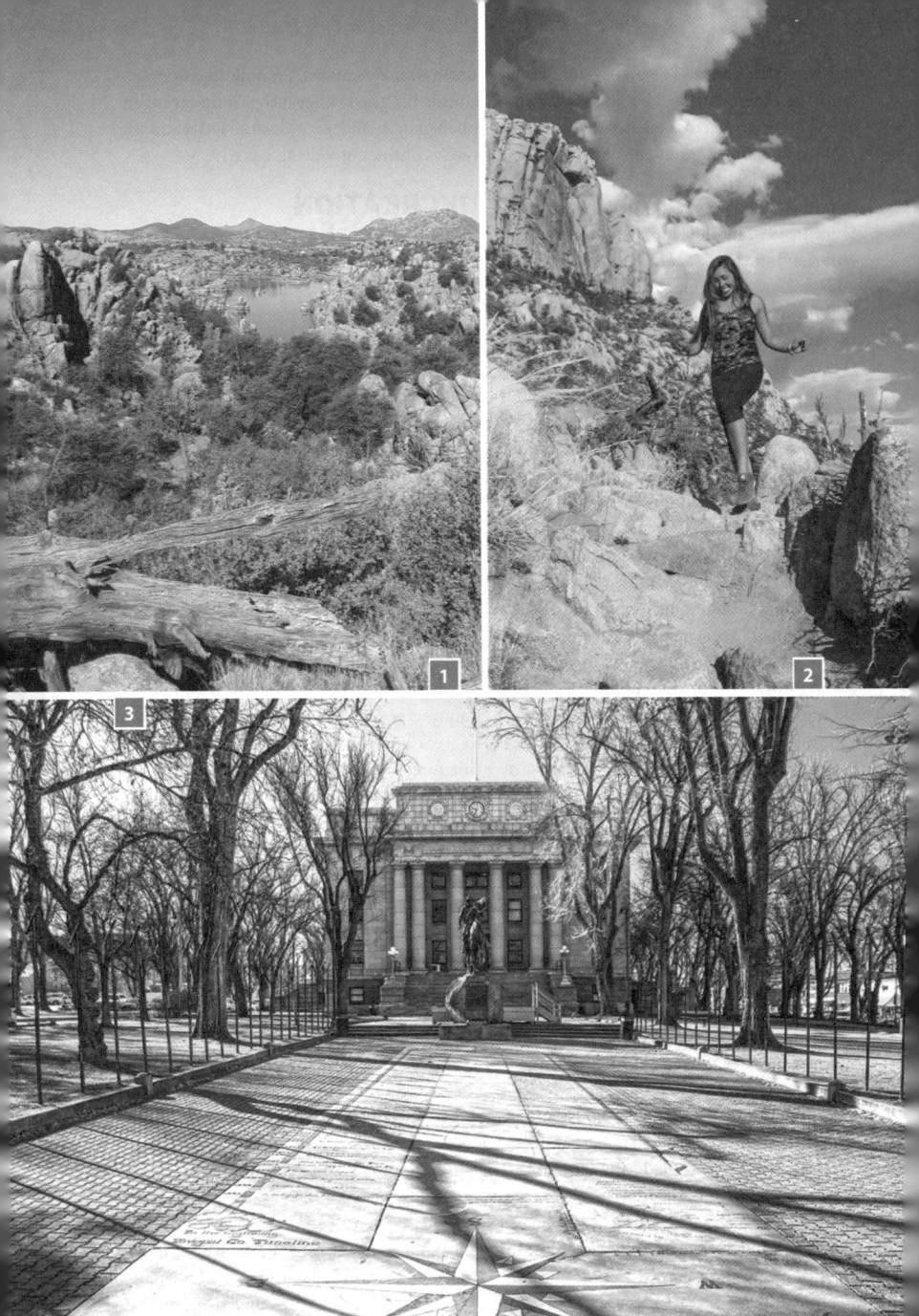

your own boat out on the lake and fish or rent a craft and gear at the **Lynx Lake Store and Marina** (928/778-0720). The surrounding forest has several hiking and biking trails. The 4.3-mile hike to **Salida Gulch** will get you to the **Gold Pan Day Use Area,** where you can engage in the occupation that put the forest around Prescott on the map. The area has two basic campgrounds (no reservations, $18).

In the forest just outside town along Senator Highway is **Goldwater Lake,** a popular place for picnicking, kayaking, and canoeing. Out along AZ 89, five miles north of downtown, **Watson Lake** is surrounded by giant otherworldly boulder piles, an area called **Granite Dells.** The five-mile **Peavine Trail,** an old railroad right-of-way that takes you through the heart of the rock piles, is a highlight of this area and can be hiked or biked with ease. If you didn't bring your mountain bike, you can rent one from **Ironclad Bicycles** (710 White Spar Rd., 928/776-1755, www. ironcladbicycles.com, 10am-5:30pm Mon.-Sat., 10am-2pm Sun., $12-16 per hour). If you forgot your canoe or kayak, or if you want to try either of these activities for the first time, call **Prescott Outdoors** (928/925-1410, www.prescottoutdoors.com, 8am-3pm Wed.-Sun. spring-fall at Watson Lake, 9am-4pm Sat.-Sun. spring-fall at Goldwater Lake).

A boulder-and-pine wilderness west of town off Iron Springs Road, **Granite Basin Recreation Area** (parking $5) is the home of 7,600-foot-high Granite Mountain, the stained sheer rock face of which is a preferred residence of peregrine falcons. The area has a small lake with fishing and a popular basic campground (no hookups or reservations, $18) as well as miles of hiking and biking trails.

Hiking and Mountain Biking

You could spend years hiking and biking the Prescott National Forest and still not get to every trail and hidden trickling-water canyon. If you've got years to spare, go down to the forest headquarters, pick up all of the handy free maps, and get hiking. If you have only a few days, however, try one of the popular and beautiful hikes described below. Most forest trails that aren't in a wilderness area are open to hikers, bikers, and horseback riders; all trails are closed to motorized vehicles unless expressly set aside for off-road recreation.

The steep but relatively easy two-mile round-trip hike up to a saddle at the base of **Thumb Butte,** Prescott's favorite natural monument, provides awesome views of the town all nestled among the pines. Several trails around the popular **Thumb Butte Picnic Area** (3 miles west of downtown, on Gurley St., which becomes Thumb Butte Rd., $3 or national park pass) lead into the forest, along creek sides, and off to highlands from which you can see the San Francisco Peaks, way up north.

The four-mile one-way hike up to the big boulders waiting atop **Granite Mountain** (3 miles west of downtown, off Iron Springs Rd., parking $2) is highly recommended for those who don't mind a steep trudge. It's one of the most popular trails in the Prescott area. Peregrine falcons nest on the mountain's rock face, so bring binoculars. The trail winds up the mountain from a manzanita and piñon forest to the pines and the rocky peak at 7,600 feet. It gets cold in early spring and fall, and there's likely to be snowpack in the higher regions in winter. This is a wilderness area, so no mountain bikes are allowed. Some of the areas around the cliff face are closed in winter and spring so the falcons can nest in peace.

The **Groom Creek Loop Trail** extends through the forest and up more than 1,000 feet to the top of Spruce Mountain, where there's a fire lookout and a few promontories to see the top of almost every tree in the land. The winding single-track heading downhill makes this a wild ride on a mountain bike, nearly worth the difficult climb up. Head out on Senator Highway via Mount Vernon Avenue, lined with intricate old Victorian homes, for six

1: Granite Dells in the Prescott National Forest **2:** hiking Granite Basin Recreational Area **3:** Yavapai County Courthouse

Granite Mountain Hotshots Memorial State Park

It happened in Yarnell, a village scattered among the boulders and scrub about 35 miles down AZ 89 from Prescott. Before the interstate, drivers passed through this old mining area on the slow drive from Phoenix to the northland, keeping a few gas stations and cafés in business. But those days were long gone by the summer of 2013, when Yarnell became synonymous with the deadliest wildfire in Arizona's history.

Sparked by lightning on June 28, 2013, the Yarnell Hill Fire took the lives of 19 elite firefighters with the Granite Mountain Hotshots, a group based in Prescott and named after the boulder mountain rising from the flatlands north of town. By the time the blaze was contained on July 10, it had burned more than 8,400 acres and changed Yarnell and Prescott forever.

Though it's not easy to visit, the **Granite Mountain Hotshots Memorial State Park** (AZ 89, 4 miles south of Yarnell, 877/697-2757, http://azstateparks.com, always open, free) tells the story of the fire and the lives it took in a powerful way, requiring of visitors a small amount of the drive and stamina needed to fight such wild and remote blazes.

The 2.85-mile one-way **Hotshots Trail** climbs and winds through brush and boulders to an observation deck above the spot where the 19 firefighters died. Along the way, plaques attached to rocks tell the story of each hotshot. From the deck you can pick up the 0.75-mile one-way **Journey Trail** down to the "fatality site," which is circled by large rock walls.

The hike is about 7 miles round-trip, and there are a few steep areas. There are no restrooms along the trail, and no shade or water. May-September it's very hot, so prepare yourself for a hard hike of four hours or more. Take water, and make sure you have your dog leashed. There are restrooms at the trailhead along with a bronze statue of a hotshot in full gear, but no visitors center.

miles until you see the sign for Groom Creek Horse Camp. The trailhead parking lot is on the east side of the road.

ENTERTAINMENT
Nightlife

Although these days there are more galleries and boutiques than saloons, gambling halls, and brothels along the short stretch of Montezuma Street known since territorial days as **Whiskey Row** (www.prescott.com/whiskey-row), downtown is still the best place to party in Prescott.

To get a sense of what it was like on this infamously raucous street back in the old days, step into **The Palace Restaurant and Saloon** (120 S. Montezuma St., 928/541-1996, www.historicpalace.com, 11am-9:30pm Mon.-Thurs., 11am-10:30pm Fri.-Sat., $12-36). In the heyday of the drunken territory, it was known as a rowdy and even dangerous place. Everybody drank at the Palace, from the Earp brothers to Steve McQueen, who made

a movie in Prescott, celebrated with several pictures on the wall. A big part of the fun of a stop here is looking at all the artifacts and memorabilia of days past. Although the old heavy-wood bar remains, and it can still get a little hectic with drinkers, the Palace is today mostly a good restaurant.

This might be the most interesting bar in the northland: **The Superstition Meadery** (120 W. Gurley St., 928/458-4256, www.superstitionmeadery.com, 11am-9pm Mon.-Thurs., 11am-10pm Fri.-Sat., 11am-6pm Sun.) serves a wide variety of complex and delicious mead and hard cider made with the help of local bees. Head down the stairs from a gift shop in a historic building downtown into the dark and romantic underground space and sample a flight of the ancient honey-wine. They also offer good tapas, including charcuterie, bruschetta, hummus, cheese plates, and the like.

You can bring your own food to **The Back-Alley Wine Bar** (156 S. Montezuma St., in the alley behind Whiskey Row, 480/570-5131, http://backalleywinebar.business.site, 2pm-9pm Mon.-Thurs., 2pm-10pm Fri.-Sat., noon-6pm Sun.), serving wine, beer, and hard cider in a casual atmosphere and with an emphasis on those made in Arizona. There's live music and karaoke on weekends.

Flying Leap's vineyard is located a few hundred miles south, in Southern Arizona's Elgin area, but its **Flying Leap Vineyards Tasting Room & Art Gallery** (124 Granite St., 888/431-5777, www.flyingleapvineyards. com, noon-6pm Wed.-Sun.) in downtown Prescott makes it easy to sample and purchase the innovative, delicious, and unforgettable Arizona-bred wines. Stop by this creek-side tasting room just west of Whiskey Row and try all the varietals while perusing local art.

The **Founding Fathers Collective** (218 N. Granite St., 928/582-9139, www. foundingfatherscollective.com) is a 14,000-square-foot former warehouse just a few blocks west of downtown along Granite Creek. In addition to a coffeehouse, a gym, a barbershop, a jiujitsu studio, a men's retail shop, and food trucks, it hosts the **City Tavern Taproom** (11am-10pm Sun.-Thurs., 11am-midnight Fri.-Sat.), "Arizona's largest self-serve beer taproom and bar," with 65 taps that you can pour yourself. It also has creative and knowledgeable bartenders.

Performing Arts
The **Historic Elks Opera House** (928/777-1370, www.prescottelkstheater.com) is on Gurley Street downtown, on Elks Hill right across from the Hassayampa Inn. The stylish old opera house, which still has a good bit of its grandeur, books acts throughout the year.

Festivals and Events
Major touring acts show up in town for the **Prescott Bluegrass Festival** (www. prescottbluegrassfestival.com, late June).

Prescott is famous, and used to be infamous, for the wild public revelry of the Fourth of July weekend, when **Prescott Frontier Days and the World's Oldest Rodeo**

(www.worldsoldestrodeo.com, July) puts the populace and the many visitors in the mood to party.

The Courthouse Plaza hosts several large shows and festivals every year, including the **Mountain Artist Guild Summer Arts and Crafts Festival** (http://prescottartfestivals. com, early Aug.) and the **Phippen Museum Western Art Show & Sale** (www. phippenartmuseum.org, May) over Memorial Day weekend, both big events in the regional Western art world.

Literary cowpunchers get together and put on readings and performances at the **Arizona Cowboy Poets Gathering** (Yavapai College, http://azcowboypoets.org, early Aug.).

SHOPPING
Prescott is a great place to find antiques, art, and that unique, indescribable item you always knew you needed but never could find. Downtown is the best place to search for such treasures. The streets flanking the Courthouse Plaza (Gurley, Montezuma, Cortez, and Goodwin Streets) and continuing on for several blocks in every direction are crowded with shops, boutiques, and galleries selling cowboy-style Western art, Mexican folk arts, handmade jewelry and crafts, gifts, Western clothing, and even contemporary furniture and home decor. **Cortez Street** especially is a kind of antiques row, with several big stores stacked with the fascinating leftovers of past generations, the members of which usually constructed their daily-life items to last—and to look beautiful and stylish while doing so.

FOOD
The ★ **Raven Café** (142 N. Cortez St., 928/717-0009, www.ravencafe.com, 7:30am-11pm Mon.-Thurs., 7:30am-midnight Fri.-Sat., 8am-3pm Sun., $9-15), with its dark-wood interior, decorative-tin ceiling, and fantastic local art on the walls, is a true Prescott original and the center of café culture in this small historic burg. All the food is fresh, and many of the ingredients are local

or regional. The breakfasts are amazing, including thick cuts of bacon, local eggs, and flavorful potatoes. The café has an excellent beer selection, top-notch coffee, free Wi-Fi, and a patio for lounging on a beautiful mile-high day. It has earned a three-star certification from the Green Restaurant Association based on the café's use of recycled materials, energy efficient equipment, and plant-based foods.

Near the small campus of Prescott College, renowned for its emphasis on environmental and social justice, **The Local** (520 W. Sheldon St., 928/237-4724, 7am-2:30pm daily, $11-16) offers a full vegan menu and gets many of its ingredients from Prescott-area farms and ranches. Open for breakfast and lunch, The Local serves familiar but Southwest-inspired dishes and one of the best veggie burgers in the known universe.

The long and fascinating menu of small plates at tiny **El Gato Azul** (316 W. Goodwin St., 928/445-1070, www.elgatoazulprescott. com, 11am-close Mon.-Fri., noon-close Sat.-Sun., $7-22) might cause you a little stress when it's time to order, but push through it and choose more than one. The dozens of creative and mouthwatering tapas, including many seafood and vegetarian selections, rarely disappoint. most plates are $2 off 4pm-6pm weekdays. They also serve delicious margaritas and sangria. Make a reservation and ask to sit on the patio as the small dining room is a bit cramped.

Locally owned restaurant and bar **Park Plaza Liquor & Deli** (402 W. Goodwin St., 928/541-9894, http://parkplazaliquor.com, 10:30am-9pm Sun.-Wed., 10:30am-10pm Thurs.-Sat., $9-19) is a casual place inside a liquor store on the edge of downtown. A favorite with locals, it represents the laid-back, beer-loving, outdoorsy vibe that pervades Prescott. Sit on the patio and enjoy the cool northland evenings and sample the excellent sandwiches, fantastic pizzas, mac-and-cheese, and burgers as well as, of course, the long list of craft brews.

If you love beer, don't miss the **Prescott Brewing Company** (130 W. Gurley St., 928/771-2795, www.prescottbrewingcompany. com, 11am-10pm daily, $8-15), right across Gurley from the Courthouse Plaza. While serving rib-sticking pub fare like bangers and mash and shepherd's pie, along with a wide assortment of lighter dishes, the brewpub offers some of the best beers in the territory.

The Peacock Room (122 E. Gurley St., 928/778-9434, http://hassayampainn.com, 7am-9pm Sun.-Thurs., 7am-9:30pm Fri.-Sat., $10-32) inside the Hassayampa Inn is a great place for a long lazy lunch or a romantic candlelit dinner. Puffy booths line the walls, art deco lines define the interior, and the chef serves up good steak, lamb, and fish dishes, along with Southwestern-tinged specials.

ACCOMMODATIONS

A tourist haven, Prescott has many chain hotels, including one or two nearly upscale; several smaller independents; and a growing number of bed-and-breakfasts. Most are along Gurley Street from one end of town to the other. The **Tourist Information Center** (800/266-7534, www.prescott.org) downtown has reams of pamphlets and brochures on various area accommodations. It's best to make reservations, especially in summer.

As historic Prescott hotels go, the ★ **Hassayampa Inn** (122 E. Gurley St., 928/778-9434, www.hassayampainn.com, $89-139) is the star. Built in 1927 atop Elks Hill, a high-class gateway to downtown, the landmark hotel has a kind of redbrick modified Spanish Colonial Revival style, with a bell tower and a covered passageway from the street to the lobby doors. Off the lobby is a great restaurant, the Peacock Room, and a cozy dark-wood lounge where a jazz band often plays. The rooms are old but classic, comfortable, and stylish. All the rooms have free Wi-Fi, TVs, and air-conditioning, which the likes of D. H. Lawrence and Greta Garbo lacked when they stayed here.

The historic **Hotel St. Michael** (205 W. Gurley St., 928/776-1999, www. stmichaelhotel.com, $109-139) is right downtown on the corner of Whiskey Row and Gurley Street, a redbrick reminder of another era. Built in 1901 with gargoyles staring down from its facade, the hotel has an excellent bistro and individually decorated guest rooms, cable TV, free Wi-Fi, and air-conditioning. The comfortable old building still operates an elevator installed in 1925. Breakfast in the bistro is included in the room rates.

The **Hotel Vendome** (230 S. Cortez St., 928/776-0900 or 888/468-3583, www. vendomehotel.com, $109-149) is a delightful, historic, and finely detailed place to stay in one of Prescott's central tree-lined neighborhoods, with beautiful relics of the Victorian heyday on every lot. Within easy walking distance to downtown, the Vendome, a registered Historic Landmark built in 1917, offers 20 guest rooms with big bathtubs and all the comforts you could ever want. There's an elegant and cozy bar on-site serving Arizona beers and wines.

A few blocks up Montezuma Street from downtown and Whiskey Row, **The Motor Lodge** (503 S. Montezuma St., 928/717-0157, http://themotorlodge.com, $129-189) is a wonderfully refurbished homage to mid-century road culture. A lot of little touches make it a fun and retro experience—like the classic cars sitting out front, the old neon, and the period furniture and knickknacks—and yet its comforts are all up-to-date and stylish, with 12 motor court-style rooms each with their own eclectic decor, free Wi-Fi, cable TV, and private porches.

The Grand Highland Hotel (154 S. Montezuma St., 928/776-9963, http://grandhighlandhotel.com, $99-189), right downtown on Whiskey Row, is a charming boutique hotel that brings back a little of what it must have felt like to a be frontier dandy in town for a spree. Sumptuous, historic, and ideally located, this is a memorable place to stay in the heart of Prescott, a few steps from bars, restaurants, and shops, and perfectly located for evening strolls around the shady courthouse square across the street.

INFORMATION AND SERVICES

The **Prescott Chamber of Commerce** (117 W. Goodwin St., 928/445-2000 or 800/266-7534, www.prescott.org, 9am-5pm Mon.-Fri., 11am-2pm Sat.-Sun.) has friendly volunteers and tons of information on the area. A volunteer offers free guided historical tours of the downtown (10am Fri.-Sun.) from the chamber building.

The Verde Valley

In the Verde Valley—an ancient oasis fed and greened by water falling headlong off the Mogollon Rim—you can't walk a mile without seeing some fallen ruins or artifact left behind by the conquistadores, miners, agriculturists, and speculators who've been drawn to this fertile valley and its surrounding mountains over the centuries. Most people came here after rumors of ore; others grew crops and orchards and raised livestock. The area continues to grow at a steady pace as more and more refugees from the Phoenix sprawl hunt out rural enclaves. It's still rather quiet, though that is likely to change in the next decade or so. The area has long been known for one set of ruins in particular, the spectacular if misnamed Montezuma Castle, a must-see.

There's a good bit of outdoor fun to be had in the valley, including tubing and boating down wild stretches of the Verde River and hiking into beautiful Sycamore Canyon. But even before you reach the valley, you'll get a chance to shop, eat, and stay in some memorable stores, restaurants, and hotels in Jerome, a former copper boomtown that is too cool to pass up. The Verde Valley is one of several regions in Arizona that produces wine, with at least seven vineyards along the Verde

River and Oak Creek. Sample and tour them on the **Verde Valley Wine Trail** (www.verdevalleywines.org); there are also tasting rooms in Jerome, Old Town Cottonwood, and Sedona.

MINGUS MOUNTAIN

The best way to start a tour of the Verde Valley is to drive up and over the mountain that watches over it from the west, 7,743-foot **Mingus Mountain,** part of the Black Hills range and Prescott National Forest. Take **AZ 89A** from the mountain's base—either from the Verde Valley on the east side or Prescott Valley on the west—and negotiate the slow switchbacks of the two-lane road, towered over by cliffs and overlooking deep pine-swept draws. It's a **scenic drive,** one of the region's most stunning, usually taking about an hour to go the 30 miles over the mountain, through the old mining metropolis of Jerome, and down the other side. The drive is understandably popular with motorcycle enthusiasts and sports-car pilots, so you might have to pull over and let some of them pass.

Near the top of the mountain is **Mingus Mountain Recreation Area** (www.fs.usda.gov), with a few basic high-forest campgrounds (no reservations, $10), and the eight-mile round-trip hike along the **Woodchute Trail** into the Woodchute Wilderness and up around to the north side of Woodchute Mountain, where boomtown Jerome got the wood to build itself. It's a pretty easy hike through an open pine and juniper forest that allows for some spectacular views. If you don't want to hike but still want to see the valley from way up high, drive three miles on the dirt road to the recreation area, where there's a granite promontory where you can sit and see mile after hazy mile spreading out in green and brown.

TOP EXPERIENCE

★ JEROME

More than 1,000 years ago the Sinagua people took minerals out of the cliffs that Jerome would one day cling to, engaging in ancient small-scale mining for precious stones and paints. This established the primary use of Cleopatra Hill, where Spanish conquistadores would dig for what was precious to them—gold and silver. But it wasn't until copper became one of the most useful metals of the modern age that the "Million Dollar Copper Camp" really got going. At its zenith in the 1920s, Jerome had about 15,000 residents.

Throughout the late 19th and early 20th centuries, Jerome was known for its moral subjectivity: prostitution and other common territorial sins were tolerated, albeit regulated, well into the 1940s. Mining of any kind is always a boom-and-bust enterprise, and by the 1950s the bust had descended. The Phelps Dodge Corporation left, never to return. The town turned ghostly around 1953, when it had fewer than 50 full-time residents and a lot of abandoned and crumbling homes, hotels, and shops.

By the 1970s, however, hippies, artists, dropouts, and crafters had found the picturesque old town and began its resurgence as a colorful hilltop village of creative people, the kind of funky tourist haven and hideaway found all over the old mining frontier. Today dozens of shops, many carrying one-of-a-kind creations made by Jerome's bevy of resident artists and artisans, line the narrow twisting streets, and saloon-esque bars, historic boutique hotels, and New American eateries occupy the old buildings that once served as saloons, hardware stores, hospitals, and hotels during the busy mining years, when the pits were worked around the clock. A couple of hours walking Jerome's streets, shopping for gifts and souvenirs, and eating at one of its excellent restaurants make for a fine way to spend an Arizona day.

Jerome Historical Mine Society Museum

The small **Jerome Historical Mine Society Museum** (200 Main St., 928/634-5477, www.jeromehistoricalsociety.com, 9am-6pm daily, $2 adults, free children) has exhibits

A Northland Road Trip

This is ideal road-trip country, its scenic treasures nearly always represented not only deep in the wilderness but right there on the roadside.

Starting from Phoenix, the most scenic road trip to hit all the wonders and sights goes first to Prescott, where you'll pick up AZ 89A, twisting up and over Mingus Mountain through Jerome and then down the other side into the Verde Valley.

After seeing the ruins and lush riverine spectacle of Verde country, continue on AZ 89A to Sedona, through Oak Creek Canyon, and up to Flagstaff, where the road becomes U.S. 89 and leads to Wupatki and Sunset Crater Volcano. Head south to I-40 and east to Walnut Canyon. Continue on I-40 to Winslow, where you'll pick up AZ 87 south through the pines to Payson and Tonto Natural Bridge, just below the Mogollon Rim.

After exploring below the Rim, take Forest Road 300 (a dirt road but easily navigable) across the Rim to AZ 260 (if you want to skip the dirt-road backcountry, pick up AZ 260 in Payson), which becomes the White Mountain Scenic Road and leads through the high forest and meadow country to U.S. 191, the Coronado Trail. Slowly twist and turn down the forest-lined two-lane road, through the tiny mountain towns, to the desert grasslands of southeastern Arizona. Then take I-10 west through Tucson and back to Phoenix.

If you don't stop too long at any one place, this road trip through the best of the region's scenery makes for a memorable and busy long weekend.

on Jerome's exciting and sometimes violent history. It has ephemera and artifacts from the town's various eras, from its boom days through the big bust in the 1950s and beyond. There's a hefty touch of the lurid, with a lot about violence, illicit sex, and the social consequences of each—the most fascinating displays in the building, naturally. There's also a small gift shop that sells books on the history of Jerome and souvenirs of the region.

Jerome State Historic Park

The Douglas family ruled mining in Jerome for decades, and in 1916 patriarch James "Rawhide Jimmy" Douglas built this palatial adobe house above his Little Daisy Mine, the better to welcome mine investors and company officials to town with the kind of style and comfort not always expected in the western wildlands. The mansion is now Jerome State Historic Park (Douglas Rd., off AZ 89A, 928/634-5381, http://azstateparks.com, 8:30am-4:45pm Thurs.-Mon., $7 adults, $4 ages 7-13, free under age 7), dedicated to Jerome's history, and it's worth a visit just to see the building. The library has been beautifully restored and evokes what it was like to

live comfortably in an otherwise rough mining town. There are several interesting displays on Jerome's history and a lot of rusty old mining equipment sitting around the grounds. A short video, narrated by a friendly ghost, tells the story of Jerome, and a cool 3-D model of the town shows what the tunnels looked like under it.

Nightlife

These days Jerome is no longer known as one of the "wickedest" places in the territory, and illegal narcotics aren't regularly ingested from the town's bar tops as in the 1970s and 1980s, Jerome's nightlife can still get rowdy—and therefore fun. The Spirit Room Bar (166 Main St., 928/634-8809, www.spiritroom. com, 11am-1am daily) offers deep cocktails and live music Saturday-Sunday afternoons and into the night.

Shopping

There are dozens of shops, boutiques, galleries, and antiques stores in Jerome, with new ones always opening as the tourist traffic increases. Along with the usual shops with gifts and crafts and a Southwestern flare, you'll find contemporary fine art, handmade wines, fudge, pottery, copper and turquoise jewelry, and all sorts of other treasures in Jerome, where shopping is really the primary activity.

Make sure to check out the amazing collection of kaleidoscopes at **Nelly Bly** (136 Main St., 928/634-0255, www.nellieblyscopes.com, 9:30am-5:30pm Sun.-Thurs., 9:30am-6pm Fri.-Sat.). Stick to Main Street to find most of the shops, although others can be found on Clark Street, Hill Street, and Jerome Avenue.

Food

Sit at one of the candlelit tables overlooking the Verde Valley at ★ **The Asylum** (200 Hill St., 928/639-3197, www.theasylum.biz, 11am-3:30pm and 5pm-9pm daily, $13-32), inside the Jerome Grand Hotel on a hill. It bills itself as "a restaurant on the fringe," meaning the cooking is on the cutting edge of New American cuisine. The menu has an interesting mix of the familiar and the exotic fused to create some delicious meals, and the wine selection is as impressive as the elegant view-centered interior.

The Clinkscale (309 Main St., 928/634-6225, http://theclinkscale.com, 8:30am-8:30pm daily, $10-30) serves an excellent daily brunch and has a great bar with Arizona beer flights and superior margaritas, plus creative sandwiches, fish tacos, mac-and-cheese, and cauliflower steaks.

The Haunted Hamburger (410 Clark St., 928/634-0554, http://thehauntedhamburger.com, 11am-9pm daily, $8-22) serves amazing specialty burgers, thick and flavorful milk shakes, hot dogs, chicken sandwiches, and a veggie wrap.

Accommodations

Jerome has several boutique hotels and bed-and-breakfast inns, most of them in refurbished historic buildings with at least one or two ghosts in residence.

★ **Jerome Grand Hotel** (200 Hill St., 928/634-8200, www.jeromegrandhotel.net, $185-295) used to be a hospital, and from the outside it has the character of an old sanatorium, perched on a hill and heavy with secrets. Inside, guest rooms are tastefully decorated and comfortable, with nice showers and tubs, TVs; some have views of the valley below.

A high-class establishment for boomtown visitors, the **Connor Hotel of Jerome** (164 Main St., 928/634-5006, www.connorhotel.com, $125-185) has been around in one form or another in this location since 1898. Today it's a charming comfortable place to stay in downtown Jerome, with 12 guest rooms, each with a TV, a minifridge, a private bath, and Wi-Fi. The rooms above the Spirit Room Bar are sometimes noisy, especially on weekends.

Information and Services

Check out the **Jerome Chamber of Commerce** (310 Hull Ave., 928/634-2900, www.jeromechamber.com, 9am-5pm Mon.-Fri.) for up-to-date information about all the goings-on in Jerome and environs.

CLARKDALE AND THE VERDE CANYON RAILROAD

Founded in 1912 by the United Verde Copper Company for workers at a nearby smelter, Clarkdale remains largely unreconstructed today, though the smelter and the company shut down long ago. It's said that the quiet town was the first master-planned community in Arizona, a state that would one day suffer from a surfeit of that breed. There's not much here save **The Verde Canyon Railroad** (300 N. Broadway, 800/582-7245, www.verdecanyonrr.com, $65-90), an excursion train that runs on tracks formerly used to bring ore from Jerome to the smelter in Clarkdale. The four-hour round-trip ride takes passengers from Clarkdale to Perkinsville Ranch and back, snaking through Verde Canyon, an inaccessible, bald eagle-populated notch with ocher cliffs towering on one side and the green river meandering on the other. It's a slow but unforgettable route,

1: Jerome State Historic Park **2:** The Clinkscale

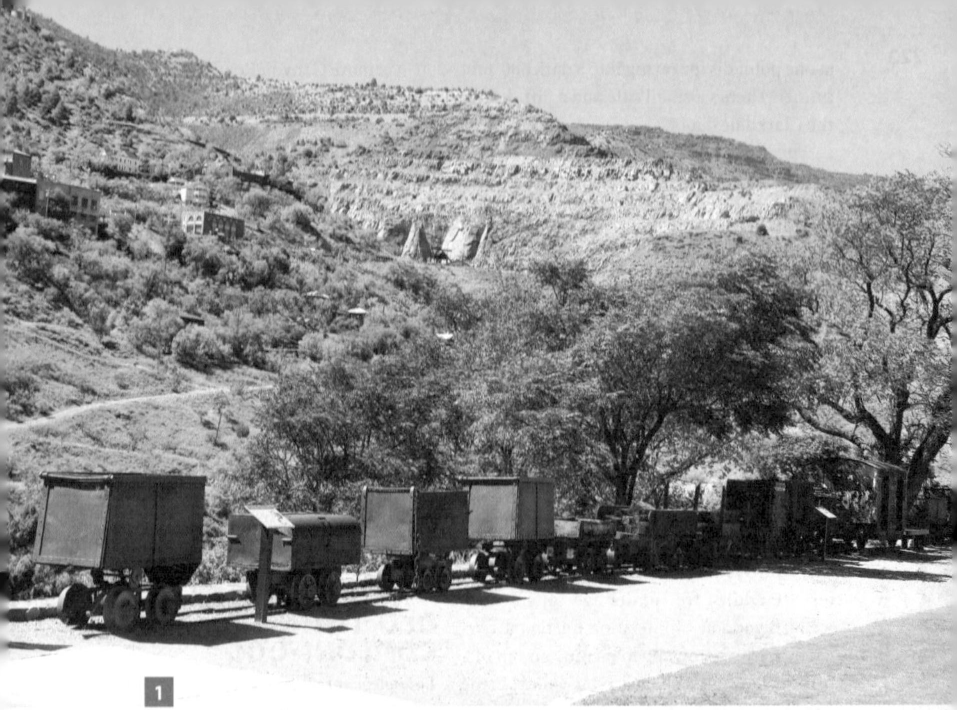

1

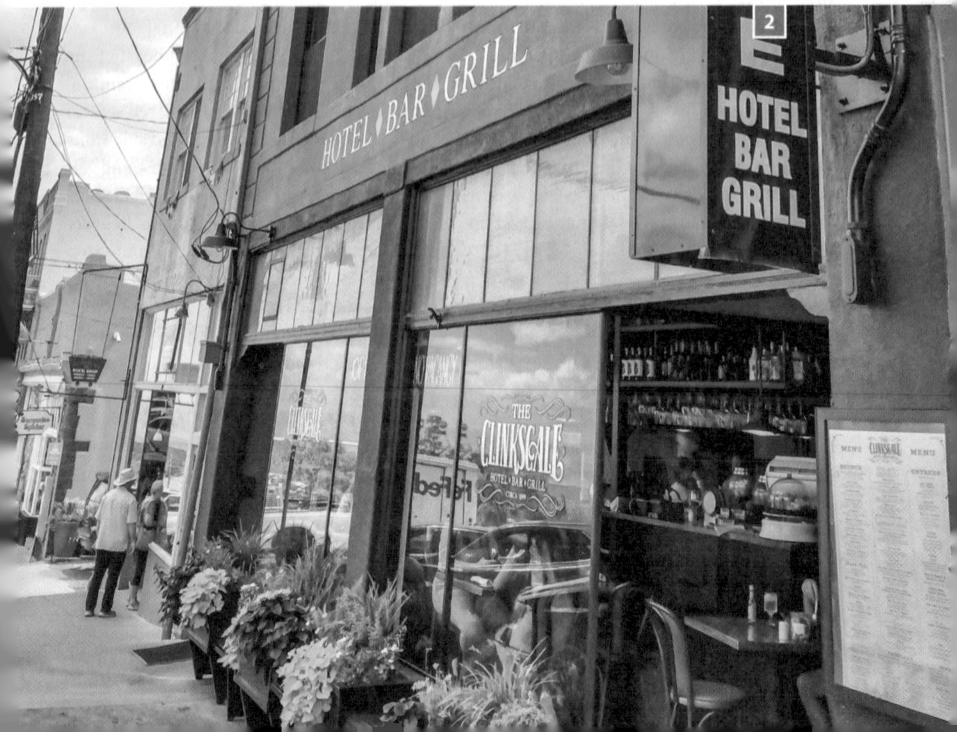
HOTEL ♦ BAR ♦ GRILL
HOTEL
BAR
GRILL
THE
CLINKSCALE
HOTEL • BAR • GRILL

2

at one point disappearing into a dark 680-foot tunnel. There's a small café and a gift shop at the Clarkdale depot.

The least expensive fare is an adult coach ticket ($65) for a basic and comfortable ride through the spectacular canyon. A first-class ticket (from $90) includes open-air viewing cars, a complimentary glass of champagne, supremely comfortable seats, and a full bar. For $129 you can book passage for special events, including wine-tasting and sunset trips.

TUZIGOOT NATIONAL MONUMENT

Just outside of Clarkdale, **Tuzigoot National Monument** (100 Main St., off Broadway between Clarkdale and Old Town Cottonwood, 928/634-5564, www.nps.gov/tuzi, 8am-6pm daily summer, 8am-5pm daily winter, $10 adults, free under age 16, entrance fee also good at Montezuma Castle), a 120-room stacked-stone pueblo ruins on top of a hill overlooking the lush river valley, is the first of three federally protected sites in the Verde Valley that preserve what remains of the disappeared Sinagua culture. A museum has some good exhibits on Sinagua culture and the natural history of the area. You can walk up to the roof of the building and see the green valley the way the Sinagua people did. The site is not as dramatic as Montezuma Castle or Well, but it is a fascinating and important place.

SYCAMORE CANYON WILDERNESS AREA

Hikers shouldn't to leave the valley before taking a jaunt into the **Sycamore Canyon Wilderness Area,** one of Arizona's most beloved and beautiful natural treasures, often called, as are other lesser canyons in the state, "the other Grand Canyon." It is the state's second-largest canyon and one of the first to gain federal wilderness protection.

You can reach the southern rim of Sycamore Canyon by taking the road to Tuzigoot, then turning left after the bridge

on Sycamore Canyon Road, and then driving about 10 miles to the rim.

The best day trip into Sycamore Canyon from this end starts at the **Parsons Trailhead** on the rim. You descend 500 vertical feet into the bottomlands, where you'll walk along the creek, with cottonwoods and willows and other water-loving flora all around. Deep still pools catch falling leaves in autumn, and the riverside shade is lifesaving in summer. Dark high walls tower over you. You can backpack the entire 11-mile canyon bottom, but the day-use portion of the Parsons Trail ends four miles in at a deep pool—the spring that feeds the creek. From here, return the way you came, climbing back up to the rim. Expect to get your feet wet crossing the creek in a few places, and expect not to want to leave the canyon bottom and return to dry reality.

OLD TOWN COTTONWOOD

This pleasant short stretch of AZ 89A (Main St.) through downtown Cottonwood, just a few miles east of the road to Tuzigoot, was once the commercial and social heart of the valley. Some of the old buildings remain; others have been rebuilt and replaced several times. Along the clean refurbished sidewalks are a few shops, antiques stores, cafés, and galleries, and a couple of really good restaurants. The Old Town area is on the National Register of Historic Places and worth a stroll and a stop for lunch or dinner. Along the Old Town's quaint row are several comfortable and stylish **Verde Valley Wine Trail** (http://vvwinetrail.com) tasting rooms.

Food and Accommodations

Jerome and Sedona offer proximity to more abundant dining and sleeping options, but a few charming hotels and some excellent restaurants are in Cottonwood's historic Old Town.

The 1950s-style **Bing's Burger Station** (794 N. Main St., 928/649-1718, www.

1: Tuzigoot National Monument 2: rock carvings at the V-Bar-V Ranch Petroglyph Site

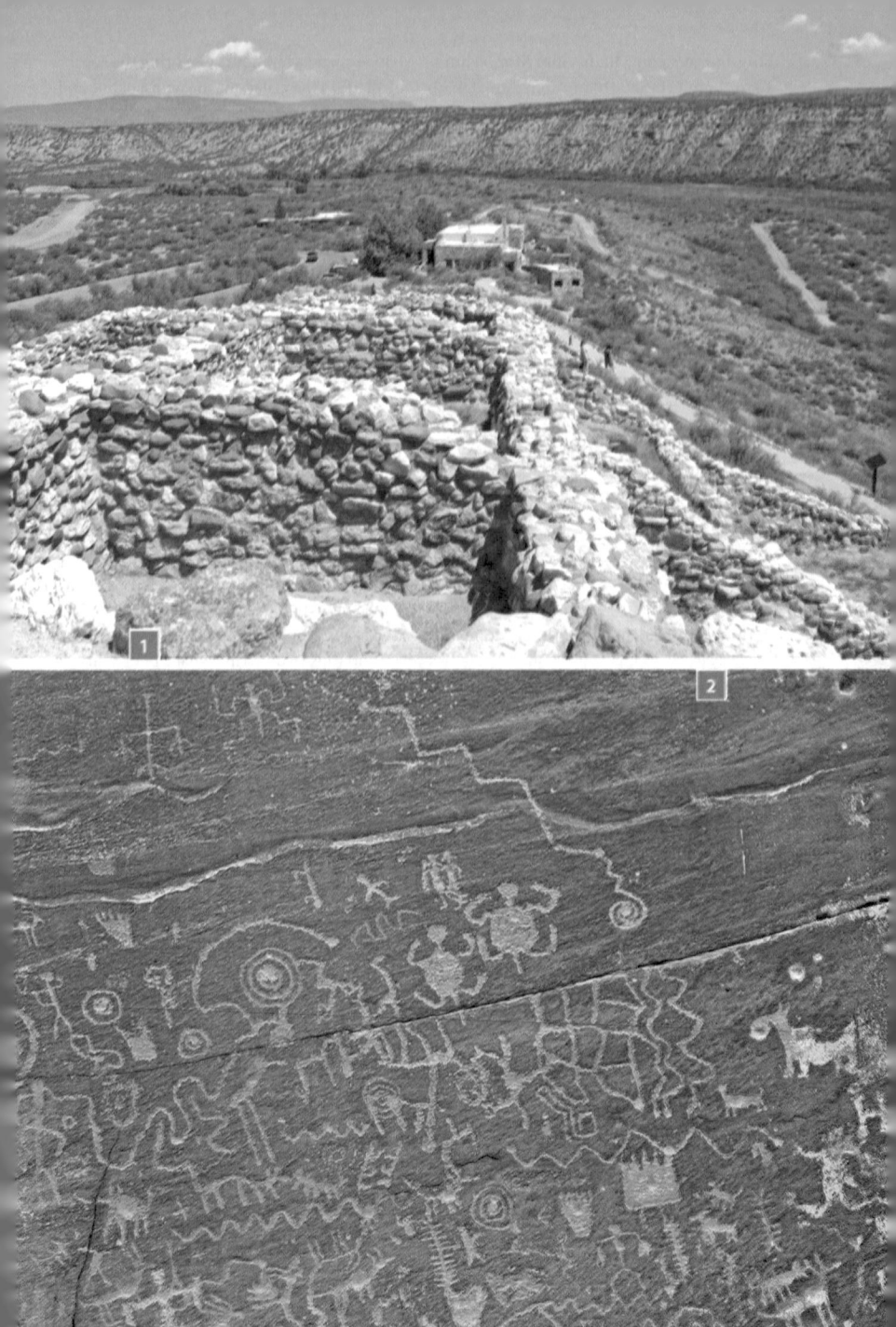

bingsburgers.com, 10am-8pm Mon.-Thurs., 10am-9pm Fri.-Sat., 10am-8pm Sun., $4.50-10.25) is in a retro gas station in Old Town and serves some of the best burgers in the region. Fans of the old-school roadhouse diner should see this place, with its road-culture antiques and simple, filling, well-prepared comfort food. The **Tavern Grille** (914 N. Main St., 928/634-6669, http://thetaverngrille.com, 11am-9pm daily, $12-24) serves an eclectic selection of burgers, sandwiches, steaks, pasta, and salads, and offers cocktails, craft beers, and wines from Arizona and elsewhere.

The **Iron Horse Inn** (1034 N. Main St., 928/634-9455, http://ironhorseoldtown.com, $119) has been a motor court-style hotel along Cottonwood's Main Street since the 1930s. It still has a good bit of retro charm, but also offers modern amenities and comforts. Guest rooms come with Wi-Fi, TVs, and refrigerators. The Iron Horse is in a great location, within walking distance of the river and Old Town's tasting rooms. A boutique hotel for the wine trail crowd, the **Tavern Hotel** (914 N. Main St., 928/634-6669, http://thetavernhotel.com, $169) is similarly located, with upscale touches and a stylish atmosphere.

DEAD HORSE RANCH STATE PARK

The near-jungle of **Dead Horse Ranch State Park** (675 Dead Horse Ranch Rd., Cottonwood, 928/634-5283, http://azstateparks.com, 8am-5pm daily, $7 per car up to 4 people), just a few blocks from Old Town Cottonwood, provides easy access to the riparian wonders of the Verde River. You can walk streamside for miles below weeping cottonwoods and hanging willows, through all kinds of teeming vines and branches, and completely forget that you are in the arid West. If you want to camp and fish one of the artificial lagoons, there are dozens of campsites ($15-55) with hookups, restrooms, and showers. But the park is best as a riverside day

trip to spend a few hours exploring the source of all life in the valley, maybe with a picnic and some bird-watching.

The best hike is the 1.5-mile loop along the **Verde River Greenway,** a six-mile stretch of lush life along the Verde between the Tuzigoot and Bridgeport bridges, meant to preserve the riparian ecosystem, one of only a few remaining in the state. Unlike the park's creepy name, the Verde River Greenway's name is perfectly descriptive—a greenway is exactly what it is, and all the more beautiful for being so rare and threatened.

FORT VERDE STATE HISTORIC PARK

One of several outposts in the central highlands from which General Crook battled the Apache and others, **Fort Verde State Historic Park** (125 E. Hollamon St., Camp Verde, 928/567-3275, http://azstateparks.com, 9am-5pm daily, $7 adults, $4 ages 7-13, free under age 7) will be of interest to history lovers and those wondering what a poor soldier's life was like on what must have felt like the edge of the world. You can stroll the grounds and look into a few old buildings set up with original fort artifacts, furniture, and items that give a sense of late-19th-century Anglo-West daily life and the officers, surgeons, and soldiers who must have wondered how they got all the way out here.

VERDE RIVER SCENIC AREA

Popular with canoers, kayakers, and other boating types, the **Verde River Scenic Area** is a wild stretch of the river. The beautiful and sometimes rough stretch from **Beasly Flat to Childs** offers a river adventure. The best way to prepare for a trip is the **Boater's Guide to the Verde River,** which you can download for free at www.fs.usda.gov. Or contact the **Verde Ranger District** (300 E. AZ 260, Camp Verde, 928/567-4121, 8am-4:30 Mon.-Fri.).

★ MONTEZUMA CASTLE NATIONAL MONUMENT

If you have time to make only one stop in the Verde Valley, make it the **Montezuma Castle National Monument** (I-17 Exit 289, 928/567-3322, www.nps.gov/moca, 8am-5pm daily winter, 8am-6pm daily summer, $10 for 7-day pass, free under age 16, entrance fee also good at Tuzigoot National Monument). The five-story, 20-room limestone structure, built about AD 1200, looks down on Beaver Creek and the former farmlands of its builders from an improbable niche in the cliff side. It resembles a castle, the home of a ruler or a god, but it was more likely the apartment-style shelter for a group of Sinagua people who found the creek and the sheltered cliffs to their liking. There's not much to do other than walk along the short trail and look up at the ruins, but it is something that should be seen. When you walk out of the small visitors center and behold the cliff side for the first time, it's a breath-catching moment.

Montezuma Well

The **Montezuma Well** (I-17 Exit 293, 928/567-4521, 8am-6pm daily June-Aug., 8am-5pm daily Sept.-May, free), a sister monument just up I-17 from the castle, is often overlooked, but it's a fascinating, quiet stop that will leave you in awe at nature's strangeness. The "well" is actually a sinkhole into which 1.5 million gallons of 74°F springwater has flowed daily for untold time, ringed by rough cliffs into which the Sinagua people built apartments. You can walk a short twisting path down to the water's edge and explore the rock-wall rooms.

BEAVER CREEK RECREATION AREA

If you find the streamside red rocks of Sedona and Oak Creek too busy, try **Beaver Creek Recreation Area** (I-17 Exit 298), a rather out-of-the-way oasis at the dirt-road southern end of Forest Road 618, about two miles from I-17. Red-rock banks and tree shade await along Wet Beaver Creek. The warm red-rock slabs make for perfect jumping into the pools along the creek, great for splashing around and soaking your feet. There's a **campground** (928/203-2900, $16) with nice creek-side spots if you can't bear to leave this beautiful spot.

FLAGSTAFF AND SEDONA
THE VERDE VALLEY

Montezuma Castle National Monument

V-Bar-V Ranch Petroglyph Site

Most of the hundreds of rock-carved symbols, animals, and mysterious beings at the **V-Bar-V Ranch Petroglyph Site** (I-17 Exit 298, www.redrockcountry.org, 9:30am-3:30pm Fri.-Mon.) were created AD 900-1300 by the Sinagua, the same people who built Montezuma Castle and other ancient sites around the Verde Valley. Here you can walk along an easy, level creek-side trail, shaded by cottonwoods and willows, and get close to the strange rock carvings. There is usually a knowledgeable docent to explain things; otherwise, there are several information panels around the site. Plan on spending an hour or more, and make sure to bring your own water. You need a Red Rock Pass ($5) to visit, which you can buy here. To reach the site, which was the V-Bar-V Ranch until it was purchased by the U.S. Forest Service in the 1990s to preserve the astonishing petroglyphs, drive two miles south on Forest Road 618 from I-17's Exit 298 and cross over Wet Beaver Creek.

Sedona

Second only to the Grand Canyon as a favorite Arizona destination, Sedona and its red rocks resemble the great canyon in several ways. Like the canyon, Sedona's rare beauty is the result of geologic circumstance—the slow work of wind, rain, trickling water, and the predictable restless rocking of the Colorado Plateau. The little resort town sits at the base of the plateau, and its red-rock monuments rise dramatically into the light blue sky.

Also like the Grand Canyon, this landscape seems so otherworldly that it's a struggle not to go a little beyond yourself. For many, other explanations fail, and the spiritual instincts come alive, which is why there are hordes of spiritual entrepreneurs here. You can stay in extreme comfort, bordering on the decadent, or rough it to a certain degree. You can purchase a world-class work of art and jostle through the backcountry in a pink Jeep. There will be crowds—some four million tourists come to the red rocks every year, searching for one thing or another. It's easy to forget that, despite its international reputation as a life-list destination, Sedona is really just a small town with only about 10,000 year-round residents. It just happens to be stuck in a geologic wonderland.

PLANNING TIPS

Sedona is a popular destination for day trips as its highlights can be seen in a few hours, and most people who visit this spectacular landscape spend only a brief time in it. Those who spend the most time here are hiking or mountain biking enthusiasts, spiritual seekers, or guests at high-end resorts. In the summer, the cool waters of Oak Creek and Wet Beaver Creek call to desert dwellers, who throng to their sandy red banks.

Uptown is the busiest and most touristy section of Sedona, making parking challenging, especially on spring and summer weekends. **West Sedona** is a more "real" town, spread out along AZ 89 in a series of shopping centers, strip malls, and stand-alone businesses. Red Rock Country is accessible from both.

Sedona can be easily and somewhat thoroughly enjoyed in an unhurried day trip; it's less than an hour from Flagstaff and just two hours from the Grand Canyon and Phoenix. The best approach is to arrive by, say, mid-morning. Drive along the **Red Rock Scenic Byway** on your way into town from I-17, take a stroll on one of the trails around **Bell Rock,** stop at the **Chapel of the Holy Cross,** and poke around Uptown before having lunch here or in West Sedona. After lunch, take the

Sedona

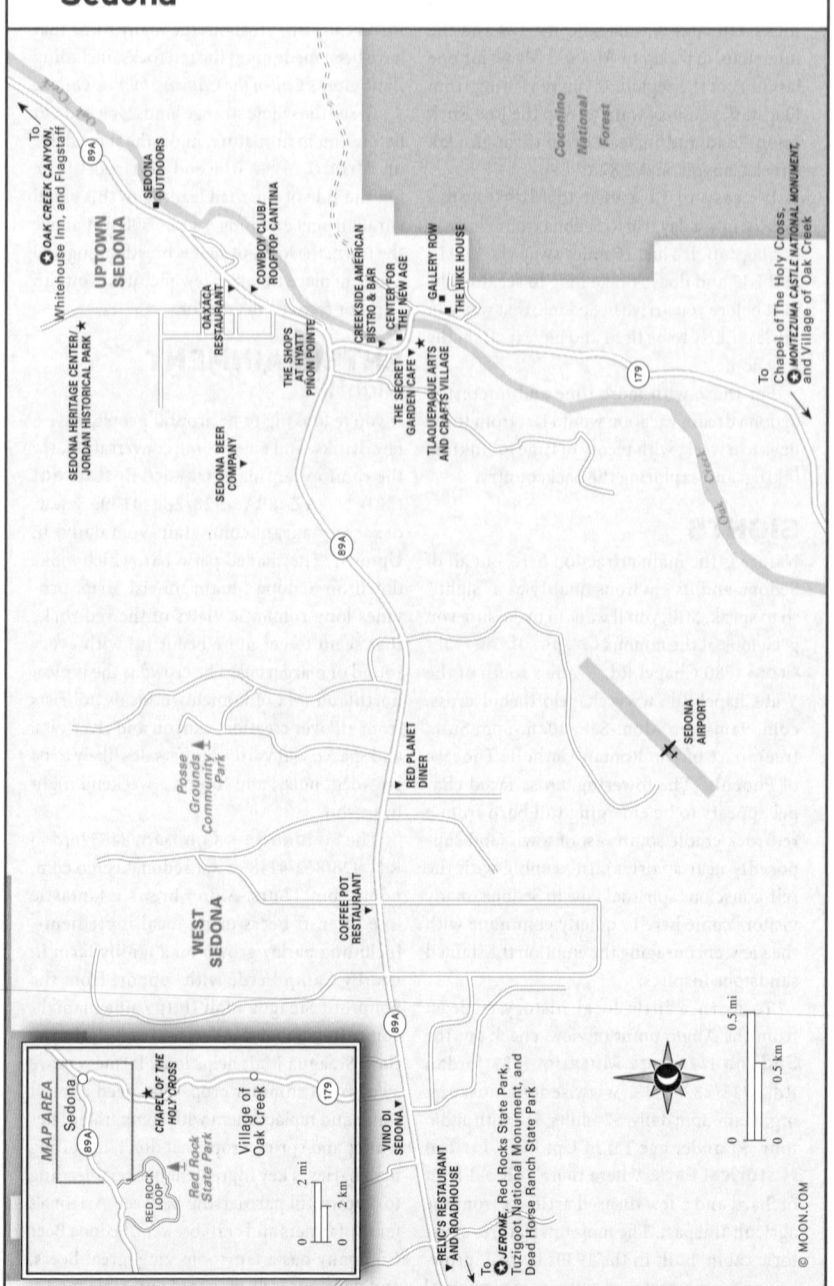

To OAK CREEK CANYON, Whitehouse Inn, and Flagstaff

SEDONA OUTDOORS

UPTOWN SEDONA

COWBOY CLUB/ ROOFTOP CANTINA

OAXACA RESTAURANT

SEDONA HERITAGE CENTER/ JORDAN HISTORICAL PARK

THE SHOPS AT HYATT PIÑON POINTE

CREEKSIDE AMERICAN BISTRO & BAR

CENTER FOR THE NEW AGE

GALLERY ROW

THE HIKE HOUSE

To Chapel of The Holy Cross, MONTEZUMA CASTLE NATIONAL MONUMENT, and Village of Oak Creek

THE SECRET GARDEN CAFE

TLAQUEPAQUE ARTS AND CRAFTS VILLAGE

SEDONA BEER COMPANY

Coconino National Forest

Oak Creek

Posse Grounds Community Park

RED PLANET DINER

SEDONA AIRPORT

WEST SEDONA

COFFEE POT RESTAURANT

VINO DI SEDONA

RELIC'S RESTAURANT AND ROADHOUSE

To JEROME, Red Rocks State Park, Tuzigoot National Monument, and Dead Horse Ranch State Park

MAP AREA

Sedona

CHAPEL OF THE HOLY CROSS

Red Rock State Park

RED ROCK LOOP

Village of Oak Creek

0.5 mi

0.5 km

0 2 mi

0 2 km

© MOON.COM

Red Rock Loop Road down to Red Rock Crossing to see the creek and the warm red rocks. On your way back to AZ 179 and the interstate, drive up to Airport Mesa for one last look at the region. If you're visiting from Flagstaff, you may want to skip the Red Rock Loop Road and instead drive through Oak Creek Canyon on AZ 89A.

It's easy to fit a visit to Montezuma Castle into a day trip to Sedona from Phoenix or Flagstaff. It's just 26 miles away via AZ 179 and I-17 and doesn't take long to see. Ideally, visit before you arrive in Sedona; that way you are less likely to be tired and blow it off on the way home.

For those with more time and interest, a Sedona dream vacation would last from three days to a week, with plenty of time for hiking, biking, and exploring the backcountry.

SIGHTS

Nature is the main attraction here, but all of Sedona and its environs qualify as a "sight," so to speak. Still, you'll want to make sure you get a look at the famous Chapel of the Holy Cross (780 Chapel Rd., 3 miles south of the Y at Chapel Rd., www.chapeloftheholycross. com, 9am-5pm Mon.-Sat., 10am-5pm Sun., free), part of the Roman Catholic Diocese of Phoenix. The towering, cross-faced chapel appears to be emerging full born from a red-rock cradle southwest of town (and supposedly near a vortex). In keeping with the self-conscious spiritual vibe in Sedona, many visitors come here to quietly commune with the view, encouraging the emotion the stained sandstone inspires.

To learn a little local history, at least from the Anglo point of view, check out the Sedona Heritage Museum (735 Jordan Rd., 928/282-7038, www.sedonamuseum. org, 11am-3pm daily, $7 adults, $10 with audio tour, $3 under age 13) in Uptown's Jordan Historical Park, where there's an old fruit orchard and a few disused artifacts from the agricultural past. The museum features a historic cabin, built in the 1930s by fruit growers and now restored with some original furnishings, and tells the story of early Sedona from the 1880s on. The best exhibit is the Movie Room, all about the many films that have been made amid the red rocks, including Zane Grey's Call of the Canyon, Johnny Guitar.

To see the whole strange landscape laid out before you in miniature, make the short drive up Airport Mesa (the end of Airport Rd.). On the side of the road leading to this small rural airport and lodge, some 500 feet above the town, the lookout spot is breathtaking and a logical place to take a few pictures. You can park for free at a nearby lot.

ENTERTAINMENT
Nightlife

If you're looking to be around people, have a few drinks, and enjoy some conversation, try the rooftop cantina at Oaxaca Restaurant (321 N. AZ 89A, 928/282-4179, www. oaxacarestaurant.com, 11am-9pm daily) in Uptown. The shaded patio bar, which looks down on Sedona's main tourist strip, provides long romantic views of the red rocks that seem to get more beautiful with every round of margaritas. The crowd is the typical northland mix of hometown locals, tourists from all over creation, canyon and river rats, and spaced-out vortex hunters. It's likely to be crowded, noisy, and fun on a weekend night in season.

The Sedona Beer Company (465 Jordon Rd., 928/862-4148, www.sedonabeerco.com, noon-9pm Thurs.-Mon.) brews a fantastic line of craft beers using local ingredients, including barley grown on a family farm in nearby Camp Verde with support from the nonprofit Sinagua Malt (http://sinaguamalt. com). To combat the Verde River's declining flow, Sinagua Malt helps local farmers move away from summer crops that need a lot of water and replace them with comparable late-winter and spring crops that don't, including malt barley, a key ingredient in beer—leading to a powerful partnership between Arizona's family farmers and craft brewers. Sedona Beer Company has a tap-room vibe, great beers, and delicious well-prepared pub-style food.

What's a Vortex... and Why Should You Care?

Hanging around the Sedona Visitor Center in the summer, one hears more than once the suggestions of local volunteers trying to get out-of-towners, especially first-time visitors, interested in the little town's story beyond the famous vortexes. "But we came out here from Boston, and we want to see the vortexes."

Well, you can't really see them. A vortex, they say, is a place with a special energy, a space in a landscape that gathers energy from all around it, concentrating it, perhaps to be manipulated by someone in touch with the earth's languages. The red rocks around Sedona are said to be rotten with them, and a hike or drive to a vortex site has become the most popular New Age activity here in recent years. Don't worry; you can still get your tarot cards read, have your aura photographed, your past lives remembered, and your crystals recharged at storefronts all over town.

The vortex movement, according to Dwight Garner of the *New York Times*, began in 1987, "the year of the Harmonic Convergence, when believers flocked to mystical places across the planet, hoping for a global awakening of harmony and love." Reportedly some 5,000 true believers descended on Sedona, understood to be one of those "mystical places," probably owing more to its unique scenery than anything else, and many of them never left. These days there's no shortage of guides who will take you out into the red rocks to introduce you to the vortexes and, perhaps, to your spiritual self. Suzanne McMillan and her staff at **Sedona Vortex Tours** (150 AZ 79, Suites 2-3, 928/282-2733 or 800/943-3266, www.sedonavortextours.com, $159-239 pp for 3-5 hours) promise to "teach you how to feel the vortex energy." McMillan has been leading tours since 1988, taking seekers out in vans or on hikes to vortexes and on Medicine Wheel Tours. Linda Summers of **Sedona Spirit Journeys** (928/282-8966, www.sedonaspiritjourneys.com, $188 pp for 2 hours) has a degree in Native American studies and guides a "Sedona Vortex Healing Journey," during which she shares the history of the vortex sites and offers "guided meditation, drumming, and a special crystal and Reiki healing energy in the beauty of nature." Cynthia Tierra of **Healing from the Heart** (928/821-0989, www.healingone.net, $100 per hour) has 25 years' experience as a holistic health practitioner and Reiki master. She will guide you to both well-known and "secret" vortexes, and she gives psychic readings as well. **Sedona Spirit Yoga & Hiking** (928/282-9900 or 888/282-9901, www.yogalife.net, $89-225 pp for 3-4 hours), run by Johanna (Maheshvari) Mosca, who calls herself "Madame Vortex," offers guided vortex hikes that include yoga sessions on the red-rock buttes.

For more on this scene, check out the **Sedona Metaphysical Spiritual Association** (928/300-7796, www.sedonaspiritual.com).

The **Oak Creek Brewery** (2050 Yavapai Dr., 928/204-1300, www.oakcreekbrew.com, noon-close daily) attracts a lot of locals and is an enjoyable place to hang out. The brewery offers some of the best microbrews in the state in a laid-back tasting-room atmosphere, with jam sessions, drum circles, dance parties, and live music throughout the week. It is a place to let loose, listen to live local music, and chow down on some fantastic tamales, quesadillas, and other Southwestern bar food. This casual place, in less touristy West Sedona, should not be confused with **Oak Creek Brewery and Grill** (336 AZ 179, 928/282-3300, www. oakcreekpub.com, 11:30am-8:30pm daily) at upscale Tlaquepaque Village, also a fun place to kick back a few of the Oak Creek-brand microbrews.

Vino Di Sedona (2575 W. AZ 89A, 928/554-4682, www.vinodisedona.com, 8pm-10pm Mon., 11am-11pm Tues.-Thurs., 11am-midnight Fri.-Sat., 11am-10pm Sun.) only works with Arizona's family-owned small-batch wineries and breweries. This fun and casual place offers live music every night along with great tapas, pizza, sandwiches, and sliders. Vino Di Sedona is also an excellent well-stocked wine store.

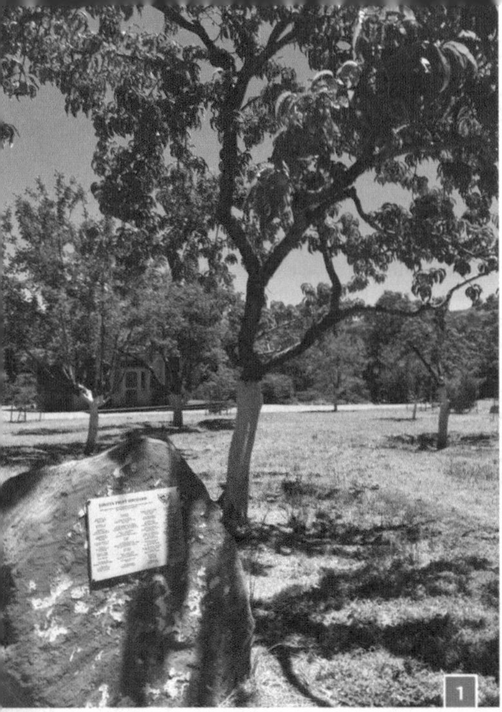
1

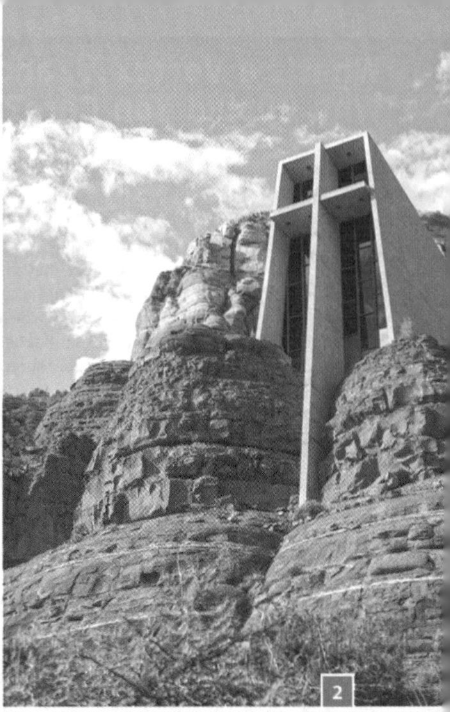
2

3

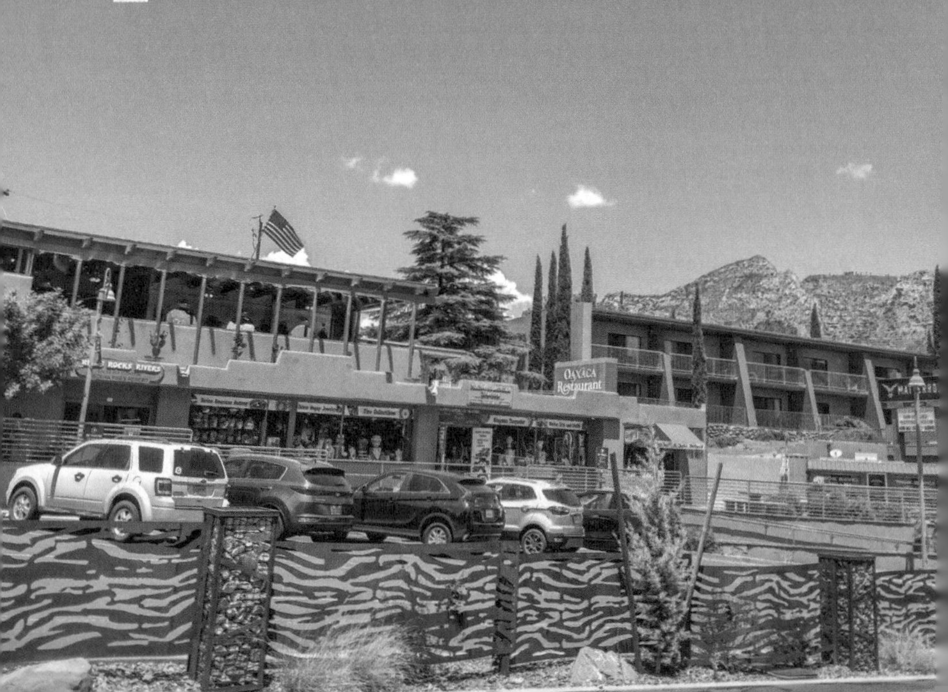

Festivals and Events

Cinephiles will enjoy drinking wine with indie film stars during the **Sedona International Film Festival** (928/282-1177, www.sedonafilmfestival.org, Feb.-Mar.), five days in late February-early March filled with cutting-edge and independent films, discussions, and workshops.

The arts take over in October, with the renowned **Sedona Arts Festival** (Sedona Red Rock High School, 995 Upper Red Rock Loop Rd., 928/204-9456, www.sedonaartsfestival.org, Oct., $12) and the **Sedona Plein Air Festival** (Sedona Arts Center, 15 Art Barn Rd., 928/282-3809 or 888/954-4442, www.sedonapleinairfestival.com, Oct.). Both feature local and national artists interpreting the painting-worthy landscapes of Sedona and the Southwest.

SHOPPING AND GALLERIES

Although there are notable exceptions, in Sedona's many shopping districts you'll find contemporary, eclectic, mid- to high-end arts and crafts with a fetish for the Southwestern, Native American jewelry and spiritual objects, Mexican colors and religious items, or a heavy-framed painting of a cowboy sleeping next to a campfire, his worn hat pulled down over his eyes. After a while, one boutique, gallery, and fancy "trading post" tends to meld into the next. Shopping is great fun and probably the second most popular activity around, just after staring at the rocks. It's doubtless even more fun if you have the wallet to afford the best pieces.

Start at the **Uptown Shops** (N. AZ 89A), the original Sedona shopping district. Both sides of AZ 89A have several levels of small touristy shops, souvenir stands, boutiques, and jewelry stores. If you feel like going hiking and didn't plan for it, look for **Sedona Outdoors** (267 N. AZ 89A, Suite 5,

928/282-0296, 9am-8pm daily), where you can get pretty much any gear you need.

The high-end **Shops at Hyatt Piñon Pointe** (AZ 89A and AZ 179, 928/204-8828, http://hyattpinonpointe.hyatt.com) are worth a stroll. Make sure to stop at **Visions Fine Art Gallery** (101 N. AZ 89A, Suite E24, 928/203-0022, www.visionsfineart.com, 11am-5pm daily), one of Sedona's best galleries.

Sedona's true shopping treasure, **Tlaquepaque Arts & Crafts Village** (336 AZ 179, 928/282-4838, www.tlaq.com) is an enchanting collection of Mexican-style courtyards with 40 unique shops and galleries and the best restaurant in town, René at Tlaquepaque. There's even a little white stucco chapel in the "village," like an upscale version of Old Mexico, with beautiful stained glass and a mural above the altar. Shops include **Feliz Navidad** (928/282-2752, www.feliznavidadsedona.com, 10am-5:30pm Sun.-Tues., 10am-7pm Wed.-Sat.), dedicated to Christmas ornaments with a Mexican aesthetic.

Across the street from Tlaquepaque is **Gallery Row** (AZ 179 and Schnebly Hill Rd.), where you'll find Sedona's best Native American art. **Kopavi** (411 AZ 179, Garland Bldg., upstairs, 928/282-4774, www.kopaviinternational.com, 10:30am-5pm Mon.-Sat., noon-5pm Sun.) has the best items made by Hopi artists. It is a good idea to call first to make sure they are open. Also check out the **Lanning Gallery** (Hozho Center, 431 AZ 179, 928/282-6865, www.lanninggallery.com, 10am-6pm Mon.-Sat., 11am-5pm Sun.) for tasteful Southwestern styles.

The **Hillside Sedona** (671 AZ 179, 928/282-4500, www.hillsidesedona.net) complex is also in this area and deserves a look, especially the **Gallery of Modern Masters** (888/282-3313, www.galleryofmodernmasters.com, 10am-5pm daily), which has some spectacular pieces by some of the all-time greats.

FOOD

★ **René at Tlaquepaque** (336 AZ 179, 928/282-9225, www.rene-sedona.com,

1: orchard in Jordan Historical Park 2: Chapel of the Holy Cross 3: Uptown Sedona

11:30am-2:30pm and 5:30pm-8:30pm daily, lunch $11-16, dinner $28-45), with its Mexican courtyard ambience and outrageously tasty food, has long been one of Sedona's top spots to dine. Try the baked French onion soup and the sweet potato ravioli, or the venison or the . . . just try the whole menu and go back again and again if you can.

A favorite with the locals, the ★ **Coffee Pot Restaurant** (2050 W. AZ 89A, 928/282-6626, www.coffeepotsedona.com, 6am-2pm daily, $8-11) is great for breakfast and lunch, with filling home-style American and Mexican food in big portions. It serves breakfast all day, with a signature list of "101 Omelettes." A few may be desperation choices: The final entry on the list comes with peanut butter, jelly, and banana. Nonetheless, there are at least 70 others worth trying. In West Sedona, not far from Coffee Pot Rock, this popular restaurant also has a shaded patio and an eclectic gift shop. Expect a crowd and a bit of a wait on weekend mornings.

A wonderful restaurant with a patio looking over babbling Oak Creek, **Creekside American Bistro & Bar** (251 AZ 179, 928/282-1705, http://creeksidesedona.com, 7:30am-9pm daily, $16-48) has chef-inspired dishes such as Southwestern-style shrimp-and-grits, great burgers, steaks, vegetarian options, and an atmosphere that is pure Sedona cool, making this a must-stop for dinner or cocktails.

The **Cowboy Club** (241 N. AZ 89A, 928/282-4200, http://cowboyclub.com, 11am-9pm daily, $14-37) in Uptown Sedona is a perennial favorite, a Western-style place with buffalo meat and rattlesnake on the menu along with great burgers and steaks. Founding members of the Cowboy Artists of America used to hang out here long ago when it was called the Oak Creek Tavern, and their memory is kept alive in the many paintings on display throughout the restaurant.

If you're headed up to Airport Mesa to view

1: Tlaquepaque Arts & Crafts Village 2: Cowboy Club in Uptown Sedona

all of Sedona spread out before you, stop by the **Mesa Grill** (1185 Airport Rd., 928/282-2400, www.mesagrillsedona.com, 7am-9pm daily, $16-26) for a bite to eat or a drink (happy hour 3pm-6pm daily). The small, sleek restaurant and bar look out on the airport's runway through large view-framing windows. The eclectic menus feature pasta dishes, hamburgers, and seafood.

As the name says, **Nick's Westside** (2920 AZ 89A, 928/204-2088, www.nickswestside.com, 7am-9pm Mon.-Sat., 8am-2pm Sun., $7-23) is in West Sedona. Popular with locals for breakfast, lunch, and dinner, this place serves exceedingly satisfying home-style ribs, brisket, burgers, sandwiches, burritos, tacos, and enchiladas. Nick's tends to be busy for breakfast on weekend mornings.

The **Oak Creek Brewery and Grill** (336 AZ 179 at Tlaquepaque Village, 928/282-3300, www.oakcreekpub.com, 11:30am-8:30pm daily, $12-24) serves excellent bar-and-grill fare, including fantastic barbecue ribs, fish-and-chips, and a large selection of pizzas. Then there's the enchanting setting within the charming confines of Tlaquepaque Village. Sit on the patio if weather permits, and it usually will. The locally brewed beer on tap is some of best in the state.

ACCOMMODATIONS

There are dozens of hotels and resorts in Sedona, some of them like little towns themselves. Many of the resorts are outlandishly well-appointed, with golf courses and all kinds of spa treatments, workshops, and spiritual rituals. Some of the most romantic and secluded spots are 2-4 miles north of Uptown Sedona on AZ 89A, in Oak Creek Canyon along the shady banks of Oak Creek.

$50-100

The clean and inexpensive **Sedona Village Lodge** (105 Bellrock Plaza, 800/890-0521, www.sedonavillagelodge.com, $69-119) is a good choice for hikers and those more interested in red rocks than gift shops. It's across from Bell Rock, a name given to an eroded mound that looks vaguely like a bell, six miles south of downtown along AZ 179—close enough but also a bit far, which is the ideal place to be. The rooms are comfortable, the hosts are friendly, and the Wi-Fi is free. It's a good idea to reserve a room far in advance.

Another great value is the Sugar Loaf Lodge (1870 W. AZ 89A, 928/282-8451 or 877/282-0632, www.sedonasugarloaf.com, $75-95), a little 15-room motel just a mile or so west of the junction of AZ 89A and AZ 179. It's close to everything and offers a clean, comfortable room with a fridge and a television. With its pool, hot tub, and budget-friendly rates, Sugar Loaf is one of the best deals in a town where bargains are often hard to find.

$100-250

In the middle of all the action in Uptown Sedona, the ★ Matterhorn Inn (230 Apple Ave., 800/372-8207, www.matterhorninn. com, $185-199) is one of the best places to stay if you're hoping to experience all that Sedona has to offer. The small hotel sits among dozens of shops and restaurants and yet still provides amazing views of the landscape. The Southwestern-style guest rooms offer comfort, free Wi-Fi, and private balconies to stare at the red rocks. Don't miss the solar-heated pool and hot tub next to a romantic outdoor sitting area with a fireplace. The Matterhorn is also one of Sedona's greener hotels: It has undergone extensive renovations with a focus on conservation, including installing low flow toilets, water-efficient faucets and showerheads, timers on outdoor lighting, dry landscaping, and on-demand hot water heaters.

An affordable and basic place to stay, the Whitehouse Inn (2986 W. AZ 89A, 928/282-6680, www.sedonawhitehouseinn.com, $115-130) offers a clean and central base for a visit without the huge price tag, mud baths, or chakra healing.

In West Sedona, away from the tourist bustle of Uptown and Tlaquepaque, the Arroyo Pinion Hotel (3119 W. AZ 89A, 928/204-1146 or 800/789-7393, www.

ascendcollection.com, $166-196) is an excellent choice for hikers and mountain bikers. The location provides easy access to backcountry roads that lead to the trails around Chimney Rock and Sugarloaf. Continental breakfast is included, and guest rooms are well appointed with flat-screen TVs, free Wi-Fi, fridges, and big comfortable beds for resting your bones after a day in the wilderness.

The Oak Creek Terrace Resort (4548 N. AZ 89A, 928/282-3562 or 800/224-2229, www.oakcreekterrace.com, $120-289) is tucked into the greenery along AZ 89A just south of Slide Rock State Park in Oak Creek Canyon. Arizonans love Oak Creek Canyon because it is one of the last easily accessible riparian areas in the state, and its green and shady nature is shocking for its rarity. It seems impossible that one could improve on the natural splendor of this place, but the folks at Oak Creek Terrace have made an honest and successful attempt. The little bungalows and cabins on this beautiful property have fireplaces, in-room hot tubs, outdoor barbecues, and kitchenettes. This is a perfect place for families looking to get out of the city and back to nature without giving up any of the comforts of home.

The Sky Ranch Lodge (1105 Airport Rd., 928/282-6400 or 888/708-6400, http://skyranchlodge.com, $124-157) offers something a little different, located on top of Airport Mesa, 500 feet above the red land, next to the small Sedona Airport. The views, especially at sunrise and sunset, are spectacular and right out your door. A variety of guest rooms includes large ones with kitchens for families and cozy romantic hideaways with fireplaces. Don't worry about noise from planes; it's a small airport that serves private planes, corporate jets, and air-tour companies. The Sky Ranch Lodge has a decent restaurant and bar, so it's conceivable that you could stay up here and never go down again.

In the Village of Oak Creek, the Wildflower Inn (6086 AZ 179, 928/284-3937 or 888/494-5335, www.sedonawildflowerinn. com, $89-199) looks out at Bell Rock and offers guest rooms with fireplaces and in-room whirlpool tubs—a little bit of decadence at relatively affordable rates.

The El Portal Sedona (95 Portal Lane, 800/313-0017, www.elportalsedona.com, from $199) is an amazing 12-room hacienda in the rustic-elegant style, with deep comfort, great food, and furniture you'll want to take home. Most guest rooms have private patios and fireplaces, and all have TVs and free Wi-Fi. This fabulous little inn is next to the Los Abrigados Resort and Tlaquepaque Village, and if you stay at El Portal, you can use the resort's pool and spa.

Over $250

★ Amara Resort and Spa (100 Amara Lane, 928/282-4828, www.amararesort.com, $326-432) is one of those Sedona places you've heard about: Lovely beyond reason and intimidatingly tasteful, this retreat on the banks of Oak Creek has a full-service spa and all the other amenities you'd expect from a five-diamond hideaway.

The enchanting Orchard Canyon on Oak Creek Lodge (8067 AZ 89A, 928/282-3343, www.garlandslodge.com, Apr.-Nov. 15, 2-night minimum, $285-385) has 16 charming and comfortable cabins of various sizes set on 10 acres along Oak Creek, on the edge of the Red Rock Secret Mountain Wilderness. The lodge has a renowned restaurant, and rates include breakfast, dinner, and tea. This wonderful place is surrounded by orchards and a lush green lawn on which they serve cocktails every evening. Some people love this place so much that they make a habit of returning year after year, so call far ahead to book a spot and you might end up on a waiting list. Something to consider: There are no TVs or phones in the guest rooms.

The Orchards Inn (254 N. AZ 89A, 928/282-2405 or 800/341-5931, www.orchardsinn.com, from $249) has a pool and a whirlpool tub plus wonderful rooms, many with fireplaces and patios with views of the red rocks. The central location in Uptown is hard to beat. Walk to all the shops and restaurants on the main AZ 89A strip and leave your car parked.

INFORMATION

The Sedona Chamber of Commerce has an energetic and organized tourism bureau that operates the well-stocked and well-staffed Visitor Information Center (331 Forest Rd., 928/282-7722 or 800/288-7336, www.visitsedona.com, 8:30am-5pm Mon.-Sat., 9am-3pm Sun.), easy to spot in the Uptown shopping area.

TRANSPORTATION

Since it's a small town with a huge visitor population, driving and parking in Sedona can be an adventure; nonetheless, it's easy to find your way around. The four distinct zones of Sedona are accessible using just two connecting roads: AZ 89A runs through the heart of town, north to Oak Creek Canyon and eventually to Flagstaff. The portion of this road north of its junction with AZ 179, the town's main intersection, called the "Y" among locals, is called Uptown. The stretch of AZ 89A west of the Y is called West Sedona. AZ 179 heads southwest from the Y and continues through the red rocks, eventually intersecting with I-17. The stretch of AZ 179 between Schnebly Hill Road and Canyon Drive is called Gallery Row. The Village of Oak Creek is five miles southwest of Sedona along AZ 179.

Car

You really need a car to see Sedona and Red Rock Country right, and ideally an SUV or a 4WD vehicle. A regular sedan will work, and if you still want to explore the inaccessible backcountry, you can book a Jeep tour.

The best and quickest way to get to Sedona from Phoenix is to take I-17 north to AZ 179, which takes you past some amazing scenery and into the small town's heart. The 116-mile drive from Phoenix to Sedona, about 90 percent of it on the interstate, takes two hours.

From Flagstaff, take AZ 89A through Oak Creek Canyon, one of the most scenic routes in the state. Much of the road is slow and twisty, so expect the 44-mile drive to take at least an hour. You can also take I-17 south from Flagstaff to AZ 179, about 90 miles or 1.5 hours. This route, though longer, is probably the safest during inclement weather.

A lot of travelers combine a visit to Sedona with stops at Montezuma Castle, the quaint old mining town of Jerome, and Prescott. The Sinagua ruins are 30 miles south of Sedona. Take AZ 179 from Sedona to I-17, and look for the Montezuma Castle sign at Camp Verde, near the casino. If you want to stay off the interstate and look around the Verde Valley on your way to Montezuma Castle, take AZ 89A southwest to Cottonwood, 19 miles, then take AZ 260 to Camp Verde, 12 miles. You can reach Prescott from Sedona, a distance of 67 miles, by taking AZ 179 to I-17, which traverses and then climbs out of the river valley for about 20 miles. As you reach the top of the hill, look for AZ 169 on the west side of the freeway. This road, also called the Cherry Cutoff, leads to AZ 69, which goes to Prescott, about 40 miles from the junction of I-17 and AZ 169. The whole trip takes about 1.5 hours. A much more scenic route to Prescott from Sedona takes you up over Mingus Mountain and through the bustling old "ghost town" of Jerome. Take AZ 89A west from Sedona and follow it to the top of the mountain, 27 miles away. Follow the road from Jerome as it twists and turns through the forest down to plains and then to Prescott, 36 miles from Jerome. The whole drive from Sedona is likely to take two hours or more despite the relatively short distance.

Public Transportation

Once you've made it to town, if you don't feel like driving around, hop on the Sedona Trolley (928/282-5400, www.sedonatrolley.com, $17 adults, $12 under age 12) for two different 55-minute "best-of" tours (10am and 4pm daily).

Red Rock Country

TOP EXPERIENCE

Red Rock Country's towering natural monuments were once a part of the Colorado Plateau, the connection eaten away by erosion, that ingenious sculptor that makes all of Arizona its medium over millions of years. High concentrations of iron oxide, or rust, in the sediment layers stain the rock statues many shades of red as a finishing flourish. The result is one of the most beautiful and sought-after landscapes on earth.

Many of the red-rock buttes, spires, and monuments around Sedona have been given names over the years. Some of the more famous rocks can be seen from the road at designated pull-offs, and most of them have relatively easy trails around them if you want to get closer. On AZ 89A heading into Sedona from the west, look for Chimney Rock off to the north, roughly around Andante Drive.

A little farther east and far off to the north around Soldiers Pass Road, look for Coffee Pot Rock. Many people recognize in a rock monument near Schnebly Hill Road and AZ 179 the shape of Snoopy relaxing with Woodstock on his nose, and thus call it Snoopy Rock.

Red Rock Pass

Before you do anything in Red Rock Country, stop by the ranger station or the Sedona visitors center and purchase a Red Rock Pass ($5 per day, $15 per week, or $20 per year), which you're required to have even if you're only going to be motoring around the rocks and stopping every now and again. The fees go to the upkeep of this heavily used national forest. An America the Beautiful Interagency Pass, the $80 federal pass to all parks, works here as well.

For all the information on driving, hiking, and biking in Red Rock Country, stop by the **Red Rock Ranger District visitors center** (8375 AZ 179, mile marker 304.7, 928/282-4119 or 928/203-2903, www.fs.usda.gov/coconino, 8am-5pm daily), six miles north of the I-17 junction.

RED ROCK SCENIC BYWAY

The best way to enter Sedona is from the south, from I-17 to AZ 179. Along this route, roughly between Wet Beaver Creek and Oak Creek, about 10 miles or so, you'll see some otherworldly scenery along both sides of the road. This short stretch, if driven slowly with stops for photographs and strolls, could take a few hours, or it could be passed at a brisk pace, mouth gaping. Either way, it is along this paved busy road that Sedona's red rocks reveal their strange splendor; if you're only passing through, do it along this stretch of AZ 179. The always busy route has a series of traffic circles as it moves through the Village of Oak Creek that must be navigated with great care. Make sure to keep extra distance between you and the car ahead; people tend to stop abruptly here.

There are two developed pullouts along the road. From the south, the first is the **Bell Rock Pathway and Vista Southern Trailhead,** on the east side of the road. Pull over for views and photographs of **Bell Rock** and **Courthouse Butte** to the east. To the southwest sit **Cathedral Rock** and **The Three Nuns.**

Just beyond the parking lot are popular and easy hiking and mountain biking trails that lead into the high-desert red land and up close to the rocks. There's a trail map and restrooms at the turnout. Just 2.6 miles up the road, again on the east side of the road, is the **Little Horse Trail and Bell Rock Pathway Northern Trailhead,** the second pullout along the route. This stop provides a different vantage point to view the rocks, and there's parking for and access to hiking trails.

There is a trail map and a restroom near the parking lot.

RED ROCK LOOP ROAD

This short loop drive is an easy way to see the red rocks, and it also provides access to beautiful Red Rock Crossing and Red Rock State Park. Most regular cars can make it with no problems; the route is paved except for one short stretch.

Head west on AZ 89A for about seven miles from Uptown and turn south on Upper Red Rock Loop Road, also called Forest Road 216, and open your eyes. There's red and green everywhere, varying in shade and mood. There are a few undeveloped scenic pullouts and many homes along this road. About 1.5 miles in you'll see signs for the **Crescent Moon Recreation Area** and **Red Rock Crossing** ($10 per car), reached by turning left on Chavez Ranch Road. This is a very popular creek-side oasis where people go to splash in Oak Creek and soak up the warmth of the red rocks. Get here early, especially on weekends in summer, if you want a picnic table. The area has restrooms and drinking fountains, but you should bring your own water. Also bring your camera: Red Rock Crossing provides some spectacular views of **Cathedral Rock,** not to mention dark green water lapping against red rock. The road continues to become Lower Red Rock Loop Road, which provides access to Red Rock State Park. It then leads back around to AZ 89A.

Red Rock State Park

The 286-acre **Red Rock State Park** (Lower Red Rock Loop Rd., 928/282-6907, http://azstateparks.com, 8am-5pm daily, visitors center 9am-5pm daily, $7 per vehicle) is a pleasant place to see Oak Creek, which runs through the park and provides water for huge cottonwoods and willows under which you can lounge and walk. There are about five miles of short streamside loop hiking trails with truly inspiring scenery.

A ranger leads an hour-long **nature walk**

(10am daily) through the riparian ecosystem. The main thrust is environmental education, and this is the best place to really get to know the ecology of the area. This is also a really good choice for families with young kids. The trails are easy and provide a kind of introductory hiking experience.

PALATKI HERITAGE SITE

Palatki Heritage Site (928/282-3854, www. fs.usda.gov/coconino, 9:30am-3pm daily), a small Sinagua cliff dwelling in the Sedona backcountry, isn't as dramatic as Montezuma Castle or the Northern Sinagua dwellings near Flagstaff, but it's still worth visiting for the beauty of the area and the amazing petroglyphs and pictographs left behind on the soft sandstone walls. The site was occupied by a small group of Sinagua people who hunted, farmed, and built unusual stone cities throughout the Verde Valley about AD 1100-1300.

A great pioneer of Southwestern archaeology, Jesse Walter Fewkes, visited Palatki, which means "Red House" in the Hopi language, as part of an archaeological expedition to Arizona in the 1890s. He described the cliff dwelling as showing a "degree of architectural skill, which, while not peculiar to the cliff dwellings of the Red-rocks, is rarely found in southern cliff houses." Not much is left, but by hiking the short but relatively steep step-trail to the dwelling you can still get an idea of how the Sinagua lived and the skill with which they built. Most visitors will find the walk of moderate difficulty; make sure you have some good walking shoes and bring along water. The view from the high dwelling of the Sedona landscape, all rust-red and pine-green, is something to remember—and photograph. Another moderately steep trail leads to the petroglyphs and pictographs, which are an essential part of a visit here.

You must purchase a Red Rock Pass ($5) to visit Palatki, and you have to call ahead to reserve a spot, as parking is limited to 20 cars. The drive to the ruins is over dirt roads, though most regular sedans can make it without problems. Take AZ 89A west from Sedona and go five miles past the last traffic light. Turn right on Forest Road 525. It's 10 miles from the turnoff to the ruins, with directional signs along the way. You'll find knowledgeable docents and a small visitors center with restrooms and a bookshop. No pets are allowed. You don't need a reservation to visit the smaller **Honanki** ruins, about five miles from Palatki. Meaning "Bear House" in Hopi, Honanki is not as well preserved as Palatki and is recommended only to those with a deep interest in the Sinagua people.

★ OAK CREEK CANYON

Arguably the most beautiful drive in the state is the twisty streamside drive north on AZ 89A through Oak Creek Canyon and back up to the plateau. Head north from Sedona, over the large bridge high over Oak Creek, and just drive and look, slowly, while not veering into oncoming traffic as you crane to see the towering red rocks, topped with white caps and greenery peppered throughout. The creek is so inviting that you may want to stop along the side of the road and put your feet in. It's illegal to park along most stretches of the road, but there are a few pullouts and several lodges and stores along the way where you can stop.

The best and easiest place to get in the creek is at **Slide Rock State Park** (6871 N. AZ 89A, 928/282-3034, http://azstateparks. com, 8am-6pm daily summer, 9am-6pm daily winter, summer $20 per vehicle, winter $10), where you can try out the 80-foot natural red-rock slide, walk around the short nature trails, picnic, or just soak in the creek and lie on the warm rocks. There will likely be crowds in the summer, including many families with children.

★ HIKING

Red Rock Country is high country, the high desert populated by evergreen junipers and piñon pines, dusted with red sand. The

---

1: Slide Rock State Park **2:** Tonto Natural Bridge State Park **3:** Pink Jeep Tours **4:** Devil's Bridge Trail

landscape holds famous rusty buttes, red slickrock, mystical slot canyons, and lush and shady creeks. It's a unique place that rewards the traveler who trades the scenic highway for rocky trails with a deeper understanding and appreciation of its natural wonders.

Several places around Red Rock Country have multiple trailheads in one place. Many trails around Sedona are open to hikers, equestrians, and mountain bikers. Trailheads often have a large map for reference, but you can also pick up a fairly comprehensive guide to the region's trails at the **Red Rock Ranger District Visitor Center** (8375 AZ 179, 928/203-2900, www.fs.usda.gov, 9am-4:30pm daily). Always take water and a hat with you.

Just south of the intersection of AZ 179 and AZ 89A (known as the Y) south of Uptown, exit the traffic circle for Schnebly Hill Road. About a mile in, you'll find the parking lot for **Huckaby & Margs Draw Trails,** with access to hikes that wind around the highlands above Uptown. A good option is **Margs Draw Trail No. 163,** an easy 2-mile one-way hike with great views of Snoopy Rock, Camel Head, and Steamboat Rock. Allow two hours for the hike. The **Huckaby Trail** is a fantastic 2.8-mile one-way hike down to Oak Creek and back up to higher land after passing beneath the dramatic Midgely Bridge. You have to cross the creek and hop over boulders, and the trail is steep in a few places. This route provides great views of Uptown Sedona, Oak Creek, and the red-rock buttes. Plan on 2.5-3 hours for the hike.

From Uptown Sedona, take AZ 179 south for about eight miles and you'll find the **Bell Rock Area Trails,** a series of mostly easy flat trails that lead around Bell Rock and Courthouse Butte, two of the most famous rocks in town. The **Bell Rock Pathway and Vista** is an easy 3.6-mile out-and-back trail that gets you close to Bell Rock and Courthouse Butte. Most of the trail is flat and wide, and mountain bikers often speed by. If you want to get better-than-average photographs of these famous eroded rocks, you

need to hike in: About 0.5 miles into the trail you'll see an offshoot for the **Courthouse Butte Loop,** a 3.6-mile loop around the hulking red rocks, moderately strenuous and a bit steep in a few places. This is a great introduction to Red Rock Country. Both trails take about 2.5 hours total to hike.

Heading west from Uptown Sedona, off the north side of AZ 89A, the **Soldier Pass Trails** can be accessed by turning right on Soldier Pass Road. A good option is the **Soldier Pass Trail No. 66,** a 4.5-mile loop that passes through the Red Rock Secret Mountain Wilderness. You'll gain some great views of Red Rock Country from the high vistas on this hike, but you have to walk up some steep and rocky trails to enjoy them. It's a moderate hike of 2.5 hours.

For sweeping in-town views, take an easy hike on the 3.3-mile round-trip **Sugarloaf/Coffee Pot Trail,** perfect for families. The trail winds through red lands and residential neighborhoods to the top of **Sugarloaf Rock,** where you can get some excellent pictures of Coffee Pot Rock and Thunder Mountain. From the Y intersection of AZ 89A and AZ 179, go west on AZ 89A for two miles to Coffee Pot Drive and turn right. Take a left on Sanborn after about 0.5 miles, then turn right on Little Elf, which ends at Buena Vista, where you'll see parking for the trailhead.

One of the most popular hikes in Sedona is the moderate hike to **Devil's Bridge,** the largest natural bridge in the area. The best way to hike here is to start at the **Mescal Trailhead.** Follow the Mescal Trail to the Chuckwagon Trail to the Devil's Bridge Trail for a moderate four-mile (round-trip) hike through the red lands. There will likely be a crowd on weekends. If you have a 4WD vehicle and want a shorter hike, you can access the **Devil's Bridge Trailhead,** where you can head out for a one-mile (one-way) climb to the bridge. The hike takes two hours round trip from the Mescal Trailhead and one hour round-trip from the Devil's Bridge Trailhead, not counting time spent standing on the natural bridge with the vast wilderness spread before you. For both trailheads, head west from Uptown Sedona on AZ 89A and turn right onto Dry Creek Road. For the Mescal Trailhead, head left at the fork onto Boynton Pass Road and then right onto Long Canyon Road. Stay on Dry Creek Road for the Devil's Bridge Trailhead.

For the **Dry Creek Trails** parking lot, continue on Boynton Pass Road past the junction with Long Canyon Road, and then turn right onto Boynton Canyon Road. The most popular trail in this area is the **Boynton Canyon Trail,** an easy five-mile round-trip to a vortex through the Red Mountain Secret Wilderness, where you'll see canyon walls more than 1,000 feet high and maybe even waterfalls if it's a wet time of year. The trailhead is just outside Enchantment Resort. Allow two hours for this hike.

For some streamside hiking, try the **West Fork of Oak Creek Trail,** 6.5 miles round-trip, which takes you through a riparian wonderland mixed with red rocks and deep-green pools. It's a popular trail, so expect crowds. The trailhead is at milepost 385 along AZ 89A in Oak Creek Canyon, north of Uptown Sedona. It's an easy, mostly flat hike that takes two or three hours, but you'll probably get your feet wet crossing the creek a few times. It costs $10 to park at the trailhead, and the parking lot and trail close when full, usually

early in the day in high season—the parking lot opens at 9am and fills by 9:30am.

MOUNTAIN BIKING

One of the best biking areas is the **Bell Rock Loops,** a series of red-dirt single-tracks among the petrified sand dunes in the rocks near the Village of Oak Creek. The northland biking authorities at **Absolute Bikes** (6101 AZ 179, 928/284-1242 or 877/284-1242, www.absolutebikes.net, 8am-6pm Mon.-Fri., 8am-5pm Sat., 8am-4pm Sun.), near the Bell Rock Loops trailhead, can give you pointers and ideas about where to go.

JEEP TOURS

One of the most famous tour companies in the Southwest, **Pink Jeep Tours** (204 N. AZ 89A, Uptown Sedona, 800/873-3662, www.pinkjeep.com, 7am-6pm daily, $95) operates under a special permit with the U.S. Forest Service to take their gaudy open-air 4WD Jeeps, filled with eager tourists, into the red lands. Founded in 1960, it's an institution, and the guides are usually friendly, entertaining, and knowledgeable. Unless you have your own 4WD vehicle, this is the best way to see the less accessible portions of the backcountry in a vehicle. There are a lot of Jeep tour companies to choose from in Sedona, but Pink Jeeps is among the oldest and certainly the most conspicuous.

Payson and Rim Country

Just a short scenic 1.5-hour drive north of Phoenix on AZ 87, also known as the Beeline Highway, you're in a different world. Payson, a small forest town of about 15,000, sits at 5,000 feet above sea level and is surrounded by the Tonto National Forest and the Sierra Ancha and Mazatzal Mountains. The town is tucked below the 7,000-foot Mogollon Rim. Visitors to this region can access the heights of the Rim via a historic dirt road 30 miles north

of Payson. The road parallels the Rim for 50 miles and ends in the White Mountains region, within the vast Apache-Sitgreaves National Forests. Along the two-lane highway between the Rim and Payson, you'll pass through a few tiny quaint forest settlements, but this area is mostly about the pine-and-aspen forest, the long sweeping views above the treetops, and the cool clean high-country air.

Founded in 1882 by miners and ranchers,

Payson, which stretches along AZ 87 about 90 miles north of Phoenix, used to be called Green Valley, and it's easy to see why. The little town is popular with Phoenicians escaping the summer heat and has several chain hotels and restaurants along the main drag, the highway. This is an inviting region if you're interested in Old West history and forest activities such as hiking, mountain biking, camping, and fishing. Otherwise, its scenic value and cool breezes, even in the summer, are enough to recommend it for a day trip from Phoenix.

SIGHTS

★ The Mogollon Rim

The 7,000-foot-high southwestern edge of the Colorado Plateau, the Mogollon (mug-ih-YOWN) Rim is a dramatic rock escarpment that runs 200 miles west to east across Arizona's high country. Also called the Tonto Rim and featured in Westerns by Zane Grey and Louis L'Amour, the escarpment's topside is covered with pine-and-aspen forests and small lakes. The easiest way to see it, and to view a sea of pine trees spread out below its heights, is to take a several-hour drive along the General Crook Trail, an ancient route across the Rim that's also known as the Rim Road.

Made from a trail that was once used by General George Crook to run supplies from Fort Verde, near Prescott, to Fort Apache in the White Mountains during the Apache Wars of the 1870s, the Rim Road (Forest Rd. 300) is not paved, but neither is it too rough; most sedans will make it just fine. The road parallels the Rim exactly in some places, and you can stop, walk right up to the edge, and feel the pine-scented wind on your face. The 51-mile one-way drive across the Rim from AZ 87 to the Mogollon Rim Visitor Center (AZ 260, 32 miles east of Payson, 27 miles west of Heber-Overgaard, 9am-3pm Thurs.-Sun. May 19-Labor Day) takes several hours. Expect the drive to take at least two hours one-way, but it could take twice that depending on stops to explore the forest. Make sure to gas up and check your tires and fluids in Payson before

you head out, and pack food and water; there's little but beautiful views along the way.

Drive north from Payson on AZ 87 (also designated AZ 260 westbound) for 29 miles until you see the sign for Forest Road 300 on the right side of the road, not far past the junction where AZ 260 separates and continues west. Turn east on Forest Road 300 and drive across the Rim to the visitors center, where there's a paved trail and some breathtaking views right at the edge of the White Mountains region, near an eastern section of AZ 260. You can make a loop back to Payson by taking AZ 260 from the Mogollon Rim Visitor Center southwest 34 miles back to the town. You could also start the trip from Payson going northeast on AZ 260 eastbound, then drive west on Forest Road 300 across the Rim to AZ 87.

Along the Rim Road you'll see the effects of the huge wildfires that have threatened this region repeatedly over the last few decades. Blackened stands of deadwood and new green growth are everywhere along the escarpment. The whole region is generally bone dry and drought-ridden, and it is usually subject to campfire restrictions in summer.

Rim Lakes

In the forest just north of the Rim along Forest Road 300 are several small pine-encircled artificial lakes that are stocked with trout and bass and offer camping spots and plenty of easy trails to the Rim's edge.

The best of these is gorgeous and popular little 55-acre Woods Canyon Lake (Apr. 1-Oct. 15), not far from the Rim Visitor Center. There are four campgrounds (Apache-Sitgreaves National Forests, Black Mesa Ranger District, Overgaard, 928/535-7300, www.fs.usda.gov/asnf, 877/444-6777, $22) near the lake with a total of 150 sites, some of which can take trailers up to 32 feet. A country store sells all kinds of supplies. There's a dump station, picnic tables, restrooms, and boat rentals. The easiest way to reach Woods Canyon Lake and the other nearby Rim lakes is to take AZ 260 northeast from Payson 30 miles to Forest Road 300, which is paved on this stretch. Then drive about four miles west and turn right on Forest Road 105. The lake is a mile farther.

INFORMATION

For more information on the Rim and its lakes and trails, try the Apache-Sitgreaves National Forests, Black Mesa Ranger District (Overgaard, 928/535-7300, www. fs.usda.gov/asnf). Another good source for information about hiking, biking, and camping in this region is the local website www. rimcountry.com.

Zane Grey Cabin

Even if you've never read any of Zane Grey's 130 books, a look at the Zane Grey Cabin (700 Green Valley Pkwy., 928/474-3483, 10am-4pm Wed.-Mon., $5) is a must when you're in the small town of Payson. The beloved writer of Westerns loved this area, which he called the Tonto Rim, and often came to write and hunt 1918-1929. The original cabin burned down in the 1990 Dude Fire, but a local group rebuilt it and furnished it according to surviving pictures. There's also a small Rim Country Museum next door with exhibits on Grey and what life was like for the Anglo pioneers who settled this piney area below the great Rim.

Tonto Natural Bridge State Park

The Tonto Natural Bridge State Park (AZ 87, 11 miles north of Payson, 928/476-4202, http://azstateparks.com, 8am-5pm daily, last entry 5pm, $7 adults, $4 ages 7-13) is the major stop in Rim Country other than the Rim itself. The strange and wondrous world's largest natural travertine bridge can be hiked to or over on short trails. The trail to the dripping moss-covered inner bridge is steep going on the back up, it's short and should be walked to get the full experience. Hike down and sit on the wet rocks, watching water drip off the bridge's arch high above. A visit typically takes about an hour but could go much longer.

Pine and Strawberry

Tucked just below the Rim, north on AZ 87 about 20 miles from Payson, the tiny towns of Pine and Strawberry have a few antiques stores, small inns and restaurants, and a historic rural atmosphere.

Pine comes first as you drive north from Payson on AZ 87. The Pine-Strawberry Museum (AZ 87, 15 miles north of Payson, 928/476-3547, www.pinestrawhs.org, 10am-2pm Wed.-Sat., $1, free under age 11) is worth a short stop. Housed in a former Mormon chapel that dates from 1917, the museum has an interesting collection of information and artifacts on the area's ancient cultures and its later settling by several hardy Mormon families in the 1880s.

Strawberry is three miles north of Pine along AZ 87. About a mile into town is Fossil Creek Road, which leads to the Verde Valley from the Rim Country. About two miles to the west on Fossil Creek Road from AZ 87 is Arizona's "Oldest Standing Schoolhouse," the pine-log cabin Strawberry Schoolhouse (10am-4pm Sat., noon-4pm Sun. mid-May-mid-June and early Aug.-mid-Oct., 10am-4pm Mon.-Sat., noon-4pm Sun. mid-June-early Aug., free). Built in 1882 to serve a few pioneer families in the area, the small pine-plank, one-room schoolhouse has been preserved and restored by locals and now presents a 19th-century frontier schoolroom as it would have looked to the kids filing in from the forest trails so long ago.

FOOD

There are a lot of chain restaurants and hotels around Payson, Pine, and Strawberry to serve Phoenicians escaping the heat, as it's a mere 1.5-hour drive from Phoenix. Most of the services are along the main road through town.

★ That Brewery (3270 AZ 87, Pine, 928/476-3349, www.thatbrewery.com, 11am-8pm Mon.-Sat., 11am-7pm Sun., $10-20), along winding AZ 87 through the dusty pine forest, deserves a stop around lunch or dinnertime for delicious pub-style food, including vegetarian and gluten-free options, as well as superior craft beers. This out-of-way gem sits among tall cool pines and has a volleyball court and a shady patio. The restaurant is serious about sustainability, with a vigorous recycling ethic that includes building and decorating a second Cottonwood location with repurposed materials and found items. They also use only grass-fed Arizona-raised beef and donate 5 percent of sales of their AZ Trail Ale brand to the nonprofit Arizona Trails Association. And, like other craft brewers in the northland, That Brewery buys its grain from a small farm in Camp Verde, helping local farmers grow a lucrative crop while using less water.

The chili and burgers at **Macky's Grill** (201 W. Main St., 928/474-7411, 10am-8pm Sun.-Wed., 10am-9pm Thurs.-Sat., http://mackysgrill.com, $10-20) are excellent, and the menu is stocked with all kinds of other dishes, including a vegetarian burger and other nonmeat options. This place is popular with locals and has a fun kitschy cowboy decor. The patio is the place to eat on a cool high-country afternoon.

ACCOMMODATIONS

Payson and the Rim work best as a drive-through or a day trip, but if you want to stay longer, there are several chain hotels along AZ 87, the main drag through town. You can't go wrong staying at the small **Majestic Mountain Inn** (602 E. AZ 260, 800/408-2442, www.majesticmountaininn.com, $119-189), with clean comfortable rooms, free Wi-Fi, in-room fridges, and a heated pool. A few of the guest rooms have hot tubs next to the bed.

The Tonto Apache Tribe operates the **Mazatzal Hotel and Casino** (AZ 87 Mile Marker 251, 800/777-7529, www.mazatzalcasino.com, from $150), which has very nice and clean all-suite guest rooms, with comfortable beds, fridges, and microwaves. Smoky and cheap, Mazatzal has the somewhat desperate and depressing atmosphere unique to gambling halls. It's a fine place to stay nonetheless, and in a great location for anything you want to do in Rim country. Eat elsewhere; the food here is overpriced.

TRANSPORTATION
Car

Payson and the Mogollon Rim are easy to visit by car from Phoenix, only 90 miles away. The best route is AZ 87, also called the Beeline Highway, usually a 1.5-hour trip, but traffic can be slow on summer weekends, when Phoenicians head to the mountains out of the heat. Fill up before you leave Phoenix, as gas is more expensive along the road.

To reach this region from the Verde Valley and Sedona, take AZ 260, east from Camp Verde 36 miles to Strawberry; then it's 30 miles south on AZ 260/AZ 87 to Payson, or only a few yards to Forest Road 300, which leads across the Rim to the White Mountains.

From Flagstaff, head south to the Verde Valley on AZ 89A, through Sedona, and then take AZ 260 to Payson from Camp Verde. Another scenic route is Forest Road 209, also known as Lake Mary Road, from Flagstaff, through the forest, past Happy Jack and Clints Well to AZ 87 near the Rim Road. The incredibly beautiful forest drive is about 100 miles and takes more than two hours. The road sometimes closes in winter.

To reach the White Mountains region from Payson, simply take AZ 260 east for 90 miles to Show Low.

The Grand Canyon and the Arizona Strip

There's a reason why Arizona's official nickname is "The Grand Canyon State." Any state with one of the true wonders of the world would be keen to advertise its good luck.

The canyon simply must be seen to be believed. If you stand for the first time on one of the South Rim's easily accessible lookouts and don't have to catch your breath, you might need to check your pulse. Staring into the canyon brings up all kinds of existential questions; its brash vastness can't be taken in without conjuring some big ideas and questions about life and humanity. Take your time here—you'll need it.

The more adventurous can make reservations, obtain a permit, and enter the desert depths of the canyon, taking a hike, or even a mule ride, to the Colorado River, or spending a weekend trekking

Highlights

Look for ★ to find recommended sights, activities, dining, and lodging.

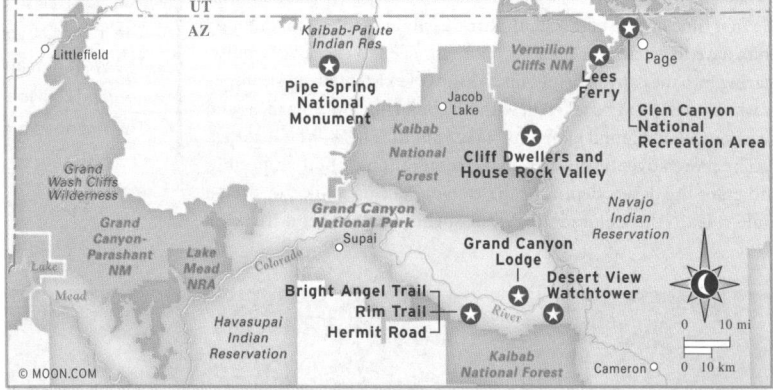

© MOON.COM

★ **Hermit Road:** Make your way west along the forested rim to the enchanting stone cottage called Hermit's Rest, stopping to see the setting sun turn the canyon walls into fleeting works of art (page 260).

★ **Desert View Watchtower:** See one of architect Mary Colter's finest accomplishments—a rock tower standing tall on the edge of the canyon (page 268).

★ **Rim Trail:** Walk along the rim on this easy, accessible trail past historical buildings, famous lodges—and the most breathtaking views in the world (page 269).

★ **Bright Angel Trail:** Hike down the South Rim's most popular trail, based on old Native American routes (page 269).

★ **Grand Canyon Lodge:** This rustic old lodge balances on the edge of the gorge, where you can sink into a chair and gaze out at the multicolored canyon (page 281).

★ **Pipe Spring National Monument:** At this wisely preserved ranch and homestead, guides will show you what life was like on the lonely 19th-century frontier (page 302).

★ **Cliff Dwellers and House Rock Valley:** Stop along the highway and walk among these strange, thrilling structures built of red rock (page 306).

★ **Lees Ferry:** This is one of the few places in the canyon lands where you can dip your toes in the mighty Colorado River without first hiking deep into the Grand Canyon (page 306).

★ **Glen Canyon National Recreation Area:** Rent a houseboat or fish the waters of Lake Powell, an artificial lake formed by the Glen Canyon Dam (page 310).

rim to rim with an overnight at the famous Phantom Ranch, deep in the canyon's inner gorge. The really brave can hire a guide and take a once-in-a-lifetime trip down the great river, riding the roiling rapids and camping on its serene beaches.

There are plenty of places to stay and eat, many of them charming and historic, on the canyon's South Rim. If you decide to go to the high, forested, and often snowy North Rim, you'll drive through a corner of the desolate Arizona Strip, which has a beauty and a history all its own.

Water-sports enthusiasts will want to make it up to the far northern reaches of the state to the Glen Canyon Recreation Area to do some waterskiing, kayaking, or maybe rent a houseboat, and anyone interested in the country's engineering prowess will want to see Glen Canyon Dam, holding back the once wild Colorado.

PLANNING YOUR TIME

The ideal South Rim-only trip lasts four days and three nights, with one day in each of the park's three major sections (Grand Canyon Village, Hermit Road, and East Rim/Desert View Drive) plus a day spent hiking into the canyon. Three days and two nights (with the first and last days including the trip to and from the rim) allow you to see all the sights on the rim, to take in a sunset and sunrise over the canyon, and even to do a day hike or mule trip below the rim. If you just have a day, five hours or so will allow you to see all the sights in Grand Canyon Village plus take a ride out to Hermit's Rest, stopping at viewpoints along the way.

If you include a North or West Rim excursion, add at least one or two more days and nights. It takes at least 4.5 hours to reach the North Rim from the South, perhaps longer if you take the daily shuttle instead of your own vehicle, and the West Rim and the Hualapai and Havasupai Indian Reservations

are some 200 miles from the South Rim on slow roads—although it makes sense if you're coming from Vegas and on your way to the South Rim anyway. A visit to the Hualapai Reservation's Skywalk should not be substituted for the South Rim, and it isn't recommended to those seeing the Grand Canyon for the first time; you have not truly seen the Grand Canyon unless you have seen the South or North Rim.

The most important thing to remember when considering a trip to the canyon is to plan far ahead, even if, like the vast majority of visitors, you're just going to spend time on the South Rim. Six months' advance planning is the norm, and longer if you are going to ride a mule down or stay overnight at Phantom Ranch in the inner canyon.

Seasons

At about 7,000 feet elevation, the South Rim has a temperate climate: warm in summer months, cool in spring and fall, and cold in winter. It rains and snows in winter, and thunderstorms, sometimes quite violent, appear in the late afternoon July-early September. Summer brings the park's busiest season, and it is *very* busy. Three million visitors from all over the world visit the South Rim each summer, offering rare opportunities for people-watching and hobnobbing with fellow tourists from the far corners of the globe. Summer (May-Sept.) temperatures often exceed 110°F in the inner canyon, which has a desert climate, but are cooler by 20-30 degrees up on the forested rims. There's no reason for anybody to hike deep into the canyon in summer. It's not fun, and it is potentially deadly. Instead, plan your epic trek in spring or fall, perfect times to visit the park: It's light-jacket cool on the South Rim and warm and not hot in the inner canyon.

October-November are the last months of the year a rim-to-rim hike from the North Rim is possible, as rim services shut down

---

Previous: the North Rim; Desert View Watchtower on the South Rim; Colorado River at Lees Ferry.

Grand Canyon and the Arizona Strip

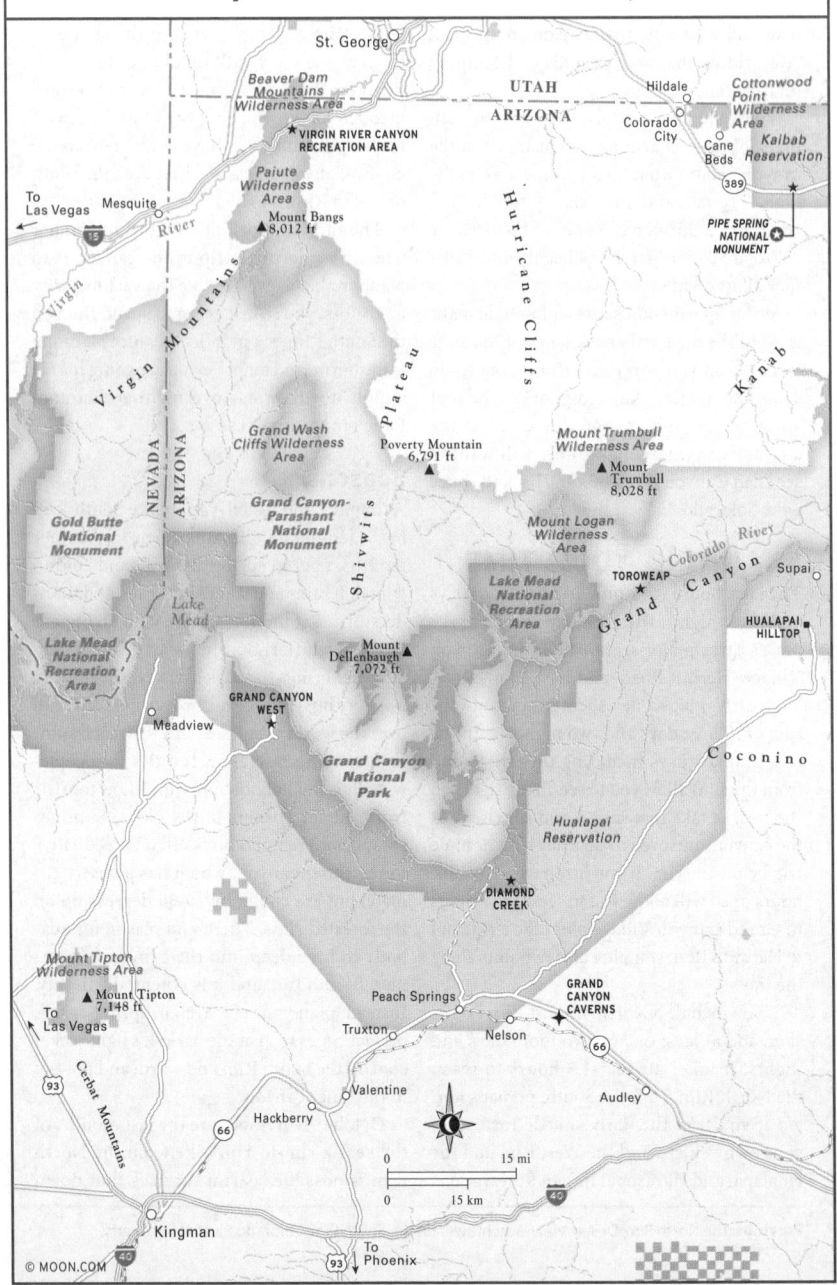

St. George

Beaver Dam
Mountains
Wilderness Area

UTAH
ARIZONA

Hildale

Cottonwood
Point
Wilderness
Area

Colorado
City

Cane
Beds

Kaibab
Reservation

VIRGIN RIVER CANYON
RECREATION AREA

389

Paiute
Wilderness
Area

To
Las Vegas

Mesquite

PIPE SPRING
NATIONAL
MONUMENT

Mount Bangs
8,012 ft

River

Virgin

Virgin Mountains

NEVADA
ARIZONA

Hurricane Cliffs

Plateau

Kanab

Grand Wash
Cliffs Wilderness
Area

Poverty Mountain
6,791 ft

Mount Trumbull
Wilderness Area

Mount
Trumbull
8,028 ft

Gold Butte
National
Monument

Grand Canyon-
Parashant
National
Monument

Shivwits

Mount Logan
Wilderness
Area

Colorado River

Lake
Mead

Lake Mead
National
Recreation
Area

TOROWEAP

Grand Canyon

Supai

HUALAPAI
HILLTOP

Lake Mead
National
Recreation
Area

Mount
Dellenbaugh
7,072 ft

Coconino

Meadview

GRAND CANYON
WEST

Grand Canyon
National
Park

Hualapai
Reservation

DIAMOND
CREEK

Mount Tipton
Wilderness Area

Mount Tipton
7,148 ft

To
Las Vegas

Peach Springs

GRAND
CANYON
CAVERNS

93

Truxton

Nelson

66

Cerbat Mountains

66

Valentine

Audley

Hackberry

0   15 mi

0   15 km

Kingman

40

© MOON.COM

93

To
Phoenix

40

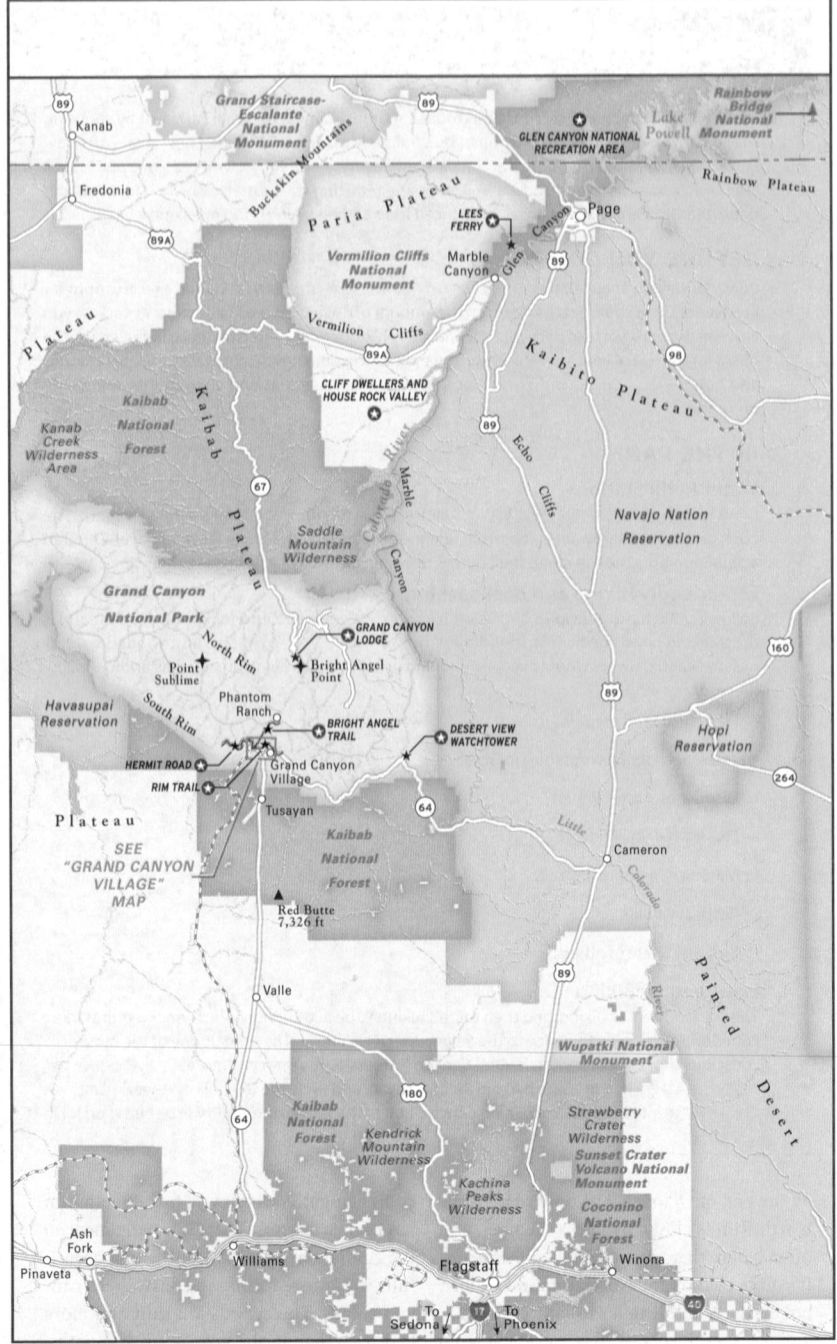

Sustainability Tips

It's not difficult to be an eco-conscious tourist at Grand Canyon National Park. Just by choosing Grand Canyon over other destinations, you've already made a good start. For several years now sustainability has been a priority at the park, and everywhere you go you see signs of this new era—water stations for refilling water bottles and reducing waste, greenway trails for bikes and pedestrians, an emphasis on locally produced food and beverages, and much more.

BEFORE YOU GO

Consider staying at one of the in-park lodges and campgrounds (make reservations far in advance). This strategy cuts down on the amount of driving you will have to do; as soon as you arrive in the park, you can park your car and walk, bike, or ride the free natural gas-fueled shuttle buses for the rest of your stay. Moreover, the park concessionaires that operate the in-park lodges and hotels—Xanterra and Delaware North—have serious and energetic sustainability programs.

IN THE PARK

Water Refill Stations

Bring your reusable water bottles along and refill them at stations across the park. The pure, delicious springwater comes from Roaring Springs near the North Rim and travels through a pipeline across the canyon to the South Rim. No throwaway plastic bottle comes close.

Eco-Friendly Hiking and Backpacking

Following the basic principles of Leave No Trace (Center for Outdoor Ethics, www.lnt.org) is the thinking hiker's bedrock responsibility. The Seven Principles take on an added seriousness in Grand Canyon, where every living thing exists in a perilous niche ruled by aridity. Follow these ideas:

- Plan ahead and prepare.

- Travel and camp on durable surfaces.

- Dispose of waste properly.

- Leave what you find.

- Minimize campfire impacts.

- Respect wildlife.

- Be considerate of others.

Eco-Friendly Biking

There's eco-friendly biking, and then there's biking to be eco-friendly. The former requires basic common sense and adherence to the Seven Principles above. The latter is one of the most eco-conscious choices an individual Grand Canyon National Park visitor can make. Leave your car outside the park in a safe parking lot in Tusayan, and cycle the 6.5-mile one-way Tusayan Greenway into the park. You, Grand Canyon, and perhaps even the world will be better off for it.

by the end of October. The only road to the North Rim is closed by late November, and often before that, due to winter snowstorms. It's quite cold on the North Rim in October, but on the South Rim it's usually clear, cool, and pleasant during the day and snuggle-up chilly at night. A winter visit to the South Rim has its own charms. There is usually snow on the rim January-March, contrasting beautifully with the red, pink, and dusty green canyon colors. The crowds are thin and more laid-back than in the busy summer months.

It is, however, quite cold, even during the day, and you may not want to stand and stare too long at the windy, bone-chilling viewpoints.

What to Take

Take an easy-to-carry receptacle to refill at the water fountains situated throughout the park. A water bottle, hydration bladder, or canteen is simply required gear for a visit; you are going to get thirsty in the high dry air along the rim. You might even bring along a cooler with cold water and other drinks, which you can leave in your car and revisit as the need arises. Consider taking a hat, binoculars, and a camera along with your water bottle. The canyon's vastness can only be considered for so long before you start to notice the details hidden in plain sight; binoculars and cameras come in handy. Bring along a light jacket, even in summer, as nights at 7,000 feet elevation can turn chilly. In winter, when it is 70-some degrees in Phoenix, the South Rim is cold and often snowy. Several layers of cold-weather clothing will serve you well October-May.

Gateways to the Canyon

Grand Canyon National Park, especially its South Rim, has some of the most interesting accommodations in the national park system, but it's not always possible to get reservations. The park's lodging rates are audited annually and generally compare favorably to those offered outside the park, but you can sometimes find excellent deals at one of several gateway towns around canyon country. Using one of these places as a base for a visit to the canyon makes sense if you're planning on touring the whole of the canyon lands and not just the park. Besides offering affordable and even a few luxurious places to stay and eat, these gateways are often interesting in their own right and deserving of some attention from the traveler, especially those interested in the history of this hard and spacious land.

Flagstaff, 79 miles southeast of the park's main South Rim entrance, was the park's first gateway town, and in many ways still the best. The home of Northern Arizona University is a fun laid-back college town with railroad and Route 66 history. In the old days, Eastern tourists detrained at Flagstaff and then faced an all-day stagecoach trip across the forest and the plains for a glimpse of the canyon and a few nights in a white canvas tent. These days, just hop in your rental car or your road-trip wagon, take U.S. 180 northwest to AZ 64, and 1.5 hours later, there you are. The route is absolutely the most scenic of all the approaches to the canyon, passing through Coconino National Forest and beneath the San Francisco Peaks, the state's ruling mountain range. (Apologies to desert rats who prefer the eastern Desert View approach.)

CAMERON

Established in 1916, the historic ★ Cameron Trading Post and Lodge (800/338-7385, www.camerontradingpost.com, $89-209) is on the Navajo Nation, 50 miles north of Flagstaff, along U.S. 89 near the junction with AZ 64 (the route to the park's east gate). The Cameron Lodge is a charming and affordable place to stay and makes a perfect base for a visit to the Grand Canyon, Indian Country, Lake Powell, and the Arizona Strip. It has a good restaurant (6am-9:30pm daily summer, 7am-9pm daily winter, $7-16) serving American and Navajo food, including excellent beef stew, heaping Navajo tacos, chili, and burgers. There's an art gallery, a visitors center, a huge trading post gift shop, and an RV park (no restrooms or showers, full hookup $35). A small grocery store has packaged sandwiches, chips, and sodas.

Guest rooms are decorated in Southwestern Native American style and are comfortable, some with views of the Little Colorado River and the old 1911 suspension bridge that spans the stream just outside the lodge. There are single-bed rooms, rooms with two beds, and a few suites that are perfect for families. The stone-and-wood buildings and the garden patio, laid out with stacked sandstone bricks with picnic tables and red-stone walkways below the open-corridor rooms, create a cozy history-soaked setting and make the lodge a memorable place to stay. The vast empty red plains of the Navajo Reservation spread out all around and create a lonely and isolated atmosphere, especially at night, but the guest rooms have cable TV and free Wi-Fi. If you're visiting in winter, the lodge drops its rates significantly.

It's about a 35-minute drive from Cameron Trading Post and Lodge to the Desert View area of the park, a good place to start a tour of the Grand Canyon. Before you reach the park, the Little Colorado drops some 2,000 vertical feet through the arid scrubby land, cutting through gray rock on the way to its marriage with the big river and creating the **Little Colorado Gorge.** Stop and get a barrier-free glimpse at this lesser chasm to prime yourself for what is to come. There are usually a few booths set up selling Navajo arts and crafts as well as lots of touristy souvenirs at two developed pullouts along the road. Starting from the East Entrance, you'll see the canyon gradually becoming grand.

WILLIAMS

This small historic town along I-40 (formerly Route 66), surrounded by the Kaibab National Forest, is the closest interstate town to AZ 64 and thus has branded itself "The Gateway to the Grand Canyon." It has been around since 1874 and was the last Route 66 town to be bypassed by the interstate, in 1984. As a result, and because of a resurgence over the last few decades owing to the rebirth of the Grand Canyon Railway, Williams, with about 3,000 full-time residents, has a good bit of small-town charm—the entire downtown area is on the National Register of Historic Places. It's worth a stop and an hour or two of strolling; there are a few good restaurants. It's only an

hour's drive to the South Rim from Williams, so many consider it a convenient base for exploring the region, though the drive is not as scenic as AZ 64 from Cameron or U.S. 180 from Flagstaff. This is the place to stay if you plan to take the Grand Canyon Railway, a highly recommended way to reach the South Rim. It's fun, cuts down on traffic and emissions within the park, and you'll get exercise walking the rim or renting a bike and cruising the park with the wind in your face.

Historic Downtown Williams

On a walk through the **Williams Historic Business District** you'll see how a typical pioneer Southwestern mountain town might have looked from territorial days until the railroad died and the interstate came. Williams wasn't bypassed by I-40 until the 1980s, so many of its old buildings still stand and have been repurposed as cafés, boutiques, B&Bs, and gift shops. Walk around and look at the old buildings; shop for Native American and Old West knickknacks, pioneer-era memorabilia, and Route 66 souvenirs you don't need; and maybe stop for a beer, cocktail, or coffee at an old-school small-town saloon or dressed-up café. The district is bounded on the north by Railroad Avenue, on the south by Grant Avenue, and on the east and west by 1st and 4th Streets. About 250 acres, the district has 44 buildings dating from 1875-1949 and an array of Route 66-era business signs and mid-century commercial architecture worth a few snapshots. Historic Route 66 is variously termed Bill Williams Avenue, Grand Canyon Avenue, and Railroad Avenue, and it splits into parallel one-way streets through the historic downtown before meeting up with the west and east.

Bearizona

Don't be surprised if a big brown bear, gone lazy from living the easy life in beautiful pine-covered **Bearizona Wildlife Park**

1: winter at the Grand Canyon **2:** Rod's Steak House in Williams **3:** downtown Williams

1

Rod's STEAK HOUSE
YOU ARE DRIVING THE WRONG WAY!
PLAZA
2

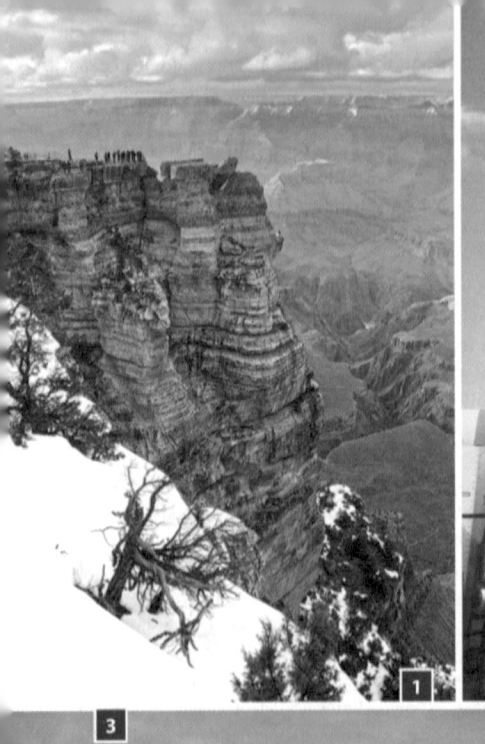

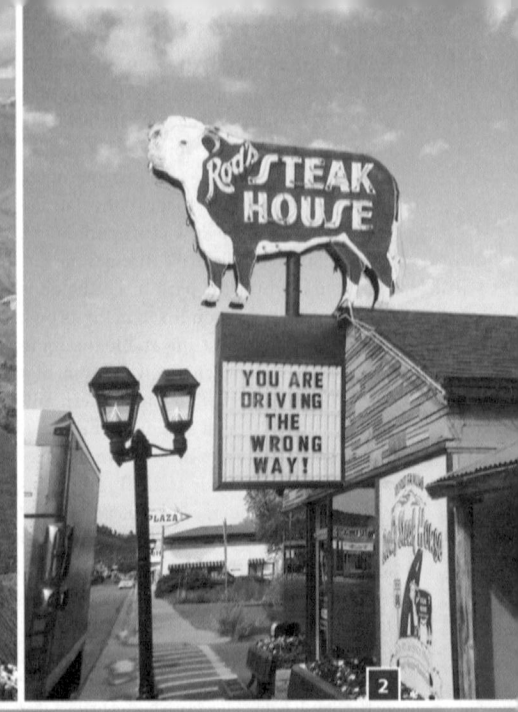

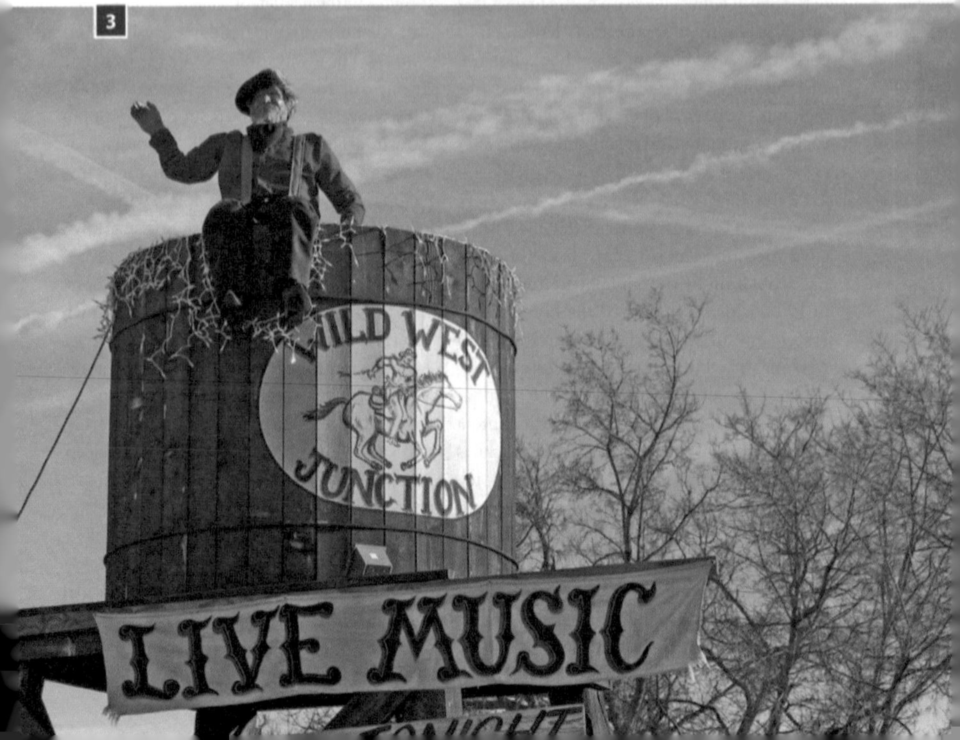
WILD WEST JUNCTION
LIVE MUSIC
3

(1500 E. Rte. 66, I-40 Exit 165, 928/635-2289, www.bearizona.com, 8am-5pm daily, $30 adults, $27seniors, $20 ages 4-12), decides to lounge on his back in front of your car; it's best to drive around the old beast, one of the many rescued animals that call this family-friendly drive-through wildlife park home. Along the three-mile drive through the forested park, which the park insists be done with windows up, you'll see many brown and black bears wrestling and lounging in the meadows, along with wolves, bison, bighorn sheep, and other classic Western animals. A walk-through section at the end of the drive called **Fort Bearizona** features adorable baby animals frolicking with innocence and wonder, as well as a few regal birds of prey that would probably like to eat all those fuzzy little morsels.

Kids absolutely love this place, and it makes for an easy side trip on the way to the Grand Canyon, located just outside Williams near the junction of I-40 and AZ 64, on the route to the South Rim. Allow two hours to visit this fun park; many of the animals have a bit of personality, and you might get hooked if you stay *too* long. Bearizona is busiest in the summer, but the park is open year-round. Hours vary according to the season and weather.

Grand Canyon Railway

The **Grand Canyon Railway** (800/843-8724, www.thetrain.com) runs daily from the original depot built by the Santa Fe Railroad back in 1908, which also housed the Fray Marcos Hotel, one of the first Harvey Houses in Arizona. The building is the oldest poured-concrete structure in the state. The original hotel inside the depot has been turned into a gift shop and offices, but across the tracks is the sprawling Grand Canyon Railway Hotel, built in 1995 to resemble the Fray Marcos; it has some of the most luxurious accommodations in the region, including a "pet resort" and an indoor pool and spa.

A fun, history-soaked, and environmentally conscious way to visit the canyon, the Grand Canyon Railway runs between the station in Williams and the South Rim depot in Grand Canyon Village. The train has several different ticket levels ($67-226 adults, $32-153 ages 2-15), including bar cars and luxury packages, and the rides feature strolling musicians, bandits, and other Old West tropes. Moving across the open highland landscape, the trip takes about 2.5 hours in each direction. Mid-June to mid-July, there are two morning departures from Williams and two afternoon departures from the South Rim; the rest of the year there is a single morning departure from Williams and a single afternoon departure from the South Rim.

Entertainment and Events

In June, classic car enthusiasts gather in Williams for the **Historic Route 66 Car Show** (www.williamshistoricroute66carshow.com), which includes a retro evening of cruising a two-mile loop around town showing off refurbished masterpieces.

Northland kids wait all year for the Grand Canyon Railway's celebration of author Chris Van Allsburg's classic holiday story *The Polar Express.* The always sold-out **Polar Express and Mountain Village Holiday** (800/848-3511, www.thetrain.com, 5:30pm and 7:30pm daily mid-Nov.-early Jan., $45-58 adults, $33-45 ages 2-15) features a one-hour nighttime pajama-party train ride, complete with cookies and hot cocoa, and a lit-up Christmas town that kids ooh and aah at from their train seats. Riders dressed up like characters in the book read the story as kids follow along in their own copies. Then Santa boards the train and gives each kid some individual attention and a free jingle bell like the one in the book. On the return trip, everybody sings Christmas carols, while the younger tykes generally fall asleep. This annual event is *very* popular, and tickets generally sell out as early as August.

Shopping

There's a gathering of boutiques and gift shops in Williams's quaint historic downtown area, bounded by Railroad, Grant, 1st, and 4th Streets.

Don't miss **Native America** (117 E. Rte. 66, 928/635-4600, 8am-9pm daily summer, 8am-6pm daily winter), a Native American-owned shop with Hopi and Navajo arts and crafts and some fun and interesting Old West kitsch sculptures holding up the front porch.

Food

A northland institution with some of the best steaks in the region, ★ **Rod's Steak House** (301 E. Rte. 66, 928/635-2671, www.rods-steakhouse.com, 11am-9:30pm Mon.-Sat., $12-25) has been operating at the same site since 1946. The food is excellent, the staff is friendly and professional, and the menus are shaped like steers.

A family-style place, the **Pine Country Restaurant** (107 N. Grand Canyon Blvd., 928/635-9718, http://pinecountryrestaurant.com, 6:30am-9:30pm daily, $8-19) serves good diner-style food and homemade pies. Check out the beautiful paintings of the Grand Canyon on the walls.

Cruiser's Route 66 Bar & Grill (233 W. Rte. 66, 928/635-2445, www.cruisers66.com, 11am-9pm daily, $15-20) offers a diverse menu of superior barbecue ribs, burgers, fajitas, pulled-pork sandwiches, and homemade chili. It has a full bar and offers live music most nights. On summer evenings the patio is lively and fun.

For something a bit more upscale and romantic, try the **Red Raven Restaurant** (135 W. Rte. 66, 928/635-4980, www.redravenrestaurant.com, 11am-2pm and 5pm-close Tues.-Sat., $11-25), a charming little place along Route 66 with big windows looking out on the bustling sidewalk and the tourists strolling by. It serves delicious and inventive dishes: steak wraps, Guinness stew, tasty lamb, sweet potato fries, and Southwest egg rolls, to name a few. The restaurant also has a deep beer list with selections mainly from Arizona and Colorado, and a good wine selection heavy on Italy and California. Make a reservation for dinner.

The vegetarian's best bet this side of Flagstaff is the **Dara Thai Café** (145 W. Rte. 66, 928/635-2201, 11am-2pm and 5pm-9pm Mon.-Sat., $7-15), an agreeable little spot in the Grand Canyon Hotel that serves a variety of fresh and flavorful Thai favorites and offers quite a few meat-free dishes.

Brewing and serving craft beers in a cavernous building near the railroad tracks, **The Grand Canyon Brewing + Distillery** (301 N. 7th St., 800/513-2072, www.grandcanyonbrewery.com, 2pm-9pm daily, $14-25) is a favorite with locals and travelers alike. It gets busy at times, especially around quitting time. Along with several excellent craft beers, they serve pub-style food and pizzas that do not disappoint.

Accommodations

Williams has some of the most affordable independent accommodations in the Grand Canyon region as well as several chain hotels.

★ **The Lodge on Route 66** (200 E. Rte. 66, 877/563-4366, http://thelodgeonroute66.com, $150-250) has stylish guest rooms with sleep-inducing pillow-top mattresses; it also has a few civilized two-room suites with kitchenettes, dining areas, and fireplaces—perfect for a family not necessarily on a budget. The motor court-style grounds, right along the Mother Road, feature a romantic cabana with comfortable seats and an outdoor fireplace. Pets aren't allowed.

It's difficult to find a better deal than the basic **El Rancho Motel** (617 E. Rte. 66, 928/635-2552 or 800/228-2370, www.elranchomotelwilliams.us, $80-143), an independently owned retro motel on Route 66 with few frills save comfort, friendliness, and a heated pool that's open in summer.

The **Grand Canyon Railway Hotel** (235 N. Grand Canyon Blvd., 928/635-4010, www.thetrain.com, $200-300) stands where Williams's Harvey House once stood. It has a heated indoor pool, two restaurants, a lounge, a hot tub, a workout room, and a huge gift shop. The hotel serves riders on the Grand Canyon Railway and offers the highest-end accommodations in Williams.

Even before the railroad arrived and made Grand Canyon tourism something not just the rich could do, the original **Grand Canyon Hotel** (145 W. Rte. 66, 928/635-1419, www.thegrandcanyonhotel. com, $79-195) opened in 1891. New owners refurbished and reopened the charming old redbrick hotel in Williams's historic downtown in 2005, and now it's an affordable friendly place with a lot of character and a bit of international flavor. Spartan single-bed guest rooms ($79) share a bath, and individually named and eclectically decorated double guest rooms with private baths ($93-105) are some of the most distinctive and affordable accommodations in the region. There are larger guest rooms with private baths and other amenities ($150-195) as well as hostel rooms ($33-38). There are no TVs in the rooms.

The **Red Garter Bed & Bakery** (137 W. Railroad Ave., 928/635-1484, www.redgarter. com, $175-249) makes much of its original and longtime use as a brothel (which, like many places in Arizona's rural regions, didn't close until the 1940s), where the town's lonely miners, lumberjacks, railroad workers, and cowboys met with unlucky women, euphemized as "soiled doves," in rooms called "cribs." The 1897 frontier-Victorian stone building, with its wide arching entranceway, has been beautifully restored with authentic charm without skimping on the comforts—big brass beds and delightful homemade baked goods, juice, and coffee in the morning. Famously, this place is haunted by some unquiet regretful soul, so you might want to bring your night-light along.

Information and Services

Stop at the **Williams-Kaibab National Forest Visitor Center** (200 W. Railway Ave., 928/635-1418 or 800/863-0546, 8am-6:30pm daily spring-summer, 8am-5pm daily fall-winter) for information about Williams, the Grand Canyon, and camping and hiking in the Kaibab National Forest.

TUSAYAN

About a mile south of Grand Canyon National Park's South Entrance, along AZ 64/U.S. 180, Tusayan is a collection of hotels, restaurants, and gift shops that has grown alongside the park for nearly a century. The village makes a decent nearby base for a visit to the park, especially if you can't get reservations at any of the in-park lodges. Although there are a few inexpensive chain hotels, a stay in Tusayan isn't cheaper than lodging in the park.

Sights

The town of Tusayan is the home of the **Grand Canyon Visitor Center** (AZ 64, 928/638-2468, www.explorethecanyon.com, 8am-10pm daily Mar.-Oct., 10am-8pm daily Nov.-Feb., IMAX $13 over age 10, $10 ages 6-10, free under age 6), not affiliated with the National Park Service. It has been a popular first stop for park visitors since the 1980s. You can purchase a park pass, reserve tours, and check out displays about the canyon, but the center wouldn't be worth the stop if not for its **IMAX Theater.** The colossal screen shows the 35-minute movie *Grand Canyon—The Hidden Secrets* every hour on the half hour. The most popular IMAX film ever (some 40 million people have reportedly seen it), the movie is quite thrilling, affording glimpses of the canyon's remote corners that almost feel like reality. This is a fun way to learn about what you'll see in the park. It's also a convenient place to book everything from helicopter tours to river rafting adventures. If you're on a budget, skip it and drive into the park, where you're likely to forget about both movies and money while staring dumbfounded into the canyon. You can also leave your car here and hop on the free shuttle bus (Tusayan Route/Purple Line) to the park.

Food

Tusayan makes a decent stop if you're hungry, but the food is just as good or better inside the park, only a mile away. A lot of tour buses stop here, so you might find yourself crowded into waiting for a table, especially during the summer high season.

If you're craving pizza after a long day exploring the canyon, try **We Cook Pizza & Pasta** (605 N. AZ 64, 928/638-2278, www.wecookpizzaandpasta.com, 11am-10pm daily Mar.-Oct., 11am-8pm daily Nov.-Feb., $10-30) for an excellent high-piled pie. It calls to you just as you enter Tusayan heading south from the park. Served in slices or whole pies, the pizza is pretty good considering the locale, and there's a big salad bar with all the fixings, plus beer and wine. It's a casual place, with picnic tables and an often harried staff. It gets really busy during summer high season.

In the center of town, **Plaza Bonita** (352 AZ 64, 928/638-8900, www.myplazabonita.com, 7am-10pm Sun.-Thurs., 7am-11pm Fri.-Sat., $10-20) serves good Mexican food and great margaritas in a pleasant family-style setting.

Inside the beautiful three-diamond Grand Hotel, on the southern side of town, the **Canyon Star Steakhouse & Saloon** (149 AZ 64, 928/638-3333, www.grandcanyongrandhotel.com, 7am-10pm daily, $11-30), with its high timber ceilings and elegant Old West aesthetic, is something of a mess hall for fancy cowboys, serving steaks, barbecue, fish, pasta, and burgers, and featuring a saloon with stools topped with old mule saddles, 24 draft beers, and live music.

Accommodations

Most of Tusayan's accommodations are of the chain variety, lining AZ 64 a mile south of the park's South Entrance. Although generally clean and comfortable, few have any character, and most are overpriced for what you get. Staying in either Flagstaff or Williams is a better choice if you're looking for an independent hotel or motel with some local color, and you can definitely find better deals in those gateways.

One of the better deals in the whole canyon region is in Valle, a tiny spot not far off AZ 64, about 30 miles south of the South Entrance. The **Red Lake Campground and Hostel** (8850 N. AZ 64, Valle, 928/635-4753, $20 pp), where you can rent a bed in a shared room, is a very basic but reasonably comfortable place on the lonely grasslands next to a gas station; it has shared baths with showers, free Wi-Fi, a common room with a kitchen and a TV, and an RV park ($25) with partial hookups. If you're going super-budget, you can't beat this place, though it is about 45 minutes from the park's south gate.

More basic than some of the other places in Tusayan, the **Red Feather Lodge** (300 AZ 64, 928/638-2414, www.redfeatherlodge.com, $182-240) is a comfortable, affordable place with a welcoming lobby with Navajo rugs on the walls, a pool, a hot tub, and separate hotel and motel complexes.

Resembling a high-end hunting lodge, the **Grand Hotel** (149 AZ 64, 928/638-3333, www.grandcanyongrandhotel.com, $200-400) is one of the more luxurious places to stay in the region, with prices to match. The sprawling sandstone-and-log hotel with a shining green metal roof appears as you enter Tusayan, and its beautiful lobby sets the craftsman wood-and-leather tone of the whole place with a fireplace lounge and large gift shop. A cowboy wilderness chic and elegant Old West hunting lodge aesthetic pervades, with heads of beasts on the walls, including a mountain lion, a bobcat, and a buffalo. The hotel has comfortable guest rooms; a pool, a hot tub, and a fitness center; and a large saloon and steak house.

Across AZ 64 from the Grand Hotel, the **Best Western Grand Canyon Squire Inn** (74 AZ 64, 928/638-2681, www.grandcanyonsquire.com, $211-289) has a fitness center, a pool and spa, a salon, a game room, a bowling alley, and so many other amenities that it may be difficult to get out of the hotel to enjoy the natural sights. The hotel offers standard and deluxe guest rooms as well as suites. The standard room has two comfy queen beds with crisp white sheets, a flat-screen TV, and a fridge and microwave. ADA-accessible and dog-friendly rooms are also available.

The South Rim

TOP EXPERIENCE

The reality of the Grand Canyon is often suspect even to those standing on its rim. "For a time it is too much like a scale model or an optical illusion," wrote Joseph Wood Krutch, a great observer and writer of the Southwest. The canyon appears at first, Krutch added, "a man-made diorama trying to fool the eye." It is *too big* to be immediately comprehended, especially to those visitors used to the gaudy lesser wonders of the human-made world.

Once you accept its size and understand that a river full of dry rocks and sand carved this mile-deep multicolored canyon into the Colorado Plateau, the awesome power and wonder of it all is bound to leave you breathless and wondering what you've been doing with your life. If there are any sacred places in the natural world, this is surely one. The canyon is a water-wrought cathedral, and no matter what beliefs or preconceptions you approach the rim with, they are likely to be challenged, cut away, and revealed—like the layers of primordial earth that compose this deep rock labyrinth and tell the history of the planet like a geology textbook. It is a story in which humans appear only briefly, if at all.

Visitors without a spiritual connection to nature have always been challenged by the Grand Canyon's size. It takes mythology, magical thinking, and storytelling to see it for what it really is. The first Europeans to see the canyon, a detachment of Spanish conquistadores sent by Coronado in 1540 after hearing rumors of the great gorge from the Hopi people, at first thought the spires and buttes rising from the bottom were about the size of a person; they were shocked, upon gaining a different perspective below the rim, to learn that they were as high or higher than the greatest structures of Seville. Human comparisons do not work here. Preparation is not possible.

Never hospitable, the canyon has nonetheless had a history of human occupation for 5,000 years, though the settlements have been small and usually seasonal. It was one of the last regions of North America to be mapped. The first expedition through, led by the one-armed genius John Wesley Powell, was completed at the comparatively late date of 1869. John Hance, the first Anglo to reside in the canyon, explored its depths in the 1880s and built trails based on ancient Native American routes. A few other tough loners tried to develop mining operations here but soon found that guiding avant-garde canyon tourists was the only sure financial bet in the canyon lands. It took another 20 years or so and the coming of the railroad before it became possible for the average American visitor to see the Grand Canyon.

Though impressive, the black-and-white statistics—repeated throughout the park on displays and interpretive signs along the rim and at the various visitors centers—do little to conjure an image that would do the canyon justice. It is some 277 river miles long, beginning just below Lees Ferry on the north and ending somewhere around the Grand Wash Cliffs in northwestern Arizona. It is 18 miles across at its widest point and an average of 10 miles across from the South to the North Rim. It is a mile deep on average; the highest point on the rim, the north's Point Imperial, rises 9,000 feet above the river. Its towers, buttes, and mesas, formed by the falling away of layers undercut by the river's incessant carving, are red and pink, dull brown, and green-tipped, though these basic hues are altered and enhanced by the setting and rising of the sun, changed by changes in the light, becoming temporary works of art that astound and then disappear.

It is folly, though, to try too hard to describe and boost the Grand Canyon. The consensus, from the first person to see it to yesterday's gazer, has amounted to "You just have to see it for yourself." Perhaps the most

The Canyon and the Railroad

It wasn't until the Santa Fe Railroad reached the South Rim of the Grand Canyon in 1901 that the great chasm's now-famous tourist trade really got going. Prior to that, travelers faced an all-day stagecoach ride from Flagstaff at a cost of $20, a high price to pay for sore bones and cramped quarters. Thanks to the railroad, even travelers of a less seasoned variety could see the wonders of the West, including the Grand Canyon, with relative ease.

The railroad's main concessionaire, the Fred Harvey Company, in those years operated Harvey House hotels, restaurants, and lunch counters all along the Santa Fe line. Widely celebrated for their high-quality fare and service, these eateries often became the nicest place in town in places that were still little more than frontier outposts. Each Harvey Company restaurant was staffed by the famous Harvey Girls, young women often recruited in cities, intensively trained as waitresses, and then sent out to work at far-flung spots along the railroad. Hard-working and efficient, they were expected

Grand Canyon Railway

to adhere to strict company rules and were held to high standards of service. Being a Harvey Girl provided the opportunity for women to be adventurous pioneers, living and working independently and helping to settle the West. There are several women who worked as Harvey Girls buried in Grand Canyon's Pioneer Cemetery.

Along with bringing its special brand of service to the South Rim, the Harvey Company in the 1920s-1930s enlisted the considerable talents of arts and crafts designer and architect Mary Colter to build lodges, lookouts, galleries, and stores on the South Rim. These treasured buildings still stand today and are considered some of the finest architectural accomplishments in the national parks system. The Harvey Company's dedication to simple elegance, and Colter's interest in understanding the architecture and lifeways of the Pueblo people, created an artful human stamp on the rim that nearly lives up to the breathtaking canyon it serves.

For half a century or more, the Santa Fe line from Williams took millions of visitors to the edge of the canyon. But finally, by the late 1960s, the country's love affair with the automobile, the rising mythology of the go-west road trip, and the interstate highway system killed train travel to Grand Canyon National Park. In the 1990s, however, entrepreneurs revived the railroad as an excursion line. Today, the Grand Canyon Railway carries more than 250,000 passengers to the South Rim every year, which has significantly reduced automobile traffic in the cramped park.

poetic words ever spoken about the Grand Canyon, profound for their obvious simplicity, came from Teddy Roosevelt, speaking on the South Rim in 1903. "Leave it as it is," he said. "You cannot improve on it; not a bit."

EXPLORING THE SOUTH RIM

The South Rim is by far the most developed portion of **Grand Canyon National Park** (928/638-7888, www.nps.gov/grca, 24 hours daily, $35 for 7-day pass for 1 vehicle with up to 15 people; $30 motorcycles; $20 walk-ins, bicycles, railroad, shuttle bus; free under age 16; rates subject to change annually) and should be seen by every American, as Teddy Roosevelt once recommended. You'll stand with people from all over the globe, each breathless as they stare into the canyon. Don't let the rustic look of the buildings fool you into thinking you're roughing it: The food here is above average for a national park. The restaurant at El Tovar offers some of the finest and most romantic dining in the state, all with one of the great wonders of the world just a few feet away.

The best way to explore the South Rim is to park your vehicle in one of the large parking lots near the main visitors center or at Market Plaza, and then take the free shuttle bus to the viewpoints and sights. It's also possible to explore on foot via the Rim Trail and greenways, or by bicycle on the roads and greenways. You can rent one at Bright Angel Bicycles, just across the plaza from the Grand Canyon Visitor Center.

As you enter the park you'll receive the *South Rim Pocket Map & Services Guide*, including a map, information about the canyon, and the shuttle schedule. It's comprehensive and will likely answer most of your questions.

Visitors Centers

While Historic Grand Canyon Village is the heart of the South Rim, Mather Point and **Grand Canyon Visitor Center** (7am-6pm daily May-Sept., 9am-4pm daily Oct.-Apr.), about 2.2 miles east of the village along the rim, provide easy and in-depth introductions to the canyon and the park.

Entering from the main South Entrance on AZ 64 from Williams or Flagstaff, keep to the South Entrance Road for 5.1 miles to reach four large parking lots around the visitors center complex. During high season and holidays, these parking lots can fill up by 9:30am, and most other days they fill up by 10am. If you can't find parking, proceed to Market Plaza and then Park Headquarters; you can then backtrack to the visitors center via the Rim Trail or the free shuttle bus.

Entering from the east through the Desert View area, turn right onto South Entrance Road at its junction with Desert View Drive, about 23 miles from the East Entrance. From the junction it's only 1 mile on the South Entrance Road to the main visitors center. After finding a spot, head directly to Mather Point, just a short walk from the visitors center parking lots.

After seeing the canyon from this famous first vantage, head back to the visitors center, where you will find a water refill station, restrooms, a bookstore with souvenirs and supplies, and a large light-filled building with information about Grand Canyon and environs. Rangers staff the center all day to answer questions and help you plan your visit, and they offer ranger-led walks, hikes, and natural-history presentations around the park most days and evenings. A 20-minute film, shown on the hour and half hour, *Grand Canyon: A Journey of Wonder,* narrated by the great Peter Coyote, depicts the canyon's dawn-to-dusk cycle of mystery and beauty, and there are several maps and other exhibitions that explain and illuminate the somewhat confusing grandeur just outside.

In Grand Canyon Village, along the rim about 2.2 miles west of Grand Canyon Visitor Center, is the smaller **Verkamp's Visitor Center** (8am-7pm daily early Mar.-mid-May and early Sept.-Nov., 8am-8pm daily mid-May-mid-Aug., 9am-8pm daily mid-Aug.-early Sept., 8am-6pm daily Dec.-early Mar.), near Hopi House and El Tovar. It began in a white-canvas tent when Grand Canyon National Park opened and was a famous curio and souvenir shop right on the rim for 100 years. Since 2015 the historic building has housed a visitors center run by the Grand Canyon Conservancy and includes books, souvenirs, and displays about the history of Grand Canyon Village.

The farthest-flung of all the park's South Rim information and visitors centers is in the **Desert View Watchtower** (9am-5pm daily), about 25 miles east of Grand Canyon Village. It is staffed with helpful rangers who have information about Desert View and the rest of the park.

Entrance Stations

The vast majority of visitors to Grand Canyon National Park enter through the **South Entrance Station** on AZ 64 from **Williams,** or via U.S. 180 to AZ 64 from **Flagstaff.** There are several lanes and generally the lines keep moving; however, on summer and holiday weekends you may experience a significant wait. The most direct route to the South Rim is AZ 64 from Williams, 60 miles of flat, dry, windswept plain, dotted with a few isolated trailers, manufactured homes, and gaudy for-sale signs offering cheap ranch land. About 20 miles longer but much more scenic is the route from Flagstaff via U.S. 180, which meets up with AZ 64 at Valle, 30 miles south of the South Entrance; it's a total of 80 miles from Flagstaff to the park gate. You can purchase your park pass ahead of time at www. recreation.gov or http://yourpassnow.com, the visitors centers in Flagstaff and Williams, the Chevron Travel Stop in Valle, or at the Grand Canyon Visitor Center in Tusayan, but doing so does not allow you to skip the lines unless you also ride the shuttle bus into the park rather than taking your car.

AZ 64 enters the park through the south but soon veers east toward the Navajo Nation and the much smaller and considerably less busy **East Entrance Station,** in the park's **Desert View** section, 25 miles east of Grand Canyon Village. This route is a good choice for a more leisurely and comprehensive look at the rim, as there are quite a few stops along the way to the village that you might not otherwise get to from the South Entrance. To reach the East Entrance Station, take U.S. 89 for 46 miles north of **Flagstaff,** across a wide big-sky landscape covered in volcanic rock, pine forests, and yellow wildflowers, to Cameron, on the Navajo Reservation. Then head west on AZ 64 for 30 miles to the entrance station. This is the best way to leave the park's South Rim section if you are heading to the Navajo or Hopi Reservations, or to the North Rim and Zion and Bryce Canyon in southern Utah.

Tours

Many tours are available, but it's easy to see and learn about everything the park has to offer without spending extra money; as in most national parks, the highly informed and friendly rangers hanging around the South Rim's sites offer for free the same information that you'll get on a tour.

MULE RIDES

Park concessionaire Xanterra offers a four-mile mule ride along the rim east of the village, with many stops and stories along the way. The **Canyon Vistas Mule Ride** (303/297-2757 or 888/297-2757, www. grandcanyonlodges.com, 8am and noon

Mather Point, near the Grand Canyon Visitor Center

Mar.-Oct., 10am Nov.-Feb., $156 pp) goes year-round and includes one hour of orientation and a two-hour ride. You must weigh less than 225 pounds fully dressed, be at least nine years old (under age 18 must be accompanied by adult), at least four-foot-nine, and in good health. Make sure to bring along a long-sleeved shirt, long pants, a hat, and closed-toe shoes. The tours start at the Mule Barn for orientation. To reach the barn, walk west 350 yards from Bright Angel Lodge across the Village Loop Drive and the train tracks (follow the smell). You can book online up to 15 months ahead. If you don't have a reservation, check to see if there's space available at the activities desk at Maswik or Bright Angel Lodges. Xanterra also offers overnight mule trips below the rim to Phantom Ranch in the inner canyon.

BUS TOURS

Xanterra, the park's main concessionaire, offers in-park interpretive **bus tours** (303/297-2757 or 888/297-2757, www. grandcanyonlodges.com). Options include sunrise and sunset tours ($33 adults, $16.50 ages 3-16) and longer tours to the eastern Desert View area ($78 adults, $39 ages 3-16) and the western reaches of the park at Hermit's Rest ($44 adults, $22 ages 3-16). This is a comfortable, educational, and entertaining way to see the park, and odds are you will come away with new friends—possibly even a new email pal from abroad. To book a tour through Xanterra, you can either plan ahead and book online, or when you arrive check at the activities desk at Maswik and Bright Angel Lodges, from which the tours begin.

AIRPLANE AND HELICOPTER TOURS

Though not ideal from the back-to-nature point of view, a helicopter or plane flight over the canyon is an exciting rare experience and can be worth the rather expensive cost—a chance to take some unique photos from a condor's perspective. Flights are only allowed in a few sections of the canyon, and most spend time over the plateau forests and the eastern canyon. Five companies offer air tours from **Grand Canyon Airport** (www. grandcanyonairport.org), along AZ 64 in Tusayan, and most offer many more flights originating in Las Vegas. All prefer reservations. Some companies offer the choice of paying a little more for a quieter EcoStar helicopter, and others use only EcoStars. Most of the companies offer narration in at least nine different languages.

One of the better operators is **Maverick Helicopters** (888/261-4414, www. maverickhelicopter.com), which offers the Canyon Spirit Tour. It departs from Grand Canyon Airport in Tusayan and soars over the Kaibab National Forest, the confluence of the Colorado River and Little Colorado River, and Marble Canyon (45 minutes, $299 pp).

Driving Tours
★ HERMIT ROAD

March-November the park's free shuttle goes all the way to architect and Southwestern-design genius Mary Colter's **Hermit's Rest,** seven miles from Grand Canyon Village along the park's western scenic drive, called the **Hermit Road.** It takes two hours to complete the loop, stopping at nine viewpoints along the way. On the return route, buses stop only at Mohave and Hopi Points. The Hermit Road viewpoints are some of the best in the park for viewing sunset. To make it in time for these dramatic solar performances, catch the bus at least an hour before sunset. There is often a long wait at the **Hermit's Rest Transfer Stop,** just west of the Bright Angel Lodge. The bus drivers usually know the times of sunrise and sunset. The route is open to cars December-February, when you can drive to most of the viewpoints and stare at your leisure. Each of the Hermit Road lookouts provides a slightly different perspective on the canyon, whether it be a strange, unnoticed outcropping or a brief view of the white-tipped river rapids far below.

The first stop along the route is the **Trailview Overlook** (1.5 miles from the village), where you can see the Bright Angel Trail twisting down into the canyon and across the plateau to overlook the Colorado River.

The next major stop along the route is **Maricopa Point** (2.7 miles from the village), which provides a vast, mostly unobstructed view of the canyon all the way to the river. The point is on a promontory that juts 100 feet into the canyon. This is the former site of the Orphan Mine, first opened in 1893 as a source of copper and silver—and, for a few busy years during the height of the Cold War, uranium.

Consider taking the 10- to 15-minute hike along the Rim Trail west through the piney rim world to the next viewing area, **Powell Point** (3.3 miles from the village). Here stands a memorial to the one-armed explorer and writer John Wesley Powell, who led the first and second scientific river expeditions through the canyon in 1869 and 1871. The memorial is a flat-topped pyramid, which you can ascend to stand tall over the canyon.

About 0.3 mile along Hermit Road from Powell Point is **Hopi Point** (2.9 miles from the village), which offers sweeping, open views of the western canyon. It is the most popular west-end point for viewing sunset. Across the canyon, look for the famous mesas named after Egyptian gods—Isis Temple to the northeast and the Temple of Osiris to the northwest.

The next viewpoint heading west is **Mohave Point** (4.2 miles from the village), where you can see the Colorado River and a few white-tipped rapids. Also visible are the 3,000-foot red-and-green cliffs that surround the deep side canyon, appropriately named the Abyss. Right below the viewpoint you can see the red-rock mesa called the Alligator.

The last viewpoint before Hermit's Rest is **Pima Point** (7.5 miles from the village), a wide-open view to the west and the east. You can see the winding Colorado River and the Hermit Trail twisting down into the depths of the canyon.

Finally you arrive at **Hermit's Rest,** a charming stone hovel built to look old and haphazard, seven miles from the village.

Inside is a gift shop and a snack bar. There are also restrooms and access to the Hermit Trail.

DESERT VIEW DRIVE

The Desert View driving tour explores the eastern portion of the South Rim; its main draw, other than expansive views of the canyon, is Mary Colter's Desert View Watchtower, the center of the area's action and appeal, about 25 miles east of Grand Canyon Village. Without stopping at the many developed viewpoints, the drive to the watchtower, campground, and small eateries takes 45-60 minutes. When you add in the many viewpoint stops, the drive could take most of the day. The viewpoints along this drive, which one ranger called the "quiet side of the South Rim," gradually change from forest to high-country desert and are typically less crowded than those that can be reached by the shuttle.

The free shuttle goes only as far as **Yaki Point,** a great place to watch the sunrise and sunset, near the popular South Kaibab Trailhead. Yaki Point is at the end of a 1.5-mile side road northeast of AZ 64. The area is closed to private vehicles, but all the other stops to the east can be reached only by private vehicle. If you want to make Yaki Point part of the Desert View driving tour, you can park your car at a small picnic area just east of the side road (2 miles from the village) and then cross the road and follow a path for about 0.5 mile through the woods to the promontory and the South Kaibab Trailhead.

Along Desert View Drive, don't miss the essential **Grandview Point,** where the original canyon lodge once stood long ago. From here the rough Grandview Trail leads below the rim. The viewpoint sits at 7,400 feet elevation, 12 miles east of the village and then 1 mile on a side road. It's considered one of the grandest views of all, hence the name; the canyon spreads out, and the sunrise in the east hits it strong and happy. To the east, look for the 7,844-foot formation called the Sinking Ship, and to the north look for Horseshoe Mesa.

East of Grandview, **Moran Point** (18 miles from the village) is just eight miles south of

Cape Royal on the North Rim and offers some impressive views of the canyon and the river. The point is named for the great painter of the canyon, Thomas Moran, whose brave attempts to capture the gorge on canvas helped create the buzz that led to the canyon's federal protection. Directly below the left side of the point you'll see Hance Rapid, one of the largest on the Colorado. It's three miles away, but if you're quiet you might be able to hear the rushing and roaring.

Farther along Desert View Drive is **Tusayan Ruin & Museum** (22 miles from the village). Stop for a self-guided walking tour of the small Ancestral Puebloan ruins and a look around the small museum with exhibits about the rim's ancient inhabitants and the descendants who still call the region home.

As the drive winds down and the trees turn from pine to piñon to scrub, **Lipan Point** (23.3 miles from the village) offers wide-open vistas and the best view of the river from the South Rim. It's one of the most popular viewpoints on the South Rim for watching the sunrise and sunset.

Finally, at Desert View, there's a large parking lot, restrooms, gift shops, a deli, a gas station, and a campground. From the patio of the amazing can't-miss **Desert View Watchtower** (25 miles from the village), you'll be able to catch a faraway glimpse of sacred Navajo Mountain near the Utah-Arizona border, the most distant point visible from within the park.

SIGHTS

You wouldn't want to make a habit of it, but you could spend a few happy hours at **Grand Canyon Village Historical District** with your back to the canyon. This small assemblage of hotels, restaurants, gift shops, and lookouts also offers some of the best viewpoints to gaze comfortably at all that splendor. From this vantage you can spot the strip of greenery just below the rim called **Indian Garden,** and follow with your eyes—or even your feet—the famous **Bright Angel Trail,**

twisting improbably down the rim's rock face. You can also see some of the most interesting and evocative buildings in the state, all of them registered National Historic Landmarks.

Bright Angel Lodge

The village's central hub of activity, rustic and charming **Bright Angel Lodge** was designed in 1935 by Mary Colter to replace the old Bright Angel Hotel, which pioneer John Hance built in the 1890s, and the Bright Angel Camp tent city near the trail of the same name. Originally meant to attract more middle-class tourists to the park, the lodge is still a romantic and comfortable place to stay, resembling a rough-hewn hunting lodge constructed of materials found nearby.

The **Bright Angel History Room,** just off the main lobby, has fascinating exhibits and artifacts telling the story of the Fred Harvey Company, architect Mary Colter, the Santa Fe Railroad, and the early years of Southwestern tourism. Spend some time learning about the legendary Harvey Girls, who hosted a golden age of train travel from Chicago to Los Angeles. You'll also see Colter's "geologic fireplace," a 10-foot-high re-creation of the canyon's varied strata. Geologists collected the stones from the inner canyon and loaded them on the backs of mules for the journey out. The fireplace's strata appear exactly like those in the canyon walls, equaling a couple of billion years of earth-building from bottom to rim.

El Tovar

El Tovar is the South Rim's first great hotel and the picture of haute wilderness style. Designed in 1905 by Charles Whittlesey for the Santa Fe Railroad, El Tovar has the look of a Swiss chalet and a log-house interior, watched over by the wall-hung heads of elk and buffalo; it is at once rustic, cozy, and elegant. This Harvey Company jewel has hosted dozens of rich and famous canyon visitors over the years, including George Bernard Shaw and presidents Teddy Roosevelt and William Howard Taft. While it is a wonderfully romantic building up close, El Tovar looks even more picturesque from a few of the viewpoints along the Hermit Road, and you can really get a good idea of just how close the lodge is to the rim by seeing it from far away. Inside you'll find two gift shops and a cozy lounge where you can have a drink or two while looking at the canyon. El Tovar's restaurant is the best in the park, and it's pleasant to sink into one of the arts and crafts leather chairs in the rustic dark-wood lobby and contemplate the animals whose majestic heads grace the walls of this enchanting building.

Hopi House

A few steps from the front porch of El Tovar is Mary Colter's **Hopi House,** designed and built in 1905 as if it sat not at the edge of the Grand Canyon but on the edge of Hopi's Third Mesa. Hopi workers used local materials to build this unique gift shop and gallery for Native American art. The Fred Harvey Company even hired the famous Hopi-Tewa potter Nampeyo to live here with her family while demonstrating her artistic talents and Hopi lifeways to visitors. This is one of the best places in the region for viewing and buying Hopi, Navajo, and Pueblo art, though most of the art is quite expensive. There are even items made by Nampeyo's descendants on view and for sale.

Lookout Studio

Mary Colter also designed the **Lookout Studio** west of the Bright Angel Lodge, a little stacked-stone house that seems to be a mysterious extension of the rim itself. The stone patio juts out over the canyon and is a popular place for taking pictures. The Lookout was built in 1914 exactly for that purpose—to provide a comfortable "indigenous" building and deck where visitors could gaze at and photograph the canyon. It was fitted with high-powered telescopes and soon became one of the most popular snapshot scenes on the rim. On many days you'll be standing elbow to elbow with other visitors clicking away. As she did with her other buildings on the rim, Colter

designed the Lookout to be a kind of amalgam of Native American ruins and backcountry pioneer utilitarianism. Her formula of using found and indigenous materials, stacked haphazardly, works wonderfully here. When it was first built, the little stone hovel was so "authentic" that it even had weeds growing out of the roof. Inside, where you'll find books and canyon souvenirs, the studio looks much as it did when it first opened. The jutting stone patio is still one of the best places from which to view the canyon.

Kolb Studio

Built in 1904 right on the canyon's rim, **Kolb Studio** is significant not so much for its design but for the human story that went on inside. It was the home and studio of the famous Kolb Brothers, pioneer canyon photographers, moviemakers, and river rafters. Inside there's a gift shop, a gallery, and a display about the brothers, who in 1912 rode the length of the Colorado River in a boat with a movie camera rolling. The journey resulted in a classic book of exploration and river-running, Emery Kolb's 1914 *Through the Grand Canyon from Wyoming to Mexico.* The Kolb Brothers were some of the first entrepreneurs at the canyon. Around 1902 they set up a photography studio in a cave near the rim and later moved it to this house. After a falling-out between the brothers, the younger Emery Kolb stayed on at the canyon until his death in 1976, showing daily the film the brothers had made of their epic river trip to generations of canyon visitors.

Viewpoints

The canyon's unrelenting vastness tends to blur the details. Viewing the gorge from many different points seems to cure this. There are 19 named viewpoints along the South Rim Road, from the easternmost Desert View to the westernmost Hermit's Rest. Is it necessary, or even a good idea, to see them all? Not really. For many it's difficult to pick out the various named buttes, mesas, side canyons, drainages, and other features that rise and fall

Grand Canyon Village

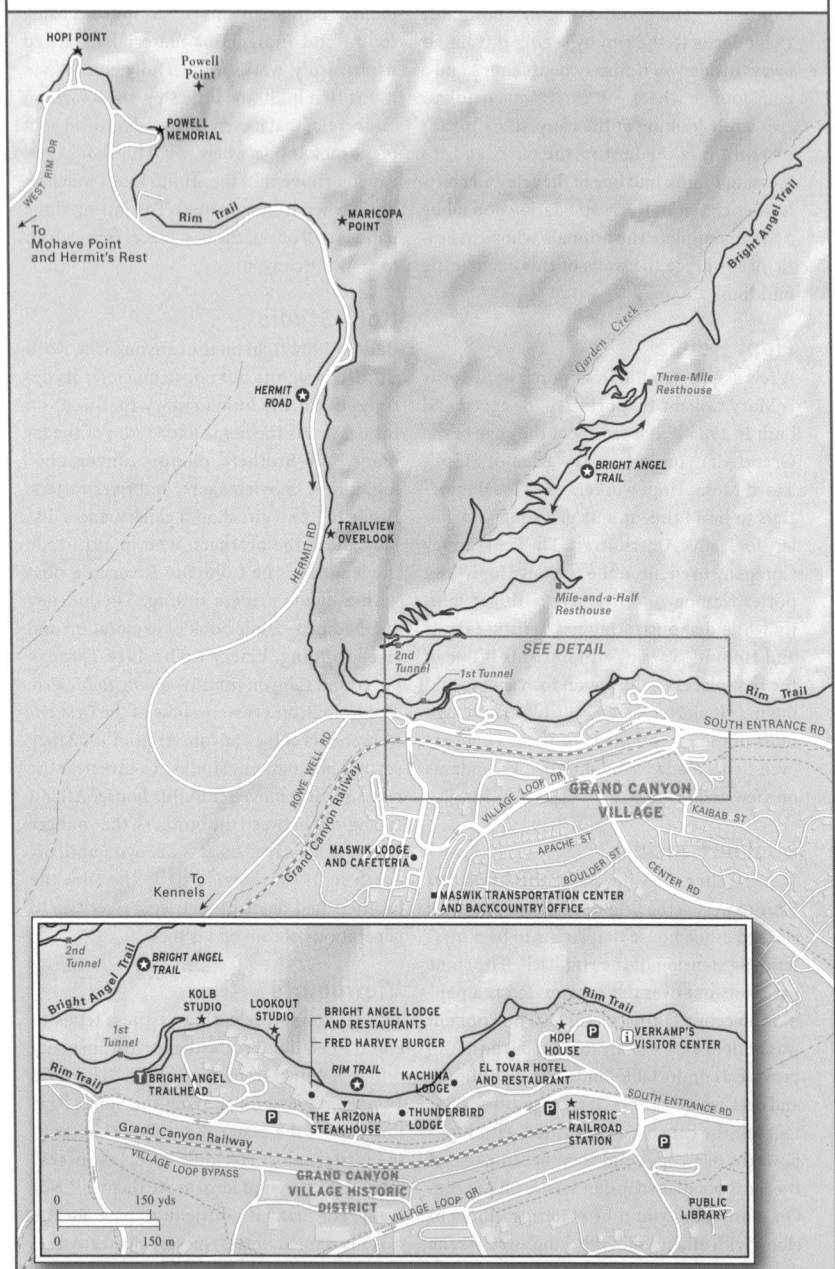

HOPI POINT

Powell
Point

POWELL
MEMORIAL

WEST RIM DR

Rim Trail

MARICOPA
POINT

To Mohave Point
and Hermit's Rest

Bright Angel Trail

Garden Creek

Three-Mile
Resthouse

HERMIT
ROAD

BRIGHT ANGEL
TRAIL

HERMIT RD

TRAILVIEW
OVERLOOK

Mile-and-a-Half
Resthouse

2nd
Tunnel

1st Tunnel

SEE DETAIL

Rim Trail

SOUTH ENTRANCE RD

ROWE WELL RD

Grand Canyon Railway

GRAND CANYON
VILLAGE

KAIBAB ST

To
Kennels

MASWIK LODGE
AND CAFETERIA

VILLAGE LOOP DR

APACHE ST

BOULDER ST

CENTER RD

MASWIK TRANSPORTATION
AND BACKCOUNTRY OFFICE

2nd
Tunnel

BRIGHT ANGEL
TRAIL

Bright Angel Trail

KOLB
STUDIO

LOOKOUT
STUDIO

BRIGHT ANGEL LODGE
AND RESTAURANTS

FRED HARVEY BURGER

Rim Trail

HOPI
HOUSE

VERKAMP'S
VISITOR CENTER

1st
Tunnel

Rim Trail

BRIGHT ANGEL
TRAILHEAD

RIM TRAIL

KACHINA
LODGE

EL TOVAR HOTEL
AND RESTAURANT

SOUTH ENTRANCE RD

THE ARIZONA
STEAKHOUSE

THUNDERBIRD
LODGE

HISTORIC
RAILROAD
STATION

Grand Canyon Railway

VILLAGE LOOP BYPASS

GRAND CANYON
VILLAGE HISTORIC
DISTRICT

VILLAGE LOOP DR

PUBLIC
LIBRARY

0   150 yds

0   150 m

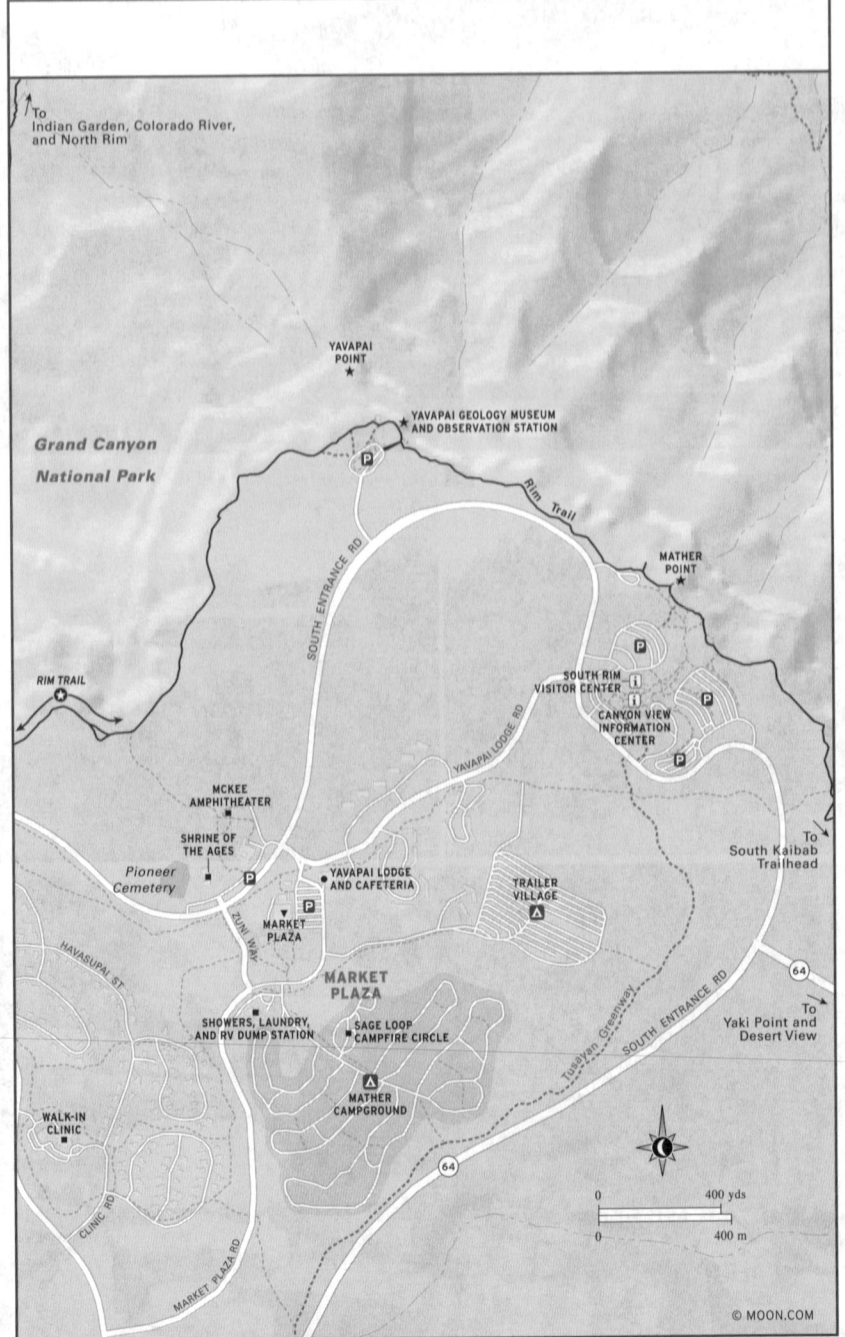

throughout the gorge, and one viewpoint ends up looking not that different from the next.

The best way to see the canyon viewpoints is to park your car and walk along the **Rim Trail.** Attempts to visit each viewpoint tend to speed up your visit and make you miss the subtleties of the different views. Consider really getting to know a few select viewpoints rather than trying to quickly hit each one. Any of the viewpoints along the **Hermit Road** and **Desert View Drive** are candidates for a long love affair. The views from just outside **El Tovar** or the **Bright Angel Lodge,** in the middle of the bustling village action, are as gorgeous as any others, and it can be fun and illuminating to watch people's reactions to what they're seeing.

There isn't a bad view of the canyon, but if you have limited time, ask the rangers at the main visitors center or Yavapai Geology Museum what their favorite viewpoint is and why. The shuttle bus drivers are also great sources of information and opinions. Try to see at least one sunset or sunrise at one of the developed viewpoints. The canyon's colors and details can seem monotonous after the initial thrill wears off (if it ever does), but the sun splashing and dancing at different strengths and angles against the multihued buttes and sheer shadowy walls makes it all new again.

Mather Point

As most South Rim visitors enter through the park's South Entrance, it's no surprise that the most visited viewpoint in the park is the first one along that route—**Mather Point,** named for the first National Park Service director, Stephen T. Mather. While crowded, Mather Point offers a typically astounding view of the canyon and is probably the view that most casual visitors take away. It can get busy, especially in summer. Park at one of the four large lots near the visitors center complex and walk the short paved path from the

---

1: the historic El Tovar lodge 2: Hopi House
3: Lookout Studio 4: the entrance to Hermit's Rest

Grand Canyon Visitor Center. At Mather Point you can walk out onto two railed-off jutting rocks to feel like you're hovering on the edge of an abyss, but you may have to stand in line to get right up to the edge.

Yavapai Point

A good way to see this part of the park is to leave your car at the visitors center and then walk a short way along the Rim Trail west to **Yavapai Point,** the best place to learn about the canyon's geology and get more than a passing understanding of what you're gazing at.

YAVAPAI GEOLOGY MUSEUM AND OBSERVATION STATION

Yavapai Geology Museum and Observation Station (928/638-7890, 8am-8pm daily summer, 8am-6pm daily winter, free) is the best place in the park to learn about the canyon's geology. This Kaibab limestone and ponderosa pine museum and bookstore is a must-visit for those interested in learning about what they're seeing. Designed by architect Herbert Maier and opened in 1928, the building itself is of interest. The stacked-stone structure, like Mary Colter's buildings, merges with the rim itself to appear a foregone and inevitable part of the landscape. It's cool in here in summer and warm in winter. It's a place where time is easily lost, where you enter the gorge's timelessness, and you may even forget that you are in a museum while staring through the large windows that face the canyon. That's because you're not really in a museum, but rather an observation station. The site for the station, originally called the Trailside Museum, was handpicked by top geologists as the best for viewing the various strata and receiving a rim-side lesson on the region's geologic history. The museum features myriad displays about canyon geology. Particularly helpful is the huge topographic relief map of the canyon—a giant's-eye view that helps you discern what you're seeing outside on the rim.

You can reach the museum by walking 0.8 mile west from the visitors center or taking the shuttle bus on the Orange Route. There's also a small parking lot and restrooms.

Hermit's Rest

The final stop on the Hermit Road is the enchanting gift shop and rest house called Hermit's Rest, designed by Mary Colter in 1914. As you walk up a path past a stacked-boulder entranceway, from which hangs an old mission bell from New Mexico, the little stone cabin comes into view. It is meant to look as if a lonely hermit dug a hole in the side of a hill and then stacked rock on top of rock until something haphazard but cozy rose from the rim—a structure from the realm of fairy tales. Inside, the huge yawning fireplace, tall and deep enough to be a room itself, dominates the warm rustic front room, where there are a few chairs chopped out of stumps, a Navajo blanket or two splashing color against the gray stone, and elegant lantern lamps hanging from the rafters. Outside, the views of the canyon and down the Hermit Trail are spectacular, but something about that little rock shelter makes it hard to leave.

Tusayan Ruin & Museum

The Tusayan Ruin & Museum (928/638-7888, 9am-5pm daily, free) has a small but interesting group of exhibits on the canyon's early human settlers. The museum is located next to an 800-year-old Ancestral Puebloan ruins with a self-guided trail and regularly scheduled free ranger walks. Since the free shuttle bus doesn't come this far east, you have to drive to the museum and ruins; it's about 3 miles west of Desert View and 22 miles east of the village. It's worth the drive, especially if you're heading to the Desert View section. The museum has displays on the history of human life in the region along with excellent artifacts of the Hopi, Navajo, Havasupai, and Paiute peoples. Don't miss Roy Anderson's fascinating 1986 painting depicting a romantic vision of life at Tusayan some 800 years ago.

While the canyon lands haven't been hospitable to humans over the eons, the oldest artifacts found in Grand Canyon date back 12,000 years. They include little stick-built animal fetishes found in caves inside the canyon and throughout the Southwest. The ancient Kayenta people constructed and occupied a small village here around AD 1185. The unreconstructed ruins consist of several "rooms" surrounded by low and mostly fallen rock walls, scattered along a 0.1-mile flat, paved, wheelchair-accessible trail through the piñon-pine forest. The ruins were first excavated in 1930 by Harold S. Gladwin. Archaeologists believe the village included apartments around a large plaza facing south toward the sacred San Francisco Peaks, which was used as a general living area for 16-20 people, along with several small storage rooms and a kiva—an underground structure used for religious ceremonies. Tusayan is thought to have been the westernmost outpost of the ancient Kayenta people and is linked to other nearby sites such as Keet Seel and White House Ruin on the Navajo Reservation to the east. Follow the short entrance road off Desert View Drive to the native-stone building and parking lot; you'll find restrooms close by.

★ Desert View Watchtower

What is perhaps the most mysterious and thrilling of Mary Colter's canyon creations, the Desert View Watchtower (built in 1932) is an artful homage to smaller Ancestral Puebloan-built towers found at Hovenweep National Monument and elsewhere in the Four Corners region, the exact purpose of which is still unknown. You reach the tower's high windy deck by climbing the steep steps winding around the open middle, past walls painted with visions of Hopi lore and religion by Hopi artist Fred Kabotie. From the deck of the watchtower, the South Rim's highest viewpoint, the whole arid expanse opens up, and you feel something like a lucky survivor at the edge of existence, even among the crowds. Such is the evocative power, the rough-edged romanticism, of Colter's vision.

RECREATION
Hiking

Something about a well-built trail twisting deep into an unknown territory can spur even the most habitually sedentary canyon visitor to begin an epic trudge. This phenomenon is responsible for both the best and worst of the South Rim's busy recreation life. It is not uncommon to see hikers a mile or more below the rim picking along in high heels and sauntering blithely in flip-flops, not a drop of water between them. It's best to go to the canyon prepared to hike, with proper footwear and plenty of water and snacks. You'll probably want to hike a little, and since there's no such thing as an easy hike into the Grand Canyon, going in prepared, even if it's just for a few miles, will make your hike a pleasure rather than a chore. Also, remember that there aren't any loop hikes here: If you hike in (down) a mile, you also must hike out (up) a mile.

★ RIM TRAIL

Distance: 12.8 miles
Duration: All day
Elevation gain: About 200 feet
Effort: Easy
Trailhead: Multiple access points, from South Kaibab Trailhead in the east to Hermit's Rest in the west
Trail conditions: Paved except the narrow packed-dirt path between Powell Point and Monument Creek Vista; some steep parts heading west from Bright Angel Lodge to Hermit's Rest

If you can manage a relatively easy 13-mile walk at an altitude of 7,000 feet, the **Rim Trail** provides the single best way to see all of the South Rim. Paved for most of its length, the trail runs from the South Kaibab Trailhead on the east, through the village, all the way to Hermit's Rest, hitting every major point of interest along the way. The path gets a little tough as it rises past the Bright Angel Trailhead just west of the village. Heading farther west, the trail becomes a thin dirt single-track between Powell Point and Monument Creek Vista, but it never gets too difficult. (You can avoid these sections by walking on the road, which is paved.) It would be considered an easy scenic walk by just about anybody, kids included. Perhaps the best thing about the Rim Trail is that you don't have to hike the whole 12.8 miles—far from it. There are at least 16 shuttle stops along the way, and you can hop on and off the trail at your pleasure. Dogs are allowed on the Rim Trail with a leash, but you can't take them on the shuttle buses.

Few will want to hike the entire way, of course. Such an epic walk would require twice the miles (or at least one long ride on the shuttle bus), as the trail is not a loop but a ribbon along the rim from west to east. It's better to pick out a relatively short stretch and take your time.

★ BRIGHT ANGEL TRAIL

Distance: 3-9.6 miles round-trip
Duration: 2-8 hours
Elevation gain: 3,040 feet from trailhead to Indian Garden
Effort: Moderate to strenuous
Trail conditions: Narrow, rocky, steep, sandy
Trailhead: Just west of Bright Angel Lodge
Shuttle Stop: Bright Angel Lodge, on Village Route (Blue)

Hiking down the **Bright Angel Trail,** you quickly leave behind the piney rim and enter a sharp and arid landscape, twisting down and around switchbacks on a path that is sometimes all rock underfoot. Step aside for the many mule trains that use this route, and watch for their droppings, which are everywhere. It doesn't take long for the rim to look very far away, and you soon feel like you are deep within a chasm, with those rim-top people mere ants scurrying about.

The Bright Angel Trail is the most popular in the canyon owing in part to it starting just to the west of the Bright Angel Lodge in the village center. It's considered by park staff to be the safest trail because it has two rest houses with water. The Bright Angel was once the only easily accessible trail from the South Rim, and for years Grand Canyon pioneer Ralph Cameron charged people $1 to use

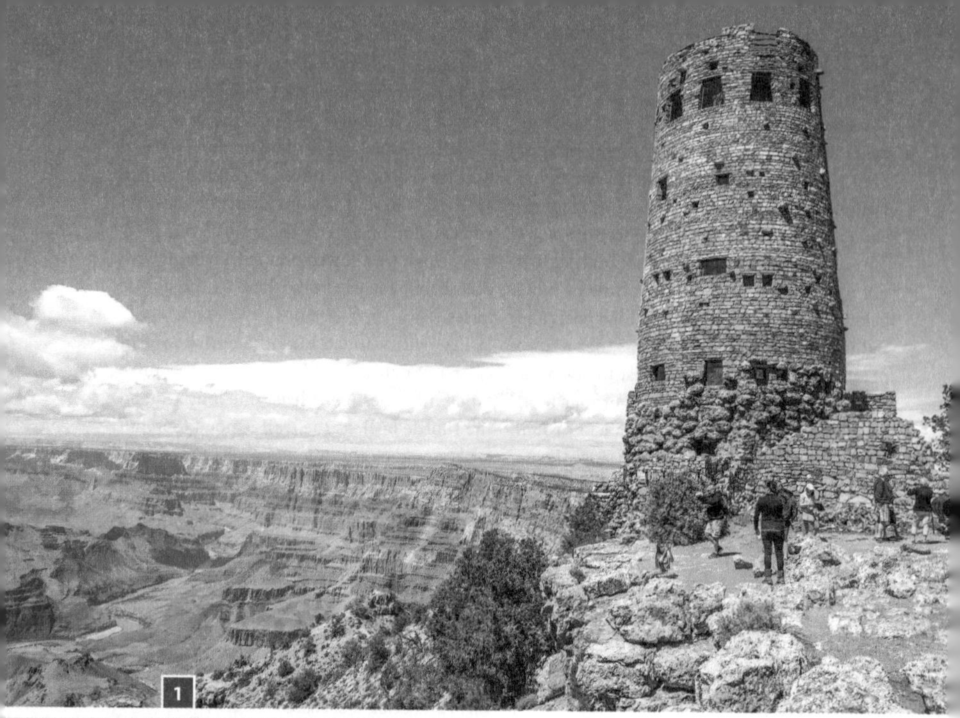
1

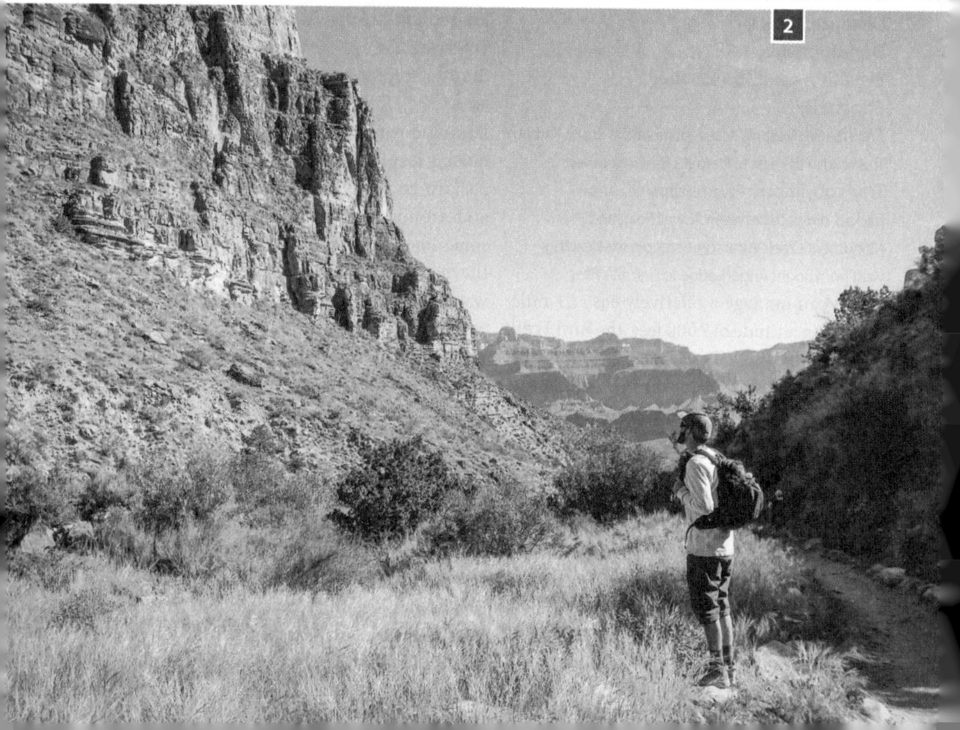
2

it. Many South Rim visitors choose to walk down the now free Bright Angel Trail a short distance just to get a feeling of what it's like to be below the rim. If you want to do something a little more structured, the three-mile round-trip hike to the **Mile-and-a-Half Resthouse** is a good introduction to the steep twisting trail. The going gets tougher on the way to **Three-Mile Resthouse,** a six-mile round-trip hike. Both rest houses have water available mid-May–mid-October, but don't rely on it; breaks in the trans-canyon waterline sometimes shuts them down. One of the best day hikes from the South Rim is the 9.6-mile round-trip to beautiful **Indian Garden,** a cool and green oasis in the arid inner canyon. This is a rather punishing day hike, not recommended in summer.

SOUTH KAIBAB TRAIL

Distance: 1.8-6 miles round-trip
Duration: 1-6 hours
Elevation gain: 2,040 feet from trailhead to Skeleton Point
Effort: Moderate to strenuous
Trail conditions: Narrow, rocky, very steep, sandy in places; mule traffic, mule leavings
Trailhead: Near Yaki Point on the East Rim
Shuttle Stop: Yaki Point, on Rim Route (Orange)

Steep but relatively short, the seven-mile **South Kaibab Trail** provides the quickest, most direct route from the South Rim to and from the river. It's popular with day hikers and those looking for the quickest way into the gorge, and many consider it superior to the often-crowded Bright Angel Trail. The trailhead is located a few miles east of the village near Yaki Point, which is closed to private vehicles; take the shuttle bus on the Kaibab/Rim Route (Orange).

The 1.8-mile round-trip hike to **Ooh Aah Point** has great views of the canyon from steep switchbacks. A common turnaround point for day hikers, **Cedar Ridge** is a 3-mile round-trip hike. If you are interested in a longer haul, the 6-mile round-trip hike to

Skeleton Point, from which you can see the Colorado River, is probably as far along this trail as you'll want to go in one day, though in summer you might want to reconsider descending that far.

There's no water anywhere along the trail, and there's no shade to speak of. Bighorn sheep have been known to haunt this trail, and you might feel akin to those dexterous beasts while hiking the rocky ridgeline, which seems unbearably steep in a few places, especially on the way back up. Deer and California condors are also regular residents of the South Kaibab Trail. This is a trail the mules use, so make sure to step aside and wait while the mule trains pass.

DRIPPING SPRING

Distance: 6.2 miles round-trip
Duration: 5-7 hours
Elevation gain: 1,600 feet
Effort: Strenuous
Trail conditions: Rock and dirt, sand in some places, narrow, steep, technical
Trailhead: just west of Hermits Rest

The 6.2-mile round-trip hike to the secluded and green **Dripping Spring** is one of the best day hikes in the canyon for midlevel to expert hikers. Start out on the **Hermit Trail's** steep, rocky, almost stair-like switchbacks. You come to the **Waldron Trail Junction** after 1.3 miles. Look for the **Dripping Spring Trailhead** after 350 yards from the Waldron Trail Junction, once you reach a more level section dominated by piñon pine and juniper. Veer left (west) on the trail, which begins to rise and leads along a ridgeline across **Hermit Basin;** the views are so awe-inspiring that it's difficult to keep your eyes on the skinny trail. After about a mile, you'll come to the junction with the Boucher Trail. Continue heading west, hiking about 0.5 mile up a side canyon to the cool and shady rock overhang known as **Dripping Spring.** And it really does drip: A shock of fernlike greenery creeps off the rock overhang, trickling cold springwater at a steady pace into a small collecting pool (don't drink the water without treating it). Get your head wet, have a picnic, and kick back in this out-of-the-way hard-won oasis. But don't stay too long. The hike back up is nothing to take lightly: The switchbacks are punishing, and the end, as it always does hiking up a trail in the Grand Canyon, seems to get farther away as your legs begin to gain fatigue weight. There's no water on the trail, so make sure to bring enough and conserve it.

GRANDVIEW TRAIL

Distance: 3.2 miles one-way to Horseshoe Mesa
Duration: 1-2 days
Elevation gain: 2,500 feet
Effort: Strenuous
Trail conditions: Narrow, rocky, steep, sandy in places
Trailhead: Grandview Point, 12 miles east of Grand Canyon Village

A steep, rocky, and largely unmaintained route built first to serve a copper mine at Horseshoe Mesa and then to entice tourists below the forested rim, the **Grandview Trail** should be left to hikers who are mid-level and above. The 6.4-mile round-trip trek to **Horseshoe Mesa** and the mine's ruins makes a difficult but fun overnight backpacking trip. Hiking back up, you won't soon forget the steep slab-rock and cobblestone switchbacks, and hiking down will likely take longer than planned as the steepest parts of the route are quite technical and require heads-up attention. There are established primitive campsites at Horseshoe Mesa, including two group sites and pit toilets, but no potable water.

Biking

There are about 13 miles of roads and greenways through the park that allow bikes, including a route from the Grand Canyon Visitor Center to Grand Canyon Village, and routes from the village to Mather Campground and Market Plaza—basically anywhere you need to go inside the park.

While the main park roads are open to bicycles, they don't have wide shoulders or bike lanes. The exception is **Hermit Road,** which is closed to cars March-November.

Seven miles one-way between the village and the western end of the park at Hermit's Rest, the Hermit Road is the best and most popular bikeway on the South Rim. The only traffic you'll have to deal with on this rolling ride of tough ups and fun downs is the occasional shuttle bus. Just pull over and let them pass.

Only experienced road cyclists should attempt the 23-mile ride along **Desert View Drive** to the park's eastern boundaries. It's a beautiful and only moderately difficult ride, but there isn't much of a shoulder and the traffic is heavy during high season.

Bikes are not allowed on the Rim Trail except for a 2.8-mile section called the **Hermit Road Greenway Trail.** The paved trail begins at Monument Creek Vista along the Hermit Road and ends close to Hermit's Rest. This is about as close as you can get to the rim on a bike, and it's a fun and beautiful stretch of trail highly recommended to bicyclists. To get to the very edge of the rim, you have to park your bike and walk, but never very far, and there are bike racks at each developed viewpoint.

You can also reach the rim by bike at Yaki Point and the South Kaibab Trailhead. Take the greenway near Grand Canyon Visitor Center to the Yaki Point Road, closed to private vehicles.

Bright Angel Bicycles and Café (10 S. Entrance Rd., 928/814-8704, www.bikegrandcanyon.com, 6am-8pm daily Apr.-Nov., 7am-7pm daily Dec.-Mar., rental adult $12.50 for 1 hour, $31.50 for 5 hours, $40 full day, child $9.50 for 1 hour, $20 for 5 hours, $31.50 full day) rents comfortable, easy-to-ride bikes as well as safety equipment and trailers for the tots. It also offers bike tours of varying length and difficulty. Bright Angel Bicycles is next to the Grand Canyon Visitor Center, near the South Entrance.

MOUNTAIN BIKING ON THE RIM

The **Tusayan Bike Trails** are a series of single-track trails and old mining and logging roads organized into several easy-moderate loop trails for mountain bikers near the park's

South Entrance. The trails wind through a forest of pine, juniper, and piñon. The longest loop is 16 miles, the shortest 3 miles. There's a map at the beginning of the trails that shows the various loops. Pick up the trails at Forest Road 605 on the west side of AZ 64 north of Tusayan. Coming south from the park, the trailhead is 0.4 mile south of the Tusayan Ranger District (176 Lincoln Log Loop, 928/638-2443, www.fs.usda.gov) sign on the west side of AZ 64. Coming from Tusayan toward the park on AZ 64, go 0.3 mile past town and turn west on Forest Road 605.

PROGRAMS

Every day at various spots the park offers many free ranger-guided hikes and nature walks as well as lectures and discussions on the animals, human history, and geology of the canyon. The programs are most numerous and varied in the high seasons, spring-fall. In January-February rangers typically offer only two programs per day—one on canyon critters and another on the geology of Grand Canyon. To make up for this, the park offers several special "Cultural Demonstrator" programs (though not daily) in winter featuring Native American artists at the Desert View Watchtower. During high season the ranger programs can get crowded, so it's best to plan ahead by checking the schedule at the visitors center, the activity desks at Bright Angel and Maswik Lodges, or online (go.nps.gov/gc_programs).

Most nights during summer there's a usually fascinating free evening ranger program at the **McKee Amphitheater** if the weather's nice and the **Shrine of the Ages** if it isn't. Night programs are generally not offered January-February, ending after Christmas and beginning again during spring break in March. This varied program of lectures and night walks, on subjects ranging from astronomy to the Colorado River to "Surviving the Apocalypse at the Grand Canyon," is usually very popular, so it's best to plan ahead. For some of the most popular programs you must get a ticket to secure a spot, starting at 7:30pm at the Shrine of the Ages venue near Park Headquarters for an 8:30pm program at either venue. The amphitheater is behind and east of the Shrine of the Ages and can be reached via a spur from the Rim Trail, about 1.4 miles east of the village.

SHOPPING

There are 16 places to buy gifts, books, souvenirs, supplies, and Native American arts and crafts at the South Rim. Nearly every lodge has a substantial gift shop in its lobby, as do Hermit's Rest, Kolb Studio, Lookout Studio, and the Desert View Watchtower.

If you check in to your in-park hotel and discover that you forget something essential, don't panic: Head to the **Canyon Village Market and Deli at Market Plaza** (1 Market Plaza Rd., 928/638-2262, 8am-8pm daily) and look around—chances are it is stocked here. A full grocery store, liquor store, hiking store, and gift shop, the general store also has a deli inside and a bank and post office nearby.

The **Grand Canyon Conservancy** (www. grandcanyon.org), the park's nonprofit partner, publishes many excellent books about the history of Grand Canyon and the region, most of them deeply researched, finely written, and sumptuously illustrated. If you're a book lover, don't miss browsing these and other books— including a substantial selection of children's readers and picture books—at the **Grand Canyon Conservancy Park Store** (8am-6pm daily), across the plaza from the main visitors center.

Whether you're a semiserious collector or a first-time dabbler, the best place on the South Rim to find high-quality Native American arts and crafts is Mary Colter's **Hopi House.** Shop here for baskets, overlay jewelry, sand paintings, kachina dolls, and other regional treasures. Don't expect to find too many great deals—most of the best pieces are priced accordingly.

FOOD

Xanterra Parks and Resorts runs most of the hotels and eateries at Grand Canyon National

Park. The company has a relatively strong sustainability program that includes creating a "single stream" trash and recycling program at the park to reduce use of local landfills, as well as efforts to save water and energy, reduce pollution, and design and retrofit buildings to make them greener.

★ **El Tovar Dining Room** (928/638-2631, ext. 6432, www.grandcanyonlodges.com, 6:30am-11am, 11:30am-2pm, and 5pm-10pm daily, $10-40, reservations strongly advised) carries on the Fred Harvey Company traditions on which it was founded in 1905. Competent staff serves fresh, creative, locally inspired and sourced dishes in a cozy mural-lined dining room that has not been significantly altered from back when Teddy Roosevelt and Zane Grey ate here. The wine, entrées, and desserts are all top-notch and would be appreciated anywhere in the world—but they always seem to be that much tastier with the sun going down over the canyon. Pay attention to the specials, which usually feature some in-season local edible; they are always the best thing to eat within hundreds of miles.

Just off the Bright Angel Lodge's lobby, ★ **Fred Harvey Burger** (928/638-2631, www.grandcanyonlodges.com, 6:30am-10pm daily, $9-22) is a perfect place for a big hearty breakfast before a day hike below the rim. It serves all the standard rib-sticking dishes amid decorations and ephemera recalling the Fred Harvey heyday. At lunch there's stew, chili, salads, sandwiches, and burgers, and for dinner there's steak, pasta, and fish dishes called "Bright Angel Traditions," along with a few offerings from the Arizona Steakhouse's menu.

Nearby is the **Bright Angel Fountain** (11am-5pm daily spring-fall), which serves hot dogs, ice cream, and other quick treats. **The Canyon Coffee House** (928/638-2631, www.grandcanyonlodges.com, 6am-10am daily, $1.60-4), just outside the Bright Angel Lodge main lobby, is open early and serves cinnamon rolls, croissants, bagels, yogurt and fruit, juice and coffee, but no espresso drinks.

Next to the Bright Angel Lodge, **Arizona Steakhouse** (928/638-2631, www.grandcanyonlodges.com, 11:30am-3pm and 4:30pm-10pm daily Mar.-Oct., 4:30pm-10pm daily Nov.-Dec., $14-36) serves locally sourced Southwestern-inspired steak, prime rib, fish, and chicken dishes in a stylish but casual atmosphere. There's a full bar, and the steaks are excellent—hand-cut and with unexpected sauces and marinades. The steakhouse is closed for dinner January-February and closes for lunch November-February.

Inside Maswik Lodge, **Maswik Food Court** (928/638-2631, www.grandcanyonlodges.com, 6am-10pm daily, $5-15) is good for a quick, filling, and delicious meal. You can find just about everything—burgers, salads, country-style mashed potatoes, french fries, sandwiches, prime rib, chili, and soft-serve ice cream, among the dozens of offerings. Grab a tray and pick your favorite, and you'll be eating in a matter of minutes.

If you get worn out from hiking the Rim Trail, look for multiple **Sustain Your Hike Carts** (11am-4pm daily, $2-7.50) near Bright Angel Lodge and other spots in the village for some jerky, trail mix, fruit, electrolyte drinks, sweets, and premade sandwiches.

ACCOMMODATIONS

The park's lodging rates are audited annually and compare favorably to those offered outside the park, but you can sometimes find excellent deals at one of several gateway towns around canyon country. Using one of these places as a base for a visit to the canyon makes sense if you're planning on touring the whole of the canyon lands and not just the park. There are six lodges within Grand Canyon National Park at the South Rim—five operated by **Xanterra** (www.grandcanyonlodges.com) and one, Yavapai Lodge, operated by **Delaware North** (www.visitgrandcanyon.com). The hotels within the park are a green and sustainable choice: both operators have robust sustainability programs aimed at conserving water and energy, reducing pollution, and increasing recycling while decreasing use of landfills. All the hotels within Grand Canyon National Park offer wheelchair-accessible guest rooms.

A stay at ★ **El Tovar** (303/297-2757 or 888/297-2757, www.grandcanyonlodges.com, standard room $217-263, suite $442-538), one of the most distinctive and memorable hotels in the state, would be the secondary highlight, after the gorge itself, of any trip to the South Rim. Opened in 1905, the log-and-stone National Historic Landmark stands 20 feet from the rim and has 78 rooms and suites. The hotel's restaurant serves some of the best food in Arizona for breakfast, lunch, and dinner, and there's a comfortable cocktail lounge off the lobby with a window on the canyon. A mezzanine sitting area overlooks the log-cabin lobby, and a gift shop sells Native American art and crafts as well as canyon souvenirs. If you're looking to splurge on something truly exceptional, there's a honeymoon suite overlooking the canyon.

When first built in the 1930s, the ★ **Bright Angel Lodge** (303/297-2757 or 888/297-2757, www.grandcanyonlodges.com, $95-210) was meant to serve the middle-class travelers then being lured by the Santa Fe Railroad, and it's still affordable and comfortable while retaining a rustic character that fits perfectly with the wild canyon just outside. Lodge rooms don't have TVs, and most have only one bed. The utilitarian "hikers" rooms have fridges and share several private showers, which have lockable doors and just enough room to dress. Bright Angel is the place to sleep before hiking into the canyon; you just roll out of bed onto the Bright Angel Trail. The lodge's cabins, just west of the main building, have private baths, TVs, and sitting rooms; these include two cabins created out of historic pioneer structures, Buckey O'Neill's Log Cabin and Red Horse Station. Drinking and dining options include a small bar and coffeehouse, the Harvey House diner, and a restaurant with big windows framing the canyon.

Standing along the rim between El Tovar and Bright Angel, the **Kachina Lodge** (303/297-2757 or 888/297-2757, www.grandcanyonlodges.com, $225-243) offers basic comfortable guest rooms with TVs, safes, private baths, and fridges. There's not a lot of character, but its location and modern comforts make the Kachina an ideal place for families. The **Thunderbird Lodge** (303/297-2757 or 888/297-2757, www.grandcanyonlodges.com, $225-243) is in the same area and has similar offerings. Both properties have some rooms facing the canyon.

Maswik Lodge (303/297-2757 or 888/297-2757, www.grandcanyonlodges.com, $215) is located on the west side of the village about 0.25 mile from the rim. The hotel has a cafeteria-style restaurant that serves just about everything you'd want and a sports bar with a large-screen TV. Guest rooms are motel-style basic but comfortable, with TVs, private baths, and fridges, located in a series of two-story buildings around a parking lot north of the main lobby building. There are no elevators.

About five miles from the park entrance at Market Plaza, **Yavapai Lodge** (11 Yavapai Lodge Rd., 928/638-4001 or 877/404-4611, www.visitgrandcanyon.com, $150-200) offers comfortable guest rooms in a central forested setting. The East Section is a two-story building featuring air-conditioned guest rooms with fridges and TVs, and the King Family Room is a great option for families, with a king bed and twin bunk beds. The West Section, a retro motel-style structure, lacks air-conditioning but has pet rooms ($25). Yavapai Lodge has a good casual restaurant and a pleasant lobby with a fireplace, a gift shop, and a tavern.

Camping

★ **Mather Campground** (877/444-6777, www.recreation.gov, $18 Mar.-Nov., $15 Dec.-Feb.) takes reservations up to six months ahead for the March-November 20 peak season and thereafter operates on a first-come, first-served basis. Near the village with more than 300 basic campsites with grills and fire pits, the campground typically fills up by about noon during the summer busy season. It has restrooms with showers and coin-operated laundry machines. The campground is open to tents and trailers but has no hookups and is closed to RVs longer than 30 feet. Even if you aren't an experienced camper, a stay at Mather is a fun and inexpensive alternative to sleeping indoors. Despite its large size and crowds, the campground gets quiet at night. Even in summer, the night takes on a chill, making a campfire not necessary but not out of the question. Bring your own wood or buy it at the store nearby. A large, clean restroom and shower facility is within walking distance of most sites, and they even have blow-dryers. Everything is coin-operated, and there's an office on-site that gives change. Consider bringing bikes along, especially for the kids. The village is about a 15-minute walk from the campground on forested paved trails, or you can take the free shuttle from a stop nearby. Pets are allowed but must be kept on a leash, and they're not allowed on shuttle buses.

About 25 miles east of the village, near the park's East Entrance, is **Desert View Campground** (877/444-6777, www.recreation.gov, first-come, first-served, May-mid-Oct. depending on weather, $12), with 50 sites for tents and small trailers only, with no hookups. There's a restroom with no showers and only two faucets with running water. Each site has a grill but little else. Pets are allowed but must be kept on a leash.

The South Rim concessionaire Delaware North operates **Trailer Village** (877/404-4611, www.visitgrandcanyon.com, $52-62), about 0.5 mile from the Mather Campground and right near Market Plaza. A clean, orderly, short tree-lined and paved area close to all the action and open year-round, Trailer Village has full hookups and pull-throughs for rolling mansions up to 50 feet long. Only charcoal fires are allowed, and there's no Wi-Fi. Dogs are welcome but must be kept on a leash. Reservations are a must during the high seasons.

GETTING THERE
Car

The majority of Grand Canyon visitors drive, reaching the South Rim from either **Flagstaff** or **Williams** and entering the park through the south or east gates. The South Entrance is usually the busiest, and during the summer traffic is likely to be backed up.

To get to the **South Entrance** from Flagstaff, take U.S. 180 through the forest past the San Francisco Peaks. The road merges with AZ 64 at Valle, for a total distance of 80 miles from Flagstaff to the park gate, which takes 1.5 hours. The drive from Williams to the South Entrance on AZ 64 is more direct but less scenic; it's 60 miles and takes an hour. To reach the **East Entrance,** take U.S. 89 north from Flagstaff to Cameron, then take AZ 64 west to the entrance. The drive is 80 miles and takes 1.5 hours. This route is recommended if you want to see portions of Navajo Country on your way to the canyon, and entering through the East Entrance will put you right at Desert View, the Desert View Watchtower, and Tusayan Ruin & Museum—sights that otherwise you'll have to travel 25 miles east from Grand Canyon Village to see.

The Grand Canyon's South Rim is 225 miles from **Phoenix,** with the closest major airport to the park, Sky Harbor International Airport. The best way to reach the canyon from out of state is to fly into Phoenix, rent a car, and drive north on I-17. Once you reach the northland, you can either take the route through Williams along AZ 64 or the Flagstaff route along U.S. 180 and AZ 64; the latter is more scenic. Expect the drive from Phoenix to take four hours, barring heavy traffic on the interstate.

The roughly five-hour, 280-mile drive from **Las Vegas** to the South Rim—a very popular trip—is relatively short by Southwestern standards. Even if you get a late-morning start and make a few stops along the way, you're likely to arrive at the park by dinnertime. Take U.S. 93 from Las Vegas to Kingman, then take I-40 to reach

Williams or Flagstaff and head north to the park. The speed limit on most sections of I-40 in Arizona is 75 mph, so all that highland forest scenery flashes by unless you stop a few times to take it in. Most summer weekends you'll find the route crowded but manageable. At all times of the year you'll be surrounded by 18-wheelers barreling across the land. If you feel like stopping overnight—and perhaps it is better to see the great canyon with fresh morning eyes—do so in Williams. It's just an hour from the park's South Entrance, has a bit of Route 66 charm, and offers several distinctive and memorable hotels and restaurants, all of which you'll miss if you breeze through in a hurry.

If you are inclined to visit the **Hualapai Reservation's Skywalk,** remember that it's only 125 miles from Las Vegas (a 2.5-hour drive), so it makes sense to include this remote side trip if you're headed to the South Rim from Vegas. To reach Grand Canyon West from Las Vegas, take U.S. 93 south for 65 miles to mile marker 42, where you'll see the Dolan Springs/Meadview City/Pearce Ferry exit. Turn north onto Pearce Ferry Road. About 30 miles in, turn east on Diamond Bar Road. Then it's 20 miles to Grand Canyon West.

To continue to the South Rim, head to Peach Springs along Historic Route 66. You can stop here for the night, at the **Hualapai Lodge,** or continue for an hour east on Route 66 to **Seligman,** which has several small hotels and a few good restaurants. Then head east on Route 66 to Ash Fork, where you can pick up I-40 east to Williams, the gateway to the South Rim.

Grand Canyon National Park's South Rim is 494 miles from Los Angeles, the capital of the American West. Most of the seven- or eight-hour drive is along I-40. It's a two-hour drive north on I-15 from L.A. to Barstow, where I-40 begins, but it's sure to take considerably longer on the weekends and during the morning and evening rush hours, which in Southern California tend to be interminable. Expect snarls and delays around Barstow as well.

PARKING

The best way to explore Grand Canyon National Park's South Rim is to park your car near a shuttle stop and use a combination of walking and riding the free shuttle to get around. First, try the four lots around the **main visitors center,** which include trailer and RV parking spots. In the high season these large parking lots generally fill up by 10am. Next, move on to **Market Plaza,** where you can park cars, trailers, and RVs in a large lot, and then the mid-size lot at **Park Headquarters** across from Market Plaza, where you can park an RV up to 22 feet long. Both of these lots usually fill up by noon. There are a number of parking spots within the village outside Bright Angel Lodge and El Tovar, but you'll be lucky to get one of these prime spots, which are typically all taken by 2pm. The **Backcountry Information Center** (928/638-7875) also has a large parking lot, the southern portion of which can accommodate RVs and trailers. This lot across the train tracks from the village typically fills by 2pm.

Air

Both Flagstaff and Williams have small airports, but most visitors fly into Sky Harbor in Phoenix, rent a car, and drive four hours north to the South Rim.

Bus

Groome Transportation aka Arizona Shuttle (928/350-8466, http://groometransportation.com) offers comfortable rides from Flagstaff to the Grand Canyon three times daily (Mar.-Oct., round-trip $60 adults). The company also runs between Phoenix's Sky Harbor International Airport and Flagstaff ($49 one-way) several times a day from Flagstaff to Sedona, the Verde Valley, and Williams ($35-43 one-way).

Train

The **Grand Canyon Railway** (800/843-8724, www.thetrain.com) runs daily between the Williams station and the South Rim depot in Grand Canyon Village, with several different ticket levels ($67-226 adults, $32-153 ages 2-15).

GETTING AROUND
Shuttle

The park operates excellent **free shuttle services** along the South Rim, with comfortable buses fueled by compressed natural gas. It's strongly encouraged you park your car for the duration of your visit and use the shuttle. It's nearly impossible to find parking at the various sights, and traffic through the park is not always easy to navigate—there are a lot of one-way routes and oblivious pedestrians that can lead to needless frustration. Make sure you pick up a free *Pocket Map,* which has a map of the various shuttle routes and stops, available at the entrance gate and at most visitors centers throughout the park. Pretty much anywhere you want to go in the park, a shuttle will get you there, and you rarely have to wait more than 10 minutes at any stop. That being said, there is no shuttle that goes all the way to the Tusayan Ruin & Museum or the Desert View Watchtower near the East Entrance. Shuttle drivers are a good source of information about the park. They are generally very friendly and knowledgeable, and a few of them are genuinely entertaining. The shuttle conveniently runs from around sunup until about 9pm, and drivers always know the expected sunrise and sunset times and seem to be intent on getting people to the best overlooks to view these two popular daily events.

Early spring-fall, the **Tusayan Route (Purple)** operates from the Grand Canyon Visitor Center and IMAX theater in Tusayan into the park, all day every day. You must have your park entrance pass before you board the shuttle. Entrance passes can be purchased at the IMAX theater as well as various other places around Tusayan, or online at www.recreation.gov. Leave your car in the parking lot in Tusayan and take the free shuttles everywhere you want to go inside the park. Shuttles from the theater begin at 8am daily, and the last trip is at 9:45pm. The Tusayan shuttle drops you off at the Grand Canyon Visitor Center; the last shuttle out of the park leaves at 9:30pm. The shuttle runs every 20 minutes and takes about 20 minutes from Tusayan to the visitors center.

The year-round **Kaibab/Rim Route (Orange)** will take you from Grand Canyon Visitor Center west to Yavapai Geology Museum and back, and east to the South Kaibab Trailhead, Yaki Point, and Pipe Creek Vista and back. Ride the year-round **Village Route (Blue)** west from the visitors center to Market Plaza, Shrine of the Ages, the Grand Canyon Railway Depot, Bright Angel Lodge, and the Hermit's Rest Route transfer area. Eastbound, the Village Route goes from the transfer area to Maswik Lodge, the Backcountry Information Center, Shrine of the Ages, Mather Campground, Trailer Village, Market Plaza, and then back to the visitors center.

The **Hermit's Rest Route (Red)** runs March-November (Hermit Road is open to private vehicles Dec.-Feb.) and is the way most visitors reach the must-see western viewpoints along the South Rim. The route starts at the Village Route transfer area at the head of Hermit Road and heads west, stopping at Trailview Overlook, Maricopa Point, Powell Point, Mohave Point, The Abyss, Monument Creek Vista, Pima Point, and Hermit's Rest. Headed back east it makes stops only at Pima Point, Mohave Point, and Powell Point before returning to the Village Route transfer.

Park shuttles have racks that fit 2-3 bikes. All shuttle buses are wheelchair accessible (up to 30 inches wide and 48 inches long), with wheelchair ramps and low entrances and exits.

If you are in a hurry to get somewhere, the free shuttle bus is not what you need. Especially during the summer and on spring and early fall weekends, expect to stand in a line and watch several buses fill and depart before you get on.

Bike

Whether you're staying in the park or just visiting for the day, consider bringing your bike along. You can park your car at the **South Rim Backcountry Information Center parking lot** (across the train tracks from the village) and ride your bike all around the park from there using the paved **Tusayan Greenway Trail**. Every hotel, restaurant, store, and sight has a bike rack; don't forget your bike lock. If you get tired, park shuttles have racks that fit 2-3 bikes. Remember, though, that the shuttles take a lot longer because they make many stops. There's a good map of all the in-park bike routes in the free *Pocket Map* guide, and staff members at **Bright Angel Bicycles and Café** (928/814-8704, www.bikegrandcanyon.com, 6am-8pm daily Apr.-Nov., 7am-7pm daily Dec.-Mar.), right next to the Grand Canyon Visitor Center near the South Entrance and Mather Point, can answer your questions and also offer bike rentals.

The North Rim

TOP EXPERIENCE

Standing at Bright Angel Point on Grand Canyon's North Rim, crowded together with several other gazers as if stranded on a jetty over a wide hazy sea, someone whispers, "It looks pretty much the same as the other rim." It's not true—far from it—but the comment brings up the main point about the North Rim: Should you go? Only about 10 percent of canyon visitors make the trip to the North Rim, which is significantly less developed than the South; there aren't many activities other than gazing, unless you are a hiker and a backcountry wilderness lover. The coniferous mountain forests of the Kaibab Plateau are themselves worth the trip—broken by grassy meadows and painted with summer wildflowers, and dappled with aspens that turn yellow and red in the fall and burst out of the otherwise uniform dark green like solitary flames. You may also catch sight of elk and mule deer. But it is a long trip, and you need to be prepared for a land of scant services—in return you'll find the simple, contemplative pleasures of nature in the raw.

EXPLORING THE NORTH RIM

It's all about the scenery here at 8,000 feet and above. The often-misty canyon, and the thick old-growth forest along its rim, command all your attention. A good portion of visitors here are hard-core hikers and backpackers waiting for early morning to hit the North Kaibab Trail for a rim-to-rim trek. You can also spend some time on the Grand Canyon Lodge's back porch and hike through highland forest on easy trails to reach uncrowded viewpoints. There are similarly lonely lookouts (at least compared to the often elbow-to-elbow scene at some the South Rim's spots) at the end of a couple of scenic drives.

A road trip to Grand Canyon's North Rim is not to be taken lightly. The Kaibab Plateau is an isolated highland country crisscrossed by rough forest roads and is sparsely populated and dormant for half the year. A road-ready vehicle is essential. Take extra water, food, and supplies even if you're staying in one of the three hotels on the plateau; being overprepared is better than the alternative.

Grand Canyon Lodge and the restaurants, shops, and visitors centers close October 31-May 15. AZ 67, the only road to the park on this side, closes December 1-May 15. During November, you can drive into the park and look around, but you can't stay overnight. From December 1, when AZ 67 closes, until May 15, the North Rim Campground remains open as a primitive campground. To stay, however, you need a backcountry permit and the energy to hike or ski 45 miles from Jacob Lake.

If you paid your park entrance fee at the South Rim, this will be honored at the North Rim as long as you go within seven days.

A North Rim edition of the park's helpful *Pocket Map* is passed out at the North Rim entrance.

Visitors Centers

The **North Rim Visitor Center** (8am-6pm daily May 15-Oct. 16, 9am-3pm daily Oct. 17-30) is next to Grand Canyon Lodge and is staffed with several rangers and volunteers who can direct you to the best sights and trails. You'll find fascinating exhibits on canyon science and lore as well as a restroom and a water station. Within the visitors center the nonprofit Grand Canyon Conservancy operates an excellent bookstore with all the essential tomes and other media about Grand Canyon and the Great Southwest. Find out the current ranger programs on offer or bombard a hard-working ranger with all your questions about the canyon and the park.

Driving Tours

CAPE ROYAL SCENIC DRIVE

This outrageously scenic drive along the rim to Cape Royal is an essential part of the North Rim experience. The paved two-lane road twists through the green, white, and fire-blackened highland forest of tall skinny quaking aspen, thick shaggy conifers, and black stumps and husks of all sizes. There are several developed viewpoints along the rim with parking, picnic tables, interpretive signs, and a few rustic benches to sit and contemplate the views. Plan on at least two hours one-way (it's 23 miles from Grand Canyon Lodge to Cape Royal), and at least another 30-40 minutes at nearby Point Imperial (a 3-mile one-way side trip; the route branches off from Cape Royal Road at mile 5.4). Several of the viewpoints are reached via short easy trails, so plan on some walking. Bring water, food, and warm clothing, and make sure that your vehicle is road-ready (no rigs over 30 feet); there are no services of any kind on this road, though there are small restrooms at Point Imperial and Cape Royal. Keep a look out for wildlife along this road, especially wild turkeys.

Get an early start and take AZ 67 north from **Grand Canyon Lodge** for 3 miles to **Cape Royal Road** and turn right. At mile 5.4 you can veer left to **Point Imperial,** a southeast-facing view of the white-rock peak **Mount Hayden** and across the red-and-green canyon to the Painted Desert on the Navajo Nation, or continue to the right and see it on the way back. Either way, Point Imperial is a stop that should not be missed. Each viewpoint provides a different perspective, so it's best to stop and spend some time at each one.

At mile 8 is **Greenland Lake,** a beautiful lush meadow with a natural sink that traps rainwater and snowmelt, making this "lake" a highly variable prospect. There's also an old ranching cabin in this peaceful clearing about 200 yards off the road, which you can reach by a short dirt trail.

At mile 10 is **Vista Encantada** ("enchanting view"), which has a gorgeous view and is a great spot for a picnic. Stop here and contemplate white-tipped attention-grabbing **Brady Peak,** just east of the picnic spot, named for Arizona pioneer Peter Brady (no relation to the Brady Bunch), who came to the territory in the 1850s and was a longtime elected official. You'll also see the often dry Nankoweap Creek etched beige against the red-and-green canyon landscape, and beyond that, on a clear day, you may see all the way to Navajo land and the Painted Desert.

Just up the road at mile 11.7 is **Roosevelt Point,** named for Teddy Roosevelt, the former U.S. president who loved Grand Canyon and spent time hunting game on the North Rim. A short loop trail (0.2 mile round-trip) provides the best views; take some time to relax on the well-placed benches. Roosevelt Point, like Point Imperial and Vista Encantada, has awesome views of the eastern canyon off the **Walhalla Plateau,** a sliver alongside the Kaibab Plateau on its southeast side. **Tritle Peak,** topped with the same white Kaibab limestone as Brady and Hayden, rises 8,300 feet to the east along a ridge that juts out into the canyon. It was named for F. A. Tritle, territorial governor 1881-1885 and an early owner of the famous Jerome Copper Mine.

At mile 17.2 is the **Cape Final Trailhead.** The trail is 4.2 miles round-trip to a spectacular viewpoint with awesome looks at **Unkar Creek,** the **Painted Desert,** and **Freya Castle.**

Just ahead at mile 18 are **Walhalla Overlook** and the ruins of **Walhalla Glades Pueblo,** occupied for about 100 years AD 1050-1150 by seasonal farmers from the **Unkar Delta** inside the canyon. A great red deposit at the confluence of Unkar Creek and the Colorado River, the Unkar Delta was inhabited and farmed from about AD 850 to AD 1200 and is visible from Walhalla Overlook. In the visitors center a pamphlet describes a self-guided tour of the ruins across the road.

To see where the farmers of Walhalla Glades likely obtained some of their water, stop at mile 19.1 and take the approximately one-mile round-trip trail into the forest to **Cliff Spring.**

Finally, at mile 19.7, is **Cape Royal,** a wonderful terminus with breathtaking views of the Colorado River and across the canyon to the South Rim, reached by an easy paved trail (1 mile round-trip) lined with cliffrose, wind-sculpted piñons and junipers, and random multicolored boulders. Along the trail you'll pass the rock arch **Angels Window,** which offers a perfectly framed view of the river.

SIGHTS
★ Grand Canyon Lodge

You don't need a reservation to enjoy the best parts of **Grand Canyon Lodge** (mid-May-mid-Oct.), the center of the North Rim universe and one of the most dramatic and enchanting railroad-built lodges in the West. Here's a plan for your first sight of Grand Canyon from this high forested rim: Park at the lodge, enter through the front doors, and proceed down a short flight of stairs to the sunroom. Through the large south-facing picture windows you will catch your first glimpse of the impossible labyrinth, accompanied by streaming sunlight and the soft sinking comfort of a couch facing the edge of world. Also in the sunroom is the adorable statue of **Brighty,** a legendary North Rim mule and the subject of a 1953 children's book, *Brighty of the Grand Canyon,* by Marguerite Henry (for sale in the gift shop). After a while, if you can bring yourself to rise, head out to the lodge's amazing veranda, sit in one of the Adirondack chairs hanging over the canyon, and explore the forest-and-desert dichotomy with the added benefit of a cool sap-scented breeze. Once you've taken in the view from these comfortable and contemplative vantages, descend the veranda stairs and walk the easy trail down to Bright Angel Point.

Viewpoints

There are three developed viewpoints at the North Rim, each offering a slightly different look at the canyon. **Bright Angel Point,** a 0.5-mile round-trip walk outside the lodge's back door, looks over Bright Angel Canyon with a view of Roaring Springs, the source of Bright Angel Creek and potable water for the North Rim and inner canyon; **Point Imperial,** at 8,803 feet the highest point on the North Rim, probably has the best all-around view of the canyon; and **Cape Royal,** a 23-mile one-way drive across the Walhalla Plateau, looks toward the South Rim.

RECREATION
Hiking

It's significantly cooler on the high forested North Rim than on the South Rim, making hiking, especially summer hiking below the rim, much less of a chore. Easy trails lead from all the developed scenic overlooks on the rim, the trailheads accessible and well marked, and several tough but unforgettable day hikes into the canyon are possible along the North Kaibab Trail. The *Pocket Map* has a comprehensive listing of the area's trails and where to pick them up. The four-mile round-trip **Transept Trail** is an easy hike through the forest from the Grand Canyon Lodge to

the campground. It has a few nice views and is a good introduction to the North Rim.

UNCLE JIM TRAIL

Distance: 5 miles round-trip
Duration: 2-3 hours
Elevation gain: 200 feet
Effort: Easy to moderate
Trail conditions: Packed dirt, rocky in parts
Trailhead: North Kaibab Trail parking lot

Take this easy flat trail through the forest to watch backpackers winding their way down the North Kaibab Trail's twisting switchbacks and maybe be passed by a mule train or two along the way. The **Uncle Jim Trail,** named for an old game warden who bragged of killing more than 500 Kaibab Plateau mountain lions, winds through old stands of spruce and fir, sprinkled with quaking aspen, to **Uncle Jim Point,** where you can let out your best roar into the tributary known as **Roaring Springs Canyon.**

WIDFORSS TRAIL

Distance: 10 miles round-trip
Duration: 4-6 hours
Elevation gain: 1,000 feet
Effort: Easy to moderate
Trail conditions: Packed dirt, sometimes rocky, dusty, undulating
Trailhead: From Grand Canyon Lodge, drive north on AZ 67 for 2.7 miles, turn left (west) onto a dirt road (Point Sublime Rd.), and follow signs to trailhead.

Named for the 1920s-1930s canyon painter Gunnar Widforss, the undulating wildflower-lined **Widforss Trail** leads along the rim of Transept Canyon and through ponderosa pine, fir, and spruce forest, with a few stands of aspen and burned areas mixed in, for five miles to **Widforss Point,** where you can stare across the great chasm and rest before heading back. The trail starts out on the edge of **Harvey Meadow,** home to an early North Rim tourist camp. Across the meadow is a cave with a doorway, which famed lion-killer Uncle Jim Owens used from time to time.

Intermediate and expert hikers will have no problem hiking the entire 10-mile round-trip route in less than four hours.

For a **shorter hike,** pick up the **free guide** to the Widforss Trail at the trailhead or the visitors center. It proposes a five-mile round-trip hike on the first half of the trail (2-3 hours) and includes a map and information on the natural and human history of the North Rim.

There is no water available along this trail, so come prepared.

NORTH KAIBAB TRAIL

Distance: 1.5-9.4 miles round-trip
Duration: 2-8 hours
Elevation gain: 3,050 feet from trailhead to Roaring Springs
Effort: Moderate to very strenuous
Trail conditions: Rocky, sandy in places, mule leavings on upper sections, dusty and technical in parts
Trailhead: 1.5 miles north of Grand Canyon Lodge on east side of AZ 67

The **North Kaibab Trail** starts out among the coniferous heights of the North Rim. The forest surrounding the trail soon dries out and becomes a red-rock desert, the trail cut into the rock face of the cliffs and twisting down improbable routes hard against the cliffs, with nothing but your sanity keeping you away from the gorge. This is the only patrolled North Rim route into the inner canyon and to the Colorado River. Sooner than you realize, the walls close in, and you are deep in the canyon, the trees on the rim just green blurs.

A good introduction to this corridor trail and ancient Indigenous route is the short 1.5-mile round-trip jog down to the **Coconino Overlook,** where, on a clear day, you can see the San Francisco Peaks and the South Rim. A 4-mile round-trip hike down will get you to **Supai Tunnel,** cut in the red rock in the 1930s by the Civilian Conservation Corps. A little more than a mile onward is **The Bridge in the Redwall** (5.2 miles round-trip), built in 1966 after a flood ruined this portion of the

---

1: Grand Canyon Lodge **2:** Transept Trail

trail. For a tough all-day hike that will likely have you sore but smiling the next morning, take the North Kaibab roughly 5 miles down to **Roaring Springs,** the source of life-giving Bright Angel Creek. The springs fall headlong out of the cliff side and spray mist and rainbows into the hot air. Just remember, you also have to go 5 miles back up.

Start hiking as early as you can no matter what the season. In summer it's not even debatable. Even on the North Rim it's still dangerously hot inside the canyon. Try to be done by 10am during the hot months. Although it's not as important from a safety perspective in spring and early fall, an early start will put you ahead of the crowds and more likely to see wildlife. The trailhead has a decent-size parking lot, though it fills up during the high season, so the earlier you get here the better. You can also arrange for a shuttle from Grand Canyon Lodge, or walk 1.5 miles from the lodge to the trailhead via the Bridle Path.

Mule Rides

Grand Canyon Trail Rides (desk inside Grand Canyon Lodge, 435/679-8665, www.canyonrides.com, 8:30am-1:30pm daily May 15-Oct. 15, $45-90), the same company that works the mules at nearby Zion and Bryce Canyon National Parks, offers three options daily during high season: a one-hour trail ride through the forest and along the rim (must be at least age 7 and 222 pounds or less, $45); a three-hour trail ride along the rim to Uncle Jim's Point (at least age 10, 200 pounds or less, $90); and a three-hour trail ride two miles down the North Kaibab Trail, 2,300 vertical feet to Supai Tunnel (at least age 10, 200 pounds or less, $90), where there are pit toilets and drinking water. If you are trying to choose between the two three-hour tours, take the ride into the canyon to Supai Tunnel. It's a whole different world below the rim, and you have a chance to see some of it on this ride. A shuttle bus picks you up at the lodge a half hour before your ride and takes you to the trailhead.

FOOD

With its native stone walls and picture windows framing the impossible vastness of the canyon, the **Grand Canyon Lodge Dining Room** must be seen even if you don't eat here. Its high ceilings, wrought-iron chandeliers, Native American symbols, and exposed wood rafters give this large, bright, open space an unforgettable atmosphere and represent the height of the National Park Service Rustic style. Reservations for dinner (928/638-8560 or gnrfbmgr@gcnr.com, 9am-4pm Mon.-Fri.) are strongly advised. All the dining options at Grand Canyon Lodge are closed mid-October-mid-May. To make reservations for spring-fall while the lodge and restaurants are closed, call Forever Resorts (877/386-4383).

The restaurant is a member of the Green Restaurant Association and serves dishes with a touch of regional and national park history made from fresh, organic, and sustainable produce, meat, chicken, and fish. Breakfast (6:30am-10am daily, $6.70-17.50, buffet $17.50 adults, $9.25 children) features all the hearty and healthy classics (yogurt, oatmeal) plus Arizona favorites like tamales and eggs and huevos rancheros. Vegetarians will like the grilled vegetable wrap and the braised portobello on offer at lunch (11:30am-2:30pm daily, $6.20-19.50), and everybody will love the fantastic soup, salad, and sandwich buffet ($17.50 adults, $9.25 children). For dinner (4:30pm-9:30pm daily, $12-34) choose between the Bright Angel Buffet with prime rib (4:30pm-6:30pm daily, $33 adults, $19 children) and a menu featuring fresh fish, grilled veggie kababs, pasta, steaks, and bison burgers.

To the left as you exit the Grand Canyon Lodge through the main doors, **Deli in the Pines** (10:30am-9pm daily) is an ultracasual eatery serving premade sandwiches, salads, pizza, chips, cookies, and more, primarily for takeout back to your cabin or to put in your backpack for a lunchtime picnic on the rim. This is the only place in the park to get a quick and relatively inexpensive bite (most items under $10). There's often a line for dinner. Grab some plastic forks and paper plates before you leave, or sit down and relax at one of the few tables inside.

Next to the lodge, a **coffee shop** (5:30am-11am daily) serves espresso and lattes, baked goods, and breakfast burritos before 11am. After that it becomes the **Roughrider Saloon** (11am-1pm), named for Teddy Roosevelt's personal fighting crew in the Spanish-American War, several volunteers for which he found in Arizona's northland. The cozy wood interiors are the perfect complement to a cold regional brew, of which there is an excellent selection on tap ($6.50). They also serve canyon-themed cocktails ($9-10), a range of bottled beer ($5), and various bar snacks.

One of the few other options within 50 miles of the park is the restaurant at the **Kaibab Lodge** (5 miles north of park entrance, AZ 67, mile marker 605, 928/638-2389), a charming knotty-pine space with picture windows, checkered tablecloths, and an old woodstove for atmosphere. The food is generally homemade, hearty, and delicious. About 18 miles north of the rim along AZ 67, the lodge serves breakfast ($6-12) and dinner ($11-30)—burgers, pasta, ribs, steaks—daily during the high season (mid-May-mid-Oct.) and is closed in the winter (mid-Oct.-mid-May). It offers gluten-free options, and for vegetarians there's a garden burger and a few pasta dishes.

ACCOMMODATIONS

The historic ★ **Grand Canyon Lodge** (877/386-4383, www.grandcanyonforever.com, mid-May-mid-Oct.) rises from the North Rim at the end of AZ 67, a rustic masterpiece of local sandstone and pine gloriously isolated at 8,000 feet elevation on what feels like the very edge of the known world. The main lodge building hangs on the rim above Bright Angel Point, the bottom of a U-shaped complex connected by porticos, and it houses the reception desk, the bright high-ceilinged dining room, and the enchanting sunroom with its huge picture windows overlooking the canyon. Cabins of various

sizes dot the forest north, east, and west of the lodge, along with two large outbuildings with motel-style rooms. The motel rooms ($148) are charming and comfortable, and some have connecting doors for families, but the stone-and-pine cabins—including some with incredible views of the canyon—are the lodge's main draw. All the cabins have private baths and romantic stone fireplaces that have been converted to gas. You'll feel like a wilderness wanderer bedded down in rare comfort. They come in three sizes: the small and basic Frontier Cabin ($163); the two-room Pioneer Cabin ($188-191), which sleeps up to six; and the larger Western Cabin ($262-301) with two queen beds and a front porch with rough-hewn rocking chairs. There are mini-fridges and coffeemakers in most of the rooms and cabins, and kids under 15 stay free (but it's an extra $15 per night if you want a rollaway bed, which are not allowed in the Frontier Cabins). To stay here, start hunting for a reservation at least 13 months ahead of your trip. Because the lodge closes in winter, there's a relatively small window to visit, so planning far ahead is the only strategy that works. Four of the Western Cabins are ADA accessible, as are two of the Pioneer Cabins and two of the Frontier Cabins. Additionally, the lodge's main lobby, sunroom, veranda, and dining room are all accessible via three lifts. Outside the main building, the gift shop, the deli, and the coffee shop and saloon are accessible via wide wheelchair-friendly walkways.

Tucked along the tree line on the edge of an expansive green meadow, 18 miles from the rim and 16 miles from the North Kaibab Trailhead, the **Kaibab Lodge** (5 miles north of park entrance, AZ 67, mile marker 605, 928/638-2389, mid-May-mid-Oct., $100-185) is a rustic wilderness haven welcoming North Rim wanderers since the late 1920s. The charming main lodge building has a warm inviting atmosphere with a fire crackling in the corner and hearty smells wafting from the restaurant. Guests and their pets stay in a variety of cabins and motel-style rooms among the pines and aspens. While all the guest rooms and cabins are generally rustic but comfortable, and all have private baths, some are more rustic than others; the older cabins and guest rooms are less expensive. There are no TVs or Wi-Fi, and cell phones don't work. The Hiker's Special is one of the best deals on the plateau: $100 for a small basic room with a double bed and a bath. Kaibab Lodge offers ADA-accessible guest rooms.

There's also a comfortable lodge at Jacob Lake, the **Jacob Lake Inn** (U.S. 89A and AZ 67, 928/643-7232, www.jacoblake.com, $128-165 rooms, $96-144 cabins), on the Kaibab Plateau about 45 miles from the North Rim.

Camping

The North Rim's warm summer days and cool star-filled nights are ideal for camping; the park's 90-site **North Rim Campground** (www.recreation.gov, mid-May-mid-Oct., $6 walk-to sites, $18-25 no hookups) typically fills up quickly in summer-early fall. Keep in mind that July-September you can expect regular late-afternoon rainstorms, often with thunder and lightning. All sites are nonelectric with picnic tables, fire rings, and grills. The campground offers tent-only sites, ADA-accessible sites, and pull-through sites for rigs up to 27 feet long. There's a dump station but

no hookups. A central complex has coin-op showers, laundry, and a drinking-water station, and there's a nearby general store with spotty Wi-Fi and a good selection of groceries and supplies. The campground spreads through an open parklike forest of pine and aspen about 1.5 miles north of the lodge, and some of the more expensive spots have rimside views. The easy Transept Trail runs along the rim from the campground to the lodge area, and the Bridle Path, the only trail in the North Rim section of the park that allows bicycles and dogs, runs to the lodge area along AZ 67. AZ 67 is closed to vehicles December 1-May 15, but the North Rim Campground remains open for primitive camping. You need a backcountry permit ($10 plus $8 pp per night), which also serves as your reservation, and the campground offers no services. In winter the campground is primarily used by rim-to-rim hikers.

About 18 miles north of the rim along AZ 67, the **DeMotte Campground** (Forest Rd. 616, 877/444-6777, www.recreation.gov, mid-May-mid-Oct., $22) has 38 campsites for tents, trailers, and small motorhomes. There are no hookups. Operated by the Kaibab National Forest, the sites have tables and fire grills, and there are drinking-water stations and vault

Grand Canyon Lodge's cabins

toilets in the campground, which is woodsy and peaceful like the rest of the plateau. You may be able to get spotty cell service, especially if you use T-Mobile.

In Jacob Lake, 45 miles north of the rim, **Kaibab Camper Village** (928/643-7804, www.kaibabcampervillage.com, mid-May-mid-Oct., $20-45) has the only sites on the plateau with full hookups. There are pull-through and back-in spots for rigs up to 40 feet as well as tent sites with tables and fire pits. The complex has chemical toilets, coin-op laundry and showers, and a store. Head south on AZ 67 from the junction with U.S. 89A for 0.25 mile and turn right on Forest Road 461, then drive 1 mile. This campground is owned and operated by the folks from the nearby Kaibab Lodge.

TRANSPORTATION

A road-ready vehicle is essential for a trip to the North Rim. Take along extra water, food, and supplies; being overprepared is better than the alternative. There is only one way into Grand Canyon National Park's North Rim section—U.S. 89A to AZ 67, a paved two-lane that closes December 1-May 15. It runs through the forest and ends at the rim and is one of the most scenic and thrilling roads in Arizona. The drive from the South Rim to the North Rim, 215 miles by car, takes about 4.5 hours. While driving on the plateau, keep an eye out for motorcycles, which proliferate during the summer, and for cyclists riding on the nonexistent shoulder. Also keep a watch out for wildlife, including elk, deer, turkeys, and all sorts of other scurrying creatures that pay little heed to the traffic.

While you really need your own vehicle to do the North Rim right, for rim-to-rim hikers the **Trans-Canyon Shuttle** (928/638-2820, www.trans-canyonshuttle.com, $90 one-way, reservation required) is also a good option. During the spring-summer high season, shuttles run twice daily from the South Rim to the North Rim (8am-12:30pm and 1:30pm-6pm) and twice daily from the North Rim to the South Rim (7am-11:30am and 2pm-6:30pm).

To get from the Grand Canyon Lodge—the park's only accommodations on the North Rim—to the North Kaibab Trailhead, take the **hikers' shuttle** ($7, $4 for each additional person), which leaves the lodge twice daily first thing in the morning. Tickets must be purchased the day before at the lodge.

The Inner Canyon

TOP EXPERIENCE

Inside the canyon is a strange desert, red and green, pink and rocky. It's those sheer rock walls, tight and claustrophobic in the interior's narrowest slots, that make this place a different world altogether. A large part of a canyon-crossing hike takes place in Bright Angel Canyon along Bright Angel Creek. As you hike along the trail beside the creek, greenery and the cool rushing water clash with the silent heat washing off the cliffs on your other side.

On any given night there are only a few hundred visitors sleeping below the rim—at either Phantom Ranch, a Mary Colter-designed lodge near the mouth of Bright Angel Canyon, or at three campgrounds along the corridor trails. Until a few decades ago visiting the inner canyon was something of a free-for-all, but these days access is strictly controlled; you have to purchase a permit ($10, plus $8 pp per night), and they're not always easy to get—each year the park receives 30,000 requests for backcountry permits and issues only 13,000.

No matter which trail you use, there's no avoiding an arduous leg- and spirit-punishing hike there and back if you really want to see the inner canyon. It's not easy, no matter who you are, but it is worth it—a true accomplishment, and a hard walk you'll never forget.

EXPLORING THE INNER CANYON

If you want to be one of the small minority of canyon visitors to spend time below the rim, stay at least one full day and night in the inner canyon. Even hikers in excellent shape find that they are sore after trekking down to the river, Phantom Ranch, and beyond. A rim-to-rim hike, either from the south or from the north, requires at least a day of rest below the rim. The ideal inner-canyon trip lasts three days and two nights.

River trips range from three days to three weeks and often include a hike down one of the corridor trails to the river. Depending on how long you want to spend on the river, plan far in advance, and consider making the river trip your only major activity on that particular canyon visit. Combining too much strenuous, mind-blowing, and life-changing activity into one trip tends to water down the experience.

Backcountry Permits

To camp overnight below the rim, you have to purchase a **permit** ($10 plus $8 pp per night). The earliest you can apply for an inner-canyon permit is 10 days before the first of the month that is four months before your proposed trip date. The easiest way to get a permit is to go to the **park's website** (www.nps.gov/grca), print out a backcountry permit request form, fill it out, and then fax it first thing in the morning on the date in question—for example, if you want to hike in October, **fax** (928/638-2125) your request May 20-June 1. On June 1 rangers will begin randomly processing all the requests for October, and they'll let you know in about three weeks. On the permit request form you'll indicate at which campgrounds you plan to stay. The permit is your reservation. For more information on obtaining a backcountry permit, call the **Backcountry Information Center** (928/638-7875, 8am-noon and 1pm-5pm daily).

HIKING
Into the Inner Canyon

Although there are many lesser-known routes into and through the canyon, most hikers stick to the **corridor trails—Bright Angel, South Kaibab,** and **North Kaibab.** A classic Grand Canyon backpacking journey begins at either the Bright Angel Trailhead or the South Kaibab Trailhead on the South Rim. Consider going up the one you don't use going down, mostly for variety's sake. Via the South Kaibab Trail, it's a seven-mile hike to the **Bright Angel Campground,** which is just a short walk from the Colorado River and also from **Phantom Ranch.** Ideally, spend at least two days (the hike-in day and one full day after that) and two nights in the Phantom Ranch area, hiking up the North Kaibab a short way to see the narrow and close walls, talking to the rangers, sitting on the beach watching the river-trippers float by, and losing yourself to the calm, quiet soul of the wilderness.

When it's time to leave the oasis that is Bright Angel Campground and Phantom Ranch, a question arises: Should you hike headlong to the rim (7 miles up on the South Kaibab or 9.5 miles up on the Bright Angel) or move on leisurely to the next oasis? Those inclined to choose the latter should stay an **extra night** below the rim at the campground at **Indian Garden,** a green and lush spot 4.7 miles up the Bright Angel Trail from the Bright Angel Campground. The small campground is primitive but charming, and the area around it is populated by deer and other creatures. After setting up camp and resting a bit, head out on the flat three-mile round-trip hike to Plateau Point and a spectacular view of the canyon and river, especially at sunset. When you wake beneath the shady trees at Indian Garden, you face a mere 4.8-mile hike to the rim.

From the North Rim, the North Kaibab is the only major corridor trail to the river and Phantom Ranch.

1: the inner canyon **2:** riding mules in the Grand Canyon

1

2

Hiking Rim to Rim... the Easy Way

One of the first things you notice while journeying through the inner canyon is the advanced age of many of your fellow hikers. It is not uncommon to see men and women in their 70s and 80s hiking at a good clip, packs on their backs and big smiles on their faces. At the same time, all over the South Rim you'll see warning signs about overexertion, each featuring a buff young man suffering from heatstroke or exhaustion, with the warning that most of the people who die in the canyon—and people die every year—are people like him. You need not be a wilderness expert or marathon runner to enjoy the rim-to-rim hike through the inner canyon. Don't let fear hold you back from what is often a life-changing trip.

Several strategies can make a canyon hike much easier than a forced march with a pack on your back:

- Don't go in summer; March-April or October-early November are cooler, though it's still warm in the inner canyon.

- Try to book a cabin or a dorm room at Phantom Ranch rather than camping. You'll need less equipment, you'll have most of your food taken care of, and there will be a shower and a beer waiting for you.

- Consider that for $76 each way, you can hire a mule to carry up to 30 pounds of gear for you, so all you have to bring is a day pack with water and snacks. Instead of suffering while you descend and ascend the trail, you'll be able to better enjoy the magnificence of this wonder of the world.

Rim to Rim

A popular way to visit the inner canyon is to backpack from rim to rim, starting at the South Rim and ending at the North Rim (or the other way around). Starting from the South Rim, you can go down either the Bright Angel Trail to see beautiful Indian Garden, or else the South Kaibab Trail, a faster, more direct route to the river. Keep in mind that, while shorter, the South Kaibab is a good deal steeper than the Bright Angel, and there is no water available. Whichever route you choose into the canyon from the South Rim, you'll connect to the North Kaibab Trail to hike out of the canyon onto the North Rim. The total rim-to-rim distance via the Bright Angel Trail is 23.9 miles, while the total via the South Kaibab Trail is 21 miles. To get the most out of this backpacking trip, hikers should plan to spend at least two nights inside the canyon, including Bright Angel Campground or Phantom Ranch. No matter how you do it, when you finally gain the final rim after a cross-canyon hike, a profound sense of accomplishment washes away at least half of the fatigue. The other half typically hangs around for a week or so.

Day Hikes Around Phantom Ranch

Some people prefer to spend their time in the canyon recovering from the hard walk or mule ride that brought them here, and a day spent cooling your feet in Bright Angel Creek or drinking beer in the cantina is not a day wasted. However, if you want to do some exploring around Phantom Ranch, there are a few popular day hikes. When you arrive, the friendly rangers will usually tell you, unsolicited, all about these hikes and provide detailed directions. If you want to get deeper out in the bush and away from other hikers, ask one of the rangers to recommend a lesser-known route.

RIVER TRAIL
Distance: 1.5 miles round-trip
Duration: 1-2 hours
Elevation gain: Negligible
Effort: Easy

Trail conditions: Dirt, rocky, narrow, dusty

Trailhead: Start at Phantom Ranch on north side of the river or at end of Bright Angel Trail on the south side.

This short hike is along the precipitous **River Trail,** high above the Colorado just south of Phantom Ranch. The Civilian Conservation Corps (CCC) blasted this skinny cliff-side trail out of the rock walls in the 1930s to provide a link between the Bright Angel and the South Kaibab Trails. Heading out from Phantom, it's a 1.5-mile loop that takes you across both suspension bridges and high above the river. It's an easy walk with fantastic views and a good way to get sore legs stretched and moving again. You are likely to see a bighorn sheep's cute little face poking out from the rocks and shadows on the steep cliffs.

CLEAR CREEK LOOP

Distance: About 1.5 miles round-trip
Duration: 1-2 hours
Elevation gain: 826 feet
Effort: Easy to moderate
Trail conditions: Dirt, rocky, narrow, dusty, steep, some sand
Trailhead: About 0.3 mile north of Phantom Ranch on North Kaibab Trail

Another popular CCC-built trail near Phantom, the 1.5-mile **Clear Creek Loop** takes you high above the river to Phantom Overlook, where there's an old stone bench and excellent views of the canyon and Phantom Ranch below. The rangers seem to recommend this hike the most. It's not tough but can be steep and rugged, especially if you're exhausted and sore. The views are, ultimately, worth the pain.

PHANTOM RANCH TO RIBBON FALLS

Distance: 11 miles round-trip
Duration: 5-6 hours to all day
Elevation gain: 1,174 feet
Effort: Easy to moderate
Trail conditions: Dirt, rocky, some sand, narrow, high canyon walls
Trailhead: North Kaibab Trail, on north side of Phantom Ranch

If you hiked in from the South Rim, and you have an 11-mile round-trip day hike in you, head north on the **North Kaibab Trail** from Phantom Ranch to beautiful **Ribbon Falls,** a mossy cool-water oasis just off the dusty trail. The falls are indeed a ribbon of cold water falling hard off the rock cliffs, and you can scramble up the slickrock and through the green creek-side foliage to stand beneath the shower. Look for the sign for Ribbon Falls on the left side of the trail 5.5 miles from Phantom. A section of this hike will also give you a chance to see the eerie claustrophobic **Box,** one of the strangest and most exhilarating stretches of the North Kaibab (the last 4 miles of the trail going from north to south). This narrow stretch through the **inner gorge** is easy and flat but low and hot, boxed in by 1.7-billion-year-old black Vishnu schist. Don't hike in the inner canyon after 10am in summer.

Guided Backpacking Trips

You certainly don't need a guide to take a classic backpacking trip into the Grand Canyon along one of the corridor trails. The National Park Service makes such a memorable expedition a relatively simple process, and while hikers die below the rim every year, the more popular regions of the inner canyon are as safe as can be expected in a vast wilderness. Then again, having some friendly, knowledgeable, and undoubtedly badass canyon-lander plan and implement every detail of your trip couldn't hurt, and would probably make the whole expedition more enjoyable. As long as you're willing to pay for it—and it is never cheap—hiring a guide is an especially good idea if you want to go places where few casual hikers dwell. There are more than 20 companies authorized by the National Park Service to take trips below the rim. If your guide does not have such a permit, do not follow him or her into the Grand Canyon. For an up-to-date list, go to www.nps.gov/grca.

The nonprofit **Grand Canyon**

Conservancy Field Institute (928/638-2481, www.grandcanyon.org, $690-815) offers several three- to five-day guided backpacking trips to various points inside the canyon, including trips designed specifically for women, beginners, and those interested in the canyon's natural history. Operating from Flagstaff, **Four Season Guides** (1051 S. Milton Rd., 928/779-6224, www.fsguides.com, $799-1,450) offers a dozen backpacking trips below the rim, from a three-day frolic to Indian Garden to a weeklong 36-mile expedition on some of the canyon's lesser-known trails. The experienced and friendly guides tend to inspire a level of strength and ambition that you might not otherwise reach. These are the ones to call if you want to experience the lonely out-of-the-way depths of the canyon but don't want to risk your life doing it alone.

MULE TRIPS

For generations the famous Grand Canyon mules have been dexterously walking the skinny trails, loaded with packs and people. Even the Brady Bunch rode them, so they come highly recommended. A descent into the canyon on the back of a friendly mule—with an often taciturn cowboy-type leading the train—can be an unforgettable experience, but don't assume because you're riding and not walking that you won't be sore in the morning.

Park concessionaire **Xanterra** offers two mule trips to Phantom Ranch, a one-night excursion and a two-night expedition. The **one-night trip** is offered **year-round** and includes accommodations at Phantom Ranch (by booking a mule trip, you automatically reserve a spot at Phantom Ranch without having to enter the lottery), dinner and breakfast in the Phantom Ranch Canteen, and a sack lunch. The cost for the one-night trip is $693 pp, $1,205 for two people, and $533 for each additional person. The **two-night trip** is offered **November-March** and includes accommodations at Phantom Ranch, meals in the canteen, and sack lunches. The cost for the two-night trip is $1,009 pp, $1,658 for two people, and $691 for each additional person. You can make a reservation (888/297-2757, www.grandcanyonlodges.com) up to 13 months in advance; book it as soon as you know your plans. There's a 225-pound weight limit.

The mule trips begin in the stone corral next to the Bright Angel Lodge and descend into the canyon via the Bright Angel Trail, stopping for a box lunch at Indian Garden. The trips ascend from the inner gorge via the South Kaibab Trail. Expect to be in the saddle for about 5.5 hours each way. You are provided with a small plastic bag about the size of a 10-pound bag of ice to carry your toiletries and other items. If you need more luggage than this, you can send a duffel bag ahead for $76 each way (maximum 30 pounds, 36 by 20 by 13 inches).

RIVER TRIPS

People who have been inside the Grand Canyon often have one of two reactions—either they can't wait to return, or they swear never to return. This is also the case for those who ride the great river, braving white-water roller coasters while looking forward to a star-filled evening—dry and full of gourmet food—camping on a white beach deep in the gorge. To boat the Colorado is one of the most exciting and potentially life-changing trips the West has to offer.

Rafting season in the canyon runs **April-October,** and there are myriad trips to choose, from a 3-day long-weekend ride to an 18-day full-canyon epic. An **upper-canyon trip** will take you from River Mile 0 at Lees Ferry through the canyon to Phantom Ranch, while a **lower-canyon trip** begins at Phantom, requiring a hike down the Bright Angel with your gear on your back. You can choose between a motorized pontoon boat (three-quarters of rafters do), a paddleboat, a kayak, or some other combination.

Expect to pay about $1,400 per person for a 3-day motor trip, $2,600 per person for a 6-day motor trip, $2,000 per person for a 6-day oar trip, and up to $5,000 per person for a 13-day oar trip. Many of the outfitters offer trips tailored to certain interests, such as trips with a naturalist or trips that make a lot of stops for hiking.

If you are considering a river trip, the best place to start is the website of the **Grand Canyon River Outfitters Association** (www.gcroa.org), a group of 13 licensed river outfitters, all monitored and approved by the National Park Service and each with a good safety record and relatively similar rates. Start planning at least **a year in advance.** Your guide takes care of all the permits needed to spend nights below the rim. After you decide what kind of trip you want, the website links to the individual outfitters for booking. Most of the companies offer trips lasting 3-18 days and have a variety of boat styles. It's a good idea to choose two or three companies, call them up, and talk to someone. You'll be putting your life in their hands, so you want to make sure that you like the spirit of the company. Also consider the size of the group. These river trips are very social; you'll be spending a lot of time with your fellow boaters. Talk to a company representative about previous trips so you can get a gauge of what kind of people, and how many, you'll be floating with.

If you are one of the majority of river explorers who can't wait to get back on the water once you've landed at the final port, remember that the National Park Service enforces a strict limit of one trip per person per year.

FOOD AND ACCOMMODATIONS

Designed by Mary Colter for the Fred Harvey Company in 1922, ★ **Phantom Ranch** (888/297-2757, www.grandcanyonlodges.com, dormitory $51 pp, 2-person cabin $149, $13 each additional person), the only noncamping accommodations inside the canyon, is a shady peaceful place that you're likely to yearn for once you've visited. Perhaps Phantom's strong draw is less about its intrinsic pleasures and more about it being the only sign of civilization in a deep wilderness that can feel like the end of the world, especially after the 14-mile hike in from the North Rim. Phantom Ranch has 11 rustic air-conditioned **cabins** and four hiker-only **dormitories.** The cabins vary in size, sleeping 2-10 people. Each cabin has a sink with cold water, a toilet, bedding, and towels. Hot-water sinks and showers are available in a separate "shower house" building, where towels, soap, and shampoo are also provided. There are two dormitories for men and two for women (families with children under age six must stay in a cabin). Each dormitory has five bunk beds, a toilet, and a shower. Bedding, towels, soap, and shampoo are provided. The dorms and the cabins are all heated in winter and air-conditioned in summer.

The lodge's center point is the **Phantom Ranch Canteen,** a welcoming air-conditioned spot selling beer and lemonade to anyone. There is no central lodge building at Phantom Ranch, but the canteen is the closest thing to it, with its family-style tables often filling up during the heat of the day with beer-drinkers and tale-tellers. The canteen offers two meals per day—a **breakfast** of eggs, pancakes, and thick slices of bacon ($24), and **dinner,** with a choice of steak ($48), stew ($30), or vegetarian ($30). The cantina also offers a **box lunch** ($21) with a bagel, fruit, and salty snacks. Reservations for meals are also difficult to come by; you must reserve at least a year ahead.

Most nights and afternoons, a ranger at Phantom Ranch will give a talk on some aspect of canyon lore, history, or science. These events are always interesting and well attended, even in the 110°F heat of summer.

Phantom is located near the mouth of Bright Angel Canyon, within a few yards of clear babbling Bright Angel Creek, and shaded by large cottonwoods, some of them planted in the 1930s by the Civilian Conservation Corps. There are several day hikes within easy reach, and the Colorado River and the two awesome suspension bridges that link one bank to the other are only about 0.4 mile from the lodge.

A **lottery system** governs Phantom Ranch **reservations** (www.grandcanyonlodges.

com/lodging/phantom-ranch/lottery). You have to enter the lottery between the 1st and 25th of the month 15 months prior to your proposed trip. You'll be notified at least 14 months before your trip if you won a stay.

Camping

To stay overnight below the rim, you must obtain a **permit** ($10 plus $8 pp per night) from the **Backcountry Information Center** (928/638-7875). March 1-November 14, you're allowed to spend up to two consecutive nights at a corridor campground (Bright Angel, Indian Garden, or Cottonwood). November 15-February 28, the limit is four consecutive nights.

There are three developed campgrounds in the inner canyon: **Cottonwood Campground,** 6.8 miles from the North Rim along the North Kaibab Trail; **Bright Angel Campground,** near Phantom Ranch; and **Indian Garden Campground,** 4.8 miles from the South Rim along the Bright Angel Trail. Your backcountry permit is your reservation. All three campgrounds offer toilets, a freshwater spigot (year-round only at Bright Angel and Indian Garden), picnic tables, food storage bins to keep the critters out, poles on which to hang your packs, and emergency phones. There are no showers or other amenities. It's a good idea to throw a roll of toilet paper into your pack just in case the campgrounds are out.

The best campground in the inner canyon is **Bright Angel Campground,** a shady, cottonwood-lined setting along cool Bright Angel Creek with 33 tent spots, each with pack poles, a picnic table, and ammo boxes to keep the raccoons out of your food. Because of its easy proximity to Phantom Ranch (about 0.4 mi), campers can make use of the Phantom Ranch Canteen, even eating meals there if they can get a reservation, and can attend the ranger talks offered at the lodge. There's nothing quite like sitting on the grassy banks beside your campsite and cooling your worn feet in the creek. Accessible from the Bright Angel Trail (9.5 miles one-way), South Kaibab Trail (7 miles one-way) and North Kaibab Trail (14 miles one-way), Bright Angel Campground has an emergency phone, a year-round potable water spigot, and restrooms with sinks and toilets. There's also a ranger on-site who will greet you once you get settled in your spot.

The West Rim and Grand Canyon West

Since the Hualapai Tribe's Skywalk opened in 2007, the remote Grand Canyon West has become a fairly busy tourist attraction on the West Rim. The Skywalk is about a two-hour drive from the Hualapai Reservation's capital, Peach Springs, along Route 66 west of Seligman. If you want to experience Grand Canyon West during your trip to the Grand Canyon National Park, remember that it is about 225 miles from the South Rim and will take at least an extra two days. Along the way, you can drive on the longest remaining portion of Route 66 and, if you have a few days extra, hike down into Havasu Canyon and see its famous fantastical waterfalls.

HAVASUPAI INDIAN RESERVATION

Heavy with lime, the waters of Havasu Creek flow an almost tropical blue green. The creek passes below the weathered red walls of the western Grand Canyon and cuts Havasu Canyon, home these many centuries to the Havasupai (Havasu 'Baaja), the "people of the blue-green water."

Thousands of travelers from all over the world flock to **Havasupai** (928/448-2121, http://theofficialhavasupaitribe.com, entry fee $50 plus $10 environmental fee) every year to see the canyon's blue-green waterfalls, to swim in the pools, and to visit one of the most remote hometowns in North America.

The Havasupai (*pai* means "people" in the Yuman language) have been living in Grand Canyon since at least the 12th century, in summer tending small irrigated fields of corn, melons, beans, and squash and small orchards of peach, apple, and apricot trees in Havasu Canyon and other spring-fed areas of Grand Canyon: Indian Garden along the Bright Angel Trail and Santa Maria Spring along the Hermit Trail. In winter they hunted and gathered on the rim. These ancient patterns were disrupted by the settling of northern Arizona in the late 19th century.

Today the Havasupai rely primarily on tourism to their little hidden oasis in Grand Canyon, and their beautiful land is known the world over for its striking waterfalls. The ease with which the internet allows images to spread inevitably brought what once was a poorly hidden secret to the attention of the globe. Now it's harder than ever to obtain a reservation in the tribe's small lodge and campground, which can only be reached via a hike into the canyon (8 miles to lodge, 10 miles to campground) or a 10-minute helicopter ride.

Reservations

The tribe requires that you **stay overnight** and have a **reservation** to visit Supai and the falls; **no day trips** are allowed. To make a reservation to camp in Havasu Canyon, you have to reserve a space online (www. havasupaireservations.com) beginning at 8am on February 1 of the year you want to go. Camping permits sell out fast. To stay at the Havasupai Lodge, make reservations far in advance (928/448-2111, www. havasupaireservations.com).

Planning Tips

A visit to Havasupai takes some planning. It's unbearably hot in the deep summer, when you can't hike except in the very early morning; the **best months** to visit are **September-October** and **April-June**. If you aren't into **backpacking,** you can hire a **pack mule** ($400 round-trip) or take the **helicopter** ($85 one-way). A popular way to visit is to hike in and take the helicopter out. It's a 10-minute thrill ride through the canyon to the rim, and the helipad is only 50 yards from the trailhead parking lot.

Most visitors stay the night at one of the motels along **Historic Route 66** before hiking in. Get an early start, especially in summer. It's a **60-mile drive** to the **trailhead at Hualapai Hill** from the junction of Route

Havasu Falls

66 and Indian Route 18, which leads to the trailhead. The closest hotel is the **Hualapai Lodge** in **Peach Springs,** seven miles west of the junction. You'll find cheaper accommodations in **Seligman,** 30 miles east of the junction.

Sights
SUPAI VILLAGE

Havasu Creek falls through the canyon on its way to the Colorado River, passing briefly by the ramshackle inner-canyon village of **Supai,** where it is not unusual to see horses running free in the dusty streets, where reggae plays all day through some community speaker, and where the supply helicopter alights and then lifts off again every 10 minutes or so in a field across from the post office. The village has a small café, a general store, and a small lodge.

THE WATERFALLS

There are two major standouts among the reservation's waterfalls. Perhaps the most famous of the canyon's blue-green falls is **Havasu Falls,** right near the campground. Few hikers refuse to toss their packs aside and strip to their swimsuits when they see Havasu Falls for the first time. The other major waterfall, **Mooney Falls,** is another mile down the trail, past the campground. It's not easy to reach the pool below; it requires a careful walk down a narrow rock-hewn trail with chain handholds, but most reasonably dexterous people can handle it.

Hiking
HAVASU CANYON TRAIL

Distance: 8 miles one-way to Supai Village; 10 miles one-way to the campground; 13 miles one-way to Beaver Falls

Duration: 3-5 hours one-way

Elevation gain: 2,000 feet

Effort: Moderate

Trail conditions: Dirt, rocky, sandy in washes, open to mules

Trailhead: Hualapai Hilltop

The eight-mile one-way hike to the **village**

of Supai from the trailhead at Hualapai Hilltop is one of the easier treks into the Grand Canyon. For the first two miles, moderately technical rocky switchbacks lead to the canyon floor, a sandy bottomland where you're surrounded by eroded humps of seemingly melted pockmarked sandstone. You'll know for sure that this is not Grand Canyon National Park when you see the trash along the trail. It doesn't ruin the hike, but it nearly breaks the spell. When you reach the village, you'll see the twin rock spires, called **Wii'Gliva,** that tower over the little farms and homes of Supai.

The trail past the village to the campground is where you'll find the waterfalls. Underwhelming by Havasu Falls standards, **Upper Navajo Falls** (1.3 miles from the village) gained steam after a flash flood in 2008 rearranged these falls closest to the village, which are also referred to as Fifty Foot Falls because they fall about 50 feet in a light-blue and foaming white rush. Just downstream is **Lower Navajo Falls,** also called Little Navajo Falls, which cascades in multiple streams about 30 feet into an inviting swimming pool. The highlight, **Havasu Falls,** appears suddenly as you near the campground, two miles from the village.

The trail then continues on to the Colorado River, seven miles down-creek through a gorgeous green riparian stretch, passing **Mooney Falls** (1 mile from the campground) and **Beaver Falls** (3 miles from the campground), somewhat underwhelming by comparison. The Havasupai Reservation ends at Beaver Falls, where Grand Canyon National Park begins.

It's difficult to hike from the village or the campground to the Colorado River in one day—it's a long, wet route with many creek crossings that's not always easy to follow, plus camping is not allowed at the river, so you must make it back by bedtime. Only experienced strong hikers should attempt the trek to the Colorado River and back. There are no water stations or toilets along the trail.

The Hualapai Nation

Before the 1850s, northwestern Arizona's small Hualapai Nation didn't really exist. It was the federal government's idea to group together 13 autonomous bands of Yuman-speaking Pai people, who had lived on the high dry plains near Grand Canyon's western reaches for eons, as the "People of the Tall Pines."

Before the colonial clampdown and the Hualapai Wars of the 1860s, the Pai bands were independent, though they "followed common rules for marriage and land use, spoke variations of one language, and shared social structures, kin networks, cultural practices, environmental niches, and so on," according to Jeffrey Shepherd's *We Are an Indian Nation: A History of the Hualapai People*, which the scholar spent 10 years researching and writing.

The U.S. Army nearly wiped out the bands during the land wars of the 1860s, and the internment of the survivors almost finished the job. But the bands persisted, and in 1883 the government established the million-acre Hualapai Reservation, with its capital at Peach Springs. Then it spent the next 100 years or so trying to take it away from them for the benefit of Anglo ranchers, the railroad, and the National Park Service.

These days the Hualapai Nation is a worldwide brand—Grand Canyon West. How did this happen? The small, isolated tribe has always been willing to take economic risks, one of the many ways, Shepherd argues, that the Hualapai have twisted colonial objectives for their own survival. A few years ago they partnered with Las Vegas entrepreneur David Jin and built the Hualapai Skywalk, a 70-foot-long glass walkway hanging from the Grand Canyon's western rim. Now you can't walk two steps along the Vegas strip without a tour guide offering to drive you to one of the most isolated sections of Arizona.

Throughout their relatively short history as a nation, the Hualapai have consistently tried to make their windy and dry reservation economically viable, sometimes with the assistance of the government but often in direct contradiction to its goals. For generations they were cattle ranchers, but they could never get enough water to make it pay. They successfully sued the Santa Fe Railroad over an important reservation spring in a landmark case for Indigenous rights. For a time in the 1980s they even hesitantly explored allowing uranium mining on their reservation. Now they have bet their future on tourism.

Food and Accommodations

The **Havasupai Lodge** (928/448-2111, $145 up to 4 people) is a small two-story wood building in a quiet corner of the village. The guest rooms are basic though relatively large, with two queen beds, air-conditioning, and private baths. The village also has a small **café** that serves decent breakfast, lunch, and dinner, and a **general store.**

Most visitors pack in and stay at the primitive **campground** (first-come, first-served, water and toilets available, $25) about two miles from the village between Havasu and Mooney Falls—an area the tribe once used to cremate the dead. The campground holds about 300 people in sites along the creek beneath shady cottonwoods.

HUALAPAI INDIAN RESERVATION

Since the Hualapai (WALL-uh-pie) Tribe's Skywalk opened, this remote region has become a fairly busy tourist attraction. There's not much in the Hualapai Reservation's capital, **Peach Springs,** other than a lodge and a few scattered houses, but it makes an obvious base for a visit to Grand Canyon West, which has several lookout points and a kitschy Old West-style tourist attraction called Hualapai Ranch, in addition to the famous Skywalk. The tribe's Hualapai River Runners also offer a one-day rafting trip on the river.

Grand Canyon West

Grand Canyon West (5001 Diamond Bar Rd., 928/769-2636 or 888/868-9378, www.

grandcanyonwest.com, 9am-sundown daily, $39, Skywalk $20 extra, meal $19 extra) is the Hualapai Reservation's tourist area, comprising several viewpoints on the western rim of Grand Canyon and the Skywalk.

A general admission ticket gets you on the free hop-on, hop-off shuttle to **Eagle Point,** where the Skywalk juts out and there's a restaurant and a café, and on to **Guano Point,** with a wonderful view of the western canyon and a café on the edge of the rim. Getting around by private vehicle is not permitted at Grand Canyon West; there is a large parking area where you leave your car and pick up the shuttle.

Book your general admission tickets and add-ons before you travel to this remote sight. If you're coming from Las Vegas, as many Grand Canyon West visitors do, you can easily find an all-inclusive tour that includes admission. Expect to spend a long day here, and the drive back to anywhere (Peach Springs or Las Vegas) takes at least two hours. Because of its remoteness and rather high cost, consider beforehand whether it is worth it to you. While the views of the Grand Canyon are spectacular along the western rim, they are less dramatic than from the South and North Rims—Grand Canyon West sits at 4,000 feet elevation, so the views of the canyon are much shallower and more uniform than in the park.

GRAND CANYON SKYWALK

The Skywalk (928/769-2636 or 888/868-9378, www.grandcanyonwest.com, $20 plus $39 Grand Canyon West admission) is as much an art installation as a tourist attraction. A horseshoe-shaped glass and steel platform juts out 70 feet from the canyon rim. It appears futuristic surrounded by the rugged canyon. It's something to see, but is it worth the long drive and the high price tag? Not really. If you have time for an off-the-beaten-path portion of your canyon trip, go to the North Rim and stand on Bright Angel Point— you'll get a somewhat similar impression, and it's cheaper. There is a thrill to the Skywalk, however. Some people can't handle it: They

walk out a few steps, look down through the glass at the canyon 4,000 feet below, and head for solid ground. It's all perfectly safe, but it doesn't feel that way if you are subject to vertigo. Another drawback of this site is that you are not allowed to take your camera out on the Skywalk. If you want a record of this adventure, you have to buy a professional photo taken by somebody else. You have to store all of your possessions, including your camera, in a locker before stepping out on the glass, with covers on your shoes.

HUALAPAI RANCH

At **Hualapai Ranch** (928/769-2636 or 888/868-9378, www.grandcanyonwest.com), you can take a zip-line ride, go horseback riding, and stay overnight in a rustic cabin.

Diamond Creek Road

You can drive to the river's edge yourself along the 19-mile **Diamond Creek Road** through a dry scrubby landscape scattered with cacti. The road provides the only easy access to the river's edge between Lees Ferry, not far from the North Rim, and Pearce Ferry, near Lake Mead. You need a permit to drive the road; obtain one at the Hualapai Lodge in Peach Springs (the road is just across Route 66 from the lodge). A tribal police officer may check it at some point along the road.

At the end of the road, where Diamond Creek meets the Colorado, there's a sandy beach by an enchanting lush oasis, and, of course, that big river rolling by.

The route is best negotiated in a high-clearance SUV; you have to cross Diamond Creek six times as the dirt road winds down through Peach Springs Canyon, dropping some 3,400 feet from its beginning at Peach Springs on Route 66. The creek is susceptible to flash floods during the summer and winter rainy seasons, so call ahead to check **road conditions** (928/769-2230).

River Rafting

Though the Skywalk may not be worth the high price of admission and the long drive, the Hualapai offer one adventure that is worth the steep price tag: the canyon's only **one-day river rafting experience,** offered by **Hualapai River Runners** (928/769-2636 or 888/868-9378, www.grandcanyonwest.com, May-Oct., $450 pp). It generally takes up to a year of planning and several days of roughing it to ride the river and the rapids through the inner gorge, making a Colorado River adventure something that the average visitor isn't likely to try. Not so at Grand Canyon West. Hualapai river guides will pick you up in a van early in the morning at the Hualapai Lodge in Peach Springs and drive you to the Colorado via the rough Diamond Creek Road, where you'll float downstream in a motorboat over roiling white-water rapids and smooth and tranquil stretches. You'll stop for lunch on a beach and take a short hike through a watery side canyon to beautiful Travertine Falls. At the end of the trip, a helicopter picks you out of the canyon and drops you on the rim near the Skywalk. It's expensive, but if you want to ride the river without a lot of preplanning and camping, this is the way to do it. Along the way the Hualapai guides tell stories about this end of the Grand Canyon, sprinkled with tribal history and lore.

Food and Accommodations

The **Hualapai Lodge** (900 Rte. 66, 928/769-2230 or 928/769-2636, www.grandcanyonwest.com, $150-170) in Peach Springs has a small heated saltwater pool, an exercise room, a gift shop, 57 comfortable newish guest rooms with soft beds, cable, free Wi-Fi, and train tracks right out the back door. This is a good place to stay the night before hiking into Havasupai, as it's only seven miles west of the turnoff to Hualapai Hill and the trailhead.

The Hualapai Lodge's restaurant, **Diamond Creek** (900 Rte. 66, 928/769-2230 or 928/769-2636, www.grandcanyonwest.com, 6am-9pm daily, $10-15), serves American and Native American dishes. The Hualapai taco (similar to the Navajo taco, with beans and meat piled high on a fluffy slab of fry bread)

and the Hualapai stew (with luscious sirloin tips and vegetables swimming in delicious hearty broth) are both recommended. The restaurant also offers a heaping plate of delicious spaghetti—great if you're carbo-loading for a big hike to Havasupai. The menu also includes a few vegetarian choices, good chili, and pizza. Otherwise, the dining scene at Grand Canyon West is not great, but three eateries have great views of the canyon. There's a restaurant and a café at Eagle Point and a café at Guano Point. To get a meal at one of the two viewpoints, you must add a $19 meal ticket to your general admission price, which gives you the choice of a burger, a veggie burger, or a chicken sandwich. Bringing outside food and beverages to Grand Canyon West is not permitted.

More food and lodging options are available in **Kingman** and **Seligman** along Historic Route 66.

TRANSPORTATION

The best way to get to **Grand Canyon West** from the **South Rim** is to take I-40 to the Ash Fork exit and then drive west on Route 66. Starting at Ash Fork and heading west to Peach Springs, the **longest remaining portion of Route 66** moves through **Seligman,** a small roadside town that's caught in the heyday of the Mother Road. The route through Seligman, which merits a stop to walk around if you have the time, is popular with nostalgic motorcyclists, and there are a few eateries and tourist-style stores in town. Once you reach **Peach Springs** (140 miles from the South Rim, a 2.5-hour drive), continue west on Route 66 for 29 miles, turn right on Antares Road and drive 32 miles, turn right onto Pearce Ferry Road and drive 3 miles, and then turn right on Diamond Bar Road and drive 21 miles. Diamond Bar Road ends at the only entrance to Grand Canyon West. The drive from Peach Springs to Grand Canyon West is 85 miles and takes about 2 hours. The total drive from the South Rim to Grand Canyon West is 225 miles and takes 4.5 hours.

To reach **Havasu Canyon** from the South Rim, take I-40 to the Ash Fork exit and then drive west on Route 66, passing through Seligman. About 30 miles past Seligman, turn north on Indian Route 18 and drive 60 miles north to a parking area at **Hualapai Hilltop,** where the **trailhead** is located. The drive from the South Rim to Hualapai Hilltop is 195 miles total and takes four hours. From here it's a moderate eight-mile **hike** in to **Supai Village** and the lodge, and another two miles to the campground. If you don't want to hike in, you can arrange to **rent a mule** (928/448-2121, 928/448-2174, or 928/448-2180, www.officialhavasupaitribe.com, $400 round-trip to the campground) or even hire a helicopter. **Airwest** (623/516-2790, 10am-1pm Sun.-Mon. and Thurs.-Fri. Mar. 15-Oct. 15, 10am-1pm Sun. and Fri. Oct. 16-Mar. 14, $85 one-way, cash or credit card) operates a helicopter service from Hualapai Hilltop to Supai.

Hualapai Reservation's Skywalk is only 125 miles from Las Vegas (a 2.5-hour drive), so it makes sense to include this remote side trip if you're headed to the South Rim from Vegas anyway. To reach Grand Canyon West from Las Vegas, take U.S. 93 out of the city, heading south for 65 miles to mile marker 42, where you'll see the Dolan Springs/Meadview City/Pearce Ferry exit. Turn north onto Pearce Ferry Road. About 30 miles in, turn east on Diamond Bar Road. Then it's 20 miles to Grand Canyon West.

Once you arrive at Grand Canyon West, you must park your vehicle and ride the free **hop-on/hop-off shuttle** between the viewpoints. There is a large parking area where you can leave your car and pick up the shuttle.

The Arizona Strip

If there is any wild loneliness left in the United States, it is on the Arizona Strip. This five-million-acre wilderness of crumbling red-rock walls, fallen boulders, and long sagebrush sweeps, humpbacked by the evergreen Kaibab Plateau, has only been accessible by highway from within Arizona since 1929 with the opening of the old Navajo Bridge across the Colorado River. Before that, only Paiutes and Latter-day Saints made a go of it here on any serious scale. The region is still inhabited primarily by ranchers, polygamists, hermits, river guides, and residents of the Kaibab Paiute Indian Reservation.

Think of the "strip" as exactly that: a narrow band of Arizona territory hemmed on the north by Utah's border, the south by the Grand Canyon, the east by the Colorado River, and the west by Nevada's border. Within that band are several semidesert grassland valleys; the long red-rock southern escarpment of the Paria Plateau, a vast tableland protected as the Vermilion Cliffs National Monument; a green and meadowy forest, smothered by deep snow in winter; and a historic human crossing point where the Paria River washes into the Colorado, the only rest in the great river's canyon-cutting ways for hundreds of miles.

The first Europeans to enter the strip were the path-finding priests of the Dominguez-Escalante expedition in 1776, looking for a northern route from New Mexico to California. In the later 1800s Mormon pioneers from Utah were encouraged by their church leaders to settle in the region. Some found the isolation of the strip to their advantage after the official LDS church outlawed polygamy in the 1890s; others raised cattle, cut wood, and fought with the Navajo and Paiute over the land's scant resources. When construction on a Mormon temple began in St. George, Utah, to the west, food from the Mormon ranch at Pipe Spring, now a national monument, were used to feed the workers, and the trees on Mount Trumbull provided

1: the Skywalk at Grand Canyon West **2:** the Vermilion Cliffs Highway

the lumber. In the years before the railroad, the red-dust wagon road across this territory was known as the Honeymoon Trail, as it was beaten and smoothed by a stream of LDS couples making the long journey from settlements along the Little Colorado River to St. George, where their unions would be officially sealed in the temple.

These days the strip isn't that different from the way it was before the bridge put Lees Ferry out of business and any Arizonan with a sedan and a canteen could explore it. It remains lonely, isolated, and mostly unpaved. There are a few exceptions, of course; 15 miles upstream from the Lees Ferry crossing, Glen Canyon Dam has stopped the old warm and muddy Colorado and impounded its water in a 186-mile canyon-flooding reservoir, where millions of boaters, anglers, and water lovers play year-round. The river that trickles out the other side of the dam is far from what it was in the old days, now running mostly clear, cold, and predictable through its great sculpted canyons.

A place of outlander history, desolate beauty, and long quiet spaces, the Arizona Strip isn't for everyone. But for those who take the time and effort to explore it, the landscape can become haunting, magnetic, and memorable.

PLANNING TIPS

The most logical way to see the Arizona Strip is to fold it into an excursion from the South Rim to the North Rim. Leave the South Rim early in the morning, cross the eastern strip, spend the night and the next day at the North Rim, and then keep heading west down the Kaibab Plateau to Pipe Spring National Monument and on to St. George, Utah. From St. George it's easy to explore western Arizona and the lower Colorado. The **Vermilion Cliffs Highway** takes you through the entire strip. If you plan on doing more than road-tripping, such as hiking the empty spaces of the Vermilion Cliffs, plan ahead and have at least a tough high-clearance SUV, if not a 4WD vehicle.

VERMILION CLIFFS HIGHWAY

This is classic road-trip territory, and if you're already in the state with a rental car or your own vehicle, consider taking time at least to drive the **Vermilion Cliffs Highway,** a paved two-lane route that runs more or less from Marble Canyon to St. George, Utah, on **U.S. 89A, AZ 389,** and **UT 59** in Utah. Along the way you'll pass through the entire strip, crossing the Colorado River, ascending, and coming back down the Kaibab Plateau. This can be done in one long day from the east or west, but if you want to stop and really see the landscape, take at least two days. Approaching from the east, the Cameron Trading Post and Lodge on U.S. 89, near the eastern entrance to Grand Canyon National Park's South Rim, makes a good starting point. If you're approaching from the west, Mesquite, Nevada, near the Virgin River Gorge, is a good starting point, and you may want to stay the night in Fredonia, Kanab, or St. George, Utah. Don't think of this scenic journey in terms of political boundaries: It is a journey over a landscape, through a region with a history that cannot be understood without seeing the formidable barriers thrown up by nature.

★ Pipe Spring National Monument

A shady watered spot on an otherwise dry and windy bunchgrass plain, **Pipe Spring National Monument** (AZ 389, 928/643-7105, www.nps.gov/pisp, 8am-5pm daily June-Aug., 8:30am-4:30pm daily Sept.-May, $7) is the Arizona Strip's best historic site. A museum and visitors center fronts a well-preserved fortified ranch house and a few historic outbuildings, built in the 1860s-1870s by Mormon pioneers who raised cattle for meat and cheese, much of it taken west weekly to feed workers building a temple in St. George. The monument is within the Kaibab Paiute Indian Reservation, and the nation operates the visitors center jointly with the National Park Service.

The excellent museum inside the visitors center has several displays telling the history of both Native American and Mormon settlement on the strip, with artifacts of both cultures. For an in-depth introduction to the history and politics of the strip, this museum can't be beat. After looking over the displays, bookstore, and gift shop, you can head out to the fort for a personal tour by a volunteer (every half hour in high season). The guide takes you through each room in the fortified home, called **Windsor Castle,** furnished with period furniture and still displaying rifle notches in the walls. The tour also includes the factorylike rooms where cheese and other provisions were made and stored, recalling the hardscrabble life on the 19th-century strip. The fort had the first telegraph in Arizona, part of which is still here. There is also a trail that goes half a mile up a rise behind the fort, where there's an expansive view of the vast plain toward lonely Mount Trumbull to the south. It is a beautiful, isolating view, and quiet except for the wind and the crunch of your feet on the rocky red ground. The rangers at Pipe Spring are excellent sources for tips on touring the area.

Pipe Spring to St. George

Past the tiny polygamist town of Colorado City-Hilldale on the Arizona-Utah border, **St. George** is the capital of Mormon expansion into southern Utah and Northern Arizona. Here you can visit the beautiful white **LDS temple** (250 E. 400 S., 435/673-5181, 9am-9pm daily, free), dedicated in 1877 and built using supplies and wood gathered on the strip. From St. George, you could head east along UT 9 to swing by the otherworldly **Zion National Park** (435/772-3256, www.nps.gov/zion, $30 per car).

Virgin River Gorge

On its way to Lake Mead and the lower Colorado, the Virgin River, the strip's only perennial stream other than the Colorado River, cuts a dramatic rock maze through the Virgin and Beaver Dam Mountains in the far northwest corner of Arizona. For several miles along I-15 between St. George, Utah, and Mesquite, Nevada, the views are towering and car crash-inducing: high and dry rock mountains, rough and jagged and molded haphazardly by the river, covered with hold-out Mojave Desert vegetation, tripped over by desert bighorn sheep and mountain lions. Few sections of the speedy interstate move through such precipitous wild scenery, and it's best to stop and look around at one of the several pullouts rather than craning your neck while trying to keep your eyes on the road. A good place to stop is Exit 18 (Cedar Pocket Interchange) at the **Virgin River Canyon Recreation Area** (435/688-3200, www.blm.gov), 20 miles southwest of St. George and halfway through the gorge. This Mojave Desert riverside preserve has a few easy sandy trails down to the river—its flow varies by season—and great views of the cliffs and mountains. It is snugged between two of the wildest wildernesses anywhere—the 19,600-acre **Beaver Dam Wilderness Area** and the 84,700-acre **Paiute Wilderness Area**—and has about 75 campsites ($8).

Grand Canyon-Parashant National Monument and Toroweap

Way off to the south and west of Pipe Spring rises the Shivwits Plateau and the vast **Grand Canyon-Parashant National Monument** (BLM Arizona Strip District, 345 E. Riverside Dr., St. George, UT 435/688-3200, www.nps.gov/para, 7:45am-5pm Mon.-Fri., 10am-3pm Sat.). There are no paved roads within this million-acre wilderness, no visitors centers, no well-stocked campgrounds, and no concessionaires—truthfully, no services of any kind. There are, however, opportunities for intrepid and well-prepared visitors to see nature in the raw.

The plateau, rising to elevations of 6,000-7,000 feet and covered by semidesert sweeps, short piñon forests, and stands of ponderosa pine on its mountains, marks the transition from the Mojave Desert basin and range province to the Colorado Plateau. It is home to one of the loneliest and most inspiring Grand Canyon views anyone with a tough vehicle and several hours of hard travel can see. In the monument's western reaches, southwest of Pipe Spring, the Toroweap Valley stretches toward the rim and **Toroweap Point** (sometimes both are called Tuweap, after an abandoned town nearby), a hard-won but amazing viewpoint, without fences or crowds, to see the canyon and the Colorado rushing by 3,000 feet below. There are a few campsites on the unhemmed rim and more at a nearby **campground** (www.nps.gov/grca, backcountry permit required), which are free but have no water or anything else. The mighty Lava Flow Rapids stir up the river just below the point, and nearby Vulcan's Throne, a volcanic remnant, rises 50 feet from the plain. There is a ranger station near the viewpoint, and a few short trails run along the rim. While this is a truly wondrous place to visit, it's not easy getting here.

There are a few different ways to get to Toroweap Point, technically within Grand Canyon National Park; all are rough, washboarded, and possibly impassable during bad weather. Make sure you take supplies, tools, and a map. The most popular route to the viewpoint is nine miles west of Fredonia, on Road 109 off AZ 389. It's about 60 miles of rough, slow travel from here, following the signs. This is an all-day, if not multiday, trip that should not be taken lightly or on a whim.

Also within the monument, Mounts Trumbull and Logan both reach around 8,000 feet and in the old days were the only source of lumber on the strip. Both rise within federal Wilderness Areas in the scrub south of Pipe Spring; you'll pass them on the way to Toroweap, and you can take a side trip to hike the short trails to both mountaintops or to walk to the half-mile trail to **Nampaweap,** a petroglyph site. For practical local advice on visiting these areas, talk to a ranger at the **North Kaibab Ranger District** (430 S. Main St., Fredonia, 928/643-7395), one of the rangers at Pipe Spring National

Monument, or the folks at the BLM office in St. George (345 E. Riverside Dr., St. George, UT, 435/688-3200, 7:45am-5pm Mon.-Fri., 10am-3pm Sat.).

KANAB, UTAH

In Utah, about seven miles north of the Arizona border along U.S. 89A, Kanab is the pleasant, relatively bustling capital of the Arizona Strip. Varied accommodations include several chain hotels and restaurants. It's a tiny rural burg, isolated on the western end of the Colorado Plateau and home to 4,000 year-round residents. It is nonetheless well set up for travelers. Kanab makes an ideal base for visiting Grand Canyon National Park's North Rim, just 80 miles or 1.5 hours away; Zion National Park, just 40 miles northwest; Bryce Canyon National Park, 77 miles northeast; and Lake Powell, 70 miles to the east.

Food and Accommodations

The **Rocking V Café** (97 W. Center St., 435/644-8001, www.rockingvcafe.com, 11:30am-10pm daily, $15-48) serves fresh and delicious food, and there's an interesting art gallery upstairs. The Rocking V makes a good burger, including a Boca burger, as well as tasty chicken and pasta dishes, veggie enchiladas, creamy mac-and-cheese, and more. A decent selection of beer and wine includes microbrews. The more upscale **Sego Restaurant** (190 N. 300 W., 435/644-5680, www.segokanab.com, 5pm-9pm Mon.-Sat.) serves regional new American dishes with a dose of international flavor using local, regional, and sustainably sourced ingredients.

The **Quail Park Lodge** (125 N. 300 W., 435/215-1447, www.quailparklodge.com, $109-129), along U.S. 89, is affordable and has a freshly painted retro motor lodge look to it that draws in the fan of road culture and popular architecture. A small pool, tasteful motel-style guest rooms with TVs and free Wi-Fi, and a location that can't be beat make this one of the best places to stay on the Arizona Strip. Right next door and owned by the same folks, the **Canyons Lodge** (236 N.

300 W., 435/644-3069, www.canyonslodge. com, $89-179) is less nostalgic, choosing instead a nattier plush-wilderness look that is warm and stylish. There's also a small pool, and the comfortable guest rooms offer flatscreens, free Wi-Fi, and crisp relaxing beds. Breakfast is included.

FREDONIA

Fredonia is a small settlement of 1,000 residents at the junction of AZ 389 and U.S. 89A about seven miles south of Kanab. It's a former polygamist holdout, these days a mostly tumbledown friendly village offering brief respite and gear storage for river guides and canyon-land explorers. The name means "free woman" in Spanish. It is Arizona's northernmost town, just four miles south of the border with Utah. It was originally settled by residents of Kanab. It has fewer services than Kanab but is a fine place to base your visit to the Arizona Strip, southern Utah, and the Grand Canyon's North Rim.

Food

The **Cowboy Butte Grill & Steakhouse** (165 N. Main St., 928/643-6848, hours vary, $13-30) serves good burgers and sandwiches, chicken-fried steak smothered in rich gravy, excellent french fries and fried chicken, pork ribs, steaks, and more—superior, home-style comfort food to fill you up and warm your soul. If you are planning on staying the night in this region, head back to Kanab.

THE KAIBAB PLATEAU

After Fredonia, U.S. 89A begins to rise into a piñon-juniper woodland that quickly becomes a ponderosa pine forest as the highway climbs the massive upsweep in the land known as the Kaibab Plateau. This islandlike highland, surrounded by arid valleys and giving way on its southern edge to Grand Canyon, measures roughly 60 miles from north to south and 45 miles east to west, ranging in elevation—and thus climate and flora—3,000-9,200 feet. In the plateau's highest ranges along AZ 67 from Jacob Lake to

the North Rim, dark evergreen forests mix with white and yellow aspens around wide green meadows. One of the state's best forest landscapes, the Kaibab has long been logged and hunted; there are old logging and Jeep trails crisscrossing the tableland, which make backcountry exploring relatively easy, though only with a 4WD vehicle and not in winter. December-mid-May AZ 67 to the North Rim is closed, but U.S. 89A usually stays open year-round, even when the plateau is covered in a thick blanket of snow.

While negotiating the steep and twisty highway on the west side of the plateau—or descending it, coming from the east—look for the sign for the **Le Fevre Overlook** and stop at the pullout for a great view.

Food and Accommodations

The main oasis on the Kaibab Plateau is the **Jacob Lake Inn** (U.S. 89A and AZ 67, 928/643-7232, www.jacoblake.com, $128-165 rooms, $96-144 cabins), 45 miles from the North Rim. It features rustic cabins greatly in need of an update, basic motel-style rooms with outside entrances, and a fairly nice hotel-style building with inside hallways, TVs, and Wi-Fi. There are also ADA-accessible rooms. The inn's restaurant offers excellent homemade bread and soups and hearty delicious scratch creations, with a few vegetarian options, including a delicious garden burger. The diner-style **counter** (6:30am-close daily, $3-15) serves breakfast and lunch, and a **dining room** (5:30pm-9pm daily, $10-25) has more formal dinner service. There's also a bakery, a gift shop, a small general store, and a gas station.

Information

The rangers at the **Kaibab Plateau Visitor Center** (928/643-7298, www.fs.usda.gov, 8am-5pm daily mid-May-mid-Oct.), next to the Jacob Lake Inn, 44 miles from the North Rim, can give you advice on hiking and exploring the plateau, and there's a good selection of books for sale and a few displays on the area's flora and fauna.

VERMILION CLIFFS NATIONAL MONUMENT

Most Arizona Strip visitors see only the southern escarpment of the Paria Plateau as they cut through the valley along U.S. 89A. That edge's high crumbling sandstone cliffs give this national monument of swirling slickrock and narrow high-walled river canyons its name. The cliffs are best viewed from an established viewpoint 10 miles east of Jacob Lake, as the highway begins to descend to the House Rock Valley.

There are no services or visitors centers at this remote monument, and much of it is within the **Paria Canyon-Vermilion Cliffs Wilderness Area** and thus can't be accessed by car. The area is best explored from the north, along U.S. 89 in Utah between Kanab, Utah, and Page, Arizona. From Page, head west on U.S. 89 for 30 miles to the BLM's **Paria Canyon-Vermilion Cliffs Wilderness Ranger Station,** where you can get advice on visiting the area; it serves as a kind of visitors center and crossroads for backpackers and day hikers. This is the kind of place you have to plan ahead for: The most popular areas require a permit, and those are given out on a lottery system.

You can also access the monument from the south on the compacted-dirt House Rock/Coyote Valley Road (Forest Rd. 1065), off the south side of U.S. 89A at House Rock, which leads to the **Coyote Buttes Permit Area.** Coyote Buttes has a north and a south section—the north is best accessed via U.S. 89 in Utah. This is a world-famous trekking area where there are several trails that lead through a strange rock world of twisted, undulating, multicolored sandstone formations, often appearing as if rough red, yellow, and pink water has been held up and petrified. Along these trails are sandstone arches, alcoves, spires, domes, amphitheaters, and buttes that make the canyon lands so exotic and enticing. A limited number of people are allowed in each day, even for day hiking, so make sure to get a permit (www.blm.gov, $5) before traveling. For more information on the monument,

talk to the folks at the BLM's **Arizona Strip Field Office** (345 E. Riverside Dr., St. George, UT, 435/688-3200, 7:45am-5pm Mon.-Fri., 10am-3pm Sat.) or the **Kanab Field Office** (435/644-4600).

★ CLIFF DWELLERS AND HOUSE ROCK VALLEY

U.S. 89A continues through the red-dirt and sagebrush **House Rock Valley** at the base of the Kaibab Plateau, overlooked by the Vermilion Cliffs. In the tiny settlement of **Cliff Dwellers,** you'll see a little sandstone-brick structure tucked beneath a fallen boulder. Like some kind of canyon-country Hobbit house, the red-rock slabs and sculpted boulder blend with the cliffs and the chipped light-blue trim paint matches the empty sky. Nearly melding into the vermilion scenery, this is one of the most enchanting structures in all of Arizona. There's usually a Navajo vendor or two selling jewelry here, and you can walk around and duck in and out of the strange rock hovels, as long as you remember this is private property. The house and other small shelters were built by Blanche and Bill Russell, the area's original homesteaders. Operating a trading post out of the little rock house, the Russells also catered to Mormon travelers moving through the valley on their way to the St. George temple.

★ LEES FERRY

Reached via a paved road past the high red buttes just east of Cliff Dwellers—look for the sign—**Lees Ferry** (www.nps.gov/glca) is the only place in hundreds of miles of canyon land where you can drive down to the Colorado River. This boat launch and fishing spot with a campground is named for a man who occupied the area briefly in the early 1870s, Mormon outlaw John D. Lee, one of the leaders of the infamous Mountain Meadows Massacre in Utah. Lee was exiled to this lonely spot after he and others attacked and murdered more than 100 westbound Arkansas emigrants moving through Utah Territory during a period when relations between the

Utah Mormons and the U.S. government were strained. One of Lee's wives, Emma Lee, ended up running the ferry more than Lee ever did; he soon lit out and lived as a kind of fugitive until he was finally arrested and sentenced to death in 1877. The proclamation was carried out by firing squad on the same ground as the massacre. To the end, and in a published memoir, Lee insisted that he was a scapegoat, and many believe Brigham Young ordered the massacre.

Long before and after Lee lent his name to the crossing, this two-mile stretch near the mouth of the Paria River was one of the few places to cross the river in southern Utah and Northern Arizona, until the bridging of the Colorado at Marble Canyon in 1929. Today the area is the starting point for thousands of river-trippers who venture into the Grand Canyon on the Colorado River every year. It's also a popular fishing spot, though the trout have been introduced and were not native to the warm muddy flow before the dam at Glen Canyon changed the Colorado's character. For guides, gear, and any other information about the area, try **Lees Ferry Anglers** (928/355-2261 or 800/962-9755, http://leesferry.com, 6am-9pm daily), located at the Cliff Dwellers Lodge. The guides at **Marble Canyon Outfitters** (800/533-7339, www.leesferryflyfishing.com) and **Kayak the Colorado** (928/856-0012, www.kayakthecolorado.com) will also take you out fishing or kayaking on the Colorado River beyond the dam, including trips to Horseshoe Bend.

Food and Accommodations

The small **Cliff Dwellers Lodge** (U.S. 89A, 928/355-2261 or 800/962-9755, http://leesferry.com, $90) is nearly drowned by the scenery around it, tucked beneath the base of the red cliffs. This lodge offers charming rustic-but-comfortable guest rooms with satellite TV. Its **restaurant** ($10-30) serves good breakfasts, lunches, and dinners, with everything from fajitas and ribs to falafel and halibut. It also serves liquor, beer, and wine.

The **Lees Ferry Lodge at Vermilion Cliffs** (U.S. 89A, 928/355-2231 or 800/451-2231, www.vermilioncliffs.com, $65) has romantic little guest rooms in a retro-West rock-built structure that blends wonderfully into the tremendous background. This lodge has undergone major renovations in recent years.

The trading post first established by Lorenzo Hubbell at **Marble Canyon Lodge** (U.S. 89A, 800/726-1789, www.marblecanyoncompany.com, $82-185) has been open for business since 1920, serving wanderers under the ever-blue sky—which is the only thing bigger out here than the wide-open landscape. This is a friendly and comfortable place to stop. Some guest rooms have kitchenettes, and the trading post has a superior selection of books about the region. The lodge also operates a gas station and convenience store just up the road, as well as has an excellent **restaurant** ($10-20) serving tasty fry bread and other Southwestern staples.

MARBLE CANYON AND NAVAJO BRIDGE

A few miles before U.S. 89A runs into U.S. 89 south toward the Navajo Nation and the Grand Canyon, two bridges span **Marble Canyon**, where the Colorado River digs deep again after surfacing at Lees Ferry. This is the exit or entrance to the heart of the strip, depending on which way you're headed. The original Navajo Bridge opened in 1929, the first to cross this part of the Colorado, putting Lees Ferry out of business. By 1995, a new bridge had opened, as the original was not up to the increased traffic along U.S. 89A. The original bridge is now open for sightseers, and you can walk over it and look down at the river flowing through magnificent Marble Canyon, here at the start of the Grand Canyon. The **Navajo Bridge Interpretive Center** (U.S. 89A, west side of Navajo Bridge, 928/355-2319, www.nps.gov/glca, 9am-5pm daily Apr.-Oct.) has a bookshop and displays about the bridge, and there are usually several booths selling Native American arts and crafts.

Glen Canyon, the lake is 186 miles long and has more than 1,000 miles of meandering desert shoreline. Its waters run through a redrock maze of narrow side canyons, like canals around an abandoned ornate sandstone city. In spring-summer the lake is crowded with sometimes rowdy Jet Skiers, water-skiers, and houseboat residents, but you could also visit the area and never get wet—the canyon-country scenery is enough to draw even the most water-averse visitors. The whole area resembles one vast salmon-pink sand dune frozen and petrified at once—it is sometimes a desolate lonely place, beautiful and sacred but also a reminder of how humans can change a seemingly unalterable landscape at their will.

Probably the most popular activity on Lake Powell is houseboating. The floating mansions chug around the buttes and spires, while their residents shoot water cannons at each other and stop at night for parties on the beaches around the lake. Some places around Lake Powell, including the nearby Navajo Reservation, are an hour later than Arizona time during daylight saving time.

GLEN CANYON DAM

Looking out at **Glen Canyon Dam** through large picture windows in Glen Canyon's **Carl** **Hayden Visitor Center** (U.S. 89, west side of the dam, 928/648-6404 or 928/608-6072, www.nps.gov/glca, 8am-5pm daily, free tours offered), it's difficult not to be impressed. The great concrete slab shimmed into the narrow Navajo-sandstone channel allows for the storage of 27 million acre-feet of water (an acre-foot is roughly the amount that a household of four uses in a year); it's a brash reclamation feat. But it is also difficult to see Lake Powell, the reservoir and playground created by the dam, and not feel that something was lost in the flooding of once-spectacular Glen Canyon and the irrevocable alteration of the Colorado River's ecosystem.

The writer and desert-country anarchist Edward Abbey, whose famous 1975 trickster-novel *The Monkey Wrench Gang* envisions the destruction of Glen Canyon Dam by a group of ecowarriors, described the long-lost canyon, waiting silent about 300 feet below Lake Powell's glassy surface, as a "once lovely wonderland of grottoes, alcoves, Indian ruins, natural stone arches, cottonwood groves, springs and seeps and hanging gardens of ivy, columbine, and maidenhair fern—and many other rare things."

Along with sinking this natural wonderland, the dam severely altered the character of

Glen Canyon Dam

the Colorado River downstream. A sediment-laden river—a characteristic of the mighty flow that allowed it to carve those famous canyons—the Colorado River once ran warm and muddy, filled with native fish and lined by beaches, sandbars, and groves of cottonwood and willow. Now that the flow stops at the dam, the once sediment-heavy river runs cool and clear on the other side, which has encouraged invasive plant and fish species to thrive to the detriment of the native flora and fauna. Beaches that are eroded don't come back easily because of the lack of sediment in the river flow, and controlled flow has replaced the natural flood cycle of the river, leading to the disappearance of an entire ecosystem.

Many people, including some who once supported the dam's construction, now believe that too much was lost for what was gained. The dam is surely an awesome sight, and it will either draw your admiration for the brave and tough laborers who built it in 1957-1964 or your disgust for the loss of a once-wild river that it changed forever. More likely, you'll feel a little bit of both, and you will agree with Abbey, who conceded that "though much has been lost, much remains."

Since the 1990s the river below the dam has been purposely flooded several times with timed releases from the reservoir. An army of scientists then moves into the canyon along the river to determine the flood's effects on the ecosystem. While these experiments have been helpful, many scientists believe they happen too infrequently to make much of a difference in combating the dam's negative influence downriver.

WAHWEAP MARINA AND LAKE POWELL RESORT

The largest marina in the recreation area and the center of Arizona-side visits to Lake Powell, the **Wahweap Marina** (928/645-2433, www.lakepowell.com) offers lodging, food, boat and other watercraft rentals, camping, RV parking, tours, and shopping, all within one area. Aramark is the main concessionaire at the marina, running the ★ **Lake**

Powell Resort and Marina (100 Lakeshore Dr., 928/645-2433, $154-250), where you can rent equipment to do just about anything on the lake. The hotel has two heated pools, a sauna, a hot tub, and a workout room. Overlooking the marina and lake, the resort is elegant but casual, with everybody walking around in flip-flops and swimsuits. Guest rooms are comfortable, stylish, and dark and cool for those overheated summer days when you've had enough of the sun.

The marina's **Rainbow Room** (100 Lakeshore Dr., 928/645-2433, 6am-2pm and 5pm-10pm daily spring-fall, 7am-1:30pm and 5pm-9pm daily winter, $10-32) at the Lake Powell Resort has lakeview tables and serves delicious fish, steak, pork chops, and pasta for dinner and a buffet at lunch. The hotel also has a stylish relaxing bar, the **Driftwood Lounge,** inside, with good drinks and tasty tapas. The marina has a sandy beach with chairs and cabanas, and it offers guided fishing tours and waterskiing instruction, among myriad other activities.

BOATING ON LAKE POWELL

If you make the drive to these remote corners of the Colorado Plateau, crossing Native American lands and canyon lands just to see the landscape, and fail to get out on the water, you are missing something. Stark and beautiful, Lake Powell offers the opportunity to kayak or Jet-Ski through a drowned labyrinth of strangely sculpted canyons.

Many otherwise landbound folks who visit Lake Powell have their own boats, including a large contingent of locals and near-locals from the surrounding region. Others become lake-top locals for a week every year, conspiring with friends to lounge in luxury under the relentless sun, blushed in a more or less perpetual buzz. You can rent a houseboat at **Wahweap Marina** (100 Lakeshore Dr., Page, 888/896-3829, www.lakepowell.com/houseboats), which also rents kayaks, Jet Skis, and powerboats.

April-October the marina offers several **boat tours** of the lake, including dinner and breakfast cruises and day trips to Rainbow Bridge and elsewhere. The red rocks grow warm and flash their deep hidden colors at sunrise and sunset, and a boat tour is a great way to experience this. There are nighttime tours of the lake for a view of the city of stars that emerges from the huge, clear sky. Depending on the length and destination, boat tours from Wahweap run $41-125. There's a booking desk inside the Lake Powell Resort at Wahweap Marina.

RAINBOW BRIDGE NATIONAL MONUMENT

Rainbow Bridge, the world's largest arched-rock span and one of the true wonders of the natural world, is a sacred site to the Navajo people, who call it *Nonnezoshi* (rainbow turned to stone). An improbable arch of reddish-orange sandstone 290 feet high, the "bridge" is one of the most popular sites in the recreation area, even with the difficulty getting there and the admonition against walking under it in deference to Navajo beliefs. You can gear up for a multiday backpacking trip across the hot rugged land to reach the wonder on foot, but most visitors take a 50-mile all-day boat tour from Wahweap Marina or take their own boat to the well-signed port of call. **Aramark** (800/528-6154, www.lakepowell.com, $122) is in charge of tours. The trip includes an easy two-mile round-trip hike from the dock to the arch.

DAM OVERLOOK

A short but mildly strenuous walk to the Dam Overlook is worth the effort to see the front of the massive dam and the Colorado River going its merry way beyond it. Catch the trailhead off U.S. 89, about 1.5 miles south of the Carl Hayden Visitor Center on Scenic View Road. It's a 940-foot walk, one-way, down some relatively steep steps.

HANGING GARDEN

For an easy introduction to this unique world of rock and water, take a hike to **Hanging Garden,** an unlikely oasis in the hard land where greenery hangs from the seeping rocks, providing a cool place to kick back and study the landscape. It's a one-mile, one-way trek on a slickrock trail that's easy and okay for kids. The trailhead is 0.5 mile from Glen Canyon Bridge on U.S. 89, on the east side of the bridge, across from the Carl Hayden Visitor Center; look for the sign.

Events

Every year on the first weekend in November, about 50 hot-air balloonists bring their colorful craft to Page for the **Page Balloon Regatta** (928/645-2741, www.pagechamber.com, early Nov.). The highlight of the event is the Balloon Glow, when the balloonists light up their balloons on the ground, creating dozens of glowing orbs. There's also a street festival and other events at this busy weekend near Lake Powell.

Food

Millions of travelers drive through Page every season to see Lake Powell and the canyon lands, and as a result the area has all the usual chain hotels and several chain restaurants—more than a typical small town in the middle of nowhere. You'll find most of Page's services along Lake Powell Boulevard, the main drag through town.

For dinner or lunch, try ★ **Strombolli's Italian Restaurant & Pizzeria** (711 N. Navajo Dr., 928/645-2605, http://strombollisrestaurant.com, 11am-10pm daily, $10-20) for toothsome Italian entrées like baked ravioli with meat sauce, calzones, New York-style pizza, chicken parmigiana, stuffed eggplant parmigiana, burgers, steaks, salads, and a decent wine list.

The Dam Bar & Grille (644 N. Navajo Dr., 928/645-2161, www.damplaza.com, 11am-11pm daily, $13-34), in the small resort town's entertainment complex, is a surf-and-turf restaurant with well-made baby back ribs, steaks, prime rib, sandwiches, and salads.

Accommodations

Most of the many chain accommodations

outside the marina are mid-range, but expect higher rates than other locations.

Canyon Colors B&B (225 S. Navajo Dr., 928/645-5979, www.canyoncolorsbandb.com, $99-159, 2-night minimum) rents two bright and homey rooms in Page and has an outdoor barbecue area and a pool, friendly hosts, and big, delectable breakfasts.

About 20 minutes from Page on the Utah side of the recreation area, the **Dreamkatcher Lake Powell Bed & Breakfast** (66 S. American Way, Big Water, UT, 435/675-5828, www.dreamkatcherslakepowell.com, $99-215) has three pleasant guest rooms with private baths, a library with views of Lake Powell, and a hot tub with a spectacular view of the canyon lands.

Information and Services

The **Page Lake Powell Tourism Bureau** (647-A Elm St., 928/660-3405, www.visitpagelakepowell.com) has all kinds of information on Page, Glen Canyon, and the rest of the region, and the staff can help you book tours. The bureau runs the **Visitor Information Center** (10am-4pm Mon.-Fri., 10am-2pm Sat.), inside the Powell Museum (6 N. Lake Powell Blvd.).

Transportation

The best way, and really the only practical way, to travel to and explore the Lake Powell region is by car. If you fly into Phoenix, it's a lonely five-hour drive from the metropolis north to Lake Powell. Take I-17 out of the valley to Flagstaff, a two-hour drive from the desert to the forest; then take U.S. 89 from Flagstaff north across the western edge of the Navajo Reservation to Page, a total of 327 miles that passes through Arizona's three great landscapes—the Sonoran Desert, the pine forest, and the Colorado Plateau.

A trip north to Lake Powell can easily be folded into a visit to the Grand Canyon's **South Rim.** Take AZ 64 east through the Desert View gate (the park's East Entrance) 30 miles to Cameron, then head north on U.S. 89 for 80 miles to Page. The total distance from the Desert View gate to Page is 110 miles and takes 2.5 hours. The **North Rim** is 154 miles from Lake Powell along U.S. 89A. It will take just as long as the drive from the South Rim; figure on 2.5 hours without stops.

If you're visiting the North Rim along with Zion National Park and Bryce Canyon National Park, consider a side trip to Lake Powell, especially if you're staying in Kanab, Utah, a central base for visiting the Arizona Strip and southern Utah. Kanab is 74 miles from Lake Powell along U.S. 89, just north of the Arizona border. The drive across the vast sagebrush plain takes about 1.5 hours. From Kayenta and Monument Valley on the Navajo Reservation, east of Lake Powell, take U.S. 160 west to AZ 98 for 100 miles, a two-hour drive. You'll reach the region right near Antelope Canyon, one of its top sights.

Navajo and Hopi Country

Here is the Arizona you often see on vintage
travel posters and in old Westerns: Monument Valley, the Painted
Desert, the railroad tracks, and Route 66. This is also the Arizona you
won't see unless you make a concerted effort to do so.

From the vast arid grasslands of the high desert to the pink and red
sandstone guardians of Indian Country, the scenery gets top billing,
but there are also comforts to be had in this region that was once a destination for generations of travelers and is still a major draw for those
looking for something a bit off the beaten path.

Here you can gaze at weather-formed canyons with rock features
that seem deliberately molded according to a strange aesthetic; hike
into Canyon de Chelly (de-SHAY), a sacred place where pueblo ruins

Highlights

Look for ★ to find recommended sights, activities, dining, and lodging.

★ **Navajo National Monument:** Stand on the edge of sacred Tsegi Canyon and gaze at an ancient city rising out of the rock (page 323).

★ **Monument Valley Scenic Drive:** Drive the red-dirt loop around a barren valley populated by crumbling stone giants, a landscape rooted deeply in the American imagination (page 327).

★ **Canyon de Chelly National Monument:** Hike to the White House Ruin along a precipitous rock trail hewn in the cliff side, circled endlessly by ravens and silence (page 332).

★ **Second Mesa:** Walk through the oldest continually inhabited village on the continent, where thousand-year-old traditions are a part of everyday life (page 338).

★ **Petrified Forest National Park:** The slickrock remains of a swampy forest are now a parched land strewn with reminders of the earth's unfathomable age (page 340).

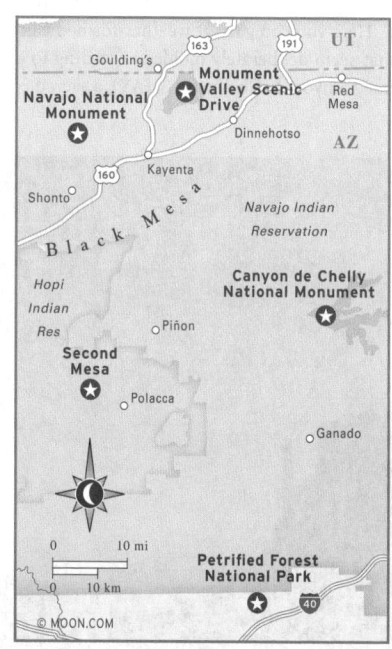

sit below sheer multicolored walls; or visit the Hopi in their remote mesa-top villages, living in some ways just as their ancestors did a thousand years ago. This place is not for the casual traveler but rather those looking for something different. The region's challenges only make a trip out here all the more memorable and meaningful.

PLANNING YOUR TIME

You could easily spend five days to a week in this region, hiking the canyons and exploring the ruins, following guides to out-of-the-way sights, searching for handmade treasures, and touring all the parks and monuments; however, a long weekend would suffice to hit all of the essentials and gain an unforgettable impression of Indian Country.

Keep in mind that the Navajo Nation recognizes **daylight saving time.** March-November, the reservation is on mountain daylight saving time (MDT), while the rest of Arizona observes mountain standard time (MST) year-round.

TRANSPORTATION

It's relatively easy to navigate Indian Country, as long as you have a reliable vehicle and a good map. Remember that distances between gas stations, much as it was in the old days of the territory, are generally long, so take advantage of off-road respite when it presents itself.

To reach the high-desert railroad towns and the sights nearby, stick to I-40, which is well signed for tourist sights. To reach the Navajo and Hopi Reservations from the west, take U.S. 89 north from Flagstaff to Cameron (53 mi, 1 hour), at the entrance to the Navajo Nation. Past Cameron, turn east on U.S. 160, which runs through Tuba City (26 mi from Cameron, 30 minutes) and Kayenta (75 mi from Tuba City, 1.25 hours), past the Navajo National Monument (63 mi from Tuba City, 1 hour). From Kayenta, head north on U.S. 163 to reach Monument Valley Navajo Tribal Park (22 mi, 30 minutes), or head east from Kayenta on U.S. 160 and then take U.S. 191 south to reach Chinle and Canyon de Chelly National Monument (71 mi, 1.25 hours). From here, take U.S. 191 farther south to Ganado and the Hubbell Trading Post (39 mi, 40 minutes), and then head east on AZ 264 to Window Rock, the Navajo Nation's capital (30 mi, 31 minutes).

If you're entering the Nation from the east via I-40, head north on U.S. 491, west on AZ 264, and then north on Indian Route 12 for Window Rock (25 mi, 30 minutes) to hit the sights.

Hopi land can be reached from the west via the gateway village of Moenkopi, at the junction of U.S. 160 and AZ 264, about 2 miles southeast of Tuba City; from the east, pick up AZ 264 at Window Rock.

The best map of this area is the American Automobile Association's (AAA) Indian Country Guide Map.

Previous: Monument Valley; Navajo National Monument; Petrified Forest National Park.

Navajo and Hopi Country

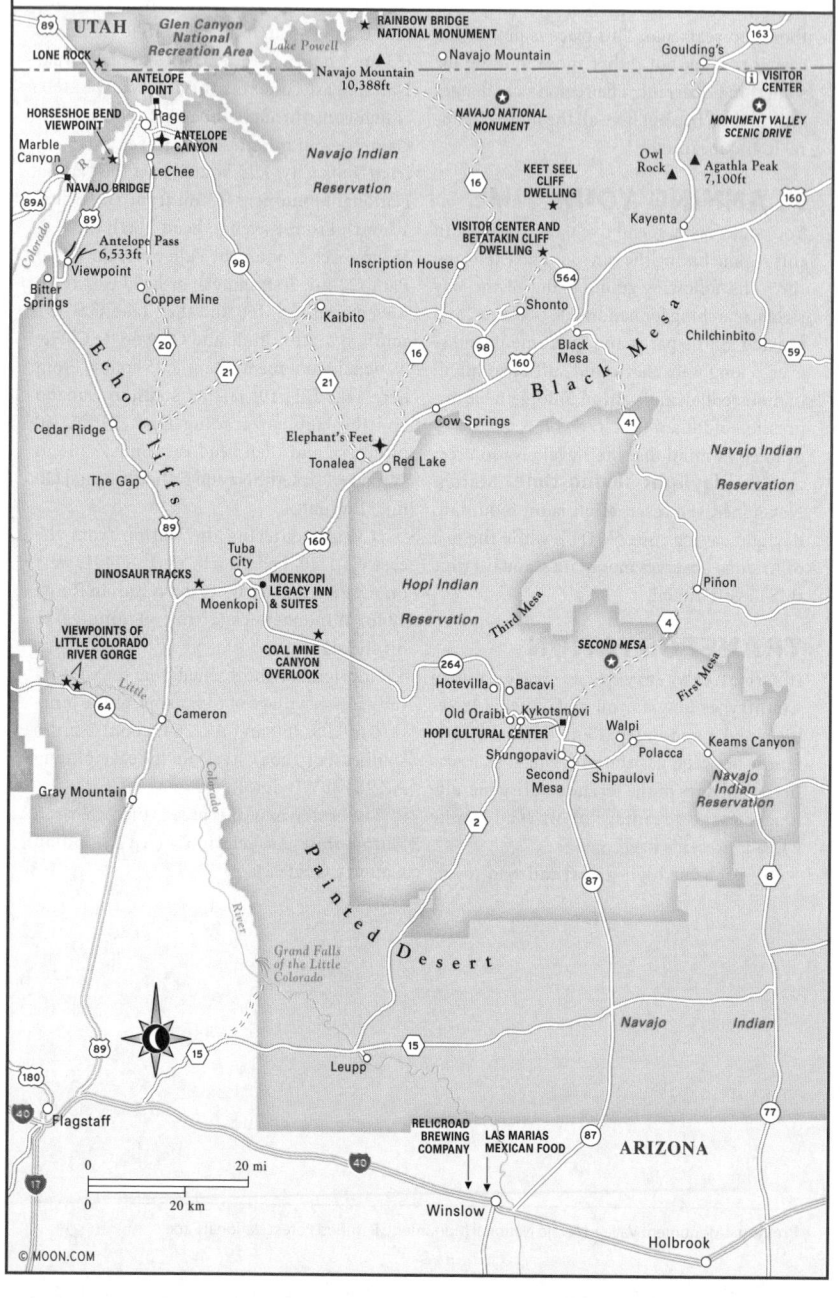

UTAH

89 LONE ROCK

Glen Canyon National Recreation Area

Lake Powell

★ RAINBOW BRIDGE NATIONAL MONUMENT

Navajo Mountain 10,388ft

○ Navajo Mountain

163

Goulding's ○

ℹ VISITOR CENTER

ANTELOPE POINT

HORSESHOE BEND VIEWPOINT

Page

✚ ANTELOPE CANYON

Marble Canyon

LeChee

NAVAJO BRIDGE

89A

89

Antelope Pass 6,533ft

Viewpoint

Bitter Springs

Copper Mine

Cedar Ridge ○

The Gap ○

89

20

21

21

16

Kaibito ○

98

Inscription House ○

NAVAJO NATIONAL MONUMENT ○

Navajo Indian

Reservation

KEET SEEL CLIFF DWELLING ★

VISITOR CENTER AND BETATAKIN CLIFF DWELLING ★

564

Shonto ○

Black Mesa ○

16

98

160

B l a c k   M e s a

Chilchinbito ○

59

Kayenta ○

Owl Rock ▲

Agathla Peak 7,100ft ▲

MONUMENT VALLEY SCENIC DRIVE

160

Echo Cliffs

Elephant's Feet ★

Tonalea ○

Red Lake ○

Cow Springs ○

41

Navajo Indian

Reservation

Piñon ○

4

Tuba City

DINOSAUR TRACKS ★

Moenkopi

MOENKOPI LEGACY INN & SUITES

160

Hopi Indian

Reservation

Third Mesa

SECOND MESA ☆

First Mesa

VIEWPOINTS OF LITTLE COLORADO RIVER GORGE

COAL MINE CANYON OVERLOOK ★

64

Cameron ○

Little

Colorado

River

Gray Mountain ○

264

Hotevilla ○

Bacavi ○

Old Oraibi ○

Kykotsmovi ■

HOPI CULTURAL CENTER

Shungopavi ○

Second Mesa

Shipaulovi ○

Walpi ○

Polacca ○

Keams Canyon ○

Navajo Indian Reservation

8

2

P a i n t e d   D e s e r t

Grand Falls of the Little Colorado

89

15

15

Leupp ○

87

Navajo   Indian

77

180

40

Flagstaff

17

0   20 mi

0   20 km

RELICROAD BREWING COMPANY

LAS MARIAS MEXICAN FOOD

87

ARIZONA

Winslow ○

Holbrook ○

© MOON.COM

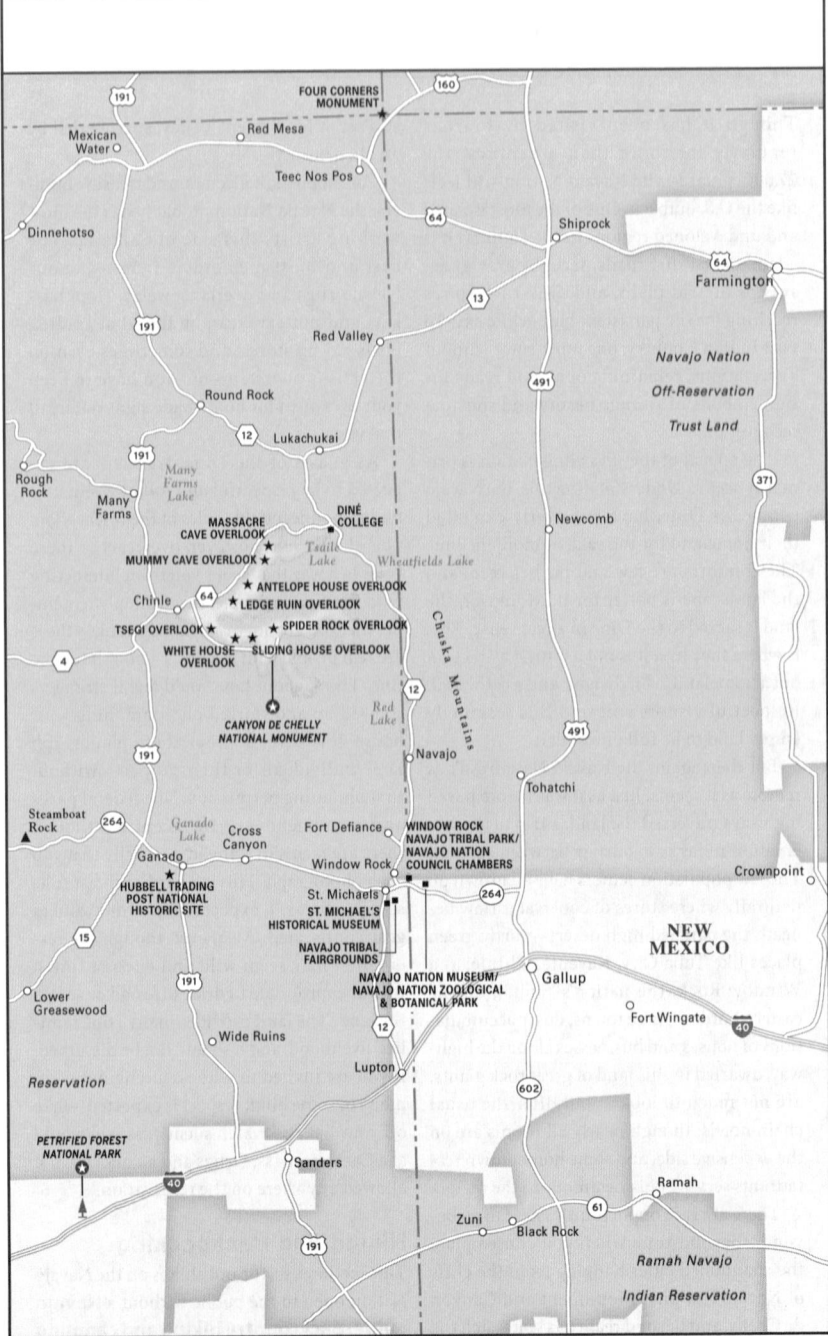

FOUR CORNERS MONUMENT
191
160
Mexican Water
Red Mesa
Teec Nos Pos
64
Shiprock
Dinnehotso
64
Farmington
191
13
Red Valley
491
Navajo Nation
371
Round Rock
Off-Reservation
12
Lukachukai
Trust Land
Rough Rock
191
Many Farms Lake
Newcomb
Many Farms
MASSACRE CAVE OVERLOOK ★
DINÉ COLLEGE
MUMMY CAVE OVERLOOK ★
Tsaile Lake
Wheatfields Lake
Chinle
64
★ ANTELOPE HOUSE OVERLOOK
★ LEDGE RUIN OVERLOOK
Chuska Mountains
TSEGI OVERLOOK ★ ★
★ SPIDER ROCK OVERLOOK
4
WHITE HOUSE OVERLOOK ★
SLIDING HOUSE OVERLOOK
12
Red Lake
491
CANYON DE CHELLY NATIONAL MONUMENT
Navajo
Tohatchi
Steamboat Rock
264
Ganado Lake
Cross Canyon
Fort Defiance
WINDOW ROCK
NAVAJO TRIBAL PARK/
NAVAJO NATION
COUNCIL CHAMBERS
Crownpoint
191
Ganado
Window Rock
264
HUBBELL TRADING POST NATIONAL HISTORIC SITE ★
St. Michaels
ST. MICHAEL'S HISTORICAL MUSEUM
NEW MEXICO
15
NAVAJO TRIBAL FAIRGROUNDS
Lower Greasewood
191
NAVAJO NATION MUSEUM/
NAVAJO NATION ZOOLOGICAL
& BOTANICAL PARK
Gallup
Fort Wingate
40
12
Wide Ruins
Lupton
602
Reservation
PETRIFIED FOREST NATIONAL PARK
40
Sanders
Ramah
191
Zuni
Black Rock
61
Ramah Navajo
Indian Reservation

The Navajo Nation

Though it has been visited by tourists regularly for more than a century, the 27,000-square-mile Navajo Nation still feels like the U.S. outback. One of the most isolated and undeveloped regions in the country, it is a land of red-dirt roads, scrubby gray-green sweeps of arid plain, and pink-rock spires reaching for the persistent blue-white sky. To visit Indian Country, one must enter without expectations, remaining open and ready for sudden bolts of strange beauty and spiritual recognition.

The appeal of the sprawling Nation is primarily scenic. Understanding this, the Navajo people, or Diné, have not overly exploited their homeland for the sake of more income. The comforts are few and far between, and the landscape is better for it. Moreover, the land is sacred to the Diné in a real sense. This is where they live; it is not a tourist attraction but a homeland, a birthright, and a cathedral. Respectful visitors will find this seemingly empty land to be full of wonder.

But then again, the Navajo Nation isn't as remote as it seems. Just as it was before paved highways traversed the land, a trip to the reservation today is a journey between springs. The few population centers have all grown up naturally where stores of cool water flow beneath the parched high desert—partly green places like Tuba City, Kayenta, Chinle, and Window Rock, the nation's capital, on the eastern border. These towns, dusty accumulations of houses and businesses along the highway, dwarfed in this land of great rock giants, are not much to look at but offer the usual chain hotels, though nearly all rooms are on the expensive side, and some homegrown restaurants serving cuisine unique to the region.

There are rare opportunities here to go beyond—beyond time when you contemplate the abandoned cities hanging from the cliffs of Navajo National Monument and Canyon de Chelly, and beyond reality as you watch the sun set at Monument Valley, surrounded by an alien beauty.

For shoppers, collectors, and treasure hunters, the Navajo Nation probably has the most working artists this side of Santa Fe. The best and most memorable items—famous Navajo rugs and overlay jewelry, Hopi baskets and pottery—can be found at trading posts, co-op stores, and sometimes even on the artist's doorstep—but you have to keep your eyes open for homemade signs out in all that vastness.

As guests of the Diné, travelers are expected to be respectful and follow a few simple but nonnegotiable rules of the reservation. One should not, however, overreact to these rules in a way that keeps you from interacting with the Navajo people. If you simply remember that you are not in a living diorama—these are real people with real lives—you should be fine. Think about how you'd feel if strangers showed up and started photographing your house. It is never appropriate to photograph Diné individuals or their property without first obtaining permission. The federal parks and monuments are an exception, though there are farms in Canyon de Chelly that you can't photograph. This is a hard-and-fast rule, so if you break it, expect to have your camera gear confiscated. Also, even though the reservation may seem wild and open at times, it's not appropriate to drive off-road or across the land. The land provides many Diné families' livelihood, and it should not be disturbed. If you are invited to witness a religious ceremony of some kind, respect is expected—take off your hat and watch silently, as you would at a Catholic mass. Drugs and alcohol are not allowed anywhere on the reservation.

Hiking and Backpacking
This section lists the only hikes on the Navajo Nation open to the public without a **Navajo guide. Backcountry hiking and camping**

The Diné

The Navajo people, also known as the Diné (the name the Navajo call themselves, meaning "The People"), are the largest and most populous Native American nation. They migrated from what is now Canada to the Colorado Plateau about a century before the Spanish arrived from the south, and lived a seminomadic life of hunting, gathering, and raiding that sometimes had them at odds with their neighbors, who were sedentary pueblo-dwelling farmers.

After contact with the Spanish and the Pueblo people, the Diné also became pastoralists and farmers, one of many occasions when these resilient people borrowed from another culture to expand their own. As the anthropologist Edward T. Hall explains: "In their natural state all people are highly adaptable, but the Navajos seem to be the most adaptable people on earth—not simply in adapting to new technologies . . . but in their ability to live with, even absorb into their society, people who are different."

The Navajo Nation's modern story is largely one of survival in the face of government antagonism and neglect. In 1863, Colonel Kit Carson was sent in to exert government control over the Navajo, loosing a brutal campaign to round up what remained of the tribe and forcibly march them 300 miles toward isolation and death at Fort Sumner, New Mexico Territory. This event, called the Long Walk, remains an indelible scar on the collective heart of the Diné, a before-and-after dividing line in the nation's modern history. About 8,000 Navajo people were interned at Fort Sumner. Four years later, when the tribe returned to Navajo land, just 5,000 remained.

After years of extreme privation, they eventually returned to their adaptive ways, becoming successful pastoralists, weavers, and artists. They were aided by the Anglo traders who found worldwide markets for high-quality Navajo crafts and brought modern goods to the remote reservation. The Diné have thrived and grown and now number 298,000, about 180,000 of whom live on the reservation.

trips on Navajo land require a permit from the tribe (http://navajonationparks.org/permits, $12 pp per day). Of the hikes below, only Keet Seel requires a permit.

CAMERON

If you're heading north on U.S. 89 from Flagstaff to the Navajo Nation, the Cameron Trading Post (466 U.S. 89, 877/221-0690), while usually crowded with folks on their way to the Grand Canyon, makes for a handy first stop for gas and snacks and a look at the beautiful old bridge that crosses Little Colorado Gorge. There's also a restaurant, a hotel, shops, and a gallery to browse.

TUBA CITY AND VICINITY

The Navajo call Tuba City Tonaneesdizi (Weaving Water or Water Scattered), due to its many life-giving underground natural springs that coax greenery out of the rocky ground and make this small town a dusty oasis. For centuries an agricultural center for the Hopi, who would move from the mesas to nearby Moenkopi to tend their corn, in the late 1800s the area was settled by Mormons. They named their town after a Hopi leader called Tuuvi, who had become a Latter-day Saint and invited others to settle here. In 1903 the federal government sent the settlers away because the town was located on part of the expanded Navajo Reservation.

Today Tuba City, with 9,000 residents, serves as the administrative and cultural center of the western part of the reservation. Its location at the junction of AZ 264 and U.S. 160, and proximity to the essential Navajo National Monument 65 miles to the northeast, makes it a natural stop for travelers. Nearby you can witness the marks ancient beasts have left on the landscape. Tuba City may not look like much, but there are a few places to eat and stay, and trading posts to browse.

Sights

Approaching Tuba City from the west (it's 80 miles from Flagstaff via U.S. 89 North and U.S. 160 East), you'll drive through a wondrous stretch of **Painted Desert**: red, dusty orange, and gray mounds rising above the washes like the humped craggy backs of buried dinosaurs, with not a shrub in sight. There are several natural turnoffs along the road to take pictures of this strange landscape. In downtown Tuba City, you'll find the **Explore Navajo Interactive Museum** (Main St. and Moenave Rd., 928/640-0684, www.explorenavajo.com, 9am-5pm Mon.-Fri. Mar.-May and Sept.-Nov., 8am-7pm Mon.-Fri., 8am-5pm Sat. June-Aug., by appt. Mon.-Fri. Dec.-Feb., $4.50 adults, $3 ages 7-12). The museum offers interesting displays on Navajo history and culture created with the assistance of Navajo scholars and artists, which explain the various stages of traditional Navajo life. It's worth it if you have a particular interest in the tribe's traditions. The museum is next to the NavajoLand Hotel and the Tuba City Trading Post.

Five miles west of Tuba City on U.S. 160, look for a sign that says **Dinosaur Tracks.** Turn north onto the dirt road and expect to be greeted by one of several Navajo guides who hang around the area, especially during the busy summer season. You can follow one of the friendly guides onto a great red sandstone slab, where eons ago raptor dinosaurs and other ancient monsters populated this land, back when it was swampy and fertile. Their birdlike tracks were sealed forever in the stone, and the guides, many of whom learned details about the tracks from Northern Arizona University archaeologists working in the area, will spray water on the dozens of claw prints to bring them out of the red rock while explaining exactly what you're seeing. Expect to tip $15-20 for the tour. Off to the northeast, look for the lush green hillsides of **Moenave,** where several Navajo families live off the natural springs for which this area is known. This is also where Mormon farmers settled in the 1870s;

for generations prior to that, it was a Hopi farming area.

Events

The **To'Nanees'Dizi Diné Fair** (aka the Western Navajo Fair, 928/283-3305, http://westernnavajonationfair.net), held annually in mid-October, is the social event of the season in this corner of the reservation. It's not easy to secure reservations during the three-day fair, which brings hundreds of Navajo families to Tuba City from around the reservation for a rodeo, parade, traditional food and ceremonies, live bands, cutest baby and Miss Western Navajo pageants, and sporting events. It's a fun and illuminating time to be in Tuba City.

Shopping

The **Historic Tuba City Trading Post** (10 N. Main St., at Moenave Rd., 928/283-5441, 8am-5pm daily) in downtown Tuba City has been selling Indigenous crafts and a vast array of staples since the 1870s. Though it has changed a lot over the decades, it offers a great assortment of handmade jewelry, rugs, and other popular Indian Country souvenirs and collectibles. **Van's Trading Post** (928/283-5343, 8am-8pm daily) along U.S. 160 is like a lesser Walmart, half grocery store and half other merchandise, like clothing and furniture. There's a coin laundry next door, and a pawn shop also operates on-site.

Food and Accommodations

The nicest hotel in Tuba City is the **NavajoLand Hotel** (10 N. Main St. and Moenave Rd., 928/283-5260, www.navajolandtubacity.com, $130-150), right next to the Historic Tuba City Trading Post. The two-story hotel has clean guest rooms decorated in a soft Southwestern style, free Wi-Fi, and free continental breakfast. On the same property is the **Hogan Restaurant** (928/283-5260, 6:30am-9pm daily, $10-30), a diner-style place that serves decent food for breakfast, lunch, and dinner, including everything from burgers and fries to Navajo tacos and mutton stew plus a few Mexican favorites. Next door you can get a cappuccino or a latte at **Hogan Espresso** (10 N. Main St., 928/283-4545, 7am-7pm Mon.-Fri., 9am-7pm Sat., 9am-4pm Sun., $5-10). The inn, restaurant, and on-site museum are all operated by the Navajo Nation Tribal Council's **Navajo Nation Hospitality Enterprise,** so the money you spend generally stays on the reservation.

A note about reserving a room: Every room in town is booked weeks before the Western Navajo Fair; expect to pay extra if you manage to find one for yourself.

Elephant Feet

On the north side of U.S. 160 at mile marker 345, about 24 miles east of Tuba City near Tonalea, you'll see the two sandstone spires called **Elephant Feet,** side by side and similarly eroded with wide red-banded bases tapering up to slender flat peaks. They really do look like elephant feet, or some great mammoth turned to stone. They are improbable landmarks, but they are merely two of the hundreds of rock formations you will see that show the random and artistic forces of erosion that formed this strange thrilling land.

★ NAVAJO NATIONAL MONUMENT

Though it's within the Navajo Reservation, beautiful **Tsegi Canyon,** an eroded pink-rock landscape carpeted with gray-green piñon pine and juniper forests, was once home to the Hisatsinom, ancestors of the Hopi. These Ancestral Puebloans are credited with building the three cliff-side villages in the canyon—some of the best-preserved and most awe-inspiring ruins in the Southwest. The Hopi, Navajo, Zuni, and Paiute peoples still consider this a sacred place, so only a few short hikes to promontories above the canyon are open to the public. If you want to explore the area more deeply, you can sign up to take guided hikes to two of the ruins with a park ranger.

Only the ruins of the village called **Betatakin** by the Navajo and Talastima by the Hopi are visible from the canyon rim,

tucked in a south-facing natural rock alcove that kept the village cool in the summer and warm in the winter; just below the village is a white-and-green aspen forest. Deeper in is **Keet Seel,** an older and larger village than Betatakin and one of the largest cliff dwellings in the Southwest. It's called Kawestima by the Hopi. **Inscription House,** or Tsu'ovi, is also perched in the canyon, but it has been closed to the public since the late 1960s.

Archaeologists believe that the Kayenta people (one of three Ancestral Puebloan subgroups, along with Chaco and Mesa Verde) lived in the canyon as early as AD 950, with major building projects getting under way around AD 1250. But by AD 1300, for reasons only guessed at, all the villages had been abandoned.

Visiting the Monument

The monument is 50 miles northeast of Tuba City and 30 miles southwest of Kayenta. Approaching from either direction on U.S. 160, take Indian Route 564 nine miles to the park entrance. Unlike most parks and monuments off the reservation, admission is free. The **visitors center** (928/672-2700, www. nps.gov/nava, 9am-5pm daily, free) has a gift shop that sells books, T-shirts, hats, and small water bottles, as well as an interesting museum featuring items used in everyday life by the Puebloans and found in their left-behind villages.

Hiking

Just outside the visitors center are three short hiking trails that provide optimum viewing of the canyon. The 1-mile round-trip **Sandal Trail** is paved and leads to an overlook for viewing the village of Betatakin/Talastima in its alcove. It's steep going back up; the hike should not be treated lightly just because it's short. Take water, especially in summer. The 0.8-mile round-trip **Aspen Forest Overlook** (easy but steep) descends vertical 300 feet to provide a good look at the forest below the village, but you can't see the ruins; the **Canyon View Trail** (easy) leads 0.6 mile round-trip to a nice view of the ruins near the Canyon View Campground. Allow 30-60 minutes for each hike.

If viewing Betatakin from the ridgetop isn't enough, you can sign up for a hike into the canyon to explore the ruins up close. The hike to Betatakin is five miles round-trip and takes three to five hours. A ranger guides you 700 vertical feet down into the canyon and then on to the ruins. It is mildly strenuous, but the outing is memorable for its scenery, not its difficulty. Two hikes are available daily May-September, leaving from the visitors center at 8:15am and 10am. The rest of the year, one hike leaves from the center at 10am daily. You must sign up beforehand with the rangers at the visitors center if you want to take the hike.

The trek to Keet Seel (which roughly translates to "shattered house") is more in-volved. One of the best-preserved ruins in the Southwest, Keet Seel was "discovered," for the Anglo world anyway, by the famous Southwestern ruin-hunter Richard Wetherill while he was chasing a runaway burro.

Reaching the ruins involves a 17-mile round-trip hike (moderate-strenuous) through the canyon bottomlands along a meandering stream—with several small wa-terfalls—that you have to cross dozens of times. You will get your feet wet early and often on this hike; there's no way to avoid it. Many hikers take along a sturdy pair of hik-ing sandals and change into them after de-scending 1,000 vertical feet into the canyon along a rock-hewn trail. When you arrive at the primitive campground within sight of the ruins, a volunteer ranger who lives in a hogan-shaped log cabin nearby will take you on an hour-long tour of the ruins, which you reach by climbing a steep ladder into a cliff-side rock alcove. They explain all about the people who once lived in this hidden canyon and usually show off a few astounding items found at the site from the everyday lives of the stone vil-lage's builders and residents. This is as close as you're likely to get to the ancients.

If you are a world-champion hiker, you could go in and out in the same day, but a stay overnight at the campground, with the ruins dark and mute just across the wash, is a memorable experience. There is no water at the campground, nor are fires allowed, but there is a compost toilet. You have to attend a short orientation meeting either the morning of your hike at 8am or the afternoon prior at 4pm. It's best to arrive the day before so you can get an early start. The best place to stay is at one of the chain hotels in Kayenta, a half-hour drive from the monument. Purchase and pack all your backpacking supplies before you arrive on the reservation, as there aren't any places to do so nearby.

Reservations and a backcountry permit are required for Keet Seel and are limited to 20 people per day. Call ahead for best results (928/672-2700). The hike is offered daily May-September, but after September 15 it's offered every second weekend of the month only.

Accommodations

Navajo National Monument (928/672-2700, www.nps.gov/nava) has two campgrounds, both free and first-come, first-served. The **Sunset View Campground** is open year-round and has 31 sites for tents and RVs up to 28 feet, with potable water but no hookups or dump stations. The **Canyon View Campground** is open April 1-November 1 and has 14 primitive tent sites with a compost-ing toilet, charcoal grills, and picnic tables.

Get supplies in either Tuba City or Kayenta before traveling to the monument for an overnight visit. The best hotel options are in Kayenta, 30 miles from the entrance to the monument.

KAYENTA AND VICINITY

Called *Tohdineeshzhee* (Water Going in Different Directions) by the Diné, Kayenta is the reservation town nearest to Monument Valley, 25 miles north, and is a good base for a visit to the northern reservation. John

1: Elephant Feet **2:** Navajo National Monument **3:** Blue Coffee Pot Restaurant in Kayenta **4:** The Three Sisters in Monument Valley Navajo Tribal Park

Wetherill, who, with his brother Richard, was one of the first Anglos to explore and exploit the Ancestral Puebloan ruins of Mesa Verde and Chaco Canyon, opened a trading post here in 1910. Today it's the only town on the reservation with a U.S.-style township government, home to 5,500 people.

Shopping

The Navajo Arts and Crafts Enterprise has a retail store at Kayenta (928/697-8611, www.gonavajo.com, 9am-7pm Mon.-Sat., noon-6pm Sun.) at the junction of U.S. 160 and U.S. 163. Operated by Navajo people, the company sells all kinds of local handmade arts and crafts, curios, rugs, silver jewelry, concha belts, bolo ties, pottery, and more.

Food and Accommodations

One of the best restaurants on the Navajo Nation, the ★ **Blue Coffee Pot Restaurant** (U.S. 160, 0.25 mile west of U.S. 163 junction, 928/697-3396, $4-12) in Kayenta serves outstanding home-style Navajo, American, and Mexican food in a hogan-shaped building just off U.S. 160. The Navajo taco is simply terrific, as are the beef ribs. The staff is friendly if a bit harried in this busy place.

The ★ **Amigo Café** (U.S. 163, 928/697-8448, www.amigocafekayenta.com, 10:30am-9pm Mon.-Fri., 8am-9pm Sat., $10-15) just north of the U.S. 160-U.S. 163 junction serves fantastic Mexican, Navajo, and American food and is popular with the locals. The **Burger King** (928/697-3534) on U.S. 160 (near the Hampton Inn) has the usual, with the added feature of a **Navajo Code Talkers** exhibit, which you can view as you chow down on your french fries.

Because it is so close to Monument Valley, there are several nice chain hotels in Kayenta, most of them along U.S. 160 as you enter town. The **Hampton Inn** (928/697-3170, $215-220) is very comfortable and offers Wi-Fi, a pool, a gift shop, a restaurant, and free continental breakfast. The **Wetherill Inn** (U.S. 163, 1000 Main St., 928/697-3231, www.wetherill-inn.com, $156) has comfortable

guest rooms, an indoor pool, Wi-Fi, a gift shop, and free breakfast.

Four Corners Monument

About 70 miles east of Kayenta on U.S. 160 is the **Four Corners Monument** (928/871-6647, 8am-5pm daily Sept.-May, 7am-8pm daily June-Aug., $5), the only place in the United States where, if you do a little bit of Twister-style contorting, you can briefly exist in four states at once—Arizona, Colorado, New Mexico, and Utah. You're not likely to stay long after you take the obligatory picture. In the summer months there are usually Navajo artisans and others selling crafts.

MONUMENT VALLEY NAVAJO TRIBAL PARK

The **scenic drive** north 22 miles from **Kayenta** along **U.S. 163** to **Monument Valley Navajo Tribal Park** (http://navajonationparks.org, $20 per car with up to 4 people) is almost as dramatic as the destination itself. About a third of the way along the paved route you'll see the aptly named **Owl Rock** to the west and the hulking jagged **Agathla Peak** to the east (also known as El Capitan), which tribal lore says marks the center of the world.

If there were any question that this is one of the most celebrated and enticing landscapes in the world, listen to the conversations around you as you visit Monument Valley—and you must visit Monument Valley, if only to know that all the images you've seen are real. Japanese, Chinese, Italian, German, British, and various Eastern European visitors gather at every lookout in this arid, dusty valley, looking for something distinctly Western, or American, in the iconic jutting red rocks.

It was the director John Ford who brought this strange remote place to the world and made it a stand-in for the West's dueling freedom and danger, most memorably in *The Searchers*. To drive around the park today is to enter a thousand Westerns, car commercials, magazine layouts, and road films, a landscape that's comfortably, beautifully familiar even if you're seeing it for the first time.

Thankfully the Navajo have not overdeveloped this sacred place—some would argue it's underdeveloped for its potential—so the only way to see the park without a Navajo guide is to drive the 17-mile unpaved **Valley Drive**, with pullouts for scenic views of the rock spires and lonely buttes. Entering the park you'll get a map of the drive with the name of each "monument"—names like Wetherill Mesa, John Ford's Point, and The Thumb. It's worth arriving an hour or so before sundown to see sunset over the valley—you'll stay until the light is gone. Be warned, though, that with the constant stream of cars driving the dry dirt road, the air tends to get dusty.

You're allowed to take photographs, but only of the natural wonders. Remember to ask permission before taking pictures of any Navajo people or their property.

Visitors Center

The park's **visitors center** (435/727-5874 or 435/727-5870, 7am-6pm daily Apr.-Sept., 8am-3pm daily Oct.-Mar.), perched on a promontory overlooking the valley and the dirt road that snakes through it and around the eroded-sandstone sculptures, is an obvious place to start your visit. There's a small museum with displays on Navajo culture and history, as well as the history of Hollywood's use of this iconic landscape, and a wall or two showing contemporary Navajo art. Staff can set you up with a guide if you want to go deeper into the valley and learn about the tribe's religious, cultural, and economic ties to it. There's a small patio outside the visitors center, right next to The View Hotel, restaurant, and trading post-gift shop, where you can sit and contemplate the natural art before you.

TOP EXPERIENCE

★ Monument Valley Scenic Drive

The best way to see the valley and its monuments on your own time is to head out into the hazy red lands via the 17-mile self-guided **Valley Drive** (6am-8pm daily Apr.-Sept., 8am-5pm daily Oct.-Mar., $20 per car with up to 4 people). The route is all dirt and a bit rough in spots. It has 11 pullouts for longer views of some of the more famous mesas, buttes, and spires. At many of these numbered stops, which otherwise have no services, you'll find Navajo families selling jewelry and souvenirs. Plan to spend at least two hours exploring the valley. If dust bothers you, so too will the Valley Drive, but try not to let that stop you: This is one of the most scenic, inspirational, and absolutely essential drives in the Southwest. Take water and food, and check your tires before you head out. The roughest part of the drive is at the start, going down a steep hill into the valley, but the rest is easy and flat. Don't follow too close behind other cars; you'll be buried in red dust. Motorcycles and RVs are not allowed on the Valley Drive.

The road into the valley starts just past the visitors center parking lot and has two lanes until Camel Butte, where it becomes a one-way loop around **Rain God Mesa.** The first stop, just as you enter the valley, provides a classic much-photographed view of the "mittens," **West Mitten Butte** and **East Mitten Butte,** named because of the spires that rise from the side of each butte to form what looks like a hand in a mitten. Just a short way up the road is **Merrick Butte,** named, according to Richard Klinck in his classic history of the valley, *Land of Room Enough and Time Enough,* for James Merrick, a soldier turned prospector who was killed near the butte for trespassing on a Navajo silver mine. The huge mesa opposite Merrick Butte is called **Mitchell Mesa.** It is said that Ernest Mitchell, Merrick's partner in trespass and violent death, died at its base.

The second stop on the drive, **Elephant Butte,** is supposed to look like the titular pachyderm. The third and fourth numbered stops, **The Three Sisters** and **John Ford's Point,** are two of the best. The sisters are side-by-side spires on the edge of Mitchell Mesa, and the point is named for the famous director who revealed this valley to the world through his Westerns. The fifth stop is **Camel Butte,** named for the stone-frozen ungulate that it resembles. Just a bit up the road from the fifth stop, a ramshackle hut and corral provides horseback tours of the backcountry (30-minute to 6-hour tours, $45-165, credit cards accepted). You can also stop and take pictures of the horses, but make sure to ask first, and be prepared to pay $5.

The sixth numbered stop on the drive provides a view of the formation called The Hub, which looks somewhat like the center of a wagon wheel, and of huge Rain God Mesa, marking the center of the valley. Here the road turns to loop around Rain God Mesa, with pullouts near Thunderbird Mesa (No. 7) and the edge of Spearhead Mesa (No. 8), from which you can see red sand dunes and, far off in the valley beyond the road, the impossibly delicate spire called the Totem Pole, which rises next to a gathering of thicker spires the Navajo call Yei Bi Chei ("dancers emerging from a hogan"). The ninth stop is at the far tip of Spearhead Mesa, where there's a short easy trail to Artist Point Overlook. The view is spectacular, and it's easy to see how the promontory got its name. Continuing on around the other side of Rain God Mesa, you'll see Cly Butte, at the base of which is buried "Old Cly," a beloved Navajo medicine man who died in 1934. Take a short side road up to the 10th stop, the North Window Overlook, which provides a breathtaking view of the valley's northern section. Return to the loop, which ends at Camel Butte, behind which rises a spire called The Thumb (No. 11). Then it's back to the visitors center along the two-lane route from Camel Butte. You'll pass the same monuments on the way back, and you can stop again.

Hiking

The only hiking you can do in Monument Valley without a Navajo guide is along Wildcat Trail, a 3.2-mile loop trail around West Mitten Butte. It's an easy quiet walk along a red-dirt path among gray-green scrub and sagebrush, with the spires and buttes looming close and lizards whipping over red

rocks. The trail starts 0.4 mile north of the visitors center. It's easy enough for kids, but there's no shade, and it can get windy. Take water with you, and plan on being out for two hours or more.

Tours

As impressive as the buttes and jutting rock castles along the main road around the valley are, they are but a small sampling; many more hulking, crumbling buttes, as well as wondrous arches, delicate spires, petroglyphs, and traditional Navajo homesteads, are scattered throughout this vast, remote land, accessible only with a Navajo guide at your side. Be sure to make reservations at least a week in advance.

There is no shortage of Navajo guides, and you can easily hire one inside the park at the visitors center. Also, the Navajo Parks and Recreation Department has a list of reputable Navajo-owned guide companies on its website (www.navajonationparks.org). Prices vary slightly among the different companies, but generally expect to pay about $50 for a 1.5-hour ride in an open Jeep around the main road, and $115-165 for an all-day backcountry immersion tour. You have to book a 2.5-hour tour or longer (generally around $75 pp) to go anywhere you can't go on your own. The View Hotel in Monument Valley also has a list of reputable guides on its website (http://monumentvalleyview.com/navajo-guided-tours).

Serious photographers should consider booking a guide, lest they return home with images not considerably different from those snapped by a cell phone. Guide Tom J. Phillips of Keya-Hozhoni Tours (928/429-0665, 928/429-0040, or 928/429-0042, www.monumentvalley.com, 3.5 hours, $125), which also offers regular Jeep and horseback tours, charges $30 an hour to show photographers the best shots outside the usual places.

Food and Accommodations

For all its fame, Monument Valley is still a considerably remote place, and there aren't a lot of services. Don't come hungry; eat in Kayenta before you head out, or bring your own food. That's not to say that there's nothing to eat at all. The View Restaurant (435/727-3468, www.monumentvalleyview. com, 7am-2pm and 5pm-8pm daily, $10-25) inside the park has decent Navajo, Mexican, and American food for breakfast, lunch, and dinner. Between meals there are only packaged sandwiches, fruit, and snacks available. At the junction of U.S. 163 and the park entrance road, there's a small shopping center where you can get snacks and fry bread, and a few gift shops sell local crafts and curios.

When the Navajo Nation developed The View Hotel (435/727-5555, www. monumentvalleyview.com, from $249), the only in-park noncamping accommodations at Monument Valley, they could have thrown up a few trailers and a kiddy pool and charged $100 per night; the location alone is the attraction, and everything else just gets in the way. But they didn't do that, thankfully. The View is instead a complement to the landscape, a low and tucked-away line of guest rooms near the Mitten Buttes, with patios facing east over the valley where the sun comes alive in the morning. The color of the hotel merges with the buttes, monuments, and vast red dunes, making it appear inevitable. Guest rooms are comfortable and decorated in generic Southwestern style. It's the view that you're paying for, and you will pay a lot, if you can get a reservation. There are no cheap rooms, especially during the spring-summer high season. The hotel also rents out cabins (sleeps 4, $199) with their own amazing views near the Wildcat Trail. These are a good option for families and groups.

CAMPING

The View Campground (435/727-5802, www.monumentvalleyview.com, $20 tent sites, $40 RV sites) is open year-round with separate RV and tent sites. Each site has a table, a grill, a ramada, and a trash can, and there are restrooms and coin-operated showers. No hookups are available, but a dump station is open during summer. Check in at the visitors center to get a campsite.

GOULDING'S LODGE

This compound just outside the park features a hotel with luxury amenities, a campground, a museum, and a trading post selling Navajo crafts. It retains the name of the first trader to settle in the valley, Harry Goulding, who opened a trading post here in 1928, exchanging staples for Navajo jewelry and rugs. The story goes that in the late 1930s Goulding himself went to Hollywood to convince John Ford to come to Monument Valley to film *Stagecoach*.

Goulding's Lodge (1000 Goulding Trading Post Rd., 866/313-9769, www. gouldings.com, $175-250) has 62 guest rooms and eight family-friendly multiroom suites with kitchenettes. There's an indoor heated swimming pool, an exercise room, Wi-Fi, and satellite TV. The Stagecoach Dining Room ($14-17) serves American and Navajo food (lamb stew, Navajo tacos, fry bread) for breakfast, lunch, and dinner. The well-equipped Goulding's Campground (435/359-0047, www.gouldings.com) offers tent sites ($19) and RV sites with full hookups ($48). There's also a convenience store, a gas station, a coin laundry, a car wash, and an indoor pool at the campground.

Goulding's offers various tours of the monument with Navajo guides (2.5 hours, about $79 pp).

MEXICAN HAT, UTAH

This very small town on the San Juan River is just 27 miles north of Monument Valley along U.S. 163, about 40 minutes from the tribal park. As such, Mexican Hat, named for a precariously balanced rock near town that looks like a sombrero, is an excellent place to base your visit, especially if you are approaching from the north or the east rather than from Phoenix. Another advantage of Mexican Hat is that it lacks the Navajo Reservation's prohibition on alcohol. The tiny conglomerate of buildings stretches along U.S. 163 near the

San Juan River for a mile or so, and there really isn't much to it. There are, however, a few places to stay and to eat, and a few scenic sites to whet your appetite for a tour of those red sandstone monuments just to the south.

The vista at **Goosenecks State Park,** eight miles or 15 minutes north of Mexican Hat, provides a jaw-dropping, head-scratching look at the San Juan River wrapping around large buttes from 1,000 feet above. The park is nothing more than the vista and has no services save for restrooms. Take U.S. 163 east from the town, turn left on UT 261 and then left on UT 316, following the signs. Along U.S. 163, look for the eponymous rock wearing a sombrero off to the east.

Another place near Mexican Hat worth a visit is the remote **Valley of the Gods,** a kind of lesser Monument Valley. You can drive through the valley and view its buttes and mesas along a 17-mile dirt road, which is a bit rough but safe for most passenger cars. There are no services, so bring your own water and food, and make sure you have enough gas. There is a gas station in Mexican Hat along U.S. 163. From Mexican Hat, take U.S. 163 east of town eight miles to Valley of the Gods Road and turn left; it's another five miles from there.

Food and Accommodations

The few accommodations in Mexican Hat are generally less expensive than the chain hotels in Kayenta and are much less expensive than The View Hotel in Monument Valley. Moreover, a few restaurants here serve alcohol, which is prohibited on the reservation.

The ★ **San Juan Inn and Trading Post** (U.S. 163 at the San Juan River, 800/447-2022, www.sanjuaninn.net, $130-145) is on the banks of the beautiful San Juan River and next to a picturesque bridge. Offering basic guest rooms with air-conditioning, TV, and free but spotty Wi-Fi, this is the best place to stay near Monument Valley for the money. It's

in a quiet and relaxing setting, with red cliffs hovering above the bushy green riverbank and the river rolling by; there are always a few other explorers around to talk to. The inn also rents out well-appointed yurts ($110) on a different property nearby. A few steps from the inn, The **Olde Bridge Bar & Grill** (2256 U.S. 163, 435/683-2322, 7am-9pm daily, $5-20), serves a big filling breakfast, tasty Mexican food, Navajo tacos, burgers, and all the other grill-style mainstays, plus a few vegetarian options. It also has a full bar and pool.

The **Mexican Hat Lodge** (U.S. 163, across from the Shell gas station, 435/683-2222, www.mexicanhatlodge.com, $98-134) has comfortable clean guest rooms with TVs and minifridges in most. The fun, laid-back, friendly vibe is more akin to a bed-and-breakfast than a regular motel. They offer free Wi-Fi, an indoor pool, and a hot tub outside. The restaurant is called **The Swinging Steak** (5pm-9pm daily Apr.-Sept., $13-40), with a pleasant patio where you can watch your steak being cooked over a swinging grill. It serves wine and beer, but it's the low-alcohol Utah variety.

CHINLE AND VICINITY

Like most town names on the arid Navajo Reservation, Ch'inlih refers to moisture, in this case "Water Flowing." There isn't much for travelers save a few chain hotels and the gateway to Canyon de Chelly. Chinle has been a center for canyon visitors since the early 20th century, when the famous trader Lorenzo Hubbell operated a stagecoach from the train stop at Gallup to bring tourists to see the ancient cliff dwellings and the other wonders of the canyon.

Food and Accommodations

Chinle is the best place to base a multiday visit to Canyon de Chelly National Monument. The town is not much to look at, but it does have two comfortable long-established chain hotels, both with good restaurants: **Best Western Canyon de Chelly** (100 Mina St., 928/674-5875, www.canyondechelly.

1: horses for Monument Valley backcountry tours 2: the rock that gave Mexican Hat its name 3: view from Spider Rock Overlook at Canyon de Chelly 4: Canyon de Chelly National Monument

com, $66-109) and Holiday Inn Canyon de Chelly (Indian Rte. 7, 928/674-5000, www. holiday-inn.com, $113-165).

Near the visitors center on Canyon de Chelly National Monument, ★ Thunderbird Lodge (Indian Rte. 7, 3.5 miles east of U.S. 191, 928/671-5841, http://thunderbirdlodge. com, $90-120) is the only hotel within the monument and feels faraway and rural with its grassy, shady grounds. The basic but comfortable guest rooms come with free Wi-Fi, fridges, and TVs. There's a decent cafeteria-style restaurant and a trading post-gift shop where you can book tours of the canyon.

Also at the monument is the free, first-come, first-served Cottonwood Campground, open year-round, with running water and flush toilets in summer only. For more information, contact the Navajo Parks and Recreation Department (928/674-2106).

★ CANYON DE CHELLY NATIONAL MONUMENT

The most visually impressive wind- and water-worn canyon in Arizona save for the one they call Grand, Canyon de Chelly (de-SHAY; the name is a Spanish approximation of the Navajo word for canyon, *tsegi*) is a labyrinth of eroded sandstone mesas, buttes, and spires, washed in pink and red and varnished with black and purple. The canyon's fertile bottomlands and safe hidden alcoves, seemingly designed to host stone cliff dwellings, have drawn people for 4,000 years. The greatest among the Southwest's ancients, the Ancestral Puebloans, built several hanging villages against the red-rock cliffs, the remains of which are still slowly crumbling in their shady alcoves.

The most beautiful, essential, intact, and wonderfully preserved ruins in the canyon is the amazing White House Ruin, which hangs above the canyon's sandy bottom and can be reached only via a 2.5-mile out-and-back hike. It's the only ruins that you can view unaccompanied by a Navajo guide.

About 40 Navajo families call the canyon and its rim home. You'll pass some of their homesites and hogans as you drive the two scenic roads along the rim. Free-roaming horses graze on the grasses and weeds along the sides of the road; they will generally ignore you until you get out of your car for a photo, when they will promptly turn and trot away. The federal monument comprises 84,000 acres of the canyon, but as with the other federal parks on the reservation, the Navajos' interests trump all others. Nearly all of the canyon is off-limits without a hired Navajo guide.

Visitors Center

Near Chinle, the visitors center (928/674-5500, www.nps.gov/cach, 8am-5pm daily, free) is a good place to start your visit. You can find out about guided tours (a ranger will give you a long list if you ask), learn about the history and science of the canyon, and browse a small bookstore well stocked with volumes on the Southwest and the Colorado Plateau. A free map of the park's scenic drives is available.

Hiking

The short but steep White House Ruin Trail (2.5 miles round-trip), a skinny trail hewn out of petrified pink sand dunes leading down to the White House Ruin, is the only route to the sandy, shady canyon bottomlands that's open to the public without a Navajo guide, and it is one of the highlights of a visit to Indian Country. The trail offers a rare chance to see Ancestral Puebloan ruins up close and on your own. Once on the canyon bottom, you pass a traditional Navajo hogan and farm, and the canyon walls, streaked with purple, black, and orange, rise hundreds of feet above. Hawks and ravens circle overhead as brown and black dots high in the bright blue sky. Cave-like hideouts built by natural forces in sandstone alcoves offer rest in their cool shade. Cottonwoods, willows, and peach trees grow in the bottomlands, while piñon pine, juniper, scrub oak, cholla, and prickly pear cling to the sides of the precipitous trail, dusty green against the reddish-pink of the de Chelly sandstone. Although you can take two scenic drives to see all the canyon's wonders, there is no substitute for hiking in. Pick up the trailhead at the White House Overlook, the fourth signed stop along the South Rim Drive, about six miles from the visitors center.

The hike is easy going down and moderate going back up, as it is steep in a few places. Allow half a day for the round-trip hike and exploring the bottomlands.

If you're on the hunt for Navajo arts, take cash with you on the hike; there are often artists sitting beneath the shady trees near the White House Ruin, offering their creations for sale.

Scenic Drives

Two paved scenic rim-side drives offer the most comprehensive look at Canyon de Chelly without hiring a guide. The visitors center has a free map of the easy drives, and both can be done in a regular car. The 37-mile round-trip South Rim Drive will take you to the Spider Rock Overlook, where you can see the eponymous 800-foot red-rock spire, a must-see on any visit to the canyon. The south drive has seven overlooks, while the 34-mile round-trip North Rim Drive has three: Antelope House Ruin, Mummy Cave Overlook, and Massacre Cave Overlook, each with a view of ruins. Many of the lookouts are at the end of a short but relatively strenuous hike, and most have no barriers between you and the edge.

Tours

You need a Navajo guide with you to travel deep into the canyon, and there are many available for hire throughout the year. Expect to pay $50-60 per hour for 1-3 people for a private Jeep tour along the canyon bottom to some of the out-of-the-way ruins, caves, and rock-art sites.

Canyon de Chelly (Unimoq) Tours (Chinle, 928/349-1391 or 928/349-1600, http://canyondechellytours.com, $75 pp) offers a three-hour group tour in a big 4WD vehicle

(you ride with 10 other passengers in the open bed). The tour takes you from Antelope House Ruin to White House Ruin.

Antelope House Tours (Chinle, 928/674-5231, www.canyondechelly.net) offers three-hour Jeep tours of all the ruins ($165 for 3 people) and three-hour hiking tours ($99 for 3 people) with guides versed in the lore and culture of the Navajo and the other peoples that lived in this spectacular place before them. Call ahead for reservations.

Tsalie and Diné College

At the end of the scenic drive along the Canyon de Chelly's north rim (Indian Rte. 64), past the last established lookout, you'll come to Diné College, a Navajo-run junior college that has been educating tribal members and preserving tribal traditions since 1968. The circular hogan-shaped campus is designed to reflect traditional Navajo philosophy. The Ned Hatathli Museum and Gallery (Diné College Tsalie campus, 1 Circle Dr./Indian Rte. 12, 928/724-6600, 8am-5pm Mon.-Fri., closed for lunch, free) is housed in a six-story glass Hogan and displays historic tribal artifacts and contemporary Navajo arts and crafts.

HUBBELL TRADING POST NATIONAL HISTORIC SITE

When you walk into the rustic building in Ganado that has housed the Hubbell Trading Post (928/755-3475, www.nps.gov/hutr, 8am-6pm daily summer, 8am-5pm daily winter, free, Hubbell Home Tour $2 over age 16) since 1876, you expect to enter a museum or a typical visitors center. Instead, you enter the "bull pen," a working trading post that looks much like it did 100 years ago, still selling jewelry, rugs, and staples and still an important commercial spot to the Diné. The area has a fascinating history, and this is the best place to learn about the impact Anglo traders—J. L. Hubbell and his family the most famous and beloved among them—had on Navajo lifeways and the reservation economy.

You can tour the homestead with a ranger or with a self-guided tour book and enter the Hubbell Home, laden with Navajo rugs, old books, and original paintings by the famous artist E. A. Burbank. There's also a small museum and bookstore operated by the National Park Service.

WINDOW ROCK

Window Rock, the capital of the Navajo Nation, is a lot like the other population centers on the Navajo Reservation: small, utilitarian, and surrounded by scenery that dwarfs the buildings. The town of 4,000 is on the Arizona-New Mexico border, just 27 miles northwest of Gallup, New Mexico (pop. 25,000), a large city by the standards of this remote corner of the world. At 8,000 feet elevation, Window Rock has a cooler climate than the lower western part of the Navajo Nation, and in winter the ponderosa pine and piñon-juniper forests that decorate the artfully eroded sandstone buttes and spires around the town are often dusted with a thin layer of snow.

It's a long drive from Phoenix (300 mi), Tucson (355 mi), or the Grand Canyon (234 mi), but it is a scenic trip and a must for anyone interested in what the Navajo Nation is all about. It has the best museum on the reservation in the Navajo Nation Museum and is a fun stop for families with small kids for its free zoo featuring the reservation's most famous and prevalent creatures.

Sights

The famous **Window Rock** that gives the town its name—a 200-foot-high red sandstone monument with an unlikely 47-foot-diameter erosion-chipped hole in it (called *Tseghahodzani* by the Navajo, roughly translating to "the rock with the hole in it")—is at the **Window Rock Navajo Tribal Park,** a short drive north on Indian Route 12 from its intersection with AZ 264. It stares down like an oracle. You can't climb it, but it is a ready-made photograph: pink-red and towering against the bright blue sky with

gnarled deep-green junipers and piñons and little yellow wildflowers stretched out in front. There's also an evocative statue of a Navajo soldier kneeling with a radio to his ear and a look of serious intensity on his face. It is the centerpiece of a **memorial to the Navajo Code Talkers** of World War II and is instantly recognizable as a depiction of those celebrated men.

Window Rock has been the center of Navajo Nation government since the 1930s, when the Civilian Conservation Corps built the rough-hewn but stylish native-stone and pinewood **Navajo Nation Council Chambers** and its surrounding buildings, which sit in the shadow of the one-eyed red rock and are used intermittently when the council is in session.

About three miles west of Window Rock in St. Michaels, a small town along AZ 264, you'll see the **St. Michael's Mission,** a Franciscan mission established in 1896 by Saint Katharine Drexel. The **St. Michael's Historical Museum** (3 mi. west of Window Rock on AZ 264, 928/871-4171, 9am-5pm Mon.-Fri. Memorial Day-Labor Day) on the mission grounds has an interesting small museum about Navajo and Catholic interactions and the history of the mission.

NAVAJO NATION MUSEUM

The tribal members could charge for a look around the sleek and informative **Navajo Nation Museum** (AZ 264 and Loop Rd., 928/871-7941, http://navajopeople.org, 10am-5pm Mon.-Sat., free), but instead they let everybody in for free. That's just the first of many surprises. Another is that there is plenty of space dedicated to contemporary reservation life—a subject that many visitors tend to overlook in favor of the romantic story-filled past. The museum's art gallery hosts revolving shows featuring Navajo artists and photographers, and throughout the museum are examples of silverwork and weaving by many living artists. The museum reaches into the past to tell the story of the harrowing Long Walk and the tribe's near fatal exile at Fort Sumner in the 1860s, showing actual artifacts and ephemera related to the events that help make the traumas suffered seem recent, as they still are from the Navajo perspective. There is also a fascinating display that explains the traditional Navajo way of life.

This is the best museum on the reservation, and it should be visited by anyone with an interest in the Navajo Nation. Even if you have no interest before entering, it's likely that you will upon exiting. Just outside the museum's front entrance, there's a traditional hogan that you are allowed to enter and examine up close; it's surprising how cool it is inside, even at the height of summer.

NAVAJO NATION ZOOLOGICAL AND BOTANICAL PARK

Tall, fat cylinders of beige-colored sandstone stand just to the north of the museum. They are called, for reasons obvious when you see them, **The Haystacks.** These photo-worthy monoliths watch over a tiny zoo run by the tribe. The **Navajo Nation Zoological and Botanical Park** (AZ 264 and Loop Rd., 928/871-6574, www.navajozoo.org, 10am-4:30pm Mon.-Sat., free) houses examples of many of the animals that share these wild open lands with the Navajos. Most occupy a sacred place in the traditional Navajo belief system. A short easy trail leads around a small open area overlooked by the Haystacks, past fenced-in habitats with raccoons, bobcats, a cougar, a black bear, prairie dogs, and other common Colorado Plateau wildlife. Along the trail are interpretive signs naming the animals and various native plants and explaining their presence and use in traditional Navajo life. You really get up close to the often playful animals, and the kids will love it here. The zoo is a short walk across from the entrance to the museum.

Events

The population of Window Rock swells every year in early September as the **Navajo Nation Fair** (http://navajopeople.org, $5-12)

brings Navajos and others to one of the largest Native American cultural fairs anywhere. The weeklong event features a rodeo; horticulture contests; pageants for babies, teens, and Miss Navajo; a parade; a midway and carnival; native foods; arts and crafts; drumming; dancing; and myriad other events. Don't count on getting a hotel room in town, or even in nearby Gallup, New Mexico, unless you book far ahead of the fair.

Shopping

The headquarters of the **Navajo Arts and Crafts Enterprises** (928/871-4090, 9am-5pm Mon.-Fri.) and a well-stocked outlet are east of the junction of AZ 264 and Indian Route 12, just across from the Quality Inn, as is the **Chi Hoo Tso Indian Market** (928/871-5443, hours vary by vendor), where there's a flea market on the weekends.

Food and Accommodations

The **Quality Inn Navajo Nation Capital** (48 W. AZ 264, 928/871-4108, $83-111) offers Wi-Fi and a full breakfast. It has comfortable guest rooms decorated in generic Southwestern style, and the staff is very friendly and helpful. This is definitely the best place to stay in town. The on-site **Diné Restaurant** (928/871-4108, $10-14) serves American and Navajo food for breakfast, lunch, and dinner and is a popular spot with the locals. Guests of the inn get access to the breakfast buffet at no additional cost, but the price is its most attractive feature.

Some visitors choose to stay in nearby Gallup, New Mexico, 27 miles to the southeast, an I-40 stop with loads of hotels and restaurants.

INFORMATION AND SERVICES

Contact the **Navajo Tourism Department** (P.O. Box 663, Window Rock, AZ 86515, 928/810-8501, www.discovernavajo.com) for advice and information about traveling in this region.

The **Navajo Area Indian Health**

Service (AZ 264 and St. Michael Rd., St. Michael, 928/871-4811, www.ihs.gov) operates six hospitals on the vast Navajo Reservation. In Arizona, the Fort Defiance Indian Hospital (928/729-8000), eight miles north of Window Rock on the eastern reservation, has a 24-hour Level 2 emergency room; on the western reservation, the Kayenta Health Center (928/697-4000), in Kayenta, has the same.

Hopi Villages

When you visit Hopi, you step out of normal time into a kind of sacred time in which the Hisatsinom still speak to their modern-day descendants, the "People of Peace," and the lessons and stories of the ancients still guide and rule life in the 21st century, the dawning of which has mostly been ignored around Hopi.

Go to Hopi if you want to have a quiet spiritual experience touring crumbling villages occupied for centuries, interacting with the friendly and creative people whose direct and well-remembered ancestors built and lived in most of the spectacular Pueblo ruins around Indian Country, and searching for artistic treasures built on patterns and narratives laid down before time began.

The Hopi do not allow any photography, sketching, or recording in the villages, and they don't like it when you enter their villages without first asking a village leader or at least someone at a crafts store or gallery. Talk to the folks at the Hopi Cultural Center on Second Mesa or the Moenkopi Legacy Inn & Suites in Moenkopi if you have any questions about the rules. Be respectful, and remember, as it is with the Navajos, the Hopi people are living their lives, not participating in an anthropological experiment. Don't bring any drugs or alcohol onto the reservation, and don't take any pottery shards off it.

Many Hopi live on three remote mesas on the southern tip of Black Mesa, a separate reservation carved out of the southwest portion of the Navajo Nation. There are 10 villages on the mesas, which are numbered east to west.

You can drive up and over the mesas and enter many of the villages, but this is not ideal, and not a very interesting way to visit Hopi. Without a bit of historical and cultural context, many of the mesa villages simply look like rundown rural outposts. But with a guide, a whole ancient hidden world that exists beneath the rather hardscrabble surface opens up, and the mesas become sacred mysterious ground.

TOURS

It's essential to call ahead to book a tour. The Hopi religious calendar is rather full, and often one village or another will close to outsiders for days at a time. Weather on the remote mesas can also cancel tours. The best place to book a tour is through the Moenkopi Legacy Inn & Suites (U.S. 160 and AZ 264, Tuba City, 928/283-4500, www.experiencehopi.com) or the Hopi Cultural Center (928/734-2401, www.hopiculturalcenter.com, 8am-5pm daily) on Second Mesa. The Moenkopi Legacy Inn's website has a comprehensive list of approved guides and their prices.

Left-Handed Hunter Tour Company (Second Mesa, 928/734-2567, $120-195 pp for 4-8 hours) offers exceedingly informative and memorable tours of the Taawaki Petroglyph Site, Moenkopi, Old Oraibi, Hotevilla, Bacavi, Kykotsmovi, Sipaulovi, and Musangnuvi, as well as visits with local artists. The Moenkopi Legacy Inn offers a highlight-filled Experience Hopi Tour

1: Coal Mine Canyon 2: Moenkopi Legacy Inn & Suites

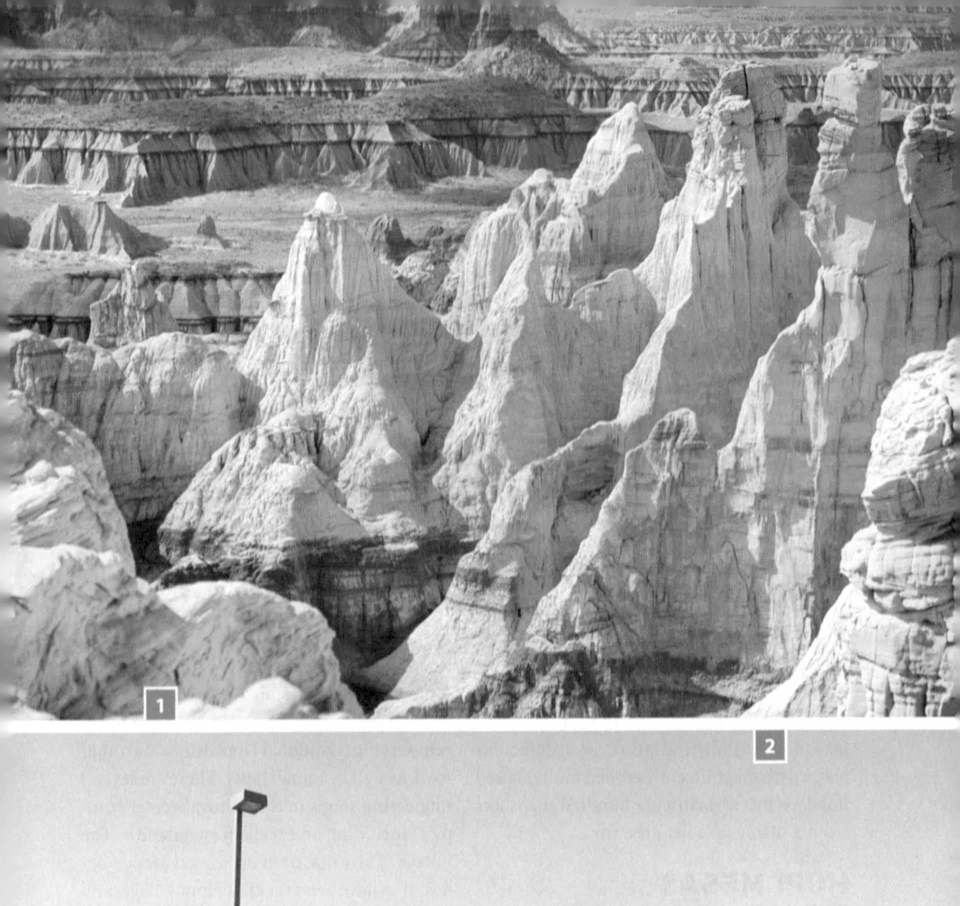
1

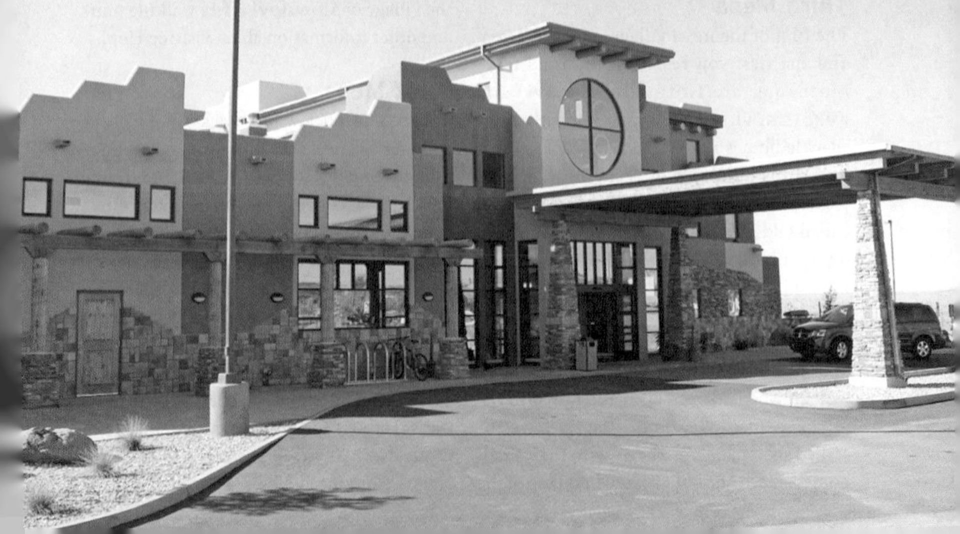
2

(www.experiencehopi.com/tours, $145 pp), which includes a comprehensive exploration of the land, people, history, and art of the Hopi, plus lunch at the Hopi Cultural Center. A guide picks you up at the hotel in the morning and brings you back in the late afternoon.

MOENKOPI

The **Moenkopi Legacy Inn & Suites** (U.S. 160 and AZ 264, Tuba City, 928/283-4500, www.experiencehopi.com, $152) in the Upper Village of Moenkopi near Tuba City, has become the gateway to visiting Hopi. The all-Hopi staff at this gorgeous hotel and visitors center can help you book a guide to take you on an unforgettable tour of the Hopi mesas.

Using Moenkopi as the gateway, it makes sense to start any tour of Hopi from the west and head east along AZ 264, which will take you to each of the mesas. From Moenkopi, Third Mesa is 45 miles, Second Mesa is 62 miles, and First Mesa is 70 miles.

About 15 miles from Moenkopi along AZ 264, look for milepost 336 and a dirt road that leads to **Coal Mine Canyon,** a spectacular gorge with magnificently eroded multicolored hoodoos that's worth a few hundred snapshots from a sitting area near the rim.

HOPI MESAS

Third Mesa

The first of the mesa villages along AZ 264, and the first you reach on the road from Moenkopi, are **Hotevilla, Bacavi,** and **Kykotsmovi.** All are a mix of mostly ramshackle homes next to ancient stacked-rock half-ruins hundreds of years old. The best place to stop on Third Mesa is **Oraibi,** also called Old Oraibi. Twenty-four families still live in the village, which sits at the edge of the mesa and looks out over the hazy flatland sea below. There's no electricity and no running water. "Our elders want no webbing above us and nothing buried in the ground," a Hopi woman who had been born and raised in the village explained. Some villagers have installed solar panels on the roofs of their small homes—each one built next to or on top of the

ruins of an older one—to bring a little modern comfort. There are several kivas in the village that look exactly like those in the Hisatsinom ruins, with their rough ladders sticking out of their trapdoor entrances, except these are still in use. A walk around this village, in which people have made lives since at least AD 1100, is a strangely humbling experience. You may come away from it wondering why most of us think we need so much stuff to live that elusive good life.

★ Second Mesa

The **Hopi Cultural Center** (928/734-2401, www.hopiculturalcenter.com, 8am-5pm daily) on Second Mesa has a small museum ($3) featuring blown-up photographs of Hopi taken in the 19th and early 20th centuries and displays on Hopi culture as well as many artifacts from around the mesas. It provides one of the few stops along the road through Hopi that can be enjoyed without a guide. The museum is an essential stop for anyone interested in Hopi culture. The center also has a restaurant serving traditional Hopi dishes and other food, as well as a small hotel. There are several interesting shops in the cultural center complex, including an excellent silversmith. The village of **Shongopavi** on Second Mesa is believed to have been the first Hopi village, and the village of **Sipaulovi** offers walking tours and other information about visiting Hopi.

First Mesa

Polacca, just below First Mesa, is one of the younger villages on Hopi, founded in 1890. There are many Hopi and Tewa potters living in Polacca. If you're interested in buying direct from the artists, keep a lookout for handmade signs outside of homes.

Next you'll come to **Hano,** founded in 1680 after the Pueblo Revolt by Tewa people from New Mexico. The Hopi said the fleeing Tewas could stay in exchange for their vigilance in keeping enemies and attackers off the mesa trails. Hano is the home of the famous Tewa potter **Nampeyo;** in the early 1900s, Fred Harvey convinced Nampeyo to move to the

Grand Canyon to demonstrate pottery making for tourists, creating a kind of living diorama at the famous Mary Colter-designed Hopi House. The area is still a center of pottery making, and artists directly related to Nampeyo—who is credited, even as a Tewa, with beginning a renaissance in Hopi pottery and thus creating a major modern art form and economy—still reside and work here, selling pottery out of their homes.

Just above Hano is **Sichomovi,** founded in 1750 by citizens of **Walpi.** This village has running water and electricity, unlike Walpi, a traditional village at the edge of the mesa founded in the 1600s when villagers moved up the mesa from their village below to escape the predations of their neighbors.

Walpi Guided Walking Tour

If you have time for just one tour, make it of **Walpi,** a traditional Hopi village where the old ways live on. You will meet several Hopi artists on the tour of Walpi, sitting on the steps in front of their rock-carved homes, carving kachina dolls from cottonwood root. The people here are remarkably friendly—everybody says hello and smiles, welcoming visitors and inviting you into their homes to show you their art. If you are at all interested in Hopi art, this is the place to buy it. Not only will the price be significantly less than at a museum store or trading post, but you'll also get to meet the artist—and maybe even watch the final stages of creation. Take cash with you. Your Hopi tour guide will take you on a slow walk around the clifftop village, a time warp on the edge of the world. You'll learn all about the traditions and history, both temporal and spiritual, of this ancient place. It's a fascinating and memorable experience. The tour takes about an hour, but you can stay around after and talk to the artists and others.

You should book a tour a day in advance if you can, and don't be surprised if the village is closed due to weather or for religious reasons. Tours run through **First Mesa Consolidated Village Office** (928/737-2670, 8am-4:30pm daily summer, 9am-3pm daily winter, last tour at 2pm daily winter, 8am-4:30pm daily summer, $20 adults, $10 under age 18), in Polacca, 71 miles from Moenkopi at the base of First Mesa, where you must stop and check in before heading up to Walpi. Take AZ 264 west to mile marker 390.8, turn north at the stop sign, and go 0.25 mile to the office, which is next to the post office.

Shopping

The Hopi are world renowned for their pottery, baskets, overlay jewelry, and kachina dolls. There are dozens of artists on the Hopi Reservation making and selling collectible, museum-quality crafts for much less than you are likely to pay in a museum store or trading post. Look for homemade signs advertising crafts for sale at homes in most villages, and take lots of cash with you.

In recent years many Hopi artists have banded together to form the **Hopi Arts Trail** (www.hopiartstrail.com), a marketing campaign that has made it easier than ever to meet and buy art from Hopi artists living on and below the mesas. A free pamphlet guide to the trail is available online or at the Moenkopi Legacy Inn. The guide features eight galleries spread around Hopi in 12 villages along AZ 264 and lists the name, phone number, and specialty of 18 different Hopi artists. An artist will typically invite you into their home, where you can view the work and learn about the process.

Another great way to meet artists on Hopi is by taking the **Walpi Guided Walking Tour** on First Mesa.

PRACTICALITIES

There are few services on Hopi, but it isn't far from any of the Navajo towns, and it's close to the high-desert towns as well.

The **Moenkopi Legacy Inn & Suites** (U.S. 160 and AZ 264, Tuba City, 928/283-4500, www.experiencehopi.com, $152), in the Upper Village of Moenkopi near Tuba City, set a new standard for accommodations on Hopi when it opened in 2010. It has luxury guest rooms with big comfortable beds, tastefully decorated with photographs of Hopi and with a patio door that opens to a heated saltwater pool and spa. There is a small eating area where continental breakfast is served, and a café at the gas station across the street (also operated by the Hopi) that serves dinerstyle fare and some Hopi dishes. Each room has free Wi-Fi and a flat-screen TV, and there are some excellent examples of Hopi arts in the beautiful lobby. This is the best hotel in Indian Country for the price.

The **Hopi Cultural Center** on Second Mesa is a hotel (Mar.-Oct., $115-120) and restaurant (6am-9pm daily, $5-12) that serves American diner- and grill-style favorites along with must-try traditional Hopi dishes such as Hopi hot beef, Hopi tacos, blue corn mush, and lamb stew. The **Hotevilla Village Co-Op Store** (928/734-2350) on Third Mesa has a convenience store with a gas station, and **The Kykotsmovi Village Store** (928/734-2456) on Third Mesa has a deli and a gas station.

The High Desert

HOLBROOK AND VICINITY

Long ago, by most accounts, Holbrook was a rough and violent cowboy town; then it profited, like everything else in this region, from the railroad and Route 66, back when tourists would by necessity stay a while. These days it's not much more than a convenient gateway and stopover for those visiting the nearby Petrified Forest National Park and Indian Country, offering several chain hotels and mostly fast food. For those interested in the history of the West, a trip to the **Navajo County Historical Society's Museum** (100 E. Arizona St., 928/524-6558 or 800/524-2459, 8am-4pm daily, free) in the 1880s Navajo County Court House is a must. Donations are encouraged and rewarded with chips of petrified wood. It's a strange and crowded place without a lot of context—you feel like you're wandering around an abandoned government building after the population died out. Sitting in the old jail, used until the 1970s and still decorated with the graffiti and sketches of its former inmates, is an eerie, thrilling experience.

Food and Accommodations

American popular architecture like that employed at the **Wigwam Motel** (811 W. Hopi Dr., Holbrook, 928/524-3048, www.

sleepinawigwam.com, $79-86) had its postwar heyday along Route 66, and like the route itself, it is mostly gone from the landscape these days in favor of cookie-cutter chains. But the kitschy tradition still has a hold on these dry high-desert plains at the Wigwam Motel in Holbrook, one of the last of many similarly designed motor courts that once lined the Mother Road. It's clean and comfortable, with all the updated amenities, but a stay here is mostly about its retro appeal. It should not be missed by Route 66 enthusiasts, road-trip scholars, chroniclers of fading Americana, and the like.

There are a number of chain hotels off I-40 in and around Holbrook, most of them located on Navajo Boulevard, the town's main drag.

★ PETRIFIED FOREST NATIONAL PARK

What once was a swampy forest frequented by ancient oversize reptiles is now **Petrified Forest National Park,** a blasted scrubland strewn with multicolored, quartz-wrapped logs some 225 million years old, each one possessing a smooth multicolored splotch or swirl seemingly unique from the rest. You can walk among the logs on several easy paved trails and view a small set of ruins and petroglyph-covered rocks (best seen with binoculars, but there are viewing scopes provided). Drive the park's 28-mile scenic road through the pastel-hued badlands of the Painted Desert, which, seen from a promontory, will take your breath away. Stop at the Painted Desert Inn Museum, a Pueblo Revival-style structure. Redesigned by Mary Colter, the great genius of Southwestern style and elegance, the inn was a restaurant and store operated by the Fred Harvey Company just after World War II, and before that it was a rustic out-of-the-way hotel and taproom built from petrified wood. There's a gift shop and bookstore at the inn now, and you can walk through it and gaze at the evocative mysterious murals, full of Hopi mythology and symbolism, painted by Fred Kabotie, the great Hopi artist commissioned by Colter. The park's proximity both to a major railroad stop at Winslow and to Route 66 have made it a popular Southwestern tourist attraction since the late 19th century, and the lore and style of that golden age of tourism pervades the park with pleasant nostalgia, adding an extra unexpected dimension to the overwhelming history all around.

Visiting the Park

Approaching Petrified Forest National Park (928/524-6228, www.nps.gov/pefo, seasonal hours daily year-round except for Nov. 25 and Dec. 25, $25 per vehicle for 7 days) from the west, take I-40 to U.S. 180 from Holbrook to the south entrance, past numerous shops featuring all things petrified. A paved road leads 28 miles north through the park, past several points of interest, back to I-40. From the east, take I-40's Exit 311 to the north entrance and then head south through the park. There are two visitors centers, one at the south entrance and one at the north, both showing a short movie about the park and passing out free maps of all the stops.

PARK ROAD DRIVING TOUR

It doesn't really matter which direction you enter the park from. To really see this understated masterpiece of a national park, you should drive the entire 28-mile route, stopping at the pullouts along the way, with time

out for short hikes into the colorful badlands. Consider starting your tour at the south entrance and the Rainbow Forest Museum, which has some amazing fossils and displays about the dinosaurs that once ruled this land.

Take a stroll on the Giant Logs Trail, an easy half-mile loop just outside the visitors center that features a few of the largest stone trees in the park. Also near the south visitors center, the Long Logs Trail is an aptly named easy 1.6-mile loop. Up the road a bit is Crystal Forest, which has a paved 0.75-mile loop trail among the petrified logs.

Strange multicolored cliffs, worn and sculpted into fantastic shapes, are the main attraction of Blue Mesa. See it via a fairly steep one-mile loop trail or a 3.5-mile loop road off the main road through the park. Farther south, the Agate Bridge pullout features a 110-foot-long bridge made of petrified logs. The Newspaper Rock petroglyphs and Puerco Pueblo ruins preserve the cultural leftovers of the people who once lived and thrived on this high-desert plain.

Cross over the usually dry Puerco River and the Santa Fe Railroad tracks, and watch for the rusted husk of a 1932 Studebaker sitting alone off the side of the road. This artifact marks the line that old Route 66 once took through the park, roughly visible now in the alignment of the power line stretching west behind the car. Now you've entered the Painted Desert section of the park. The views are long, subtle, colorful, and barren. It is a wondrous exotic landscape. Make sure to stop at the Painted Desert Inn Museum, where you'll see one of the most dramatic petroglyphs in the state—a large stylized mountain lion etched into a slab of rock. Free Wi-Fi is available here and at the Painted Desert Visitor Center.

PRACTICALITIES

Both visitors centers have excellent gift shops, and rangers are always on hand to answer your questions. The only place to get a meal in the park is the south entrance's Fred Harvey Company restaurant, ★ Painted Desert

Diner (928/524-3756, 8am-4pm daily, $5-10), which serves delicious fried chicken, Navajo tacos, burgers, and other road-food favorites in a cool Route 66 retro dining room. The south entrance visitors center has snacks for sale, but consider bringing your own food and especially water, as the park is spread out and it is a 28-mile drive between visitors centers.

WINSLOW AND VICINITY

Stop at this small, ex-Route 66, ex-railroad town if you happen to be in the area. Much of its historic downtown remains intact, if not too busy, and there are a few off-track treasures to be found if you have time to walk around. The town seems committed to celebrating the fact that its name appeared in the song "Take It Easy," an Eagles hit co-penned by Jackson Browne. There are reminders in nearly every business, and there's even **Standin' on the Corner Park** along the town's main street, featuring a statue of a man doing just that. The primary reason to stop in Winslow is to see **La Posada,** Southwestern architect Mary Colter's masterpiece and a place where Fred Harvey-style outback elegance is kept alive.

Sights

The **Old Trails Museum** (212 Kinsley Ave., 928/289-5861, www.oldtrailsmuseum.org, 10am-4pm Tues.-Sat., free) in downtown Winslow is a treasure trove of strange and thrilling artifacts, photographs, and stories about life in the high desert, with a special emphasis on the region's Route 66 past and its connection with the stylish railroad era of the Fred Harvey Company. The museum also has a fine collection of Navajo arts and crafts, and all kinds of weird and forgotten items that take on new historical meaning and emotional color simply by virtue of being old and saved. It's a small museum but definitely worth a stop for anyone interested in Route

66, the railroad, and Fred Harvey, and a visit here should be paired with a look around the restored Harvey House, **La Posada.**

Food

The independently operated ★ **Turquoise Room** (303 E. 2nd St., 928/289-2888, www.theturquoiseroom.net, 7am-9pm daily, $11-36), just off La Posada's main lobby, serves Southwestern- and Native American-inspired twists on prime rib, lamb, steak, pasta and fish dishes in an elegant space that riffs on the great Fred Harvey days. Chef John Sharpe does his best to find his largely organic ingredients semi-locally from central Arizona, the Valley of the Sun, and nearby New Mexico. In a nod to the Hopi people who live on the mesas just north of Winslow, Sharpe serves piki bread, a traditional Hopi staple, made by a Hopi baker from Second Mesa, along with a hummus prepared with tepary beans grown on the Hopi Reservation. This is the best restaurant in the region and one of the best in the state. Reservations are required for dinner.

Slowly but surely over the long years since the La Posada Hotel put this small town back on the map, Winslow's downtown has been crawling toward becoming a tourist draw, and it has made mighty progress lately. These days there's even the obligatory brewpub just across the street from Standin' on the Corner Park. **RelicRoad Brewing Company** (107 W. 2nd St., 928/224-0045, 11am-10pm daily, $8-15) brews terrific beers and serves mouthwatering burgers, salads, tacos, and other delicious brewpub staples. **Las Marias Mexican Food** (122 E. 2nd St., 928/289-6496, $6-15) serves fantastic and authentic fare in a casual downtown setting filled with locals.

Accommodations

There are several chain hotels and fast-food places off the interstate at Winslow for those in a hurry.

People travel to this lonely ramshackle high-desert town just to stay at ★ **La Posada** (303 E. 2nd St., 928/289-4366, www.laposada.org, $137-177) and eat at the **Turquoise**

1: Painted Desert in Petrified Forest National Park 2: a 1932 Studebaker along old Route 66 in Petrified Forest National Park

The Last of the Fred Harvey Railroad Hotels

Now owned by Allen Affeldt and the brilliant painter Tina Mion (whose paintings fill the arched hallways of the hotel), La Posada has been beautifully restored and is a reminder of the days when Indian Country was a chic travel destination for the rich and famous.

This was largely the result of the genius of Fred Harvey. He and his "Harvey Girls"—well-trained professional young women imported to the West to serve train passengers at Harvey's restaurants along the Santa Fe Railroad's right-of-way—made a trip to this barren underdeveloped high desert an experience beyond merely comfortable. The Harvey Company lunch counters and hotel restaurants offered fine dining and fresh gourmet food prepared by European chefs, along with the unmatched service of the Harvey Girls, many of whom ended up marrying their customers. Using the talents of Mary Colter, the Southwest's greatest designer and architect, Harvey built fine hotels in decidedly out-of-the-way places, allowing passengers on the Santa Fe's

La Posada

popular Chicago-to-Los Angeles line to live well even when stopping in Needles, California, and Winslow, Arizona.

Harvey also hired attractive educated young women who knew their history, anthropology, ethnology, and art as tour guides. Intrepid tourists who could pay, in 1936, about $45 per person were packed into tough but comfortable limousines, along with gourmet box lunches, and driven in style deep into Indian Country. These trips were famously called "Indian Detours"—three days of adventure and exoticism billed, according to surviving marketing pamphlets, as "the most distinctive motor cruise service in the world . . . off the beaten path in the Great Southwest."

The crowning achievement of the Harvey-Colter partnership came just before the 1929 stock market crash with the construction of La Posada (The Resting Place) at Winslow, the headquarters of the Santa Fe Railroad and the gateway to Arizona's Indian Country. Howard Hughes, Frank Sinatra, Albert Einstein, Bob Hope, and the crown prince of Japan all stayed in Colter's masterpiece, along with many other luminaries. They'd hop off the train right outside the hotel, tour the Hopi Mesas and Navajo land, and then return to the Spanish hacienda-inspired hotel and enjoy supreme comfort in a land that knew little of that luxury.

Eventually train travel fell off, and Route 66 gave way to the interstate. Not long after that, everything was the same, and the interstate became the province of chain hotels and those restroom machines that blow hot air on your hands. La Posada closed in the 1950s and sat disused until 1997, when Affeldt and Mion saved it. Now the old hotel has been restored beyond even its original glory, and it's often booked up with guests from all over the world. The hotel is especially popular these days with Europeans, many of whom rent motorcycles and ride the remainders of Route 66, searching for a lost version of the "America Road." Affeldt said recently that the irony of this phenomenon was not lost on a modern-day celebrity visitor to La Posada: the "Easy Rider" himself, Peter Fonda.

Room, so it's essential to call ahead for a reservation. Built in 1929 and obsessively restored by its current owners, the hacienda-style hotel is truly an Arizona treasure. Guest rooms all have that rare touch of retro style, and each is named for some famous person who visited the hotel back in the golden age of train travel. They also have up-to-date amenities, including deep tubs and heavenly beds. You could spend two full days exploring this hotel—walking its tiled and arched corridors, looking at co-owner and artist Tina Mion's gallery of strange and thrilling paintings, eating locally sourced Fred Harvey-inspired meals at the Turquoise Room, sitting outside on the back platform watching the trains go by, or taking a long and peaceful stroll through the hotel's large and surprisingly lush grounds. Over the years the owners have attempted not only to restore the gardens and grounds but to expand them based on original architect Mary Colter's vision of a desert-adapted oasis. The native dryland plant communities throughout the beautiful grounds create a sustainable explosion of green on this otherwise high and dry desert—just one of the many reasons why it's hard to leave this special place.

Information and Services

The Winslow Visitor Center & Hubbell Trading Post (523 W. 2nd St., 928/289-2434, http://winslowarizona.org, 9am-5pm daily) has much useful information about traveling these high desert plains and driving the remains of the Mother Road. The visitors center is in a historic building that was once a Hubble Trading Post and the center of the world for the pioneers of these lonely grasslands.

METEOR CRATER

Meteor Crater (I-40 and Meteor Crater Rd., 928/289-4002, www.meteorcrater.com, 7am-7pm daily summer, 8am-5pm daily fall-spring, $22 adults, $20 seniors, $13 ages 6-17), though impressive, is perhaps best viewed prior to a visit to, say, Canyon de Chelly or the Grand Canyon. Compared to those nearby attractions, built over eons by wind and water, this pockmark has trouble looking like more than the hole in the ground it is, isolated on the plain off I-40.

But the crater is an interesting hole nonetheless, born from the collision of an asteroid with the high-desert grasslands about 50,000 years ago. A small museum examines this and other meteor sites and explores the role the crater and its owner played in the study of meteors and in the U.S. space program. There's a 10-minute film about the crater, and rangers offer short interpretive hikes but insist that you have closed-toe shoes to tag along. A Subway restaurant on-site sells sandwiches and drinks. Unlike most of the outdoor sights in Arizona, Meteor Crater is run by a private corporation. The $15 adult entrance price is, truthfully, a bit steep for what you get.

HOMOLOVI RUINS STATE PARK

Here in the grasslands south of the Hopi mesas, along the banks of the Little Colorado River, the ancient Hisatsinom settled for a time in the 1200s-1300s before moving northward to Black Mesa. A few crumbling rock aggregations and beds of shattered pottery, what remains after decades of looting, sit on dry promontories. It's a beautiful place, windy and desolate, but the ruins aren't as impressive as others nearby. This is a good place to start a trip to Indian Country and its ancient structures; afterward, it pales in comparison to what you've already seen. The **visitors center** (AZ 87, 928/289-4106, http://azstateparks.com, 8am-5pm daily, $7 per car), east of Winslow on I-40 and then north on AZ 87, has one of the best selections of books on Southwestern archaeology in the region and offers a chance to converse with Hopi artists. There are picnic tables and trails in the park, plus a 53-site campground ($25) with hookups and showers.

The White Mountains and the Gila Valley

The high pine forests of eastern Arizona's White

Mountains have for generations been a cool summer getaway for the state's lowlanders and city dwellers.

It was in these still largely unbroken stands of evergreens, high on the Colorado Plateau, that the idea of wilderness for its own sake began in the United States, with the great conservationist and writer Aldo Leopold. He arrived in Springerville in 1909, a young man starting out in the newly created U.S. Forest Service. Still moved years later by these mountains, forests, and meadows, he would write of them in his 1949 classic *A Sand County Almanac,* one of the prime movers of a then-nascent campaign to preserve the West's wild places. Leopold predicted the fate of Arizona as a state and its slow ongoing

Highlights

Look for ★ to find recommended sights, activities, dining, and lodging.

★ **White Mountain Trail System:** Hike, bike, or ride a horse through thick cool green forests on this renowned series of trails (page 352).

★ **Apache Cultural Center and Museum:** Learn about the lifeways and history of the Western Apache (page 355).

★ **Sunrise Park Resort:** In winter, slide down dozens of ski runs on three forested peaks. In summer, do the same on a mountain bike (page 357).

★ **Casa Malpais Indian Ruins and Archaeological Park:** Explore a basalt-rock village built by the ancestors of the Hopi and Zuni peoples (page 361).

★ **The Coronado Trail:** Drive 120 miles of twisting two-lane switchbacks from the desert to the high pine forests (page 364).

★ **Gila Box Riparian National Conservation Area:** Hike beside the slow lazy flow of the Gila River, watching wildlife hiding out in the cool shade (page 371).

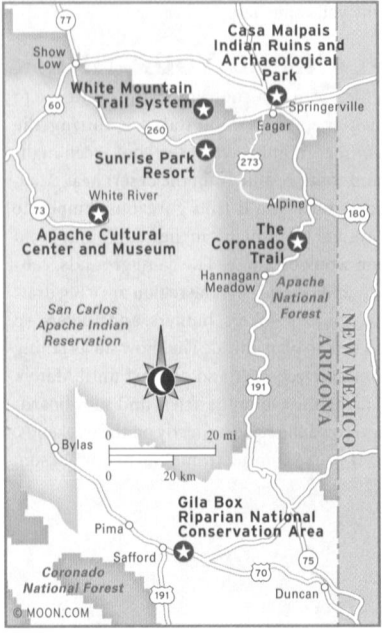

departure from a mining, ranching, and logging economy when he wrote of the predator control agent who killed the last known grizzly bear in the state around 1910: "He did not foresee that within two decades the cow country would become tourist country, and as such would have greater need of bears than of beefsteaks."

Now, just over a century since Leopold rode these forests on horseback, his observations still ring true. The White Mountains are known today as a wilderness playground, a place where the real Old West—the Old West not of gunfights and cardsharps but of wilderness, solitude, and natural beauty—lives on. The region still lacks grizzlies, but the wolf has returned. On a dark quiet night in these ancient forests, all snuggled up and safe in your rented-cabin bed, you might happen to hear a long-forgotten howl at the moon from deep in the rural darkness—then you'll know why you came here.

PLANNING YOUR TIME

Unless you're a snow lover, the best time to visit the White Mountains is during the summer months, when the cool green highlands offer respite from the desert heat. May-September you'll find gorgeous temperate days and nippy nights in the high country, and you won't be alone. The campgrounds, cabins, and lakesides of the region are a big draw for campers, hikers, hunters, and anglers, so it's best to plan ahead. The snow starts falling around December and can last until March. During these months skiers and snowboarders crowd the region, mostly on the weekends.

If you're coming from Phoenix or Tucson, a weekend is enough to see the glorious mountains and forests of the region. This is the perfect destination for a road trip—cruising slowly along twisty mountain roads, taking in the scenery, and keeping a sharp eye for wildlife.

The Gila Valley's charms are less obvious. It's hot in this desert river valley in summer but cool and temperate in fall and winter. The best way to see the Gila Valley is to drive through it on your way to the mountains along the Coronado Trail. It's a slow winding route, but one that won't soon be forgotten.

If you have more time—say, five days to a week—consider renting a cabin beside one of the high-country lakes or setting up a camp deep in the forest and sampling the White Mountains' many trails for hikers and mountain bikers. Or grab your kayak or canoe and float down the remaining wild sections of the Gila River. If you're interested in seeing the huge telescopes that scan the heavens from the heights of the Gila River Valley's Mount Graham, make sure you reserve a spot far in advance and plan to be in the region for at least one full day and night.

TRANSPORTATION

You really must have your own car to visit this out-of-the-way mountainous playground. Pinetop-Lakeside, the capital village of the White Mountains region, sits 200 miles northeast of Phoenix, a scenic drive from the desert to the cool mountain pines. Plan on at least 3.5 hours, longer on weekends. Take U.S. 60 east to Mesa, pick up AZ 87 north to the Mogollon Rim, and then head east on AZ 260 to Show Low, near Pinetop-Lakeside.

Previous: hiking in the White Mountains; the Gila River; Sunrise Park Resort.

The White Mountains and the Gila Valley

© MOON.COM

The Hopi and Zuni peoples have ancient ties to these mountains, the highest of which is Mount Baldy, at 11,409 feet the second-highest in Arizona. Mormons settled the region from the north along the Little Colorado River in the 1870s and still have a major presence here. The towns are small but set up for tourists. Bring your hiking boots, your fishing rod, your mountain bikes, your skis, your snowboard, and your kayak, and don't forget your binoculars and your camera. This region is very popular with Arizona's hunters and anglers, and the culture in many of the small towns here is geared more toward the hunter than the hiker.

SHOW LOW

The largest town in the White Mountains region, with 11,000 residents, Show Low stretches along U.S. 60, which becomes Deuce of Clubs as it passes through the one-strip town. Surrounded by the Apache-Sitgreaves National Forests at 6,400 feet elevation, Show Low has average temperatures 25-30 degrees lower than in the desert 175 miles to the south. It's a popular place for summer homes and getaway cabins. It makes a good base for a White Mountains excursion, but the resort town of Pinetop-Lakeside, just 10 miles to the southeast along White Mountain Road (AZ 260), has a greater diversity of accommodations.

The town, founded in 1870, got its unique name from a card game played for its spoils. Two early settlers, the story goes, decided that the town site wasn't big enough for both of them and so played a hand of seven-up to decide who would stay and who would move on. Whoever could "show low," that is, the lowest card, would win the site. There's a sculpture depicting the card game at the **Festival Marketplace** (Deuce of Clubs Ave. and E. Cooley St., between 9th St. and 11th St.).

Events

The **Show Low Main Street Farmers' Market & Art Walk** (Festival Market Place, Deuce of Clubs Ave. and E. Cooley St., between 9th St. and 11th St., www.showlowmainstreet. org, 9am-1pm Sat. late May-early Oct.) showcases local artists, artisans, horticulturists, and ranchers every Saturday in the warm months. Locally grown produce, locally raised beef, all manner of folk art, and the typical farmers market wares are sold from 60 booths set up at the Festival Market Place.

Accommodations

Just 10 miles southeast of Show Low in Pinetop-Lakeside are several excellent motels, hotels, and cabins. Show Low and Pinetop-Lakeside have many sprawling chain hotels, a lot of them relatively new. In Show Low, try the **Best Western Paint Pony Lodge** (581 W. Deuce of Clubs Ave., 928/537-5773, $116-129), with 50 standard guest rooms, free Wi-Fi, and continental breakfast included.

Information and Services

There's a well-stocked **visitors center** (81 E. Deuce of Clubs Ave., 928/537-2326, 9am-5pm Mon.-Fri.) on the main drag that has a lot of information on the White Mountains region.

Summit Healthcare Regional Medical Center (2200 Show Low Lake Rd., 928/537-4375, www.nrmc.org) has a 24-hour emergency room with a Level 4 trauma center.

FOOL HOLLOW LAKE RECREATION AREA

Fool Hollow Lake Recreation Area (1500 Fools Hollow Rd., Show Low, 928/537-3680, http://azstateparks.com, 5am-10pm daily, ranger station 8am-4:30pm daily Apr.-mid-Oct., 8am-11am and 3:30pm-4:30pm daily mid-Oct.-Mar., $7 per car Mon.-Thurs., $10 per car Fri.-Sun., $3 bicyclists), with its jewel-like blue highland lake surrounded by tall

The White Mountains

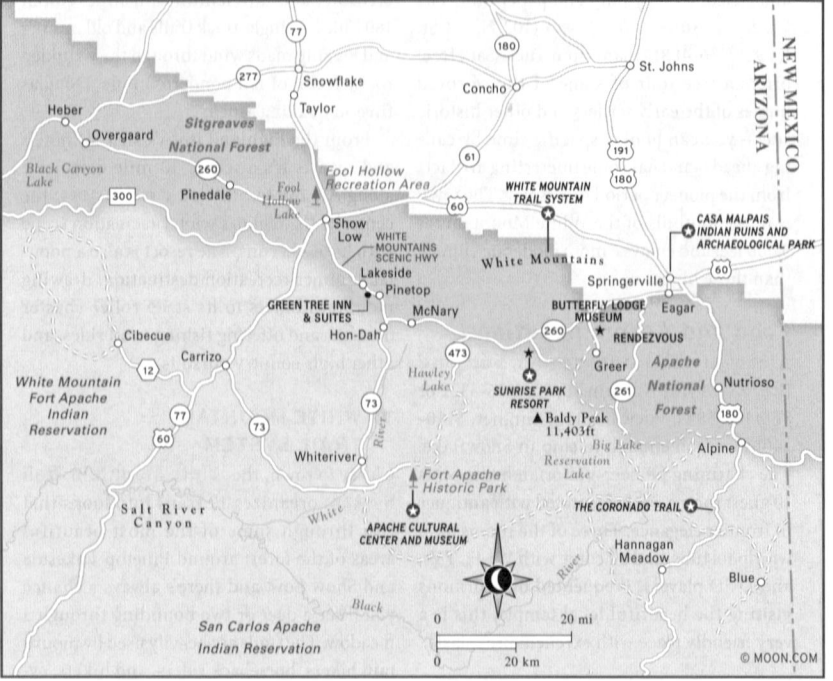

pines, offers fishing, camping, picnicking, swimming, and hiking. A dam at the meeting of Show Low Creek and Fool Hollow Wash (so named because people said the original settlers were fools to attempt to farm here) created the 150-acre lake in 1957, and it has since become a popular spot for outdoor types, especially in summer. The 1.5-mile trail along the south and west sides of the lake is worth a stroll.

This is a family-oriented place with a playground and interpretive programs on natural history and wildlife. There always seem to be a lot of parents and kids fishing together for rainbow trout, large- and smallmouth bass, sunfish, catfish, and other species. Only gas-powered motorboats (10 hp or less) are allowed. Canoe and kayak rentals are available at the East Dock from **J&T's Wild-Life Outdoors** (928/892-9170, www.jtwildlifeoutdoors.com,

9am-5pm Mon.-Thurs., 8am-6pm Fri.-Sat., 8am-4pm Sun., $20-25 per hour).

Camping

Fool Hollow is an ideal spot for **car camping** (electricity available, $33-35), as it's just a few miles from Show Low and only 15 miles from Pinetop-Lakeside and the area's best trails and restaurants. There are 31 tent sites tucked among the evergreens, with fire rings and picnic tables, and 92 RV spots for rigs up to 40 feet long. All the sites have water and are just a short walk from relatively clean restrooms and showers.

SNOWFLAKE

Founded in 1878 by Mormon pioneers sent south from Utah by Brigham Young to establish colonies throughout the arid west, this small roadside village 18 miles north of

Show Low on AZ 77 is home to the Latter-day Saints' 108th temple (there are 133 total) and Arizona's only pulp and paper mill. The Stinson Pioneer Museum (102 N. 1st St. E., 928/536-4881, 10am-4pm Tues.-Sat., free) offers a free tour of some of the restored homes of the early settlers and other historic sites—you can book a specific time by calling ahead—and has some interesting artifacts from the pioneer period on display. The town is in the foothills of the White Mountains at 5,600 feet and enjoys a more moderate climate than those higher up.

Food and Accommodations

A stay at the Heritage Inn Bed and Breakfast (161 N. Main St., 928/536-3322 or 866/486-5947, www.heritage-inn.net, $110-140) is reason enough to stop in Snowflake. The charming pioneer-Victorian home rents 10 guest rooms, each decorated with antiques in frontier elegance. Three of the rooms have whirlpool tubs, and all come with Wi-Fi, TVs, and DVD players. Frequented by Mormons visiting the beautiful local temple, this is a very friendly place with excellent breakfasts.

PINETOP-LAKESIDE

This small resort village marks the beginning of the White Mountain Scenic Road, otherwise known as AZ 260. One incorporated community, Pinetop-Lakeside, stretches out along the highway at more than 7,000 feet, a high-forest getaway with just 4,000 year-round residents. When the snow melts, however, more than 35,000 call this place home, mostly on summer weekends. This is the White Mountain region's tourism capital, and there are quite a few distinctive shops and restaurants. This burgeoning mountain village offers forest-and-meadow trails beside glimmering lakes, country comfort food, and adorable little antiques shops run by friendly senior citizens and big-city runaways.

Recreation

Surrounded by the Apache-Sitgreaves National Forests, Pinetop-Lakeside offers a pine needle-paved antidote to hikers and mountain bikers who are sick of saguaros, creosote, and unrelenting sunshine. About 180 miles of single-track trails and old mining and logging roads wind through the wrinkled rocky forest of tall ponderosa pine, Douglas fir, and quaking aspen.

From the highland town's strip of hotels and resorts it's a scenic 30-mile drive east along AZ 260 to Sunrise Park Resort, the center of the region's winter recreation scene with its 65 ski runs. The resort is also a popular summer recreation destination, drawing mountain bikers to its steep roller-coaster descents and offering fishing, trail rides, and other high-country pursuits.

★ WHITE MOUNTAIN
TRAIL SYSTEM

Closer to town, the White Mountain Trail System organizes 19 trails into loops that run through some of the most beautiful areas of the forest around Pinetop-Lakeside and Show Low, and there's always a chance you'll see a deer or two bounding through a meadow. The trails are heavily used by mountain bikers, horseback riders, and hikers, especially in the summer. They can get muddy during the late-summer rainy season. The trails range 1.5-14 miles, and several wind along babbling brooks with spongy green banks and up highland ridgeways overlooking the pines.

TRACKS (www.tracks-pinetop-lakeside.org), the heroic local group that organized the trail system in response to development encroaching on the forest, keeps a guide to the trails on its website. The Lakeside Ranger District (W. White Mountain Blvd., 928/368-5111, www.fs.usda.gov/asnf) sells a paperback guide to the trail system ($2) that has detailed directions on how to get to the trailheads, and the rangers are usually happy to provide advice. Cycle Mania (100 N. White Mountain Rd., Show Low, 928/537-8812, http://cyclemaniaaz.com, 10am-6pm Tues.-Fri., 11am-3pm Sat.) has bike equipment, repairs, and rentals.

WOODLAND LAKE PARK

The small **Woodland Lake Park** (Pinetop-Lakeside Parks and Recreation, 928/368-6700, sunrise-10pm Apr.-Oct., sunrise-sunset Nov.-Mar., free) offers the best of the White Mountains in miniature, and it's an ideal place to hike around and get a deep impression of the forest if you don't have the time to mount a major expedition. The little reservoir attracts wildlife and anglers, and the trails are easy—especially the 1.25-mile **Lake Loop Trail,** a paved route around the lake that's perfect for families with young children. Hiking the two-mile **Hitching Post Loop Trail** is an excellent way to introduce yourself to the forest, and there's a side trail off the loop that leads to the marshy meadow of the **Big Springs Environmental Study Area.** The park has restrooms, picnic tables, and charcoal grills. To get here, take AZ 260 south to Woodland Lake Road.

Entertainment and Events

Wine Mountains (1746 E. White Mountain Blvd., 928/414-1188, www.winemountains. com, 3pm-8pm Thurs.-Sat., noon-5pm Sun.), an inviting tasting room with a patio, is dedicated to promoting Arizona wines and has knowledgeable helpful staff. It offers revolving flights of Arizona and California wines and a small menu of creative small plates and flatbreads, and draws a fun friendly mix of locals, travelers, and summer residents.

The place for live music in the White Mountains is **The Lion's Den Bar & Grill** (2408 E. White Mountain Blvd., 928/367-6050, www.thelionsdenpinetop.com, 11am-10pm Mon.-Tues. and Thurs., 11-midnight Wed., 10am-midnight Fri.-Sat.), a fun old-school bar-and-grill where you can meet the locals. It also has a big pet-friendly backyard with and lots of games and seats for lounging and offers 20 draft beers, 17 TVs for sports, and a food menu of hamburgers, sandwiches, fish-and-chips, and other pub-style eats, plus a Bloody Mary bar on Sunday.

Over July 4-7 every year, artists and artisans congregate in Pinetop and sell their creations at the **4th of July Arts and Crafts Festival** (480/816-4165, www.highcountryartgallery. com). The long-running juried festival features more than 75 booths with unique arts and crafts, live music, and food from Charlie Clark's, a legendary local bar and grill. The artisans set up in The Orchard, a cool grassy area behind the restaurant and saloon to retire for a cool one.

In fall the quaking aspens turn red and

Wine Mountains tasting room

yellow, flashing like flames from their evergreen surroundings. This inspiring time of year brings the **Pinetop-Lakeside Fall Artisans Festival** (Orchard at Charlie Clarks, 1701 E. White Mountain Blvd., 928/367-4290, www.pinetoplakesidechamber.com, late Sept.) to the Mountain Meadow Recreation Complex, with more than 150 artists and artisans selling their unique wares. The festival includes the **Run to the Pines Car Show** and antiques and quilt shows—all around a great weekend to be in Pinetop.

Shopping

There are a number of antiques stores, boutiques, gift shops, and galleries scattered along AZ 260 through Pinetop-Lakeside, one of the sure signs that you're in a resort community. As such, the scene tends to be seasonal: If you're planning a visit in the dead of winter, you could find some places closed, as many stores are open only April-October.

Stop at the **High Country Art Gallery and Gift Shop** (592 W. White Mountain Blvd., 928/367-3916, www.highcountryartgallery.com, 10am-5pm Tues.-Sun.) to check out paintings, jewelry, clothing, pottery, and other arts and crafts for sale by local artists.

The **Red Door Consignment Shops** (2701 N. Porter Mountain Rd., 928/368-2477, 10am-5pm Tues.-Sat.) has 6,000 square feet of resale furniture, antiques, clothes, jewelry, and all manner of treasures waiting to be found. There's also a coffee bar and hot dog stand inside.

If you're up for something truly unique, have the "master chainsaw artist" at **The Burly Bear** (1545 S. Adair Dr., at White Mountain Blvd., 928/367-2327, www.theburlybear.com, 10am-5pm Mon.-Sat.) carve you a 15-foot-tall cuddly faced wooden bear or some one-of-a-kind furniture.

Food

More and more varied restaurants are opening in Pinetop-Lakeside all the time, it seems, and the area has more food choices than any other White Mountains community. You'll find pizza and other Italian food, Thai food, seafood, fast food, and many others as you drive through the one-strip town spread out along AZ 260. The places listed below are the leading lights of this moderately bustling food scene—local favorites, many of which have been serving the townies and travelers alike for generations.

The oldest continually operating restaurant in the White Mountains, **Charlie Clark's Steakhouse** (AZ 260, 928/367-4900, www.charlieclarks.com, 11am-3pm and 5pm-10pm daily, $11-32) serves some of the best steaks, barbecue beef, and prime rib in the area on a site that disguised a distillery during Prohibition. A casual Western-style place that's popular with visitors and locals alike, Charlie's has been open since the late 1930s. Lunch is served daily in the saloon and enclosed log cabin patio, and there's a garden-style bar out back called **The Orchard.** For lunch, a full menu of sandwiches and salads is served, along with some really excellent fish tacos and other specials. Sitting in the saloon, you'll hear regulars and cowboys joshing each other. Make sure to check out all the cartoon caricatures that line the walls depicting favored customers throughout the years.

Darbi's Café (235 E. White Mountain Blvd., 928/367-6556, http://darbiscafe.com, 6am-2pm Sun.-Tues., 6am-8pm Wed.-Sat., $7-16) is a favorite among locals for big breakfasts—for which there's often a wait, especially on weekends—and burgers, sandwiches, soups, and salads for lunch, all at a fair price.

A favorite spot for locals since the early 1960s, **El Rancho Restaurant** (1523 E. White Mountain Blvd., 928/367-4557, www.elranchorestaurantpinetop.com, 11am-8:30pm Mon.-Sat., noon-8pm Sun., $8-20) serves reliably tasty and filling Mexican favorites like enchiladas, burritos, and fajitas, and has a fairly extensive selection of tequila and brain-freezing margaritas.

Accommodations

There are more than 40 hotels, motels, and country-cabin resorts in this tiny sylvan burg—so many that it seems like the whole town is for rent by the night. Rates fluctuate according to season, with the prices highest during summer months (roughly mid-May-Sept.) and the ski season (late Dec.-Mar.). Make reservations far in advance, especially for cabin rentals.

Part of a small Southwestern chain of boutique hotels with a fairly extensive sustainability mission, ★ **GreenTree Inn & Suites** (431 E. White Mountain Blvd., 928/367-6077, www.greentreeinn.com, $113-135) is sleek, fresh, and comfortable, with an indoor pool and hot tub, free Wi-Fi, and immaculate guest rooms with fridges and microwaves. You'll eat your free hot breakfast with compostable plates, cups, cutlery, and napkins, and the hotel has tailor-made recycling program. Tasteful LED lighting illuminates the guest rooms and corridors, and you'll find only waste-reducing pump dispensers in the shower and at the sink.

The **Antlers Inn** (1023 E. White Mountain Blvd., 928/367-4146, www.antlersinnpinetop.com, $89-104) is a basic motor lodge-style hotel with affordable, clean, and comfortable guest rooms with free Wi-Fi, a fridge, a TV, a microwave, and free breakfast. The little courtyard has mini golf and barbecue grills. This is a great place to base your hiking or mountain-biking weekend.

At the **Moonridge Lodge** (596 W. White Mountain Blvd., 928/367-1906, $129-199) you can rent your own one- to three-bedroom cabin, a few of which also have lofts. The three-bedroom can hold groups or families of up to 12. Cabins have pinewood interiors, comfy old chairs and couches, and TVs; many have covered porches and picnic tables, and all are surrounded by the whispering forest and are close to restaurants, shopping, and trailheads. This place is pet-friendly, allowing dogs for no extra charge.

The **Hidden Rest Resort** (3448 White Mountain Blvd., 928/368-6336, www.hiddenrest.com, $89-129) rents 11 country-quaint and comfortable knotty pine-paneled cabins on a forested property along AZ 260.

Four of the cabins have in-room whirlpool tubs, and most will sleep up to four. All the cabins have private baths, a gas or wood fireplace, and a stocked kitchen. Pets are allowed for a fee.

Information and Services

The **Pinetop-Lakeside Chamber of Commerce Visitor Center** (102-C W. White Mountain Blvd., 800/573-4031, www.pinetoplakesidechamber.com, 8:30am-4:30pm Mon.-Fri., 8:30am-2:30pm Sat.-Sun.) has all the information you will need on visiting this area.

WHITE MOUNTAIN APACHE INDIAN RESERVATION

The homeland of the White Mountain bands of the Western Apache, who call themselves the Ndee (The People), comprises 2,600 square miles of tall pines and lush green flower-strewn meadows in and below the White Mountains. Established in the 1880s, the reservation is home to 12,000 of the tribe's 15,000 members. There's not much to see save for beautiful high-elevation forests and a few scattered, often dilapidated homes and trailers, most of them with a corral and several perfectly posed horses peeking through the screen of pine trees along the highway. The tribe operates two of the region's top stops— **Hon-Dah Resort and Casino** and **Sunrise Park Resort.** The reservation is also home to **Salt River Canyon,** a 2,600-foot-deep wild mountain gorge, and the sacred 11,409-foot Mount Baldy, the second-highest mountain in Arizona. The reservation begins just south of Pinetop along AZ 260, and its capital is the tiny roadside village of **Whiteriver,** along AZ 73 about 30 miles south of Pinetop.

★ Apache Cultural Center and Museum

The Western Apache preserve and interpret their history at the **Apache Cultural Center and Museum** (Indian Rte. 46, 5 miles south of Whiteriver, 928/338-4625, www.fortapachearizona.org, 8am-5pm Mon.-Fri., 11am-3pm Sat. summer, 8am-5pm Mon.-Fri. winter, $5 adults, $3 children) in Whiteriver, part of **Fort Apache Historical Park** (7am-sunset daily).

Called **Nohwike' Bágowa** (House of Our Footprints), the cultural center and museum has a fascinating collection of Apache artifacts and historic photographs and features revolving exhibits on Apache history and culture. Apache artists-in-residence show their work here, and a gift shop sells locally made baskets, beadwork, Crown Dancer figures, and books about the tribe. You'll come away from this small but well-managed museum with an introductory understanding of the tribe's hard-fought and often tragic history, especially if you spend some time perusing the exhibit "Ndee Bike'/Footprints of the Apache," which traces the tribe's epic journey from creation to the present day.

The surrounding 288-acre historical park is a National Register Historic District; a self-guided tour reveals something of what it was like to be a soldier at this far-flung mountain outpost of the Apache Wars of the 1870s. The oldest building is the 1871 log General Crook's Cabin, where the exhibit **The Fort Apache Legacy** explains the history of the fort. There's even a historic cemetery, and a 1.4-mile loop trail through a small canyon past an old scout camp.

Four miles west of the park, the **Kinishba Ruins National Historic Landmark** preserves the ruins of a small Pueblo occupied until about 1400. Admission to the historic park includes the ruins. Apache tour guides are sometimes available to take you around if you call in advance.

Scenic Drive

AZ 73 through the reservation's western section becomes the **Whiteriver Scenic Road** as it winds through the lumpy green landscape and hooks up with U.S. 60/AZ 77 south through **Salt River Canyon** toward Globe and the desert. This is the most scenic route out of the region, and a stop at the pullout about an hour south of Whiteriver provides a breathtaking view of Salt River Canyon. Make sure to gas up and fill up first: After Whiteriver, where gas is expensive, and there's nothing much to eat past the casino, there are no gas stations until Globe, almost 100 miles.

One of the more impressive roadside natural wonders in a state chock-full of them, the Salt River Canyon was once used as a hideout by the Apache during the Indian Wars. The 2,600-foot-deep jagged desert gorge is where the Salt River runs free and wild. There's a parking area before the bridge where you can learn about the canyon and take pictures, and easy paved trails lead down to the flowing river. If you've got a 4WD vehicle, you can take a riverside Jeep trail and explore the canyon in more depth. The traffic along AZ 77 near the canyon bridge can get heavy and frustrating, especially on weekends. The canyon is 60 miles from Whiteriver and 40 miles north of Globe.

Events

Thousands head to the tiny town of Whiteriver in late August-early September for the **White Mountain Apache Fair and Rodeo** (S. Chief Ave. and Mint Rd., 928/338-4346, early Sept., $3-5) at the White Mountain Apache Rodeo Grounds, which started in 1925. Apache people of all ages compete and watch bull riding, roping, barrel racing, and other rodeo events, and there's a fry bread-making competition, traditional dancing, food, and handmade local arts and crafts.

Recreation

Elk, deer, black bears, bobcats, wild turkeys, and a host of other beasts share these coniferous mountains with the Apache people, and hunters from all over the Southwest fill the region's campgrounds in all seasons. The same goes for anglers, as the reservation has 12 stocked lakes and 800 miles of cold-water trout streams renowned for giving up various river monsters, including the Apache trout, Arizona's official state fish.

The tribe operates the Southwest's largest ski resort at Sunrise Park, where the temperate summer months find mountain bikers whipping down the runs and hikers and horseback riders taking a slower tack through the highland forests and meadows. The still and the patient have a reasonable chance of seeing a group of deer, heads lowered to graze in some flowery meadow, and maybe, if you're really lucky, a chubby black bear waddling toward the tree line. If you do see a bear, take your obvious good luck and your hard-earned money straight to the tribe's Hon-Dah Resort and Casino and see how the one-armed bandits and the blackjack tables react.

PERMITS

You must purchase a recreation permit (fishing $9 per day; camping $8 per day; boating $5; hiking, mountain biking, sightseeing $15 per day; rafting $20 per day) from the tribe to do just about anything within the boundaries of the reservation. **White Mountain Apache Wildlife & Outdoor Recreation** (100 West Fatco Rd., 928/338-4385, www.wmatoutdoors.org) in Whiteriver controls outdoor recreation on the reservation and issues the permits; state fishing and hunting licenses hold no authority here. You can secure a permit online (www.wmatoutdoors.org) or at **Hon-Dah Ski and Outdoor Sport** (787 AZ 260, 928/369-7669, www.hon-dah.com, 7am-5pm daily), where you can also rent and buy equipment and get local advice. The shop also organizes rafting and canyoneering trips deep into Salt River Canyon and other remote corners of the reservation. Hunters should contact the tribe's recreation department or check the website for detailed information on elk, deer, small game, and predator hunt permits. The tribe offers guided hunts, but you can also go out on your own.

Permits are available throughout the region, including at **Pinetop Sporting Goods** (747 E. White Mountain Blvd., 928/367-5050, 8am-5pm Tues.-Fri., 8am-noon Sat.) and **Sportsman's Warehouse** (4421 S. White Mountain Rd., Show Low, 928/537-0800,

9am-8pm Mon.-Thurs., 9am-9pm Fri.-Sat., 10am-6pm Sun.).

★ Sunrise Park Resort

Like drunken migratory birds, skiers and snowboarders from the desert flock north to the White Mountains every winter to slide down the 65 high-mountain (10,700-11,100 feet) ski runs scratched into Sunrise, Cyclone, and Apache Peaks. **Sunrise Park Resort** (AZ 273, 4 miles south of AZ 260, 928/735-7669, http://sunriseskiparkaz.com), 30 miles east of Pinetop and usually at least ankle deep in snow by January, has a separate **Terrain Park** for snowboarding, with a half-pipe, wood and metal rails, and jumps. The trails, the longest of which is the 1.2-mile Sidewinder from 10,700-foot Sunrise Peak, are somewhat diverse, with 20 percent strictly for expert skiers. A fair number of runs are for beginners and a few are just for kids. Cross-country trails through the high pine forests are for those strange folks who prefer a cardio workout to a whooshing rush. The park has 10 ski lifts ($23-49). If you are willing to throw yourself down a mountain but lack the necessary equipment, there are rentals available at the Sunrise Park Lodge, or you can go to the folks at **Hon-Dah Ski and Outdoor Sport** (787 AZ 260, 928/369-7669, www.hon-dah.com/sos.html) at the casino for your gear.

The lifts creak to life 10am-4pm Thursday-Monday Memorial Day-Labor Day. A slow cool-breeze ride up one of the three peaks ($19), high above the green-carpeted land on a summer's day, is a romantic and relaxing way to spend an hour or so. Also on summer weekends, the park welcomes **mountain bikers** for the most fun you can have on two wheels. Sunrise is one of the few places in Arizona where the obvious benefits of going down can be had without a lot of heart-pounding ground work: Bikers can attach their rides to the **lift chairs** ($36.50 all-day pass) for an easy ride up the peaks and a high-speed roller-coaster ride down.

Summer also finds anglers vying for a spot along the shore of **Sunrise Lake,** the state's largest cold-water lake, stocked with big fat trout and other species and the only lake on the reservation that allows gas-powered motorboats (10 hp or less). The park's **Snowy Mountain Stables** (928/205-7607, half hour-all day $22-180) offer horseback rides through the cool forests and meadows during the summer months.

Hon-Dah Resort and Casino

On a rainy day in the White Mountains, **Hon-Dah Resort and Casino** (AZ 260 and AZ 73, 928/369-0299, www.hon-dah.com) can seem a bit dour, with dead-eyed RV gypsies and chain-smoking octogenarians watching emotionless as a bleeping and blinking machine takes their retirement money. At other times it seems a bit brighter, but it rains quite a bit here. Hon-Dah, which means "welcome" in the Apache language, has a good restaurant (with a casino-style buffet Thurs.-Sun.), a store and gas station, an RV park, and a lodge with clean basic guest rooms, but in truth it offers little for those not drawn to games of chance. It's relatively clean and features the usual slot machines, poker, and blackjack. Middling Las Vegas-style music acts, many of them with a country-western bent, play to the dance floor at the **Timbers Lounge and Showroom** Tuesday-Saturday.

Food and Accommodations

Hunters and anglers, the reservation's primary block of annual visitors, prefer to rough it in fishing cabins, tent camps, and RVs. For a comprehensive list of the reservation's **camping** options, reach out to the tribe's recreation department (928/338-4385, www.wmatoutdoors.org). Camping permits cost $8 per day, and most sites on the reservation are first come, first served. Ice fishing is popular on reservation lakes in winter, but not all the campgrounds are open and accessible during the snowy months.

The **Hawley Lake Recreation Area** (928/369-1753) rents out rustic but reasonably

comfortable cabins along the shores of the reservation's highest lake. At 8,200 feet elevation, the 300-acre mountain lake is stocked with trout and a popular spot for serious solitary anglers and families alike. The tribe rents cabins that sleep 2-14 people ($125-300) as well as a few two-person motel rooms ($65). There's also a large campground around the lake and an RV park. There are no phones, TVs, or microwaves in the cabins, but they are fully furnished with dishes, pans, utensils, coffeemakers, and toasters. There's a small store, a lunch counter, and a gas station on-site, but it's best to come prepared with food and drinks just in case. To reach Hawley Lake from Pinetop-Lakeside, take AZ 260 through McNary to AZ 473, then turn right on AZ 473/Hawley Lake Road. From here it's nine miles to the lake.

Hon-Dah Resort and Casino (AZ 73 and AZ 260, www.hon-dah.com, $109-199) offers standard, clean, comfortable guest rooms with free Wi-Fi, room service, and a swimming pool. Check the website for special ski and fishing packages. Guest rooms are nothing special but are a half-notch above the region's decidedly mid-range knotty-pine rental cabins, and the **Indian Pine Restaurant** (928/369-0299, 6am-10pm daily, $10-35) serves a fair plate of eggs, potatoes, and bacon for breakfast, along with omelets and other staples, and sandwiches, pizzas, calzones, salads, and, of course, Indian fry bread for lunch. At dinner, the menu features tasty pizzas and calzones, prime rib, burgers, and ribs.

The tribe's **Sunrise Park Lodge** (928/735-7669 or 800/772-7669, www.sunriseskipark.com, $89-250 Mon.-Fri. winter, $124-295 Sat.-Sun. winter) sits at the base of the three-peaked ski-scape. There's nothing like rolling out of bed onto the slopes; otherwise you waste precious downhill time driving 30 icy-road miles from Pinetop. In 2021, the lodge was undergoing a remodel; check for updates.

1: Whiteriver Scenic Road through Salt River Canyon **2:** the White Mountains near Greer **3:** Hawley Lake Recreation Area **4:** Rendezvous restaurant in Greer

GREER

Turn south off AZ 260 onto AZ 273 to reach the little village of Greer (www.greerarizona. com), a log-cabin hamlet nestled in the forest and green meadows around 7,000-9,000 feet elevation, below the peaks of the White Mountains, through which flows the Little Colorado River. The area is outlandishly beautiful and picturesque. It could just as well be snuggled in the Alps, and the babbling forks of the river support a lush riparian belt with overgrowing greenery and flat narrow trails along the moss-covered waterway. In spring-summer, Greer is perfect for hiking, horseback riding, and lying around in highland meadows, surrounded by colorful wildflowers. In winter the snow comes, and Greer makes a good base for trips to the ski hills and for cross-country expeditions into the forest.

Sights

While the forests and meadows tend to push everything else of interest off the radar, the strange and quaint Butterfly Lodge Museum (AZ 373 and County Rd. 1126, 928/735-7514, http://butterflylodgemuseum. org, 10am-5pm Thurs.-Sun. Memorial Day-Labor Day, $2 adults, $1 ages 12-17, free under age 12) is worth a look if you're in Greer during summer. The little log house was once the hunting lodge of James Willard Schultz, an early-20th-century writer of adventure stories about the West for magazines, known primarily for his 1907 book *My Life as an Indian*. The home was later used as a studio by Schultz's equally interesting son, Hart Merriam Schultz, or Lone Wolf, a famous Indian painter and artist. The home is set up with all kinds of artifacts and everyday items that show what life was like in this remote green mountain valley years ago. Several of Lone Wolf's paintings are on display, and a gift shop sells the elder Schultz's nostalgic writings.

On a guided tour of the Little House Museum (928/333-2286, www. xdiamondranch.com, reservation required, $15) and the Little Bear Archaeological Site, you'll get an entertaining course on the whole long history of human habitation in the White Mountains region, from the proto-Pueblo inhabitants to the tough pioneers, ranchers, and cattle rustlers. The museum, a cluster of restored pioneer-style buildings filled with all kinds of strange and wonderful Old West and pioneer-era furniture, household items, and collectibles, is on the grounds of the X Diamond Ranch and is only accessible with a reservation. The museum tour includes a jaunt out to the Little Bear site, where the rubble of several dwellings dates back to AD 500. A tour of the museum without the ruins is $8.

Recreation

The best hiking in Greer is along the forks of the Little Colorado River. Pick up several trailheads where Main Street enters the National Forest on the south end of Greer. Head south until the end of the main road and follow the well-worn footpaths along the river. In some places the ground is so spongy and overgrown with greenery that it seems like a rain forest. But walking is so lowland: Here, not 20 miles from where John Wayne himself raised prize Hereford cattle on the 26 Bar Ranch, consider letting a mountain-bred horse take you deep into the pines. The X Diamond Ranch (928/333-2286, www. xdiamondranch.com, $30-155) offers guided rides ranging from one hour to all day, and on occasion they'll let a greenhorn do some ranch work à la *City Slickers*. The historic ranch, started by White Mountain pioneers John and Molly Butler in the early 1900s, also operates a catch-and-release fly fishery on the Little Colorado ($40 pp half day, $50 full day).

Food and Accommodations

There are several lodges in Greer and a host of cabins for rent, for the night or the season. For a complete list, check out the official town website (www.greerarizona.com).

Make reservations for a memorable lunch at ★ Rendezvous (117 Main St., 928/735-7483, 8am-3pm Wed.-Mon., $9-15), which is often crowded, especially on summer weekends—you'll know you've arrived when you see all the cars parked along the street. This small restaurant serves some of the best food in the White Mountains, offering a creative array of sandwiches, burgers, and salads as well as a popular Friday fish fry and famous green bean "fries." Sit on the cool and shady patio or inside the small historic home with its quirky country style.

The historic **Molly Butler Restaurant and Bar** (109 Main St., 928/735-7226 or 866/288-3167, www.mollybutlerlodge.com) is a fantastic beloved restaurant that's been serving hearty mountain food since 1910. It's open for dinner (5pm-9pm daily, $13-30), serving excellent fish, steaks, chili, prime rib, and more. The restaurant is also open for lunch (11am-2:30pm Mon.-Sat.) and brunch (10am-2pm Sun.). Reservations are advised.

The **X Diamond Ranch** (928/333-2286, www.thexdiamondranch.com, $140-175), where Molly Butler once lived and raised cattle in the early 1900s, rents out seven comfortable and scenically placed cabins along the Little Colorado River. Each cabin is a unique structure surrounded by the outlandish grandeur of the area. All sleep up to four people and can accommodate eight, and all have kitchens and fireplaces.

SPRINGERVILLE-EAGAR

The Round Valley opens up at the base of the mountains near the junction of U.S. 191 and U.S. 60; nestled there at about 7,000 feet elevation are the sister villages of Springerville and Eagar. The ancestors of the nearby Zuni and Hopi peoples found this Little Colorado River valley to their liking in the 1250s, and Basque settlers arrived in 1870 and gave the area its moniker, Valle Redondo. By 1879 ranchers and farmers from New Mexico and Utah had trickled in to homestead and raise cattle and crops to supply nearby Fort Apache. A dramatic reminder of the frontier beginnings of these rural Arizona towns is the **Madonna of the Trails** statue, dedicated in 1928 on Main Street in Springerville, across the street from

the post office. John Wayne was famously a partial owner of the 26 Bar Ranch in Eagar, where the Duke and his partners raised high-quality Herefords in the 1960s and 1970s. The Hopi purchased the ranch in the late 1990s in a campaign to reclaim their ancestral lands in the Little Colorado River region.

A short drive north of Springerville on U.S. 191/180 leads to the vast and lonely **Springerville Volcanic Field.** Covering 1,200 square miles of basaltic badlands, the field, whose activity dates from more than 3 million to 13,000 years ago, has 405 vents, some of which look like giant anthills rising out of the sweeping plains strewn with black rocks. A pamphlet guide for a driving tour of the volcanic field, the third largest in North America, is available at the **Springerville-Eagar Regional Chamber of Commerce** (7 W. Main St., 928/333-2123, www.springerville-eagarchamber.com, 9am-5pm daily).

★ Casa Malpais Indian Ruins and Archaeological Park

The volcanic badlands around Springerville and Eagar were once home to several stone-built villages occupied by the ancestors of New Mexico's Zuni and Arizona's Hopi people. The upper Little Colorado River region was occupied on and off from at least AD 900 until about 1400, with the largest villages constructed 1275-1400. The remains of one of these basalt outposts overlooking the river are preserved by the city of Springerville at **Casa Malpais Indian Ruins and Archaeological Park** (418 E. Main St., 928/333-5375, www.casamalpais.org, tours 9am and 1pm Tues.-Sat. Mar.-Nov. weather permitting, advance reservations required, $10). The "house of badlands" had about 50 rooms, a square kiva (a structure used for rituals), and an accurate solar calendar. It was constructed in the late 1270s-early 1280s and occupied for about 50 years. Archaeologists believe that most of its residents had left the area by 1400 and settled at Zuni, 140 miles northeast, while some moved to the Hopi villages, 180 miles

The Wolves of the White Mountains

"We reached the old wolf in time to watch the fierce green fire dying in her eyes," wrote renowned conservationist and author Aldo Leopold in his classic *A Sand County Almanac*. Leopold, a founding hero of the wilderness movement in America, did his first tour of duty as a U.S. Forest Ranger in the White Mountains in 1909, back when the only good wolf in Arizona was a dead wolf. "I was young then, and full of trigger itch," Leopold continued. "I thought that because fewer wolves mean more deer, that no wolves would mean hunters' paradise. But after seeing that green fire die, I sensed that neither the wolf nor the mountain agreed with such a view."

Ahead of his time in the early 20th century, Leopold's hard-learned lesson—that a healthy ecosystem needs predators as well as prey to remain so—is today accepted scientific fact (though a few rural ranchers would disagree). And the wolves, gone from these mountains and forests since the 1970s, have returned.

In 1998, several Mexican gray wolves were reintroduced into the White Mountains region in the **Blue Range Wolf Recovery Area,** near **Hannagan Meadow** along the **Coronado Trail,** and in a nearby New Mexico wilderness. According to the Mexican Wolf Interagency Field Team, as of January 2020 there were a minimum of 163 wolves in the reintroduction area, including 76 in Arizona and 87 in New Mexico.

northwest. When Coronado came through in 1540 searching for the Seven Cities of Cibola, he found no permanent residents in the valley. A tour here, which lasts two hours and requires walking up a steep and rocky trail, is a fascinating and memorable way to learn more about the early settlers of this beautiful harsh land, and the museum preserves some of the artifacts that they left behind.

Recreation

A popular site for fishing, boating, and camping, the **Big Lake Recreation Area** is open May-November and has several campgrounds around the 400-acre **Big Lake** and nearby **Crescent Lake,** 19 miles southwest of Eagar off AZ 261. At 9,000 feet elevation, the highlands can get cold, even in the summer. Still, it's one of the most popular fishing and camping areas in the region and is often crowded with families during summer. **Big Lake Tackle and Supply** (U.S. 191 and U.S. 180, Alpine, 928/339-4338, www.biglakeaz. com) has all the bait, tackle, and other supplies you'll need for a day fishing on Big Lake. They also rent four- and five-person rowboats, motorboats, and kayaks ($16-43 per hour).

Serious hikers should not miss a trek up Arizona's second-highest mountain, 11,409-foot **Mount Baldy.** The high peak is sacred to the Apache people, and the actual top of Mount Baldy is closed to the public. You can make it to within a quarter mile or so of the peak, which most agree is good enough once they see the sweeping views. There are a couple of routes up the mountain, but the most scenic is the 13.5-mile round-trip **West Fork Trail,** which follows the Little Colorado River for several miles through thick old-growth forests and high green meadows. The grade is mostly moderate, though you climb more than 2,000 vertical feet from the bottom to the top, which is above the tree line and rocky and cold, with short gnarled subalpine trees and a blasting wind. To reach the trailhead, drive 3.1 miles west from Eagar on AZ 260, then south on AZ 261 for 18.2 miles to AZ 273. Then head 7.2 miles northwest on AZ 273, cross the river, and drive 1 mile to Mount Baldy Wilderness Trailhead. From Pinetop-Lakeside, take AZ 260 for 26 miles east to AZ 273 (toward Sunrise Ski Resort), turn right on AZ 273, and head south for 11 miles.

Shopping

At the retro-rural **Western Drug & General Store** (106 E. Main St., 928/333-4321, www.westerndrugstore.com, 9am-7pm Mon.-Fri., 9am-6pm Sat., 9am-5pm Sun.) on Springerville's main drag you can buy a deer rifle, pick up a bag of chips and a soda, and fill a prescription. Even if you need none of these things, this 1934 precursor to Walmart is worth a stop, if only to wonder at the bagged-and-stuffed menagerie featuring a mountain lion, an elk, a bighorn sheep, and other Arizona wildlife frozen in mid-grandeur by a loving taxidermist.

Food and Accommodations

Family-owned since the 1970s, **Booga Red's Restaurant and Cantina** (521 E. Main St., 6am-9pm daily, cantina 10am-11pm daily, $6-11) serves delicious, familiar Mexican and American fare from passed-down recipes. This place is a favorite with locals.

Goob's Pizza (211 S. Mountain Ave., 928/333-1502, www.goobspizzas.com, 11am-8pm Tues.-Wed., 11am-9pm Thurs.-Sat., $13-30) serves top-notch pizza, wings, and breadsticks, and has a salad bar. It's in the Safeway Shopping Plaza in Springville and is a great place to fill up after a day outdoors. Along with mouthwatering specialty pizzas and create-your-own options, Goob's offers a small pizza with gluten-free dough.

There are a few small motels along the main route through Springerville and Eagar. You could do worse for a base, as the Round Valley is just 23 miles east of Sunrise Park, 17 miles from Greer, at the junction of U.S. 60 and U.S. 191. **Reed's Lodge** (514 E. Main St., 928/333-4323, http://reedslodge.com, $85-120) has been welcoming travelers since 1949, and, reportedly, the Duke played cards here on occasion back when he owned the nearby 26 Bar Ranch. You probably won't see any celebrities these days, but there's a gallery featuring work by local artists and lots of Old West memorabilia, collectibles, and books. There's a big fireplace in the lobby; the rooms have free Wi-Fi, microwaves, and fridges; and outside there's a hot tub to soak your road-weary bones.

CAMPING

Five campgrounds in the **Big Lake Recreation Area** (www.fs.usda.gov/asnf) offer hundreds of sites (reservations www.recreation.gov) for monster RVs to pup tents. **Apache Trout Campground** ($26 per vehicle, $42 with hookup) has full hookups and can handle big RVs, while **Rainbow Campground** ($20-22 per vehicle) and **Grayling Campground** ($20 per vehicle) can hold small RVs and cars but don't have hookups. The campgrounds offer restrooms and showers a short walk from your site, and there's a store nearby. **Brookchar Campground** ($16 per vehicle), with 12 sites right on the water, is for tent camping only, as is **Cutthroat Campground** ($16 per vehicle).

At most of the campgrounds on Big Lake (Springerville Ranger Station, 928/333-6200, www.fs.usda.gov) you can rent an old-school white canvas tent cabin ($55), just like the ones homesteaders in the area used while they built their cabins, complete with cots, lanterns, and a stove.

Services

The **White Mountain Regional Medical Center** (118 S. Mountain Ave., 928/333-4368, www.wmrmc.com) in Springerville has a 24-hour emergency room.

LYMAN LAKE STATE PARK

North of Springerville-Eagar along U.S. 191/180, the landscape flattens out and opens wide as the crumpled mountains give way to high desert. About 11 miles south of the small town of St. Johns, 1,500-acre **Lyman Lake,** a reservoir formed by damming the Little Colorado River, is stocked with bass and catfish and is one of the only lakes in the region with no boat restrictions. The lake is the centerpiece of the large **Lyman Lake State Park**

(928/337-4441, http://azstateparks.com, $7 per vehicle) where you can camp lakeside in a small log cabin ($65) with electricity and air-conditioning. There are also regular campsites and RV spots (electric, water, and sewer hookups available, $28-33).

At a mere 6,000 feet elevation, Lyman Lake State Park has a more temperate climate than the mountain towns, and it gets relatively hot here in the summer. The **visitors center** (8am-5pm daily May-Sept., 9am-4pm daily Oct.-Apr.) has lots of information and a few displays about the prehistory of the area and its natural history. A small store in the park sells ice, snacks, and fuel, but you should bring all your food with you.

There are a number of ancient mysterious petroglyphs etched into boulders throughout the park, some of which can be seen on the 0.25-mile self-guided **Peninsula Petroglyph Trail** near the campground. You'll need a boat to reach the spectacular **Ultimate Petroglyph Trail,** a 0.5-mile trail on the lake's eastern shore, but it's worth the trip over to see the rocks covered with those cryptic figures.

Apache County Historical Museum

Woolly mammoth tusks, frontier fashions, pioneer-era farming equipment and household items, rock slabs covered in petroglyphs, refurbished historic log cabins, and all manner of other artifacts and ephemera from prehistory to the near present are preserved at the **Apache County Historical Museum** (180 W. Cleveland St., St. Johns, 928/337-4737, 8am-4pm Mon.-Fri., free). It's worth a stop to learn about the people's history of northeastern Arizona—from proto-Pueblo people to Mormon homesteaders and beyond. St. Johns has just 3,000 residents but has an outsize historical presence in the state because it's the hometown of the Arizona Udall clan, Mormon Democrats who produced two national politicians: congressman (1961-1991) and presidential candidate (1976) Mo Udall and secretary of the interior (1961-1969) Stewart Udall.

★ THE CORONADO TRAIL

When Francisco Vazquez de Coronado spurred his prancing mount north from Compostela, Mexico, in 1540, he had reason to believe that the vast unknown northern lands into which he would lead his crowded retinue held riches and glory quite beyond those even of Mexico itself. A few years later he returned, after having traversed what is now the U.S. Southwest, with nothing but saddle sores and a secure place in the history of North American exploration and conquest.

Nobody knows for sure the exact route the Coronado expedition took on its way north in search of the sadly nonexistent Seven Cities of Cibola, but scholars believe that he passed through, or at least nearby, the White Mountains, perhaps following the San Francisco River drainage along what is now the border between Arizona and New Mexico. And they aren't just guessing: Ranching families, homesteaders, and other longtime residents of the region have been digging up and tripping over left-behind and discarded items from the Spanish colonial era for generations.

So it is not wholly unreasonable, as you slowly negotiate the switchbacks and hairpins along the twisty two-lane U.S. 191 from the desert grasslands to the high pinelands, to feel a certain connection to the hard-bitten Spanish explorer. The 120-mile route from the copper mines of Clifton to the U.S. 60 junction near Springerville, which takes 3-5 hours, is often as deserted as it must have been when there was no road at all, the haunt of more wildflowers than vehicles.

Along the way you'll pass the tiny settlements of **Alpine, Nutrioso,** and **Hannagan Meadow,** and to the east, between Clifton and Hannagan Meadow, is the vast **Blue Range Primitive Area,** a coniferous wildland cut through by the Blue River. The scenery is really the attraction; it's best to take it slow, stopping often at the lookouts and

1: Big Lake in the White Mountains **2:** Blue Range Primitive Area along the Coronado Trail

1

2

Blue Range Primitive Area

pullouts set up along the route, marveling at the deep green meadows splashed with yellow, red, and purple in spring-summer. With so much beauty it's hard to keep your eyes on the road, so be careful, and watch for motorcycles; the route is understandably quite popular with that growing group.

Don't take this route if you're in a hurry to hit the lakes or the slopes (indeed, don't take it in winter at all), if you are an impatient driver, or if you're susceptible to car sickness.

Recreation

Most of the Coronado Trail is surrounded by the **Apache-Sitgreaves National Forests.** As you drive along U.S. 191 you'll see a number of trailhead signs on both sides of the road. The helpful folks at the **Alpine Ranger Station** (42634 U.S. 191, Alpine, 928/339-5000, www.fs.usda.gov/asnf) give away a handy 66-page guide to the hiking, mountain biking, and equestrian trails along the Coronado Trail and environs that has detailed descriptions of nearly 20 different trails and information on the area's many lakes.

The best hike in this section of the White Mountains, and one that serious hikers should not miss, is the **Escudilla National Recreation Trail** to the top of **Escudilla Mountain,** a storied regional landmark and the state's third-highest peak. The six-mile round-trip hike takes you through aspen groves and deep stands of fir and spruce, through wide green mountain meadows, and into the Escudilla Wilderness Area (no bicycles allowed). The hike is relatively easy, especially compared to the monumental trek up Mount Baldy, Escudilla's big-sister peak to the west. When you reach the top, at about 10,900 feet above sea level, you'll see the **Escudilla Lookout,** a fire lookout that offers an even higher view of the green land spreading out below. To reach the trailhead, take U.S. 191 north from Alpine for 5.5 miles to Forest Road 8056, then turn right and drive 3.6 miles to Terry Flat. Take the left fork past Toolbox Draw about 0.5 miles to the trailhead.

Just three miles east of Alpine on U.S.

180, the 154-acre **Luna Lake** is stocked with trout and a popular camping, fishing, hiking, and biking spot. A few loop trails around the lake, which attracts bald eagles and other exotic wildlife, offer easy hiking and biking for families with children.

If you're dead set on seeing some of the region's abundant but typically shy wildlife, the best place is the **Sipe White Mountain Wildlife Area** (928/367-4281, www.azgfd. com, visitors center 8am-5pm daily mid-May-mid-Oct.). Two miles south of Eagar off the Coronado Trail, this 1,362-acre former Hereford ranch has been converted by the Arizona Game and Fish Department into a prime wildlife-viewing area with several easy trails and developed lookouts. Bring your binoculars to spot elk, deer, bald eagles, hawks, wild turkeys, and other wildlife. This is another ideal place to bring the kids, as the trails are relatively flat, easy, and short, and everybody knows that kids love animals. The visitors center, open only in the summer months, has displays about the area's natural history. It's all free, and you can bring your horse or your bike along, but the best way to see wildlife is to sit still and quiet, waiting.

Food and Accommodations

Most of the services along the Coronado Trail are in the tiny mountain village of **Alpine,** 94 miles north of the scenic byway's beginnings in Clifton. If you're headed up the trail from the desert, there isn't much in the way of food or even gas between Clifton and Alpine, a drive that could take three hours. But once you reach the tiny highland settlement, at 8,050 feet elevation near the headwaters of the San Francisco River, there are several excellent restaurants to choose from for a leisurely lunch or dinner after a long day of driving and forest play. Alpine, six miles west of the New Mexico border, has a few rustic rural hideaways, and dozens of cabins are for rent throughout the area. Some of the restaurant owners in Alpine also rent cabins, and the **Alpine Area Chamber of Commerce** (928/339-4330, www.alpinearizona.com)

has information about rentals on its website. Many of the businesses in Alpine have seasonal hours and are often closed in winter.

A pleasant and cozy little place close to the junction of U.S. 180 and the Coronado Trail at Alpine, **Foxfire at Alpine** (42661 U.S. 180, 928/339-4344, http://foxfireatalpineaz.com, 4pm-8pm Mon.-Thurs., 11am-8pm Fri.-Sun., $10-25) serves delicious burgers, sandwiches, salads, soups, pasta, and pizza, all with a homemade touch and care for details. It offers vegetarian, vegan, and gluten-free dishes.

Open since 1926 and right off the trail, **Hannagan Meadow Lodge** (U.S. 191, mile marker 232, 928/339-4370, www. hannaganmeadow.com, $85-165), 22 miles south of Alpine, is a historic cozy forest getaway with a backcountry atmosphere and antique country-style decor. Rates vary by season by $5-10 and are lowest in winter (early Nov.-Apr.) and fall (mid-Aug.-early Nov.), slightly higher in spring (May-early June), and highest in summer (early June-mid-Aug.). The lodge rents seven suites named for figures from Arizona history, and there are cabins named for luminaries of local history. It also has a **country-comfort dining room** (8am-8pm daily, $6-30).

The Gila Valley

Only about 40,000 people live in the Gila (HEE-la) Valley, where the Sonoran and Chihuahuan Deserts meet near Arizona's border with New Mexico. Tiny towns, many of them moribund long ago, stand dusty and forgotten along the Old West Highway (U.S. 70). Former Supreme Court justice Sandra Day O'Connor grew up near Duncan, the last station before New Mexico, on the Lazy B Ranch. The whole lonely region is watched over by the largest of Southern Arizona's sky islands, Mount Graham, where telescopes scour the heavens for signs and wonders. Hot springs bubble up from beneath the hot sand, and the Gila River, a once mighty Southwestern river now dammed to oblivion and sucked mostly dry, still runs year-round here in a few lush riparian oases.

SAFFORD AND VICINITY

Safford, a rural town of 8,000 inhabitants near the Gila River, has been a farming, mining, and ranching area since the 1870s. Cotton is still grown in this hot desert valley, and a mighty chunk of the nation's copper is ripped from the ground just to the northeast. Safford still has a quaint downtown strip, an old courthouse building, and some residential neighborhoods with historic bungalows, but most of the town is a jumble of chain stores, restaurants, hotels, and strip malls strung along U.S. 70 between the New Mexico border (45 miles east) and the San Carlos Apache Reservation (60 miles west). Safford is the bright light of the upper Gila Valley, to which all the outliers, holding tight to something in the nearly empty old communities of Pima and Thatcher to the west and Solomon, Duncan, and Clifton-Morenci to the east, look toward for company and supplies. As such, it makes a good base for your Gila Valley adventures.

Sights

Not even the dust kicked up by all that uninterrupted open-pit mining less than 50 miles to the northeast can spoil the clear dark rural skies, and the 10,720-foot sky island peak that hems the valley to the southwest, Mount Graham, holds a few of the world's most powerful telescopes. **Eastern Arizona College's Discovery Park Campus** (1651 W. Discovery Park Blvd., Safford, 928/428-6260, www.eac.edu/discoverypark, 8am-5pm Mon.-Fri., 4pm-9:30pm Sat., free) celebrates and explains the area's astronomical benefits, the science of astronomy, the beginnings of life, and the mysteries of the universe at its

Governor Aker Observatory. It costs nothing to take a look at the sun through a telescope equipped with eye-saving filters, or to listen to the eerie sounds of space. The highlight of a visit is a ride on the **Space Shuttle Polaris** simulator, in which you tour the solar system after buzzing Mount Graham. This is a great place to take kids. The grounds have several trails along which the public can stroll at will during business hours; the campus shows off the desert at its best, with a restored riparian area alive with birds and, if you are patient, maybe a few other animals. You can also book an all-day tour of the Mount Graham International Observatory.

For a more down-to-earth, human-centric view of the valley, visit the **Eastern Arizona Museum and Historical Society** (2 N. Main St., Pima, 928/485-9400, www.easternarizonamuseum.com, 10am-3pm Thurs.-Sat.), which preserves relics and stories from the valley's long history of habitation, from hunter-gatherer tribes to the Apache people, Mormon pioneers, cotton farmers, and cattle ranchers.

An even deeper look at the valley's history is offered on the **Graham County Historic Walking and Driving Tour,** a self-guided tour of U.S. 70 through Solomon, Safford, Thatcher, and Pima. Along the way you'll see just about every old building of note in the tiny old towns as well as Safford's 1916 neocolonial courthouse and several historic homes. The **Graham County Chamber of Commerce** (1111 Thatcher Blvd., Safford, 928/428-2511 or 888/837-1841, www.visitgrahamcounty.com, 9am-5pm Mon.-Fri.) has a free 11-page booklet describing the tour, along with a plethora of other information about the area.

Festivals and Events

The whole valley celebrates its Mexican restaurants and heritage with **SalsaFest** (www.salsatrail.com) in late September, when local chefs compete in salsa-making competitions, eaters try to outdo one another in a jalapeño-eating contest, children bounce around in castles, and bands play to crowds stuffed with food and fun.

Food

The Gila Valley has some of the finest Mexican restaurants in Arizona, most of them small casual family-owned spots along U.S. 70 and frequented by locals. Some valley restaurants have grouped together to form **The Salsa Trail,** a marketing campaign to draw visitors and diners to this lonely region. One

the Old Safford Bridge in Gila Box Riparian National Conservation Area

can hardly imagine a more worthy public service. Uniformly first-rate, the member eateries serve fresh and familiar Mexican fare with local and familial twists, and many offer American dishes as well. There is no reason to eat anywhere else, and the non-Mexican choices in Safford are mostly chains and fast food. A brochure and map of the Salsa Trail are available at the **Graham County Chamber of Commerce** (1111 Thatcher Blvd., Safford, 928/428-2511 or 888/837-1841, www.visitgrahamcounty.com, 5am-9pm Mon.-Fri.) or at any of the eateries listed below.

In Safford's retro and quiet old downtown, **El Coronado** (409 W. Main St., 928/428-7755, 7am-8pm Mon. and Wed.-Fri., 7am-5pm Sat.-Sun., $8-11) has superlative breakfasts: big fat burritos stuffed with egg, potato, cheese, and peppers, legendary huevos rancheros, or a simple plate of eggs and bacon if you're not into early morning spice. The Mexican dishes are delicious and, of course, filling.

For tortillas that might convince you to buy a trailer in Safford just to be nearby, visit the famed **Mi Casa Tortilla Factory** (621 S. 7th Ave., 928/428-7915, www.micasatortilla.com, 10am-6pm Mon.-Fri., 10am-4pm Sat., $5-10). Fresh and hot, simple and handmade, these tortillas are known far and wide. Buy a few dozen to chomp on in the car as you head out to the river or up to Mount Graham. Also try the beans, chips, and salsas.

Valley locals love **El Charro** (601 W. Main St., 928/428-4134, www.elcharrogrill.com, 11am-8:30pm Mon.-Thurs., 11am-9:30pm Fri.-Sat., $8-11) in downtown Safford because it's been open and serving pretty much the same food since 1955; it's the oldest restaurant in the region. The enchiladas, red- and green-chili burritos, and other standard dishes are tasty and fresh, and the special *chalaca,* a fried masa bowl stuffed with beans and chili meat, is worth a try if you're in the mood for something slightly different.

Accommodations

The **Cottage Bed & Breakfast** (1104 S. Central Ave., Safford, 928/428-5118 or 800/814-5118, www.cottagebedandbreakfast.com, $90) in Safford has the most distinctive and drive-worthy accommodations in town. This very small bed-and-breakfast, in a red-brick Western Colonial Revival home on the National Register of Historic Places, has a pleasant kind of Old West ambience. A wonderful bakery on-site serves homemade bread and pastries, espresso, and tea.

Nothing beats Duncan's **Simpson Hotel** (116 Main St., Duncan, 928/359-3590, www.simpsonhotel.com, $80-109), about 40 miles east of Safford on U.S. 70, for that rural-West atmosphere. The owner has beautifully restored an old hotel first opened in 1915 and decorated its small cozy guest rooms (including one named for writer Cormac McCarthy) with a tasteful country simplicity. The breakfasts are worth waking up for, made with all-natural and often local ingredients. Birders will want to walk a short loop trail nearby along the Gila River; ask the host for a birding checklist.

The **Essence of Tranquility Natural Hot Spring** (6047 S. Lebanon Loop, Safford, 928/428-9312, www.azhotmineralspring.com), in the shadow of 10,720-foot Mount Graham, offers clothing-optional hot spring baths where you can soak away all your stress and troubles. The baths are charmingly decorated and private; a bigger communal bath requires clothing. A bit on the rustic side, Essence of Tranquility is a wonderful place to visit if you love hot springs and want to meet like-minded soakers. If you want to stay the night or longer, you can camp ($15), which includes use of a communal kitchen and barbecue area and unlimited use of the tubs. Rustic but comfortable casitas ($50-70) are also available. You can make a reservation for ear coning (an alternative-medicine method of cleaning and detoxifying the ears), shiatsu, and Swedish massage, or a detoxifying sweat wrap. If you're just going for the day, expect to pay $8-10 per person to use the baths. While most of the baths are clothing optional, the owners don't allow any "open nudity." They also discourage bringing children.

Services

The **Mount Graham Regional Medical Center** (1600 S. 20th Ave., Safford, 928/348-4000, www.mtgraham.org) in Safford has a full-service 24-hour emergency room with 17 treatment bays.

ROPER LAKE STATE PARK

Desert-valley **Roper Lake State Park** (101 E. Roper Lake Rd., Safford, 928/428-6760, http://azstateparks.com, $10 per car) has decent fishing in a 30-acre reservoir and rents small but comfortable (more than a tent, anyway) log cabins (reservations required, $65-70) that sleep up to six. The lake is stocked with trout and bass, and there are clean showers and both electric ($30) and nonelectric ($20) campsites.

Roper Lake is also a fun spot to stop for a day of swimming from its sandy swimming beach and soaking in its stone-lined hot tub filled by underground hot springs. Five miles of mostly flat easy desert trails around the park include a two-mile loop trail at nearby **Dankworth Pond,** a unit of the park three miles south on U.S. 191, that winds around a recreated village from the Paleo-Indian and Mogollon periods.

HOT WELL DUNES RECREATION AREA

Another developed hot spring bubbles up deep in the desert 35 miles southeast of Safford in the middle of 2,000 acres of shifting sand dunes at **Hot Well Dunes Recreation Area.** This is a stark and hot landscape popular with off-road vehicle enthusiasts, who crowd the dunes fall-spring to tear around on their sand rails and ATVs. The recreation area is often quite busy for being so remote, and if you're just looking to soak in the three developed fenced-in tubs fed by a warm artesian well, it's not a good idea to go out on the weekends during the beautiful months. In summer it's blistering hot and not too welcoming. There's no electricity, drinking water, food, gas, or phones, so bring all your own

supplies. Several developed camping spots have fire rings and picnic tables, or you can camp in undeveloped spots. There are toilets on-site. A recreation use fee ($3 per day) is required, and if you're planning to rip around the dunes you also need an OHV decal ($25). From Safford, head 7 miles east on U.S. 70, then turn south on Haekel Road; from here it's 25 miles to the recreation area.

Despite the distance and isolation of the dunes, if you're a natural hot spring enthusiast, you should make the effort. The artesian well, discovered in 1928 by workers drilling for oil (you can still see the ancient drilling equipment nearby), spews 250 gallons of 106°F water every minute. It fills two developed tubs and overflows into a pond to make a cooler third pool.

For more information contact the **Safford BLM office** (711 14th Ave., 928/348-4400, www.blm.gov/az). You can purchase an OHV decal at www.servicearizona.com.

PINALEÑO MOUNTAINS AND MOUNT GRAHAM

The largest of Southern Arizona's sky islands, the Pinaleño range guards the upper Gila Valley from the west, an often-snowcapped Olympus for the lowlanders in the desert scrub below to ponder. The range has seven peaks, all of them over 7,000 feet but none as high as 10,720-foot Mount Graham, which residents here often use to refer to the entire range, its influence over the valley below being that strong.

Mount Graham, atop which astronomers scan the universe with some of the most powerful telescopes in the world, can be reached by just about any vehicle via the Civilian Conservation Corps-constructed **Swift Trail Parkway** (AZ 366, off U.S. 191 about 8 miles south of Safford). The steep twisting two-lane road rises from the scrubby desert floor at 3,000 feet elevation to over 9,000 feet near the top of Mount Graham. Along the way it passes through most of the state's major ecosystems, finally reaching the high evergreen forest, where the air is cool and thin. Swift

Trail Parkway is 35 miles one-way and takes about two hours. You'll twist past old summer cabins, trailheads, campgrounds, lookouts, and picnic tables, and it's essential to stop along the way and take your time, noticing as the scrub gives way to oak woodlands, which give way to tall and thin pines, which pass on to majestic stands of fir and spruce. Snow usually closes the Swift Trail by November 14; it opens for the driving season on April 15. Most passenger cars can navigate the 22 miles of the route that are paved and the 13 miles that are graded dirt. At the end of the trail you'll see Riggs Lake, a small highland fishing hole stocked with trout. The Safford Ranger Station (711 14th Ave., Suite D, Safford, 928/428-4150, 8am-4pm Mon.-Fri.) has a lot of information on traveling, hiking, and camping in the mountains, including a booklet on driving the Swift Trail. The folks at the Columbine Visitor Information Station, three-quarters of the way up the road, are also helpful.

Operated by the University of Arizona in Tucson, the Mount Graham International Observatory sits near the top of Mount Graham, its powerful telescopes pointed at the heavens. Indeed, the Vatican Advanced Technology Telescope may literally be aimed heavenward. Also scanning the galaxy and beyond are the Heinrich Hert Submillimeter Radio Telescope and the Large Binocular Telescope, humankind's strongest eye on the great unknown. Eastern Arizona College's Discovery Park Campus (1651 W. Discovery Park Blvd., Safford, 928/428-6260, http://mgio.arizona.edu/visiting-public) organizes infrequent tours of the observatory complex Friday-Saturday May-October, when the mountain weather cooperates. The tour, in groups of six or more, lasts all day (9am-4:30pm, no children under 8, $40 pp) and includes a sack lunch and a fair bit of the natural and human history of the area as well as an in-depth look at the observatory. You ride in a van along the Swift Trail to the top, and the guide points out all the interesting sights along the way. The tour begins in Safford at Discovery Park. Call far ahead to make a reservation.

★ GILA BOX RIPARIAN NATIONAL CONSERVATION AREA

You can't visit the Gila Valley without at least a glimpse at the sad river that drew, in turn, Apaches, trappers, and Mormon farmers to this area long ago. The Gila was once a mighty desert river, but Phoenix's thirst, along with the irrigation needs of the valley's farmers, has dammed and sucked the Gila to death. In a few places it still runs wild and free through wilderness that isn't too different from that seen by Native Americans and pioneers. One of those places is the BLM-monitored Gila Box Riparian National Conservation Area (BLM Safford Field Office, 711 14th Ave., 928/348-4400, www.blm.gov/az, recreation fee $3 per day), a 23,000-acre nature preserve off U.S. 70 just 20 miles northeast of Safford.

A popular spot for kayakers and other river runners, the Gila Box offers streamside hiking, cool riparian coves, and a chance to see a few bighorn sheep clinging to rocky cliffs. Cottonwood stands, mesquite bosks, and sandbars line the mud-brown flow, hemmed by high beige cliffs. The best way to see the river and possibly some wildlife is to take Sanchez Road off U.S. 70, five miles east of Safford (you'll see signs) to the Spring Canyon Picnic Area, nine miles from the turnoff; along the way you'll pass an entrance kiosk. From here you can walk along the river on the two-mile Cottonwood Trail loop through the Riverview Campground and past the Kearny Monument, a tribute to General Stephen Watts Kearny, who led 300 soldiers along the Gila River, camping nearby at Bonita Creek, to California during the Mexican-American War. Then it's on to the Bonita Creek Watchable Wildlife Area, which has interpretive signs about the area's animals. You can also drive through the area on dirt roads, and there are two developed campgrounds ($5). If you're a floater,

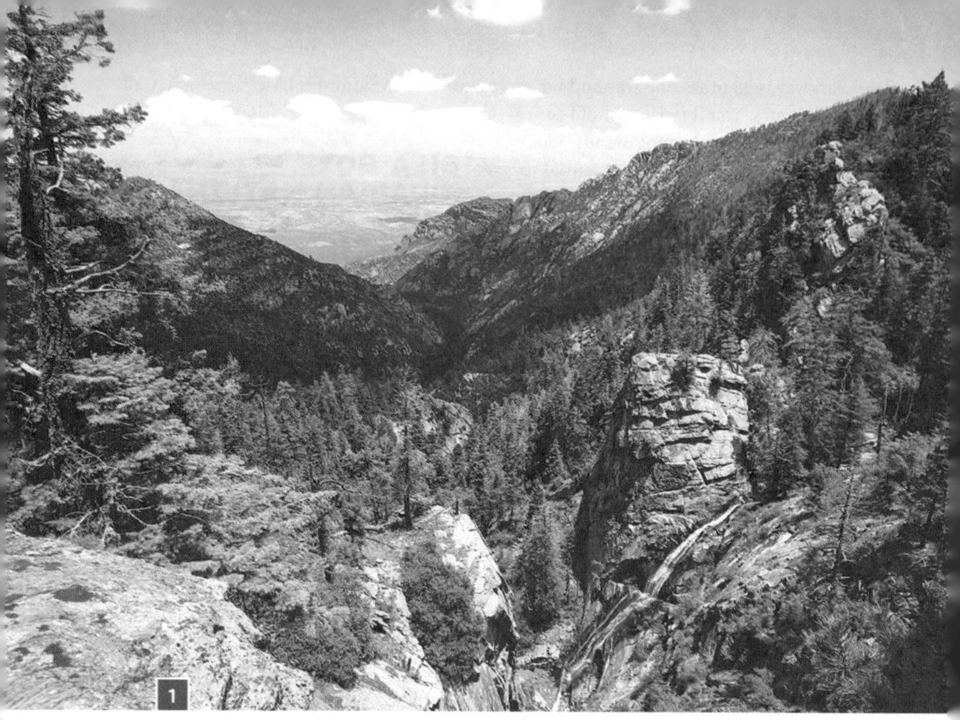
1

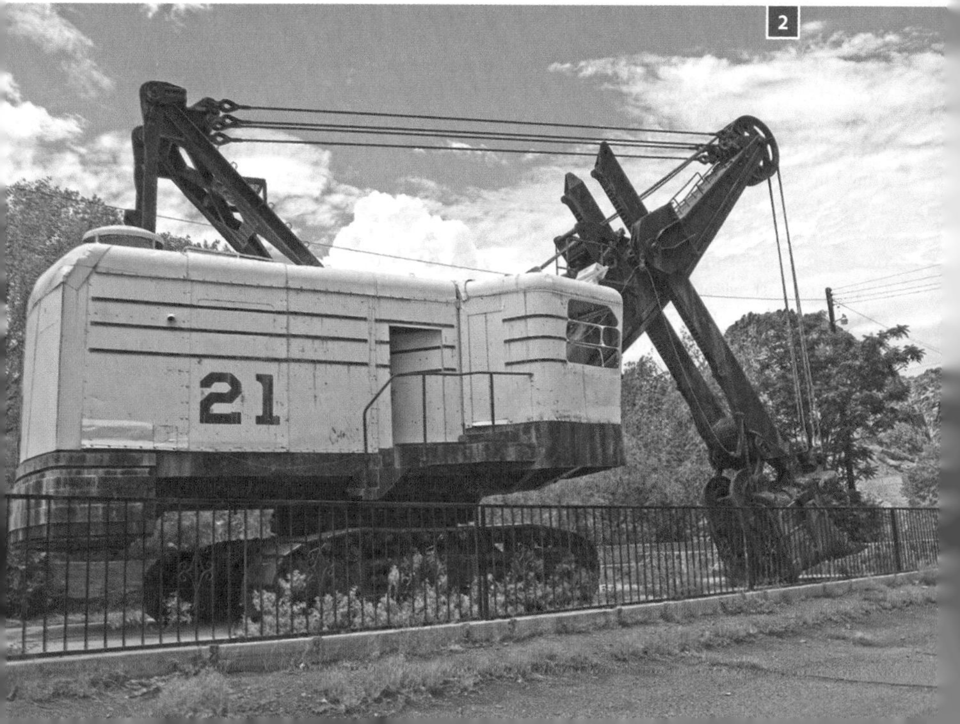

2

make sure to check out the website for more information.

A rugged and scenic alternative route to the river is the **Black Hills Back Country Byway,** a 21-mile bumpy dirt road that passes over the river at the historic concrete **Old Safford Bridge,** built in 1918. You don't reach the river until 17 miles in, but along the way the dry scrublands provide sweeping lonely views, including the postapocalyptic Morenci Mine. There's a picnic area and campground with a restroom below the bridge. This is also a popular place for boaters to put in. The byway ends just outside Morenci at U.S. 191 and makes a good scenic detour.

CLIFTON AND MORENCI

These two small towns along U.S. 191, bisected by the lazy San Francisco River and marking the start of the Coronado Trail into the White Mountains, were founded in the late 1800s as a copper mining complex, and they remain so today.

Clifton, with only 2,000 residents, is full of boarded-up old buildings from the late 19th-early 20th centuries. Drive around slowly and wonder at the fix-up potential of these grand old structures. There's a small local-history museum and some cool old buildings in the old downtown and several across the bridge on the east side of the river. The town's old jail, chunked out of the cliff side, is still visible along the highway, and on the east side of the bridge is a huge old digger that helped open up the pit. Up the hill a few miles in **Morenci** is Freeport-McMoran's Morenci Mine, the nation's largest, producing 800 million pounds of metal every year. There's a turnout five miles north of town to view the monumental hole in the ground that is the result. Two-thirds of the 4,500 residents of the two towns work for the mine, which moans day and night. Driving up or down the twisting road through Morenci at night, while the

lit-up mine is working, is an unsettling—and thrilling—experience.

SAN CARLOS APACHE RESERVATION

Before 1871, the Western Apache bands that call this 1.8-million-acre reservation along the Gila River northwest of Safford home used to live and migrate across the valley's desert grasslands, creek sides, and oak woodlands, hunting game and gathering the land's many edibles. These days the San Carlos Apache Tribe welcomes visitors for recreation on their sparsely populated lands, and they operate a casino-resort complex with a golf course. To hike, fish, swim, and drive the backcountry, you need to purchase a permit from **San Carlos Apache Tribe Recreation & Wildlife Department** (U.S. 70 and Geronimo Rd., San Carlos, 928/475-2343 or 888/475-2344, www.scatrecreation.org, $10 per day). Permits are also sold at the Apache Gold Casino's convenience store and at the Express Stop in Globe.

The **San Carlos Apache Culture Center** (U.S. 70, milepost 272, 928/475-2894, www.sancarlosapache.com, 9am-5pm Mon.-Fri.) has interesting displays about the tribe's history and culture. You can also see and purchase examples of the locally made peridot jewelry. The world's largest deposit of the August birthstone is located near the reservation capital of **San Carlos,** and there are a few places in the small town that sell jewelry, Apache burden baskets, cradle boards, and other local arts and crafts. The culture center has a good gift shop selling all of these items and more, as does the Apache Gold Casino.

Apache Gold Casino

Apache Gold (U.S. 70, 5 miles east of Globe, 800/272-2438, www.apache-gold-casino.com) is the center of activity on the reservation, offering the usual slots, blackjack, poker, bingo, and live entertainment. The resort also offers accommodations, restaurants, a gift shop, and a golf course. In 2021 it was undergoing renovations; check for updates.

1: Pinaleño Mountains **2:** a mining tractor at Morenci Mine

The Western Apache and the Settlers

All over Southern and Central Arizona, where the Western Apache people once wandered unchallenged according to a seasonal schedule held deep in their cultural memories, there is food: acorns, agave, wild spinach, wild onions, mesquite beans, cactus fruit, and more—all integral to the diverse Apache larder.

Once settlers—Spanish, then Mexican, then American—began claiming this land as their own, the Western Apache found it increasingly difficult to gain unfettered access to their traditional gathering grounds, and they drew the unending ire of the new arrivals when they stole livestock, which many Apache saw as little different from hunting any other ungulate grazing in the desert.

Really, the Western Apache never had much of a chance. Their lifeways were about thin-line subsistence, living lightly so as to conserve the resources of the desert for future generations. The capitalist settlers couldn't have been more different. They wanted wealth, surplus, and the power that comes with it. The settlers also never really got that not all Apaches were the same. The Western Apache, one of the few agricultural-minded bands in Apacheria, were often blamed for the depredations of the less sedentary Chiricahua Apache, who claimed Geronimo as one of their leaders.

These circumstances, building over generations, led to the Camp Grant Massacre in 1871, an infamous slaughter of more than 100 Western Apache people, mostly women and children, who were peacefully camped close to a U.S. Army fort near Aravaipa Canyon, south of San Carlos Lake on the San Carlos Apache Reservation.

The outrage was planned and perpetrated by the leading lights of Tucson's business community and justified by the half-mad screeds of *Tucson Citizen* editor John Wasson. In the aftermath of the largely unprovoked massacre, Tucson's murderous elite didn't even bother to attempt to name the victims for the laughable trial that saw all the perpetrators acquitted; instead, they listed them as John Doe Apache or Mary Doe Apache—names that reveal just how unknown the Western Apache were to their new neighbors.

San Carlos Lake

Formed by the damming of the Gila River, **San Carlos Lake** is a large reservoir with 158 miles of desert shoreline surrounded by the jagged Gila, Mescal, and Santa Teresa Mountains. It has good fishing, and there's a tackle shop with snacks and other supplies on-site. The nearby **Coolidge Dam,** dedicated by its namesake Commander-in-Chief Calvin Coolidge in 1930, is a feat of engineering that's worth seeing. Follow the signed road south from U.S. 70 at Peridot to the **San Carlos Reservoir Recreation Area** (928/475-2343, recreation permit $10 per day), where you can boat and swim, water-ski, fish, camp, and walk around the rocky scrublands.

The Lower Colorado River

The great river is the chief draw of this region, with much to see and do in the small resort communities along its banks—especially if you like getting wet.

Here you can marvel at the engineering audacity of Hoover Dam, which sought to tame the Colorado and bring hydroelectricity, irrigation, and predictable flows to the desert. Spend hot lazy days by the water at Lake Havasu City and stroll across London Bridge, rebuilt here in the desert in the 1970s. Discover the Old West in Yuma and the history of U.S. road culture in Kingman, Seligman, and along the lonely remains of old Route 66.

Hikers, bikers, desert rats, and winter bird-watchers can explore several vast desert wildlife refuges as well as nine wilderness areas

Highlights

Look for ★ to find recommended sights, activities, dining, and lodging.

★ **Hoover Dam:** One of the largest concrete dams in the world holds back the Colorado River in a barren desert canyon (page 380).

★ **Driving Historic Route 66:** On the longest remaining stretch of the old Mother Road, nostalgia rules (page 387).

★ **Seligman:** This small town is a throwback to the Route 66 era—and one of the models for the town of Radiator Springs in the Disney-Pixar film *Cars* (page 394).

★ **London Bridge:** The picturesque bridge that once spanned the Thames now reaches across the Lake Havasu channel (page 399).

★ **Yuma Territorial Prison State Historic Park:** Witness how the rapscallions and outlaws of Arizona's wild territorial days lived in this legendary Old West prison (page 404).

within Lake Mead National Recreation Area. The shifting sand dunes outside of Yuma will make you wonder if you've wandered into the Sahara.

This region is often the hottest in the state, if not the country, but the cool waters of the Colorado make it a resort destination for thousands of water-loving visitors every year.

PLANNING YOUR TIME

A week is sufficient to tour "Arizona's west coast" (a half-serious nickname that refers to the region's river-centric lifestyle) in depth, but a scenic drive-through with a stop for a dip in the river, a boat tour, and a visit to all the essentials can be done in a long weekend.

TRANSPORTATION

It's best to start at one end and drive south or north, hitting towns and sights along the river. From the north, start at Lake Mead National Recreation Area (or in Las Vegas, just an hour or so to the northwest) and move south on U.S. 93 to Kingman. Along the way, visit the recreation area and Hoover Dam, an absolutely essential stop in this region. From Kingman, take Historic Route 66 over Sitgreaves Pass and through the little Old West reenactment town of Oatman, with its friendly semiwild burros. If you want to gamble or splash in the Colorado, from Oatman head west to AZ 95 and Bullhead City-Laughlin; if you want to skip Route 66 altogether and head straight back to the river, take AZ 68 west from Kingman. If you're more

interested in desolate stretches than river play, you can keep south on Route 66 from Oatman to Topock and the Havasu National Wildlife Refuge. A brief tug east on I-40 and then south through the seemingly empty land along AZ 95 will take you into Lake Havasu City, where you can stroll beneath London Bridge and maybe rent a boat or book a cruise up to wild Topock Gorge.

Keep heading south through the sparse, jagged desert around Parker and Quartzsite and then on to Yuma, the southern end of the tour. A short drive west into California on I-8 will take you to the strange and thrilling Algodones Dunes, where you can imagine that you're floating above the Dune Sea in *Return of the Jedi.* Just west of U.S. 95, north of Yuma, you'll find Martinez Lake, where you can book a boat tour into the Imperial National Wildlife Refuge. To reach the refuge on your own, take I-10 from Quartzsite to Blythe, California, and then CA 78 south. Also just a bit north of Yuma along U.S. 95 you'll pass the huge Kofa National Wildlife Refuge, where you can take a short hike into Palm Canyon to see the state's only native palm trees. If you're starting from Yuma in the south, which makes sense if you're coming from either Tucson or Phoenix, reverse the route, taking U.S. 95 north across the desert, following it when it becomes AZ 95 at Quartzsite through Bullhead City-Laughlin, veering west briefly onto I-40, and then taking Old Route 66 northeast and then U.S. 93 northwest to Hoover Dam.

Previous: Hoover Dam; Yuma Territorial Prison State Historic Park; Historic Route 66 Motel in Seligman.

The Lower Colorado River

UTAH

NEVADA

Kaibab National Forest

Grand Canyon National Park

Havasupai Indian Reservation

To Flagstaff

Williams

Kaibab National Forest

Prescott National Forest

Grand Canyon Village

Ash Fork

180

HISTORIC RTE 66

SELIGMAN

DRIVING HISTORIC ROUTE 66

Colorado River

Hualapai Indian Reservation

DIAMOND CREEK RD

40

St. George

Lake Mead National Recreation Area

Grand Canyon National Park

Peach Springs

Truxton

Valentine

66

Hualapai Mountain

93

Virgin River

BUCK AND DOE RD

SEE "KINGMAN" MAP

Cherum Peak 6,983ft

Kingman

Hualapai Peak 8,416ft

Wabayuma Peak 7,601ft

Lake Mead National Recreation Area

GRAND WASH

GUANO POINT

WINDY POINT

BORIANA MINE RD

Dolan Springs

25

Overton

Lake Mead National Recreation Area

ECHO BAY

Lake Mead

TEMPLE BAR

Chloride

KATHERINE LANDING

93

68

Goldroad

Havasu National Wildlife Refuge

169

CALLVILLE BAY

KINGMAN WASH

143

WILLOW BEACH

93

Colorado River

Bullhead City

Oatman

95

OVERTON BEACH

169

167

Nelson

165

ELDORADO CANYON

DAVIS DAM

163

Laughlin

Fort Mohave Indian Res

40

Needles

LAS VEGAS BAY

BOULDER BEACH

ALAN BIBLE VISITOR CENTER

Boulder City

HOOVER DAM

COTTONWOOD COVE

Lake Mohave

95

147

93

Las Vegas

SEE "DRIVING HISTORIC ROUTE 66" MAP

15

Searchlight

95

164

15

To Los Angeles

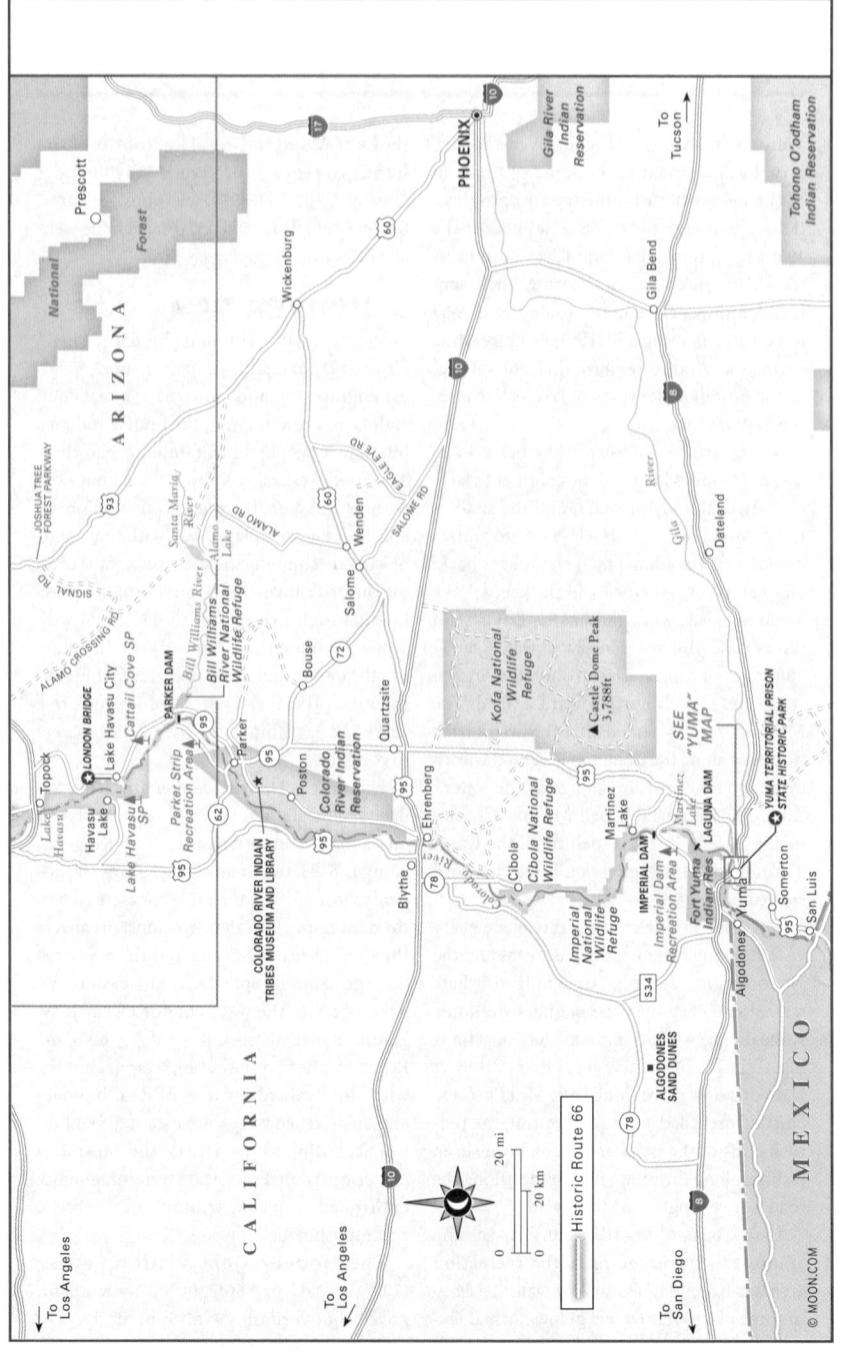

THE LOWER COLORADO RIVER

© MOON.COM

Lake Mead National Recreation Area

Water spreads like fingers over the dry scrubby land, molding a wet playground out of the necessities of industry and progress. It wasn't enough for those reclaimers of the 1930s to stop the Colorado River dead in its tracks and impound all the water the imagined Southwestern empire would need. Why not create a boating and fishing empire while we're at it? And so we have this 290-square-mile 2.5-million-acre national recreation area, the nation's first.

There are two desert lakes here: Lake Mead, 112 miles long and the continent's largest artificial body of water, and the smaller Lake Mohave (moh-HAH-vee), 67 miles downriver. Two dams hold the waters back: Hoover Dam, 70 stories high, keeps Lake Mead in check, while the smaller Davis Dam forms Lake Mohave. The placid waters lap at 700 miles of Mojave Desert shoreline in two states and stretch north toward a third. The Mojave Desert is named after the desert tribe that lived along the Colorado River—the word means something like "alongside the water." The folks that established Mohave County in 1864 used a variant spelling of the word. Throughout this region you'll see the word spelled both ways.

Millions of revelers find this place every year, flocking from nearby Las Vegas and the Arizona cities. There is excellent fishing here no matter the season, plus boating, swimming, scuba diving, sunbathing, and houseboat touring. If you're not a water type, a tour of Hoover Dam or a slow drive along Lake Mead's scenic Northshore Road—the sun igniting the red-rock cliffs of the Bowl of Fire, bighorn sheep picking along the rough rock spines along the road—are enough to justify a visit.

Due to prolonged drought in the Southwest, in recent years the recreation area has been plagued by low water levels—in some places it is 60 feet below normal levels—causing the closure of a few areas. Call the **Lake Mead National Recreation Area headquarters** (601 Nevada Way, Boulder City, NV, 702/293-8907, www.nps.gov/lame, $25 per vehicle for 7 days) or check the website before making plans.

★ HOOVER DAM

Once the largest dam of its kind anywhere, **Hoover Dam** is still one of the nation's greatest engineering and construction feats and stands as a testament to the brawn and ambition of a people set on taming a wild river. The Southwest as we know it would not exist without this dam. During its construction, an epic human story played out, with thousands of workers climbing the sheer rock walls of an overheated canyon in the middle of nowhere, holding back a river with concrete and will. Some say more than 700 workers died during the dam's construction (a number higher than the official estimates), which took five years and 3.2 million cubic yards of concrete to complete.

Not only is Hoover Dam engineering audacity of the highest order, it's a rather stylish one at that. Heading northwest from Kingman along U.S. 93, the walls of Black Canyon suddenly close in, and the huge concrete slab of the dam comes into view. You must drive over the dam to reach Nevada and the **parking garage** (8am-5:15pm daily, $10, cash only), passing along the way sculptor Oskar J. W. Hansen's soaring work *Winged Figures of the Republic*. The two 30-foot-high bronze angels, with the strained muscles of dam builders and upstretched wings, are meant to symbolize, according to the artist, "the enormous power of trained physical strength, equally enthroned in placid triumph of scientific accomplishment."

The **Hoover Dam Visitor Center** (702/494-2517 or 866/730-9097, www.usbr.gov/lc/hooverdam, 9am-5pm daily, $10 without tour) has numerous exhibits on the building of the dam and the scientific and social justifications behind the enormous undertaking. There's a short movie and an elevator to the roof, the best overview of the dam complex and the river flowing beyond it to Lake Mohave. If you're already here, it's worth taking one of the two tours offered. The **Powerplant Tour** ($15 adults, $12 ages 4-16) lasts about 30 minutes and gives a comprehensive view of the dam and an explanation of how it works. The **Hoover Dam Tour** (minimum age 8, $30) lasts about one hour and goes deep into the dam, revealing the inner workings of the huge complex. This tour is highly recommended and worth the extra cost; it includes a booklet about the dam for each participant. You get to walk the rounded and brightly lit low-ceilinged corridors inside the dam works and view the lazy river from high up in the dam. This tour also provides a chance to see all the beautiful art deco touches folded into the design of the dam complex in the 1930s, an arguably more stylish era than our own. The entire inner complex is floored with gray Italian marble flecked with reds and yellows, and there are stylized Native American-inspired designs etched into the floor in even the most out-of-the-way corners. In summer, the first tour begins at 9am, and

the last tour at 5:15pm. In winter, the last tour begins at 4:15pm. The last tickets are sold an hour before the last tour. There's a standard gift shop near the parking garage and a little café that serves good but expensive hamburgers, sandwiches, hot dogs, and other tasty eats.

Hoover Dam Bypass/ Colorado River Bridge

The Colorado River Bridge spans Black Canyon about 900 feet above the Colorado River just south of Hoover Dam. Officially named the **Mike O'Callaghan-Pat Tillman Memorial Bridge** (after Nevada governor Mike O'Callaghan and Pat Tillman, a former Arizona Cardinals player and Army Ranger killed by friendly fire in Afghanistan), it is one of the longest and highest arch bridges in the western hemisphere. On the Nevada side there's a path and viewing area where you can stop and look at the dam and the river rushing by far below.

LAKE MEAD

The larger of the two lakes in the recreation area is **Lake Mead.** When full—which it hasn't been since the early 1980s due to prolonged drought—the lake is 112 miles long and 500 feet deep, with 247 square miles of

Hoover Dam

surface area. The Colorado River's low-water woes have hit this reservoir particularly hard in recent years, and you may experience closed boat launches, beaches, and even marinas. It is very hot in the summer, despite all the splashing and frolicking going on in the water. There is little shade in the Mojave Desert, and the sun is incessant and unforgiving. The vegetation is sparse—nothing but rocks, scrub, and sharp and jagged barren red, pink, and blue hills. The native terrain seems out of touch with the artificial oases around the lake, with their imported palm trees and other assorted lush touches, creating a contradictory atmosphere that is strange and thrilling. Throngs flood the lake country with speedboats, kayaks, and fishing gear in tow on any spring or summer weekend. April-October the high temperatures are generally in the 80s, then the 90s, then the triple digits in deep summer, then back down to the 90s and then 80s. November-March the weather is cooler, though certainly not cold during the day. Water temperatures range 45°F in winter to 85°F in summer. One of the least crowded times of year to visit is January-February, though you might not want to get in the water during this time.

The best place to start is the **Lake Mead Visitor Center** (10 Lakeshore Rd., 4 miles northeast of Boulder City, NV, 702/293-8990, www.nps.gov/lame, 8:30am-4:30pm daily, $25 per vehicle for 7 days, boats and other vessels $16) just west of Hoover Dam along U.S. 93. Here you'll find helpful rangers and volunteers with all the information and maps you'll need for your visit.

Northshore Road

If you're only going to be in the area for a day or so, or if you're not the water sports type, the best way to see the recreation area's natural wonders is to take a slow scenic drive along Lake Mead's **Northshore Road.** From the entrance station near the Lake Mead Visitor Center, head north on Lakeshore Road, which turns into Northshore Road. You'll pass all the major west- and north-end bays and beaches,

and you can turn off at any point and stop. The road extends 50 miles along the shore and eventually becomes NV 169 near Overton, Nevada.

Try to make it as far as the spectacular **Bowl of Fire** at the base of the Muddy Mountains, 25 miles from the entrance. The Bowl of Fire is named for the deep red rocks jutting up from the desert, which light up as if ablaze, especially as the sun is dropping in the west. Climb up about 0.5 mile to the overlook on the **Northshore Summit Trail** (it's well signed at the trailhead) for one of the best views in the region. Keep your eyes open along the rocky spines of the mountains on both sides of the road, as you're likely to see a few bighorn sheep negotiating the rugged terrain.

Recreation
HIKING AND BIKING

The Lake Mead Visitor Center offers free and comprehensive information about trails around the lake, most of which are quite short and lead to overlooks or scenic features. Be careful hiking here, especially in the heat of summer; the best time for hiking is November-March, when the weather is nearly perfect most days. There are also 800 miles of backcountry dirt roads through the Mojave Desert in the recreation area, perfect for touring on a mountain bike. The visitors center can give you a map of backcountry roads.

Just outside the visitors center is the trailhead for the **Railroad Tunnel Trail,** which leads along the disused right-of-way built during the construction of Hoover Dam and through five spooky old train tunnels. From the visitors center to the entrance of the fifth tunnel is two miles one-way, and through all five tunnels to the dam is three miles one-way. This trail is also good for biking.

Birders and families with kids may enjoy the **Wetlands Trail,** a 1.2-mile round-trip walk through a dry wash that runs into the Las Vegas Wash and a wetland that attracts desert wildlife. Another good option for families with kids is the easy **Redstone Trail,** a 1.1-mile loop among red sandstone hills with displays about the region's geology. For both trailheads, head north from the visitors center on Lakeshore Road, then east on Northshore Road; just past the junction is the Wetlands Trailhead, while the Redstone Trailhead is farther east down Northshore Road at the Red Stone Picnic Area (mile marker 27).

One of the tougher hikes in the recreation area will take you to natural hot springs in a slot canyon below Hoover Dam. The hike to **Arizona Hot Springs,** in White Rock Canyon, is a six-mile round-trip moderately rough trek to the Colorado River and into a side canyon with nearly vertical walls and the spare and rocky landscape typical of this inhospitable but strangely beautiful land. This isn't for the casual hiker—you have to climb down a 20-foot ladder stuck in the rocks to reach the best pools, and the walk back to the car can be a tough trudge. To reach the trailhead, go east from the visitors center about eight miles, four miles past Hoover Dam on U.S. 93, to a dirt parking lot at the head of White Rock Canyon (the trailhead is on the map you'll get when entering the recreation area). The trail is closed during summer.

BOATING

You can rent boats for fishing, exploring, waterskiing, and living the easy lake-top life at **Callville Bay** (702/565-8958, www.callvillebay.com)—everything from 16-foot fishing craft to big patio cruisers and 18-foot speedsters. Rates range $25-95 per hour for wakeboard boats, pontoon boats, Jet Skis, and kayaks.

A leisurely sightseeing cruise around Lake Mead on the *Desert Princess,* a replica of an old Mississippi paddleboat, is a popular way to take in the stark scenery. **Lake Mead Cruises** (866/292-9191, www.lakemeadcruises.com, $35-79) offers several different options, including brunch and dinner cruises.

You can rent a **houseboat** for three days or up to a week ($750-4,000); most sleep 6-14 people and come with all kinds of extras, depending on how much you want to spend. Contact **Forever Houseboats** (800/255-5561, www.foreverhouseboats.com).

If you're more into a guided tour or skimming across the water on your own power, look into **Black Canyon/Willow Beach River Adventures** (268 Lakeshore Rd., Boulder City, NV, 800/455-3490, 10:30am-5pm Mon.-Fri., www.blackcanyonadventures.com). It offers group raft trips on the Colorado River, along the starkly beautiful **Black Canyon National Water Trail,** which stretches from Hoover Dam to Willow Beach, with several stops at beaches for swimming and frolicking and a waterside box lunch (1.5-hour trip $69 pp, 3-hour tour with lunch $114 pp). You can rent kayaks and canoes at the **Willow Beach Marina** (928/767-4747, www.willowbeachharbor.com, 2 hours $50-79 plus deposit, minimum 2 hours).

SWIMMING AND SCUBA DIVING

The best place to swim and scuba dive is around **Boulder Beach,** not far from the visitors center, which has a cordoned swimming area that's popular with families. Lately the area has been adversely affected by low water levels, but swimming remains viable. There's a **Dive Park** at North Boulder Beach that's a great place for beginners and experts alike, and a few watercraft have been deliberately submerged for exploring and pretending. **Boulder Islands,** large concrete tanks that were used to store water during the construction of the dam, are also a popular area for scuba enthusiasts. More experienced and adventuresome scuba divers have many options around the two lakes. Check out **Lake Mead's website** (www.nps.gov/lame) for more scuba information.

FISHING

Sport anglers launch on Lake Mead in search of striped and largemouth bass, rainbow trout, channel catfish, and other fish. The biggest striped bass in Lake Mead have been known to weigh up to 50 pounds. Each of the marinas has fishing gear for sale and rent, boats for rent, fishing guides, and information. **Lake Mead's website** (www.nps.gov/lame) has an up-to-date fishing report.

Food and Accommodations

The food options are scarce around Lake Mead National Recreation Area, and it's a good idea to bring your own with you. There are restaurants, snack bars, bars, and small stores at the marinas on Lake Mead and Lake Mohave, but they are far apart and should not be relied on for sustenance while visiting the park. Remember that restaurants at the marinas have seasonal hours, open daily roughly Memorial Day-Labor Day, and then truncated hours after that.

On the Arizona side of the lake, **Temple Bar Marina Restaurant** (31409 N. Temple Bar Rd., 928/767-3211, 7am-8pm daily Mar.-Sept., 8am-5pm Fri.-Sun. Oct., 8am-3pm Fri.-Sat. Nov., $9-18) is a typical and decent bar-and-grill serving burgers, sandwiches, pizzas, and the like. **Harbor House Café** (490 Horsepower Cove, Boulder City, NV, 7am-8pm Sun.-Thurs., 7am-10pm Fri.-Sat., $8-15), at Las Vegas Boat Harbor on the Nevada side of the lake, is another decent restaurant also serving bar-and-grill-style food and offering a nice lakeside view for breakfast, lunch, or dinner.

The **Temple Bar Resort and Marina** (928/767-3211, www.templebarlakemead.com, $65-150), near the eastern part of the lake, offers standard guest rooms, fishing cabins, and suites with kitchens, some with lake views and some with desert views.

There are hundreds of **camping** spots around Lake Mead ($20-45). The campgrounds—with showers, tables, grills, and all the other amenities a camper needs—are at **Boulder Beach** (148 sites), **Callville Bay** (52 sites), **Temple Bar** (71 sites), and **Las Vegas Bay** (89 sites). Those driving RVs and campers will find 52 sites at **Callville Bay Resort** (702/565-8958, www.callvillebay.com, $20), with restrooms, running water, and dump stations.

LAKE MOHAVE

This lake doesn't really seem like a lake at all but more like the river it's filled with.

Lake Mohave is thin and runs long through Black Canyon, widening at Arizona Basin and Cottonwood Basin. The scenery around Lake Mohave is similar to Lake Mead: spare and rocky, ruled by creosote and other scrub, with sandy beaches and hidden coves. The recreation opportunities are similar as well—fishing and waterskiing, houseboating and floating in the calm warm water.

A boat launch and placid waters ringed by ragged rock cliffs make **Willow Beach** a fine place for an easy day on the water with your canoe, fishing near a fish hatchery, or just lounging and picnicking on the hot desert beach. Waterfowl and other birds abound. Take U.S. 93 west toward Hoover Dam and turn at the sign for Willow Beach.

Food and Accommodations

Lake Mohave has two major marinas, both with small hotels with basic and clean lakeside rooms, stores, restaurants, bars, and boat and watercraft rentals (including houseboats)—everything you'll need for a perfect time on the water.

On the Arizona side, at the Lake Mohave marina at Katherine Landing, the **Tail O' the Whale** (8am-5pm Mon.-Thurs., 8am-9pm Fri.-Sat., 8am-8pm Sun. Memorial Day-Labor Day, $8-20) has pretty good food and offers a full bar with views of the lake while you eat.

A modest waterside stop with plenty of boat rentals and water activities, **Lake Mohave Resort at Katherine Landing** (2690 E. Katherine Spur Rd., Bullhead City, 928/754-3245, www.katherinelanding.com, $145 summer, $115 winter) is a popular place for families with kids. Make sure to ask for one of the remodeled rooms, as the older ones reek of stale smoke.

Cottonwood Cove Resort & Marina (702/297-1464, www.cottonwoodcoveresort.com, $150 summer, $89 winter) is on the Nevada side and has a nice little lodge and campground, plus a great swimming beach popular with kids.

Kingman and Vicinity

Spread across a dry desert basin below pine-topped mountains and cut through by I-40, Kingman and its environs have long been a stopover for those traveling the two famous American trails along the 35th Parallel: the Santa Fe Railroad and Route 66. Indeed, the town, mostly a transportation hub and county government center these days, has secured its place in Americana, along with a few other Arizona towns, by appearing in the song "Route 66," certainly one of the most frequently covered tunes of all time, written in 1946 by Bobby Troup and first recorded by the great Nat King Cole.

Kingman's identity, at least for the sake of tourism, is wrapped up in being the "Heart of Route 66," and there are a few nostalgic sights harking back to a time when cross-country travel was slower and, in a sense, more meaningful than it is today. The town, which isn't much to look at, sits near the junction of two scenic drives that will show you an unvarnished Arizona, rolling through large swaths of left-alone desert and old mining ghost towns taken over by artisans and actors, up over mountain passes held together by strange cacti, across bridges swaying high above dry arroyos, and past abandoned outposts and tourists traps, the rusted shells of long-dead vehicles, and all those tiny white roadside crosses remembering road-weary tragedies.

SIGHTS

Peruse museums and stores featuring the artifacts and stories of the heyday of Route 66 travel, then hop in your car and drive the rough and lonely remains of the Mother Road, through squat-cactus forests and old lost towns still pining for the region's long-gone gold- and silver-mining days. Paying $4 for one museum gets you into all three local museums.

Historic Route 66 Museum

The serious-faced mannequins that populate the life-sized dioramas at the small **Historic Route 66 Museum** (Powerhouse Visitors Center, 120 W. Andy Devine Ave., 928/753-9889, www.route66museum.net, 9am-5pm daily, $4 adults, free under age 13) are a bit unsettling, but they create an evocative picture of how Arizona was influenced, and to a major degree populated, by one long strip of road. Plastic pioneers, decked out in authentic frontier-era outfits, walk beside real wagons, while sad dust-bowl migrants gather their possessions and their children into a rickety truck and look plaintively toward a new life in the gardens of California. The curators have stuffed a lot of history and a good deal of local artifacts and ephemera into a relatively small space, using detailed scenes to depict the historic movement of people and culture along the 35th Parallel—from the Native Americans to Lieutenant Edward Beale's 1857 trek across what was then a wagon road, at the helm of a company of 25 camels, to the well-remembered golden age of postwar car culture.

One of the museum's best scenes recreates the style and design of 1950s Route 66, the heyday of the cross-country family road trip that brought so many easterners to the still-wild West to see the Grand Canyon and the Petrified Forest. Much of the road romance found in those eras is gone now, but thanks to this excellent little museum we can relive it a little. Those interested in American car culture and road culture should not miss this sight.

Mohave Museum of History and Arts

A diverse local history museum, the **Mohave Museum of History and Arts** (400 W. Beale St., 928/753-3195, www.mohavemuseum.org, 9am-4:30pm Mon.-Fri., 1pm-5pm Sat., $4

Kingman

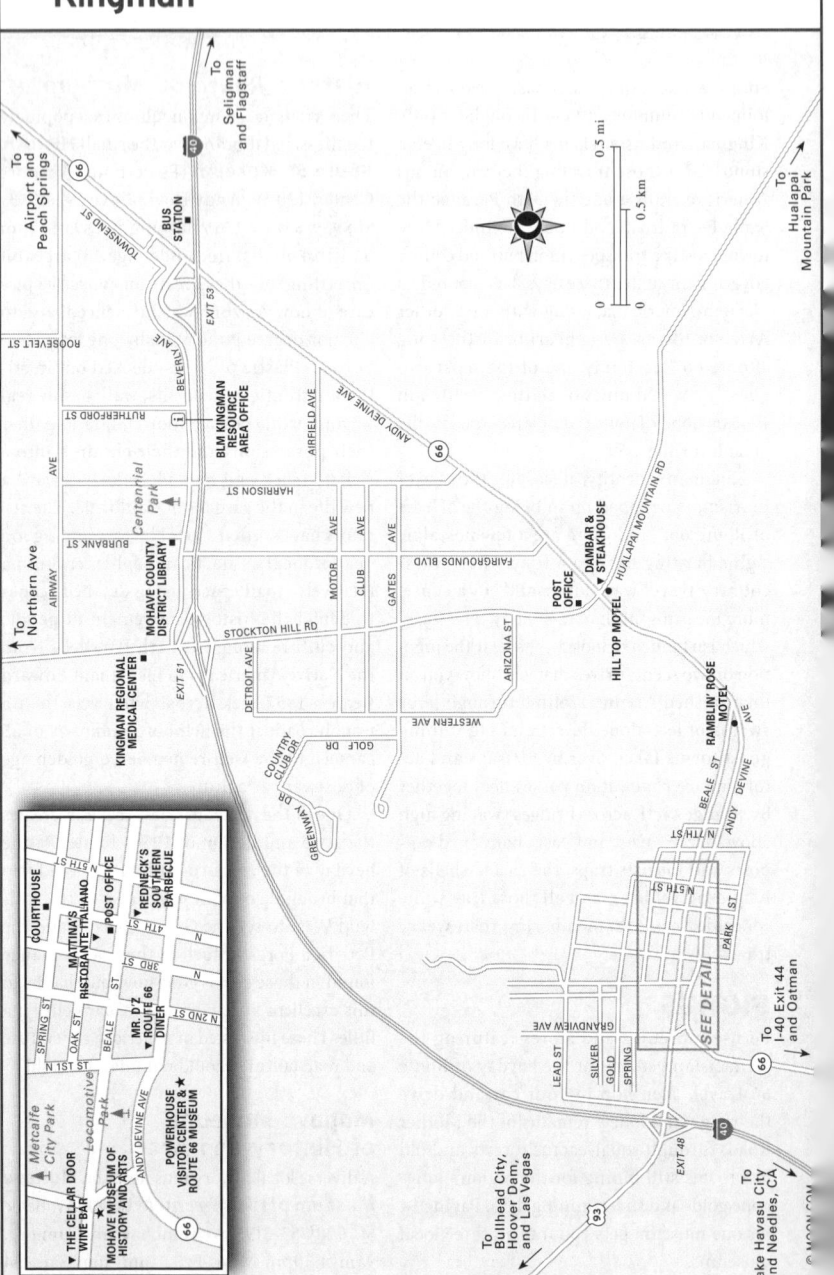

adults, free under age 12) has a lot to look at, including a detailed display on the life and career of Kingman's favorite son, actor Andy Devine (there are even original telegrams sent by the famous screen cowboy on display here). About a block from the Powerhouse Visitors Center, the museum has several rooms crowded with the history of northwestern Arizona as well as a gallery of portraits depicting each U.S. president and first lady and some stuffed examples of the region's wildlife. Other displays explain the history of mining and ranching in the area, and there are some first-rate examples of Hualapai basketry and locally mined turquoise. You could spend a few hours lost among the eclectic collections. Southwestern artist Roy Purcell, a former director of the museum, painted the museum's wonderful murals showing life as it used to be in this forgotten frontier, and a gallery features the work of a rotating group of local artists.

Bonelli House

A pioneer Mormon family that settled in Kingman in the 1890s, the Bonellis built this territorial-era home after their first home burned down in 1915. They rebuilt better and stronger, using tufa stone from the rocky hills nearby to create an interior that was cool in summer and warm in winter. Local history buffs have restored the Bonelli House (430 E. Spring St., 928/753-1413, 11am-3pm Mon.-Fri., included in admission to Mohave Museum) with exacting detail, giving visitors an authentic look at what middle-class family and home life was like on the high-desert frontier.

TOP EXPERIENCE

★ Driving Historic Route 66

The longest remaining stretch of Route 66 runs through the dry grasslands, cholla forests, and barren rocky mountains of northwestern Arizona, 165 miles between Ash Fork on the east and Topock on the Colorado River to the west. Ash Fork is just off I-40, about 94 miles east of Kingman. From here, head west to the Colorado River, following the Route 66 signs. Or start from Topock, near the Havasu National Wildlife Refuge, and drive east, ending at Ash Fork. Either way, you'll pass through sleepy Peach Springs, capital of the Hualapai Indian Reservation, and the nearly abandoned Truxton and Valentine, with a few buildings dating from the 1930s-1950s moldering along the road. You'll pass Hackberry, with its famous and much photographed Hackberry General Store, and climb up a scrubby, rocky mountain, where the road is like a washboard and steep and curvy beyond reason, passing old abandoned houses, mine shafts, and a few sprawling junkyard compounds. Then climb up over Sitgreaves Pass and down the other side of the mountain to Oatman, home of the wild burros of Route 66, each descended from the beasts of burden that helped prospectors fight these desert hills more than a century ago.

HACKBERRY GENERAL STORE

Try not to stop at this picture-ready old store and junkyard museum; it can't be done. Maybe it's the cherry-red 1957 Corvette parked conspicuously out front. Maybe it's because it's the only sign of life for miles in either direction along this forgotten stretch of the old Mother Road. Maybe it's the root beer. Cluttered with Route 66 and American road culture memorabilia, including several rusting old cars that once made their way along the route, the Hackberry General Store (11255 E. Rte. 66, Hackberry, 928/769-2605, www.hackberrygeneralstore.com, 8am-6pm daily summer, 9am-5pm daily winter) looks like it belongs to another era. Inside you'll find cold sodas, snacks, souvenirs, and a lot to look at, including some really cool road-map murals on the walls by artist Bob Waldmire. The owners, who bought the place on a whim years ago while driving Route 66, encourage visitors to walk around the property, examine the memorabilia, and take pictures. The store is 28 miles east of Kingman and 60 miles west of Seligman.

Driving Historic Route 66

© MOON.COM

COOL SPRINGS STATION

Twenty miles west of Kingman and 16 miles east of Oatman, on the way up over the Black Mountains, **Cool Springs Station** (8275 W. Oatman Hwy., 928/768-8366, 10am-5pm Tues.-Sun., free) is a photogenic replica of a gas station that served this stretch of Route 66 in the 1920s. The station eventually fell to ruins and later played a fiery role in the 1990s film *Universal Soldier*. New owners built a detailed replica of the old station in 2004, and now it's a small museum and gift shop worthy of a brief stop.

OATMAN

Between 1904 and 1931 about $36 million in ore, mostly gold and silver, came out of these dry rocky hills. At its peak the town of Oatman had 10,000 residents. It went ghostly for a while after the mines shut down, but, as with so many mining towns in the Southwest, Oatman was rediscovered in the 1960s-1970s as a tourist stop along one of the roughest stretches of Historic Route 66. There are a few resale shops and gift boutiques, a restaurant or two, and a saloon. Some latter-day gunfighters will stage

1: Historic Route 66 **2:** semi-wild burro in Oatman **3:** Oatman, originally a mining camp **4:** Cool Springs Station

Who Is Andy Devine?

Kingman's favorite son was one of those great American character actors that most of us recognize but often can't name. His strained, gravelly, but high voice, the result of a childhood accident that permanently damaged his vocal cords, and his size—a former football star, he was corpulent his entire adult life—make Andy Devine (1905-1977) stand out more than most.

While film buffs will remember Devine as the driver in John Ford's 1939 Western classic *Stagecoach*, John Wayne's breakout film made partly in Monument Valley, or as one of the soldiers in John Huston's *The Red Badge of Courage* in 1951, his career was long and diverse, encompassing radio, both A- and B-grade movies, and television. He started out as a bit player in silent films during the 1920s and went on to entertain several generations.

Those of us who grew up in the 1970s-1980s will likely remember Devine by his voice alone, which became that of the gentle and funny Friar Tuck in Disney's animated *Robin Hood* in 1973. Those who grew up in the 1950s-1960s remember Devine as Jingle Jones from the Western television series *Wild Bill Hickok* or as the host of Saturday morning show *Andy's Gang*. If you remember the 1930s-1940s, you'll recognize that voice again as a regular on the Jack Benny radio show, where his greeting "Hiya, Buck!" made him famous, and of course you'll know Devine as the funny sidekick in many Roy Rogers westerns.

Though Devine was born in Flagstaff, a couple of hours northeast of Kingman, where his father worked for the railroad, he moved to Kingman when he was just one year old. An on-the-job accident had taken the elder Devine's leg, and a settlement with the railroad helped the family buy the Beale Hotel in Kingman, where Devine grew up and is celebrated in the local museum and during an annual festival and parade.

duels in the street on most days, and you can check out the old Oatman Hotel, where Clark Gable and Carole Lombard spent their honeymoon. But the real fun in Oatman—which is a touch kitschy and has few genuinely authentic buildings left—is to feed and commune with wild burros. They're not really "wild" anymore—they'll walk right up and say hello, letting you pet their heads and feed them snacks sold by various vendors in town. There are usually a few baby burros milling around.

Leaving Oatman and descending along Route 66 to the desert floor just east of the river, the foothills are covered with cholla, which blooms, along with a few dormant wildflowers, in the spring and adds a bit of shocking bright color to the landscape, making those warm and clear months the perfect time for a visit.

Keepers of the Wild Nature Park

Though tawny cougars are known to occasionally haunt these windy high-desert plains, and some stretches of Historic Route 66 could stand in for a sweeping African savanna, one doesn't expect to encounter a shaggy-maned lion, or for that matter a flitting lemur or a thoughtful baboon—except at this hospital, retirement home, and haven for abused, neglected, and abandoned exotic animals. Keepers of the Wild Nature Park (13441 E. Rte. 66, milepost 87, www.keepersofthewild.org, 9am-5pm Wed.-Mon., all-day pass $20, $12 over age 12) has tigers, a bear, a wolf, a whole village full of squealing playful monkeys, and much more. The animals live in large fenced-in habitats, with big boulders and pools and mostly native trees and shrubs. Two miles of easy paths take you through the park, but there isn't a lot of shade, so bring a hat. The whole park is wheelchair accessible, and there's a gift shop with snacks and drinks. They encourage picnicking, so feel free to bring a basket. The last tickets are sold at 4pm. For $10 per person more, a guide will take you on a driven "safari" tour of the park that lasts about an hour and a half (10am,

1pm, and 3:30pm). This is an ideal stop for families with kids. Most of the animals here have cute names and sad life stories, so you run the risk of falling in love.

RECREATION
Hiking and Camping

If you missed North-Central Arizona's pinelands, head to northwest Arizona's answer at sap- and campfire-scented 2,300-acre Hualapai Mountain Park (6250 Hualapai Mountain Park, 928/681-5700, www.mcparks.com), 12 miles from Kingman, high in the pines overlooking the scrub valley. The titular mountain range rises from the plain southeast of town to 5,000-8,500 feet, cloaked in the conifers typical of such elevations in Arizona. There are 19 cabins that sleep 2-12 for rent through the Mohave County Parks Division (877/757-0915, www.mcparks.com, $70-150), built of stacked stone and wood by the Civilian Conservation Corps in the 1930s, most with rustic old fireplaces—but also with kitchens and electricity. You can camp here too or park your RV among the pines; most of the camping spots ($20-35) don't have water and are first-come, first-served.

The park's trail system leads high into the mountains for some inspiring views. There will be ATV riders, so be forewarned. The trails are well-worn and forested, with huge slabs and half-buried outcroppings of granite everywhere as if there had been a rock fight among giants long ago. The 8,417-foot Hualapai Peak is the highest point in the park and in the region. The 4.3-mile round-trip Potato Patch Loop Trail is a moderate and representative hike, running through ponderosa pines, aspens, and high stands of spruce and fir, strewn with needles and cones and watched over by boulders covered in dry lichen. Start out on the switchbacks of the Aspen Springs Trail and then after about a mile meet the loop at the Aspen Springs-Potato Patch Junction. You climb about 800 vertical feet in the first 1.5 miles, but it levels out on the loop. A map of the trail system, which has 16 miles of developed and undeveloped trails, is available at the park office. There's really no time of year to stay away from this pleasant heavily used mountain park. It's hot in summer but with the breezy moderation that its elevation allows. It's cold and sometimes snowy in the winter, but not to an uncomfortable degree.

ENTERTAINMENT AND EVENTS

A focal point of Kingman's downtown, Cellar Door Beer & Wine Bar (414 E. Beale St., 928/753-3885, 4pm-10pm Tues.-Wed., 1pm-11pm Thurs.- Sat.) adds a bit of city class to this rural region. It offers wine, beer, live music, and fun events. Bring your food and sit at the tasteful bar listening to a laid-back local musician, or bring your bottle with you.

Thousands of Route 66 nostalgists and classic-car lovers flock to the old stretch of the Mother Road from Seligman to Topock for the Historic Route 66 Fun Run (928/753-5001, www.azrt66.com, late Apr.-early May). Far-flung drivers in a riot of old and new vehicles—many of them gorgeous and classic, and many of their owners in 1950s wear—gather in Seligman for the kickoff of this popular regional event. After eating and dancing to the live bands, a host of roaring two- and four-wheelers makes its slow way along Historic Route 66 west to Kingman, where they park en masse for show-and-tell in the parking lot of the Powerhouse Visitors Center. In downtown Kingman there's more eating, bands and other entertainment, and vendors. Come Sunday morning, hangover or not, everybody gets up, climbs back behind the wheel, and heads east to Topock and the end of the road, stopping to give some love to the burros in Oatman.

In late September, Kingman celebrates itself and its favorite son during Andy Devine Days Parade & Community Fair (928/757-7919, late Sept.), which features food vendors, arts and crafts, and entertainment in the town's historic, if usually a bit desolate, downtown.

SHOPPING

There are two shops in the Powerhouse Visitors Center (120 W. Andy Devine Ave., 928/753-6106, 9am-5pm daily) where you'll find items you might not be able to get too many other places. For Route 66 and American road-culture gifts and souvenirs, check out the Historic Route 66 Association of Arizona Gift Shop inside the Powerhouse.

If you're into finding the treasures that other people have given up, there are a few antiques and resale shops along East Beale Street in the historic old town area that are definitely worth wandering through.

FOOD

It is widely known throughout this flat and windy region that the retro Route 66 drive-in ★ Mr. D'z Route 66 Diner (105 E. Andy Devine Ave., 928/718-0066, 7am-9pm daily, $9-18) serves the best burger in town, but it also has a large menu with all manner of delectable diner and road food, like chili dogs, pizza, hot sandwiches, baby back ribs, chicken-fried steak, and a big plate of spaghetti. Breakfast is served all day. Portions are big, but save room for a thick shake or a root-beer float. Don't leave your camera in the car; the turquoise-and-pink interior and the cool old jukebox here are snapshot-ready.

A local favorite that serves great steaks, prime rib, lobster, cowboy beans, and burgers is the Dambar & Steakhouse (1960 E. Andy Devine Ave., 928/753-3523, www. dambarsteakhouse.com, 11am-10pm daily, $15-33). The bar has excellent regionally brewed beers, and the sawdust on the floor, cowboy kitsch, and Route 66 memorabilia add character to this popular place. They offer patio seating in the summer and live country music on the weekends.

Mattina's Ristorante Italiano (318 E. Oak St., 928/753-7504, http:// mattinasristorante.com, 5pm-9pm Tues.-Sat., $14-38) serves expertly prepared Italian food, including outstanding beef medallions and rack of lamb. It's difficult to choose among the diverse and outlandishly appetizing selection of pasta dishes, but it's equally difficult to pass up the lobster ravioli or the thick creamy fettuccini alfredo. Don't leave without trying the tiramisu or key lime pie, and consider sampling liberally from the well-stocked wine cellar.

In Kingman's small downtown, Floyd & Co. (420 E. Beale St., 928/757-8227, 11am-8pm Tues.-Sat., www.floydandcompany.com, $7-25) serves excellent wood-fired pizza and tasty barbecue plates and sandwiches, as well as fantastic sweet potato fries, corn nuggets, and other scrumptious sides. Six taps have Arizona-made beer.

Beale Street Brews Coffee Shop (510 E. Beale St., 928/753-1404, 7am-3pm Wed.-Mon., 7am-6pm Tues.) has coffee, pastries, wine, beer, and cocktails as well as free Wi-Fi, poetry readings, local art on the walls, local music in the air, and a cool old art deco building—perfect for relaxing the day away.

ACCOMMODATIONS

There are several very affordable basic hotels on Andy Devine Avenue, Route 66, in Kingman's downtown area, some with retro road-trip neon signs and Route 66 themes. There are a good many chain hotels in town as well.

The Ramblin' Rose Motel (1001 E. Andy Devine Ave., 928/753-4747, $42-48) doesn't look like much beyond another roadside place to park and snooze. It's inexpensive and clean, with big comfy beds, fridges, and free Wi-Fi.

Welcoming Route 66 travelers since 1937, El Trovatore Motel (1440 E. Andy Devine Ave., 928/753-6520, www.eltrovatoremotel. com, $59, with breakfast $79) is a fun and comfortable place to stop for the night. You can't miss its huge Route 66 mural. It offers Hollywood-themed motor-lodge style guest rooms, an optional big breakfast in the morning, and free Wi-Fi.

Along Hualapai Mountain Road on the

1: Grand Canyon Caverns, west of Seligman
2: Delgadillo's Snow Cap Drive-In

GRAND CANYON
CAVERNS
CAVERNS
ENTRANCE
2015
HISTORIC
ROUTE
66
CURIO SHOP
1

DELGADILLO'S
SNOW CAP
BURGERS
HISTORIC
ROUTE
66
·MALTS· Creamy Root Beer ·SHAKES
KEEP
FEET &
HANDS
OFF WALL
100 ANNIVERSARY
WELCOME
TO OUR WORLD
2

way up to the piney mountains, the **Hualapai Mountain Resort** (4525 Hualapai Mountain Rd., 928/757-3545, www.hmresort.net, $99-179) rents eight rustic but comfortable and clean guest rooms in a quiet secluded setting. It has an on-site **restaurant** (11am-8pm Wed.-Thurs., 11am-10pm Fri., 8am-10pm Sat., 8am-8pm Sun., $10-31) serving steaks, burgers, and wild game—including mountain lion—as well as salads and sandwiches.

INFORMATION AND SERVICES

Built in 1907 to supply power to the region's mines, the **Powerhouse Visitors Center** (120 W. Andy Devine Ave., 928/753-6106, 9am-5pm daily) has information on all the sights, accommodations, and attractions in Kingman and environs, plus a model train circling the inside perimeter.

Kingman Regional Medical Center (3269 Stockton Hill Rd., 928/757-2101, www.azkrmc.com) has a full-service emergency room.

★ SELIGMAN

This tiny roadside settlement 87 miles east of Kingman holds tight to its Route 66 heritage. Fewer than 500 full-time residents live in this old ranching hub, railroad center, and Route 66 stop, but often twice that number of tourists drive through and stop for a bite to eat and a look around the gift shops, especially on summer weekends. On occasion tour buses and large gangs of motorcycling Europeans stop and crowd the one-strip town, as Seligman has become in recent years one of the top stops for a burgeoning subculture of classic car nuts, fortysomething *Easy Rider* role players, and lovers of mid-20th-century commercial architecture and road culture, all of whom prefer to eschew the interstate and take to the back roads.

John Lasseter, codirector of the 2006 Disney-Pixar film *Cars,* has said that he based the movie's fictional town of **Radiator Springs** partly on Seligman, which, like Radiator Springs, nearly died out when it was bypassed by I-40 in the late 1970s.

Sights

Stop in at the **Route 66 Gift Shop & Visitor's Center** (217 E. Rte. 66, 928/422-3352, www.route66giftshop.com, 8am-6pm daily) to buy a Route 66 souvenir and learn about the history of the area from Angel and Vilma Delgadillo, longtime residents who are largely responsible for keeping Seligman on the map.

In 2005, Seligman's commercial center, a three-block area off of Chino Street (Historic Route 66) that's hemmed by 1st Street on the west, Lamport Street on the east, Picacho Street on the north, and Railroad Avenue on the south, made the National Register of Historic Places as "an important reminder of how transportation systems influenced the development of communities in the American West." Pick up a pamphlet for the self-guided tour of the **Seligman Historic District** (www.nps.gov/nr/travel/route66) at the **Historic Seligman Sundries** and other places in town, and walk the district with your camera, snapping shots of all the retro signs and buildings from the pre-interstate era.

About 25 miles west of Seligman along Historic Route 66, **Grand Canyon Caverns** (Rte. 66, mile marker 115, 928/422-3223, www.gccaverns.com, 8am-6pm daily summer, 10am-4pm daily winter, $21-29 adults, $11-18 ages 6-12) offers guided underground tours of North America's largest dry cave, where crystals and other strange rock formations hide in the darkness. The main tour lasts 45 minutes and takes you 0.75 mile through the limestone cavern, but not before you descend 21 stories (210 feet) beneath the earth in an elevator. There's a lot of history here: During the Cold War the cavern served as a bomb shelter, packed with enough food and water to sustain hundreds of blast-weary survivors if the unthinkable occurred. The friendly folks at this old-school Route 66 tourist trap (in the best sense of the phrase) also offer an off-trail tour

($99) that goes much deeper into the caverns. They'll also be happy to take you out into the nearby ranch lands on horseback or in a Jeep.

Shopping

Inside the turquoise-and-pink 100-year-old **Historic Seligman Sundries** (22495 Rte. 66, 928/853-0051, www.seligmansundries. com, 8am-7pm daily Apr.-Oct.), you'll find a plethora of Route 66 memorabilia as well as motorcycle- and car-culture items, Native American jewelry, cowboy kitsch, and really good coffee and malts. There's a small museum, and the walls are covered with old advertisements and other reminders of the mid-20th-century heyday of American popular culture.

That sprawling building with all the dressed-up mannequins on the roof, and Elvis kicking back on the bumper of a classic pink roadster, is **The Rusty Bolt** (115 E. Rte. 66, 928/422-0106, www.rustybolt66.com, 8am-4pm daily), where they sell the usual local Route 66 memorabilia and a large selection of items for motorcyclists.

Food

A majority of the Route 66 argonauts who slide through Seligman stop at ★ **Delgadillo's Snow Cap Drive-In** (301 E. Chino Ave., 928/422-3291, 10am-6pm daily, $5-10), a famous food shack whose family of owners have been dedicated to feeding, entertaining, and teasing Route 66 travelers for generations. They serve a mean chili burger, a famous "cheeseburger with cheese," hot dogs, malts, soft ice cream, and much more, but the food's not really the point. Originally built in 1953 out of found lumber, the Snow Cap has become one of the stars of the back-to-Route 66 movement. There's a lot to look at outside: a 1936 Chevy and other old cars (all of them with big eyes on their windshields, à la Disney-Pixar's 2006 homage to Route 66, *Cars*); railroad junk; and several very silly signs. Inside, the walls are covered with the business cards of customers from all over the world. Don't come here if you're grumpy: There will likely be a stand-up wait, especially on summer weekends, and you *will* be teased, especially if you have a question that requires a serious answer.

The **Roadkill Café** (502 W. Rte. 66, 928/422-3554, 7am-9pm daily, $8-24) is more than just a funny name: It's a popular place for buffalo burgers, steaks, sandwiches, and other typical Old West-themed bar-and-grill eats. Have a few drinks in the **OK Saloon** and a look around at the cluttered interior.

The majestic stuffed mountain lion that watches over diners at **Westside Lilo's Café** (415 W. Chino Ave., 928/422-5456, www. westsidelilos.com, 6am-9pm daily, $8-23), a popular diner-style eatery complete with counter service, was shot not far from the restaurant by a member of the owners' family. It's just one of the backcountry touches that add to the ambience. They serve good burgers, excellent homemade potato salad, and other standard American fare, as well as the famous carrot cake, which is moist and flavorful.

Accommodations

There are several small locally owned motels in Seligman, many of them with historic retro signs and, of course, a Route 66 theme. The accommodations here are nothing special, though they are typically quite affordable.

Named for the nearby Grand Canyon-bottom village inhabited by the Havasupai tribe, the **Supai Motel** (134 W. Chino St., 928/422-4153, $69-82) has clean and comfortable rooms at fair rates. The **Historic Route 66 Motel** (22750 W. Rte. 66, 928/422-3204, $77-87) offers free Wi-Fi and fridges in clean comfortable guest rooms.

The **Canyon Lodge** (114 E. Chino St., 928/422-3255, www.route66canyonlodge. com, $70-100) has free Wi-Fi in its themed guest rooms (posters on the walls of James Dean, Marilyn Monroe, John Wayne, and other pop-culture icons), along with fridges and microwaves. A free continental breakfast is served.

U.S. HIGHWAY 93

Though not as popular as Route 66, U.S. 93 between Wickenburg, an hour north of Phoenix, and Hoover Dam, about an hour northwest of Kingman, has 200 miles of spectacular desert scenery. Just north of AZ 71, before the town of Wikieup, U.S. 93 becomes the **Joshua Tree Forest Parkway;** look out your window and you'll see why.

A few miles north of Kingman, Mohave County Road 125 leads to **Chloride** (4 miles east of U.S. 93), an old mining town turned tourist trap in the foothills of the Cerebat Mountains. You can browse some shops and galleries; explore the ruins of mine shafts and a brothel; watch gunfights (high noon 1st and 3rd Sat. July-Aug., noon every Sat. Sept.-June); and look at all the artwork and found art in town, including famous rockface murals by renowned Southwestern artist Roy Purcell.

Food

As you pass through the wide spot in the road known as Wikieup, stop at **Luchia's** (15797 U.S. 93, Wikieup, 928/765-2229, 9am-5pm Sun.-Fri., $5-20), where tasty American and Mexican dishes are served on a lush and shady outdoor patio. It's known for homemade pies (when in doubt, get the apple) and also sells Native American jewelry, rugs, pottery, kachinas, and baskets.

Bullhead City and Laughlin

You pretty much have to be interested either in river games or games of chance to get anything out of a visit to Laughlin or Bullhead City, often two of the hottest spots in the nation during the summer months. In August 1983, the shade temperature in Bullhead City reached 132°F—the hottest on record. However, if you'd like nothing more than to spray around the river on a Jet Ski during the day and play poker and slots when the unforgiving sun finally dips away, follow the many families from Phoenix and elsewhere who head for this desert playground several times a year, with their kids, speedboats, and Jet Skis in tow. Bullhead City, which otherwise has little to offer, is also a good choice for river rats, though without the gambling and Vegas aesthetic of Laughlin. (It has more of a strip-mall aesthetic, unfortunately.) It borders Lake Mead National Recreation Area and is near Lake Mohave, with its marinas and boat rental shops, and has one of the best river parks in the region at Davis Camp.

CASINOS

There are nine resorts and 13 casinos in Laughlin, most of them relatively affordable.

The best of the bunch stretch along the river's west bank, and there's a riverside walkway between them with streetlights, public art, and boat docks. Room rates vary, but you can often find a relatively nice bed on the river for under $50. Prices generally go up on holidays. Most of the resorts offer a variety of packages that include meals and river cruises. These aren't the Native American casinos that you've seen in Arizona; Laughlin's gambling halls are pure Vegas clones. With the heat and the desert, it's possible to forget you're not in Sin City, especially if you've been head-down at the blackjack table for two days straight. But then you look out the window and see that blue river, and you know exactly where you are.

The **New Pioneer Hotel and Gambling Hall** (2200 S. Casino Dr., 800/634-3469, www.pioneerlaughlin.com) is a step or two down from the likes of the Aquarius and the other newer luxury places in town but has the usual slots, poker, blackjack, roulette, and more. This is a good overnight choice for folks with boats and other watercraft because you can park close to your room.

The first casino built in Laughlin, way back in 1966, the **Riverside Resort Hotel** and Casino (1650 S. Casino Dr., 800/227-3849, www.riversideresort.com) has been built up mightily since then, with a movie theater, a classic car collection, a bowling alley and game room, and two swimming pools. The 80,000-square-foot casino has slots, blackjack, table games, and more, and a concert venue hosts music, comedy, and burlesque shows.

A nonfloating replica of a 19th-century Mississippi paddlewheel, the **Colorado Belle Hotel and Casino** (2100 S. Casino Dr., 877/460-0777, www.coloradobelle.com) is a wonder of popular architecture. It has a swimming pool and spa and a huge casino with the usual games. It's right on the river walk.

The **Aquarius Casino Resort** (1900 S. Casino Dr., 800/662-5825, www.aquariuscasinoresort.com) has slots, blackjack, poker, keno, and a variety of table games and offers frequent concerts in its pavilion (Foreigner, ZZ Top, Carrie Underwood, Rascal Flatts). There's a big pool on the roof with cabanas and some amazing views of the stark desert cut through by that shining band of blue river.

RECREATION

People come here for the river: to float on it, speed over it, and swim in it. Every other truck barreling down the melting blacktops around here tows a speedboat, and the kids walk around in their life vests because they are rarely out of the water long enough to bother removing them.

Davis Camp

If you're not staying in one of the casino resorts, the best place to spend a day playing in the river and seeing if your boat still floats is **Davis Camp** (2251 AZ 68, 928/754-7250, www.mcparks.com, dawn-dusk daily, $10 per car, $15 if launching watercraft) in Bullhead City, which was built in the 1940s to house workers building nearby Davis Dam. You can fish, ride your Jet Ski (or rent one), and swim and lounge in the sun on the park's sandy beaches, which all have charcoal grills

and picnic tables. The 1.5 miles of shoreline here is the easiest and most convivial way to get a taste, though hopefully not a mouthful, of the Colorado. Just east of the park's boat dock, **BestJetz** (702/789-9514 or 702/298-0757, http://bestjetzrentals.com, 9am-11pm daily, reservations advised, $69 per hour, $189 per day) rents Jet Skis and kayaks. Prices are higher Friday-Sunday.

Boat Tours

Along the river walk in Laughlin and in many of the casino resorts, you can book speedboat tours of the river. One of the best is **London Bridge Jet Boat Tours** (888/505-3545, http://laughlinboattours.com, 9:30am to 4:30pm, $95 adults, $55 under age 13). The fully enclosed boats run 58 miles downriver to London Bridge in Lake Havasu City, along the way passing through spectacular **Topock Gorge,** with its bighorn sheep dancing on the cliffs above. The trip takes all day—two hours each way and a two-hour layover at the bridge for lunch and sightseeing—but is worth the time away from the casino for all the beautiful scenery.

EVENTS

In late April, thousands of Harley-Davidson enthusiasts gather in the desert along the river for the **Laughlin River Run** (714/694-2800 or 800/357-8223, http://laughlinriverrun.com, late Apr.), which includes concerts, festivals, and all sorts of general revelry.

In early August, just as the hot dog days take hold, thousands of revelers gather from both sides of the river for the **River Regatta Roundup** (855/924-6882, www.bullheadregatta.com, early Aug.), a floating party of tubers and boaters and other floaters, all drifting together along the Colorado River in one big traffic jam.

SHOPPING

Nearly all of the casino resorts in Laughlin have several retail and gift shops selling local souvenirs and T-shirts with silly slogans, cowboy gear, and the necessities of river play.

If you're more inclined to drop your money at the shoe store than in a slot machine, check out the Laughlin Outlet Center (1955 S. Casino Dr., 702/298-3650, www.laughlinoutletcenter.com, 9am-8pm Mon.-Sat., 10am-7pm Sun.). The 68 outlet stores in this air-conditioned mall across the street from the Aquarius will keep bargain hunters busy and out of the heat and sun.

FOOD

For a good time in Laughlin, reserve a table at Guy Fieri's El Burro Borracho (2900 S. Casino Dr., 702/298-6898, www.guyfieri.com, 4pm-10pm Sun.-Mon. and Thurs., 4pm-11pm Fri.-Sat., $11-24) in Harrah's casino; it's as colorful and exciting as the celebrity chef himself. Order one the big specialty margaritas ($14-15) or a tequila flight before trying out the top-notch creative Mexican food. At Laughlin's New Pioneer, Bumbleberry Flats (2200 S. Casino Dr., 800/634-3469, www.laughlinpioneer.com, 8am-midnight daily, $12-26) serves American comfort food, like a heaping plate of chicken and waffles, excellent burgers, and a flavorful jambalaya, as well as big beautiful Bloody Marys. It also serves a juicy prime rib on weekends.

Across the river in Bullhead City, head to Mohave Steakhouse (2430 AZ 95, 928/704-6878, http://mohavesteakhouse.com, 11am-8pm Sun.-Thurs., 11am-9pm Fri.-Sat., $20-50) for something upscale and splurge-worthy out here in the desert, with amazing hand-cut steaks by master griller and cutter Jesse Godinez.

ACCOMMODATIONS

In Laughlin, your best bet for accommodations is the casinos. The New Pioneer Hotel and Gambling Hall (2200 S. Casino Dr.,

800/634-3469, www.laughlinpioneer.com, $109-159) has some of the most affordable guest rooms in Laughlin, many looking over the river walk and the river with the hotel's landmark "River Rick" sign looking down from high above. This is a good choice for visitors with boats and other watercraft because you can park close to your room. The rooms at the Riverside Resort Hotel and Casino (1650 S. Casino Dr., 800/227-3849, www.riversideresort.com, $99-109 plus $17 per night resort fee), many of them high in the sky and overlooking the dry land and the river, are standard, clean, and comfortable. The 80,000-square-foot casino has slots, blackjack, table games, and more. The Aquarius Casino Resort (1900 S. Casino Dr., 800/662-5825, www.aquariuscasinoresort.com, $79-170) has elegant guest rooms with river views and an adults-only tower. There's a large pool on the roof with cabanas and amazing views of the desert.

Several chain hotels are in Bullhead City, but you can probably find a better deal and a nicer, more entertaining place to stay across the river in Laughlin. But Davis Camp (2251 AZ 68, 928/754-7250, www.mcparks.com), right on the river, rents rustic 1940s-era two- and three-bedroom bungalows ($150-215) perfect for a weekend family getaway. There are also dry campsites ($20) and an RV park ($30). Make reservations for a bungalow far in advance.

INFORMATION AND SERVICES

Stop in at the Laughlin Visitor Information Center (1555 Casino Dr., 702/298-3321, www.visitlaughlin.com, 8am-4:30pm Mon.-Fri.) for information on Laughlin and the surrounding area.

Lake Havasu City and Vicinity

This riverside haven for snowbird retirees and boat-cruising vacationers sprang up from the hot and sandy desert in 1963. A few years later, Havasu's developer, Robert McCulloch Sr., secured the master-planned community's place in history by bringing a bit of history to its brand-new shores. He purchased the London Bridge and shipped it to Arizona, where he installed it brick by brick across the channel at Pittsburgh Point, a peninsula now referred to locally as "the island." McCulloch also hired a former Disneyland designer to help create an "English Village" in the bridge's shadow, and the whole package has been a popular tourist draw ever since. These days, the state parks and walkways and beaches along the reservoir are crowded most weekends in spring and even summer—when the triple digits rule for three months or more—with boaters, anglers, and Jet Ski enthusiasts. During the annual college spring break bacchanalia, hordes of bikini- and board short-clad students descend on the town, while at other times it seems as though everyone is over 60.

Lake Havasu City, like many other once-sleepy communities along the state's west coast, has grown immensely over the last decade or so, and there are more working families living here now, and thus more chain stores and restaurants. For the visitor, however, it is still Lake Havasu—born from the building of Parker Dam and holding water that travels across the desert in canals to Phoenix and Tucson—that is the main draw. If you're not into water sports and if you wilt easily in the sun, consider spending no more than an afternoon here, strolling over and beneath the bridge and along the walkway next to the channel, watching the ducks dip and bob. If you want to get to know the reservoir, there are all manner of wet and cool things to do here.

SIGHTS AND RECREATION

If you're not boating, fishing, swimming, or generally worshipping the sun here, you may find things a bit dull. The water is the place to be, but you can easily get on it without getting wet. All along the main walkway under the bridge are boat rentals, fishing guides, excursion cruises, and even a singing gondola ride. There are also unique shopping opportunities near the lake, and a few great places to eat. This is where you'll want to go first—just follow the signs to London Bridge, where the parking is generally free.

★ London Bridge

London Bridge (McCulloch Blvd., 928/453-8883, free) began its long life in 1831, spanning the Thames River in London. First, horses pulled carriages across it, then the first cars chugged its length, and then, inevitably, the modern world caught up with it. By the early 1960s the old bridge no longer had what it takes to serve such a busy crossing, so the City of London sold it to Robert McCulloch, a chainsaw manufacturer just then entering the lucrative trade of master-planned retirement and resort communities. Now it spans an artificial channel of the Colorado River, walked and driven over by millions of sun-baked tourists every year. It's a strange sight, the old-world urban structure stuck out here in the middle of the desert. The best views are from below, where the scene has a bit of a picturesque old London look to it—but not quite. The bridge's seeming incongruity isn't as strange as it appears, however. In the 19th century, the lower Colorado and the Arizona Strip, not far north of this region, were settled by Mormon pioneers from Salt Lake City, many of whom were English. That has little to do with the bridge's travels, though. Take a half hour or so to walk across and under

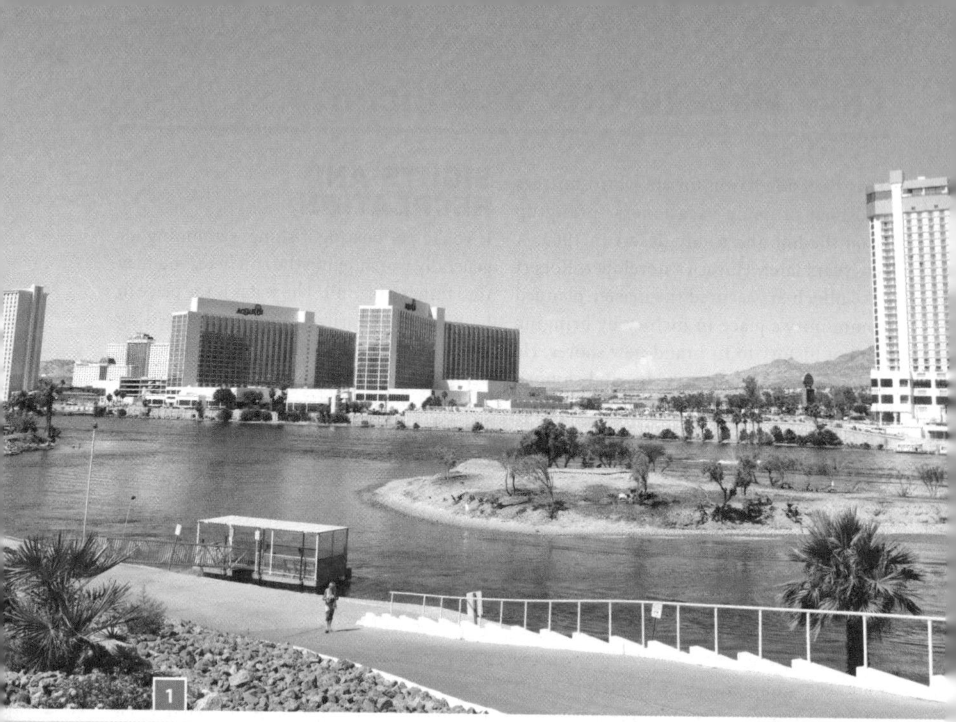

1

2

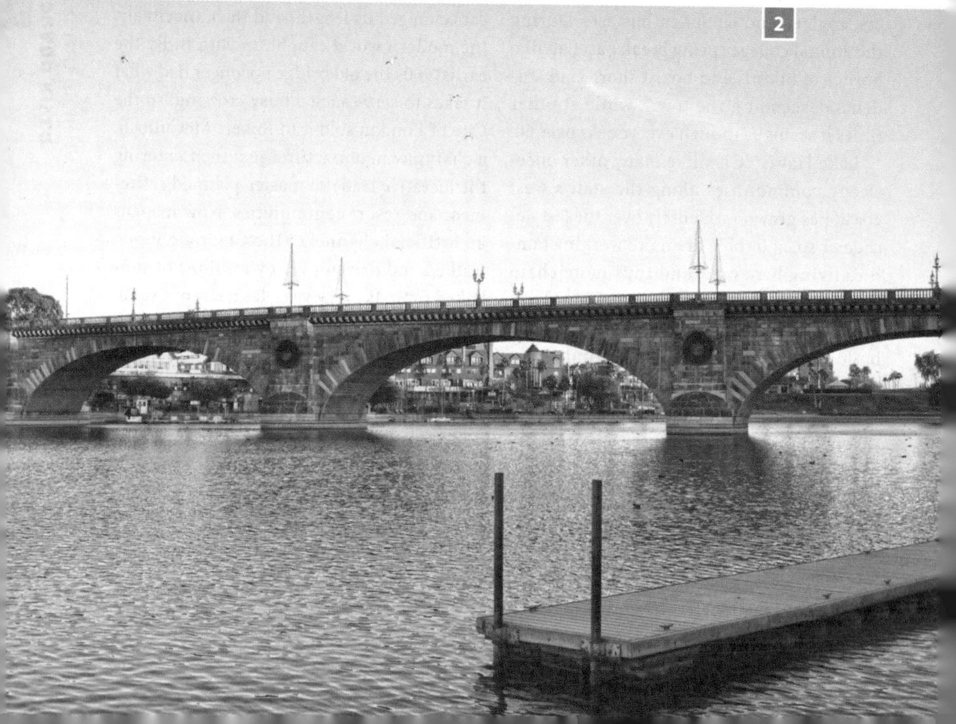

it, and read the plaques placed at either end that explain how these bricks from across the Atlantic wound up stacked here in the desert.

Lake Havasu State Park

Popular Lake Havasu State Park (99 London Bridge Rd., 928/855-2784, http:// azstateparks.com, 24 hours daily, visitors center and store 6am-6pm daily Apr.-Sept., 7am-5pm Oct.-Mar., $15 per car Mon.-Thurs., $20 per car Sat.-Sun. and holidays, camping $35-40) stretches along the river north and south of the bridge and includes Windsor Beach, an excellent riverside campground and sunning and swimming spot. If you're looking to laze around on the beach for a while and watch the people and the waterfowl, Windsor Beach is the place to do it.

Cattail Cove State Park

About 15 miles south of the bridge, the telltale cattails that give Cattail Cove State Park (AZ 95, 928/855-1223, http://azstateparks. com, sunrise-10pm daily, $10 per car Mon.-Fri., $15 Sat.-Sun. and holidays, camping $30-35) its name rise from the water. Here you'll find camping, boating, and fishing opportunities just outside the main town area, along with several primitive campsites along the shores accessible only by boat. There's a nice beach and good swimming—a perfect place for a laid-back day or overnight riverine outing with the family.

Havasu National Wildlife Refuge

Protecting 30 river miles of Colorado River habitat from Needles, California, to Lake Havasu City, Arizona, Havasu National Wildlife Refuge (317 Mesquite Ave., Needles, CA, 760/326-3853, www.fws.gov) is where one of the last remaining natural sections of the lower Colorado River flows through the 20-mile-long spectacle that is Topock Gorge, where you might see bighorn sheep and other native animals.

Watercraft Rentals

One of the better outfitters is London Bridge Watercraft Tours and Rentals (928/453-8883, http://londonbridgewatercraft. com, 10am-5pm daily), which operates out of Crazyhorse Campgrounds (1534 Beachcomber Blvd., 928/855-4033, www. crazyhorsecampgroundsaz.com, $35 day use) on "the island" on the west side of the bridge. A number of other rental places are along the walkway beneath the bridge offering all-day and dining excursions, fishing trips, expeditions into the Lake Havasu Wildlife Refuge upriver, and paddleboats and canoes for sticking closer to shore. Rental prices fluctuate seasonally, with spring break and other busy times ushering in higher fees. All of the rental spots require a deposit, typically taken care of by handing over your credit card number.

Several concessionaires beneath the bridge in Lake Havasu City offer guided tours of Topock Gorge, a gorgeous river canyon with towering walls and dramatic formations. It's essential to prebook at least a day ahead and plan to be gone for several hours. Bluewater Jet Boat Tours (926/855-7171, www. coloradoriverjetboattours.com, 10:30am and 1:30pm daily Oct.-May, $50 pp, $30 ages 6-12) offers a 2.5-hour air-conditioned excursion into the gorge in a 49-passenger speedboat.

EVENTS

Not surprisingly, most of Lake Havasu's annual events have to do with the water. The biggest event of the year is spring break, which happens throughout March-April. The population skews young during this time, and if you're not looking for a party and crowds, you might want to stay away. In late February the Mark Hahn Memorial Havasu 300 APBA National Team Endurance Race (www.pwcoffshore.com, late Feb.) brings together the nation's best Jet Ski pilots for a big race. April brings the Lake Havasu Marine Associations Annual Boat Show

---

1: Laughlin, a mini-Vegas on the Colorado River
2: London Bridge in Lake Havasu City

(928/453-8833, Apr.), a three-day event featuring the best in watercraft, food, concerts, and all sorts of other fun.

SHOPPING

Stick around the water to find distinctive gifts and souvenirs at the English Village Shoppes (1477 Queens Bay, 928/855-0888, hours vary by shop). Under the bridge and across the channel you'll find the Island Mall & Brewery (1425 McCulloch Blvd., 928/855-6274, hours vary by shop), a two-story enclosed mall.

Away from the bridge and water area, the Main Street in the Uptown District (upper McCulloch Blvd., 1 mile east of London Bridge) has more than 200 shops, including Shambles Village, which has all kinds of antiques galleries.

FOOD AND ACCOMMODATIONS

For those who've worn themselves hungry playing on the river, Juicy's River Café (42 Smoketree Ave. S., 928/855-8429, www.juicysgreatfood.com, 7am-9pm Mon.-Sat., 7am-7pm Sun., $12-40) serves delectable breakfasts, sandwiches, and homemade comfort fare such as ribs and fish-and-chips.

Shugrue's (1425 McCulloch Blvd., 928/453-1400, www.shugrueslakehavasu.com, 11am-close daily, $15-42) has great views of the water and bridge; delicious seafood, burgers, and other American fare; plus homemade pastries and bread.

The nicest and most popular place to stay in town is the London Bridge Resort (1477 Queens Bay, 928/855-0888, www.londonbridgeresort.com, $159-359 plus $30 per night resort fee), right near the bridge and overlooking the lake. It has a beautiful lobby with a replica of the "queen's carriage," comfortable suite-style guest rooms with bridge and channel views, a good restaurant, and a lot of extras, like a waterslide for the kids.

The boutique Heat Hotel (1420 McCulloch Blvd., 928/854-2833, www.heathotel.com, $250-350 plus $15 per night

resort fee) is bringing a bit of badly needed style to this desert waystation. Many of the bright guest rooms have wonderful views of the water and feature natural light and sleek modern furnishings. The outdoor but covered Heat Bar off the lobby is a great place to drink and watch the boats go by, and if you brought your own boat, the hotel has its own docks.

INFORMATION AND SERVICES

The Lake Havasu City Convention and Visitors Bureau (314 London Bridge Rd., 928/453-3444 or 800/242-8278, www.golakehavasu.com, 8am-5pm Mon.-Fri.) can help with all your questions and provide plenty of literature on sights and events in Lake Havasu. There's also a Visitor Information Center (422 English Village, 9am-5pm daily).

PARKER AND THE PARKER STRIP

The small resort town of Parker looks out on 16 miles of swift-flowing Colorado River called the Parker Strip, where retirement and vacation homes line the banks between the town and Parker Dam to the north. Most of the land below and around Parker comprises the Colorado River Indian Reservation, 270,000 acres that include the beautiful 16,400-acre Swansea Wilderness Area, 25 miles northeast of town. This is one of the best stretches of the lower Colorado, packed with boaters and other river lovers most weekends in season. Again, if you're not a river rat or trying to be one, there's not much of an incentive to stop.

Sights and Recreation

The small Colorado River Indian Tribes Museum and Library (1007 Arizona Ave., Parker, 928/669-8770, www.crit-nsn.gov, 8am-5pm Mon.-Fri., 10am-2pm Sat., free) has some interesting exhibits and artifacts of these often-overlooked tribes.

Buckskin Mountain State Park (5476

AZ 95, 928/667-3231, http://azstateparks. com, $10 per car) and its River Island Unit (5200 AZ 95, 928/667-3386), 12 miles north of Parker, have excellent camping, fishing, and boating opportunities.

You can also drive over Parker Dam (AZ 95, 760/663-3712) just north of the town; it's open to passenger vehicles only (5am-11pm daily). On the California side of the dam, there's a rough but scenic drive that will take you along the river and past a few historic sites and shoreline oases.

Just north of Parker, the Bill Williams River flows from the east into the Colorado River. A beautiful thin ribbon of water moving through a marshy forest of cattails announces the Bill Williams River National Wildlife Refuge (60911 AZ 95, Parker, 928/667-4144, www.fws.gov), which protects a thick cottonwood-willow forest and has excellent bird-watching and kayaking opportunities. The refuge is on AZ 95 between mileposts 160 and 162, about 17 miles south of Lake Havasu City.

Food and Accommodations

The place to be in the Parker area is the Colorado Indian Tribe's BlueWater Resort & Casino (AZ 95, 928/669-7000, www. bluewaterfun.com, $115-140), which has affordable and clean, but chilly, guest rooms that look over the river and the marina, where you can rent boats and Jet Skis and park your own craft. Inside the hotel there's a buffet, slots, blackjack, and poker, along with a multitiered pool and waterslide that the kids won't want to leave behind. There's also a movie theater and a sports bar.

QUARTZSITE

This quiet desert spot where AZ 95 becomes U.S. 95, between Parker and Yuma and right off I-10, is nearly deserted in summer, when temperatures reach 120°F fairly regularly. When the mercury dips, however, this wide spot in the road becomes crowded with itinerant retirees, roaming bands of gem and mineral dealers, and other assorted swapmeet entrepreneurs. Throughout January-February, the streets in town are lined with booths and tables selling all manner of gems and jewelry and just about anything else you can think of, and into the winter RV retirees and nomads makes Quartzsite a temporary boomtown.

Even if it's summer and 110°F in the shade, if you happen to be passing through this settlement around lunch or dinnertime, make sure to stop at the ★ Grubstake Social Club (725 AZ 95, 928/927-4485, www. grubstakeaz.com, 11am-2pm and 4pm-8pm Thurs.-Sun., $15-30), which serves delicious bar-and-grill-style food and has karaoke, pool tables, live bands, and a fun local vibe.

Yuma and Vicinity

Yuma has long been an important place. For centuries the area where the once wild Colorado and Gila Rivers merged was a natural crossing point for Native Americans, and during the great gold rush of 1849 the riverside desert became a crucial crossing and lifeline for all those prospectors and adventurers going to California. For a time, steamboats chugged up and down the Colorado, docking at Yuma to unload supplies important to the settling of the Southwest. Some of the Wild West's most despicable characters found themselves sweltering in the hell of the Yuma Territorial Prison. In the era of reclamation, Yuma became an important agricultural center, and it still is, producing winter lettuce and other crops. In 1915 Yuma became an important link in the nation's commercial scene with the opening of the famous Ocean-to-Ocean Highway Bridge over the Colorado River. To most Arizonans who don't live near the state's western border, Yuma is known

Yuma

mostly as a place to stop and get gas on the way to the cool ocean breezes of San Diego.

Today, Yuma is a growing city of about 105,000 people with an economy based on agriculture and the service industry. November-March the city's population swells by 90,000, many of them retirees and snowbirds seeking the easy life in one of Yuma's more than 80 RV and mobile home parks. While the town boasts sunny skies 95 percent of the year, and winter temperatures are often in the 70s and even the 80s, it is not a place that you want to visit during the height of summer: Many days the temperature hovers around 110°F, cooling off very little at night. Consequently, some businesses and attractions truncate their hours or shut down altogether when the heat reigns.

SIGHTS

★ Yuma Territorial Prison State Historic Park

They say Yuma Prison wasn't as bad as its reputation suggests, that the more than 3,000 outlaws, polygamists, gunfighters, robbers, and murderers housed here 1876-1909 were afforded three squares a day, health care, and education, conveniences many of their pioneer counterparts on the outside sorely lacked. But spend a little time exploring popular **Yuma Territorial Prison State Historic Park** (100 Prison Hill Rd., 928/783-4771, http:// azstateparks.com, 9am-5pm daily, $8 adults, $4 ages 7-13) and you'll likely come to a different conclusion: This wasn't a place where you'd want to spend any time, especially in an era before air-conditioning. If you think it's hot in Yuma today, just imagine being confined to a dark airless cell, the heat as incessant as the din from the cell block, with constant tubercular coughing.

There's not much left of the original buildings; Yuma citizens used the old prison as a kind of free lumberyard for years before it was made into a state park. During the Great Depression the cells served as temporary homes for some. But the real interest here is the lore of the lawless territorial days, and there is much of it in the museum, where you'll learn all about the various people who once called the dark cells home as well as the doctors and prison administrators who managed the place. You can climb up to the large guard tower, look over the slowly meandering Colorado River as it snakes through wetlands below, and feel what it was like (sort of, anyway) to be confined to a prison cell way out in the middle of the desert, far from home and grace. Plan on spending an hour or two, as there is much to discover in the stories and artifacts of crime and punishment on the Southwestern frontier.

Colorado River State Historic Park

A small park on Yuma's main drag, **Colorado River State Historic Park** (201 N. 4th Ave., 928/329-0471, http://azstateparks.com, 9am-5pm daily, $6 adults, $4 ages 7-13), formerly **Yuma Quartermaster Depot State Historic Park,** preserves the history of the U.S. Army's presence in Yuma 1864-1883,

when riverboat steamers brought supplies up from the mouth of the Colorado to serve army outposts throughout the region. Before the railroad entered the Southwest, a six-month supply of food, clothing, ammunition, and other staples was quartered here for distribution to forts in Arizona, Utah, Nevada, and New Mexico. At the park you can see the old commanding officer's quarters and a few other historic buildings and artifacts related to the army's long occupation of the wild open West.

The most interesting story told at the park is about the construction of the audacious Yuma Siphon, an engineering project that would seem ambitious even today. Using old Captain Nemo-style diving gear, workers built a concrete tunnel underneath the Colorado River to divert the river for use in agriculture, changing the fate of Yuma forever and securing the town's survival beyond being a way station for goods and people headed to California. At the park some excellent displays explain the project, along with a few of the old diving suits and other artifacts of this incredible reclamation feat.

Sanguinetti House Museum & Gardens

The history of Yuma is on display at the **Sanguinetti House Museum & Gardens** (240 S. Madison Ave., 928/782-1841, www. arizonahistoricalsociety.org, 10am-4pm Tues.-Sat., $8 adults, $4 ages 7-13) in the city's quiet historic downtown. Named after the home's former owner, pioneer merchant E. F. Sanguinetti, the little adobe house has informative displays on the history of the lower Colorado region from prehistory through modern times, with period rooms and a shady garden patio and aviary with talking birds in cages. If you're really interested in the history of the region, make sure to converse with one of the volunteer docents who staff the main desk; they are usually locals and can provide personal context to the historical displays. A separate adobe next door, formerly the residence of a riverboat captain, houses an excellent local- and regional-history bookshop.

Historic Downtown

Yuma's downtown has been going through a planned rebirth for a few decades now, and there are some cool old buildings from various eras still standing, including the art deco Yuma Theatre, built in 1936. It has been restored and now shows movies. Nearby, the Yuma Downtown Art Center has four galleries showing the work of local and regional artists. Other buildings show the influence of Spanish Colonial Revival style, and there are even a few old adobes still standing from the territorial days. It's easy to walk around the downtown. Start at Main Street Plaza and just explore—there are a few shops, antiques stores, galleries, and boutiques along the narrow streets, and on the edges of downtown you'll see a few old historic homes. That being said, on most days the downtown is a bit quiet and deserted, especially in summer. Still, it's a good place to get a feel for what Yuma used to be.

Algodones Dunes

Desert country neophytes might be a little disappointed with the relative lushness of the typical Arizona desert landscape, which defies with its diversity the daydream of Sahara-esque dunes with nothing but white sand for miles. If you were hoping for a "real desert," something on the order of Luke Skywalker's home planet of Tatooine, head across the bridge into California for a look at the southeastern end of the great shifting stretch of sand known as the Algodones Dunes, also called the Imperial Dunes. About 17 miles west of Yuma on I-8, take the Gray's Well exit to a parking lot on the edge of the dunes near the Midway campground, part of the Imperial Dunes Recreation Area. Here you can park and witness the 45-mile-by-6-mile dunes—but don't go far. There is literally nothing here but sand and then more sand. If you think it looks like Tatooine, that's because it is: George Lucas filmed portions of Return of the Jedi near here in the 1980s. These days the dunes are popular with motorcycle and ATV enthusiasts, who tear around nearby Glamis on holiday weekends in a great rumbling and rolling party. A few miles west on the frontage road from Gray's Well (follow the signs) you can see what remains of the old Plank Road, a movable highway of wooden planks once placed on top of the dunes so early car travelers could pass without sinking into the sand, in a time before highway technology advanced enough to build the interstate that now bisects the area. It's not recommended to go here in summer, nor should you take off across the dunes on foot. Just look, or maybe scamper up a tall dune near the parking lot and see what an expanse of nothing looks like—it's preternaturally beautiful, and a good place for meditating on, well . . . nothingness.

RECREATION

The lighted and paved riverfront trail follows the Colorado River past wetlands and historic sites, parks, and Yuma's downtown. There are several interesting stops along the way, including a wetlands park, a small plaza marking the spot where in 1877 the first railroad car passed into Arizona, and Gateway Park, a riverside greenspace with great views of the Ocean-to-Ocean Highway Bridge. A walk or bike ride (no rentals are nearby, so you'll need to bring your own) is a perfect way to get a sense of what the river is like and how important it has been to the history of the Yuma. The trail begins at Joe Henry Memorial Park (23rd Ave. and 1st St.) and goes to Pacific Avenue/Avenue 2E.

A popular and fun way to see the river and the refuge is to take a boat tour with Yuma River Tours (1920 Arizona Ave., 928/783-4400, www.yumarivertours.com, $38-89). Call ahead in summer, as they have limited hours during the hot months. The best tour is the four- to five-hour 32-mile boat trip to Norton's Landing ($75 pp, includes lunch), an old steamboat port and mining ghost town. The tour takes you deep into the refuge, and the guides are expert at spotting and pointing out birds and mammals along the way. Reservations are required. Yuma River Tours also offers day and dining cruises ($48-63 pp) on an old stern-wheeler and overnight guided kayak and canoe trips.

About 35 miles north of Yuma on U.S. 95 is **Martinez Lake,** where you can fish, boat, and view wildlife, among other activities. The Imperial National Wildlife Refuge is just north of the lake and extends 30 miles upriver, teeming with water-loving birds and other wildlife. At **Fisher's Landing** (928/782-7049, www.fisherslandingresort.com) on Martinez Lake you can rent a boat for the day ($50). You can also rent or buy fishing gear and book a guide to show you the best hide-outs of bass, crappie, bluegill, stripers, and flathead catfish. There's a restaurant serving burgers, sandwiches, fish, and steaks ($5-18) and a general store. The boat shop and a gas dock are open 8am-4pm daily. Other facilities at Fisher's Landing are open daily but hours vary seasonally, so call ahead.

Wildlife Refuges

While the many dams built along the Colorado River during the era of reclamation in the 1930s-1940s made it possible for the Southwest to grow and thrive as a habitat for humans, the loss of the river's natural and wild flow ruined much of the essential riparian habitat downstream. In an effort to restore what was lost and hold on to what remains, the U.S. Fish and Wildlife Service has established a number of wildlife refuges in western Arizona. These are wild and rugged places, not for the unprepared or the uninitiated. But for those looking for something far off the beaten track, these protected lands provide some of the best bird-watching, wildlife-viewing, and nature communing—especially of the desert and riverine kind—in the entire state.

Two of the refuges—Imperial and Havasu—feature well-established tour companies that will take you along the river and point out all there is to see.

Just north of Yuma on U.S. 95, the ruggedly beautiful **Kofa National Wildlife Refuge** (356 W. 1st St., Yuma, 928/783-7861, www.fws. gov) includes 665,400 acres of rough desert landscape, home to the dexterous bighorn and legions of reptiles who couldn't live anywhere else but this dry and sharp-rock land. Within

Kofa National Wildlife Refuge

the refuge is Palm Canyon, in the west end of the Kofa Mountains, are the only native palm trees in Arizona, a state that probably has more than its fair share of palms imported to its city streets. The 0.5-mile hike into Palm Canyon to see the trees is one of the region's best. Along U.S. 95 north of Yuma, watch for the Palm Canyon sign, then follow the dirt road east for nine miles toward the mountains and the trailhead.

Heading west to the river, you will find the 25,768-acre Imperial National Wildlife Refuge (Martinez Lake, 928/783-3317, www. fws.gov), a 30-mile desert-meets-wetland landscape renowned as a stop for migratory bird species and full of desert mammals, including bighorn sheep, mountain lions, bobcats, deer, wild horses, and burros. There's a visitors center, a rough-and-tumble scenic drive through an unvarnished Sonoran Desert stretch, and a few awesome lookouts with views of the river valley. The 1.3-mile Painted Desert Trail leads to a grand view as well. Yuma River Tours (1920 Arizona Ave., 928/783-4400, www.yumarivertours.com) offers boat tours into the refuge.

Farther upriver is the Cibola National Wildlife Refuge (66600 Cibola Lake Rd., Cibola, 928/857-3253, www.fws.gov), with some of the best birding in the region. Just outside the visitors center is the short scenic Canada Goose Drive, along which you can stop and hike the one-mile loop nature trail, moving through a beautiful riparian habitat of cottonwood, willow, and mesquite forests. In winter, thousands of Canada geese, snow geese, ducks, and sandhill cranes are usually visible from an observation deck here.

The Cabeza Prieta National Wildlife Refuge (1611 N. 2nd St., Ajo, 520/387-6483, www.fws.gov), 90 miles east of Yuma, is a forbidding landscape hugging the U.S.-Mexico border. If you're looking for the Sonoran Desert in the raw, you'll find it here. The Cabeza Prieta (meaning "dark head" in Spanish, for the area's volcanic coloring) is a hot and sparse land, covered in cacti and creosote and in spring by wildflowers and

other blooming desert show-offs. The refuge provides 860,010 acres of habitat for desert creatures to roam, including bighorn sheep and the cactus-pollinating lesser long-nosed bats. There's a small visitors center and short interpretive trail at the refuge office, where you have to stop first to pick up a permit to explore. Most of the refuge is within the airspace of the Barry M. Goldwater Air Force Range, so there are often low-flying aircraft in the area, crossing the refuge on their way to the bombing ranges to the north. Somewhere out in that sublimely wild swath of Sonoran Desert, that great advocate of wild desert, author Edward Abbey, is said to be buried in an unmarked grave.

ENTERTAINMENT AND EVENTS

For Vegas-style entertainment and games of chance, head to Quechan Paradise Casino (450 Quechan Dr., 888/777-4946, www.paradise-casinos.com), where popular bands of yesteryear often play, and there are slots, blackjack, poker, and lots of food and drinks. Take I-8 to the 4th Avenue exit, then go north on Imperial County Route S-24.

In early January, Yuma's historic downtown hosts the Old Town Jubilee, with artisans, entertainment, and activities for the whole family. If you're in town in mid-February, when the weather in Yuma is perfect, don't miss Yuma River Daze and the Yuma Crossing Days Festival, three days celebrating local history and culture that includes river races, swimming, and a block party downtown.

FOOD

The must-visit restaurant in downtown Yuma is ★ Lute's Casino (221 S. Main St., 928/782-2192, www.lutescasino.com, 9am-8pm Mon.-Thurs., 9am-9pm Fri.-Sat., 10am-6pm Sun., $5-15), popular with locals and visitors alike. Even if you aren't hungry, you'll enjoy sitting at one of the tall tables and drinking a brew, your neck craning to look at all the strange and hilarious—and even a bit bawdy—pictures covering the walls. The menu offers everything from burgers and hot dogs to burritos and tacos, all served in huge portions. If you like hot dogs, don't miss Bob's Polish Kraut Dog—it's awesome. Lute's is also a good place to enjoy some nightlife with the locals.

On the site where the first airplane landed in Yuma, the ★ Yuma Landing Restaurant (195 S. 4th Ave., 928/782-7427, www.yumalanding.com, 6am-9pm Sun.-Thurs., 6am-midnight Fri.-Sat., $14-30) has all sorts of memorabilia about that and other town history on the walls. It serves an eclectic mix of salads, sandwiches, steaks, prime rib, and Mexican dishes and has a bar with a good happy hour.

The River City Grill (600 W. 3rd St., 928/782-7988, www.rivercitygrillyuma.com, 11am-2pm and 5pm-10pm Mon.-Fri., 5pm-10pm Sat.-Sun., $18-35) serves top-notch seafood, beef, chicken, and vegetarian dishes in a cool contemporary setting, with a great patio for dining in the warmth of winter. It also has a fairly large selection of vegetarian and vegan options.

A great place for breakfast, lunch, and a relaxing coffee or tea, The Press Café & Bistro (121 E. 24th St., 928/726-2960, www.thepressyuma.com, 7am-4pm daily, $5-10) serves an assortment of pressed sandwiches—including the Yuman, with avocado dressing, romaine lettuce, and pepper jack—as well as creative and filling salads for lunch, and breakfast burritos and homemade biscuits for breakfast. The Press uses all-recyclable, compostable, or biodegradable paper products.

ACCOMMODATIONS

Yuma has all the chain hotels and motels a town its size would ever want. Many are just off I-8 or along 4th Avenue, the town's main commercial thoroughfare.

The best independent hotel in town is the historic Coronado Motor Hotel (233 4th Ave., 928/783-4453, www.coronadomotorhotel.com, $150-200). Built in 1938, this retro road-culture gem has comfortable guest rooms with free Wi-Fi and fridges. The staff is very friendly and helpful, and it's within minutes of the Yuma's historic downtown and the river. Breakfast at Yuma Landing comes with the room.

INFORMATION AND SERVICES

Downtown, the Visitor Information Center (264 S. Main St., 928/783-0071 or 800/293-0071, www.visityuma.com, 10am-6pm Tues.-Sun. Apr.-Sept.) has all kinds of pamphlets and advice for enjoying Yuma and the lower Colorado River region.

TRANSPORTATION

Yuma International Airport (YUM, 2191 E. 32nd St., 928/726-5882, www.yumaairport.com) offers a few flights each day to Phoenix, but you really need a car to explore this region and to get around Yuma. The main road in and out of the city is I-8, and going north along the river, U.S. 95.

Background

The Landscape

The Arizona landscape is more varied than most, with rises in elevation changing from hot cactus-choked **deserts** to scrubby bushlands to open **ponderosa pine forests** to coniferous snowy highlands. Dry **grasslands** and long stretches of sagebrush plains spread across the higher deserts.

While it snows and rains much more in the high country than it does in the desert belt, the entire state is subject to what Lawrence Clark Powell called a "wrinkled dryness." Aridity is a constant no matter where you go. Spread thinly across the land, a few life-giving river

ways and riparian areas are treasured as oases and predictably exploited.

Arizona has 114,000 square miles, making it sixth in size among the states. Large tracts of wild open land remain and likely always will.

GEOGRAPHY AND GEOLOGY

When dinosaurs roamed the earth, this desert was a swampy and wet place. Over the eons different portions of Arizona were covered by shallow seas that flowed in, flourished, and then retreated and dried up. Eventually the Arizona you see took shape—mountains rose, volcanoes burst and created new land, and plates slid apart and crashed into each other, creating upland plateaus and digging deep canyons with the erosional help of rivers, wind, and aridity.

Mountains

Few places have such extremes in elevation: You could travel from sea level along the lower Colorado to the 12,600-foot peak of Mount Humphreys, part of the volcanic San Francisco Mountain Range above Flagstaff, in a matter of a day or so. The White Mountains in the central-eastern part of the state tower higher than 10,000 feet and are often snow-capped. The Santa Catalinas, north of Tucson, rise to similar heights and feature the nation's southernmost ski run. A bit south of Tucson toward the U.S.-Mexico border, the Santa Rita Mountains tower above the Santa Cruz Valley, and just to the east the Huachuca Mountains do the same over the San Pedro Valley. Farther east the Pinaleño range rises above 10,000 feet, with towering Mount Graham watching over the Gila Valley. Many of these high Southern Arizona mountain ranges have important international observatories on their high reaches, so the cities and towns around them, Tucson included, are encouraged to keep their street lights and other "light noise" to a minimum so as to keep the sky dark and

clear. These southern ranges are often referred to as sky islands because they are exactly that: islands of biological diversity surrounded, and isolated, by vast seas of harsh hot desert. In these sky islands can be found flora and fauna that exist in few other places in North America. Subtropical birds and other animals use these mountains as the northern reaches of their ranges, so it's not uncommon to find quetzal-like birds and even jungle-loving jaguars flitting and stalking around the misty creek sides of these forested ranges.

The central and north-central region of Arizona is also very mountainous, though the ranges here are somewhat smaller and older than those in the south. Around Prescott the Bradshaws and the Sierra Prieta reach to 9,000 feet and are covered in pine. They were once, and perhaps still are, strewn with the precious minerals that became the impetus for one of the state's first mining booms. Throughout the state there are several other ranges and many detached lonely peaks, many of them high and timbered and others midsize and rocky, covered in cactus, creosote, and old mining tunnels.

The Colorado Plateau

The plateau country dominates the northern portion of the state, covering about two-fifths of its area; its nearly 200-mile southern edge, the Mogollon Rim, borders the scrub-and-pine belt of the transition zone. Below that is the basin and range province of the desert country, stretching from the western to the eastern border and south to Mexico. Elevations in the basin and range swing from sea level to about 4,000 feet, though several large mountain ranges dot the lowlands and rise above 9,000 feet. In the uplands of the plateaus, deep canyons plunge into the layers of ancient rock. The bottom of the Grand Canyon, which is cut into the Colorado Plateau, is a low hot desert. The highest points in the plateau country reach

---

Previous: blooming cactus in the Superstition Mountains.

above 12,000 feet and are dominated by tundra and bare cold boulders.

It is the contrast between the plateau and the basin and range provinces that makes Arizona such a rare landscape. Both have their origins deep in geologic time. The plateau country began to form in its current shape around 600 million years ago, when the continent was relatively flat and layer after layer of limestone, sandstone, siltstone, and shale were deposited by tropical seas moving in and then receding, leaving behind dunes and stream deposits and eroding the older layers for some 300 million years. Then the dune deposits started to harden and petrify, creating the strange swirling rock-dune sandstone one sees all over the plateau region. Volcanic eruptions around the plateau added to the great piling of sediment while rivers and lakes and inland seas flushed in and then dried up or receded. But the plateau itself, while it was eroded and cut and sculpted and formed, remained relatively stable in contrast to the other lands around it, which changed mightily. About 70 million years ago the land all around the Southwest began to rise, pushing the plateau from about sea level to more than 10,000 feet above it. Great mountains were thrust up out of the ground all around the region, and the earth stretched with underground tension to create the basin and range province to the west and south of the plateau. According to the U.S. Geological Survey, about 20 million years ago a "great tension developed in the [earth's] crust . . . and the basin and range province broke into a multitude of down-dropped valleys and elongated mountains" similar to what we see today in Arizona's desert lands. But the Colorado Plateau remained stable and eventually rose nearly a mile higher than the basin and range. The Colorado River fell through the plateau and cut deep into the rock, carving the Grand Canyon—a process that started less than six million years ago.

The Grand Canyon

A visit to the Grand Canyon reveals much of the story of the continent's geologic formation. The top layers of rock, through which the Colorado first cut, called the Kaibab Formation, are around 270 million years old, while the gneiss and schist of the inner canyon are about 1.8 billion years old. Many geologists believe that the lower 2,000 feet or so of the canyon was cut and eroded just in the last 750,000 years—on geological time scales, the blink of an eye. The canyon was formed by the great cosmic need of all water to return to the sea from whence it came. Water falls, and huge torrents of water carrying loads of dry rocky sediment fall hard and fast, cutting deep into the rocks of an uplifted plateau. As the cuts get deeper, the land around it gives way and falls apart, thus creating the deep, wide, and wonderful hole in the plateau that has made Arizona famous.

Deserts

Arizona is the only state where three major deserts converge: The **Sonoran Desert** stretches across the southern portion of the state and includes the Phoenix and Tucson areas, while the **Mojave Desert** dominates the western reaches. The **Chihuahuan Desert** of Mexico stretches north into southeastern Arizona.

The Sonoran Desert comprises about 120,000 square miles across the southwestern and south-central parts of Arizona. It is a woody desert, full of mesquite and paloverde trees, creosote bushes, and, of course, the famous saguaro cactus. A small portion of the Mojave Desert dominates northwestern Arizona and is marked by creosote and other small bushes, cholla cacti, and Joshua trees. The Chihuahuan Desert spreads out through southeastern Arizona and into Mexico, dominated by arid grasslands.

Rivers

The state's rivers, though many of them are dry for much of the year these days, have made human culture possible in Arizona. The **Gila River,** nearly dead today, was the main east-west waterway, stretching from the mountains of New Mexico to the lower Colorado, which forms the state's western border. The banks of the Gila's tributaries—the Verde, the San Pedro, the Salt, and the Santa Cruz—saw the rise of several complex and creative cultures over the centuries, including the Hohokam, the Salado, the Sinagua, and the Mogollon peoples. The state's main river, the **Colorado River,** drains the vast Colorado Plateau and stretches from Wyoming to Mexico. Much of the river through Arizona, about half its total length, has historically been difficult to access because it flows deep within intricately carved canyons. Tributaries of the Colorado, like the Little Colorado in the northeastern portion of the state and the Bill Williams River in the central-west portion, have also been important to human settlement. The Little Colorado provided a reasonable water supply for the early Puebloan cultures that settled on the high plains and, much later, was the source of life for Mormon pioneers in the 19th century.

Most of the state's rivers are no longer wild, having been dammed and controlled, a process that started on a major scale in the late 19th-early 20th centuries with the era of reclamation. Because wild desert rivers like the Gila, Salt, and Colorado were subject to intense flooding and severe drought, it was difficult for European settlers to rely on their quirky flows for agriculture. The federal government was also eager to harness the rivers' power to create hydroelectricity and to build vast reservoirs of water that could be sent to the growing agricultural and urban areas of Arizona, California, and elsewhere. Beginning at the turn of the 20th century with the building of Roosevelt Dam on the Salt River, which helped make Phoenix and the Valley of the Sun first an agricultural boomtown and then an urban megalopolis, the era of reclamation saw most of the state's rivers dammed, ending with the damming of the Colorado River at Glen Canyon in the mid-20th century. Earlier, the biggest dam of them all, Hoover, was constructed in Black Canyon on the Colorado River at the Arizona-Nevada border, creating the world's largest artificial lake, **Lake Mead,** and making possible the agricultural blunder called the Imperial Valley in California.

The damming of any river changes it irrevocably; the damming of the Colorado at Glen Canyon altered the stretch of the West's greatest river that created the Grand Canyon so much that it is unrecognizable compared to its previous form. Even the color of the river is different. The red Colorado used to flow muddy and warm through the canyon, hence its name, "Colored River," because it was full of the sediment that helped cut the great gorge. Since the dam was built, most of that sediment has been deposited behind the dam in the reservoir known as **Lake Powell,** and the river flows cool and green through the inner gorge. This has led to a complete change in the river's downstream ecosystem, as the ancient cycles of flood and drought have changed to a predictable constant flow, thus altering the very character of the river and making it difficult for native species to survive.

CLIMATE

Contrary to popular belief, many regions of Arizona experience four seasons. Even on the desert, while summers are long and hot below 5,000 feet elevation, the sky island mountain ranges experience little pockets of seasonally based weather.

Spring is the best time to be on Arizona's lowland deserts. Late February-May temperatures are typically in the high 70s and 80s from the lower Colorado River region across the desert belt to the New Mexico border.

The highland summer is warm—even hot—during the day and cool at night, ranging from the mid- to high 80s to the low 60s at night. In late summer the smell of wet pine needles precedes each late-afternoon monsoon rainstorm, and a mist rises when the cold raindrops hit the warm rocks.

While it also rains during the late summer on the deserts, during the beloved monsoon season, the storms only serve to make an already unbearable heat humid as well. Summers in the desert are intensely hot

The Desert at Risk

Many scientists in the Southwest these days are busy researching how climate change and prolonged drought will affect the region's arid life zones over the long term. One of these scientists is Travis Huxman, director of the University of California, Irvine's Huxman Lab, which studies ecology and evolution of plant functional traits.

For many years Huxman has been interested in how plants translate climate into ecosystem behavior—how plants respond to temperature fluctuation, carbon dioxide concentration, animals, and microbes, and how a plant's interaction with all these elements affects how an ecosystem processes water, which is probably the single most important question here in the arid thirsty Southwest.

"Plants can tell us a lot about ourselves, especially in the desert," Huxman says. "Deserts are very sensitive to change; you see big impacts in deserts before you might see them somewhere else." Huxman and others argue that, because of climate change, big representative species of the Sonoran Desert, most notably the mighty saguaro, are living under a very real threat. We could lose the saguaro and other celebrities of the desert because of fires sparked by invasive grasses, the spread of which is a direct impact of global climate change. It's happening in North America's other deserts as well. In the Mojave Desert to the west, the great Joshua tree is similarly threatened, according to Huxman.

"I don't have a projection for how long it would take, but you can hardly drive a freeway through the North American deserts and not see this change and the impact of fire on these landscapes," Huxman says. "It's fairly obvious."

So far in Arizona, such changes are most evident in the high deserts of the state's north-central pine belt. There, the largest ponderosa pine forest in North America is on the verge of total collapse. The conifers are stressed due to drought, and that stress allows bark beetles and other killers to dig in, which in turn leaves this typically fire-resistant species ready to burn. And once they're gone, will they grow back, or has the ecosystem changed irrevocably?

But that's not even the biggest problem, Huxman says. What we don't know yet is how the water cycle will react if a single dominant species like the ponderosa pine is no longer part of the ecosystem. "That's the big research question," he says. "How will all this affect water?" And that, according to Huxman, points to the most important fact we can learn from plants: what he calls the water-energy problem.

"Plants take up carbon dioxide in order to grow, but to do so they have to lose water to the atmosphere," he explains. "That's our problem on many different scales: How water and energy are related. So the most important thing we can do now is to remember that when we are thinking about energy efficiency, we are also thinking about water efficiency at the same time."

and listless. The daytime highs range from the high 90s to 110°F or even 120°F at their worst, while at night the lows rarely fall below the 80s. In Tucson and Phoenix it is not uncommon to experience several months straight of 100°F or higher temperatures with little or no rainfall.

The monsoon season, which, to be strictly correct, should be called simply the summer rainy season, occurs when shifting winds from the south encourage late-afternoon downpours, often attended by thunder and lightning, nearly every day July-September. During this time of year, the dry washes and riverbeds throughout the state are subject to flash flooding as torrents of rain flow through the channels from the uplands to the desert. Never stop or park in a dry wash at this time of year—it could become a raging river rather quickly, even if the sun is shining overhead. Monsoon storms are highly localized—so much so that it is sometimes raining in the backyard and not in the front yard. Hiking up a canyon during this time of year can also be dangerous and sometimes deadly; you never know if it's raining in the mountains above you, and that water could show up anytime, falling off the mountain and rushing through the canyon, taking hikers with it. Washes fill up quickly during the rainy season, and trapped drivers necessitate rescues that are expensive and dangerous for first responders. Never venture into a flooded wash, no matter how shallow it appears. However, unless you visit Arizona during the two months or so of the summer rainy season, or during the couple months in winter when it may be snowing in the highlands and raining intermittently on the deserts, you're not likely to experience anything but sunshine.

In the highlands during spring, you'll encounter cool days and cold nights, and it has even been known to snow across the pine belt in April or later. Depending on the length and strength of the winter, there will typically be snow in the north-central high country in February and even March.

Fall (Oct.-Dec. or Jan.) comes on cold and barren in the highlands, and the ground crunches with fallen leaves. The "second spring" begins in the desert. The weather gets perfect again, from the high 60s to the 80s, with cool light-jacket nights. This is the time of year when the snowbirds arrive from the Midwest to set up camp until it starts to get hot. After December, the winter rains come to the desert, and it starts to snow in the high country. For a very brief couple of weeks, everybody in the state is cold and housebound.

Winter temperatures can fall below freezing in the highlands and regularly reach lows of 20°F or below and highs in the 40s and 50s. On the deserts during this time, highs fall to the low 60s and even into the 50s, and lows regularly fall below 30°F. Only a few places in the state receive significant snowfall—Flagstaff, the Kaibab Plateau, and the White Mountains. In these places the snow can be deep enough to close roads and halt normal life.

ENVIRONMENTAL ISSUES

With its delicate and finely balanced biomes and some of the most dramatic and exotic scenery on earth, Arizona has over the generations been a haven, a laboratory, and a rallying point for environmentalists and ecologists. One of the biggest threats to the state's extremely varied ecosystems is simple growth; much of the desert has been paved over and crowded with homes, while the upland forests host droves of overbuilt homes just waiting for a wildfire to burn them to their foundations. It may seem strange that a land so naturally inhospitable to human occupation is, year after year, listed as one of the top two or three fastest-growing states in the nation. There are no signs that this trend is going to let up soon. Over the years the constant influx of people has led to environmental problems far beyond the mere paving of deserts and clearing of forests. Growth and the state's founding impetus to glean profit from the land have led to the overpumping of groundwater and the damming and taming of most of the state's rivers. This has altered the green riverways so completely that many species of native fish are now as good as gone, and nonnative plants line the mostly dry riverbeds, crowding out native riverine flora like cottonwoods and willows.

Climate change, scientists say, is likely to increase the state's environmental woes and, coupled with an ongoing drought that has been eating away at the state for more than a decade, may lead to shortages on the Colorado River, water from which the vast majority of urban Arizonans depend. Some scientists have recently predicted that Lake Mead may dry up by 2025, while others believe that one day in the future, the current human culture in Arizona may suffer the same collapse as did the Ancestral Puebloans, the Hohokam, and other complex societies that have tried to make a go of it here, leaving behind the ambitious ruins of their rise and fall but not much else.

There are numerous organizations fighting to save Arizona and its rare natural beauty from destruction and overuse, and over the last few decades the state, many local governments, and especially the diverse citizenry have taken a more proactive approach to conservation. Visiting neighborhoods in Tucson, Phoenix, and elsewhere in the desert gives the best evidence of this, where one can see a slowly increasing number of homes with solar panels on their roofs and rainwater tanks rising from behind their fences. The federal government, which controls many of the state's most famous environmental treasures, has over the last several years set aside more and more of the remaining open and wild lands as wilderness areas and national monuments. However, as ever the fluctuating price of copper and energy lead to periodic renewed explorations and plans to dig strip mines on public lands. These familiar debates over resource conservation have been raging for decades. Groups like the Nature Conservancy and the Tucson-based Sky Island Alliance and Center for Biological Diversity are using a variety of methods, including simple capitalism, science-based advocacy, and the federal courts to make sure that large swaths of Arizona remain open and wild.

Visitors to Arizona can help keep the state beautiful and clean by adhering to a few simple commonsense rules. First of all, as always, pack out what you pack in. Always stay on the trails, don't feed wild animals, and never take any vehicle off the road or the trail, including a bike. If you're an off-highway vehicle (OHV) enthusiast, stick to the set-aside off-road areas in the national forests (identified through the U.S. Forest Service's Arizona websites or at the local offices). Also, if you're visiting any of the state's many national forests during summer, there are likely to be campfire and smoking restrictions enforced throughout the state due to high temperatures and ongoing drought. Make sure that you are familiar with these restrictions and that you follow them to the letter. Nearly all of the state's huge catastrophic wildfires in recent years have been caused by humans.

Plants and Animals

PLANTS

The state's flora, like the land itself, is extremely diverse, ranging from weird desert rarities to tall thick evergreens.

If you pay attention to your elevation—and the "wrinkled" nature of the state assures that you are changing elevation all the time—you can generally predict what the weather will be like and which plants you are likely to see; of course, it's not all strictly delineated, and the various life zones often bleed into one another. Between 4,500 and 7,000 feet elevation you're in the **Upper Sonoran zone,** characterized by scrub oak, piñon pine, juniper, manzanita, and sagebrush grasslands; this zone is often called the chaparral. The midlands of the state, at around 6,000 feet and higher, are marked by the **transition zone,** a scrubby land of short dry bushes stretching into the ponderosa pines. Above 8,500 feet, thick stands of evergreen conifers and white aspen are common. Above 9,500 feet, a height reached in Arizona primarily by climbing up towering mountains, the **subalpine zone** has tough Engelmann spruce and bristlecone pine, and above that it's all barren rocks and tundra.

Trees and Bushes

The official Arizona state tree is the paloverde, a green-skinned desert dweller that can grow up to 25 feet tall. The tree proliferates throughout the Lower Sonoran zone and is often a close neighbor to the saguaro, the baby buds of which use the paloverde's cover to hide and grow. Other common desert trees are the ubiquitous mesquite, which has often been used for firewood and building and whose beans have nourished people and animals alike. Both the mesquite and the paloverde bloom yellow in spring.

Ironwood trees, drought-resistant evergreens, grow along slopes and washes in the desert. Bushy plants crowd the desert as well: Creosote is everywhere, as are stickery, catclaw, and rabbitbrush, all of which bloom yellow. Adding a little red to the bloom time is the ocotillo, which is everywhere in the desert and resembles a sprouting group of pipe cleaners. Throughout the desert and into the chaparral of the transition zones you'll see several sword-cluster species of agave, an important plant to the human population in that it can be turned into mescal and tequila. The *Agave parryi*, or century plant, blooms only once with a tall stalk of yellow flowers.

In the scrublands and chaparral and higher you'll see scrub oak, piñon pine, juniper, manzanita, and other brushy trees. In the high country, above 6,000 feet elevation, you'll see mainly ponderosa pine. Higher still, in the mountain forests near the North Rim of the Grand Canyon, the White Mountains, and elsewhere, fir, spruce, and aspen forests dominate. Along many waterways you'll see big cottonwoods and willows and sycamores.

Cacti

The most famous of Arizona's cacti, the saguaro, looks like it does because it is perfect: Every form has a function. Its green skin allows for photosynthesis, normally the job of leaves on less individualistic plants. Its spongy flesh and ribbed contours encourage water storage; the saguaro can collect and store up to 200 gallons of water from a single rainfall, which can maintain it throughout the year. Its telltale needles protect it from the incessant gnawing of hungry desert creatures. Its splashy white blossoms (seen April-June—the blossoms are Arizona's official state flower) and its juicy red fruit (eaten for eons by the desert's native inhabitants) assure the rising of another generation. The best place to

commune with these perfectly adapted desert plants is Saguaro National Park near Tucson.

You'll see various species of cactus throughout the Lower and into the Upper Sonoran zones. Most cacti are easily recognizable if you know their names: organpipe, barrel, beavertail, claret cup, and hedgehog cacti generally look like their so-briquets suggest, albeit spiky and standoffish versions. The famous prickly pear cactus can be identified by its red fruit-blooms, which are turned into jellies and even margarita mix.

Wildflowers

In the early spring, especially after a rainy winter, the desert *bajadas*, the sloping flatland that stretches out from the desert mountain ranges, and valleys bloom with color as dormant wildflowers burst back to life. Various shades of photogenic whites, yellows, blues, reds, and purples contrast with the uniform rich green of the well-watered springtime desert to create truly beautiful but ephemeral scenery. Some of the most common bloomers are the light-purple Arizona lupine, the deep yellow Mexican gold poppy, the dark pink Parry's penstemon (or Parry's beardtongue), and the virginal white desert lily. In summer the northland meadows and grasslands bloom with wild color as well. The best and most accessible places to see wildflowers in the spring are Picacho Peak State Park between Phoenix and Tucson and the Superstition Mountains east of Phoenix. You'll also see the desert in bloom in places like Saguaro National Park near Tucson and throughout the Santa Cruz Valley south of Tucson.

ANIMALS
Mammals

Arizona's official state mammal is the ringtail, a relative of the raccoon often called a ringtailed cat or a miner's cat because of its rodent-eating proclivities. Its huge, bushy, white-and-black-ringed tail is its identifying feature, but it's not likely you'll see one unless you're nocturnal. The mountain lion, or cougar, is found, and hunted, throughout Arizona; smaller **bobcats** are often seen lounging near water features in Sonoran Desert backyards, and scrawny **coyotes** can be spotted quickly crossing highways throughout the state. In the western deserts a few **bighorn sheep** still cling to the dry rocky cliffs.

A few different species of **jackrabbit** can be found all over, and **white-tailed deer** and **mule deer** live from the bottom of the Grand Canyon to the mountain heights and most places in between. **Pronghorn** live on the high grasslands in herds. The **collared peccary** or **javelina,** which resembles a wild pig, is everywhere in the desert and the transition zone, so much so that they are generally considered pests. The **black bear** lives in the mountains throughout the state, and various species of **bats** come out in the Arizona night, responsible for pollinating and continuing the state's signature cactus forests.

Birds

The small flitting **cactus wren,** which lives among the spiky plants, is the Arizona state bird, while the tall **roadrunner** may be its most recognizable. The **red-tailed hawk** proliferates in the desert sky, hunting rodents. The **California condor** has been reintroduced into the wild around Grand Canyon country. Though the condor is not a native to the state, the jagged canyon country was deemed a perfect place to acclimate the threatened prehistoric-looking bird into the wild.

Waterbirds, including the elegant **great blue heron,** hang around the state's riparian areas, and **wild turkeys** are somewhat common in oak and pine woodlands. One of the most common birds in the desert is the **Gambel's quail,** which can often be seen crossing streets followed by a ragged line of tiny offspring. The **turkey vulture** is constantly soaring slowly in the ever-blue dryland sky. Various owl species are common in the woodlands and the deserts, and the **gila woodpecker** and the **acorn woodpecker** are always tapping away at some tree or woodland home.

Southern Arizona is a mecca for bird enthusiasts, who stalk the region's sky island mountain ranges looking for rare subtropical birds like the **elegant trogon,** a green, red, white, and black bird related to the jungle-loving quetzal.

cactus wren

Fish

The apache trout, a gold-and-black native Arizona species, is the official state fish. Because of changes to the ecosystem and other factors, 28 of the state's 31 native fish are threatened, endangered, or as good as extinct. Still, in the mountain streams and lakes popular with anglers, you'll find rainbow and brown trout, bass, and others. In the lowland lakes there's bass, crappie, sunfish, catfish, and trout.

Reptiles

The desert is known as the home of the rattlesnake, seen more and more these days as the suburban attack on the desert continues. A few species of rattlesnake are found in Arizona. The western diamondback, which has lent its name to the state's world-champion professional baseball team, lives in the desert and the mountains and has deadly venom. Its skin is gray with brown diamond-shaped splotches along the back and a series of black-and-white bands just above its rattle. As with nearly all animals, the diamondback will leave you alone if you afford it the same courtesy. The light-brown western rattlesnake lives throughout the state, and the Arizona ridge-nosed rattlesnake lives in the woodlands of southeastern Arizona, a reddish-brown or gray hunter of rodents and lizards.

Several different species of lizard can be seen all over the lowlands, doing push-ups on hot rocks. The desert's most recognizable residents, these tiny leftover dinosaurs come in many shapes and sizes. One of the biggest is the fat and venomous Gila monster, with its beady skin and languid looks. The monster can be seen sunning itself sometimes in and around Tucson. The only venomous lizard in the United States should be given a wide berth if encountered.

The slow and wise desert tortoise hides out from the desert sun in its burrow, and if it makes it past its soft-shell youth—when it's a favorite of predatory birds—it can live up to a hundred years or more. Frogs and toads in Arizona include the Arizona tree frog, a lime-green forest resident, and the western spadefoot toad, blotchy greenish-brown with gray tints; it lives in the desert in a burrow.

Insects and Arachnids

The bark scorpion is the crabby pinching demon of the desert underworld; its venom is dangerous if it finds its way to the blood. The grand western cicada makes a racket in the woodlands on summer evenings. The hirsute desert tarantula looks much meaner than it is, cruising about in the early morning and early evening. You're bound to encounter gnats, mosquitoes, and other tiny pests in desert riparian areas and around upland lakes.

History

ANCIENT CULTURES

Small bands of ice-age migrants were probably moving through North America 20,000 years ago, but the pioneer Southwesterners are still widely considered to be the Clovis people (named for their spear points, first found in Clovis, New Mexico), who hunted big game in what is now Arizona 10,000-16,000 years ago. Climate change and the overexploitation of the mammoths and great ground sloths of the Pleistocene ended this epoch by about 8,000 BC. From then until pottery-making cultures began to rise around 2,000 years ago, the Archaic-era hunter-gatherers made a long successful go of it here, moving between the forested highlands and the deserts seasonally to hunt and gather wild foods. By the late Archaic period these bands were living in semipermanent camps in pit houses and were growing corn likely introduced by migrants from Mesoamerica.

The first millennium AD saw the rise of

several sophisticated and mostly sedentary cultures in Arizona, the most successful of which were the Ancestral Puebloans on the Colorado Plateau, the Sinagua in the Verde Valley and volcano lands around Flagstaff, the Mogollon in eastern Arizona and New Mexico, the Salado in the region around the Little Colorado River, and the Hohokam in the river valleys of the Sonoran Desert. These cultures would rise and fall in stages, with rises generally coinciding with wet times and falls subsequent to droughts.

By AD 700 the Ancestral Puebloans were building above-ground rock-and-mud urban-like villages that would become known as pueblos, from the Spanish word for town or city. The Ancestral Puebloan culture would briefly rise to become an empire in the plateau country, with New Mexico's Chaco Canyon as its ruling capital.

A separate culture, related in many ways to the Ancestral Puebloans, flourished in the Flagstaff and Verde Valley regions around AD 500-1425. Called the Sinagua, which means "without water" in Spanish, the group mostly lived around Sunset Crater near Flagstaff until AD 700, when several bands migrated below the Mogollon Rim to live along the Verde River and among the red rocks of Sedona. The Sinagua built impressive cliff dwellings and huge sandstone apartment-style pueblos that can still be seen and visited today. The Sinagua culture survived the eruption of Sunset Crater in 1064 and thrived as part of an important regional trade route for centuries.

Known for their elegant black-and-white Mimbres pottery, the Mogollon people lived in scattered villages in the pine forests of West-Central New Mexico and East-Central Arizona around AD 150-1400, when they are thought to have been absorbed into the Ancestral Puebloan regime. The Salado people lived in the Tonto Basin northeast of Phoenix from about AD 1150 to the 1400s. One of their cliff dwellings above the Salt River can still be seen today at Tonto National Monument. In the low deserts, the Hohokam constructed a network of irrigation canals in the river valleys around what are now Phoenix and Tucson and lived in complex hierarchical agricultural societies that built adobe great houses and ceremonial ball courts.

Around AD 1150 many of the dramatic cliff dwellings, built by various cultures and scattered from the desert to the pines to the rocky lands of the Colorado Plateau, began to appear throughout the Southwest. These cultures had mostly run their course by AD 1450 due to a variety of factors—ecological, climatic, and social. For generations the monuments and ruins they left behind have fascinated scientists and travelers alike.

Sometime in the 1400s or before, the Athapaskan culture migrated south to the area from the far north of what is now Canada; these tribes would later become known as the Apache and the Navajo. These tribes were not related to any of the cultures living in the region at the time they arrived. The Apache eventually moved to southeastern Arizona, where they would have an epochal battle for supremacy with the U.S. Army in the late 19th century, while the Navajo stayed in the Colorado Plateau area and learned about dryland farming from their Puebloan neighbors while also spending a good amount of time raiding those same neighbors. They would eventually be nearly killed off by the U.S. Army under the direction of Kit Carson. After a long and brutal internment outside their harsh but beloved Four Corners lands, the Navajo signed a treaty with the United States in 1868 that allowed them to return to the plateau country, where they remain today and have grown to become North America's largest tribe. The Hopi, who live on a small reservation on three mesas in the middle of the Navajo Nation, are the descendants of the Ancestral Puebloans who lived in the region's dramatic cliff dwellings and pueblos. They were never forced off their homeland—the same harsh and seemingly inhospitable mesas they still live on today—but along with the Navajo and Apache, they were subject to periodic attempts by the federal government to "Americanize" them by sending their children to government-run schools off the reservation, forcing them into a cash and labor economy very different from their subsistence lifestyle, and converting them to Christianity. A large number of Navajo today are Christians, and there are churches throughout the reservation.

EUROPEANS ARRIVE

The impenetrable northern reaches of the Spanish Empire in Mexico were essentially unexplored by Europeans when Álvar Núñez Cabeza de Vaca found himself shipwrecked and lost in the grasslands and deserts of what is now the southwestern United States and northern Mexico in the 1520s. And though he and his companions—one of them, Estevan, was an enslaved or indentured Moor—probably never made it to Arizona proper, the tales they told of their adventures when they finally returned to Mexico City inspired subsequent explorations in the great north. In 1539 Fray Marcos de Niza and Estevan trekked north to search for the Seven Cities of Cibola, rumors of which Estevan and Cabeza de Vaca had heard during their ordeal. Estevan scouted ahead and was killed by the Zuni, who lived not in golden cities but in regular old mesatop pueblos not too different from those that still exist on the Hopi reservation in Arizona and in the Rio Grande Valley of New Mexico. Nevertheless, de Niza's report suggested that the golden cities might indeed be a reality, and that was enough to inspire an ambitious expedition in 1540 led by Francisco Vázquez de Coronado in search of the reported riches. Coronado found none, but his expedition moved through what is now eastern Arizona. In the 1690s Jesuit priest Eusebio Francisco Kino began his journeys into Southern Arizona and Sonora, bringing cattle to the region for the first time and establishing several long-lasting missions, including San Xavier del Bac near Tucson, to this day still celebrating mass in its dark cool interior. By the 1750s the Spanish crown had established a presidio or fort at Tubac, which was moved to the Santa Cruz Valley near Tucson in 1775. Southern Arizona comprised the northern reaches of the Spanish New World empire, though it was sparsely populated and was a violent, dangerous place to live. Spanish cattle ranchers and other hardy settlers fought Apaches and others for the resources of the region, but for decades the north would remain too isolated and too dangerous to develop much. The Mexicans won their independence from Spain in 1821 and took over administration of the vast northlands. The wilderness was exploited somewhat for its resources, used for cattle ranching and placer mining by tough Mexican explorers, but mostly it was too far from the center of power and too dangerous to be of much worth to the new nation.

In the late 1820s, trappers, hunters, and mountain men like James Ohio Pattie, Antoine Leroux, and Pauline Weaver became some of the first Anglo Americans to venture through Arizona, in search of beaver pelts. Such men would in turn guide the Army of the West and the Mormon Battalion through the state in 1846-1847 during the Mexican-American War, which was fought primarily in Mexico. After the war ended in 1848, much of what is now the Southwest became part of the United States, and in 1850 a huge area that included Arizona and New Mexico became the New Mexico Territory. In 1854 the land between the Gila River and the Mexican border—Southern Arizona, basically—was added to the territory through the Gadsden Purchase.

In 1849 and for several years afterward, thousands of Americans passed through Arizona headed for gold and glory in California. Those hard-rock, hard-luck miners would return east to the state a few years later in search of the gold and silver most of them had failed to find farther west. Several boundary, land, railroad, and scientific surveys of Arizona and the West during the 1850s brought this far corner of the continent greater attention and interest from the East.

TERRITORIAL YEARS

It was the increasing mining activity in the state that, among other factors, led President Lincoln to establish the Arizona Territory in 1863, disconnecting it from the huge conglomerate of land called New Mexico. The capital was established at Prescott, in the state's mineral-laden midlands, and the East's economic exploitation of the land, albeit on a much smaller scale than it would become, commenced. During the Civil War, Tucson was a Confederate hotbed for a time before being occupied by the U.S. Army. After the Civil War ended, immigration and exploration of the Southwest picked up considerably. Still, when **John Wesley Powell** completed the first river run through the Grand Canyon in 1869, the population of the territory was under 10,000.

Settlers trickled in over the subsequent years, spurred to find treasure, to cure their tuberculosis, and for adventure, science, and cheap land made available by the federal Homestead and Desert Land Acts. Despite this, the territory remained a wild and dangerous place for most. The Apache, Navajo, and other tribes didn't feel they should have to give up the land they had conquered to settlers, many of whom were looking to get rich quick by exploiting the land and then leave. From 1871 until **Geronimo**'s final surrender in 1886, the U.S. Army fought a brutal war with the Apache and other tribes. The Apache were eventually defeated at a high cost to both parties, and some bands were sent to Oklahoma, where they became prisoners of war for many years. They struggled to hold to their traditional ways and remain a strong culture, but privation and the machinations of a government that did not understand them took their toll. Eventually the Apache were allowed to return to Arizona to reservations that include parts of their traditional homelands, and today they operate successful casinos and resorts.

With the end of the Apache Wars the territory moved one step closer to large-scale settlement and development. In the 1880s the railroad arrived and transformed the region, bringing in more people and materials than ever before. By 1889 the Phoenix area had already begun to dominate the territory, and with the construction of Roosevelt Dam on the Salt River in 1911, the valley's agricultural boom was on the horizon. In 1912, Arizona entered the union as the 48th state.

STATEHOOD AND BEYOND

The first half of the 20th century in Arizona was dominated by the era of reclamation. The federal government used taxpayer money to develop the state's water resources, damming rivers for irrigation, water storage, and hydroelectric power, creating a huge agricultural industry in the process. Phelps Dodge and other mining giants ripped huge holes in the land to extract low-grade copper, while Anglo owners and managers on the whole treated the Mexican and Native American miners and those who worked in the agricultural industry as seasonal laborers—without whom Arizona agriculture would not have been possible—poorly, even criminally on many occasions.

At the same time, more residents and visitors began to realize that there was more to the fantastic Arizona landscape than profit and loss, and this era saw the rise of national parks and monuments, national forests, and state-level protection of important lands. Beginning around the 1920s, boosters in Phoenix, Tucson, and elsewhere began to see the economic benefits of attracting tourists to the sunny state, and by 1950 or so tourism had replaced the extractive industries in importance. During the two world wars the federal government set up training bases and military installations in the state that led to a growth spurt, and the advent of swamp coolers and air conditioners stimulated a population boom in Arizona that has yet to let up.

Government and Economy

GOVERNMENT

Arizona's government has had a contrary relationship with the federal establishment since before statehood. The state's entrance into the union was delayed for some time because the legislature, backed by a majority of the public, refused to give up a section of its constitution that allowed for the popular recall of judges. Today the bickering between the two continues over public land issues and border control. The truth is that the federal government made Arizona, and it still controls a large portion of the land in the state. With history as an example, it's easy to see that had the federal government not protected huge portions of the state as national forests, monuments, parks, and wilderness areas, Eastern economic interests would have used that land for their own profit, as they have the majority of Arizona's natural resources since long before statehood.

The state's government for most of its history has been interested, like nearly everybody else, in developing and taking from the land, and the various land-hungry interests who at one time or another were in favor—be they mining, agricultural, ranching, or military—have dictated policy. This is not as true today as it has been in the past, however.

While Arizona is known today as a somewhat conservative state, it has not always been that way. Progressive Democrats ruled the state for a few generations until **Barry Goldwater** and the conservative revolution found success here and on the national stage in the 1960s. However, in recent years the state's demographics have been changing, and the voter rolls are swelling not with Republicans and Democrats but with Independents. Evidence of this slow purpling of Arizona came in 2018 when Arizona elected Kyrsten Sinema to the U.S. Senate, the first Democrat since 1995 to hold the seat, and again in 2020

when voters elected a second Democratic senator, former astronaut Mark Kelly, husband of Gabrielle Giffords, a gun control advocate and former U.S. Representative of Arizona who was seriously injured in a 2011 mass shooting in Tucson.

ECONOMY

Arizona's economy in the past was ruled by the boom-and-bust realities of the extractive and agricultural industries. Worldwide prices, the fickleness of the market, and the constant threat of a destructive act of nature made economic life here before World War II a wild ride. Booms in the cattle industry in the 1890s and cotton before and during World War I created large industries in the state virtually overnight. The overgrazing of an arid open range and monocultural agriculture took their individual tolls, and both of these members of the state's well-known "Five C" economy (cotton, cattle, copper, citrus, and climate) actually influenced life here on a major scale for a relatively short time. The other members of the Five C's have fared better than cotton and cattle, both of which are now very minor elements of the state's economy. Copper mining, the state's claim to fame in economic circles for several generations, faces an ever-precarious future. The extractive and agricultural industries are no longer the primary economic engines of Arizona and the western states and haven't been for some time. According to a report by the Tucson-based Sonoran Institute, fewer than 5 percent of the West's counties have more than 20 percent of employment in traditional extractive industries.

A boom in single-family housing and urban and suburban development has enraptured the state for several decades, but the deep truth of the Arizona economy, and

Native American Arts and Crafts

Native American artists abound in Arizona, many of them of the Hopi and Navajo Nations in the far northeastern corner of the state. These artists often sell their work at markets and fairs held throughout the year in Phoenix, Tucson, Flagstaff, and elsewhere, and their silverwork, kachinas, pottery, rugs, and paintings have been highly desired since territorial days.

Many people approach this art with preconceived notions, especially about authenticity and tradition. People expect every Native American artist and artisan to adhere to some ancient set of guidelines, a method that washes each squash-blossom necklace and kachina doll carving with some undeniable spiritual patina. As with most artistic movements, however, the provenance of the Southwestern Indian Arts and Crafts tradition is far more complex.

Think of these artists as working within similar confines as did painters and sculptors of the Western European tradition during the Renaissance. Such artists were bound more often than not to paint and sculpt imagery from the Bible or Greek and Roman mythology, and they could count on their public immediately recognizing the scenes and characters they depicted. However, within this rather narrow tradition there existed astonishing variety.

Consider, as an example, the story of how silverwork was introduced to the Navajo people. In the 1850s, Navajo ironworker Atsidi Sani (Old Smith) added silver to the Navajo tradition of making jewelry out of shell and stone. The oral tradition says the Southwest's Indigenous inhabitants were taught metalwork in general by the Europeans; Atsidi Sani is said to have learned silversmithing from a smith called Nakai Tsosi or "Thin Mexican." More and more Navajo people learned the art during the tribe's tragic imprisonment at Fort Sumner at Bosque Redondo, and the Navajo then taught their Pueblo neighbors, mostly the Hopi and the Zuni, to work silver.

The silver in the early days and for a long time after mostly came from Mexican and U.S. coins. Reservation traders like John Lorenzo Hubbell, at Ganado, paid the Navajo to teach each other, then sold the products to tourists. Some of the best silversmiths gave up raising livestock and farming and were able to become full-time artisans, a pattern that still plays out today.

It was during the golden age of Southwestern tourism that the authenticity of Native American jewelry became an issue. The artists were, of course, encouraged to create work specifically for tourists, who flocked to the reservations and pueblos on the Fred Harvey Indian Detours. Writer and trader Mark Bahti writes that these pieces were often lightweight, with "horses, tipis, arrows, thunderbirds . . . designed to fit the tourist notion of what Indian jewelry was *supposed* to look like." But, as Bahti points out, what was Indian jewelry actually "supposed" to look like? Nobody could really say, and they still can't. By the 1920s manufactured copies were being made outside the Southwest and then shipped in to be sold as authentic, spurring the artists to join together in co-ops and guilds, many of which are still in operation and training new artists.

The 1970s brought a boom in the market for Pueblo and Navajo jewelry, and today there is a really diffuse sense of what is traditional and what is innovative. Innovation—the artist responding not only to tradition but to the world around them—can be seen everywhere at Native American markets throughout Arizona.

one that holds for the entire West, is that the service industry, much of it tourism-related, with its low wages and transient workers, is the hottest-running economic engine and has been for many years. All over the West, non-labor income like investments, disability, and retirement payments come in a close second to the service industry as a top economic driver.

The median household income in Arizona is about $56,000, with 2.6 people per household. Some 15 percent of Arizonans live below the poverty line.

Local Culture

Most Arizona residents are immigrants to the state, and most have lived here a relatively short time. The majority of the state's 6.7 million residents live in Pima and Maricopa Counties, in and around the two large cities of Tucson and Phoenix. About a million people live in Pima County, and some four million live in Maricopa. About 18 percent of Arizonans are 65 and over, but 23 percent are under 18. The number of seniors is expected to rise significantly as more and more baby boomers retire and move to the sunbelt, just as their parents did in the 1960s and 1970s. About 87 percent of Arizonans are high school graduates, and 30 percent have at least a bachelor's degree. Some 64 percent of Arizonans own their homes.

Arizonans who identify as Latino or Hispanic represent about 31 percent of the state's population, according to the U.S. Census, and have a significant and growing influence on the state's politics, economy, and culture, especially in Phoenix, Tucson, and other parts of Southern Arizona. Their cultural influences can be seen throughout the state—in much of the finest art, music, and food to be found in Arizona.

Native Americans make up about 4 percent of the population; the largest tribe, the Navajo Nation, has some 350,000 members. Other tribes include the O'odham people, formerly called the Papago and Pima. The Tohono O'odham (the Desert People) live on a large reservation southwest of Tucson and operate casinos near the city. In the Phoenix area, the Akimel O'odham (the River People), or the Gila River Indian Community, live on a reservation and operate casinos as well. Other tribes in the state include the Hopi, the Yavapai near Prescott, the Western Apache bands, and the Colorado River tribes of western Arizona. Most of the state's Native American tribes have compacts

allowing them to operate casinos, and those casinos are popular.

Unlike many of the other Native American nations on the continent, Arizona's tribes are still living today on their ancestral homelands, albeit smaller portions of that homeland set aside by the federal government under the reservation system. Arizona's Native Americans have made important contributions to the artistic, cultural, political, and economic life of the state. The finest artists to come out of Arizona are Native American, and many are known the world over for their arts and crafts based on traditional designs and patterns but adapted and evolved to speak to a contemporary world.

RELIGION

Religious life in Arizona is diverse and complex. Catholicism is popular among Latino/Hispanic residents and with many Anglos as well, while the Church of Jesus Christ of Latter-day Saints, or the Mormons, has been established in some rural areas of the state since the 19th century.

A Pew Forum survey in 2014 found that 20 percent of Arizonans identified as Catholics, and 25 percent identified as Evangelical Protestants. Mainline Protestants make up about 15 percent of the religious population, and LDS adherents constitute about 4 percent. A surprising 22 percent see themselves as "unaffiliated." Members of historically Black Protestant churches make up 2 percent of the population, 2 percent are Jewish, and 1 percent is Buddhist. Jehovah's Witnesses also make up 1 percent of the population.

LANGUAGE

The majority of Arizonans speak English, though 27 percent of residents speak a language other than English at home (mostly Spanish), according to the U.S. Census

Bureau. From time to time over the years there have been calls for and votes on making English the official language of the state, usually attending some new round of anger and fear over illegal immigration, which, owing more than anything else to Arizona's proximity to Mexico, is an ever-present political issue. The reality is that Spanish is used throughout the state. You'll see and hear it everywhere. You may also hear several Native American languages as you travel around the state, including the intricate Hopi language and the Navajo tongue, which was used by the famous code talkers of World War II—one of the only "codes" never to be broken.

THE ARTS

Most of the prominent non-Native American artists and writers associated with Arizona were émigrés. **Edward Abbey,** author of the *Monkey Wrench Gang* and many other books, continues, nearly two decades after his death, to influence writing and environmental politics in the state. Tucsonan **Charles Bowden** had a national reputation as a nonfiction writer and produced some of the best books ever about the disaffection and dark ironies of sunbelt culture. Tucson resident **Leslie Marmon Silko** wrote an Arizona epic: her *Almanac of the Dead* examines the ancient and contemporary Southwest and the confluence of the two. The prolific **Zane Grey,** one of the progenitors of the Western genre, spent a lot of time in Arizona's Rim Country and based many of his books in the state.

German painters **Max Ernst** and **Dorthea Tanning** came to Arizona in 1946, settling in Sedona and painting the state's surrealistic landscapes in the manner they deserved. Some of Ernst's work is on display at the **Phoenix Art Museum.** There are hundreds of painters and sculptors living and working in Arizona today. Many of them congregate in Sedona, Tucson, Tubac, Bisbee, and Jerome. Each of these towns and cities has many galleries dedicated to individual artists, styles, and groups. The famed **Cowboy Artists of America** group was founded in Sedona in 1965, and the aesthetic traditions of the group are still highly visible in the state's galleries and museums.

Arizona has produced a few pop stars, most notably **Linda Ronstadt,** whose family has deep roots in Tucson. **Alice Cooper** grew up in the Valley of the Sun and still resides here, operating a popular downtown rock-and-jock-themed restaurant and bar. The Tempe music scene had a minor worldwide reputation in the 1990s thanks to bands like the **Gin Blossoms** and the **Refreshments.** Singer **Stevie Nicks** is from the Phoenix area, as is **Wayne Newton.**

Thanks to its desert scenery and always clear skies, Arizona has had a vibrant moviemaking scene on and off since the silent era. Classic films like *Arizona, Stagecoach,* and *Oklahoma* were filmed in the state, along with *The Planet of the Apes, The Three Amigos,* and hundreds of others. The fortunes of Arizona's film industry tend to rise and fall with the popularity of the Western.

Essentials

Transportation

AIR

If you're flying into Arizona, you'll likely find yourself at **Phoenix Sky Harbor International Airport** (PHX, 3400 E. Sky Harbor Blvd., 602/273-3300, www.skyharbor.com). One of the Southwest's largest airports, Sky Harbor has three terminals served by many domestic and international airlines. The airport is just three miles east of downtown Phoenix and easy to find. There's a free shuttle system to take you between terminals.

The only other serious choice is Tucson International Airport (TUS, 7250 S. Tucson Blvd., 520/573-8100, www.flytucson.com), which hosts a few airlines and offers daily flights to both coasts and other destinations. If you book a flight to Tucson, it may be slightly more expensive than flying into Sky Harbor in Phoenix, and you probably won't get a direct flight; in many cases, you'll have to fly into Sky Harbor, switch planes, and then fly south to Tucson—just a 1.5-hour drive on I-10. If you're renting a car anyway, it's probably a better idea to fly into Phoenix and then drive from there, unless you are just going to Tucson and Southern Arizona; then a direct flight into Tucson makes more sense.

Flagstaff, Prescott, Tusayan near the Grand Canyon, Yuma, and other towns have airports, though they are small and offer mostly regional routes. There are also several smaller regional airports around the Valley of the Sun, offering regional flights to Southwestern and West Coast ports. If you're coming from the West Coast or some other Southwestern city, you might look into regional flights to your Arizona destination; otherwise, Sky Harbor and then a rental car are your best bet no matter where you're headed in Arizona.

TRAIN

The *Southwest Chief* route of Amtrak, which mirrors the old Santa Fe Railway's *Super Chief* route of the grand Fred Harvey days, stops twice daily (one eastbound, one westbound) at Flagstaff's classic downtown depot (1 E. Rte. 66, 800/872-7245, www.amtrak.com), the former Santa Fe headquarters and also the town's visitors center (800/842-7293). The route crosses the country from Chicago to Los Angeles, dipping into the Southwest through northern New Mexico and Northern Arizona. There are long-term plans for a high-speed railroad between Phoenix and Tucson, and possibly to other parts of the state, though such

a project is likely a generation or more away from being realized. The Southwest, while built and populated largely by the railroads, continues to hold strong to the car culture, and that isn't going to change anytime soon.

CAR

You need a personal vehicle to get around in Arizona. A significant part of the fun of a visit to the great Southwest is the road trip, and there's just too much scenery and too many spur-of-the-moment stops to go any other way. Reserve a rental car before you travel, but don't rent it at the Phoenix Sky Harbor International Airport; the airport charges exorbitant taxes and fees that make a short taxi ride to an off-airport rental place well worth it.

If you'd like to carry your home with you on the Arizona road, or if you want to relive a favorite sitcom moment or two, look into renting an RV. All over the state you'll see rented RVs touring the monuments and landscapes, packed with families and groups of friends. In Phoenix, check out Arizona Camper Van (480/382-0764, http://arizonacampervan.com) and Cruise America RV Rental (11 W. Hampton Ave., Mesa, 480/464-7410, http://cruiseamerica.com).

From Los Angeles: The major road routes to and through the state are I-10, I-40, and I-8. I-10 is the best and only practical way to get from Los Angeles to Phoenix (373 miles, 5 hours) and Tucson, (488 miles, 7 hours). To reach Flagstaff and the Grand Canyon from Los Angeles, take I-40 to Flagstaff (486 miles, 7 hours), with another 78 miles (1.5 hours) to the Grand Canyon. I-40 also passes Williams (431 miles, 6 hours), another gateway to the Grand Canyon, 60 miles (1 hour) to the South Rim.

From Las Vegas: The main route from Las Vegas to Flagstaff, Williams, and the Grand Canyon is U.S. 93 to I-40. The popular South Rim section of Grand Canyon National

Park is 277 miles from Las Vegas: 4 hours from Las Vegas to Flagstaff, then 1.5 hours to the Grand Canyon.

The drive across the rocky jagged desert from Las Vegas to Phoenix is 300 miles (5 hours). Most of the drive, save for a short stretch on I-40 near Kingman, is on U.S. 93, a scenic desert highway that moves through some of the most ruggedly beautiful wildlands in the Southwest and crosses the Colorado River near Hoover Dam.

From Phoenix: To reach Arizona's northland (Flagstaff, the Grand Canyon, Prescott, the Mogollon Rim, and Sedona) from Phoenix, take I-17 north out of the valley. I-17 goes to Flagstaff (150 miles, 2 hours), where it meets I-40.

BUS

Greyhound (www.greyhound.com) provides bus service between major towns, mostly along the interstate highways. This isn't a very efficient way to travel around Arizona. Check out the website for schedules and station locations.

BIKE

The most bike-friendly towns in Arizona are Tucson and Tempe, in the southern desert portion of the state, and Flagstaff, in the cool mountainous pine forest. They have large and active biking communities that consistently push for more trails and lanes. Each has hundreds of miles of bike paths and bike lanes, making it possible to live in these cities with just a bike for transportation. However, for three months of the year it is either too hot in Tucson and Tempe or too cold in Flagstaff to ride much.

Grand Canyon National Park's South Rim has become increasingly bike-friendly in recent years. You can take your own bike or rent one inside the park. Biking is actually an ideal way to see the park—much better than driving to each of the lookouts and having to park and get out of the car. It's mostly a summertime activity, however, considering the park's relatively high elevation; from early November you'll likely find it too cold to enjoy the ride.

TOURS

If you're looking for the knowledgeable assistance of an expert, you can hire Open Road Tours (602/997-6474, http://openroadtoursusa.com) to guide and shuttle you in comfort all over the state. Such tours are only recommended for those who enjoy groups. Arizona's tourist track is well established and easy to negotiate, and a tour guide is not necessary. Most of the best sights are controlled by the federal government, specifically the National Park Service, and rangers are always on hand to answer questions and give free informative tours.

Food and Accommodations

FOOD

Mexican food reigns supreme in Southern Arizona, but the local-food revolution shows throughout the state in numerous restaurants dedicated to using local and all-natural ingredients, harking back to a simpler time when we knew more about our food. In the old mining towns of Bisbee in Southern Arizona and Jerome in Northern Arizona, you'll find a few high-style restaurants serving an eclectic blend of Southwestern and haute cuisine. In Scottsdale, Phoenix, and throughout the Valley of the Sun, your head will spin from all the options, most highly creative and dedicated to fusion of the native and the new. Head to either the Navajo or Hopi Reservation, and you can sample Indigenous cuisine, centered mainly around mutton and corn and a kind of Mexican-Native American amalgam called the Navajo (or Hopi) taco—a delicious hunk

Clothing-Optional Accommodations

There's something about the powerful Arizona sun, especially when it shines hard on the desert country, that makes one want to wear as little clothing as possible. While this usually isn't recommended, what with society's conventions and the danger of overexposure to the dastardly rays, those who enjoy the popular world of naturism will want to check out the clothing-optional resort in the desert just north of Phoenix. **Shangri La Ranch** (44444 N. Shangri La Rd., New River, 623/465-5959, www.shangrilaranch.com, office 9am-5pm daily, daily fee $20 pp, $70-100 guest rooms, $10 camping, $15 RV hookup) is a family-oriented nudist resort with guest rooms, camping, and an RV park. It offers numerous activities, a huge swimming pool, and friendly staff. Although no bathing suits are allowed in the pool, the philosophy of Shangri La seems to be live and let live, so you can "ease into" the nudist lifestyle if you're not already a committed naturist. The setting is gorgeous, way out in the scrubby desert 45 minutes north of Sky Harbor International Airport off I-17 near New River. This is most definitely a family place, so be respectful and adhere to the rules of conduct.

of fry bread piled high with meat and beans. If you're looking for gluten-free options, many of the best restaurants in Phoenix and Tucson offer choices or will make a gluten-free version for you. As you move into rural areas, which is most of Arizona, the choices dwindle, but it never hurts to ask. Some venues in Arizona's small towns offer gluten-free dishes, and their numbers appear to be growing.

ACCOMMODATIONS

Arizona is famous for its luxury resorts. The best of these all-inclusive upscale spa-resorts in Phoenix, Scottsdale, Tucson, and Sedona are listed in the chapters for those cities.

The state is also fortunate to have a number of historic hotels still in operation, though updated and remodeled, and there are many boutique hotels and bed-and-breakfasts operating in historic buildings that used to serve some important territorial function. If you're just looking for a place to flop between adventures, there is an abundance of chain hotels in every major city and town, and in small towns near national parks and monuments and off the interstates.

Travel Tips

In many ways Arizona was saved by tourism. If travelers didn't love the state's scenery and history so much, the Grand Canyon may have long ago been strip-mined and the last of the desert paved over. Instead, the natural wonders have largely been preserved indefinitely, and a vibrant and busy tourism industry has grown up here. Because of this, it's easy to be a tourist in Arizona. Below are a few tips to make it even easier.

TIME ZONES

Arizona is in the mountain time zone (MST) and is one of the few places in the country that does not switch to daylight saving time in summer. The Navajo Nation in northeastern Arizona, spread across three states, does switch to daylight saving time from the second Sunday in March to the first Sunday in November, adding even a time change to complete the foreign-country feel of that region.

INTERNATIONAL TRAVELERS

The many national parks and monuments in Arizona are well equipped for international tourists. All offer guides and other literature in major languages and are used to working with international travelers. Arizona and the Southwest in general are popular destinations for European, Japanese, and Chinese travelers, and in summer, no matter where you're from, you could very well meet one of your compatriots on the South Rim or at Monument Valley.

The U.S. government's Visa Waiver Program allows tourists from a number of countries to visit without a visa for up to 90 days. To check if your country is on the list and for requirements, go to http://travel.state.gov. Even with a waiver, you still need to bring your passport and present it at the port of entry.

ACCESS FOR TRAVELERS WITH DISABILITIES

Many of the best sights in Arizona are accessible to travelers with disabilities in one way or another. The Grand Canyon and most of the other major federal parks have accessible trails and viewpoints. For advice and links to other helpful internet resources, go to www.disabledtravelers.com, based in Arizona and full of accessible travel information, though it's not specific to the state. For questions specific to Arizona, contact the state Department of Administration's Office for Americans with Disabilities (100 N. 15th Ave., Suite 361, Phoenix, 602/542-6276 or 800/358-3617, TTY 602/542-6686).

SENIOR TRAVELERS

The best thing those age 62 or older can do before visiting Arizona is to purchase an America the Beautiful—National Parks and Federal Recreational Lands Senior Pass. This golden ticket will get you and up to three adults into every national park and monument for the rest of your life (non-seniors can buy an America the Beautiful Pass as well, but that version is only valid for one year). It costs $80, paid once in person at any federal park. In Arizona, where most of the best attractions and sights are under federal control, this adds up to big savings.

Road Scholar (800/454-5768, www.roadscholar.org) offers guided trips to Grand Canyon, Sedona, the Navajo Reservation, and elsewhere in Arizona.

TRAVELERS OF COLOR

Arizona's population of 7.2 million is not what you would call diverse: About 53 percent of Arizonans are white, according to the 2020 U.S. Census, and the largely rural state tends to be politically and culturally conservative. But Arizona's culture also greatly benefits from its large Latino and Hispanic population (about 31 percent of the state's population), as well as its small but significant Native American population (about 4 percent)—indeed, these communities are part of the very fabric of the Southwest. The most diverse areas in the state are Phoenix and the Valley of the Sun and Tucson and Southern Arizona's border region. A strong and vocal minority of more liberal wilderness lovers and runaway hippies also exists in nearly every forest and desert town of any size, and the college towns of Flagstaff and Tempe also tend to be more liberal. Additionally, as a major tourist destination, Arizona draws diverse travelers from around the country and the world.

Much of the best of a trip to Arizona and the Southwest involves getting outdoors and exploring a wilderness like no other in the world. Groups such Outdoor Afro (http://outdoorafro.com) and Latino Outdoors (http://latinooutdoors.org) promote inclusion in the country's outdoor culture and organize group hikes and backpacking trips. Both have active groups based in the Phoenix and Tucson areas.

Green Travel

Arizona's sights, restaurants, and accommodations offer the traveler plenty of opportunities to consider the state's fragile arid environment. The challenges inherent in keeping that environment healthy amid the frenzy of consumerism and growth are in your face and hard to miss: The rivers are dry; the city is hotter than it used to be; the freeways are choked with cars carrying a single passenger. But don't get discouraged or overwhelmed. There are ways to leave fewer footprints in this desert country.

Your green-travel strategy begins with planning and packing. Look for hotels that list their sustainable practices on their website or in their literature. Businesses that are serious about the environment want you to know about it. Consider staying in an independent, locally owned hotel or motel that has made new use of an old space rather than wasting nonrenewable resources to build yet another shining tower. You will find several such quirky and enchanting accommodations in Tucson, Phoenix, Jerome, Prescott, and Flagstaff. There are also about 20 hotels, many of them high-end resorts in Tucson, Phoenix, and Scottsdale, that have been Certified Green under the Arizona Hotel & Lodging Association's fairly new Green Lodging Program. To earn the certification, hotels and motels work through a long list of criteria that include stepping up recycling and energy and water saving and generally reducing their impact on the state's environment. You will find many of these Certified Green options in this guidebook.

Once you've chosen your ecofriendly hotel, the first item you should pack is a reusable water bottle—and then you should use it all the time. All of Arizona's national parks and monuments have water stations for refills.

One of the most meaningful, and difficult, green choices you can make while traveling in Arizona is to drive less. It's actually possible these days in Phoenix and Tucson to use public transportation most of the time, as long as you confine yourself to just a few areas. In Tucson, if you stay in a hotel downtown and seek to go no farther afield than the University of Arizona campus, you could ride the SunLink Modern Streetcar all around the city's historic core. In the Valley of the Sun, you could explore the essential parts of central Phoenix, Tempe around the university, downtown Mesa, and downtown Scottsdale via the Valley Metro light rail system.

Tucson, Flagstaff, Prescott, and other Arizona towns make it easy to get around on a bike, as does Tempe and a few parts of Phoenix. If you're visiting Arizona's national parks, consider taking a bike along and parking your car. This is especially easy to do in Grand Canyon National Park, whose South Rim section has excellent paved trails leading into and out of the park. If you don't have your bike with you, there's a place to rent one in the park.

When it's time for breakfast, lunch, and dinner, consider a locally owned eatery that uses locally sourced ingredients and humane practices. Or skip the meat and eat at plant-based restaurants, of which there are several in Arizona. Back at the hotel, ask housekeeping not to wash your bedding for the duration of your stay, within reason, of course.

Finally, when you are out in the deserts, pine forests, and red rocks, pack out what you pack in, stay on the trail, and leave wild animals alone.

LGBTQ TRAVELERS

The gay community is strong and diverse in both Phoenix and Tucson, the state's two major cities. There aren't really LGBTQ districts, though in Phoenix the Melrose District, on 7th Avenue between Camelback and Indian School Roads, is sometimes considered one. In Tucson, www.gaytucson.com has news and information about the local offerings.

The Greater Phoenix Gay & Lesbian Chamber of Commerce (P.O. Box 2097, Phoenix, AZ 85001, 602/266-5055, www.gpglcc.org) has lists of the state's LGBTQ and LGBTQ-friendly accommodations. The Valley of the Sun's Echo Magazine (602/266-0550, www.echomag.com) is an excellent source of news and culture for the community.

TRAVELING WITH CHILDREN

A family trip around Arizona is necessarily a road trip. Is there such a thing as an entirely kid-friendly road trip? At any rate, Arizona is an ideal place for an active outdoor vacation involving the whole family. Most major sights, especially the national parks and monuments, cater to families and offer a host of fun and educational programs for kids. Phoenix and Tucson both have excellent zoos, both of them kid-centric. Rangers at parks and monuments are usually eager to explain and illuminate the sights for kids, and the Junior Rangers program, offered at most of the parks, is a fun and educational way to get kids engaged with nature—it even includes a photo-ready swearing-in ceremony. Children under 16 are admitted free to federal parks, monuments, and recreation areas.

CONDUCT AND CUSTOMS

On the Navajo, Hopi, Western Apache, and other Native American reservations throughout the state, don't take pictures without asking first, and don't drive off the road for any reason—that's somebody's land and livelihood. On the Hopi Reservation, don't enter a village without first stopping at a store or a village office to ask permission. It's a good idea to hire a guide to take you around, as there are many places that are off limits without one.

Health and Safety

THE ARIZONA SUN

Whether you're hiking deep into Grand Canyon, walking sun-splattered paths through a saguaro forest, or simply strolling through the Phoenix Zoo, you must be aware that the incessant sun, the driving reason for most visits to Arizona, can quickly become a dangerous threat to your health. Practice moderation and prevention. Rather than worship, the sun requires timidity: Stay in the shadows, covered from head to toe. If you're not willing to do this, as most aren't, then at least wear a hat with a wide brim, use high-SPF sunscreen, cover your neck, and, preferably, wear long sleeves. This applies not only to backcountry desert adventurers and hikers; mere sightseers, especially those with fresh-faced children in tow, are just as susceptible to sun- and heat-related health issues—the less fit you are, the greater the danger.

The least of what the sun can do to you is not to be taken lightly. A sunburn, which comes on quicker than you'd think, can lead to skin cancer and death. If you get a sunburn, there's little you can do except try to make yourself more comfortable. Stay out of the sun, of course, and try to keep cool and hydrated. There are dozens of over-the-counter balms available, but simple aloe works as well as anything. A popular home remedy is to gently dab the burned areas with vinegar. If the burn starts to blister, reaching the dreaded third-degree stage, skin cancer becomes a very real threat. Again, the best way to avoid sunburn is to stay out of the sun; barring that, cover up and follow common sense. Those with fair skin and children should be even more cautious.

Hikers, shoppers, sightseers, golfers, and anybody else exerting themselves under high-heat conditions should watch out for dehydration. When your body becomes dangerously depleted of fluids, you'll notice first that you are not urinating regularly and your saliva has dried up. You may become irritable and confused; your skin may turn gray, and your pulse may race. Children especially can become dehydrated quickly. The best way to avoid dehydration is to limit your exertion during the hottest part of the day and to drink a lot of water. If you feel the symptoms of dehydration coming on, get to a cool comfortable place, take in fluids, and rest.

Hikers should take along a few packets of electrolyte powder, similar to Gatorade and the like, and a separate water bottle to mix it in—these can be lifesavers. If you exert yourself in the heat and sun and fail to replace the fluids flowing out, your body can become depleted of electrolytes and fluids. Such is the path to **heat exhaustion,** a dangerous condition that can turn fatal if not treated. You begin to feel nauseated, dizzy, and weak, and your muscles cramp. Again, if you experience any of these symptoms, get to a cool comfortable place quickly and drink water and something with sodium and potassium in it, like an electrolyte drink.

Dehydration and heat exhaustion, while dangerous and unpleasant, pale when compared to **heatstroke,** sometimes called sunstroke or heat hyperpyrexia, a severe, dangerous health threat that is frequently fatal or changes a victim's future health significantly and irrevocably. Heatstroke occurs when the body's temperature-regulating capacity fails; this can be caused by either relatively short exposure to extremely high heat—like, say, a short, strenuous run on a 120°F July afternoon in Yuma—or prolonged exposure to relatively high temperatures, as in a 15-mile hike in 90°F heat. And that's only if you're in good shape. It would take far less to cause heatstroke in most of us. The first and most important sign of heatstroke is a lack of sweating. If you stop sweating in a situation where you *should* be sweating, take notice. Sweating is your body's way of regulating its temperature, so it stands to reason that if you stop sweating, there may be something wrong with your body. Your heart rate will speed up noticeably, and your skin will become dry; you'll get a headache and become confused. At its worst, heatstroke leads to

unconsciousness, convulsions, and death. Once you notice you're not sweating, you must get help immediately: Get to an emergency room as soon as possible.

ALTITUDE SICKNESS

The mountains in Arizona rarely reach 12,000 feet elevation, and more frequently reach 10,000 feet. Most visitors won't be going that high, but you should be aware that a few of the state's mountain towns sit at 5,000-8,000 feet above sea level. Lowlanders in relatively good shape may get headaches, a little dizziness, and shortness of breath while walking around Flagstaff or other mountain towns, but few will experience serious altitude sickness—the result of not getting enough oxygen, and therefore not enough blood flow to the brain. Still, take it easy at higher elevations if you begin to feel tired and out of breath, dizzy, or euphoric. If you have heart or lung problems, you need to be more aware at higher elevations; the best thing to do is to get a prescription for oxygen from your doctor and carry it with you if you plan on spending a lot of time in the mountains.

HIKING SAFETY

Most hiking safety is based on common sense: Take enough water, wear a hat and good shoes, take along something to eat, don't go alone, and make sure somebody knows where you're going and when you're planning on being back. In the desert, such common sense takes on added meaning. It's best to avoid taking long strenuous hikes in the desert May-September. You probably won't enjoy it anyway, and it can get very dangerous very fast. If you do go out in the summer, however, don't go during the hottest part of the day—stick to early morning or evening, though even at these times the heat can be brutal.

Besides the usual hiking gear that every hiker should have—water, food, a hat, shoes—Arizona hikers should carry a **tourniquet** with them; if you happen to get bitten by a

Coronavirus in Arizona

At the time of writing in early 2022, Arizona was moderately impacted by the effects of the coronavirus, but the situation is constantly evolving. Arizona has struggled throughout the pandemic to strike a balance between the need for public safety measures and the state's traditionally libertarian political culture. Stay attentive, as rules and regulations can vary widely among federal sites, Native American lands, and state sites and venues.

Now more than ever, Moon encourages its readers to be courteous and ethical in their travel. Be respectful to local residents and mindful of the situation in your chosen destination when planning your trip.

BEFORE YOU GO

- Check websites (listed below) for local restrictions and the overall health status of the destination. If you're traveling to or from an area that is currently a COVID-19 hot spot, you may want to reconsider your trip. Moon encourages travelers to get vaccinated if their health status allows and to take a coronavirus test with enough time to receive the results before departure if possible.

- If you plan to fly, check with your airline and the local health authorities for updated travel requirements. Some airlines may be taking more steps than others to help you travel safely; check their websites before buying your ticket. Consider a very early or very late flight to limit exposure. Flights may be more infrequent, with increased cancellations.

- Check the website of any venues or sights you wish to patronize, such as museums and Native American sites, to confirm that they're open, if their hours have been adjusted, and to learn about any specific visitation requirements, such as mandatory reservations or limited occupancy.

- Pack hand sanitizer, a thermometer, and plenty of face masks. Consider packing snacks, bottled water, a cooler, or anything else you might need to limit the number of stops along your route. Be prepared for possible closures and reduced services over the course of your travels.

- Assess the risk of entering crowded spaces, joining tours, and taking public transit.

- Expect general disruptions. Some tours and venues may require reservations, enforce limits on the number of guests, or operate during different hours than the ones listed. Some may be closed entirely. Events may be postponed or cancelled. Some services at the state's national parks and monuments may be curtailed.

RESOURCES

- CDC: The U.S. Centers for Disease Control and Prevention (www.cdc.gov)

- State of Arizona: Arizona Department of Health Services (www.azdhs.gov/covid19)

- Native American Nations: Havasupai (http://theofficialhavasupaitribe.com), Hopi (www.hopi-nsn.gov), Hualapai (http://hualapai-nsn.gov), Navajo (www.navajo-nsn.gov), Tohono O'odham (www.tonation-nsn.gov)

- Grand Canyon National Park: National Park Service at the Grand Canyon (www.nps.gov/grca)

- U.S. Forest Service: Southwestern Region (www.fs.usda.gov/r3)

rattlesnake or a scorpion—not a very likely occurrence at all—you'll want to tie the tourniquet around the area to slow the blood flow, and the venom, until you can get to a hospital and the antivenin. The best way to avoid a snakebite is to avoid snakes. They are not going to bother you unless you bother them or surprise them. Keep an eye on the ground while you're hiking; if a snake, rattler or otherwise, is in your general vicinity, leave the area. Cover your ankles, keep your hands and feet out of dark holes, and don't put your hands on a rock without looking at it first.

OTHER CONCERNS

West Nile virus and the hantavirus are unlikely threats to your health in Arizona, and both can be avoided by taking precautions. Use insect repellent to ward off the mosquitoes that transmit West Nile virus, and simply stay away from rodents and their nests and droppings to avoid hantavirus.

Threats from humans come in all the usual forms. Lock your vehicle wherever you go, even in the remotest locations. Don't pick up hitchhikers anywhere.

Information and Services

MAPS AND TOURIST INFORMATION

The Arizona Office of Tourism (1110 W. Washington St., Suite 155, Phoenix, 866/275-5816, www.visitarizona.com) will send you a free print or electronic version of the official state guide, and its website is full of information and lists of accommodations, events, and restaurants throughout the state.

If you're planning to spend a lot of time in the state's national forests, you can get maps and information beforehand from the National Forest Service, Southwestern Region (333 Broadway SE, Albuquerque, NM, 505/842-3292, www.fs.usda.gov/r3), or from the websites for the individual forests, listed in the chapters in which they appear.

The Arizona BLM State Office (1 N. Central Ave., Suite 800, Phoenix, 602/417-9200, www.blm.gov) also has a lot of information on the state's wildlands, and the Arizona State Parks Department (1300 W. Washington St., Phoenix, 602/542-4174, http://azstateparks.com) has information on all the parks managed by the state. For state and federal parks, passes can be obtained and reservations and made online or at the parks themselves.

COMMUNICATIONS

Arizona has five telephone area codes. For eastern Maricopa County, including Tempe, Mesa, and most of Scottsdale, dial 480; for Phoenix proper, dial 602; for western Maricopa County, dial 623; for all of Southern Arizona, including Tucson, dial 520; and for all of Northern Arizona, including Prescott, Flagstaff, Jerome, the Grand Canyon, and western Arizona (including Yuma and Lake Havasu City), dial 928.

Your cell phone will work in most parts of Arizona, though there are large swaths of the Navajo and Hopi Reservations where cell service is spotty at best and mostly nonexistent. Cell phones don't usually work in the backcountry, but it's worth taking them along just in case.

You'll find high-speed wireless internet service throughout the state at the majority of hotels and motels and in cafés and libraries everywhere. Even the remote reservation lands are wired in.

MEDIA

Arizona has just two major daily newspapers, the *Arizona Republic* in Phoenix and the *Arizona Daily Star* in Tucson. The

Republic is more a statewide newspaper, while the *Star* focuses on Southern Arizona. You'll find the *Republic* at newsstands and newspaper vending machines throughout the state, while the *Star* is typically available only in Southern Arizona. In North-Central Arizona, the daily *Prescott Courier* and the *Daily Sun* in Flagstaff cover the northland well, including all the happenings at the Grand Canyon and the Navajo Nation. In western Arizona, the *Yuma Sun* is the only daily newspaper.

For alternative news, commentary, and arts and entertainment coverage, check out the free weekly *Phoenix New Times,* covering the Valley of the Sun. In Tucson, the free *Tucson Weekly* offers in-depth coverage of the news and art and entertainment scene in Southern Arizona. Both weeklies publish annual "best of" issues, which list readers' picks of the best restaurants, bars, shops, and attractions in the state's two major urban areas.

Tucson and Phoenix both have network television affiliates, as does Flagstaff. Outside Southern Arizona, which looks to Tucson for its television news, you'll mostly see the local news from Phoenix.

All three of the state's universities operate National Public Radio stations (Phoenix: KJZZ FM 91.5; Tucson: KUAZ FM 89.1; Flagstaff: KNAU FM 88.7), which offer public radio news programs throughout the day.

MONEY

Despite its largely rural character, Arizona is set firmly in the 21st century. Even in the most out-of-the-way areas, you'll be able to use your credit or debit card with impunity. However, it's always a good idea to carry some cash, especially if you're headed to the Navajo and Hopi Reservations, where it is not uncommon for phone lines, and therefore credit card machines, to go down, and you may find yourself in need of gas but with no way to pay for it.

Foreign travelers can exchange their money at banks throughout the state; check the website www.xe.com for up-to-date exchange rates.

If you cross the border into Mexico and remain in the tourism and shopping areas, you don't need to exchange your money. Shops and restaurants in Nogales and other border towns are happy to take your U.S. dollars.

BUSINESS HOURS

While the majority of businesses in Arizona keep regular hours, in many areas the business hours change with the season. In Tucson, Phoenix, Yuma, and all the other desert cities and towns, you may find some places closed during July-August. Call ahead, and don't take anything for granted if you're planning a trip to the desert during those infernal hottest summer months. In winter, some of the small towns of the White Mountains go into hibernation, and many businesses close for weeks or months at a time. Again, it's best to call ahead.

Resources

Suggested Reading

HISTORY

Armstrong, William Patrick. *Fred Harvey: Creator of Western Hospitality*. Bellmont, AZ: Canyonlands Publications, 2000. A slim introduction to Harvey and his accomplishments. Available at many Grand Canyon bookstores, it puts a positive spin on the "Civilizer of the West" and the marketing of the Southwestern style.

Bandelier, Fanny, trans. *The Journey of Alvar Nuñez Cabeza de Vaca*. Chicago: Rio Grande Press, 1964. This strange first-person account follows a conquistador who spent years of privation with various Native American tribes after being shipwrecked near Florida in the late 1520s before finally finding his way back to Mexico and inspiring later explorations of the Southwest by the Spanish.

Corel, Edwin. *The Gila: River of the Southwest*. New York: Holt, Rinehart and Winston, 1951. Using Arizona's once-mighty east-west riverway as his hub, Corel jumps off in many directions, exploring human history and culture under the influence of the Gila, which, along with its major tributaries—the Salt, the Santa Cruz, the San Pedro, and the Verde—has been the main artery of Arizona civilization for centuries.

Hall, Sharlot M. (Crampton, C. Gregory, ed.). *Sharlot Hall on the Arizona Strip: A Diary of a Journey Through Northern Arizona in 1911*. Flagstaff: Northland Press, 1975. Hall, a famous regional writer of the frontier and early statehood, took an arduous trip to the isolated Arizona Strip and lived to write about it. The editor's notes provide a short but thorough introduction to the human history of the region.

Jones, Billy M. *Health-Seekers in the Southwest 1817-1900*. Norman, OK: University of Oklahoma Press, 1967. A scholarly but readable study of health migration in the 19th century. It turns out, according to Jones, that the Wild West was really a "health frontier" full of reluctant settlers who ventured west to cure TB and other ailments.

Limerick, Patricia Nelson. *The Legacy of Conquest: The Unbroken Past of the American West*. New York: Norton, 1987. An unromantic reconsideration of the history of the Western frontier. Limerick finds that it was a distinctly American hunger for resources, profit, and real estate that built and ruled the West, not the six-gun and its stoic free-shooting hero.

Luckingham, Bradford. *The Urban Southwest*. El Paso, TX: Texas Western Press, 1982. A study of the rise of four major Southwestern cities, including Phoenix and Tucson.

Martin, Douglas D. *An Arizona Chronology: The Territorial Years, 1846-1912*. Tucson: University of Arizona Press, 1962.

Martin, Douglas D. (Patricia, Paylore, ed.). *An Arizona Chronology: Statehood 1913-1936*. Tucson: University of Arizona Press, 1966. A retired journalist, Douglas spent years searching through old Arizona newspapers, gathering the major headlines from 1846 to 1936. The series provides a general and surprisingly entertaining understanding of the march of Arizona history.

Powell, Lawrence Clark. *Arizona: A History*. Albuquerque, NM: University of New Mexico Press, 1990. A more recent edition of the book first published in 1976, Powell's history is not a definitive blow-by-blow but rather a series of essays on various chapters in Arizona's history and culture. A much-admired Southwestern writer, librarian, and scholar, Powell lived in Tucson for many years. His *Southwest: Three Definitions* (Benson, AZ: Singing Winds Bookshop, 1990) is an excellent trilogy of essays on the landscape and culture of the Southwest.

Sheridan, Thomas. *Arizona: A History*. Tucson: University of Arizona Press, 1995. A very well-written and informative general history.

Sonnichsen, C. L. *Tucson: The Life and Times of an American City*. Norman, OK: University of Oklahoma Press, 1982. A thorough telling of the Old Pueblo's long history from its founding in 1776 as a presidio up to the early 1980s.

Waters, Frank. *The Colorado*. New York: Holt, Rinehart and Winston, 1951. The great Western writer known for his novel *The Man Who Killed the Deer*, Waters was also a master of nonfiction. Though he penned this book about the Colorado River and all that it influences in the 1940s, in a Southwest unrecognizable from what it is today, the greater part of his story still seems true—a classic of that "sense of place" all writers seek.

NATIVE AMERICANS, ANTHROPOLOGY, AND ARCHAEOLOGY

Dentdale, Jennifer Nez. *Reclaiming Diné History: The Legacies of Navajo Chief Manuelito and Juanita*. Tucson: University of Arizona Press, 2007. A compelling account of the Navajo Nation written by the first Navajo woman to earn a PhD in history. Dentdale gives the oral history of her people just as much credence as the mostly Anglo-written accounts that claim to be official and complete. This method reveals, among other things, that women played a much larger role in traditional Navajo society than colonial records credit.

Hall, Edward T. *West of the Thirties: Discoveries Among the Navajo and Hopi*. New York: Doubleday, 1994. The great anthropologist tells stories about his work with the Navajo and Hopi during the Great Depression, evoking a time when the remote Indian Country was practically inaccessible.

Houk, Rose. *Sinagua*. Tucson: Western National Parks Association, 1992. Pick up this short volume at any of the national parks or monuments you're sure to visit in Arizona; it's a concise introduction to the Sinagua and their land, part of a series sold throughout the state.

Kosik, Fran. *Native Roads: The Complete Motoring Guide to the Navajo and Hopi Nations*. Tucson: Rio Nuevo, 2005. Kosik knows the reservation lands well and includes a lot of fascinating historical tidbits; recommended to anyone wanting to go deeper than most into Indian Country.

Lamb, Susan. *A Guide to Navajo Rugs*. Tucson: Western National Parks Association, 1992.

Lamb, Susan. *A Guide to Pueblo Pottery*. Tucson: Southwest Parks and Monuments

Association, 1996. These handy guides, available at park and monument bookshops and most of the gift shops and tourist attractions in Indian Country, explain the basics of rug and pottery identification—just enough to hook you in and whet your appetite for collecting the arts and crafts of the Navajos and Pueblos.

Waters, Frank. *Book of the Hopi*. New York: Penguin, 1963. Though this history of the Hopi and retelling of their myths and legends sometimes gets a cold shoulder from scholars, Waters's book has a narrative thrust that makes the Hopi story seem immediate and meaningful not just to the Hopi and a few anthropologists but to all of us.

Wright, Barton. *The Complete Guide to Collecting Kachina Dolls*. Flagstaff: Northland Press, 1977. A classic guide to the kachina spirits and what they mean.

GRAND CANYON

Ghiglieri, Michael P., and Thomas M. Myers. *Over the Edge: Death in Grand Canyon*. Flagstaff: Puma Press, 2001. A popular collection of macabre stories about tumblers, jumpers, drowning victims, and killers in the Grand Canyon. One of the few books of its kind that is updated quite regularly.

Grattan, Virginia L. *Mary Colter: Builder upon Red Earth*. Grand Canyon: The Grand Canyon Association, 1992. A very readable account of architect Mary Colter's life and career. Colter seems to be little known outside the Southwest, though she deserves a wider reputation for her fanciful Grand Canyon creations and the rustic arts and crafts elegance of her Harvey Houses.

Hughes, Donald. *In the House of Stone and Light*. Grand Canyon Natural History Association, 1978. A relatively short well-written account of the human history of the Grand Canyon, concentrating mainly on the Anglo development of the South Rim and the evolution of Grand Canyon National Park.

Powell, John Wesley. *The Exploration of the Colorado River and Its Canyons*. New York: Dover, 1961. A reprint of Powell's 1895 classic *Canyons of the Colorado*, this firsthand account of two journeys through the canyon on the Colorado River is essential reading (and it is surprisingly readable) for anyone interested in the continuing story of the confluence of humans and Grand Canyon.

Schullery, Paul. *The Grand Canyon: Early Impressions*. Boulder, CO: Colorado Associated University Press, 1981. Includes essays by John Muir and others, showing that writers and other visitors have struggled mightily to describe and comprehend the canyon since people have been visiting it.

THE ENVIRONMENT AND NATURAL HISTORY

Carter, Jack L., et al. *Common Southwestern Native Plants: An Identification Guide*. Silver City, NM: Mimbres Press, 2003. A thorough but easy-to-use guide to plants you're likely to see in Arizona; includes common species of the deserts, the forested mountains, and the plateau country.

Grubbs, Bruce. *Desert Sense: Camping, Hiking & Biking in Hot, Dry Climates*. Seattle: The Mountaineers Books, 2004. If you're going to be hiking or riding a bike in the desert, especially if you're doing it in the summer, consider picking up this or a similar book to familiarize yourself with desert survival beyond the basics of bringing water and wearing a hat.

Kavanagh, James, ed. *The Nature of Arizona*. Blaine, WA: Waterford Press, 1996. A useful all-in-one guide specific to the state; most guides attempt to lump everything together under "Southwest." Lists and provides illustrations of the state's flora and fauna, including mammals, snakes, fish, birds, and spiders.

Logan, Michael F. *The Lessening Stream: An Environmental History of the Santa Cruz River.* Tucson: University of Arizona Press, 2002. A professor paints an attractive and elegiac portrait of what the river used to be like and explains why it isn't like that anymore.

Olin, George. *50 Common Mammals of the Southwest.* Tucson: Western National Parks Association, 2000. An introduction to Arizona's mammals; slim with attractive illustrations, part of a series available throughout the state.

Quinn, Meg. *Wildflowers of the Southwest.* Tucson: Rio Nuevo, 2000. If you're going to be hiking in the desert in spring, pick up this guide to the many wildflowers that bloom throughout the state.

HIKING

Berkowitz, Alan. *Grand Canyon North Kaibab Trail Guide.* Grand Canyon Conservancy, 2005.

Menconi, Lilia. *Moon Take a Hike Phoenix: Hikes within Two Hours of the City.* Berkeley, CA: Avalon Travel, 2013.

Thybony, Scott. *Grand Canyon Bright Angel Trail Guide.* Grand Canyon Conservancy, 2004.

Thybony, Scott. *Grand Canyon Hermit Trail Guide.* Grand Canyon Conservancy, 2005.

Thybony, Scott. *Grand Canyon South Kaibab Trail Guide.* Grand Canyon Conservancy,

2006. Pick up these small, inexpensive guides to the major Grand Canyon trails at most canyon-area bookstores. They contain a lot of information for being so small, and several color photos show you what's ahead. Each guide also includes an interesting history of the trail.

Tessmer, Martin. *50 Hikes in Arizona.* Woodstock, VT: The Countryman Press, 2004. An excellent guide to the best hiking trails in the state, with detailed descriptions of each trail and precise directions to the trailheads. Includes all regions of the state.

Warren, Scott S. *100 Classic Hikes in Arizona.* Seattle, WA: The Mountaineers Press, 2000. Has 50 more hikes than *50 Hikes in Arizona.* For those looking not only for the best and most popular hikes but also the less known and little used.

LITERATURE

Abbey, Edward. *One Life at a Time, Please.* New York: Henry Holt, 1987. Abbey was the Southwest's resident poet-provocateur, a major influence on a few generations of Western writers and environmentalists. It has yet to be decided if he was writing literature disguised as polemics or the other way around, but he is an essential voice in the long project to justify the ways of the West to the rest of the country. This volume of essays from the late 1970s-1980s includes his thoughts on Lake Powell.

Bowden, Charles. *Blue Desert.* Tucson: University of Arizona Press, 1986.

Bowden, Charles. *Frog Mountain Blues.* Tucson: University of Arizona Press, 1987. Bowden's voice is overwhelming once you get into it. His essays, reportage, and nature writing chronicle the darker side of the sunbelt.

Internet Resources

TOURISM SITES

Arizona Office of Tourism
www.visitarizona.com
The official site for the state's Office of Tourism has basic information on the state's regions and lists various possible itineraries.

Discover Navajo
www.discovernavajo.com
The official site of the Navajo Nation's tourism group has basic information about visiting the nation—where to stay, what to do, and what not to do. It has a large number of links to tour companies.

**Flagstaff Convention
and Visitors Bureau**
www.flagstaffarizona.org
This site has general information on visiting Flagstaff, the northland, and the Grand Canyon along with helpful listings.

Grand Canyon National Park
www.nps.gov/grca
The Grand Canyon's official website has basic information on the park; go here for information about backcountry permits. For reservations and information on the park's accommodations, go to the **Xanterra South Rim** site (www.grandcanyonlodges.com).

**Greater Phoenix Convention
& Visitors Bureau**
www.visitphoenix.com
The official site for Phoenix and the Valley of the Sun has a comprehensive list of restaurants and hotels in the valley.

**Metropolitan Tucson Convention
and Visitors Bureau**
www.visittucson.org

This is Tucson and Southern Arizona's official tourism site.

Sedona Chamber of Commerce
www.visitsedona.com
The official site for Sedona tourism has general information on Sedona, Oak Creek Canyon, Red Rock Country, and the Verde Valley.

Yuma Visitors Bureau
www.visityuma.com
The official site for Yuma and the lower Colorado River region.

NEWS AND CULTURE

Arizona Daily Star
www.azstarnet.com
Tucson's morning daily is free on this site, with news and information on all of Southern Arizona.

Arizona Republic
www.azcentral.com
The state's largest newspaper is free online every day, and the site has a robust Arizona travel guide and a useful dining and entertainment section.

Phoenix New Times
www.phoenixnewtimes.com
This site is the best place to go for entertainment and cultural listings and alternative news and commentary about life in the Valley of the Sun.

Tucson Weekly
www.tucsonweekly.com
Southern Arizona's best source of alternative news, political blogs, and cultural and entertainment news and listings.

Index

D

E

454

List of Maps

Photo Credits

Title page: Devil's Bridge in the Sedona area © Tim Hull
All interior photos © Tim Hull, except page 3 © Children's Museum of Phoenix; page 6 © (top right) Markskalny | Dreamstime.com; page 7 © (top) Zrfphoto | Dreamstime.com, (bottom right) Rinus Baak | Dreamstime.com; page 9 © (top) © Volodymyr Tverdokhlib | Dreamstime.com; (bottom right) Rinusbaak | Dreamstime.com; page 10-11 © Sepavo | Dreamstime.com; page 12 © (top) Hpbfotos | Dreamstime.com; page 13 © (top) Derrick Neill | Dreamstime.com; (bottom) Rapidshooter | Dreamstime. com; page 14 © Billvorasate | Dreamstime.com; page 15 © (top) Cheri Alguire | Dreamstime.com; (middle) Larisamystock | Dreamstime.com; (bottom) Desertsolitaire | Dreamstime.com; page 20 © (bottom) Entrance to the Heard Museum featuring "Earth Song" by Allan Houser, photo by Craig Smith © Heard Museum; page 22 © Gloria P. Meyerle | Dreamstime.com; page 26 © Thomas Vieth | Dreamstime.com; page 27 © (top) Studiobarcelona| Dreamstime.com; page 30 © Salaverría Calahorra | Dreamstime.com; page 31 © (top) Derrick Neill | Dreamstime.com; page 32 © Phartisan | Dreamstime.com; page 33 © (top left) Diomedes66 | Dreamstime.com; (top right) © Heard Museum; page 41 © (bottom) Heard Museum; page 43 © (bottom) Children's Museum of Phoenix; page 48 © (top left) Nylakatara2013 | Dreamstime.com; (top right) Gregoryeclifford | Dreamstime.com; (bottom left) Gregoryeclifford | Dreamstime.com; (bottom right) Adogslifephoto | Dreamstime.com; page 62 © (top) Neilld | Dreamstime.com; page 85 © (top) Davepmorgan | Dreamstime.com; (right middle) Phartisan | Dreamstime.com; page 99 © Iprintezis | Dreamstime.com; page 103 © (top) Cottingham | Dreamstime.com; page 106 © Irina Kozhemyakina | Dreamstime.com; page 115 © (top right) Glenn Nagel | Dreamstime.com; page 120 © (top) Ken Wolter | Dreamstime.com; (left middle) Florence McGinn/123rf.com; page 127 © (top) Martha Marks | Dreamstime.com, (bottom) Tryder | Dreamstime.com; page 137 © (bottom) Mdurson | Dreamstime.com; page 147 © Olgany | Dreamstime. com; page 164 © (top) Mati Parts | Dreamstime.com; page 170 © (bottom) Visions of America LLC/123rf.com; page 183 © Kaye Oberstar | Dreamstime.com; page 184 © (top left) Msfj4w | Dreamstime.com; (top right) Chris Putnam/123rf.com; page 190 © (top) Fotoluminate | Dreamstime.com; (left middle) Christopher Durot | Dreamstime.com; (right middle) Fainagur | Dreamstime.com; page 210 © (top right) Fotosforthought | Dreamstime.com; (bottom) Chris Putnam/123rf.com; page 219 © (top) Nylakatara2013 | Dreamstime.com; page 221 © (bottom) Christopher Fell/123rf.com; page 228 © (top right) Jack Aiello/123rf.com; page 244 © (top right) trekandshoot | Dreamstime.com; page 251 © (top left) Songquan Deng/123rf.com; (bottom) Elizabeth Jang; page 257 © Scott Griessel | Dreamstime.com; page 270 © (top) Milosk50 | Dreamstime. com; page 282 © (top) Jesse Kraft | Dreamstime.com; page 289 © (bottom) Studiobarcelona | Dreamstime. com; page 301 © (top) Robert Wilson/123rf.com; (bottom) Chee-Onn Leong/123rf.com; page 315 © Frank Bach | Dreamstime.com; page 316 © (top left) Lizziemaher | Dreamstime.com; (top right) Fotoluminate | Dreamstime.com; page 325 © (left middle) Joerg Hackemann/123rf.com; (bottom) Zakaz86 | Dreamstime. com; page 337 © (top) MNStudio | Dreamstime.com; page 347 © (top right) Daniel Raustadt | Dreamstime. com; page 359 © (top left) Steve Estvanik | Dreamstime.com; page 372 © (top) Derrick Neill/123rf.com; page 375 © Sean Pavone | Dreamstime.com; page 376 © (top right) Mikekarcher | Dreamstime.com; page 381 © Kobby Dagan/123RF.COM; page 389 © (left middle) Miroslav Liska/123RF.COM; page 393 © (bottom) Littleny | Dreamstime.com; page 400 © (bottom) 12Fish/123RF.COM; page 407 © Designpics/ 123RF.COM; page 410 © Info102828 | Dreamstime.com; page 418 © William Wise | Dreamstime.com; page 427 © Kapu | Dreamstime.com

MOON

Arizona
& THE GRAND CANYON

MOON

PHOENIX, SCOTTSDALE & SEDONA

BEST HIKES • LOCAL SPOTS • WEEKEND GETAWAYS

MOON

NEVADA

SCOTT SMITH

MOON

TAHOE & RENO

LOCAL SPOTS • GETAWAY IDEAS • HIKING & SKIING

MOON

New Mexico

MOON

SANTA FE, TAOS & ALBUQUERQUE

MOON

UTAH

With Zion, Bryce Canyon, Arches, Capitol Reef & Canyonlands National Parks

W. C. McRAE & JUDY JEWELL

MOON

SALT LAKE, PARK CITY
& THE WASATCH RANGE

MAYA SILVER

LOCAL SPOTS • GETAWAY IDEAS • HIKING & SKIING

MOON

TEXAS

MOON

AUSTIN
SAN ANTONIO & THE HILL COUNTRY

JUSTIN MARLER

GETAWAY IDEAS • ROAD TRIPS • BBQ & TEX-MEX

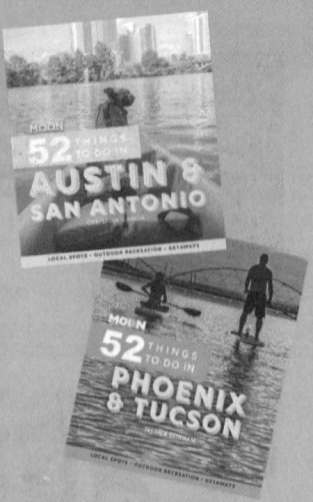

MOON

52 THINGS TO DO IN
AUSTIN & SAN ANTONIO

LOCAL SPOTS • OUTDOOR RECREATION • GETAWAYS

MOON

52 THINGS TO DO IN
PHOENIX & TUCSON

LOCAL SPOTS • OUTDOOR RECREATION • GETAWAYS

Explore local spots and day trips with Moon's **52 Things**, or make the most of short trips to top national parks with our **Best Of Parks** travel guides.

MOON

- BEST OF -
GRAND CANYON

MAKE THE MOST OF ONE TO THREE DAYS IN THE PARK

TOP SIGHTS, TOP HIKES, TOP SCENIC DRIVES

TIM HULL

MOON

- BEST OF -
ZION & BRYCE

MAKE THE MOST OF ONE TO THREE DAYS IN THE PARKS

TOP SIGHTS, TOP HIKES, TOP SCENIC DRIVES

JUDY JEWELL & W. C. McRAE

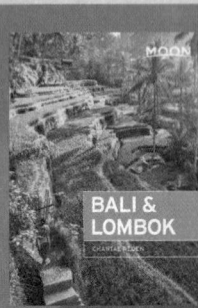

BAHAMAS

DOMINICAN REPUBLIC

JAMAICA

PUERTO RICO

AMALFI COAST

AMSTERDAM
BRUSSELS & BRUGES

EGYPT

GREEK ISLANDS & ATHENS

ICELAND

IRELAND

ISRAEL
& THE WEST BANK

MOROCCO

NORMANDY & BRITTANY

ROME,
FLORENCE
& VENICE

Scotland

SOUTHERN ITALY

ROAD TRIP GUIDES

MOON
BLUE RIDGE PARKWAY
Road Trip

WITH SHENANDOAH & GREAT SMOKY
MOUNTAINS NATIONAL PARKS

JASON FRYE

MOON
CALIFORNIA
Road Trip

SAN FRANCISCO, YOSEMITE, LAS VEGAS,
GRAND CANYON, LOS ANGELES,
& THE PACIFIC COAST HIGHWAY

STUART THORNTON

MOON
NASHVILLE TO NEW ORLEANS
Road Trip

NATCHEZ TRACE PARKWAY • MEMPHIS •
TUPELO • MISSISSIPPI BLUES TRAIL

MARGARET LITTMAN

MOON
NEW ENGLAND
Road Trip

SEASIDE SPOTS, MAJESTIC MOUNTAINS &
FALL FOLIAGE, COZY GETAWAYS

MILES HOWARD

MOON
NORTHERN CALIFORNIA
Road Trips

DRIVES ALONG THE COAST, REDWOODS, AND MOUNTAINS
WITH THE BEST STOPS ALONG THE WAY

STUART THORNTON & KAYLA ANDERSON

MOON
OREGON TRAIL
Road Trip

HISTORIC SITES, SMALL TOWNS, AND
SCENIC LANDSCAPES ALONG THE LEGENDARY
WESTWARD ROUTE

KATRINA EMERY

MOON
PACIFIC COAST HIGHWAY
Road Trip

CALIFORNIA,
OREGON & WASHINGTON

IAN ANDERSON

MOON
PACIFIC NORTHWEST
Road Trip

OUTDOOR ADVENTURES AND CREATIVE CITIES
FROM THE COAST TO THE MOUNTAINS

ALLISON WILLIAMS

MOON
ROUTE 66
Road Trip

JESSICA DUNHAM

MOON.COM | ROADTRIPUSA.COM

MOON

SOUTH FLORIDA & THE KEYS
Road Trip

WITH MIAMI, WALT DISNEY WORLD, TAMPA & THE EVERGLADES

JASON FERGUSON

MOON

SOUTHERN CALIFORNIA
Road Trip

DRIVES ALONG THE BEACHES, MOUNTAINS, AND DESERTS WITH THE BEST STOPS ALONG THE WAY

IAN ANDERSON

MOON

SOUTHWEST
Road Trip

LAS VEGAS, ZION & BRYCE, MONUMENT VALLEY, SANTA FE & TAOS, AND THE GRAND CANYON

TIM HULL

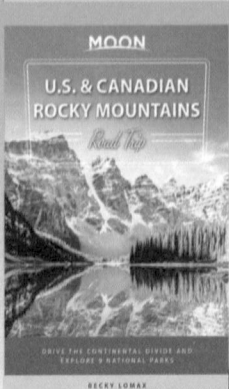

MOON

U.S. & CANADIAN ROCKY MOUNTAINS
Road Trip

DRIVE THE CONTINENTAL DIVIDE AND EXPLORE 9 NATIONAL PARKS

BECKY LOMAX

MOON

VANCOUVER & CANADIAN ROCKIES
Road Trip

VICTORIA, BANFF, JASPER, CALGARY, THE OKANAGAN, WHISTLER & THE SEA-TO-SKY HIGHWAY

CAROLYN B. HELLER

MOON

YELLOWSTONE TO GLACIER NATIONAL PARK
Road Trip

JACKSON HOLE, CODI, THE GRAND TETONS & THE ROCKY MOUNTAIN FRONT

CARTER G. WALKER

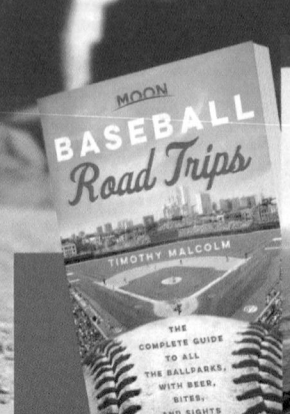

MOON

BASEBALL
Road Trips

TIMOTHY MALCOLM

THE COMPLETE GUIDE TO ALL THE BALLPARKS, WITH BEER, BITES, AND SIGHTS NEARBY

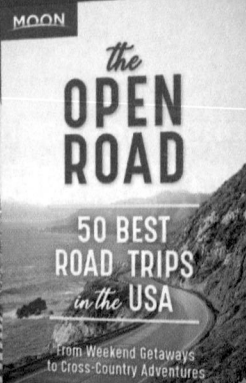

MOON

the OPEN ROAD

50 BEST ROAD TRIPS *in the* USA

From Weekend Getaways to Cross-Country Adventures

JESSICA DUNHAM

MOON

Road Trip USA

25TH ANNIVERSARY EDITION

CROSS-COUNTRY ADVENTURES ON AMERICA'S TWO-LANE HIGHWAYS

Get inspired for your next adventure

Follow @**moonguides** on Instagram or
subscribe to our newsletter at **moon.com**

MAP SYMBOLS

Highway	○ City/Town	ⓘ Information Center	♠ Park
Primary Road	◉ State Capital	Ⓟ Parking Area	⚑ Golf Course
Secondary Road	⊛ National Capital	⛪ Church	✛ Unique Feature
Unpaved Road	◉ Highlight	🍇 Winery/Vineyard	✛ Unique Feature Hydro
Trail	★ Point of Interest	Trailhead	Waterfall
Ferry	• Accommodation	⛺ Camping	▲ Mountain
Railroad	▼ Restaurant/Bar	Train Station	Ski Area
Pedestrian Walkway	■ Other Location	✈ International Airport	Glacier
Stairs		✈ Regional Airport	

CONVERSION TABLES

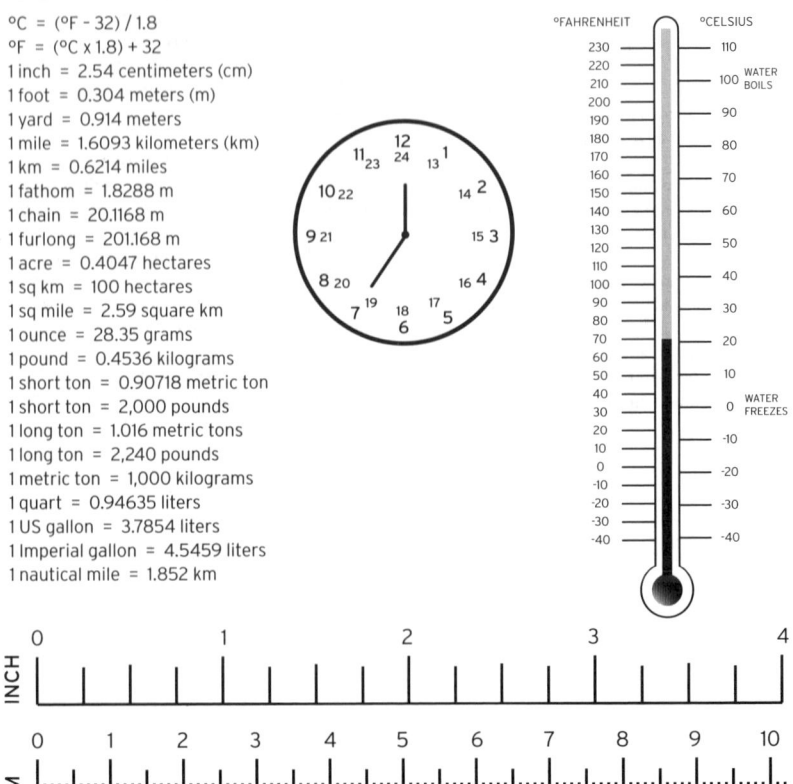

°C = (°F - 32) / 1.8
°F = (°C x 1.8) + 32
1 inch = 2.54 centimeters (cm)
1 foot = 0.304 meters (m)
1 yard = 0.914 meters
1 mile = 1.6093 kilometers (km)
1 km = 0.6214 miles
1 fathom = 1.8288 m
1 chain = 20.1168 m
1 furlong = 201.168 m
1 acre = 0.4047 hectares
1 sq km = 100 hectares
1 sq mile = 2.59 square km
1 ounce = 28.35 grams
1 pound = 0.4536 kilograms
1 short ton = 0.90718 metric ton
1 short ton = 2,000 pounds
1 long ton = 1.016 metric tons
1 long ton = 2,240 pounds
1 metric ton = 1,000 kilograms
1 quart = 0.94635 liters
1 US gallon = 3.7854 liters
1 Imperial gallon = 4.5459 liters
1 nautical mile = 1.852 km

°FAHRENHEIT °CELSIUS

230 —
220 — — 110
210 — — 100 WATER BOILS
200 —
190 — — 90
180 — — 80
170 —
160 — — 70
150 —
140 — — 60
130 — — 50
120 —
110 — — 40
100 —
90 — — 30
80 —
70 — — 20
60 —
50 — — 10
40 —
30 — — 0 WATER FREEZES
20 —
10 — — -10
0 —
-10 — — -20
-20 — — -30
-30 —
-40 — — -40

INCH 0   1   2   3   4

CM 0 1 2 3 4 5 6 7 8 9 10

MOON ARIZONA & THE GRAND CANYON

Avalon Travel
Hachette Book Group
1700 Fourth Street
Berkeley, CA 94710, USA
www.moon.com

Editor: Kristi Mitsuda
Series Manager: Kathryn Ettinger
Copy Editor: Christopher Church
Graphics and Production Coordinator:
  Lucie Ericksen
Cover Design: Toni Tajima
Map Editor: Albert Angulo
Cartographer: John Culp
Indexer: Greg Jewett

ISBN-13: 9781640496514

Printing History
1st Edition — 1986
16th Edition — September 2022
5 4 3 2 1

Text © 2022 by Tim Hull.
Maps © 2022 by Avalon Travel.

Front cover photo: Grand Canyon viewed from Sinking Ship Summit © RooM the Agency / Alamy Stock Photo
Back cover photo: Arizona desert © Danny Raustadt | Dreamstime.com

Printed in Malaysia for Imago